Preparing Hearts For His Glory

A Learning Program for Ages 8-10

(with extensions for older students)

Written by Carrie Austin, M.Ed.

Editor:	Cover Designer:
Julie Grosz	Merlin DeBoer

Heart of Dakota Publishing
www.heartofdakota.com

Special Thanks to:

Our Lord and Savior, Jesus Christ, for giving us the vision to train up our children in the Lord. May He be glorified through this work.

My parents, Ken and Marlene Mellema, for their faithful example of living for Christ and their steadfast commitment to family that has lasted a lifetime. I am so blessed by their unwavering support as they have attended conventions with me and have lovingly watched over my children as I've finished this book. I can only hope to live up to their example.

Julie Grosz for her countless hours of editing, her teaching expertise and knowledge, her listening ear, and her eye for detail. I am so thankful for her steadfast support and encouragement and her enthusiasm for using our programs with her own children. God blessed me with Julie.

Dave and Cindy Madden for forging a new path by homeschooling their seven precious children. We are so thankful that they have gone before us and are showing all of us a better way to live our lives for Christ. I am blessed to call Cindy my sister and my friend.

Mike Austin for his unending support and love, his patient encouragement, and consistent hard work without complaint. I am blessed by his faithful commitment to prayer. He is the love of my life and a cherished father to our four boys. Without him, there would be no Heart of Dakota Publishing.

Cole, Shaw, and Greyson, (and Beau) Austin, my sons, for posing for the cover of this book. They are truly an inspiration to me and are wonderful blessings from our Father in heaven.

Heart of Dakota Publishing, Inc.
1004 Westview Drive
Dell Rapids, SD 57022

Website: www.heartofdakota.com
Phone (605) 428-4068

Printed in the U.S.A.
ISBN 0-9747695-9-2

Table of Contents

Introduction

Complete Plans

Preparing Hearts for His Glory features 35 units with complete daily plans. Each unit lasts 4 days, which gives you the 5th day of each week to use as you wish. The 4-day plan can be stretched to cover 5 days if needed. This guide is meant to save you time planning, so you can instead spend your time teaching and enjoying your children. Activities are rotated daily, so you can cover many areas that might often be neglected, without lengthening your school day. These plans are designed to provide an academic, well balanced approach to learning.

Easy to Use

Simple daily plans are provided on each two-page spread. The subjects can be done in any order. Each day of plans is divided into the following 2 parts: "Learning Through History" and "Learning the Basics". Each segment of plans is further designated as "Teacher Directed = T", "Semi-Independent = S", or "Independent = I". Dividing the plans in this manner is meant to help you gradually move your children toward more independent work. Easy to follow daily plans are divided into 10 boxes, which can be spaced throughout the day as time allows.

Learning Through History

The "Learning Through History" part of the program is told in story form and provides a one-year overview of world history from creation to the late 1900's. Biblical stories are interwoven with other stories from world history to show that the flow of history is really one continuous story. Students will be led to see that all of history belongs to God, and is actually "His" story. The following areas are linked with the history stories: corresponding read alouds, oral narration practice, written narration lessons, oral comprehension and opinion questions, Biblical applications, geography quick-finds, timeline entries, vocabulary study, research questions, history projects, notebooking assignments, copywork, and corresponding independent literature assignments.

Learning the Basics

The "Learning the Basics" part of the program focuses on language arts, math, Bible, and science. It includes dictation practice and passages, a choice of scheduled grammar and writing texts, reading choices, creative writing from the poetry of Robert Louis Stevenson, oral narrations, a choice of math texts, a Bible study of the Psalms, and scheduled science readings with lessons.

Quick Activities

Preparing Hearts for His Glory was written with the busy homeschool teacher in mind. It provides a way to do great activities without all of the usual planning and preparation. Quick and easy activities require little or no preparation and use materials you're likely to have on hand.

Fun Ideas

Engaging daily lessons take approximately 4 hours to complete. More time will be needed if you linger on activities or draw out discussions. The activities are filled with ideas that get kids thinking, exploring, and learning in a meaningful way.

Balanced

Each day's lessons are carefully planned to provide a balance of oral, written, and hands-on work. In this way, oral narration is practiced daily, but in a variety of subject areas. Written work is required daily, but care is taken to balance it with other forms of assessment. Hands-on experiences are provided in each day's plans, but they do not require overwhelming amounts of time.

Flexible

Lesson plans are written to allow you to customize the program to suit your child's needs. A choice of resources is provided. Resources noted in the plans with a 'star' are considered necessary to do the box of the plans in which the resource appears. Resources noted in the plans with a 'checkmark' provide a text or music connection to the activity. An Extension Pack Schedule in the Appendix extends the area of history to include more advanced reading material. This allows your older students to learn along with your younger students.

Resources

All of the 'star' and 'checkmark' resources noted in *Preparing Hearts for His Glory* are available from Heart of Dakota Publishing. Order resources online at www.heartofdakota.com, by mail using the printable online order form, or by telephone at (605) 428-4068. Resource titles are listed below.

History 'Star' Resources (Required)

**A Child's History of the World* by Virgil M. Hillyer (Calvert Education Services, 1997) Note: This text is available in several different versions, but only the 1997 version matches with the page numbers in this guide and includes the additional end chapters needed for this study.

**Grandpa's Box* by Starr Meade (P&R Publishing Co., 2005)

**Life in the Great Ice Age* by Michael and Beverly Oard (Master Books, 1996)

**Hero Tales: Volume I* by Dave and Neta Jackson (Bethany House Publishers, 1996)

Science 'Star' Resources (Required, unless you have your own science)

**One Small Square: Arctic Tundra* by Donald M. Silver (McGraw-Hill, 1997)
**One Small Square: Cactus Desert* by Donald M. Silver (McGraw-Hill, 1997)
**The Great Dinosaur Mystery and the Bible* by Paul S. Taylor (David C. Cook Publishing, 2005)
**Find the Constellations* by H.A. Rey (Houghton Mifflin, 2006)
**One Small Square: Coral Reef* by Donald M. Silver (McGraw-Hill, 1997)
**Columbus* by Ingri and Edgar Parin D'Aulaire (Beautiful Feet, 1996)
**Who Was Leonardo da Vinci?* by Roberta Edwards (Penguin Group, 2005)
**Pasteur's Fight Against Microbes* by Beverley Birch and Christian Birmingham (Barron's Educational Series, 1996)
**Albert Einstein: Young Thinker* by Marie Hammontree (Simon & Schuster Children's Publishing, 1986)

'Star' Resource Choices (Considered to be necessary choices)

*If your child is an independent reader, choose one of the following options:

1. *Drawn into the Heart of Reading: Level 2/3* or *Level 4/5* by Carrie Austin (Heart of Dakota Publishing, 2000)
2. Your own program

*Choose one of the following English options to use with this program:

1. *Beginning Wisely: English 3* by Rod and Staff Publishers (Rod and Staff Publishers, 1991)
2. *Building with Diligence: English 4* by Rod and Staff Publishers (Rod and Staff Publishers, 1992)
3. Your own program

*Choose one of the following math options to use with this program:

1. *Singapore Primary Mathematics 2A/2B: U.S. Edition* by Singapore Ministry of Education (Times New Media, 2003)
2. *Singapore Primary Mathematics 3A/3B: U.S. Edition* by Singapore Ministry of Education (Times New Media, 2003)
3. *Singapore Primary Mathematics 4A/4B: U.S. Edition* by Singapore Ministry of Education (Times New Media, 2003)
4. Your own program

*Choose the following CD to aid in memorizing the Psalms scheduled in this guide:

1. *Lead Me to the Rock* by Kelly Crawford (Hearts for Family, 2007)

Note: Since resources sometimes go out of print or undergo changes, you may check the "Updates" portion of our website at www.heartofdakota.com for any needed replacement texts and schedules pertaining to our products.

"Learning Through History" Components

Reading About History

The "Learning Through History" part of the program is told in story form and provides a one-year overview of world history from creation to the late 1900's. Biblical stories are interwoven with other stories from world history to show that the flow of history is really one continuous story. Students will be led to see that all of history belongs to God, and is actually "His" story.

History stories are scheduled to be read aloud to the students each day using the following resources: *A Child's History of the World* by Virgil M. Hillyer, *Grandpa's Box* by Starr Meade, *Life in the Great Ice Age* by Michael and Beverly Oard, and *Hero Tales: Volume I* by Dave and Neta Jackson. These stories provide the focus for this part of the plans. If your children are able to read these stories well on their own, you may encourage them to do the readings independently. The areas that follow are linked to the daily stories:

*Day 1: questions guide reflection about the day's readings; questions range from comprehension to evaluation and are based on the levels of Bloom's Taxonomy (The level of each question is noted in parentheses.)

*Day 2: a Bible passage which connects to the history story is shared and discussed

*Day 3: oral narration is practiced by retelling the story

*Day 4: guided instruction is provided for writing a written narration

These books along with the *Preparing Hearts for His Glory* guide are sold as an **Economy Package**, or individually, at www.heartofdakota.com.

Storytime

Daily storytime sessions are linked to the "Reading About History" box of the plans by a similar historical time period. These books provide the historical backdrop for each time period, or a panoramic view of history, while the "Reading About History" readings provide a more factual view. These scheduled read-alouds are highly recommended, unless you need to economize. Complete listings and book descriptions for these books can be found in the Appendix. These books are sold as a set in the **Basic Package**, or sold individually, at www.heartofdakota.com:

- *The True Story of Noah's Ark* by Tom Dooley
- *Tirzah* by Lucille Travis
- *Classic Treasury of Aesop's Fables* by Don Daily
- *A Triumph for Flavius* by Caroline Dale Snedeker
- *Fountain of Life* by Rebecca Martin

"Learning Through History" Components
(continued)

- *Viking Quest I: Raiders of the Sea* by Lois Walfrid Johnson
- *The Door in the Wall* by Marguerite De Angeli
- *The Wonderful Winter* by Marchette Chute
- *The Family Under the Bridge* by Natalie Savage Carlson
- *Twenty and Ten* by Claire Huchet Bishop and Janet Joly

Each unit includes the following activities in coordination with the "Storytime" read-aloud assignments:

*Day 1: personal connections are shared that relate to the story
*Day 2: differences between the characters' lives and the students' lives are identified based upon the historical time period of the story
*Day 3: the main character's faith is evaluated for its impact on the character's life and the story
*Day 4: oral narration is practiced by retelling the story

Research Skills

One day in each unit requires students to use beginning research skills on a topic inspired by the history stories. Students are asked to research a specific topic using one source and orally answer one or more of the provided questions. The purpose of the research activity is to train students to use an index or a search engine, to skim to find answers, and to formulate an answer from the information they've gathered. One or more comprehensive history encyclopedias (in print form, on CD, and/or on the internet) is recommended for use with the lessons.

Vocabulary

One day in each unit includes a vocabulary activity that uses 3-5 words from the unit's history stories. The purpose of the vocabulary activities is to train students in the use of contextual clues, alphabetization, and dictionary skills. A Webster's dictionary is recommended for use with the lessons. Students need a vocabulary notebook or index cards and a card file for their words.

Geography Quick-Finds

One day in each unit includes geography quick-finds that directly relate to the history stories. Studying geography in this manner helps students recognize how geography has impacted history. Provided questions connect history with geography by directing students to find various locations from long ago on the globe, while also discussing what those locations are called

"Learning Through History" Components
(continued)

today; by tracing the routes of explorers, while also discussing the information they had about the world at that time; by identifying how countries and boundaries have changed, while also noting how nations rose and fell in power; by noticing geographical features, while also recognizing that they have remained unchanged by the passage of time; and by locating bodies of water, while also noting how important they were for travel and commerce; and so on.

The following standard geographical concepts are also reviewed on a rotating basis: continents, oceans, cardinal directions, hemispheres, latitude, longitude, zones (tropical, temperate, and arctic), and time zones. A world map or globe is needed for the geography activities.

Timeline Entry

To understand the flow of history, students keep a basic timeline of the major events studied throughout the year. Students will need 32 small index cards cut in half for their timeline. They will be making a staircase timeline, like the one shown on p. xvii of *A Child's History of the World*. Each row of cards will represent approximately one thousand years of history. Cards may **either** be taped to the back of a door **or** be taped side-by-side and accordion-folded to be stored. Plan for 4 rows of cards. The longest row will have 18 cards. Rows will need to be angled to fit properly on a door.

History Project

Three days in each unit are devoted to a meaningful, hands-on project that is designed to bring the history stories to life. Each project is scheduled to be easily completed by the student semi-independently in three short stages. Projects require little or no preparation and use materials you are likely to have on hand. Projects correlate closely with the history stories and provide an important creative outlet for students to express what they've learned. Projects range from painting cave art, to carving a clay cartouche; from creating a flip-book, to designing a denarius coin; from constructing a paper mosaic, to mixing perfume; from making a Viking brooch, to baking a medieval trencher; from designing a pendent, to etching an engraving, and much more!

Independent History Study

Daily independent history assignments are scheduled using real books that correspond with the historical time periods being studied. These books are contained in the Deluxe Package. This is an optional package, but it greatly

"Learning Through History" Components
(continued)

enhances the study of history. The Deluxe Package gives your child 12 incredible books to read independently, using the self-study plans in *Preparing Hearts for His Glory*. Reading material is meant to be easy and short enough for children to complete on their own. Complete listings and book descriptions for these books can be found in the Appendix. These books are sold as a set in the **Deluxe Package**, or individually, at www.heartofdakota.com.

Oral narration, copywork, notebook entries, and Biblical connections round out the independent readings. At this age, notebook entries are limited to copying, tracing, and drawing from a model. Accuracy and attention to authentic detail are encouraged. Entries are meant to be factual and to provide a finished product that gives an overview of the history topics studied throughout the year. Reminders are given for copywork to be done in cursive.

Students need a place to store their notebook entries. Either use a 3-ring binder with plastic page protectors or a bound sketchbook with unlined pages. Students also need a *Common Place Book* for their copywork. A *Common Place Book* is often a bound composition book with lined pages. It provides a common place to copy anything that is timeless, memorable, or worthy of rereading. It is for copying text and not for original writing. Bible verses, classic poetry, and passages from excellent literature with beautiful or vivid wording are often included. Students will add to the *Common Place Book* throughout the year.

Independent History Study for Older Students

An Extension Package Schedule in the Appendix extends the area of history to include more advanced reading material. This allows your older students to learn along with your younger students. A schedule of daily independent readings for these books is provided in the Appendix of *Preparing Hearts for His Glory*. Books are at a mid-fifth to upper seventh grade reading level. Complete listings and book descriptions for these books can be found in the Appendix. These books are sold as a set in the **Extension Package**, or individually, at www.heartofdakota.com. This package is an optional part of *Preparing Hearts for His Glory*.

"Learning The Basics" Components

Handwriting/Copywork

Daily practice of cursive handwriting is scheduled from a variety of copywork sources. By copying from a correctly written model, students gain practice in handwriting, spelling, grammar, capitalization, punctuation, and vocabulary. Copywork also prepares students to eventually write their own compositions. Work should be required to be done neatly and correctly. It is more important for students to produce careful, quality work, rather than a large quantity that is carelessly done. If your student has had no formal instruction in cursive handwriting, you may want to use one of the recommended cursive handwriting options from *Bigger Hearts for His Glory*.

Grammar, Mechanics, Usage, and Writing

Daily lessons from **either** *Beginning Wisely: English 3* **or** *Building with Diligence: English 4* focus on grammar, mechanics, and usage for the purpose of improving writing. Systematic lessons focus on one rule or concept per lesson. In order to keep the lessons short, you may want to do most of the lesson orally or on a white board, requiring only one set of practice exercises to be written by the student each day. The Teacher's Manual is considered to be necessary at this level. See the "Table of Contents" in either *Beginning Wisely: English 3* or *Building with Diligence: English 4* for a scope and sequence. Students need a lined composition book or notebook for their written work.

Dictation

Studied dictation to practice spelling skills is scheduled three days in each unit. Three different levels of dictation passages are provided in the Appendix. The dictation passages are for use with students who have mastered basic spelling words. If your student is not ready for dictation, you may want to use the spelling lists provided in the Appendix of *Beyond Little Hearts for His Glory* or *Bigger Hearts for His Glory*, or use another spelling program instead.

Special instructions for the dictation passages are included in the Appendix. The Charlotte Mason method of studied dictation is used. In this method, students study the passage prior to having it dictated. This is an important step in learning to visualize the correct spelling of words. All items in the passage must be written correctly, including punctuation marks, before going on to the next passage. Studied dictation focuses on the goal of using correct spelling within the context of writing.

"Learning The Basics" Components
(continued)

Permission is granted for you to make copies of the "Dictation Passages Key" to log your children's progress in dictation. A lined composition book is needed for dictation.

Poetry and Rhymes

A different classic poem written by Robert Louis Stevenson is introduced in each unit. Each poem was chosen for its enduring quality and its ability to withstand the test of time. Each unit includes the following poetry study activities:

*Day 1: questions and discussion related to the meaning of the poem
*Day 2: creative writing lesson based upon the poem's style, content, pattern, or poetic devices
*Day 3: personal connections with the poet and the poem
*Day 4: suggested ways to share the poem with another person
*Each 12 week term: memorization of a previously studied Robert Louis Stevenson poem of the student's choice

You are granted permission to make copies of the poems in the Appendix if needed for the lessons in this guide.

Reading

Three days in each unit recommend using *Drawn into the Heart of Reading* for literature study. This reading program is multi-level and is designed to use with any books you choose. It is available for students in levels 2-8. It is divided into nine literature units, which can be used in any order.

Drawn into the Heart of Reading is based on instructions and activities that work with any literature. It can be used with one or more students of multiple ages at the same time because it is structured around daily plans that are divided into three levels of instruction. *Drawn into the Heart of Reading* is intended for use year after year as you move students through the various levels of instruction. It is designed to teach students to evaluate characters using a Christian standard that is based on Godly traits.

In order to use *Drawn into the Heart of Reading* with your independent reader, you need the *Drawn into the Heart of Reading* Teacher's Guide and the *Level 2/3* or *Level 4/5 Student Book.* You may also choose whether to purchase these optional resources: *Level 2 Book Pack, Level 3 Book Pack,* or the *Sample Book Ideas List.* Packages for *Drawn into the Heart of Reading* are available at www.heartofdakota.com.

"Learning The Basics" Components
(continued)

Bible Study

Memory work from the book of Psalms is introduced in each unit. Students memorize entire passages from the Psalms through repetition, copywork, actions, and music. Musical selections from *Lead Me to the Rock* by Kelly Crawford correspond with the Bible memory verses in the program. Ten Psalms, taken directly from the KJV Bible, are beautifully performed with simply orchestrated music. Each unit includes the following Bible study activities:

*Day 1: discuss a portion of a Psalm using heartfelt questions that encourage students to read and reflect upon God's word (Note: The questions work best with the KJV of the Bible.)
*Day 2: identify the mood and purpose of the Psalm, and pray about the Psalm
*Day 3: have a personal quiet time filled with prayer and praise based on a portion of a Psalm
*Day 4: copy the Scripture memory selection in a *Common Place Book* (Note: See the description of a *Common Place Book* in the "Bible Study" box of the plans for Day 4 in each unit.)

Corresponding Music

Musical selections from *Lead Me to the Rock* by Kelly Crawford correspond with the Bible memory work in each unit. While this is an optional resource, this CD can be a powerful aid to your children committing large portions of Scriptures to heart.

Math Exploration

A math instruction reminder is listed in the plans daily. *Preparing Hearts for His Glory* offers a choice of *Singapore Primary Mathematics 2A, 2B, 3A, 3B, 4A,* or *4B*. Each of these choices covers one semester of instruction, so both an "A" and a "B" set are needed for a full year of math instruction. Sets include both a textbook and a workbook. Text pages for all of these options are listed in the Appendix of *Preparing Hearts for His Glory*. For further help with math placement, go to www.singaporemath.com and click "placement" for a free math placement test. If you have a different math program that you are already comfortable using, feel free to substitute it for the math portion of the plans.

“Learning The Basics” Components

(continued)

Independent Science Exploration

Daily independent science readings are scheduled using real books contained in the Science Add-On Package. Reading material is meant to be easy and short enough for children to complete on their own. Complete listings and book descriptions for these books can be found in the Appendix.

These books are sold as a set in the **Science Add-On Package**, or individually, at www.heartofdakota.com. This package includes these 9 engaging resources:

- *One Small Square: Arctic Tundra* by Donald M. Silver
- *One Small Square: Cactus Desert* by Donald M. Silver
- *The Great Dinosaur Mystery and the Bible* by Paul S. Taylor
- *Find the Constellations* by H.A. Rey
- *One Small Square: Coral Reef* by Donald M. Silver
- *Columbus* by Ingri and Edgar Parin D’Aulaire
- *Who Was Leonardo da Vinci?* by Roberta Edwards
- *Pasteur’s Fight Against Microbes* by Beverley Birch and Christian Birmingham
- *Albert Einstein: Young Thinker* by Marie Hammontree

These stories provide the focus for this part of the plans. The areas of life science, physical science, and earth science are each addressed. “Science Exploration” topics loosely correspond with the history topics being studied in the “Learning Through History” part of the plans.

While students read about the Israelites wandering in the desert in history, they will study about the desert habitat in science. When students are reading about seafaring explorers in history, they will study the coral reef in science.

As students move into the history time periods in which Columbus, daVinci, Pasteur, and Einstein lived, they will study these great men’s lives and scientific contributions in science. Studying science in this manner helps it flow with the study of history and allows for natural connections to be made between the two areas.

“Learning The Basics” Components
(continued)

Each unit includes the following science activities in coordination with the read-aloud assignments:

*Day 1: create a science notebook entry
*Day 2: practice oral narration by retelling the science story
*Day 3: write answers to five provided questions (including one Biblical application question) based on the science reading
*Day 4: conduct an experiment related to the reading and log it in a science notebook or on a copy of the “Science Lab” form found in the Appendix

The students need a place to store their notebook entries, written answers, and science experiment results. Use either a 3-ring binder with plastic page protectors or a bound sketchbook with unlined pages for the notebook assignments and science experiment results. An optional “Science Lab” form is provided in the Appendix and may be reproduced for students to log their science experiment results. Use a lined composition book or a lined notebook for the written answers on Day 3.

Learning through History
Focus: Creation to Noah

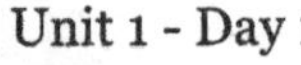
Unit 1 - Day 1

Reading about History — T

Read about history in the following resource:

★ *Grandpa's Box: Ch. 1* p. 9-14
Note to Parents: You may also wish to read p. 281-282 for more information.

After today's reading, say, *Tell me what you learned about Grandpa from today's story.* (comprehension) *Where did Grandpa get his yellow, wooden box?* (knowledge) *How does Grandpa use the yellow box?* (application) *Decide what war Grandpa could be talking about.* (evaluation) *Predict who might be the enemy Grandpa mentioned.* (synthesis)

Key Idea: Marc and Amy enjoyed visiting their Grandpa at his shop. Grandpa brought out his yellow box of carved figures. He was preparing to tell Amy and Marc some war stories.

History Project — S

In this unit you will be designing a shield of faith and your own coat of arms to place on it. From a 9 x 12 sheet of white paper, cut out a paper shield. You will use this paper shield to draw your coat of arms.

What are some symbols of faith? (i.e. cross, dove, empty tomb, crown, Easter lily, etc.) On the white paper shield that you cut out, sketch with pencil a design using symbols of faith to be your coat of arms. Do not color the design. Save the design for Day 2.

Key Idea: Grandpa was talking about a spiritual war. In a spiritual war, we need the full armor of God to protect us.

Storytime — T

Read aloud the following assigned passage:

★ Ephesians 6:10-20
Discuss today's reading in a "conversational way". Share about a person, time, event, or emotion from your life that today's passage brought to mind. Next, have your child share a connection.

Key Idea: Connect personally to the passage.

Research — S

Ephesians 6:10-17 talks about the armor of God. In verse 16, what piece of armor is mentioned? A shield often had a coat of arms on it. What is a **coat of arms**? Where could you look to discover more about a coat of arms? A dictionary will give you a definition of a coat of arms. An encyclopedia will tell you what a coat of arms is and show you a picture of it. Use a reference book or an online resource like www.wikipedia.org to look up *coat of arms*. Depending on the resource you use, you will have to type *coat of arms* in the search or look it up in the index.

Orally answer one or more of the following questions from your research: *What is a coat of arms? Which types of designs were used to make a coat of arms? What color patterns were used when making a coat of arms? Who designed the coat of arms?*

Key Idea: The shield of faith protects Christians from the arrows of the enemy. A shield's coat of arms identifies a soldier. Can people identify that you are a Christian?

Independent History Study — I

★ Read *Draw and Write Through History* p. 4-5. Follow the directions given on p. 6-7 to draw and color plants and trees on white paper. Either store completed drawings in a 3-ring binder with plastic page protectors or use a sketchbook with half blank and half lined pages.

Key Idea: The history of Earth began with creation, which shows God's mighty power.

Learning the Basics

Focus: Language Arts, Math, Bible, and Science

Unit 1 - Day 1

Poetry

T

Read aloud to the students the poem *"The Swing"* (see Appendix). Ask, *What does the poem say about swinging? Describe what the child sees as he/she swings. What feeling do the last two lines of the poem give you?* Read the poem again with the students.

Key Idea: Read and appreciate a variety of classic poetry.

Language Arts

S

Have students complete the first studied dictation exercise (see Appendix for directions and passages).

Help students complete one lesson from the following reading program:

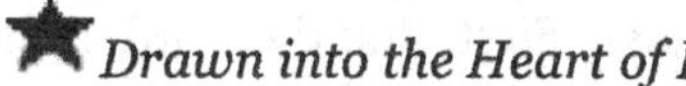

★ *Drawn into the Heart of Reading*

Work with the students to complete **one** of the English options listed below:

★ *Beginning Wisely:* Lesson 2

★ *Building with Diligence:* Lesson 1

★ Your own grammar program

Key Idea: Practice language arts skills.

Bible Study

T

Say, *Find Psalm 1:1-2 in your Bible. This is the memory selection for this unit. Read the verses out loud.* Ask, *In Psalm 1:1, what kind of man does it say is blessed? What does it mean to counsel someone? Can a good man still give ungodly counsel? Why is it important to receive counsel from those that are faithful to God? What does it mean to mock or scorn someone? How does living an ungodly life mock or scorn God? What does Psalm 1:2 say is the delight of a Godly man? How does the word of God show us His law? Explain what it means to meditate. Why is it important to meditate on God's word?* Have students say the verse 3 times, adding hand motions to help remember the words.

✔ *Lead Me to the Rock* CD
Track 4; Song: "His Delight" (vs. 1-2)

Key Idea: A Godly man is faithful and delights in studying God's word.

Math Exploration

S

Choose **one** of the math options listed below (see Appendix for details).

★ *Singapore Primary Mathematics 2A/2B, 3A/3B*, or *4A/4B*

★ Your own math program

Key Idea: Use a step-by-step math program.

Science Exploration

I

★ Read *One Small Square: Arctic Tundra* p. 3-5. Day 1 of each unit includes a science notebook assignment. Store completed notebook entries in a 3-ring binder with plastic page protectors or a bound sketchbook with unlined pages. At the top of an unlined paper, copy Genesis 8:22 in cursive. Beneath the verse, draw or trace the map from p. 48 of *One Small Square: Arctic Tundra.* Color the tundra blue. Copy the first sentence of text from p. 48 next to your picture. Look on a real globe to see where the tundra is found.

Key Idea: The arctic tundra is known for its long, cold winters and chilly summers. The tundra is located within the Arctic Circle where the Sun is farthest away from the Earth.

Learning through History
Focus: Creation to Noah

Unit 1 - Day 2

Reading about History T

Read about history in the following resource:

★ *Grandpa's Box: Ch. 2* p. 15-20

After today's reading, read aloud Romans 5:12-21. Ask, *In Romans 5:12, how does it say that sin and death entered the world? What does Romans 5:14 tell you about death and the law? In Romans 5:14, what pattern does it say Adam set that all mankind follows? Have we followed in the pattern of sinfulness? How does the law help us see our sin? Since we are all sinful, we will all die someday, but what gift does Romans 5:15 say we are given? What act of righteousness does Romans 5:18 say brought life to all men? According to Romans 5:20, can we ever be good enough to save ourselves? Then, how does Romans 5:21 say we can be saved?*

Key Idea: Grandpa pointed out to Marc and Amy that God cannot be taken by surprise. He knew Adam and Eve would sin.

History Project S

Take out the coat of arms that you saved for your shield of faith from Day 1. Choose one or two main colors to brightly color your symbols of faith. Cut out your symbols when you are finished coloring. Save the symbols for Day 3.

Key Idea: We have all sinned like Adam and Eve, so each of us can only be saved by grace through faith in Christ Jesus. Our faith in Jesus is our shield or defense against Satan.

Storytime T

Read aloud the following assigned passage:

★ Genesis 3:1-24

Ask, *In today's reading, how were people's lives different from your life? What would you have enjoyed or found difficult about living during that time?*

Key Idea: Compare and contrast the historical time period of the reading to your own life.

Vocabulary S

You will need a place to write and store your vocabulary words this year. Use either a card file with index cards and alphabetical tabs or a composition notebook with 2 pages labeled for each letter of the alphabet. You may choose 3-5 of the following vocabulary words from *Grandpa's Box* to use: *memorials* (p. 15), *warfare* (p. 16), *allies* (p. 17), *traitor* (p. 17), and/or *rebel* (p. 18). First, find the word in the text and read the sentence containing the word. Think about possible meanings. Next, find the word in a dictionary and select the correct meaning. Write the word at the top of an index card or at the top of the corresponding letter page in the notebook. Underneath the word, copy the correct definition from the dictionary. Then, use the word correctly in a sentence. The sentence may be copied from the text or be one of your own creation. Last, draw a small picture to show the word's meaning. If you used an index card to record your word, file it under the correct alphabetical tab in the file.

Key Idea: God had a plan for dealing with man's sin. He warned us there would be pain and sadness, but He also promised a Savior.

Independent History Study I

★ On white paper, follow the directions in *Draw and Write Through History* p. 8 to draw and color a dinosaur. Store your completed drawing in the place you have chosen for it.

Key Idea: When sin entered the world, death entered the world too. All of creation was affected.

Learning the Basics

Focus: Language Arts, Math, Bible, and Science

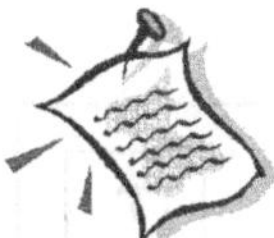

Language Arts

T

Work with the students to complete **one** of the English options listed below:

★ *Beginning Wisely:* Lesson 3

★ *Building with Diligence:* Lesson 2

★ Your own grammar program

Say, *You will be doing a writing activity based on the poem, "The Swing"* (see Appendix). Ask, *What does the child in the poem see as he's going up in the air? What does the child in the poem see as he's looking down?* At the top of a markerboard or a paper, make 2 columns: *"Going Up in the Air"* and *"Coming Down"*. Ask students to look out the window and imagine they are swinging in the yard. Ask, *What would you see on the way up in the air?* Write down the students' ideas. Repeat the activity for *"Coming Down"*.

Say, *You will use the list we made to help you rewrite lines 7, 8, 9, and 10 of "The Swing"*. Read the first 6 lines of the poem together. On paper, write, "____ and ____ and ____ and all". This will be line 7. Have students fill in the blanks with 3 things from the list that they would see on the way up. For line 8, have students write one more thing they would see. For line 9, write "Till I look down on the ____". Have students fill in the blank with something from the list that they would see on the way down. For line 10, write, "Down on ____". Have students fill in the blank with one more thing they would see on the way down.

Read the poem with the new lines. Students may copy or type the changed poem if desired.

Key Idea: Write creatively from classic poetry.

Bible Study

T

Have students say Psalm 1:1-2 using the hand motions they added on Day 1. Say, *A mood is a feeling, a sensation, or a state of mind. What is the mood of Psalm 1:1-2?* (Some examples of moods include frightened, worried, happy, peaceful, hopeful, sad, unhappy, angry, thankful, prayerful, joyful, and lonely.) Ask, *When would this Psalm help you, or when would you go to this Psalm?* (i.e. as a reminder of whom to seek counsel from, to know that we must seek God's word when making a decision, to assure us of what is right in God's eyes, to remind us of the right attitude to have as we study God's word.) Last, pray with your children that they will delight in the word of the Lord and desire His word more and more. Pray that if they need counsel they will seek out Christians and that they may enjoy God's favor.

✔ *Lead Me to the Rock* CD
Track 4; Song: "His Delight" (vs. 1-2)

Key Idea: The Psalms reflect the many emotions and moods we have. They are a wonderful place to seek counsel from the Lord.

Math Exploration

S

Choose **one** of the math options listed below (see Appendix for details).

★ *Singapore Primary Mathematics 2A/2B, 3A/3B,* or *4A/4B*

★ Your own math program

Key Idea: Use a step-by-step math program.

Science Exploration

I

★ Read *One Small Square: Arctic Tundra* p. 6-7. Orally retell or narrate to an adult the portion of text that you read today. Use the *Narration Tips* in the Appendix for help as needed.

Key Idea: In the Arctic tundra, animals and plants need special adaptations to stay alive. Even trees do not grow to their full-size on the frozen tundra.

Learning through History
Focus: Creation to Noah

Unit 1 - Day 3

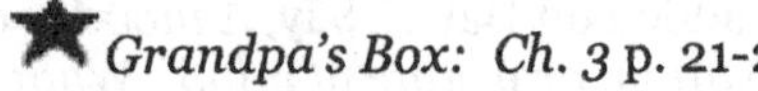

Reading about History — T

Read about history in the following resource:

★ *Grandpa's Box: Ch. 3* p. 21-26

After today's reading, have your students orally narrate or retell the portion of today's text that you read. Use the *Narration Tips* in the Appendix as needed.

Key Idea: After Cain and Abel were born, Satan used Cain's sinful nature to stir up hatred for Abel. God spoke to Cain about his anger and warned him that it could destroy him. Did Cain listen?

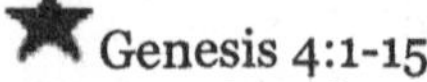

Storytime — T

Read aloud the following assigned passage:

★ Genesis 4:1-15

Ask, *In what does the main character place his faith? How would the story be different if the main character put his faith in God? Share a character, a story, or a verse from the Bible that you are reminded of by today's reading.*

Key Idea: Share a Biblical connection.

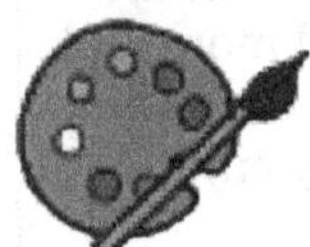

History Project — S

Get the symbols you cut out for your shield of faith on Day 2. A coat of arms often used a contrasting color for the background to make the design really stand out. To see which combinations of colors contrast the most, set out the following 6 colored sheets of paper: blue, green, red, orange, yellow, and purple. Place your symbols in the center of each sheet of paper until you narrow your choices down to the three best contrasting colors. Then, choose the colored background you like the best. Once you have selected the color for the background, cut it out in the shape of a shield. Glue on your symbols. You have created a coat of arms. Glue your coat of arms on a larger piece of paper or tagboard cut in the shape of a shield. Add a handle out of paper or tagboard to the back .

Key Idea: Cain should have listened when God warned him. Do we listen when we are wrong?

Geography — S

You will need a globe or a world map for the geography lessons this year. Each unit will feature geography quick finds and questions related to the day's history reading. One review quick find will also be included each unit for extra practice on key concepts.

Using a map or globe, have an adult help you find the location of the city where you were born. Answer the following questions: *In what state or province is the city where you were born located? In what country is it located? On what continent is it found?*

Review the following concept: *Point to and name the 7 continents.*

Key Idea: Grandpa remembered the special day when Amy and Marc's father was born. Adam and Eve must have always remembered the day their first son, Cain, was born. God knew the date and place of your birth before you were ever born.

Independent History Study — I

★ On lined paper, copy in cursive the **first** paragraph of *Draw and Write Through History* p. 12. You will copy the other two paragraphs on a different day. Store your completed copywork with your completed drawings in the place you have chosen for them.

Key Idea: God had a plan for all of creation. It did not happen accidentally. God is in control.

Learning the Basics

Focus: Language Arts, Math, Bible, and Science

Unit 1 - Day 3

Poetry

T

Read aloud with the students the poem *"The Swing"* (see Appendix). Say, *Describe a time you have been somewhere like this or felt like this. What can you learn about the poet, Robert Louis Stevenson, from the poem?* Say, *Did you know, Robert Louis Stevenson was a sickly child and often had to stay in bed? He longed to be outside, playing in the carefree way he describes in his poems.* Have the students read the poem again on their own.

Key Idea: Read and appreciate classic poetry.

Language Arts

S

Have students complete one studied dictation exercise (see Appendix for directions and passages).

Help students complete one lesson from the following reading program:

★ *Drawn into the Heart of Reading*

Work with the students to complete **one** of the English options listed below:

★ *Beginning Wisely:* Lesson 4

★ *Building with Diligence:* Lesson 3

★ Your own grammar program

Key Idea: Practice language arts skills.

Bible Study

T

Say, *You will be having your own quiet time with God today. Choose a quiet place for this special time, where you can be alone with God. Then, do the following things:*

1. Read Psalm 1:1-2 in your Bible.
2. Pray about the Psalm using the following beginning for your prayer: *Thank you for placing Godly people in my life like ___________. I know that you call men and women blessed who _________. Help me to _________.*
3. Recite Psalm 1:1-2 using the hand motions you added on Day 1.
4. Sing Psalm 1:1-2 along with the CD at the end of your quiet time.

✔ *Lead Me to the Rock* CD
Track 4; Song: "His Delight" (vs. 1-2)

Key Idea: You can have a close relationship with God when you delight in the study of His word and seek to do His will.

Math Exploration

S

Choose **one** of the math options listed below (see Appendix for details).

★ *Singapore Primary Mathematics 2A/2B, 3A/3B,* or *4A/4B*

★ Your own math program

Key Idea: Use a step-by-step math program.

Science Exploration

I

★ Read *One Small Square: Arctic Tundra* p. 8-9. Write the answer to each numbered question on lined paper. You do not need to copy the question. Use the listed page to help you answer each question.

1. What do the hares' and the birds' bodies grow to prepare them for cold weather? (p. 9)
2. How do white fur and white feathers protect the animals? (p. 9)
3. Make a sketch of a Ptarmigan's foot. (p. 8)
4. Describe what makes a ptarmigan's foot special. (p. 8)
5. What does Job 12:7-10 say you can learn from the animals, birds, and fish?

Key Idea: The arctic animals have adaptations like white fur and white feathers to camouflage them.

Learning through History
Focus: Creation to Noah

Unit 1 - Day 4

Reading about History T

Read about history in the following resource:

★ *Grandpa's Box: Ch. 4 p. 27-32*

After today's reading, say, *On Day 4 of each unit, you will be writing a narration about part of the day's history reading. In order to remember the details very well, you will need to reread the part of today's reading from the second paragraph on p. 30 to the bottom of p. 31 (on your own if possible).*

After students have finished reading the passage, ask them the questions below. If the students do not know the answers, help them find the answers in the passage they just read. Ask, *In order to make a new start, what did God send on earth? Why did God send a flood to cover the earth? What reason is given for God saving Noah? How did God save Noah and his family? In what way is Jesus like the ark? What promise did God keep through Noah?*

After the questions have been answered, have students dictate a one to three sentence narration about the main idea of the reading. Write the sentences on a markerboard or paper. Direct the students to read the sentences out loud. Ask, *Did you include* ***who*** *the reading was mainly about? Did you include* ***what*** *important thing(s) happened? Did you include* ***how*** *it ended? If not, how could you add those things?*

Then, have the students copy the sentences on paper. A bound composition notebook works well for written narrations.

Key Idea: When God sent the flood to wipe out mankind, He gave all sinners a chance to be saved. But, no one believed except Noah.

Storytime T

Read aloud the following assigned passage:

★ *The True Story of Noah's Ark* p. 4-21

Say, *Transport yourself back to the time of this story. Become one of the characters. Tell me what you see and do. (Make sure to use the word, "I", and to tell only what happened in today's reading.)*

Key Idea: Practice oral narration skills.

Timeline S

You will need 32 index cards cut in half for your timeline this year. You will be making a staircase timeline like the one shown on p. xvii of *A Child's History of the World.* Each row of cards will represent approximately one thousand years of history. You may **either** tape your cards to the back of a door to display your timeline **or** choose to tape the cards side-by-side to each other and accordion-fold them to store. Plan for 4 rows of cards. The longest row will have 18 cards. Rows will need to be angled to fit properly on a door. On your first card, draw and color a tree. Write, *Creation (approximately 4000 B.C.).* Note: If you are not of the young earth philosophy, you may wish to omit the date on the card. This may be a good time to discuss your family's view on the age of the earth.

Either tape the card to the back of a door (near the bottom of the door and on the left side) **or** store your card in a ziploc bag.

Key Idea: As time passed, man became more and more sinful, until God decided to destroy His Creation. But, God kept Noah faithful.

Independent History Study I

★ On white paper, follow the directions on p. 9-10 of *Draw and Write Through History* to draw people. Wait to color your drawing until next time. Store your drawing in the place you have chosen for it.

Key Idea: The Bible says that man is created in the image of God. That makes us very special.

Learning the Basics

Focus: Language Arts, Math, Bible, and Science

Unit 1 - Day 4

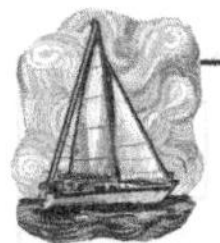

Poetry

T

Read aloud with the students the poem *"The Swing"* (see Appendix). Have students share this poem in a special way. Suggestions for sharing the poem include recording it to play for someone, reading it to someone on the telephone, photocopying the poem and adding illustrations, reading it to someone at home, putting the poem to a melody and singing it, using an instrument to tap out the meter or rhythm of the poem while reading it, or copying the poem on paper.

Key Idea: Share a variety of classic poetry.

Language Arts

S

Have students complete one dictation exercise.

Guide students to complete one reading lesson.

★ *Drawn into the Heart of Reading*

Help students complete **one** English lesson.

★ *Beginning Wisely:* Lesson 5

★ *Building with Diligence:* Lesson 4

★ Your own grammar program

Key Idea: Practice language arts skills.

Bible Study

T

Have students say Psalm 1:1-2 using the hand motions from Day 1. Have students copy in cursive Psalm 1:1-2 onto a clean page in their *Common Place Book*. Students should leave the rest of the page blank to add to next week. Note: A *Common Place Book* is often a bound composition book with lined pages. It provides a common place to copy anything that is timeless, memorable, or worthy of rereading. It is for copying text and not for original writing. Bible verses, classic poetry, and passages from excellent literature with beautiful or vivid wording are often included. Students will add to the *Common Place Book* throughout the year.

✔ *Lead Me to the Rock* CD
Track 4; Song: "His Delight" (vs. 1-2)

Key Idea: Copy in cursive a portion of a Psalm.

Math Exploration

S

Choose **one** math option listed below.

★ *Singapore Primary Mathematics 2A/2B, 3A/3B,* or *4A/4B*

★ Your own math program

Key Idea: Use a step-by-step math program.

Science Exploration

I

★ Read *One Small Square: Arctic Tundra* p. 10-11. Use the same binder or sketchbook you have chosen for science notebooking. Make a science experiment section. At the top of a blank page, write: *How do layers help to keep animals warm?* Under the question, write: *'Guess'*. Write down your guess.

Run hot water from a faucet into a cup. Place 2 coins in the hot water for 2 minutes. While the coins are heating, get out 2 ziploc bags. Place a wadded up tissue inside one bag. Leave the other bag empty. Fill a sink partway with cold water. Next, pour the hot water off of the coins. Place one coin in each bag, making sure one coin is inside the wadded up tissue. Zip both bags closed and place them in the cold water for 5 seconds. Take the bags out. Open the bags and feel each coin. What do you notice? Why would the coin without the tissue be colder? Next, on the paper write: *'Procedure'*. Draw a picture of the experiment. At the bottom of the paper, write: *'Conclusion'*. Explain what you learned from the experiment.

Key Idea: In the Arctic, animals like the musk ox and tundra birds have layers to help trap their body heat.

Learning through History
Focus: Life After the Flood

Unit 2 - Day 1

Reading about History

T

Read about history in the following resource:

★ *Life in the Great Ice Age* p. 4-9

After today's reading, ask, *How does the caveman fit in with the Bible?* (application) *Explain some of the problems that people faced after the flood.* (comprehension) *Describe how the weather changed after the flood, according to Grandpa.* (knowledge) *Why might the weather have changed?* (analysis) *What have you learned about Jabeth and his family?* (comprehension)

Key Idea: The descendents of Noah were very intelligent. Since the world had changed after the flood, it took time to adjust to the new land.

History Project

S

In this unit you will be studying warm and cool colors and using them to paint a rainbow. Red, yellow, and orange are warm colors. Green, blue, and purple are cool colors. Divide a piece of white paper in half. Label one side *warm colors*. Label the other side *cool colors*. Use a magazine to find swatches of colors that fall into the 2 categories. Cut the swatches out and glue them onto the correct side of the paper to create a warm-colored collage and a cool-colored collage. Compare the two collages. How do they each make you feel? Why might the cool colors make you feel calm, peaceful, or cool? Why might the warm colors make you feel energized, cheerful, or warm? Read the last paragraph on p. 8 of *Life in the Great Ice Age*. How is Jabeth describing the sunset?

Key Idea: We all descended from Noah.

Storytime

T

Read aloud the following assigned passage:

★ *The True Story of Noah's Ark* p. 22-37

Discuss today's reading in a "conversational way". Share about a person, time, event, or emotion from your life that today's reading brought to mind. Next, have your child share a connection.

Key Idea: Connect personally to the passage.

Research

S

The Bible tells the story of the worldwide flood in Genesis 7:1-24. Almost all cultures have some sort of **flood** story. Why do you think that is true? Since mankind was almost wiped out by the flood, except for Noah and his family, we all descended from Noah. Why do you think there are so many different versions of the "flood" story? Since these stories were passed down by word of mouth, over time this would result in variations. Where can you find an accurate retelling of the flood story? The Bible has the only accurate retelling. Read Genesis 7:1-24. Then, use a reference book or an online resource like www.wikipedia.org to find another retelling of the flood story, if possible from another culture. Depending on the resource you use, you will have to type *worldwide flood* or *Noah's ark* in the search or look it up in the index. Orally answer one or more of the following questions from your research: *Did the 2 retellings of the flood stories you read match? Explain. How does the fact that many cultures have a flood story help show that there was a worldwide flood?*

Key Idea: Most cultures have a "flood story".

Independent History Study

I

★ Take out the people you drew in Unit 1 – Day 4. Follow the example given on p. 11 of *Draw and Write Through History* to color your people. Store your completed picture in the place you have chosen for it.

Key Idea: Since people are created in God's image, we are given intelligence and the ability to reason.

Learning the Basics

Focus: Language Arts, Math, Bible, and Science

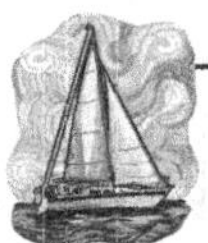

Poetry

T

Read aloud to the students the poem *"Bed in Summer"* (see Appendix). Ask, *What difference between winter and summer is the poet pointing out in the first stanza? How does the number of daylight hours change with the seasons? Why is it more difficult to go to bed in the summer than in the winter?* Read the poem again with the students.

Key Idea: Read and appreciate a variety of classic poetry.

Language Arts

S

Have students complete the first studied dictation exercise (see Appendix for directions and passages).

Help students complete one lesson from the following reading program:

 *Drawn into the Heart of Reading*

Work with the students to complete **one** of the English options listed below:

- ★ *Beginning Wisely:* Lesson 6
- ★ *Building with Diligence:* Lesson 5
- ★ Your own grammar program

Key Idea: Practice language arts skills.

Bible Study

T

Say, *Find Psalm 1:1-3 in your Bible. This is the memory selection for this unit. Read the verses out loud.* Ask, *In Psalm 1:3, to what is the man who delights in the Lord compared? What does it mean to be fruitful or to bring forth fruit? How can Christians bear good fruit in their lives? What does it mean to prosper? Is being wealthy or having a lot of money the only way to be prosperous? How can the results of our actions make us prosperous in God's eyes?*

Have students say the verse 3 times, adding hand motions to help remember the words.

 *Lead Me to the Rock* CD
Track 4; Song: "His Delight" (vs. 1-3)

Key Idea: A faithful Christian is like a tree that bears fruit over time. By delighting in the Lord and His word, we can act in a way that honors God.

Math Exploration

S

Choose **one** of the math options listed below (see Appendix for details).

 *Singapore Primary Mathematics 2A/2B, 3A/3B*, or *4A/4B*

★ Your own math program

Key Idea: Use a step-by-step math program.

Science Exploration

I

Today you will add to your science notebook. At the top of an unlined paper, copy 1 Corinthians 15:39 in cursive. Beneath the verse, draw and color **either** the circled picture of the musk ox fur from p. 11 **or** the circled picture of the bird feathers from p. 10 of *One Small Square: Arctic Tundra.* Then, copy the matching paragraph of text found under the circled picture you chose from p. 10 or 11.

Key Idea: God gave the musk ox layered fur and the birds inner and outer feathers in order to survive the cold, harsh weather in the Arctic tundra. Man, beasts, birds, and fish are each created with special features to help each of them to survive.

Learning through History

Focus: Life After the Flood

Unit 2 - Day 2

Reading about History **T**

Read about history in the following resource:

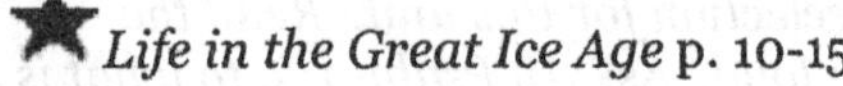

★ *Life in the Great Ice Age* p. 10-15

After today's reading, read aloud Genesis 6:5-22. Ask, *How does Genesis 6:11-12 describe man at the time of Noah? In Genesis 6:6, how does it say the Lord felt about this? What did the Lord say in Genesis 6:7? Then, what happened in Genesis 6:8? How is Noah described in Genesis 6:9? Was Noah perfect? What was God's plan in Genesis 6:13 and 6:17-18? In Genesis 6:15-16 and 6:19-21, what does God tell Noah? How did Noah respond to God in Genesis 6:22?*

Key Idea: At the time of Noah, the earth was full of violence and evil. God was grieved and planned a worldwide flood. He also planned to save Noah and his family.

History Project **S**

On white paper, paint a background for your rainbow using **either** warm colors **or** cool colors. Warm colors are red, yellow, and orange. Cool colors are blue, green, and purple. You may paint a scene or just a sky for the background. Let your background dry. Set it aside for use on Day 3.

Key Idea: When the Flood was over, God placed a rainbow in the sky as a promise that He would never again send a flood to cover the whole earth.

Storytime **T**

Read aloud the following assigned passage:

★ *The True Story of Noah's Ark* p. 38-53

Ask, *In today's reading, how were people's lives different from your life? What would you have enjoyed or found difficult about living during that time?*

Key Idea: Compare and contrast the historical time period of the reading to your own life.

Vocabulary **S**

You may choose 3-5 of the following vocabulary words from *Life in the Great Ice Age* to use for this lesson: *ancient* (p. 10), *ancestor* (p. 11), *generations* (p. 11), *barge* (p. 12), and/or *sulfur* (p. 13). First, find the word in the text and read the sentence containing the word. Think about possible meanings. Next, find the word in a dictionary and select the correct meaning. Write the word at the top of an index card or at the top of the corresponding letter page in the notebook. Underneath the word, copy the correct definition from the dictionary. Then, use the word correctly in a sentence. The sentence may either be copied from the text or be one of your own creation. Last, draw a small picture to show the word's meaning. If you used an index card to record your word, file it under the correct alphabetical tab in the card file.

Key Idea: Jabeth heard the stories of his ancestors from his Grandfather. Stories were told rather than read. This is how Jabeth learned that climate and hunting had changed.

Independent History Study **I**

★ On lined paper, copy in cursive the **second** and **third** paragraphs of *Draw and Write Through History* p. 12. Store your completed copywork with your completed drawings in the place you have chosen for them.

Key Idea: Man is special because he can reason and think. However, only Jesus can save us.

Learning the Basics
Focus: Language Arts, Math, Bible, and Science

Unit 2 - Day 2

Language Arts
T

Work with the students to complete **one** of the English options listed below:

★ *Beginning Wisely:* Lesson 7

★ *Building with Diligence:* Lesson 6

★ Your own grammar program

Say, *You will be doing a writing activity based on the poem, "Bed in Summer"* (see Appendix). Ask, *What does the child in the poem see as he's going to bed? What does the child in the poem hear as he's going to bed?* At the top of a markerboard or a paper, make 2 columns: "*See*" and "*Hear*". Ask students to look out the window and imagine they are going to bed while it is still daylight. Ask, *What would you see out your bedroom window?* Write down the students' ideas under the *"See"* column. Repeat the activity for the *"Hear"* column.

Say, *You will use the list we made to help you rewrite lines 6, 7, and 8 of "Bed in Summer".* Read the first 5 lines of the poem together. Clap out the number of syllables in each line of the poem (i.e. In/win/ter/I/get/up/at/night). Ask, *What do you notice about the number of syllables in each line?* Say, *Since there are 8 syllables in each line of the poem, we will need an 8 syllable line to replace line 6. Look at your list of things you see to help you rewrite line 6. You may also want to rhyme line 6 with line 5, since the rhyming pattern in the poem is in couplets.* Repeat the activity for lines 7-8 using the list of things students "hear". These two lines may also rhyme. Read the poem with the new lines. Students may copy or type the changed poem if desired.

Key Idea: Write creatively from classic poetry.

Bible Study
T

Have students say Psalm 1:1-3 using the hand motions they added on Day 1. Say, *A mood is a feeling, a sensation, or a state of mind. What is the mood of Psalm 1:1-3?* (Some examples of moods include frightened, worried, happy, peaceful, hopeful, sad, unhappy, angry, thankful, prayerful, joyful, and lonely.) Ask, *When would this Psalm help you, or when would you go to this Psalm?* (i.e. as a reminder of what God considers important, as an example of how to honor God with our lives, to encourage us as we wait for our actions to bear fruit.)

Last, pray with your children that they will delight in the word of the Lord and will follow it with their actions. Pray that your children's lives may bear good fruit for the Lord.

✔ *Lead Me to the Rock* CD
Track 4; Song: "His Delight" (vs. 1-3)

Key Idea: The Psalms reflect the many emotions and moods we have. They are a wonderful place to seek counsel from the Lord.

Math Exploration
S

Choose **one** of the math options listed below (see Appendix for details).

★ *Singapore Primary Mathematics 2A/2B, 3A/3B,* or *4A/4B*

★ Your own math program

Key Idea: Use a step-by-step math program.

Science Exploration
I

★ Read *One Small Square: Arctic Tundra* p. 12-13. Orally retell or narrate to an adult the portion of text that you read today. Use the *Narration Tips* in the Appendix for help as needed.

Key Idea: In the Arctic tundra, there is no daylight for half of the year. However, the Moon still reflects the Sun's light, and the aurora borealis or the "Northern Lights" light up the sky.

Learning through History
Focus: Life After the Flood

Unit 2 - Day 3

Reading about History — T

Read about history in the following resource:

★ *Life in the Great Ice Age* p. 16-19

After today's reading, have your students orally narrate or retell the portion of today's text that you read. Use the *Narration Tips* in the Appendix as needed.

Key Idea: When Jabeth's tribe met the Beetle-Brows, they weren't sure whether the tribe was friendly and trustworthy. The Beetle-Brows looked different and spoke another language.

Storytime — T

Read aloud the following assigned passage:

★ *The True Story of Noah's Ark* p. 54-71

Ask, *In what does the main character place his faith? How would the story be different if the main character put his faith in something other than in God? Share a character, a story, or a verse from the Bible that you are reminded of by today's reading.*

Key Idea: Share a Biblical connection.

History Project — S

Get out the painted background from Day 2. Set out a paintbrush, a cup of water for rinsing, a plate or palette for mixing paint, and red, yellow, and blue paint. First, on your painted background, use red paint to make a sweeping outer edge for your rainbow. Next, on your palette, dab yellow paint and add a little red to make orange. Paint an orange arc under the red one on your rainbow. Next, paint a yellow arc under the orange one on your rainbow. Now, on your palette, dab yellow paint and add a little blue to make green. Paint a green arc under the yellow one on your rainbow. Paint a blue arc under the green one on your rainbow. Now, on your palette, dab red paint and add a little blue to make violet. Leave an arc of white space beneath the blue arc and paint a violet arc beneath the white space. On your palette, add more blue paint to the violet to make indigo. Paint an indigo stripe in the white space between the blue and violet arcs.

Key Idea: Noah saw the first rainbow. When you see a rainbow, remember God's promise.

Geography — S

Use a globe for today's activities. *Demonstrate how the Earth rotates. What is the name of the imaginary line on which the Earth rotates? How many times does the Earth rotate on its axis in 24 hours? Due to the curving shape of the Earth, which parts of the Earth are farthest away from the sun? Where is the North Pole? Where is the South Pole? Why is it so cold at the poles?*

Review the following concept: *Point to and name the 7 continents.*

Key Idea: Living mainly under shelter, in a cold climate, with very little sunshine, and mostly meat for food, would affect how people looked over time. During the Ice Age, some tribes, like the fictional Beetle-Brows we read about, would have lived in this manner. It most likely changed their appearance.

Independent History Study — I

★ On white paper, follow the directions on p. 14 of *Draw and Write Through History* to draw and color Noah's ark. Store your drawing in the place you have chosen for it.

Key Idea: After the Flood, some people like Jabeth's tribe remained faithful to God, but others didn't.

Learning the Basics
Focus: Language Arts, Math, Bible, and Science

Unit 2 - Day 3

Poetry

T

Read aloud with the students the poem *"Bed in Summer"* (see Appendix). Say, *Describe a time you have felt like this. What can you learn about the poet, Robert Louis Stevenson, from the poem?* Say, *Did you know, Robert Louis Stevenson had a terrible cough as a child that kept him awake at night? Since he had a hard time falling asleep, he often wrote about things he saw outside his window.* Have the students read the poem again on their own.

Key Idea: Read and appreciate classic poetry.

Language Arts

S

Have students complete one studied dictation exercise (see Appendix for directions and passages).

Help students complete one lesson from the following reading program:

 *Drawn into the Heart of Reading*

Work with the students to complete **one** of the English options listed below:

★ *Beginning Wisely:* Lesson 8

★ *Building with Diligence:* Lesson 7

★ Your own grammar program

Key Idea: Practice language arts skills.

Bible Study

T

Say, *You will be having your own quiet time with God today. Choose a quiet place for this special time, where you can be alone with God. Then, do the following things:*

1. Read Psalm 1:1-3 in your Bible.
2. Pray about the Psalm using the following beginning for your prayer: *Thank you for bringing me close to you through __________. Help me as I'm learning __________, which is hard for me. Show me how you can use me to do your work.*
3. Recite Psalm 1:1-3 using the hand motions you added on Day 1.
4. Sing Psalm 1:1-3 along with the CD at the end of your quiet time.

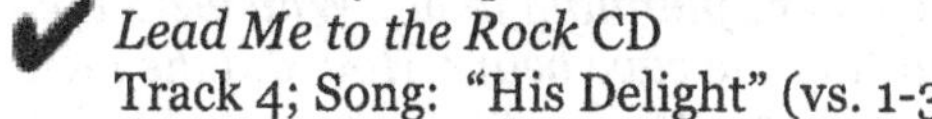

✔ *Lead Me to the Rock* CD
Track 4; Song: "His Delight" (vs. 1-3)

Key Idea: You can know God better if you read His word, pray, and seek to do His will.

Math Exploration

S

Choose **one** of the math options listed below (see Appendix for details).

★ *Singapore Primary Mathematics 2A/2B, 3A/3B,* or *4A/4B*

★ Your own math program

Key Idea: Use a step-by-step math program.

Science Exploration

I

★ Read *One Small Square: Arctic Tundra* p. 14-15. Write the answer to each numbered question on lined paper. You do not need to copy the question. Use the listed page to help you answer each question.

1. How do lemmings and voles survive in the Arctic tundra? (p. 14-15)
2. What types of predators hunt lemmings and voles? (p. 15)
3. How does the snow help the animals and plants? (p. 15)
4. Describe how the ground squirrel hibernates. (p. 15)
5. What does Psalm 104:19-22 show you about how predators must depend on God for their food?

Key Idea: Animals like the Arctic fox and the ermine are predators. They must hunt for prey in the snow.

Learning through History
Focus: Life After the Flood

Unit 2 - Day 4

Reading about History [T]

Read about history in the following resource:

★ *Life in the Great Ice Age* p. 20-23

After today's reading, say, *You will be writing a narration about part of the day's history reading. In order to remember the details very well, you will need to reread p. 20-21 (on your own if possible).*

After students have finished reading the passage, ask them the questions below. If the students do not know the answers, help them find the answers in the passage they just read. Ask, *Who is Jabeth? What mood was Jabeth in at the beginning? Why? Explain what the men were planning to do. Why were the men hunting the cave bear? How did the men prepare for the hunt? At the end of today's reading, what was the mood? Explain.*

After the questions have been answered, have students orally dictate a one to three sentence narration about the main idea of the reading. Write the sentences on a markerboard or a piece of paper. Direct the students to read the sentences out loud. Ask, *Did you include* ***who*** *the reading was mainly about? Did you include* ***what*** *important thing(s) happened? Did you include* ***how*** *it ended? If not, how could you add those things?*

Then, have the students copy the sentences on paper. Store the written narration in the place you have chosen for it.

Key Idea: Jabeth woke up eager to go on his first, dangerous hunt. The cave bear had become increasingly dangerous to the tribe. Since the Beetle-Brows were expert hunters, the tribes worked together to hunt the bear.

Storytime [T]

Read aloud the following assigned passage:

★ Genesis 9:1-17

Say, *Transport yourself back to the time of this story. Become one of the characters. Tell me what you see and do. (Make sure to use the word, "I", and to tell only what happened in today's reading.)*

Key Idea: Practice oral narration skills.

Timeline [S]

You will be adding to your staircase timeline today. On a new timeline card, draw and color an ark. Write, *The Great Flood (approximately 2300 B.C.).*

Note: If you are not of the young earth philosophy, you may wish to omit the date on the card. This may be a good time to discuss your family's view on the age of the earth.

If you decided to tape your timeline cards to the back of a door, then add *The Great Flood* card to the right of the *Creation* card from Unit 1. If you decided to tape the timeline cards side-by-side to accordion-fold them, then use clear packing tape to tape *The Great Flood* card next to the *Creation* card and accordion-fold the timeline to store it.

Key Idea: The flood changed the Earth. It was harder to survive for both animals and people. As the animals struggled to find food, they probably became more aggressive. Man and animals would now hunt one another.

Independent History Study [I]

★ On white paper, follow the directions on p. 15-16 of *Draw and Write Through History* to draw a giraffe. Wait to color your drawing until next time. Store your drawing in the place you have chosen for it.

Key Idea: When the floodwaters pushed up mountains and changed the face of the Earth, life for both man and animal changed too.

Learning the Basics

Focus: Language Arts, Math, Bible, and Science

Unit 2 - Day 4

Poetry

T

Read aloud with the students the poem *"Bed in Summer"* (see Appendix). Have students share this poem in a special way. Suggestions for sharing the poem include recording it to play for someone, reading it to someone on the telephone, photocopying the poem and adding illustrations, reading it to someone at home, putting the poem to a melody and singing it, using an instrument to tap out the meter or rhythm of the poem while reading it, or copying the poem on paper.

Key Idea: Share a variety of classic poetry.

Language Arts

S

Have students complete one dictation exercise.

Guide students to complete one reading lesson.

★ *Drawn into the Heart of Reading*

Help students complete **one** English lesson.

★ *Beginning Wisely:* Lesson 9

★ *Building with Diligence:* Lesson 8

★ Your own grammar program

Key Idea: Practice language arts skills.

Bible Study

T

Have students say Psalm 1:1-3 using the hand motions from Day 1. Have students copy in cursive Psalm 1:3 beneath last unit's Psalm 1:1-2 in their *Common Place Book.* Students should leave the rest of the page blank to add to next week. Note: A *Common Place Book* is often a bound composition book with lined pages. It provides a common place to copy anything that is timeless, memorable, or worthy of rereading. It is for copying text and not for original writing. Bible verses, classic poetry, and passages from excellent literature with beautiful or vivid wording are often included. Students will add to the *Common Place Book* throughout the year.

✔ *Lead Me to the Rock* CD
Track 4; Song: "His Delight" (vs. 1-3)

Key Idea: Copy in cursive a portion of a Psalm.

Math Exploration

S

Choose **one** math option listed below.

★ *Singapore Primary Mathematics 2A/2B, 3A/3B,* or *4A/4B*

★ Your own math program

Key Idea: Use a step-by-step math program.

Science Exploration

I

★ Read *One Small Square: Arctic Tundra* p. 16-19. Turn to the science experiment section in your science binder or sketchbook. At the top of a blank page, write: *What causes ice to melt?* Under the question, write: *'Guess'.* Write down your guess.

Get 2 ice cubes that are the same size. Place one cube back in the freezer for later. Place the other cube in a cup. It is your job to get the ice cube to melt as quickly as possible. Think of some different ways to get your ice to melt. Then, set the timer and try your ideas. When your cube is completely melted, write down how long it took. Try the experiment again with your second ice cube. See if you can change things to make your ice cube melt faster. Next, on the paper write: *'Procedure'.* Draw a picture of the experiment. At the bottom of the paper, write: *'Conclusion'.* Explain what you learned from the experiment.

Key Idea: In the Arctic, the summer Sun's heat slowly melts the ice through radiation. As the ice and snow melt, birds and caribou return to the tundra to have their babies.

Reading about History [T]

Read about history in the following resource:
★ *Life in the Great Ice Age* p. 24-27

After today's reading, ask, *How did the tribes celebrate the successful bear hunt?* (knowledge) *In what ways did the women prepare the bear meat for winter?* (comprehension) *Why was Grandfather asked to tell the story of the hunt?* (analysis) *Who was praised for the success of the hunt?* (knowledge) *Do you think all tribes praised the Lord after their hunts? Why, or why not?* (evaluation)

Key Idea: The tribes had a feast to celebrate the successful hunt. They praised God for the hunt's success. Grandfather told the story of the hunt as everyone listened.

History Project [S]

In this unit you will be making a cave art painting. Cut the front or back section out of a paper bag. This will be your cave wall. (If you do not have a paper bag, use white construction paper.) Crumple and uncrumple the paper, working it with your hands until the paper feels soft. Then, fill a bowl with several inches of water. Dip a tea bag in the water or add coffee grounds to give the water a brown color. Next, dip your paper in the water. Then, hold it gently over the bowl, letting the excess water drip back into the bowl. Last, lay your paper flat to dry. Save the paper for Day 2.

Key Idea: Cave art may have been one way of celebrating or remembering a hunt.

Storytime [T]

Read aloud the following assigned passage:
★ *Life in the Great Ice Age* p. 54-55
Discuss today's reading in a "conversational way". Share about a person, time, event, or emotion from your life that today's passage brought to mind. Next, have your child share a connection.

Key Idea: Connect personally to the passage.

Research [S]

Life in the Great Ice Age discusses cave art on p. 54. What is **cave art**? Do the paintings on p. 54 look like they were painted by men who were very simple-minded? How can you tell that the painters were talented? Where could you look to discover more about cave art? Use another reference book or an online resource like www.wikipedia.org to view other examples of cave art. Depending on the resource you use, you will have to type *cave painting* or *cave art* in the search or look it up in the index.

Orally answer one or more of the following questions from your research: *What colors were used in cave art paintings? Name some animals usually shown in cave art. Where have cave art paintings been found? Why would it take skill and intelligence to create cave art?*

Key Idea: Cave paintings have been found in many places in the world. The paintings are often of animals that were hunted at that time. We can wonder and learn about people's lives as we study their cave art.

Independent History Study [I]

★ Take out the giraffe you drew in Unit 2 – Day 4. Follow the example given on p. 16 of *Draw and Write Through History* to color your giraffe. Store your completed picture in the place you have chosen for it.

Key Idea: After the flood, people and animals slowly spread out across the whole Earth.

Learning the Basics

Focus: Language Arts, Math, Bible, and Science

Poetry

T

Read aloud to the students the poem *"Rain"* (see Appendix). Ask, *What pictures did the poem paint in your mind? How did the poem make you think differently about rain?* Say, *Read the first line and clap out the syllables* (i.e. The/rain/is/rain/ing/all/a/round). Write the number of syllables at the end of the first line (8). Repeat the activity with the next 3 lines of the poem to see a pattern emerge (8,6,8,6). This is called the meter of the poem. Read the poem again with the students.

Key Idea: Read and appreciate a variety of classic poetry.

Language Arts

S

Have students complete the first studied dictation exercise (see Appendix for directions and passages).

Help students complete one lesson from the following reading program:

★ *Drawn into the Heart of Reading*

Work with the students to complete **one** of the English options listed below:

★ *Beginning Wisely:* Lesson 10

★ *Building with Diligence:* Lesson 9

★ Your own grammar program

Key Idea: Practice language arts skills.

Bible Study

T

Say, *Find Psalm 1:1-4 in your Bible. This is the memory selection for this unit. Read the verses out loud.* Ask, *What are the ungodly compared to in Psalm 1:4? When grain was harvested, the chaff (or the outer shell), was removed by crushing the grain and throwing it into the air. The chaff blew away, while the grain fell to the Earth. How is an ungodly person like chaff? Why is it wrong to be drifting through life without any real direction or faith in God? How can you guard against becoming like chaff? Where should your direction come from?*

Have students say the verse 3 times, adding hand motions to help remember the words.

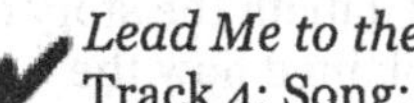

✔ *Lead Me to the Rock* CD
Track 4; Song: "His Delight" (vs. 1-4)

Key Idea: It is important for us to go to God and His word for direction so that we can live purposefully for the Lord each day.

Math Exploration

S

Choose **one** of the math options listed below (see Appendix for details).

★ *Singapore Primary Mathematics 2A/2B, 3A/3B*, or *4A/4B*

★ Your own math program

Key Idea: Use a step-by-step math program.

Science Exploration

I

★ Read *One Small Square: Arctic Tundra* p. 21-23. Today you will add to your science notebook. At the top of an unlined paper, copy Isaiah 40:8 in cursive. Beneath the verse, draw and color the circled picture of the thawed soil and the permafrost from p. 22 of *One Small Square: Arctic Tundra*. Then, copy the matching paragraph of text found under the circled picture on p. 22. Next, draw and color the circled picture showing the tree line from p. 6 of *One Small Square: Artic Tundra*. Then, copy the matching paragraph of text found under the circled picture on p. 6.

Key Idea: Even in the summer months, the ground stays muddy in the Arctic tundra. This is due to the permafrost under the ground that remains permanently frozen. Water can't soak deeply into the ground.

Reading about History T

Read about history in the following resource:

★ *Life in the Great Ice Age* p. 28-31

After today's reading, read aloud Genesis 9:1. Ask, *What does God tell Noah and his sons to do in Genesis 9:1?* Read aloud Genesis 9:18-19. Ask, *How do we know that all people across the earth came from Noah's sons? Did they scatter across the earth?* Read Genesis 11:1-4. Ask, *Why did the people wish to build a tower? How was this going against God's command?* Read Genesis 11:8-9. Ask, *What did God do in Genesis 11:8-9 so that the people acted according to His plan? Are God's plans always carried out? Explain.*

Key Idea: Grandfather told Jabeth the story of the Tower of Babel. He explained how the tribes scattered in search of new lands.

History Project S

Take out the paper that you saved to be your cave wall from Day 1. You will be painting a wild bull and a mammoth on your 'cave wall'. Today, you will only paint the bull. Save room on your 'wall' to add the mammoth. Choose one of the paintings shown on p. 11, 24, or 54 of *Life in the Great Ice Age* to help you as you paint your wild bull. First, lightly sketch the outline of the bull in pencil. Then, use a permanent black marker or black paint to outline your sketch. Last, use brown and black paint to finish your bull. Lay your painting flat to dry. You will add the mammoth on Day 3.

Key Idea: Many tribes moved with the herds of animals until the tribe found a place to settle.

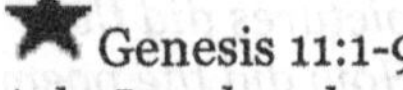

Storytime T

Read aloud the following assigned passage:

★ Genesis 11:1-9

Ask, *In what does the main character place his faith? How would the story be different if the main character put his faith in God? Share a character, a story, or a verse from the Bible that you are reminded of by today's reading.*

Key Idea: Share a Biblical connection.

Vocabulary S

You may choose 3-5 of the following vocabulary words from *Life in the Great Ice Age* to use for this lesson: *sought* (p. 28), *stalking* (p. 30), *hulking* (p. 30), *imbedded* (p. 30), and/or *North Star* (p. 30). First, find the word in the text and read the sentence containing the word. Think about possible meanings. Next, find the word in a dictionary and select the correct meaning. Write the word at the top of an index card or at the top of the corresponding letter page in the notebook. Underneath the word, copy the correct definition from the dictionary. Then, use the word correctly in a sentence. The sentence may either be copied from the text or be one of your own creation. Last, draw a small picture to show the word's meaning. If you used an index card to record your word, file it under the correct alphabetical tab in the card file.

Key Idea: Grandfather told Jabeth about mountains that spit out fire and smoke, and ash that covered the sun. He told Jabeth about the Great Wall of Ice. The Bible tells stories of the upheaval on the earth after the Flood.

Independent History Study I

★ On lined paper, copy in cursive the **first** paragraph of *Draw and Write Through History* p. 18. Store your completed copywork with your completed drawings in the place you have chosen for them.

Key Idea: The worldwide Flood was God's punishment for man's disobedience, violence, and wickedness. God spared Noah and his family, because Noah was righteous, and Noah found grace in the Lord's eyes.

Learning the Basics

Focus: Language Arts, Math, Bible, and Science

Unit 3 - Day 2

Language Arts

T

Work with the students to complete **one** of the English options listed below:

★ *Beginning Wisely:* Lesson 11

★ *Building with Diligence:* Lesson 10

★ Your own grammar program

Say, *You will be doing a writing activity based on the poem, "Rain"* (see Appendix). At the top of a markerboard or a paper, make 2 columns: "*Rain*" and "*Snow*". Ask, *What things does the child in the poem imagine rain falling upon?* Write students' responses under the "Rain" column. Ask, *What might you imagine snow falling upon?* Write student responses under the "Snow" column.

Say, *You will use the list we just made to help you write a poem about snow.* On paper, write the following 4 lines, one under the other:

The snow is ____ all around.
It falls on ____ and ____.
It snows on the ____ here
And on the ____ ____ ____.

Have students use their list of ideas in the "Snow" column to help them complete the poem. Use the following hints as needed: Students will need an action verb for line 1. Two nouns are needed for line 2. Line 3 needs a noun naming something located nearby. Line 4 needs a noun naming something far away. Students may follow the meter of the "Rain" poem if they desire (8,6,8,6).

Students may also copy or type the changed poem if desired.

Key Idea: Write creatively from classic poetry.

Bible Study

T

Have students say Psalm 1:1-4 using the hand motions they added on Day 1. Say, *A mood is a feeling, a sensation, or a state of mind. What is the mood of Psalm 1:1-4?* (Some examples of moods include frightened, worried, happy, peaceful, hopeful, sad, unhappy, angry, thankful, prayerful, joyful, and lonely.) Ask, *When would this Psalm help you, or when would you go to this Psalm?* (i.e. as a reminder that we need to get our direction from God and His word, as a warning about how God views the ungodly, as a help to stand firmly for what we believe .)

Last, pray with your children that they will not be easily swayed by unbelievers. Pray that your children's lives may show their faith in God, and that they will remain anchored in His word.

✔ *Lead Me to the Rock* CD
Track 4; Song: "His Delight" (vs. 1-4)

Key Idea: The Psalms reflect the many emotions and moods we have. They are a wonderful place to seek counsel from the Lord.

Math Exploration

S

Choose **one** of the math options listed below (see Appendix for details).

★ *Singapore Primary Mathematics 2A/2B, 3A/3B,* or *4A/4B*

★ Your own math program

Key Idea: Use a step-by-step math program.

Science Exploration

I

★ Read *One Small Square: Arctic Tundra* p. 24-25. Orally retell or narrate to an adult the portion of text that you read today. Use the *Narration Tips* in the Appendix for help as needed.

Key Idea: Plants in the Arctic tundra grow very slowly. They hug the ground and grow in bunches to conserve heat. Insects bask in the sunniest spots to keep warm.

Learning through History
Focus: People Spread Out

Unit 3 - Day 3

Reading about History — T

Read about history in the following resource:

★ *Life in the Great Ice Age* p. 32-35

After today's reading, have your students orally narrate or retell the portion of today's text that you read. Use the *Narration Tips* in the Appendix as needed.

Key Idea: When a herd of woolly mammoths was seen, plans for the hunt began. The hunt had to be carefully planned in order to protect the hunters from being hurt. Jabeth's tribe needed the mammoth meat for survival.

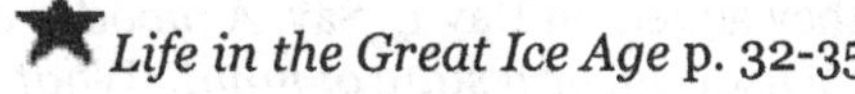

Storytime — T

Read aloud the following assigned passage:

★ *Life in the Great Ice Age* p. 56-57

Ask, *In today's reading, how were people's lives different from your life? What would you have enjoyed or found difficult about living during that time?*

Key Idea: Compare and contrast the historical time period of the reading to your own life.

History Project — S

Take out your cave painting of the wild bull from Day 2. Today, you will be adding a mammoth to your cave painting. Look at the pictures of the mammoths shown on p. 33, 35, and 37 of *Life in the Great Ice Age* to help you as you paint your mammoth. First, lightly sketch the outline of the mammoth in pencil on your 'cave wall'. Then, use a permanent black marker or black paint to outline your sketch. Last, use brown and black paint to finish your mammoth. Lay your painting flat to dry.

Key Idea: As colder weather approached, Jabeth's tribe hunted woolly mammoths. They needed larger animals for food during the long, cold winter when hunting would be scarce. The cold temperatures would freeze the mammoth meat and keep it from spoiling, so Jabeth's tribe would have enough food for winter.

Geography — S

Use a globe for today's activities. *Point to where the Earth's axis is found. Remember the axis is an imaginary line that runs through the earth from the North Pole to the South Pole. The Earth turns slowly on its axis once every 24 hours. What is the name of the imaginary line that runs around the center of the Earth? Run your finger along the Equator. Why is it so hot along the Equator? Remember, since the Earth curves outward at the Equator that this part of the Earth is closer to the sun, making it much hotter.*

Review the following concept: *Point to and name the 7 continents.*

Key Idea: Jabeth's tribe was preparing for the cold winter. During the winter, the Earth is tilted away from the sun, making the climate much colder.

Independent History Study — I

★ On lined paper, copy in cursive the **second** paragraph of *Draw and Write Through History* p. 18. Store your completed copywork with your completed drawings in the place you have chosen for them.

Key Idea: The Flood caused the climate to change all over the Earth. It could have caused the Ice Age.

Learning the Basics
Focus: Language Arts, Math, Bible, and Science

Unit 3 - Day 3

Poetry

T

Read aloud with the students the poem *"Rain"* (see Appendix). Say, *Describe a time you were caught in a rain shower. What can you learn about the poet, Robert Louis Stevenson, from the poem?* Say, *Did you know, Robert Louis Stevenson's father (and grandfather) built lighthouses? Robert sometimes went with his father to inspect them. You'll notice he often mentions ships and the sea in his poems.* Have the students read the poem again on their own.

Key Idea: Read and appreciate classic poetry.

Language Arts

S

Have students complete one studied dictation exercise (see Appendix for directions and passages).

Help students complete one lesson from the following reading program:

★ *Drawn into the Heart of Reading*

Work with the students to complete **one** of the English options listed below:

★ *Beginning Wisely:* Lesson 12

★ *Building with Diligence:* Lesson 11

★ Your own grammar program

Key Idea: Practice language arts skills.

Bible Study

T

Say, *You will be having your own quiet time with God today. Choose a quiet place for this special time, where you can be alone with God. Then, do the following things:*

1. Read Psalm 1:1-4 in your Bible.
2. Pray about the Psalm using the following beginning for your prayer: *Thank you for always being here for me when I ________. Please help me to stay faithful to you by ________. Help me to surround myself with others who are faithful to you.*
3. Recite Psalm 1:1-4 using the hand motions you added on Day 1.
4. Sing Psalm 1:1-4 along with the CD at the end of your quiet time.

✔ *Lead Me to the Rock* CD
Track 4; Song: "His Delight" (vs. 1-4)

Key Idea: It is important to surround yourself with Christians who are also seeking God's will.

Math Exploration

S

Choose **one** of the math options listed below (see Appendix for details).

★ *Singapore Primary Mathematics 2A/2B, 3A/3B,* or *4A/4B*

★ Your own math program

Key Idea: Use a step-by-step math program.

Science Exploration

I

★ Read *One Small Square: Arctic Tundra* p. 26-29. Write the answer to each numbered question on lined paper. You do not need to copy the question. Use the listed page to help you answer each question.

1. Why do animals come to the Arctic tundra for the summer? (p. 26)
2. During which months does the tundra have no night? (p. 28)
3. What is one problem that all mammals and birds have on the Arctic tundra? (p. 29)
4. Draw the life cycle of an adult snow mosquito. (p. 29)
5. What does Job 12:7-10 say the beasts, fish, fowl, and Earth can teach us about God?

Key Idea: Animals come to the tundra for the plentiful food, long days, places to nest, and fewer enemies.

Reading about History [T]

Read about history in the following resource:

★ *Life in the Great Ice Age* p. 36-39

After today's reading, say, *You will be writing a narration about part of the day's history reading. In order to remember the details very well, you will need to reread the part of today's reading from the second paragraph on p. 36 to the bottom of p. 36 (on your own if possible).*

After students have finished reading the passage, ask them the questions below. If the students do not know the answers, help them find the answers in the passage they just read. Ask, *Who was going to paint a picture of the hunt? Why did Soren want to paint a picture of the mammoth hunt? Who offered to show Soren a place for the painting? Where did the boys take Soren? Which color of paint did Soren say was special? Why was it special? Describe how Soren made the mammoth painting.*

After the questions have been answered, have students orally dictate a three to five sentence narration about the main idea of the reading. Write the sentences on a markerboard or a piece of paper. Direct the students to read the sentences out loud. Ask, *Did you include **who** the reading was mainly about? Did you include **what** important thing(s) happened? Did you include **how** it ended? If not, how could you add those things?*

Then, have the students copy the sentences on paper. Store the written narration in the place you have chosen for it.

Key Idea: Soren was a gifted artist. He signed the painting with his handprint.

Storytime [T]

Read aloud the following assigned passage:

★ *Life in the Great Ice Age* bottom of p. 51-53

Say, *Transport yourself back to the time of this story. Pretend you lived at this time. Tell me what you see and do. (Make sure to use the word, "I", and to tell only what was described in today's reading.)*

Key Idea: Practice oral narration skills.

Timeline [S]

You will be adding to your staircase timeline today. On a new timeline card, draw and color the Tower of Babel. Write, *The Tower of Babel.*

Note: We will not place a date on this card, as the Bible does not provide enough information to place an accurate date on this event.

If you decided to tape your timeline cards to the back of a door, then add *The Tower of Babel* card to the right of *The Great Flood* card from Unit 2. If you decided to tape the timeline cards side-by-side to accordion-fold them, then use clear packing tape to tape *The Tower of Babel* card next to the *The Great Flood* card and accordion-fold the timeline to store it.

Key Idea: The people spread out across the Earth from the Tower of Babel. Some tribes lived in caves to protect themselves from the cold climate. Life was hard for these people, yet they were able to survive with God's help.

Independent History Study [I]

★ On white paper, follow the directions on p. 17 of *Draw and Write Through History* to draw and color a woolly mammoth. Store your drawing in the place you have chosen for it.

Key Idea: Soren painted a woolly mammoth on the cave wall to remind the tribe of God's blessings.

Learning the Basics
Focus: Language Arts, Math, Bible, and Science

Unit 3 - Day 4

Poetry

T

Read aloud with the students the poem *"Rain"* (see Appendix). Have students share this poem in a special way. Suggestions for sharing the poem include recording it to play for someone, reading it to someone on the telephone, photocopying the poem and adding illustrations, reading it to someone at home, putting the poem to a melody and singing it, using an instrument to tap out the meter or rhythm of the poem while reading it, or copying the poem on paper.

Key Idea: Share a variety of classic poetry.

Bible Study

T

Have students say Psalm 1:1-4 using the hand motions from Day 1. Have students copy in cursive Psalm 1:4 beneath last unit's Psalm 1:1-3 in their *Common Place Book*. Students should leave the rest of the page blank to add to next week. Note: A *Common Place Book* is often a bound composition book with lined pages. It provides a common place to copy anything that is timeless, memorable, or worthy of rereading. It is for copying text and not for original writing. Bible verses, classic poetry, and passages from excellent literature with beautiful or vivid wording are often included. Students will add to the *Common Place Book* throughout the year.

✔ *Lead Me to the Rock* CD
Track 4; Song: "His Delight" (vs. 1-4)

Key Idea: Copy in cursive a portion of a Psalm.

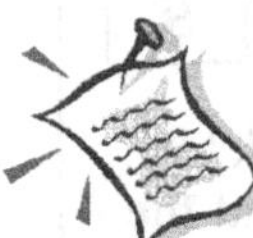

Language Arts

S

Have students complete one dictation exercise.

Guide students to complete one reading lesson.

★ *Drawn into the Heart of Reading*

Help students complete **one** English lesson.

★ *Beginning Wisely:* Lesson 13

★ *Building with Diligence:* Lesson 12

★ Your own grammar program

Key Idea: Practice language arts skills.

Math Exploration

S

Choose **one** math option listed below.

★ *Singapore Primary Mathematics 2A/2B, 3A/3B,* or *4A/4B*

★ Your own math program

Key Idea: Use a step-by-step math program.

Science Exploration

I

★ Read *One Small Square: Arctic Tundra* p. 30-35. Turn to the science experiment section in your science binder or sketchbook. At the top of a blank page, write: *How do caterpillars and insects keep from freezing to death during the winter?* Under the question, write: *'Guess'.* Write down your guess. Get an empty ice cube tray. Pour an equal amount of water into 3 compartments. Stir ½ teaspoon salt into one compartment. Label the outside of that compartment with masking tape that says, *salt.* Next, stir ½ teaspoon sugar into a different compartment. Label the outside of that compartment with masking tape that says, *sugar.* Place the tray in the freezer. After 15 minutes, poke a toothpick into each compartment. What do you notice? Check every 15 minutes for 1 hour. Next, on the paper write: *'Procedure'.* Draw a picture of the experiment. At the bottom of the paper, write: *'Conclusion'.* Explain what you learned.

Key Idea: The salt in the water works like antifreeze, because it lowers the temperature at which the water freezes. In the Arctic tundra, caterpillars and insects make chemicals in their bodies that act like antifreeze to keep them from freezing to death during the winter months.

Learning through History
Focus: The Climate Changes

Unit 4 - Day 1

Reading about History [T]

Read about history in the following resource:

★ *Life in the Great Ice Age* p. 40-43

After today's reading, ask, *How are the Beetle-Brow people different from Jabeth's tribe?* (comprehension) *Why is Grandfather able to translate or understand what Ungar is saying?* (analysis) *Describe some of the new things the Beetle-Brows have seen.* (knowledge) *Can you explain why the hunting seems to be getting more difficult?* (analysis) *Do you think the Beetle-Brows will stay with Jabeth's tribe? Explain.* (evaluation)

Key Idea: Ungar told about the Beetle-Brows' travels when they saw a great salty lake and hunted strange new animals. Later, they traveled back toward the Great Wall of Ice.

History Project [S]

In this unit you will be creating a map of the area where Noah's Ark landed and the Tower of Babel was most likely located. Place a ½-inch thick layer of clay on the bottom of a container that has an airtight lid. Use the tip of a pencil or the end of a paperclip to carve out the rivers and seas shown on p. 17 of *A Child's History of the World*. Place the airtight lid on the container and save it for Day 2.

Key Idea: Since all people are descended from Noah, it would take time after the flood for people to spread out and fill the earth. Genesis 10 lists the clans of Noah's sons, from which all nations come.

Storytime [T]

Read aloud the following assigned passage:

★ *Life in the Great Ice Age* p. 50-middle p. 51

Discuss today's reading in a "conversational way". Share about a person, time, event, or emotion from your life that today's passage brought to mind. Next, have your child share a connection.

Key Idea: Connect personally to the passage.

Research [S]

What is an ice age? Where could you look to discover more about the **Ice Age**? Look at the map on p. 62-63 of *Life in the Great Ice Age*. Compare the map to a globe to see where the Ice Age glaciers were found. Was the area where you live covered by glaciers at one time? Read the first paragraph under the heading *Cause of the Ice Age* on p. 62 of *Life in the Great Ice Age*. What explanation is given for the cause of the Ice Age? Do you think scientists agree on when and how the Ice Age occurred on Earth? Why not? Read from the paragraph at the top of the right side of p. 63 – the first column on p. 64 in *Life in the Great Ice Age*. What other possible explanations are there for the Ice Age? In light of the Bible, which idea makes the most sense to you?

Key Idea: As people spread across the Earth, the climate was ever-changing. After the Flood, Earth would have been in upheaval for quite some time. Volcanoes erupted, earthquakes shook the Earth, and ash blotted out the Sun. Life during the Ice Age would have been difficult for both man and animals.

Independent History Study [I]

★ On white paper, follow the directions on p. 20 of *Draw and Write Through History* to draw the Tower of Babel. Wait to color your drawing until next time. Store your drawing in the place you have chosen for it.

Key Idea: When God confused the languages at Babel, the people spread out across the Earth.

Learning the Basics

Focus: Language Arts, Math, Bible, and Science

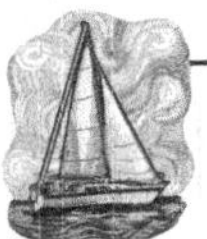

Poetry

T

Read aloud to the students the poem *"To Any Reader"* (see Appendix). Ask, *What was the poet probably remembering from his own childhood as he wrote this poem? Why won't the child in the poem hear you? What do the last 2 lines of the poem mean? How will you be like the child in the poem someday?* Read the poem again with the students.

Key Idea: Read and appreciate a variety of classic poetry.

Language Arts

S

Have students complete the first studied dictation exercise (see Appendix for directions and passages).

Help students complete one lesson from the following reading program:

 *Drawn into the Heart of Reading*

Work with the students to complete **one** of the English options listed below:

 *Beginning Wisely:* Lesson 14

 *Building with Diligence:* Lesson 13

 Your own grammar program

Key Idea: Practice language arts skills.

Bible Study

T

Say, *Find Psalm 1:1-6 in your Bible. This is the memory selection for this unit. Read the verses out loud.* Ask, *In Psalm 1:5, what does it say about the ungodly? When the final judgment day comes, why will the sinners not be in the congregation of the righteous? Since we are all sinners, how can we be righteous in God's eyes? Why do we need Jesus as our Savior? Even though God has permitted the ungodly to prosper on Earth for a time, what does Psalm 1:6 say will happen to the ungodly? How does what we do in this life affect where we will spend eternity?*

Have students say the verse 3 times, adding hand motions to help remember the words.

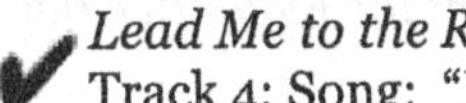

Lead Me to the Rock CD
Track 4; Song: "His Delight" (vs. 1-6)

Key Idea: It is important to study God's word and to heed the warnings that He gives us about ungodly behavior.

Math Exploration

S

Choose **one** of the math options listed below (see Appendix for details).

 *Singapore Primary Mathematics 2A/2B, 3A/3B,* or *4A/4B*

 Your own math program

Key Idea: Use a step-by-step math program.

Science Exploration

I

Read *One Small Square: Arctic Tundra* p. 36-37. Today you will add to your science notebook. At the top of an unlined paper, copy Revelation 4:11 in cursive. Beneath the verse, write, *Classifying Living Things*. Make 5 columns and label them from left to right: *Vertebrates (with backbones), Invertebrates (without backbones), Monera and Protists (single-celled organisms), Fungus,* and *Plants*. In the column labeled "Vertebrates", draw and label one mammal, one bird, one fish, and one amphibian from p. 40-41 of *One Small Square: Arctic Tundra*. Under the remaining 4 columns, draw and label one plant or animal to match each column's heading from p. 42-43 of *One Small Square: Arctic Tundra*.

Key Idea: God created plants and animals that can survive in the cold, harsh climate of the Arctic tundra.

Learning through History
Focus: The Climate Changes

Reading about History [T]

Read about history in the following resource:

★ *Life in the Great Ice Age* p. 44-49

After today's reading, read aloud Genesis 1:27. Ask, *How do we know that man was created to be able to think, to reason, and to have morals and values? Does this sound like the cave man that is pictured in many history books? What is the difference?* Read aloud Genesis 1:28. Ask, *How do we know that man did not come from beasts* (i.e. like apes eventually turning into people)? Read Genesis 1:29-30. Ask, *What does it say that man and beasts were given to eat?* Read aloud Genesis 9:2-3. Ask, *What changed after the Flood? Why was it alright to hunt for food after the Flood?*

Key Idea: Grandfather told Jabeth about the changes in the climate. The summers were getting hotter, and the winters were growing colder.

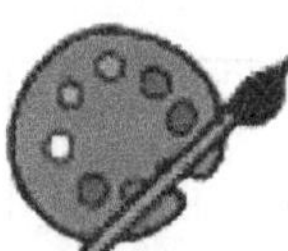

History Project [S]

Take out the clay map in the airtight container from Day 1. Make paper labels with the names of the locations shown on the map on p. 17 of *A Child's History of the World*. Attach the labels to toothpicks to make flags. Stick each flag in its correct location on your clay map. Place the airtight lid on your container and save it for Day 3.

Key Idea: The Beetle-Brows liked to hunt. They were going to a place where the hunting was better and the winters weren't as cold.

Storytime [T]

Read aloud the following assigned passage:

★ *Life in the Great Ice Age* p. 66-top of p. 67

Ask, *In today's reading, how were people's lives different from your life? What would you have enjoyed or found difficult about living during that time?*

Key Idea: Compare and contrast the historical time period of the reading to your own life.

Vocabulary [S]

You may choose 3-5 of the following vocabulary words from *Life in the Great Ice Age* to use for this lesson: *firebreak* (p. 44), *turmoil* (p. 45), *mammoth* (p. 46), *bogs* (p. 47), and/or *clan* (p. 48). First, find the word in the text and read the sentence containing the word. Think about possible meanings. Next, find the word in a dictionary and select the correct meaning. Write the word at the top of an index card or at the top of the corresponding letter page in the notebook. Underneath the word, copy the correct definition from the dictionary. Then, use the word correctly in a sentence. The sentence may either be copied from the text or be one of your own creation. Last, draw a small picture to show the word's meaning. If you used an index card to record your word, file it under the correct alphabetical tab in the card file.

Key Idea: Grandfather told Jabeth that dust storms and flooding were becoming common. Jabeth wondered whether there would be enough large animals left for him to hunt when he grew older. Today, mammoths are extinct.

Independent History Study [I]

★ Take out the Tower of Babel that you drew on Day 1. Follow the example given on p. 19 and the directions given in step 7 on p. 21 of *Draw and Write Through History* to color the tower. Store your completed picture in the place you have chosen for it.

Key Idea: As tribes left the Tower of Babel, some hunted, some farmed, and some became war-like.

Learning the Basics

Focus: Language Arts, Math, Bible, and Science

Unit 4 - Day 2

Language Arts

T

Work with the students to complete **one** of the English options listed below:

 *Beginning Wisely:* Lesson 15

★ *Building with Diligence:* Lesson 14 (half)

★ Your own grammar program

Say, *You will be doing a writing activity based on the poem, "To Any Reader"* (see Appendix).

Say, *Imagery means using words that paint a picture or an image in the reader's mind. What are some of the lines in the poem that paint a picture in your mind?* Write student responses on a markerboard or a piece of paper. It will be helpful if you have students share their favorite lines in the order that they appear in the poem or if you number the lines in sequence after the students have shared.

Say, *Use the phrases that we listed to write your own retelling of the poem. You may write your retelling as a poem, or as a one or two paragraph summary. Add some of your own words or phrases to the retelling to reflect your own style of writing.*

Have students share their completed poem or summary by reading it aloud.

Key Idea: Write creatively from classic poetry.

Bible Study

T

Have students say Psalm 1:1-6 using the hand motions they added on Day 1. Say, *A mood is a feeling, a sensation, or a state of mind. What is the mood of Psalm 1:1-6?* (Some examples of moods include frightened, worried, happy, peaceful, hopeful, sad, unhappy, angry, thankful, prayerful, joyful, and lonely.) Ask, *When would this Psalm help you, or when would you go to this Psalm?* (i.e. as a reminder that God despises wicked behavior, as a comfort that the Lord is watching over us, as an explanation of what will happen to the ungodly one day.)

Last, pray with your children that their actions and attitudes will honor God. Pray that they will stay away from wickedness and will use God's word as a guide for how to live their lives.

✔ *Lead Me to the Rock* CD
Track 4; Song: "His Delight" (vs. 1-6)

Key Idea: The Psalms reflect the many emotions and moods we have. They are a wonderful place to seek counsel from the Lord.

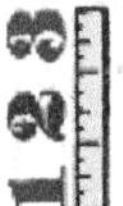

Math Exploration

S

Choose **one** of the math options listed below (see Appendix for details).

 *Singapore Primary Mathematics 2A/2B, 3A/3B,* or *4A/4B*

 Your own math program

Key Idea: Use a step-by-step math program.

Science Exploration

I

★ Read *One Small Square: Arctic Tundra* p. 38-43. Orally retell or narrate to an adult the portion of text that you read today. Use the *Narration Tips* in the Appendix for help as needed.

Key Idea: The Arctic tundra can be found in Canada, Alaska, and Siberia. Mammals and birds can make their own body heat, which keeps them active even in freezing cold weather. Fish, amphibians, and insects cannot make their own body heat.

Learning through History
Focus: The Climate Changes

Unit 4 - Day 3

Reading about History T

Read about history in the following resource:

★ *A Child's History of the World: Ch. 4* p. ~~16-19~~ 22-26

After today's reading, have your students orally narrate or retell the portion of today's text that you read. Use the *Narration Tips* in the Appendix as needed.

Key Idea: Each group of people had their own language, culture, and foods. They traded with one another, and over time they spread out farther and farther across the earth.

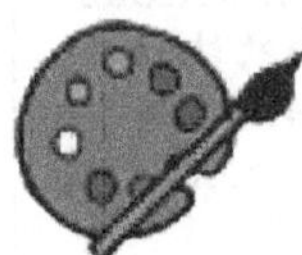

History Project S

Get the clay map in the container from Day 2. Add a small amount of water to your clay map to fill the seas and the rivers. Refer to the map on p. 17 of *A Child's History of the World* to remind you which areas should be filled with water. Place ice cubes above and to the left of the Black Sea and the Mediterranean Sea to be the Wall of Ice. Place a small strip of ice between the Caspian Sea and the Black Sea. Look at the map on p. 58 of *Life in the Great Ice Age* to see the location of the Wall of Ice. The Caspian Sea is found on the right side of the map on p. 58. You may also wish to compare the map on p. 58 of *Life in the Great Ice Age* to the map on p. 17 of *A Child's History of the World.*

Key Idea: Early civilizations sprung up in the areas near Mount Ararat and the Tower of Babel.

Storytime T

Read aloud the following assigned passage:

★ Genesis 10:1-2, 5-6, 8-10, 18-22, 30-32

Ask, *Do you think all of the people in today's passage put their faith in God? Explain. How would history be different if they had? Share a character, a story, or a verse from the Bible that you are reminded of by today's reading.*

Key Idea: Share a Biblical connection.

Geography S

For today's activities you will need a globe and the map on p. 17 of *A Child's History of the World.* Find the answers to the following questions: *Where are the Tigris and the Euphrates Rivers located? Find these 2 rivers in Iraq on the globe. Where is the Persian Gulf located? Find the modern countries that surround the Persian Gulf on the globe (Iran, Iraq, Kuwait, Saudi Arabia, and the United Arab Emirates). Where is the Nile River located? Find the Nile River in Egypt on the globe. On which continent is Egypt located?*

Review the following concept: *Point to and name the 7 continents.*

Key Idea: At the time that God created the Garden of Eden, two of the rivers named in the Bible that flowed out of Eden were the Tigris and the Euphrates Rivers. After the Flood, we do not know if these rivers were located in the same place. But, we do have rivers with those same names today.

Independent History Study I

★ On lined paper, copy in cursive **the first half** of the text of *Draw and Write Through History* p. 21. You will copy the other half on Day 4. Store your completed copywork with your completed drawings in the place you have chosen for them.

Key Idea: Even after the Flood, man still continued to sin and to disobey God. Babel is an example of this.

S E

Learning the Basics

Focus: Language Arts, Math, Bible, and Science

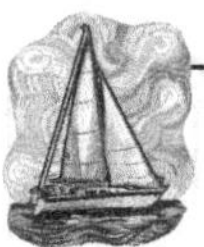

Poetry

T

Read aloud with the students the poem *"To Any Reader"* (see Appendix). Say, *Describe a time you were playing outside in the garden or by the trees. What can you learn about the poet, Robert Louis Stevenson, from the poem?* Say, *Did you know Robert Louis Stevenson had many cousins? As a boy, he enjoyed playing with them in the garden during the summer days that he was well enough.* Have the students read the poem again on their own.

Key Idea: Read and appreciate classic poetry.

Language Arts

S

Have students complete one studied dictation exercise (see Appendix for directions and passages).

Help students complete one lesson from the following reading program:

★ *Drawn into the Heart of Reading*

Work with the students to complete **one** of the English options listed below:

★ *Beginning Wisely:* Lesson 16

★ *Building with Diligence:* Lesson 14 (half)

★ Your own grammar program

Key Idea: Practice language arts skills.

Bible Study

T

Say, *You will be having your own quiet time with God today. Choose a quiet place for this special time, where you can be alone with God. Then, do the following things:*

1. Read Psalm 1:1-6 in your Bible.
2. Pray about the Psalm using the following beginning for your prayer: *Thank you for giving me your word, the Bible, to show me how to live my life. Help me to stay away from the sins of_______ because_______. Forgive me for_______.*
3. Recite Psalm 1:1-6 using the hand motions you added on Day 1.
4. Sing Psalm 1:1-6 along with the CD at the end of your quiet time.

✔ *Lead Me to the Rock* CD
Track 4; Song: "His Delight" (vs. 1-6)

Key Idea: It is important to ask God to forgive you when you sin and to ask for His help.

Math Exploration

S

Choose **one** of the math options listed below (see Appendix for details).

★ *Singapore Primary Mathematics 2A/2B, 3A/3B*, or *4A/4B*

★ Your own math program

Key Idea: Use a step-by-step math program.

Science Exploration

I

★ Use the Index on p. 44-47 of *One Small Square: Arctic Tundra* to help you answer today's questions. Write the answer to each numbered question on lined paper. You do not need to copy the question.

1. What is a protist? (p. 46)
2. How is a protist different from a monera? (p. 46)
3. How does the caribou's foot described on p. 18 act like the snowshoe pictured on p. 47?
4. Describe the difference between the dwarf willow on p. 24 and the black willow on p. 47.
5. What does Isaiah 55:9-11 show us about the way God designed creation and His plan for mankind?

Key Idea: Just as God sends the rain and the snow, He has a plan for all of His creation.

Learning through History
Focus: The Climate Changes

Unit 4 - Day 4

Reading about History [T]

Read about history in the following resource:

★ *A Child's History of the World: Ch. 5* p. ~~20-24~~ 21-33

After today's reading, say, *You will be writing a narration about part of the day's history reading. In order to remember the details very well, you will need to reread the part of today's reading from the third paragraph on p. 23 to p. 24 (on your own if possible).*

After students have finished reading the passage, ask them the questions below. If the students do not know the answers, help them find the answers in the passage they just read. Ask, *Where did people in ancient times often choose to settle? Why did people in ancient times settle next to rivers?* After students have answered, pause to allow them to write one sentence about the two questions you just discussed. The sentence should begin, *In ancient times, people...* After students have written the sentence, ask, *Eventually, what did the people do to band together and to trade?* Pause to allow students to answer this question orally and to write a sentence about it. Next, ask, *How did governments begin?* Pause to allow students to answer this question orally and to write a sentence about it. Then, ask, *In what way do we find out about how people lived in ancient times?* After students have answered the question orally, have them write one final sentence about it.

See the *Written Narration Skills* in the Appendix to guide students in editing their narrations. Remember to work on only one new skill at a time.

Key Idea: People in ancient times settled near rivers for water, trade, and transportation.

Storytime [T]

Read aloud the following assigned passage:

★ Genesis 12:1-9

Say, *Transport yourself back to the time of this story. Become one of the characters. Tell me what you see and do. (Make sure to use the word, "I", and to tell only what happened in today's reading.)*

Key Idea: Practice oral narration skills.

Timeline [S]

You will be adding to your staircase timeline today. On a new timeline card, draw and color a glacier. Write, *Ice Age*.

Note: We will not place a date on this card, as we do not have enough information to place an accurate date on this event.

If you decided to tape your timeline cards to the back of a door, then add the *Ice Age* card to the right of *The Tower of Babel* card from Unit 3. If you decided to tape the timeline cards side-by-side to accordion-fold them, then use clear packing tape to tape the *Ice Age* card next to the *The Tower of Babel* card and accordion-fold the timeline to store it.

Key Idea: As the Ice Age came to a close, the climate on Earth probably became more stable. Civilizations would have begun to flourish.

Independent History Study [I]

★ On lined paper, finish copying in cursive the **last half** of the text from *Draw and Write Through History* p. 21. Store your completed copywork with your completed drawings in the place you have chosen for them.

Key Idea: We can learn much about ancient civilizations by reading their various forms of writing.

Learning the Basics

Focus: Language Arts, Math, Bible, and Science

Unit 4 - Day 4

Poetry

T

Read aloud with the students the poem *"To Any Reader"* (see Appendix). Have students share this poem in a special way. Suggestions for sharing the poem include recording it to play for someone, reading it to someone on the telephone, photocopying the poem and adding illustrations, reading it to someone at home, putting the poem to a melody and singing it, using an instrument to tap out the meter or rhythm of the poem while reading it, or copying the poem on paper.

Key Idea: Share a variety of classic poetry.

Language Arts

S

Have students complete one dictation exercise.

Guide students to complete one reading lesson.

★ *Drawn into the Heart of Reading*

Help students complete **one** English lesson.

★ *Beginning Wisely:* Lesson 17

★ *Building with Diligence:* Lesson 15

★ Your own grammar program

Key Idea: Practice language arts skills.

Bible Study

T

Have students say Psalm 1:1-6 using the hand motions from Day 1. Have students copy in cursive Psalm 1:5-6 beneath last unit's Psalm 1:1-4 in their *Common Place Book.*

Note: A *Common Place Book* is often a bound composition book with lined pages. It provides a common place to copy anything that is timeless, memorable, or worthy of rereading. It is for copying text and not for original writing. Bible verses, classic poetry, and passages from excellent literature with beautiful or vivid wording are often included. Students will add to the *Common Place Book* throughout the year.

✔ *Lead Me to the Rock* CD
Track 4; Song: "His Delight" (vs. 1-6)

Key Idea: Copy in cursive a portion of a Psalm.

Math Exploration

S

Choose **one** math option listed below.

★ *Singapore Primary Mathematics 2A/2B, 3A/3B,* or *4A/4B*

★ Your own math program

Key Idea: Use a step-by-step math program.

Science Exploration

I

★ Read *One Small Square: Cactus Desert* p. 3-5. Turn to the science experiment section in your science binder or sketchbook. At the top of a blank page, write: *How do the spines and the shape of the desert cactus help to keep it cool?* Under the question, write: *'Guess'*. Write down your guess.

Use playdough or clay to make a model of a cactus like the one shown on *One Small Square: Cactus Desert* p. 43. Next, break toothpicks into thirds and place them in your cactus to be the spines. Then, shine a flashlight on your cactus to be the Sun. Do you notice the shadows the spines make on the cactus? How could the shadows help the plant stay cooler? Now, turn your cactus so that the thin, narrow side of the cactus is facing the Sun (flashlight). How would the direction the cactus is facing affect how much sun the cactus gets? On the paper write: *'Procedure'*. Draw a picture of the experiment. At the bottom of the paper, write: *'Conclusion'*. Explain what you learned.

Key Idea: The Sun's rays heat the desert air and sand. Desert cactuses adapt to survive and keep cool.

Learning through History
Focus: Egyptian Civilization

Unit 5 - Day 1

Reading about History [T]

Read about history in the following resource:

★ *A Child's History of the World: Ch. 6* p. 25-28

After today's reading, ask, *What are hieroglyphics?* (knowledge) *How was the Rosetta Stone used to help read hieroglyphics?* (application) *Why was the flooding of the Nile River a good problem to have?* (analysis) *Just because the Pharaoh Menes declared he was a god, did it really make him God? Explain.* (evaluation) *What does having hundreds of gods and goddesses show you about the Egyptians?* (analysis)

Key Idea: The Egyptian civilization is one of the oldest civilizations in the world. It developed along the Nile River.

History Project [S]

In this unit you will be making a clay cartouche of the lady Pharaoh Hatshepsut's name in hieroglyphic writing. Today, you will make the air-dry clay needed to make the cartouche. In a bowl, mix ½ cup salt with ¾ cup warm water. Add 2 cups flour to the mixture and stir to combine. With your hands, knead the clay for 5 minutes or more. Place the clay in an airtight container with a lid for Day 2.

Key Idea: The Rosetta Stone had the same text written in 3 languages. Jean-Francois Champollion cracked the Rosetta Stone code in 1922. This discovery allowed hieroglyphic writing to be read, providing a better understanding of the Egyptian way of life.

Storytime [T]

Read aloud the following assigned passage:

★ Genesis 12:10-20

Discuss today's reading in a "conversational way". Share about a person, time, event, or emotion from your life that today's passage brought to mind. Next, have your child share a connection.

Key Idea: Connect personally to the passage.

Research [S]

Early Egyptian writing used hieroglyphics. What are **hieroglyphics**? Where could you look to discover more about hieroglyphics? A dictionary will give you a definition of hieroglyphics. An encyclopedia will tell you what hieroglyphics are and show you a picture of them. Use a reference book or an online resource like www.wikipedia.org to look up *hieroglyphics*. Depending on the resource you use, you will have to type *hieroglyphics* in the search or look it up in the index.

Orally answer one or more of the following questions from your research: *What are hieroglyphics? Who used hieroglyphics? Where have hieroglyphics been found? Why was the discovery of the Rosetta Stone so important in helping us learn to read hieroglyphics? Who figured out the code for reading hieroglyphics? Why was this so important?*

Key Idea: The Egyptians developed a form of writing called hieroglyphics. Over time, no one knew how to read this kind of writing anymore.

Independent History Study [I]

★ Read *The 5,000-Year-Old Puzzle* Introduction-p. 9. On white paper, follow the directions on p. 23 of *Draw and Write Through History* to draw and color a pyramid. Store your drawing in the place you have chosen for it.

Key Idea: The Egyptians built pyramids as tombs for their kings or pharaohs.

Learning the Basics
Focus: Language Arts, Math, Bible, and Science

Unit 5 - Day 1

Poetry

T

Read aloud to the students the poem *"A Good Play"* (see Appendix). Ask, *What is the first stanza of the poem describing? What did the children use to make their ship? Tea was a time in the late afternoon when people drank tea and had a snack. What clues does the poem give you about how long the boys were planning to play? Did the children really sail on for days and days? What does that mean then?* Read the poem again with the students.

Key Idea: Read and appreciate classic poetry.

Language Arts

S

Have students complete the first studied dictation exercise (see Appendix for directions and passages).

Help students complete one lesson from the following reading program:

 *Drawn into the Heart of Reading*

Work with the students to complete **one** of the English options listed below:

 *Beginning Wisely:* Lesson 18

 *Building with Diligence:* Lesson 16

 Your own grammar program

Key Idea: Practice language arts skills.

Bible Study

T

Say, *Find Psalm 127:3-4 in your Bible. This is the memory selection for this unit. Read the verses out loud.* Ask, *How does Psalm 127:3 describe children? What is a heritage? How are children a "heritage from the Lord"? What are children compared to in Psalm 127:4? How can children be like arrows in the hand of a mighty man? What can we learn about how God views children from this Psalm?*

Have students say the verse 3 times, adding hand motions to help remember the words.

 *Lead Me to the Rock* CD
Track 6; Song: "Children Are a Heritage" (vs. 3-4)

Key Idea: Children are a blessing from the Lord. Parents are responsible to train children and teach them the Lord's ways, so they will be like an arrows flying straight and true.

Math Exploration

S

Choose **one** of the math options listed below (see Appendix for details).

 *Singapore Primary Mathematics 2A/2B, 3A/3B,* or *4A/4B*

 Your own math program

Key Idea: Use a step-by-step math program.

Science Exploration

I

Today you will add to your science notebook. At the top of an unlined paper, copy Job 38:25-27 in cursive. Beneath the verse, write, *What's living in a cactus desert?* You will be drawing and coloring a desert scene over the next 4 units, so save room on your page to add plants and animals each unit until your scene is complete. Today you will begin your desert scene by drawing and coloring two or more mammals from p. 40 of *One Small Square: Cactus Desert*. Page through the book to make sure you are drawing the mammals the correct size. When you are finished coloring, file your paper in the place you have chosen.

Key Idea: Animals and plants need special adaptations to be able to survive in the hot, dry cactus desert.

Learning through History
Focus: Egyptian Civilization

Unit 5 - Day 2

Reading about History — T

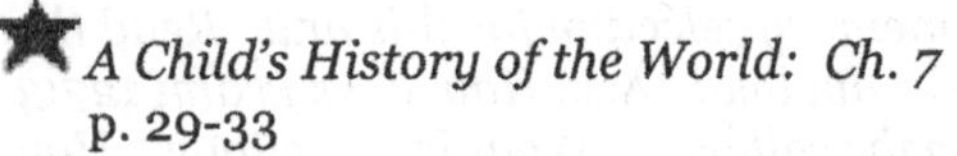

Read about history in the following resource:

★ *A Child's History of the World: Ch. 7* p. 29-33

After today's reading, read aloud Leviticus 18:1-5. Note: Make sure to stop at verse 5, as the verses after it are about sexual immorality, which is not appropriate for children this age. Say, *When God speaks to Moses, what does He say about the Egyptians? How can you tell that God is displeased by the Egyptians' worship of many gods?* Say, *In Egypt, the Pharaoh was considered to be a god.* Read aloud Ezekiel 28:1-9 to see what God thinks of that. Ask, *How does God feel about men who think they are gods?*

Key Idea: The Egyptians worshiped many gods, but we know there is only one true God.

History Project — S

Take out the air-dry clay that you saved for your cartouche from Day 1. Place a piece of waxed paper on your work surface. Place half of your clay in the middle of the waxed paper. Flatten your clay into an oval shape that is about 6" wide and 11" long. Your oval should not be very thick, or it will take a long time to dry. Use the pointed end of a pencil or the sharp end of a paperclip to etch out Hatshepsut in hieroglyphics as shown on p. 25 of *A Child's History of the World*. Etch an oval line around the outside. Leave the cartouche out to air-dry for Day 3.

Key Idea: Hatshepsut was a female pharaoh.

Storytime — T

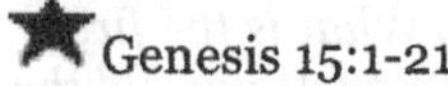

Read aloud the following assigned passage:

★ Genesis 15:1-21

Ask, *In today's reading, how was Abraham's life different from your life? What would you have enjoyed or found difficult about living during that time?*

Key Idea: Compare and contrast the historical time period of the reading to your own life.

Vocabulary — S

You may choose 3-5 of the following vocabulary words from *A Child's History of the World* to use for this lesson: *mummy* (p. 29), *classes* (p. 30), *monuments* (p. 30), *derricks* (p. 30), and/or *Sphinx* (p. 31). First, find the word in the text and read the sentence containing the word. Think about possible meanings. Next, find the word in a dictionary and select the correct meaning. Write the word at the top of an index card or at the top of the corresponding letter page in the notebook. Underneath the word, copy the correct definition from the dictionary. Then, use the word correctly in a sentence. The sentence may be either copied from the text or be one of your own creation. Last, draw a small picture to show the word's meaning. If you used an index card to record your word, file it under the correct alphabetical tab in the card file.

Key Idea: The Egyptians built huge pyramids, temples, and palaces. They decorated these places with brightly colored paintings and statues.

Independent History Study — I

★ Read *The 5,000-Year-Old Puzzle* p. 10-17. On lined paper, copy in cursive the **first** paragraph of *Draw and Write Through History* p. 28. You will copy the other paragraph on a different day. Store your completed copywork with your completed drawings in the place you have chosen for them.

Key Idea: The Egyptians preserved the body after death by mummifying it.

Language Arts

T

Work with the students to complete **one** of the English options listed below:

★ *Beginning Wisely:* Lesson 19

★ *Building with Diligence:* Lesson 17

★ Your own grammar program

Say, *You will be doing a writing activity based on the poem, "A Good Play"* (see Appendix). Say, *Robert Louis Stevenson wrote many poems about his memories of childhood. What are some things that you can remember building to use for pretend play?* (i.e. castle, fort, ship, store, house, car, bus, spaceship, airplane, train) List students' responses on a markerboard or a piece of paper.

Say, *You will choose* **one** *idea off the list we just made to help you write a poem about your memories of pretend play.* On paper, write the following lines, one under the other:
We built...
All made of...
And...
To...

We....
And had the very best of plays;
But....
So there was no one left but me.

As they write, have students refer to stanzas one and three in *"A Good Play"* for ideas. Students may also choose to add a 4-line second stanza to insert in the middle if desired.

Have students share the completed poem by reading it aloud.

Key Idea: Write creatively from classic poetry.

Bible Study

T

Have students say Psalm 127:3-4 using the hand motions they added on Day 1. Say, *A mood is a feeling, a sensation, or a state of mind. What is the mood of Psalm 127:3-4?* (Some examples of moods include frightened, worried, happy, peaceful, hopeful, sad, unhappy, angry, thankful, prayerful, joyful, and lonely.) Ask, *When would this Psalm help you, or when would you go to this Psalm?* (i.e. to remind you how much the Lord values you, to know that you are a blessing, as a reminder that your actions and behavior are looked upon as a reflection of your parents' teaching.)

Last, pray with your children, thanking the Lord for blessing you with them. Pray for help teaching your children what the Lord wants them to know. Pray for your children to listen.

✔ *Lead Me to the Rock* CD
Track 6; Song: "Children Are a Heritage" (vs. 3-4)

Key Idea: The Psalms reflect the many emotions and moods we have. They are a wonderful place to seek counsel from the Lord.

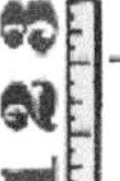

Math Exploration

S

Choose **one** of the math options listed below (see Appendix for details).

★ *Singapore Primary Mathematics 2A/2B, 3A/3B, or 4A/4B*

★ Your own math program

Key Idea: Use a step-by-step math program.

Science Exploration

I

★ Read *One Small Square: Cactus Desert* p. 6-7. Orally retell or narrate to an adult the portion of text that you read today. Use the *Narration Tips* in the Appendix for help as needed.

Key Idea: A cactus desert can be a dangerous place to explore due to the high temperatures, poisonous animals, spiny plants, and threat of floods when it rains. Yet, the desert is home to fascinating creatures.

Reading about History **T**

Read about history in the following resource:

 *A Child's History of the World: Ch. 8* p. 34-39

After today's reading, have your students orally narrate or retell the portion of today's text that you read. Use the *Narration Tips* in the Appendix as needed.

Key Idea: People in Babylonia were known to study and worship the sun, moon, and stars. We know that we are only to worship the Creator and not to worship creation.

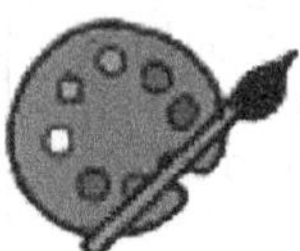

History Project **S**

Get the clay cartouche you made on Day 2. Place it carefully on a paper towel. Use a paintbrush and brown paint to cover the clay, working the paint into the etchings. Then, use a wadded-up paper towel to dab gently across the clay. Dab carefully so as not to break the clay. Much of the paint should come off, leaving darker-colored paint in the etchings. Let the clay and the paint dry. You have completed your cartouche.

Key Idea: We know the names of some leaders of long ago from early writings. We know Hatshepsut was a lady pharaoh. The Egyptians wrote in hieroglyphics. We also know that Sargon I was an early king of Babylonia. The Babylonians wrote in cuneiform.

Storytime **T**

Read aloud the following assigned passage:

 Isaiah 47:10-15

Ask, *In what had the people of Babylon placed their faith? How would the story be different if they had put their faith in God? Share a character, a story, or a verse from the Bible that you are reminded of by today's reading.*

Key Idea: Share a Biblical connection.

Geography **S**

For today's activities you will compare the modern-day globe to the map of the Ancient World on p. 35 of *A Child's History of the World.* Remember, the Tigris and the Euphrates Rivers are found in modern-day Iraq. Answer the following questions: *What modern-day country is located where Babylonia used to be? In what modern-day country is Mt. Ararat located? Point to Mt. Ararat in the country of Turkey. What modern-day country is where Axum used to be? Point to Africa. Is modern-day Egypt located in the same place as ancient Egypt?* Review the following concept: *Point to and name the 5 oceans.* Note: Many texts list the Southern Ocean at the South Pole as a 5th ocean.

Key Idea: At the time that God created the Garden of Eden, two of the rivers named in the Bible that flowed out of Eden were the Tigris and the Euphrates Rivers. After the Flood, we do not know if these rivers were located in the same place. But, we do have rivers with those same names today.

Independent History Study **I**

★ Read *The 5,000-Year-Old Puzzle* p. 18-23. On white paper, follow the directions on p. 24-26 of *Draw and Write Through History* to draw a sarcophagus. Wait to color your sarcophagus until Day 4. Store your drawing in the place you have chosen for it.

Key Idea: A pharaoh's mummy was placed in a beautifully decorated sarcophagus overlaid with gold.

Learning the Basics

Focus: Language Arts, Math, Bible, and Science

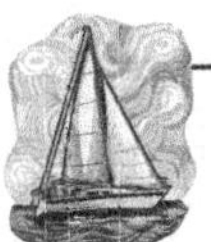

Poetry

T

Read aloud with the students the poem *"A Good Play"* (see Appendix). Say, *Describe a time you have done something like this. What can you learn about the poet, Robert Louis Stevenson, from the poem?* Say, *Did you know Robert Louis Stevenson had a full-time nurse when he was a child? He often mentions his nurse and the nursery in his poems. The nursery refers to young children's rooms.* Have the students read the poem again alone.

Key Idea: Read and appreciate classic poetry.

Language Arts

S

Have students complete one studied dictation exercise (see Appendix for directions and passages).

Help students complete one lesson from the following reading program:

★ *Drawn into the Heart of Reading*

Work with the students to complete **one** of the English options listed below:

★ *Beginning Wisely:* Lesson 20

★ *Building with Diligence:* Lesson 18

★ Your own grammar program

Key Idea: Practice language arts skills.

Bible Study

T

Say, *You will be having your own quiet time with God today. Choose a quiet place for this special time, where you can be alone with God. Then, do the following things:*

1. Read Psalm 127:3-4 in your Bible.
2. Pray about the Psalm using the following beginning for your prayer: *Thank you for making me and for giving me another day of life. Help me to listen to ________ and to learn about _________ to honor you. I praise you for _________.*
3. Recite Psalm 127:3-4 using the hand motions you added on Day 1.
4. Sing Psalm 127:3-4 along with the CD at the end of your quiet time.

✔ *Lead Me to the Rock* CD
Track 6; Song: "Children Are a Heritage" (vs. 3-4)

Key Idea: You are a blessing from the Lord.

Math Exploration

S

Choose **one** of the math options listed below (see Appendix for details).

★ *Singapore Primary Mathematics 2A/2B, 3A/3B,* or *4A/4B*

★ Your own math program

Key Idea: Use a step-by-step math program.

Science Exploration

I

★ Read *One Small Square: Cactus Desert* p. 8-9. Write the answer to each numbered question on lined paper. You do not need to copy the question. Use the listed page to help you answer each question.

1. Describe a saguaro cactus. (p. 9)
2. Why shouldn't you put your hand inside a saguaro cactus? (p. 8)
3. What makes the holes in the saguaro cactus? (p. 9)
4. Name some of the animals that make their home in the saguaro cactus. (p. 9)
5. What picture does Job 38:37-38 paint in your mind of the Lord watering the dry Earth?

Key Idea: The saguaro cactus often grows as tall as a tree. It becomes a home for many desert creatures.

Reading about History T

Read about history in the following resource:

★ *Grandpa's Box: Ch. 5* p. 33-38

After today's reading, say, *You will be writing a narration about part of the day's history reading. In order to remember the details very well, you will need to reread the part of today's reading from the middle of p. 36 to p. 38 (on your own if possible).*

After students have finished reading the passage, ask them the questions below. If the students do not know the answers, help them find the answers in the passage they just read. Ask, *Whom did God speak to in this story? What did God tell Abram to do? How could you write that as a sentence?* The sentence should begin, *When God spoke to Abram...* After students have answered, pause to allow them to write one sentence. After students have written the sentence, say, *Explain what Abram did. Why did he listen to God? How could you write that as a sentence?* Pause to allow students to answer this question orally and to write a sentence about it. Next, ask, *How was God going to use Abram?* Pause to allow students to answer this question orally and to write a sentence about it. Then, have students read their narration aloud to you.

See the *Written Narration Skills* in the Appendix to guide students in editing their narrations. Remember to work on only one new skill at a time.

Key Idea: Abram followed God because God chose him. He left Ur, and went to the land God chose for him. Through Abram, God was continuing the promise He'd made to Adam and Eve. A Savior would come from Israel.

Storytime T

Read aloud the following assigned passage:

★ *Tirzah: Ch.1* p. 7-17

Say, *Transport yourself back to the time of this story. Become one of the characters. Tell me what you see and do. (Make sure to use the word, "I", and to tell only what happened in today's reading.)*

Key Idea: Practice oral narration skills.

Timeline S

You will be adding 3 new cards to your staircase timeline today. On the first new timeline card, draw and color a pyramid. Write, *Ancient Egypt*. Note: We will not place a date on this card, as we do not have enough information to place an accurate date on it. On the second new card, draw stars. Write, *Abraham (approximately 1900 B.C.)*. On the third new card, draw and color a clay tablet with cuneiform writing on it. Write, *Hammurabi, Babylonia (1770 B.C.)*.

If you decided to tape your timeline cards to the back of a door, then add the *Ancient Egypt* card to the right of *The Ice Age* card. Then, begin a new row above the row you just made (like a staircase). On the right side, tape the *Abraham* card, and to the left of it tape the *Hammurabi* card. If you decided to tape the timeline cards side-by-side to accordion-fold them, use clear packing tape to tape the cards as described above.

Key Idea: God chose Abram to be the start of a great nation, the Israelite nation.

Independent History Study I

★ Read *The 5,000-Year-Old Puzzle* p. 24-29. Take out the sarcophagus that you drew on Day 3. Follow the directions given in step 8 on p. 26 of *Draw and Write Through History* to color the sarcophagus. Store your completed picture in the place you have chosen for it.

Key Idea: Abram was different from his idol-worshiping neighbors. He worshiped the one, true God.

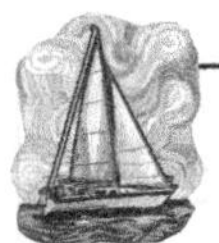

Poetry

T

Read aloud with the students the poem *"A Good Play"* (see Appendix). Have students share this poem in a special way. Suggestions for sharing the poem include recording it to play for someone, reading it to someone on the telephone, photocopying the poem and adding illustrations, reading it to someone at home, putting the poem to a melody and singing it, using an instrument to tap out the meter or rhythm of the poem while reading it, or copying the poem on paper.

Key Idea: Share a variety of classic poetry.

Language Arts

S

Have students complete one dictation exercise.

Guide students to complete one reading lesson.

★ *Drawn into the Heart of Reading*

Help students complete **one** English lesson.

★ *Beginning Wisely:* Lesson 21

★ *Building with Diligence:* Lesson 19

★ Your own grammar program

Key Idea: Practice language arts skills.

Bible Study

T

Have students say Psalm 127:3-4 using the hand motions from Day 1.

Have students copy in cursive Psalm 127:3-4 on a new page in their *Common Place Book.* Students should leave the rest of the page blank to add to next week.

Students will add to the *Common Place Book* throughout the year.

✔ *Lead Me to the Rock* CD
Track 6; Song: "Children Are a Heritage" (vs. 3-4)

Key Idea: Copy in cursive a portion of a Psalm.

Math Exploration

S

Choose **one** math option listed below.

★ *Singapore Primary Mathematics 2A/2B, 3A/3B,* or *4A/4B*

★ Your own math program

Key Idea: Use a step-by-step math program.

Science Exploration

I

★ Read *One Small Square: Cactus Desert* p. 10-13. Turn to the science experiment section in your science binder or sketchbook. At the top of a blank page, write: *How does the waxy covering of the desert cactus help it store water?* Under the question, write: *'Guess'.* Write down your guess.

Cover a cookie sheet with aluminum foil. Fold a paper towel in half. Draw a cactus-shaped plant on the paper towel. When you cut it out, you should have 2 identical cactuses. Dip both paper towel cactuses in water. They should be damp but not dripping wet. Lay the 2 cactuses flat on the cookie sheet. Wrap one cactus in waxed paper to be the waxy covering that cactuses have. Set the cookie sheet in a sunny place. After an hour or more, feel the two cactuses. Leave your cactuses setting in the sun to check again later in the day. What do you notice? Next, on the paper write: *'Procedure'.* Draw a picture of the experiment. At the bottom of the paper, write: *'Conclusion'.* Explain what you learned.

Key Idea: The waxy covering on the saguaro cactus prevents the cactus from drying out so quickly.

Learning through History
Focus: The Israelites in Egypt

Unit 6 - Day 1

Reading about History T

Read about history in the following resource:

★ *Grandpa's Box: Ch. 6* p. 39-45
After today's reading, say, *What 3 things did God promise Abraham?* (knowledge) *Why do you think God's promises were so important to Abraham?* (analysis) *Explain how God tested Abraham's faith in His promises.* (comprehension) *How did Abraham's actions show that he trusted God completely?* (evaluation) *In what way does the story of Abraham and Isaac help us understand God's sacrifice of Jesus better?* (synthesis)

Key Idea: God fulfilled His promises to Abraham. Abraham did gain land and had a son named Isaac, from whom a great nation would come. Yet, God asked Abraham to sacrifice Isaac, his only son.

Storytime T

Read aloud the following assigned passage:

★ *Tirzah: Ch. 2-3* p. 18-36
Discuss today's reading in a "conversational way". Share about a person, time, event, or emotion from your life that today's passage brought to mind. Next, have your child share a connection.

Key Idea: Connect personally to the passage.

History Project S

In this unit you will be designing a crook. Take out a sheet of white, construction paper. Starting at one corner, roll the sheet of paper into a tube and tape it together. Tear off a 14 inch sheet of aluminum foil. Roll the sheet of foil around the end of your paper tube. Tape that end of the foil to the end of the tube. Fashion the other end of the foil into a crook or a hook-shape. Save the crook for Day 2.

Key Idea: Abraham was a shepherd. God blessed him with wealth through land, sheep, and cattle. In the story of the sacrifice of Isaac, we see Abraham's great faith and glimpse God's incredible sacrifice of His Son, Jesus.

Research S

As a shepherd, Abraham would have carried a crook. What is a **crook**? Where could you look to discover more about a crook? Use a reference book or an online resource like www.wikipedia.org to look up *crook*. Depending on the resource you use, you will have to type *crook* in the search or look it up in the index.

Orally answer one or more of the following questions from your research: *What is a crook? Who used a crook? How was a crook used? What do the crook and the flail have to do with ancient Egypt?* Note: See p. 26 of *Draw and Write Through History*. *Why would Pharaoh hold a crook? In the Bible, who else is portrayed as a good shepherd, with a crook to rescue His sheep?*

Key Idea: The image of a shepherd and the symbol of the crook were important in past times. Shepherds were known for watching over, leading, and caring for their flocks.

Independent History Study I

★ Read *The 5,000-Year-Old Puzzle* p. 30-35. On lined paper, copy in cursive the **second** paragraph of *Draw and Write Through History* p. 28. Store your completed copywork with your completed drawings in the place you have chosen for them.

Key Idea: Egypt was a great nation, but the Egyptians believed in many gods. God promised a great nation would come from Abraham. This nation was to believe in the one true God.

Learning the Basics

Focus: Language Arts, Math, Bible, and Science

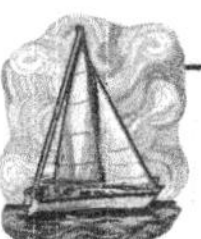

Poetry

T

Read aloud to the students the poem *"Summer Sun"* (see Appendix). Ask, *How does the poet make the Sun seem like a person? What parts of the body are given to the Sun in the poem?* (i.e. fingers, face, footing) *Explain what kind of mood or feeling this poem gives you. Which places are touched by the Sun's rays in this poem? Why is "Gardener of the World" a good way to describe the Sun?* Read the poem again with the students.

Key Idea: Read and appreciate classic poetry.

Language Arts

S

Have students complete the first studied dictation exercise (see Appendix for directions and passages).

Help students complete one lesson from the following reading program:

 *Drawn into the Heart of Reading*

Work with the students to complete **one** of the English options listed below:

 *Beginning Wisely:* Lesson 22

 *Building with Diligence:* Lesson 20

 Your own grammar program

Key Idea: Practice language arts skills.

Bible Study

T

Say, *Find Psalm 127:3-5 in your Bible. This is the memory selection for this unit. Read the verses out loud.* Ask, *What is a quiver? How is a quiver full of arrows compared to the blessing of children in Psalm 127:5? Once an arrow is out of the hand, can you direct it? Why is it important that children be directed to the right mark when they are young? After a child has gone into the world, will it be hard to direct him/her then? Why is it important that children be trained according to God's word?* Have students say the verse 3 times, adding hand motions to help remember the words.

 *Lead Me to the Rock* CD
Track 6; Song: "Children Are a Heritage" (vs. 3-5)

Key Idea: It is important for children to be trained according to God's word so that when they go out into the world, God can direct them.

Math Exploration

S

Choose **one** of the math options listed below (see Appendix for details).

 *Singapore Primary Mathematics 2A/2B, 3A/3B,* or *4A/4B*

 Your own math program

Key Idea: Use a step-by-step math program.

Science Exploration

I

Today you will add to your science notebook. Find the notebook page you began in Unit 5 titled, *What's living in a cactus desert?* You will add to your desert scene by drawing and coloring a barrel cactus along with the diagram showing its layers from p. 13 of *One Small Square: Cactus Desert*. Make sure to label the layers of the cactus as shown on p. 13. Next, draw and color roots under your cactus along with a roundworm, red velvet mite, bacteria, and green algae which are pictured in the circle on p. 14 of *One Small Square: Cactus Desert*. You will continue adding to your desert scene over the next few units.

Key Idea: The spines on the cactus protect it from animals that are hungry or thirsty. The shallow roots find water near the surface before the water evaporates.

Learning through History
Focus: The Israelites in Egypt

Unit 6 - Day 2

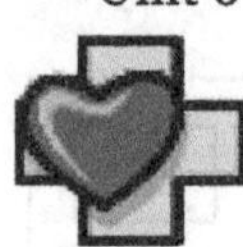

Reading about History [T]

Read about history in the following resource:

★ *Grandpa's Box: Ch. 7* p. 46-51

After today's reading, read aloud Genesis 25:27-34. Ask, *What can we learn about Esau from this passage? Would he really have died of hunger? How important was the birthright to Esau? How important was the birthright to Jacob?* Read Genesis 28:1-9. Ask, *What had Esau done that was displeasing to his father, his mother, and to God? Did Jacob obey Isaac when he told him not to marry a Canaanite woman? Why was marrying a Canaanite woman so displeasing to Isaac?* Read Hebrews 12:16-17. Ask, *How does God feel about Esau? What can we learn from Esau?*

Key Idea: From the beginning, Esau and Jacob were opposites. Both Esau and Jacob had many flaws, yet God chose Jacob to carry out His plan. Through the Scriptures, we can see that Esau's choices greatly displeased God.

History Project [S]

Take out the crook that you made on Day 1. Paint blue and gold (or yellow) stripes around the paper tube, alternating blue and gold. Lay the crook out to dry.

Key Idea: Jacob grew up to be a shepherd, like his father Isaac, and his grandfather Abraham had been. God blessed Jacob with much wealth through his livestock of sheep and cattle.

Storytime [T]

Read aloud the following assigned passage:

★ *Tirzah: Ch. 4-5* p. 37-53

Ask, *In today's reading, how were people's lives different from your life? What would you have enjoyed or found difficult about living during that time?*

Key Idea: Compare and contrast the historical time period of the reading to your own life.

Vocabulary [S]

You may choose 3-5 of the following vocabulary words from *Grandpa's Box* to use for this lesson: *requirements* (p. 46), *skilled* (p. 47), *scoundrel* (p. 48), *vowed* (p. 49), and/or *flee* (p. 49). First, find the word in the text and read the sentence containing the word. Think about possible meanings. Next, find the word in a dictionary and select the correct meaning. Write the word at the top of an index card or at the top of the corresponding letter page in the notebook. Underneath the word, copy the correct definition from the dictionary. Then, use the word correctly in a sentence. The sentence may either be copied from the text or be one of your own creation. Last, draw a small picture to show the word's meaning. If you used an index card to record your word, file it under the correct alphabetical tab in the card file.

Key Idea: There were consequences for both Jacob's and Esau's actions that both men lived with all of their lives. Yet, God's promise was carried out through Jacob.

Independent History Study [I]

★ Read *The 5,000-Year-Old Puzzle* p. 36-40. On white paper, follow the directions on p. 27 of *Draw and Write Through History* to draw and color the Sphinx. Store your completed picture in the place you have chosen for it.

Key Idea: The Sphinx was thought to be the guardian of the pyramids in Egypt. One day, Jacob would be living in Egypt, after discovering his long-lost son Joseph was there.

Learning the Basics

Focus: Language Arts, Math, Bible, and Science

Unit 6 - Day 2

Language Arts

T

Work with the students to complete **one** of the English options listed below:

★ *Beginning Wisely:* Lesson 23

★ *Building with Diligence:* Lesson 21

★ Your own grammar program

Say, *You will be doing a writing activity based on the poem, "Summer Sun"* (see Appendix). At the top of a markerboard or a paper, make 2 columns labeled: *"Sun"* and *"Moon"*. Say, *Personification means giving human actions to things to make them seem like a person. What are some examples of human actions given to the Sun in "Summer Sun"?* Write down the phrases the students share in the *"Sun"* column (i.e. showers his rays, slips his golden fingers through, maketh glad, smiles, has a golden face, sheds a warm and glittering look, pleases the child, paints the rose).

Next, say, *Use the ideas in the "Sun" column to help you list some phrases that describe the Moon by giving it human qualities.* Write down the ideas the students share under the *"Moon"* column. If needed, give the following examples to get them started: bathes the Earth with _____ (moonbeams), slips her _____ across the ground (moonlit tendrils), gives the Earth a _____ look (silvery or shimmering), soothes the _____ to sleep (child), slips away as _____ (dawn arises).

Then, have students use the list to write a paragraph using personification to describe the Moon. Ask, *What would be a good first sentence, based on the first line of "Summer Sun"? What would be a good ending sentence based on the last line of "Summer Sun"?*

Key Idea: Write creatively from classic poetry.

Bible Study

T

Have students say Psalm 127:3-5 using the hand motions they added on Day 1. Say, *A mood is a feeling, a sensation, or a state of mind. What is the mood of Psalm 127:3-5?* (Some examples of moods include frightened, worried, happy, peaceful, hopeful, sad, unhappy, angry, thankful, prayerful, joyful, and lonely.) Ask, *When would this Psalm help you, or when would you go to this Psalm?* (i.e. to remind you that children are a blessing from the Lord, to help you listen to your parents as they train you knowing you will be thankful for their guidance one day, to know it is important to study God's word in order to know right from wrong.) Last, pray with your children, thanking God for blessing you with them. Pray for God's word to soak into their hearts and for them to know right from wrong. Pray that they will remain close to God throughout their lives.

✔ *Lead Me to the Rock* CD
Track 6; Song: "Children Are a Heritage" (vs. 3-5)

Key Idea: The Psalms reflect the many emotions and moods we have. They are a wonderful place to seek counsel from the Lord.

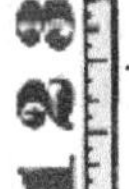

Math Exploration

S

Choose **one** of the math options listed below (see Appendix for details).

★ *Singapore Primary Mathematics 2A/2B, 3A/3B,* or *4A/4B*

★ Your own math program

Key Idea: Use a step-by-step math program.

Science Exploration

I

★ Read *One Small Square: Cactus Desert* p. 14-15. Orally retell or narrate to an adult the portion of text that you read today. Use the *Narration Tips* in the Appendix for help as needed.

Key Idea: The desert temperatures can get to be almost 120 degrees F (or 50 degrees C)! The ground can get to be more than 170 degrees F (or 77 degrees C)! There is no shade, and there are no clouds.

Learning through History
Focus: The Israelites in Egypt

Unit 6 - Day 3

Reading about History T

Read about history in the following resource:

★ *Grandpa's Box: Ch. 8* p. 52-57

After today's reading, have your students orally narrate or retell the portion of today's text that you read. Use the *Narration Tips* as needed.

Key Idea: As time passed, Jacob had 12 sons. The older sons were jealous of Jacob's favorite son, Joseph. So, they sold Joseph into slavery in Egypt. When famine struck in the land and there was nothing to eat, Jacob sent his older sons to Egypt to buy food.

Storytime T

Read aloud the following assigned passage:

★ *Tirzah: Ch. 6-7* p. 54-63

Ask, *In what does the main character place his faith? How would the story be different if the main character put his faith in God? Share a character, a story, or a verse from the Bible that you are reminded of by today's reading.*

Key Idea: Share a Biblical connection.

History Project S

When Joseph's brothers came to buy food in Egypt, Joseph served his brothers a meal. The Egyptians were known for their bread. Today, we will make Egyptian pastries. In a bowl, mix together 1½ cups flour, ½ tsp. salt, and 1 tsp. baking powder. Next, cut 4 Tbsp. butter and add it to the mixture. Rub the butter into the mixture with your fingers until the mixture feels like fine crumbs. Add ½ cup honey and 3 Tbsp. milk. Stir until dough forms. Place the dough on a floured surface. Divide the dough into 3 parts. Roll each part into long strips. Then, coil each strip into a spiral to make 3 separate pastries. Place each pastry on a greased baking sheet. Use honey to glaze the tops of the pastries. Then, sprinkle with caraway seeds. Bake the pastries at 355 degrees for 20 minutes. Let the pastries cool, and then enjoy eating them.

Key Idea: The crook and the flail symbolized Pharaoh's position as protector and leader of his people.

Geography S

For today's activities you will need a globe and the map on p. 35 of *A Child's History of the World*. Follow these instructions: *Point to the land of Canaan on p. 35. Walk your fingers from the land of Canaan to Egypt. Point to Goshen.* Note: This is where Joseph had his father, Jacob, and his brothers settled. *Find the same area on the globe. Point to the Red Sea on p. 35.* Note: The Red Sea will be very important in the coming stories. *Look on the globe to see if the Red Sea is still located there in modern times.*

Review the following concept: *Point to and name the 5 oceans.* Note: Many texts list the Southern Ocean at the South Pole as a 5th ocean.

Key Idea: God prepared Joseph to be in the right place at the right time to save his entire family from starvation. Although Joseph's brothers intended to harm Joseph, God intended it for good. God placed Joseph in Egypt for such a time as this.

Independent History Study I

★ On white paper, follow the directions on p. 36-37 of *Draw and Write Through History* to draw Joseph. Wait to color Joseph until Day 4. Store your drawing in the place you have chosen for it.

Key Idea: Joseph must have wondered why God allowed so many seemingly bad things to happen to him. But, God had the overall plan, which Joseph couldn't see. Yet, Joseph remained faithful to God.

Learning the Basics

Focus: Language Arts, Math, Bible, and Science

Unit 6 - Day 3

Poetry

T

Read aloud with the students the poem *"Summer Sun"* (see Appendix). Say, *Describe a memory that the poem brought to mind. What can you learn about the poet, Robert Louis Stevenson, from the poem?* Say, *Since Robert Louis Stevenson spent much time in bed as a child, he needed to find ways to pass the time. Having time to carefully watch things in nature helped him write such enduring poems.* Have the students read the poem again alone.

Key Idea: Read and appreciate classic poetry.

Language Arts

S

Have students complete one studied dictation exercise (see Appendix for directions and passages).

Help students complete one lesson from the following reading program:

 *Drawn into the Heart of Reading*

Work with the students to complete **one** of the English options listed below:

★ *Beginning Wisely:* Lesson 24

★ *Building with Diligence:* Lesson 22

 Your own grammar program

Key Idea: Practice language arts skills.

Bible Study

T

Say, *You will be having your own quiet time with God today. Choose a quiet place for this special time, where you can be alone with God. Then, do the following things:*

1. Read Psalm 127:3-5 in your Bible.
2. Pray about the Psalm using the following beginning for your prayer: *Thank you for the blessing of people who love me like ______ and ______. Help me to be a blessing to my parents by ______. Guide me to pass on a Godly heritage to my own children one day by ______.*
3. Recite Psalm 127:3-5 using the hand motions you added on Day 1.
4. Sing Psalm 127:3-5 along with the CD at the end of your quiet time.

✔ *Lead Me to the Rock* CD
Track 6; Song: "Children Are a Heritage" (vs. 3-5)

Key Idea: You can be a blessing to others.

Math Exploration

S

Choose **one** of the math options listed below (see Appendix for details).

★ *Singapore Primary Mathematics 2A/2B, 3A/3B,* or *4A/4B*

 Your own math program

Key Idea: Use a step-by-step math program.

Science Exploration

I

★ Read *One Small Square: Cactus Desert* p. 16-17. Write the answer to each numbered question on lined paper. You do not need to copy the question. Use the listed page to help you answer each question.

1. Explain why the collared lizard faces the setting Sun. (p. 16)
2. Why does the desert go from hot to chilly after the Sun goes down? (p. 16)
3. What do desert honey ants eat? (p. 17)
4. Describe a honeypot ant. (p. 17)
5. What does Psalm 19:1-6 say about the Sun? Be sure to use vs. 6 to help you answer the question.

Key Idea: After the Sun sets, the desert heat quickly cools. Many animals come out to hunt at night.

Learning through History
Focus: The Israelites in Egypt

Unit 6 - Day 4

Reading about History [T]

Read about history in the following resource:

★ *Grandpa's Box: Ch. 9* p. 58-64

After today's reading, say, *You will be writing a narration about part of the day's history reading. In order to remember the details very well, you will need to reread the part of today's reading from the sixth paragraph on p. 60 through the second paragraph on p. 62 (on your own if possible).*

After students have finished reading the passage, ask them the questions below. If the students do not know the answers, help them find the answers in the passage they just read. Ask, *Who was upset about the Hebrew people in this story? Why was Pharaoh worried about the Hebrew people? What did Pharaoh do first to the Hebrews? Next, what did Pharaoh do? Last, what did Pharaoh do?*

After the questions have been answered, have students write the following sentence starters down the left side of a piece of paper. *Pharaoh was worried that..., First..., Next..., Last...,* Have students complete the sentence starters to write a narration about today's reading. Then, have students read their narration aloud to you.

See the *Written Narration Skills* in the Appendix to guide students in editing their narrations. Remember to work on only one new skill at a time. Store the written narration in the place you have chosen for it.

Key Idea: Over time, the Israelite nation grew larger and larger in Egypt. The new pharaoh was worried that the Hebrews would take over Egypt, so he made them slaves.

Storytime [T]

Read aloud the following assigned passage:

★ *Tirzah: Ch. 8-9* p. 64-78

Say, *Transport yourself back to the time of this story. Become one of the characters. Tell me what you see and do. (Make sure to use the word, "I", and to tell only what happened in today's reading.)*

Key Idea: Practice oral narration skills.

Timeline [S]

You will be adding a new card to your staircase timeline today. On a new timeline card, draw and color a coat of many colors. Write, *Joseph in Egypt (approximately 1700 B.C.).*

If you decided to tape your timeline cards to the back of a door, then add the *Joseph* card to the left of the *Hammurabi* card. If you decided to tape the timeline cards side-by-side to accordion-fold them, use clear packing tape to tape the cards as described above. Then, accordion-fold the timeline to store it.

Key Idea: After Joseph died, the next pharaohs forgot how Joseph had saved Egypt from a famine. As the Hebrews continued to grow and prosper, the new Pharaoh thought of ways to stop the Hebrew people from getting any stronger. He thought of different ways to kill their boy babies. But, God was raising up a deliverer, and his name was Moses.

Independent History Study [I]

★ Take out your picture of Joseph. Follow the directions on p. 37 of *Draw and Write Through History* to color Joseph. Then, on lined paper, copy in cursive the **first** paragraph on p. 48 of *Draw and Write Through History*. Store your completed picture and copywork in the place you have chosen.

Key Idea: Even after Joseph died, God did not forget about His people in Egypt. He had a plan for them.

Learning the Basics

Focus: Language Arts, Math, Bible, and Science

Unit 6 - Day 4

Poetry

T

Read aloud with the students the poem *"Summer Sun"* (see Appendix). Have students share this poem in a special way. Suggestions for sharing the poem include recording it to play for someone, reading it to someone on the telephone, photocopying the poem and adding illustrations, reading it to someone at home, putting the poem to a melody and singing it, using an instrument to tap out the meter or rhythm of the poem while reading it, or copying the poem on paper.

Key Idea: Share a variety of classic poetry.

Language Arts

S

Have students complete one dictation exercise.

Guide students to complete one reading lesson.

★ *Drawn into the Heart of Reading*

Help students complete **one** English lesson.

★ *Beginning Wisely:* Lesson 25

★ *Building with Diligence:* Lesson 23

★ Your own grammar program

Key Idea: Practice language arts skills.

Bible Study

T

Have students say Psalm 127:3-5 using the hand motions from Day 1.

Have students copy in cursive Psalm 127:5 beneath last unit's Psalm 127:3-4 in their *Common Place Book.* Students should leave the rest of the page blank to add to next week.

Students will add to the *Common Place Book* throughout the year.

✔ *Lead Me to the Rock* CD
Track 6; Song: "Children Are a Heritage" (vs. 3-5)

Key Idea: Copy in cursive a portion of a Psalm.

Math Exploration

S

Choose **one** math option listed below.

★ *Singapore Primary Mathematics 2A/2B, 3A/3B,* or *4A/4B*

★ Your own math program

Key Idea: Use a step-by-step math program.

Science Exploration

I

★ Read *One Small Square: Cactus Desert* p. 18-19. Turn to the science experiment section in your science binder or sketchbook. At the top of a blank page, write: *How do bats help the saguaro cactus to produce seeds?* Under the question, write: *'Guess'.* Write down your guess. Today you will make your own saguaro flower and experiment with sipping nectar like a bat. Dip the rim of a tall glass in a bowl of water. Then, dip the wet rim in sugar or decorative candy sprinkles until the rim of the glass is coated. This will be **pollen**. Trace around the bottom of the glass on a coffee filter. Cut out the circle you traced. Slide the filter around the outside of the glass to be the cactus flower's **petals**. Pour a small amount of juice in the bottom of the glass to be **nectar**. Cut a short piece off a straw to be your bat-like tongue called a **probiscus**. Use your short straw to sip nectar from the saguaro flower like a bat. You may have to tip the flower toward you. What was stuck on your face after sipping the nectar? When the bat sips nectar from a different flower, how is the pollen spread? On the paper write: *'Procedure'.* Draw a picture of the experiment. At the bottom of the paper, write: *'Conclusion'.* Explain what you learned.

Key Idea: Bats help cactuses make seeds by carrying pollen from male flower parts to female flower parts.

Learning through History
Focus: Moses Leads Israel Out of Egypt

Unit 7 - Day 1

Reading about History [T]

Read about history in the following resource:

★ *Grandpa's Box: Ch. 10* p. 65-71

After today's reading, say, *When Moses was living in the desert, how was God preparing him for what was to come?* (synthesis) *What was Moses' reaction when God told Moses His plan for the Israelites?* (knowledge) *Describe Pharaoh's answer to Moses, when Moses told Pharaoh, "God says, 'Let my people go'!"* (comprehension) *How did God show Pharaoh that there is only one true God?* (analysis) *As Pharaoh was approaching with his army, why would God lead the Israelites to the Red Sea?* (evaluation)

Key Idea: God prepared Moses for what was to come, by allowing him to be raised and taught in Pharaoh's palace and then by training him for life in the desert.

Storytime [T]

Read aloud the following assigned passage:

★ *Tirzah: Ch. 10-11* p. 79-93

Discuss today's reading in a "conversational way". Share about a person, time, event, or emotion from your life that today's passage brought to mind. Next, have your child share a connection.

Key Idea: Connect personally to the passage.

History Project [S]

In this unit you will be making a 3-dimensional pyramid. In the center of a white paper, draw a diamond that is 4" long on each side. The diamond will also be a square when the paper is turned. From each edge of the diamond, draw a triangle coming out. Each side of each triangle also needs to be 4" long. Cut the shape out following the outer edges of the 4 triangles. Then, fold each triangle in toward the center, leaving the diamond shape in the center to be the base of the pyramid. Tape the edges of the pyramid together and save it for Day 2.

Key Idea: Even though the Egyptians built amazing pyramids that are still standing, God is greater than anything that man can build.

Research [S]

In ancient times, Egyptian rulers were called **pharaohs**. Where could you look to discover more about the pharaohs? Use a reference book or an online resource like www.wikipedia.org to look up *pharaoh*. Depending on the resource you use, you will have to type *Egyptian pharaoh* in the search or look it up in the index.

Orally answer one or more of the following questions from your research: *What does pharaoh mean? How did a person get to be pharaoh? Who were some of the more famous pharaohs? What did the pharaoh usually wear? What monuments did the pharaohs build that are still standing today? Why did pharaohs build pyramids?*

Key Idea: In Egypt, the pharaoh had more power than anyone. He was considered to be a god. Many pharaohs built huge pyramids as symbols of their greatness and as tombs for their bodies. The Bible warns men against trying to become like God. We are told to worship only the one, true God.

Independent History Study [I]

★ On white paper, follow the directions on p. 38-39 of *Draw and Write Through History* to draw Moses. Wait to color Moses until Day 2. Store your drawing in the place you have chosen for it.

Key Idea: God saved Moses to lead the Israelites out of Egypt, just as God had promised Abraham.

Learning the Basics

Focus: Language Arts, Math, Bible, and Science

Unit 7 - Day 1

Poetry

T

Read aloud to the students the poem *"Foreign Lands"* (see Appendix). Ask, *How do you know the poem is told from a child's point of view? What sights does the child see up in the cherry tree? Why do you think the poet mentions a fairy land? How do children sometimes use their imaginations to pretend their play things are "alive"? What is a far away place you would like to visit one day?* Read the poem again with the students.

Key Idea: Read and appreciate classic poetry.

Language Arts

S

Have students complete the first studied dictation exercise (see Appendix for directions and passages).

Help students complete one lesson from the following reading program:

 *Drawn into the Heart of Reading*

Work with the students to complete **one** of the English options listed below:

 *Beginning Wisely:* Review One p. 66-67

 *Building with Diligence:* Lesson 24

 Your own grammar program

Key Idea: Practice language arts skills.

Bible Study

T

Say, *Find Psalm 9:9-10 in your Bible. This is the memory selection for this unit. Read the verses out loud.* Ask, *What is a refuge? How is the Lord our refuge in times of trouble? Does being a Christian mean we will not have times of trouble? Why will there always be trouble as long as there is sin in the world? In Psalm 9:10, who does it say will trust in the Lord? What does it mean to know someone? What does Psalm 9:10 say about the Lord? Why is it important to seek the Lord? What promise is given to us in Psalm 9:10?* Have students say the verse 3 times, adding hand motions to help remember the words.

 *Lead Me to the Rock* CD
Track 10; Song: "I Will Trust in You"
Note: This song goes with the history theme this week, but it does not sing the words of a Psalm. Just listen and enjoy the song.

Key Idea: We need to trust in the Lord.

Math Exploration

S

Choose **one** of the math options listed below (see Appendix for details).

 *Singapore Primary Mathematics 2A/2B, 3A/3B,* or *4A/4B*

 Your own math program

Key Idea: Use a step-by-step math program.

Science Exploration

I

Today you will add to your science notebook. Find the notebook page you began in Unit 5 titled, *What's living in a cactus desert?* You will add to your desert scene by drawing and coloring the circled diagram about the yucca moth and the yucca flower from p. 19 of *One Small Square: Cactus Desert*. Make sure to label the parts of the cycle as shown in the diagram on p. 19. Under your drawing, copy the paragraph of text about the yucca moth found next to the circled diagram on p. 19. Save your desert scene for Unit 8.

Key Idea: The yucca moth and yucca flower need one another. Yucca moths can only eat yucca flowers. The yucca flower also needs the yucca moth to carry its pollen to another flower, so it can make seeds.

Learning through History
Focus: Moses Leads Israel Out of Egypt

Unit 7 - Day 2

Reading about History [T]

Read about history in the following resource:

★ *A Child's History of the World: Ch. 9* p. 40-44

After today's reading, read aloud Exodus 6:1-8. Ask, *How was Abraham different from his neighbors, the Babylonians? How did the Israelites come to be in Egypt? Why was it important for the Israelites to leave Egypt?* Read aloud Joshua 24:14-15. Ask, *In what way did God want the Israelites to be different from their neighbors? How can you tell that the Lord hated the idol-worship of the Egyptians? What choice did the Lord give the people?*

Key Idea: The Lord kept His covenant with Abraham, and the great nation of Israel came from him. Just as God had prophesied to Abraham, the Israelites were enslaved in Egypt for 400 years.

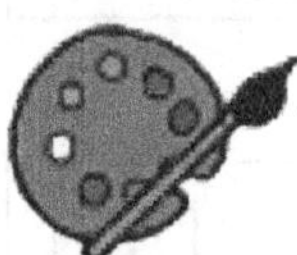

History Project [S]

Take out your pyramid that you made on Day 1. Since the pyramids were originally covered with white limestone, leave your pyramid white. Thin glue by mixing it with water. Lightly, paint the outsides of the 4 triangles with the glue mixture. Then, sprinkle salt or sugar on the outside of your pyramid to make it sparkle. Gently shake off the excess salt or sugar in the garbage. Let your pyramid dry.

Key Idea: God sent Moses to deliver a message to Pharaoh. God said, *Let my people go!*

Storytime [T]

Read aloud the following assigned passage:

★ *Tirzah: Ch. 12-13* p. 94-105

Ask, *In today's reading, how were people's lives different from your life? What would you have enjoyed or found difficult about living during that time?*

Key Idea: Compare and contrast the historical time period of the reading to your own life.

Vocabulary [S]

You may choose 3-5 of the following vocabulary words from *A Child's History of the World* to use for this lesson: *famine* (p. 41), *foreign* (p. 42), *enslaved* (p. 42), *hostile* (p. 42), and/or *Exodus* (p. 42). First, find the word in the text and read the sentence containing the word. Think about possible meanings. Next, find the word in a dictionary and select the correct meaning. Write the word at the top of an index card or at the top of the corresponding letter page in the notebook. Underneath the word, copy the correct definition from the dictionary. Then, use the word correctly in a sentence. The sentence may either be copied from the text or be one of your own creation. Last, draw a small picture to show the word's meaning. If you used an index card to record your word, file it under the correct alphabetical tab in the card file.

Key Idea: God told Moses that He had heard the Israelites' groaning, and He was ready to deliver them from Pharaoh's hand. The stage was set for the Lord to show His power.

Independent History Study [I]

★ Take out your picture of Moses, and color it following the directions on p. 39 of *Draw and Write Through History*. Then, on lined paper, copy in cursive the **second** paragraph of p. 48 from *Draw and Write Through History*. Store your completed picture and copywork in the place you have chosen for them.

Key Idea: God gave Moses a difficult task. Moses wasn't sure he could do what God asked.

Learning the Basics

Focus: Language Arts, Math, Bible, and Science

Unit 7 - Day 2

Language Arts

T

Work with the students to complete **one** of the English options listed below:

★ *Beginning Wisely:* Review Two p. 68-69

★ *Building with Diligence:* Lesson 25

★ Your own grammar program

Say, *You will be doing a writing activity based on the poem, "Foreign Lands"* (see Appendix). Say, *What are some of the things that you would see, if you were looking down from a tree near the place where you live?* (i.e. lawns, roads, housetops, ditches, cars, fences, fields, etc.) List students' responses on a piece of paper or a markerboard. On paper, write the lines listed below, one under the other. Say, *Use the ideas off the list we just made to help you finish the missing lines from the following poem:*

Up into the cherry tree
Who should climb but little me?
I held the trunk with both my hands
And looked abroad on foreign lands.

I saw...
...before my eyes
And...
That I had never seen before.

I saw....
And...
The....
With...

If I could find a higher tree
Farther and farther I should see,
To where the grown-up river slips
Into the sea among the ships.

Key Idea: Write creatively from classic poetry.

Bible Study

T

Have students say Psalm 9:9-10 using the hand motions they added on Day 1. Say, *A mood is a feeling, a sensation, or a state of mind. What is the mood of Psalm 9:9-10?* (Some examples of moods include frightened, worried, happy, peaceful, hopeful, sad, unhappy, angry, thankful, prayerful, joyful, and lonely.) Ask, *When would this Psalm help you, or when would you go to this Psalm?* (i.e. as a comfort during times of trouble, as a reminder that the Lord is always with us, to remember that the Lord will never forsake us.)

Last, pray with your children that they might turn to the Lord when they are in trouble. Thank the Lord for never forsaking us and for always being there when we call upon Him.

✔ *Lead Me to the Rock* CD
Track 10; Song: "I Will Trust in You"
Note: This song goes with the history theme this week, but it does not sing the words of a Psalm. Just listen and enjoy the song.

Key Idea: The Psalms are a source of comfort.

Math Exploration

S

Choose **one** of the math options listed below (see Appendix for details).

★ *Singapore Primary Mathematics 2A/2B, 3A/3B,* or *4A/4B*

★ Your own math program

Key Idea: Use a step-by-step math program.

Science Exploration

I

★ Read *One Small Square: Cactus Desert* p. 20-21. Orally retell or narrate to an adult the portion of text that you read today. Use the *Narration Tips* in the Appendix for help as needed.

Key Idea: In the evening animals like the wood rat, mule deer, kangaroo rat, and porcupine come out to get food. Insects such as termites, grasshoppers, ants, and crickets come out in search of food too.

Learning through History
Focus: Moses Leads Israel Out of Egypt

Unit 7 - Day 3

Reading about History **T**

Read about history in the following resource:

★ *Grandpa's Box: Ch. 11* p. 72-77

After today's reading, have your students orally narrate or retell the portion of today's text that you read. Use the *Narration Tips* in the Appendix as needed.

Key Idea: After God miraculously saved the Israelites at the Red Sea, it was time to give the people His commands. Moses reminded the people of all that God had done to save them. The people agreed to obey God's commands.

Storytime **T**

Read aloud the following assigned passage:

★ *Tirzah: Ch. 14-15* p. 106-120

Ask, *In what do the main characters place their faith? How are the two sides of the story different based on whom the main characters place their faith in? Share a character, a story, or a verse from the Bible that you are reminded of by today's reading.*

Key Idea: Share a Biblical connection.

History Project **S**

Get out your pyramid from Day 2. Roll tape under it to tape it in the center of a white sheet of paper. Turn off the lights. Use a flashlight or an overhead light to be the sun. Shine the light on the pyramid at an angle from the top right corner of the paper. Use your pencil to shade the triangular shadow you see on the ground to the left of the pyramid. Then, turn on the lights. Lightly shade the rest of the ground with light yellow and light brown colored pencils. Make the shadowed-area darker. Since there is some evidence that suggests that the tip of the Great Pyramid of Giza was once covered in gold, you may paint only the tip of your pyramid in gold or yellow.

Key Idea: In Egypt, the Israelites were used to being surrounded by examples of Pharaoh's power and greatness. At Mt. Sinai, they were shown how much greater God's power is than any earthly power.

Geography **S**

For today's activities you will need a globe and the maps on p. 17 and 35 of *A Child's History of the World.* Follow these directions: *Find Ur on p. 35. Who left Ur at God's command? Find the modern-day city near the Persian Gulf in Iraq that is located near the spot where Ur once was. Did you find Basra in Iraq? Point to Mt. Sinai on p. 17. Then, find Mt. Sinai on the globe. It is located in Egypt by the Red Sea. Point to the Black Sea, the Caspian Sea, and the Mediterranean Sea on p. 17. Look on the globe to see if these 3 seas are still there in modern times.*

Review the following concept: *Point to and name the 5 oceans.* Note: Many texts list the Southern Ocean at the South Pole as a 5th ocean.

Key Idea: Mt. Sinai was located near the Red Sea. This is the spot where God talked with Moses to give the Israelites His commands. The mountain shook and was covered with smoke, and the people were afraid.

Independent History Study **I**

★ On white paper, follow the directions on **either** p. 40 **or** p. 41-42 **or** p. 43 of *Draw and Write Through History* to draw and color **either** a frog **or** a locust. Store your drawing in the place you have chosen for it.

Key Idea: God used the plagues to show Pharaoh and the Israelites His power over all created things.

Learning the Basics
Focus: Language Arts, Math, Bible, and Science

Unit 7 - Day 3

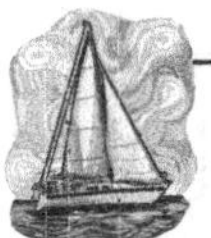

Poetry

T

Read aloud with the students the poem *"Foreign Lands"* (see Appendix). Say, *Describe a memory that the poem brought to mind. What can you learn about the poet, Robert Louis Stevenson, from the poem?* Say, *Did you know, that even though his health was often poor, Robert Louis Stevenson was still very adventurous? He canoed and camped and took trips to see the world.* Have the students read the poem again on their own.

Key Idea: Read and appreciate classic poetry.

Language Arts

S

Have students complete one studied dictation exercise (see Appendix for directions and passages).

Help students complete one lesson from the following reading program:

★ *Drawn into the Heart of Reading*

Work with the students to complete **one** of the English options listed below:

★ *Beginning Wisely:* A Poem to Enjoy p. 71

★ *Building with Diligence:* Lesson 26 (Half)

★ Your own grammar program

Key Idea: Practice language arts skills.

Bible Study

T

Say, *You will be having your own quiet time with God today. Choose a quiet place for this special time, where you can be alone with God. Then, do the following things:*

1. Read Psalm 9:9-10 in your Bible.
2. Pray about the Psalm using the following beginning for your prayer: *Thank you for always hearing me when I pray. Right now, I am worried about ________ because ________. Help me know what I can do to make it better.*
3. Recite Psalm 9:9-10 using the hand motions you added on Day 1.
4. Listen to the song on the CD at the end of your quiet time.

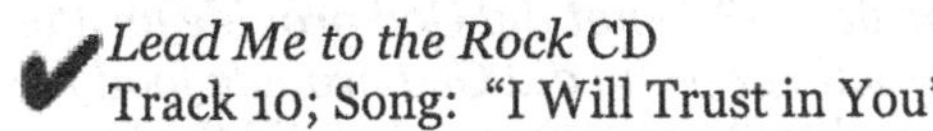

✔ *Lead Me to the Rock* CD
Track 10; Song: "I Will Trust in You"

Key Idea: The Lord always hears our prayers.

Math Exploration

S

Choose **one** of the math options listed below (see Appendix for details).

★ *Singapore Primary Mathematics 2A/2B, 3A/3B,* or *4A/4B*

★ Your own math program

Key Idea: Use a step-by-step math program.

Science Exploration

I

★ Read *One Small Square: Cactus Desert* p. 22-25. Write the answer to each numbered question on lined paper. You do not need to copy the question. Use the listed page to help you answer each question.

1. Who are some of the poisonous animals that live in the desert? (p. 22)
2. How does the rattlesnake "smell" its prey? (p. 23)
3. Draw the pupils of the snake's eyes as they would look during the day and at night. (p. 23)
4. How do some animals stay warm as the desert becomes cold at night? (p. 24)
5. What does the story of Paul and the poisonous snake in Acts 28:1-10 show you about God's power?

Key Idea: There are many poisonous animals in the desert, making it a dangerous place to be at night.

Reading about History T

Read about history in the following resource:

★ *Grandpa's Box: Ch. 12* p. 78-84

After today's reading, say, *You will be writing a narration about part of the day's history reading. In order to remember the details very well, you will need to reread the part of today's reading from the second paragraph on p. 80 to the bottom of p. 81 (on your own if possible).*

After students have finished reading the passage, ask them the questions below. If the students do not know the answers, help them find the answers in the passage they just read. Ask, *What was one of the biggest problems in the desert? What did God provide for the Israelites? How did God provide food for the Israelites? Over time, what did the Israelites begin to do? What did the Israelites' complaints about the manna show God?*

After the questions have been answered, have students write a 3-4 sentence narration that begins, *When the Israelites were in the desert...* When students have finished their narration, direct them to read the sentences out loud. Ask, *Did you include **who** the reading was mainly about? Did you include **what** important thing(s) happened? Did you include **how** it ended? If not, how could you add those things?*

See the *Written Narration Skills* in the Appendix to guide students in editing their narrations.

Key Idea: In the desert, there wasn't enough food or water. Yet, God miraculously provided water and manna to take care of their needs.

Storytime T

Read aloud the following assigned passage:

★ *Tirzah: Ch. 16-17* p. 121-131

Say, *Transport yourself back to the time of this story. Become one of the characters. Tell me what you see and do. (Make sure to use the word, "I", and to tell only what happened in today's reading.)*

Key Idea: Practice oral narration skills.

Timeline S

You will be adding to your staircase timeline today. On a new timeline card, draw and color the Red Sea parting. Write, *The Exodus (approximately 1500 B.C.).* Note: New information on the dates of the Exodus place it closer to 1500 B.C., so that is the information we'll use (as opposed to the 1300 B.C. date in Hillyer).

If you decided to tape your timeline cards to the back of a door, then add *The Exodus* card to the left of the *Joseph* card from Unit 6. If you decided to tape the timeline cards side-by-side to accordion-fold them, then use clear packing tape to tape *The Exodus* card next to the *Joseph* card and accordion-fold the timeline to store it.

Key Idea: Even after their miraculous escape from Egypt, the Israelites rebelled against God again and again. There were always consequences for the people's rebellion, but God forgave them over and over. Aren't you glad that God forgives you over and over too?

Independent History Study I

★ On white paper, follow the directions on p. 44-45 of *Draw and Write Through History* to draw and color a quail. Store your completed picture in the place you have chosen for it.

Key Idea: God provided quail in the desert for the Israelites when they were hungry.

Learning the Basics

Focus: Language Arts, Math, Bible, and Science

Unit 7 - Day 4

Poetry

T

Read aloud with the students the poem *"Foreign Lands"* (see Appendix). Have students share this poem in a special way. Suggestions for sharing the poem include recording it to play for someone, reading it to someone on the telephone, photocopying the poem and adding illustrations, reading it to someone at home, putting the poem to a melody and singing it, using an instrument to tap out the meter or rhythm of the poem while reading it, or copying the poem on paper.

Key Idea: Share a variety of classic poetry.

Language Arts

S

Have students complete one dictation exercise.

Guide students to complete one reading lesson.

★ *Drawn into the Heart of Reading*

Help students complete **one** English lesson.

★ *Beginning Wisely:* Lesson 26

★ *Building with Diligence:* Lesson 26 (Half)

★ Your own grammar program

Key Idea: Practice language arts skills.

Bible Study

T

Have students say Psalm 9:9-10 using the hand motions from Day 1.

Have students copy in cursive Psalm 9:9-10 on a clean page in their *Common Place Book.*

Students will add to the *Common Place Book* throughout the year.

✔ *Lead Me to the Rock* CD
Track 10; Song: "I Will Trust in You"
Note: This song goes with the history theme this week, but it does not sing the words of a Psalm. Just listen and enjoy the song.

Key Idea: Copy in cursive a portion of a Psalm.

Math Exploration

S

Choose **one** math option listed below.

★ *Singapore Primary Mathematics 2A/2B, 3A/3B,* or *4A/4B*

★ Your own math program

Key Idea: Use a step-by-step math program.

Science Exploration

I

★ Read *One Small Square: Cactus Desert* p. 26-27. Turn to the science experiment section in your science binder or sketchbook. At the top of a blank page, write: *How does dew form on rocks or cactuses in the desert?* Under the question, write: *'Guess'*. Write down your guess. Put several ice cubes in a glass. Pour water that is at room temperature into the glass. Add a few drops of food coloring. Wait several minutes. What do you notice forming on the outside of the glass? These very tiny water droplets are called condensation or dew. Wipe the outside of the glass with a paper towel. Is the water on the outside of the glass colored? Since it isn't colored like the water inside the glass, where do you think the water on the outside of the glass came from? Next, try the "Dew It" experiment on p. 26 of *One Small Square: Cactus Desert*. Then, on the paper write: *'Procedure'*. Draw a picture of the experiments. At the bottom of the paper, write: *'Conclusion'*. Explain what you learned.

Key Idea: As night comes in the desert, the rocks and cactuses get cooler as they lose their heat into the air. When the temperature of the rocks or cactuses drops below the dewpoint of the surrounding air, water condenses on their surfaces forming dew.

Learning through History
Focus: The Israelites in the Promised Land

Unit 8 - Day 1

Reading about History — T

Read about history in the following resource:

★ *Grandpa's Box: Ch. 13* p. 85-90

After today's reading, say, *How do you think Joshua may have been feeling as he was preparing to lead the Israelites into the Promised Land?* (explain) *What stranger did Joshua meet? Describe the meeting.* (comprehension) *Explain the instructions the Lord gave the Israelites for conquering Jericho.* (knowledge) *List the contents of the ark of the covenant.* (knowledge) *Why might these things have been chosen to go in the ark?* (evaluation) *In what ways did the Lord show everyone that He was fighting on the side of Israel?* (synthesis)

Key Idea: Joshua was chosen to lead Israel after Moses died. God gave Joshua the battle plan, and Joshua obeyed. He knew that God is in control.

History Project — S

In this unit you will make a map of the 12 tribes of Israel. Look in the back of your Bible or in a Bible atlas to see a map of the "Land of the Twelve Tribes". On white paper, draw the map of the twelve tribes' land and label each tribe. The tribe of Manasseh was split into 2 areas of land. Joseph's two sons, Ephraim and Manasseh, were each given land. Wait to color the map until Day 2.

Key Idea: God gave the Israelites the land He had promised them in Canaan. Each tribe had to fight for their land, but God was with them.

Storytime — T

Read aloud the following assigned passage:

★ *Tirzah: Ch. 18-19* p. 132-143

Discuss today's reading in a "conversational way". Share about a person, time, event, or emotion from your life that today's passage brought to mind. Next, have your child share a connection.

Key Idea: Connect personally to the passage.

Research — S

God promised Abraham, and then Isaac, and then Jacob that a great nation would come from them one day. Jacob had 12 sons that eventually became the 12 tribes. Where could you look to discover more about the **12 tribes of Israel**? Use a Bible, a reference book, or an online resource like www.wikipedia.org to look up *12 tribes of Israel.*

Orally answer one or more of the following questions from your research: *What are the names of the 12 tribes of Jacob (or Israel)? Who were the mothers of each of the 12 tribes? Since Joseph was one of Jacob's 12 sons, why isn't there a tribe named Joseph? What were the names of Joseph's two sons? Why are there tribes named for Joseph's two sons? How was it decided how much land each tribe would receive?*

Key Idea: God kept His promise to Abraham, Isaac, and Jacob when their descendants entered the Promised Land. Each of the tribes descended from Jacob's 12 sons received a portion of land for their tribe (or family).

Independent History Study — I

★ On white paper, follow the directions on p. 46-47 of *Draw and Write Through History* to draw and color the Ark of the Covenant. Store your completed picture in the place you have chosen for it.

Key Idea: The Ark of the Covenant carried the Ten Commandments, a jar of manna, and Aaron's staff. It went before the Israelites to remind them that they were God's people.

Learning the Basics

Focus: Language Arts, Math, Bible, and Science

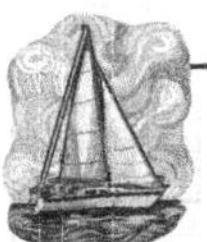

Poetry

T

Read aloud to the students the poem *"Looking-Glass River"* (see Appendix). Ask, *At the beginning of the poem, how does the poet describe the river? In the middle of the poem, what happens to change the appearance of the river? How does the poet describe the river then? What do the last 4 lines of the poem mean? Why is it necessary for water to be very still in order to reflect well?* Read the poem again with the students.

Key Idea: Read and appreciate classic poetry.

Language Arts

S

Have students complete the first studied dictation exercise (see Appendix for directions and passages).

Help students complete one lesson from the following reading program:

★ *Drawn into the Heart of Reading*

Work with the students to complete **one** of the English options listed below:

★ *Beginning Wisely:* Lesson 27

★ *Building with Diligence:* Lesson 27

★ Your own grammar program

Key Idea: Practice language arts skills.

Bible Study

T

Say, *Find Psalm 34:1-3 in your Bible. This is the memory selection for this unit. Read the verses out loud.* Ask, *If we follow David's example in Psalm 34:1, when should we bless the Lord? Is it easy to bless the Lord at all times? Why not? How can God's praise be continually in our mouth? In Psalm 34:2, why is it good for our soul to boast in the Lord? How is this different from boasting about ourselves? What does it mean to be humble? Why would the humble be glad to hear people boasting about the Lord's goodness?*

Have students say the verse 3 times, adding hand motions to help remember the words.

✔ *Lead Me to the Rock* CD
Track 5; Song: "O Magnify the Lord" (vs. 1-3)

Key Idea: Praise for the Lord should continually be heard from our lips.

Math Exploration

S

Choose **one** of the math options listed below (see Appendix for details).

★ *Singapore Primary Mathematics 2A/2B, 3A/3B,* or *4A/4B*

★ Your own math program

Key Idea: Use a step-by-step math program.

Science Exploration

I

Today you will add to your science notebook. Find the notebook page you began in Unit 5 titled, *What's living in a cactus desert?* You will add to your desert scene by drawing and coloring at least one "reptile" from p. 41 and at least one "Other Invertebrate" from p. 42 of *One Small Square: Cactus Desert.* Make sure to label your reptile and other invertebrate with their names. You may wish to look at p. 22-23 for larger views of some of the reptiles. You will continue adding to your desert scene over the next few units.

Key Idea: Reptiles have backbones and dry scaly skin. Invertebrates do not have bones. There are some reptiles and some invertebrates that are poisonous.

Learning through History

Focus: The Israelites in the Promised Land

Unit 8 - Day 2

Reading about History — T

Read about history in the following resource:

★ *Grandpa's Box: Ch. 14* p. 91-97

After today's reading, read Judges 6:1-16. Ask, *In Judges 6:1, why did the Lord give the Israelites over to the Midianites? How did the Midanites treat the Israelites in Judges 6:2-5? What did the Israelites do in Judges 6:6? What did the prophet say to the people in Judges 6:8-10? What reasons did God give for the Israelite's oppression by Midian? When God chose Gideon in Judges 6:12-13, how did Gideon respond? In Judges 6:14, how does the Lord respond to Gideon? What excuses does Gideon give in Judges 6:15? What can we learn from God's response in Judges 6:16?*

Key Idea: After Joshua died, the people forgot God and started worshiping idols! God allowed the Israelites to be overtaken by their enemies.

History Project — S

On your map of the 12 tribes, make a key in the bottom right corner. In the key, write *Leah, Rachel, Bilhah,* and *Zilpah*. Make a different colored square next to each name. On the map, color each tribe's land the matching color of the name in the key that the tribe descended from. Leah had Reuben, Simeon, Levi, Judah, Issachar, and Zebulun. The Levites were priests, so they did not own land. Rachel had Joseph and Benjamin. Joseph's 2 sons Ephraim and Manasseh were both given land. Rachel's servant Bilhah had Dan and Naphtali. Leah's servant Zilpah had Gad and Asher.

Key Idea: Gideon was from Manasseh's tribe.

Storytime — T

Read aloud the following assigned passage:

★ *Tirzah: Ch. 20-21* p. 144-159

Ask, *In today's reading, how were people's lives different from your life? What would you have enjoyed or found difficult about living during that time?*

Key Idea: Compare and contrast the historical time period of the reading to your own life.

Vocabulary — S

You may choose 3-5 of the following vocabulary words from *Grandpa's Box* to use for this lesson: *regiment* (p. 92), *bayonet* (p. 92), *lapped* (p. 95), *pantomimed* (p. 96), and/or *host* (p. 96). First, find the word in the text and read the sentence containing the word. Think about possible meanings. Next, find the word in a dictionary and select the correct meaning. Write the word at the top of an index card or at the top of the corresponding letter page in the notebook. Underneath the word, copy the correct definition from the dictionary. Then, use the word correctly in a sentence. The sentence may either be copied from the text or be one of your own creation. Last, draw a small picture to show the word's meaning. If you used an index card to record your word, file it under the correct alphabetical tab.

Key Idea: Gideon wasn't especially brave. Yet, God used him to defeat the Midianites. Gideon trusted in God and His strength, and God gave Gideon a great victory.

Independent History Study — I

★ Copy Hebrews 9:2-4 in cursive onto a clean page in your *Common Place Book*. You will continue to add copywork to your *Common Place Book* throughout the year.

Key Idea: The Ark of the Covenant was kept in the Most Holy Place. Only the high priest could enter this place. God was separated from the people in this way, yet the ark traveled with them to show that God was always with them.

Learning the Basics

Focus: Language Arts, Math, Bible, and Science

Unit 8 - Day 2

Language Arts

T

Work with the students to complete **one** of the English options listed below:

★ *Beginning Wisely:* Lesson 28

★ *Building with Diligence:* Lesson 28

★ Your own grammar program

Say, *You will be doing a writing activity based on the poem, "Looking-Glass River"* (see Appendix). Say, *Imagery means using words that paint a picture or an image in the reader's mind. What are some of the lines in the poem that paint a picture of the river in your mind?*

Next, say, *Today you will be using imagery to write a paragraph about the desert. Let's make a list of phrases that will help the reader "see" the desert through the words of your poem.* In the center of a markerboard or a piece of paper, draw a circle with spokes coming out of it. As students share phrases, write each one on a different spoke. Students may refer to *One Small Square: Cactus Desert* for ideas. If needed, give the following examples to get them started: blazing sun, scorching heat, sand dunes, cactus country, poisonous fangs and sharp stingers, saguaro cactus giants with sharp spines, chilly night air, and predators stalking their prey.

Then, have students use the list to write a paragraph with imagery that describes the desert. Discuss possible opening sentences. As students finish their paragraph, discuss possible ways to wrap-up the paragraph.

Have students share their paragraphs by reading them aloud.

Key Idea: Write creatively from classic poetry.

Bible Study

T

Have students say Psalm 34:1-3 using the hand motions they added on Day 1. Say, *A mood is a feeling, a sensation, or a state of mind. What is the mood of Psalm 34:1-3?* (Some examples of moods include frightened, worried, happy, peaceful, hopeful, sad, unhappy, angry, thankful, prayerful, joyful, and lonely.) Ask, *When would this Psalm help you, or when would you go to this Psalm?* (i.e. to remind us to bless the Lord in all circumstances, to help us to remember to be humble, to show that we should be praising our Lord with our mouths in song and by telling others of His goodness.)

Last, pray with your children, praising the Lord for the blessing of children. Thank God for His goodness and His mercies. Pray that each of you will remember to bless the Lord in joyful times and in hard times.

✔ *Lead Me to the Rock* CD
Track 5; Song: "O Magnify the Lord" (vs. 1-3)

Key Idea: The Psalms reflect the many emotions and moods we have. They are a wonderful place to seek counsel from the Lord.

Math Exploration

S

Choose **one** of the math options listed below (see Appendix for details).

★ *Singapore Primary Mathematics 2A/2B, 3A/3B,* or *4A/4B*

★ Your own math program

Key Idea: Use a step-by-step math program.

Science Exploration

I

★ Read *One Small Square: Cactus Desert* p. 28-29. Orally retell or narrate to an adult the portion of text that you read today. Use the *Narration Tips* in the Appendix for help as needed.

Key Idea: In the desert, rain doesn't come for months! When it does, roots near the surface of the ground quickly soak up any water that soaks in. Much of the water runs off the hard-packed Earth.

Learning through History
Focus: The Israelites in the Promised Land

Unit 8 - Day 3

Reading about History **T**

Read about history in the following resource:

★ *Grandpa's Box: Ch. 15* p. 98-104

After today's reading, have your students orally narrate or retell the portion of today's text that you read. Use the *Narration Tips* in the Appendix as needed.

Key Idea: Naomi and her husband Elimelech moved to Moab to find food during a time of famine. When Naomi's husband and both her sons died, Naomi decided to go back to her own land. Ruth chose to go with Naomi.

History Project **S**

Get out your map of the 12 tribes of Israel that you colored on Day 2. Cut apart the map, following the lines you drew between each tribe. Then, reassemble the map like a puzzle. When the puzzle is complete, either glue it on paper or place it in a ziploc bag to store for use later or as a keepsake.

Key Idea: Naomi and her husband were from the tribe of Judah. One day, Jesus would be born from the line of Judah.

Storytime **T**

Read aloud the following assigned passage:

★ Ruth 1:3-18; 4:9-17

Ask, *In what does the main character place his faith? How would the story be different if the main character put his faith in something other than in God? Share a character, a story, or a verse from the Bible that you are reminded of by today's reading.*

Key Idea: Share a Biblical connection.

Geography **S**

For today's activities you will need a globe and the map on p. 35 of *A Child's History of the World*. Follow these directions: *Find Moab on the globe in the modern-day country of Jordan, east of the Dead Sea. At the time of Naomi and Ruth's story, Moab was located just south of the Israelite tribe of Rueben. So, Moab was a neighboring country to the Israelite nation. It was a pagan country. Find the city of Bethlehem on the globe just south of Jerusalem in Israel. Ruth and Naomi returned to Bethlehem, which was Naomi's home. Look at the land of Canaan near the Red Sea on p. 35. What modern-country is the land of Canaan located in today? It is still a part of Israel!*

Review the following concept: *Point to and name the 5 oceans.* Note: Many texts list the Southern Ocean at the South Pole as a 5th ocean.

Key Idea: Ruth chose to make Naomi's country her own, and Naomi's God her God.

Independent History Study **I**

★ On white paper, follow the directions on p. 52-53 of *Draw and Write Through History* to draw David. Wait to color David until Day 4. Store your drawing in the place you have chosen for it.

Key Idea: The son of Boaz and Ruth was Obed. Obed was King David's grandfather. Jesus was later born from the line of King David. So, Ruth, the foreigner from Moab, is in the line of Christ.

Learning the Basics

Focus: Language Arts, Math, Bible, and Science

Poetry

T

Read aloud with the students the poem *"Looking-Glass River"* (see Appendix). Say, *Describe a time you have been somewhere like this. What can you learn about the poet, Robert Louis Stevenson, from the poem?* Say, *Did you know that Robert Louis Stevenson's first full-length book was about a slow trip he took down a French River? He must have had plenty of time to study the river on that trip!* Have the students read the poem again alone.

Key Idea: Read and appreciate classic poetry.

Language Arts

S

Have students complete one studied dictation exercise (see Appendix for directions and passages).

Help students complete one lesson from the following reading program:

 *Drawn into the Heart of Reading*

Work with the students to complete **one** of the English options listed below:

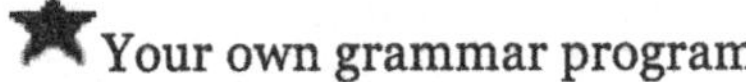

★ *Beginning Wisely:* Lesson 29

★ *Building with Diligence:* Lesson 29

★ Your own grammar program

Key Idea: Practice language arts skills.

Bible Study

T

Say, *You will be having your own quiet time with God today. Choose a quiet place for this special time, where you can be alone with God. Then, do the following things:*

1. Read Psalm 34:1-3 in your Bible.
2. Pray about the Psalm using the following beginning for your prayer: *Thank you for creating me to glorify you. Help me to remember to bless you with the words of my mouth by ________. Forgive me for ______, which I know doesn't bless you. Help me to remember to praise you all day.*
3. Recite Psalm 34:1-3 using the hand motions you added on Day 1.
4. Sing Psalm 34:1-3 along with the CD at the end of your quiet time.

✔ *Lead Me to the Rock* CD
Track 5; Song: "O Magnify the Lord" (vs. 1-3)

Key Idea: We need to praise the Lord often.

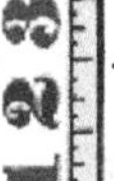

Math Exploration

S

Choose **one** of the math options listed below (see Appendix for details).

★ *Singapore Primary Mathematics 2A/2B, 3A/3B,* or *4A/4B*

★ Your own math program

Key Idea: Use a step-by-step math program.

Science Exploration

I

★ Read *One Small Square: Cactus Desert* p. 30-31. Write the answer to each numbered question on lined paper. You do not need to copy the question. Use the listed page to help you answer each question.

1. What do spadefoot toads do after it rains? (p. 30)
2. Draw the life cycle of a spadefoot toad. (p. 30)
3. Name some of the animals that you would see in the desert after a rain. (p. 30-31)
4. What do algae do after it rains? (p. 31)
5. What does Jeremiah 10:12-13 show us about God's power over the rain?

Key Idea: After it rains, animals like the spadefoot toad, algae, millipedes, and fairy shrimp come to life.

Learning through History
Focus: The Israelites in the Promised Land

Unit 8 - Day 4

Reading about History [T]

Read about history in the following resource:

★ *Grandpa's Box: Ch. 16* p. 105-111

After today's reading, say, *You will be writing a narration about part of the day's history reading. In order to remember the details very well, you will need to reread the part of today's reading from the second paragraph on p. 109 to the middle of p. 110 (on your own if possible).*

After students have finished reading the passage, ask them the questions below. If the students do not know the answers, help them find the answers in the passage they just read. Ask, *Where did God send Samuel? When God sent Samuel to anoint the next king, whom did God choose? What did God show Samuel when He chose David? Whom did David fight first? What did David understand about the fight with Goliath? How was David different from Saul?*

After the questions have been answered, have students write a 3-5 sentence narration that begins with, *God sent Samuel to...* When students have finished their narration, direct them to read the sentences out loud. Ask, *Did you include* ***who*** *the reading was mainly about? Did you include* ***what*** *important thing(s) happened? Did you include* ***how*** *it ended? If not, how could you add those things?*

See the *Written Narration Skills* in the Appendix to guide students in editing their narrations.

Key Idea: The Israelites wanted a king, so God gave them Saul. Israel needed to realize God was their king. Next, God gave them David.

Storytime [T]

Read aloud the following assigned passage:

★ 1 Samuel 16:1-13; 17:17-51

Say, *Transport yourself back to the time of this story. Become one of the characters. Tell me what you see and do. (Make sure to use the word, "I", and to tell only what happened in today's reading.)*

Key Idea: Practice oral narration skills.

Timeline [S]

You will be adding to your staircase timeline today. On a new timeline card, draw and color a stone wall. Write, *The Fall of Jericho (approximately 1400 B.C.).*

If you decided to tape your timeline cards to the back of a door, then add *The Fall of Jericho* card to the left of the *Exodus* card. If you decided to tape the timeline cards side-by-side to accordion-fold them, use clear packing tape to tape the cards as described above. Then, accordion-fold the timeline to store it.

Key Idea: God had helped the Israelite nation take the land of Canaan, starting with the battle of Jericho. But, the Israelites kept falling back into idol worship. Even though King Saul started out as a good king, he turned away from God and took matters into his own hands. So, God rejected Saul as king and chose David.

Independent History Study [I]

★ Take out your picture of David. Follow the directions on p. 53 of *Draw and Write Through History* to color David. Store your drawing in the place you have chosen for it.

Key Idea: After Saul, God gave Israel David as their next king. He was a man "after God's own heart".

Learning the Basics

Focus: Language Arts, Math, Bible, and Science

Poetry

T

Read aloud with the students the poem *"Looking-Glass River"* (see Appendix). Have students share this poem in a special way. Suggestions for sharing the poem include recording it to play for someone, reading it to someone on the telephone, photocopying the poem and adding illustrations, reading it to someone at home, putting the poem to a melody and singing it, using an instrument to tap out the meter or rhythm of the poem while reading it, or copying the poem on paper.

Key Idea: Share a variety of classic poetry.

Language Arts

S

Have students complete one dictation exercise.

Guide students to complete one reading lesson.

★ *Drawn into the Heart of Reading*

Help students complete **one** English lesson.

★ *Beginning Wisely:* Lesson 30

★ *Building with Diligence:* Lesson 30

★ Your own grammar program

Key Idea: Practice language arts skills.

Bible Study

T

Have students say Psalm 34:1-3 using the hand motions from Day 1.

Have students copy in cursive Psalm 34:1-3 on a clean page in their *Common Place Book*. Students should leave the rest of the page blank to add to next week.

Students will add to the *Common Place Book* throughout the year.

✔ *Lead Me to the Rock* CD
Track 5; Song: "O Magnify the Lord"
(vs. 1-3)

Key Idea: Copy in cursive a portion of a Psalm.

Math Exploration

S

Choose **one** math option listed below.

★ *Singapore Primary Mathematics 2A/2B, 3A/3B,* or *4A/4B*

★ Your own math program

Key Idea: Use a step-by-step math program.

Science Exploration

I

★ Read *One Small Square: Cactus Desert* p. 32-35. Turn to the science experiment section in your science binder or sketchbook. At the top of a blank page, write: *How does the design of a seed help it travel?* Under the question, write: *'Guess'*. Write down your guess. Seeds travel by sailing on the wind, floating on the water, getting stuck in animal fur as "hitchhikers", and being eaten and passed through the animal's body onto the ground. You will design 4 different seeds to travel the 4 different ways. Use one sheet of white paper, markers, tape, glue, waxed paper, and Velcro (or a piece of rough fabric like wool). Hint: The seed that travels by air will need to be parachute-like. The seed that travels by water will need to be waterproof and float. The seed that travels by hitchhiking will need to be rough to stick to animal fur. The seed that gets eaten will need to be bright and colorful to be noticed and look good to eat. After you create your seeds, test them in the following ways: 1) Drop them into the air. 2) Hide them in a room and have someone find them. 3) Rub against them. 4) Float them in water. Write: *'Procedure'*. Draw a picture of the experiment. At the bottom of the paper, write: *'Conclusion'*. Explain what you learned.

Key Idea: God designed each seed to travel in a special way. The rain makes the seeds sprout.

Learning through History

Focus: The Greeks at the Time of King David

Unit 9 - Day 1

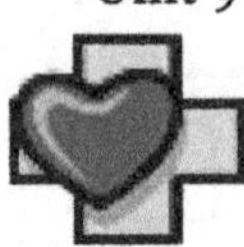

Reading about History [T]

Read about history in the following resource:

★ *Grandpa's Box: Ch. 17* p. 112-117

After today's reading, say, *Describe what God said was special about David.* (knowledge) *Tell about the promise God made to King David.* (comprehension) *After David sinned, how did God show him that what he'd done was wrong?* (analysis) *Why did David repent?* (evaluation) *What can you learn from Psalm 51?* (application)

Key Idea: God knew that David would sin. God filled David's heart with sorrow and repentance over the sin. David's sin had consequences, but God forgave David.

History Project [S]

In this unit you will make a sign to hang on the door to your room that describes you and your name. Use colorful markers and decorative lettering to write your name and its meaning in the center of a white sheet of paper (i.e. Joshua means "God saves".) Save your sign for Day 2.

Key Idea: David means "beloved". Even though David sinned, he was still loved by God. Aren't you glad that God still loves us even though we sin?

Storytime [T]

Read aloud the following assigned passage:

★ *Aesop's Fables* p. 6-12

Discuss today's reading in a "conversational way". Share about a person, time, event, or emotion from your life that today's reading brought to mind. Next, have your child share a connection.

Key Idea: Connect personally to the passage.

Research [S]

In Bible times, the meaning of a name was very important. Names might describe a feeling or an event from the time of the child's birth, or describe the family, or signify a hope for the child to fulfill. When Jacob's wives named their sons in Genesis 29:31-35 and Genesis 30: 1-24, each of the son's names described how the mother was feeling. Use an online source like www.babynamesworld.com or a baby name book to find the meaning of the names Jacob, Moses, Joshua, and/or Ruth. Then, find the meaning of your first and middle name. Depending on the resource you use, you will have to type each name in the search or look each name up in the index. Orally answer one or more of the following questions from your research: *What is the meaning of the name Jacob? What does the name Moses mean? Explain the meaning of the name Joshua. What is the meaning of the name Ruth? How does the meaning of those names match what you know about the person from the Bible? What is the meaning of your name? Was your name chosen for its meaning?*

Key Idea: Names are important.

Independent History Study [I]

★ On white paper, follow the directions on p. 54 of *Draw and Write Through History* to draw and color a sheep. Store your completed drawing in the place you have chosen for it.

Key Idea: God used David's years as a shepherd to train him to be a fighter and a protector.

Learning the Basics

Focus: Language Arts, Math, Bible, and Science

Unit 9 - Day 1

Poetry

T

Read aloud to the students the poem *"Autumn Fires"* (see Appendix). Ask, *What season is this poem written about? How does the poet help you picture the autumn fires? Why might you see fires in the autumn? How do the last 4 lines make you feel? What rhyming pattern do you notice in the poem?* Read the poem again with the students.

Key Idea: Read and appreciate classic poetry.

Language Arts

S

Have students complete the first studied dictation exercise (see Appendix for directions and passages).

Help students complete one lesson from the following reading program:

★ *Drawn into the Heart of Reading*

Work with the students to complete **one** of the English options listed below:

★ *Beginning Wisely:* Lesson 31

★ *Building with Diligence:* Lesson 31

★ Your own grammar program

Key Idea: Practice language arts skills.

Bible Study

T

Say, *Find Psalm 34:1-5 in your Bible. This is the memory selection for this unit. Read the verses out loud.* Ask, *In Psalm 34:4, what does David say happened when he sought the Lord? Is it possible to trust the Lord even when you are in a scary or difficult situation? Does this mean that He will always take the situation away? Then, how can the Lord deliver us from our fears, even though the situation around us may remain difficult? In Psalm 34:5, what does David say he could see in the faces of those who trusted in the Lord? How can we be comforted, encouraged, and uplifted by our hope in the Lord even in times of trouble?* Have students say the verse 3 times, adding hand motions to help remember the words.

✔ *Lead Me to the Rock* CD
Track 5; Song: "O Magnify the Lord"
(vs. 1-5)

Key Idea: The Lord is there if we seek Him.

Math Exploration

S

Choose **one** of the math options listed below (see Appendix for details).

★ *Singapore Primary Mathematics 2A/2B, 3A/3B,* or *4A/4B*

★ Your own math program

Key Idea: Use a step-by-step math program.

Science Exploration

I

Today you will add to your science notebook. Find the notebook page you began in Unit 5 titled, *What's living in a cactus desert?* You will add to your desert scene by drawing and coloring at least one "bird" from p. 41 and at least one "plant" from p. 43 of *One Small Square: Cactus Desert.* Make sure to label your bird and plant with their names. You may wish to look at p. 32-33 for larger views of some of the birds and flowering plants as you are drawing. This is your last entry in your desert scene.

Key Idea: In the desert, wildflowers bloom quickly to make seeds after a rain. Birds help carry the seeds to other places. The seeds are not harmed by cold nights or hot days. They sprout when it rains.

Learning through History

Focus: The Greeks at the Time of King David

Unit 9 - Day 2

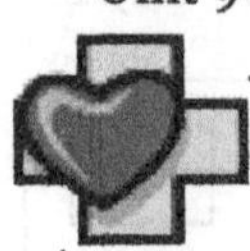

Reading about History [T]

Read about history in the following resource:

★ *A Child's History of the World: Ch. 10* p. 45-50

After today's reading, read aloud Acts 14:8-18. Ask, *In Acts 14:9, what reason is given for the lame man's healing? In whom did the man have faith in order to be healed? What did the people in Lystra do in Acts 14:11-13 when they saw what had happened? What did Paul and Barnabas say was wrong with the people's reaction in Acts 14:11-15? In Acts 14:17, what examples did Paul and Barnabas give as a testimony or evidence of God's care and greatness? In spite of what Paul and Barnabas said, what did the people still wish to do in Acts 14:18? Why was this wrong?*

Key Idea: The Greeks made up many stories of gods and goddesses. Later, the Romans adopted many of these gods. In the Bible we are commanded not to worship any other gods.

History Project [S]

Look on p. 46-47 of *A Child's History of the World* to see why the people in Acts 14:12 called Barnabas, Zeus; and Paul, Hermes? How do the planets Jupiter, Neptune, Mars, Mercury, Venus, and Pluto fit the descriptions of the Roman gods with those names on p. 46-47? Get the sign with your name on it. Draw small colorful pictures around your name to show your talents, hobbies, and favorite things.

Key Idea: The names of the Greek gods are still used today. Yet, the evidence of the one true God surrounds us in all of Creation.

Storytime [T]

Read aloud the following assigned passage:

★ *Aesop's Fables* p. 13-19

Ask, *What did today's fables remind you of from your own life? Explain. What can be learned from the fables? How can that help you in your life?*

Key Idea: Compare and apply the morals of the fables to your own life.

Vocabulary [S]

You may choose 3-5 of the following vocabulary words from *A Child's History of the World* to use for this lesson: *juts* (p. 45), *divine* (p. 45), *immortal* (p. 46), *omen* (p. 49), and/or *oracle* (p. 50). First, find the word in the text and read the sentence containing the word. Think about possible meanings. Next, find the word in a dictionary and select the correct meaning. Write the word at the top of an index card or at the top of the corresponding letter page in the notebook. Underneath the word, copy the correct definition from the dictionary. Then, use the word correctly in a sentence. The sentence may either be copied from the text or be one of your own creation. Last, draw a small picture to show the word's meaning. If you used an index card to record your word, file it under the correct alphabetical tab.

Key Idea: The Greeks believed in many gods. They made up stories about each god to show the god's personality and power. We do not need to make up stories about the one true God. We have His word the Bible that tells the truth about Him.

Independent History Study [I]

★ On lined paper, copy in cursive the **second** paragraph of *Draw and Write Through History* p. 55. Store your completed copywork with your completed drawings in the place you have chosen for them.

Key Idea: God chose David to be the next king over Israel after Saul. Saul and David lived near the time the Greeks were writing their tales of gods and goddesses.

Learning the Basics
Focus: Language Arts, Math, Bible, and Science

Language Arts

T

Work with the students to complete **one** of the English options listed below:

★ *Beginning Wisely:* Lesson 32

★ *Building with Diligence:* Lesson 32

★ Your own grammar program

Say, *You will be doing a writing activity based on the poem, "Autumn Fires"* (see Appendix). At the top of a markerboard or a piece of paper, list the name of the present season. Say, *You will be writing a poem or a paragraph about* ______ (name your present season). *Let's make a list of the things that we see during this season.* Write students' responses under the seasonal heading on the markerboard or paper. For example, for spring, you might list flowers blooming, rain showers, budding trees, grass growing, and birds returning.

Say, *You will use the list we just made to help you write a poem or a paragraph about this season.* Then, have students use the list to write a 4-8 line poem or a 4 sentence paragraph about the season.

To end their poem or paragraph, students may wish to copy the last 4 lines of the poem *"Autumn Fires"*, changing the last line of the poem to match the season that they are writing about.

Have students share the poem or paragraph by reading it aloud.

Key Idea: Write creatively from classic poetry.

Bible Study

T

Have students say Psalm 34:1-5 using the hand motions they added on Day 1. Say, *A mood is a feeling, a sensation, or a state of mind. What is the mood of Psalm 34:4-5?* (Some examples of moods include frightened, worried, happy, peaceful, hopeful, sad, unhappy, angry, thankful, prayerful, joyful, and lonely.) Ask, *When would this Psalm help you, or when would you go to this Psalm?* (i.e. as a reminder that we must seek the Lord, to give us hope and encouragement when we are fearful, to help us trust in the Lord and turn to Him even more during difficult times.)

Last, pray with your children that they will seek the Lord in good times and in bad times. Pray that the Lord will deliver them from their fears and will fill their hearts with comfort when they need it.

✔ *Lead Me to the Rock* CD
Track 5; Song: "O Magnify the Lord" (vs. 1-5)

Key Idea: The Psalms reflect the many emotions and moods we have. They are a wonderful place to seek counsel from the Lord.

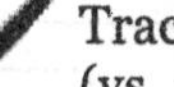

Math Exploration

S

Choose **one** of the math options listed below (see Appendix for details).

★ *Singapore Primary Mathematics 2A/2B, 3A/3B,* or *4A/4B*

★ Your own math program

Key Idea: Use a step-by-step math program.

Science Exploration

I

★ Read *One Small Square: Cactus Desert* p. 36-37. Orally retell or narrate to an adult the portion of text that you read today. Use the *Narration Tips* in the Appendix for help as needed.

Key Idea: Saguaro cactuses grow in the Sonoran Desert where there are only 2 rainy seasons. One season is in the summer and one is in the winter. The desert gets less then 10 inches of rain a year!

Learning through History

Focus: The Greeks at the Time of King David

Unit 9 - Day 3

Reading about History — T

Read about history in the following resource:

★ *A Child's History of the World: Ch. 11* p. 51-54

After today's reading, have your students orally narrate or retell the portion of today's text that you read. Use the *Narration Tips* in the Appendix as needed.

Key Idea: We are not sure how much of the legend of the Trojan War is true, but two famous poems written by the Greek poet Homer tell the story of this war. Often stories in ancient times were based on legends that changed over time as they were retold. However, God's word has not changed over time. It is still true today.

History Project — S

On p. 53 of *A Child's History of the World,* what explanation is given of where the names the *Iliad* and the *Odyssey* came from? Color the pictures that you drew on your name sign on Day 2. Then, hang your sign on your bedroom door.

Key Idea: The *Iliad* and the *Odyssey* are two famous poems that can still be read today. It's hard to know how much of the poems are true. But, we never have to wonder how much of God's word is true, because it's all true.

Storytime — T

Read aloud the following assigned passage:

★ *Aesop's Fables* p. 20-25

Ask, *In what does the main character place his faith? How would the story be different if the main character put his faith in God? Share a character, a story, or a verse from the Bible that you are reminded of by today's reading.*

Key Idea: Share a Biblical connection.

Geography — S

Use a globe for today's activities. *Find Hellas (or Greece) on the globe. Notice how Greece juts into the Mediterranean Sea. Find Troy on p. 35 of A Child's History of the World. Then, find the area where Troy would be in modern-day Turkey on the globe. Helen was carried off from Sparta across the Aegean Sea to Troy. Find Sparta on p. 35 of A Child's History of the World. Then, find the area where Sparta would be in modern-day Greece on the globe. What 3 seas surround modern-day Greece? Find the Mediterranean Sea, the Ionian Sea, and the Aegean Sea. On the globe, trace Helen's path from Sparta in Greece across the Aegean Sea to Troy (in modern-day Turkey).*

Review the following concept: *Point to and name the 5 oceans.* Note: Many texts list the Southern Ocean at the South Pole as a 5th ocean.

Key Idea: The story of Helen and the Trojan War is a Greek legend.

Independent History Study — I

★ Read *The Trojan Horse* p. 5-22. Then, copy Psalm 96:3-5 in cursive onto a clean page in your *Common Place Book.*

Key Idea: The Greek gods were idols. The Lord who made heaven and Earth is the one true God.

Learning the Basics
Focus: Language Arts, Math, Bible, and Science

Unit 9 - Day 3

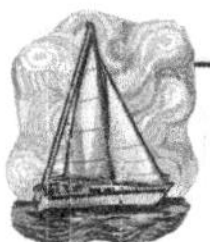

Poetry

T

Read aloud with the students the poem *"Autumn Fires"* (see Appendix). Say, *Describe a memory that the poem brought to mind. What can you learn about the poet from the poem?* Say, *Did you know that Robert Louis Stevenson grew up in Scotland in the mid-1800's? Many of his poems come from his childhood memories. Yet, the poems seem timeless, as we still enjoy them over 120 years later.* Have the students read the poem alone.

Key Idea: Read and appreciate classic poetry.

Language Arts

S

Have students complete one studied dictation exercise (see Appendix for directions and passages).

Help students complete one lesson from the following reading program:

★ *Drawn into the Heart of Reading*

Work with the students to complete **one** of the English options listed below:

★ *Beginning Wisely:* Lesson 33

★ *Building with Diligence:* Lesson 33

★ Your own grammar program

Key Idea: Practice language arts skills.

Bible Study

T

Say, *You will be having your own quiet time with God today. Choose a quiet place for this special time, where you can be alone with God. Then, do the following things:*

1. Read Psalm 34:1-5 in your Bible.
2. Pray about the Psalm using the following beginning for your prayer: *Thank you for always hearing me when I pray. Deliver me from my fear of______. Help me to trust in you instead. Help my face look______, so others can see I am comforted by you.*
3. Recite Psalm 34:1-5 using the hand motions you added on Day 1.
4. Sing Psalm 34:1-5 along with the CD at the end of your quiet time.

✔ *Lead Me to the Rock* CD
Track 5; Song: "O Magnify the Lord" (vs. 1-5)

Key Idea: When we seek the Lord, He always hears us. He can deliver us from our fears.

Math Exploration

S

Choose **one** of the math options listed below (see Appendix for details).

★ *Singapore Primary Mathematics 2A/2B, 3A/3B,* or *4A/4B*

★ Your own math program

Key Idea: Use a step-by-step math program.

Science Exploration

I

★ Read *One Small Square: Cactus Desert* p. 40-43. Write the answer to each numbered question on lined paper. You do not need to copy the question. Use the listed page to help you answer each question.

1. How can you tell which animals are mammals? (p. 40)
2. Explain how the skin of a reptile and the skin of an amphibian are different. (p. 40)
3. Which types of animals would you need a microscope to see? (p. 42)
4. Draw a fungus. (p. 43)
5. What does Matthew 6:26-34 show you about how God cares for all of His creation?

Key Idea: God cares for all of His creation and knows our needs. We can trust Him to care for us.

Learning through History
Focus: The Greeks at the Time of King David

Unit 9 - Day 4

Reading about History (T)

Read about history in the following resource:

★ *A Child's History of the World: Ch. 12* p. 55-58 79-83

After today's reading, say, *You will be writing a narration about part of the day's history reading. In order to remember the details very well, you will need to reread the part of today's reading from the last paragraph on p. 56 through the first sentence on p. 58 (on your own if possible).*

After students have finished reading the passage, ask them the questions below. If the students do not know the answers, help them find the answers in the passage they just read. Ask, *Who became King of Israel after David? When Solomon became King of Israel, what did he build? What words can be used to describe the temple and palace? Who came to see Solomon? What was Solomon known for? Where did Solomon get his wisdom?*

After the questions have been answered, have students write a 3-5 sentence narration that begins, *After David, Solomon...* When students have finished their narration, direct them to read the sentences out loud. Ask, *Did you include **who** the reading was mainly about? Did you include **what** important thing(s) happened? Did you include **how** it ended? If not, how could you add those things?*

See the *Written Narration Skills* in the Appendix to guide students in editing their narrations.

Key Idea: God chose David to be King of Israel after Saul. David's son Solomon was king next.

Storytime (T)

Read aloud the following assigned passage:

★ *Aesop's Fables* p. 26-33

Say, *Transport yourself back to the time of this story. Become one of the characters. Tell me what you see and do. (Make sure to use the word, "I", and to tell only what happened in today's reading.)*

Key Idea: Practice oral narration skills.

Timeline (S)

You will be adding 3 new cards to your staircase timeline today. On the first new card, draw and color the Trojan Horse. Write, *Trojan War (approximately 1200 B.C.).* On the second new card, draw and color a sling. Write, *King David (1040 B.C.).* On the third new card, draw a golden temple. Write, *Solomon Builds the Temple (967 B.C.).*

If you decided to tape your timeline cards to the back of a door, then add the *Trojan War* card to the left of *The Fall of Jericho* card. To the left of the *Trojan War* card, add the *King David* card. Then, begin a new row above the row you just made (like a staircase). On the left side, tape the *Solomon* card. If you decided to tape the timeline cards side-by-side to accordion-fold them, use clear packing tape to tape the cards as described above. Then, accordion-fold the timeline to store it.

Key Idea: At the time of the Greeks, the Israelites were still fighting for the land of Canaan. David was a soldier and a fighter. His son, Solomon, was chosen to build the temple.

Independent History Study (I)

★ Read *The Trojan Horse* p. 23-30. On white paper, follow the directions on p. 50-51 of *Draw and Write Through History* to draw the Trojan Horse. Wait to color your horse until Unit 10. Store your drawing in the place you have chosen for it.

Key Idea: Legends exaggerate or stretch the truth of a real story or an event. The Trojan Horse is a legend.

Learning the Basics
Focus: Language Arts, Math, Bible, and Science

Poetry
T

Read aloud with the students the poem *"Autumn Fires"* (see Appendix). Have students share this poem in a special way. Suggestions for sharing the poem include recording it to play for someone, reading it to someone on the telephone, photocopying the poem and adding illustrations, reading it to someone at home, putting the poem to a melody and singing it, using an instrument to tap out the meter or rhythm of the poem while reading it, or copying the poem on paper.

Key Idea: Share a variety of classic poetry.

Language Arts
S

Have students complete one dictation exercise.

Guide students to complete one reading lesson.

★ *Drawn into the Heart of Reading*

Help students complete **one** English lesson.

★ *Beginning Wisely:* Lesson 34

★ *Building with Diligence:* Lesson 34

★ Your own grammar program

Key Idea: Practice language arts skills.

Bible Study
T

Have students say Psalm 34:1-5 using the hand motions from Day 1.

Have students copy in cursive Psalm 34:4-5 beneath last unit's Psalm 34:1-3 in their *Common Place Book.* Students should leave the rest of the page blank to add to next week.

Students will add to the *Common Place Book* throughout the year.

✔ *Lead Me to the Rock* CD
Track 5; Song: "O Magnify the Lord" (vs. 1-5)

Key Idea: Copy in cursive a portion of a Psalm.

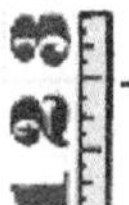

Math Exploration
S

Choose **one** math option listed below.

★ *Singapore Primary Mathematics 2A/2B, 3A/3B,* or *4A/4B*

★ Your own math program

Key Idea: Use a step-by-step math program.

Science Exploration
I

★ Read *One Small Square: Cactus Desert* p. 38-39. Turn to the science experiment section in your science binder or sketchbook. At the top of a blank page, write: *Why does water disappear so quickly in the desert after it rains?* Under the question, write: *'Guess'*. Write down your guess.

Get out a rectangular pan. Inside the pan, spread a thin layer of either clay or peanut butter on half of it. Sprinkle either sand or dry cereal over the clay or peanut butter. Use the bottom of a cup to press the sand or cereal pieces into the layer beneath it. Together these layers will be your hard desert "soil". Next, use either a strainer, a watering can, or a paper cup with large holes poked in the bottom to water your desert. What happened to the water? Why did it have a tough time soaking into your desert soil? Tip the pan and watch what happens next. Why did most of the water run off of the soil? On your paper, write: *'Procedure'*. Draw a picture of the experiment. At the bottom of the paper, write: *'Conclusion'*. Explain what you learned.

Key Idea: In the desert, the Sun bakes the sand until it's hard, making it difficult for rainwater to soak in.

Learning through History

Focus: Early Greece and Rome

Unit 10 - Day 1

Reading about History T

Read about history in the following resource:

★ *A Child's History of the World: Ch. 13* p. 59-62 84-89

After today's reading, say, *Why do we call the ABC's the alphabet?* (knowledge) *List some of the things for which the Phoenicians were known.* (comprehension) *Contrast how the Jewish religion was different from the Phoenicians.* (analysis) *Where did King Solomon get the cedar wood needed to build God's temple?* (knowledge) *Over time, even King Solomon began worshiping idols. How did this happen?* (evaluation)

Key Idea: King Solomon used cedar trees from the Phoenicians to build God's temple. The Phoenicians and the Israelites were neighbors. Yet, the Phoenicians worshiped idols, and the Israelites worshiped the one true God.

History Project S

In this unit you will make a scytale message like the Spartan army used in ancient Greece. Cut strips of white paper that are each 1 inch wide. Tape the ends of the strips together to make one long strip that is at least 36 inches long. Save the long strip of paper for Day 2.

Key Idea: The Phoenicians were a strong civilization at the same time that the ancient Greeks were building their civilization. The Phoenicians descended from the Canaanites and were eventually conquered by Assyria. The Phoenicians were known for their cedar trees, their shipbuilding, and their purple cloth.

Storytime T

Read aloud the following assigned passage:

★ *Aesop's Fables* p. 34-39

Discuss today's reading in a "conversational way". Share about a person, time, event, or emotion from your life that today's reading brought to mind. Next, have your child share a connection.

Key Idea: Connect personally to the passage.

Research S

In ancient Greece, the Spartan army used a method called scytale to pass secret military messages. Where could you look to discover more about the **scytale** method? A dictionary will give you a definition of scytale. An encyclopedia will tell you what scytale is and show you a picture of a message sent that way. Use a reference book or an online resource like www.wikipedia.org to look up *scytale*. Depending on the resource you use, you will have to type *scytale* or *cryptography* in the search or look it up in the index.

Orally answer one or more of the following questions from your research: *What is scytale? What did the Spartans use scytale or cryptograms for in wartime? How is scytale used? How would this method help keep messages secret? Why wouldn't the enemy be able to read messages sent using the scytale method? What would you have to have in order to read the message?*

Key Idea: The Phoenicians were great sailors. Their merchant ships traded in far away places.

Independent History Study I

★ Read *The Trojan Horse* p. 31-37. Take out your picture of the Trojan Horse. Follow the directions on p. 51 of *Draw and Write Through History* to color the horse. Store your drawing in the place you have chosen for it.

Key Idea: By the time of the Trojan War in 1200 B.C., the Phoenicians had become very powerful traders.

Learning the Basics

Focus: Language Arts, Math, Bible, and Science

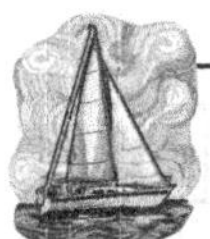

Poetry

T

Read aloud to the students the poem *"My Shadow"* (see Appendix). Ask, *How is the shadow different from a "proper child"? What causes the shadow to shoot up tall or to shrink very small? Why does the child call his shadow a "coward"? In the last stanza, where is the shadow? Why isn't the shadow up yet? How does Robert Louis Stevenson make the shadow seem like a person?* Read the poem again with the students.

Key Idea: Read and appreciate classic poetry.

Language Arts

S

Have students complete the first studied dictation exercise (see Appendix for directions and passages).

Help students complete one lesson from the following reading program:

★ *Drawn into the Heart of Reading*

Work with the students to complete **one** of the English options listed below:

★ *Beginning Wisely:* Lesson 35

★ *Building with Diligence:* Lesson 35

★ Your own grammar program

Key Idea: Practice language arts skills.

Bible Study

T

Say, *Find Psalm 34:1-6 in your Bible. This is the memory selection for this unit. Read the verses out loud.* Ask, *In Psalm 34:6, what is the poor man doing? How is David feeling in this Psalm if he is "crying out" to the Lord? What does Psalm 34:6 say the Lord did? How can the Lord save a man from all of his troubles? Is anything too difficult for the Lord?*

Have students say the verse 3 times, adding hand motions to help remember the words.

✔ *Lead Me to the Rock* CD
Track 5; Song: "O Magnify the Lord" (vs. 1-6)

Key Idea: In times of trouble, we should cry out to the Lord. He always hears our prayers and can save us from our fears.

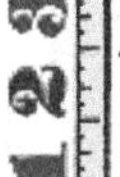

Math Exploration

S

Choose **one** of the math options listed below (see Appendix for details).

★ *Singapore Primary Mathematics 2A/2B, 3A/3B,* or *4A/4B*

★ Your own math program

Key Idea: Use a step-by-step math program.

Science Exploration

I

★ Read *The Great Dinosaur Mystery and the Bible* p. 9-13. At the top of an unlined paper, copy John 1:3 in cursive. Beneath the verse, copy the following text:

Problems with Fossils:

1. Fossils are often incomplete. Bones can be missing or damaged.
2. Different creatures might be mixed together.
3. We are guessing what the creature looked like, which means our information isn't based on fact.
4. We have never seen a live one, so we're not sure about the fossil's skin, flesh-type, and color.

Key Idea: God made everything from nothing! We are just guessing about how things are put together.

Learning through History

Focus: Early Greece and Rome

Unit 10 - Day 2

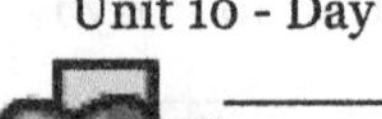

Reading about History — T

Read about history in the following resource:

★ *A Child's History of the World: Ch. 14* p. 63-66 90-95

After today's reading, read aloud 1 Corinthians 1:20-25. Say, *What is Paul saying about the wisdom of the world in 1 Corinthians 1:20? What does 1 Corinthians 1:22 say that the Greeks looked for or valued? In 1 Corinthians 1:23, since the Greeks believed in powerful mythological gods, how would the crucifixion of Christ be a stumbling block to them believing that Jesus was God's son? Even though believing in Christ seems foolish to the world, what does 1 Corinthians 1:24-25 say? What message is there in 1 Corinthians 1:25 about the two things that the Greeks prized, wisdom and strength?*

Key Idea: We should prize God above all.

Storytime — T

Read aloud the following assigned passage:

★ *Aesop's Fables* p. 40-45

Ask, *What did today's fables remind you of from your own life? Explain. What can be learned from the fables? How can that help you in your life?*

Key Idea: Compare and apply the morals of the fables to your own life.

History Project — S

Get the long strip of paper that you made on Day 1. Wrap the long strip of paper in a spiral around a rolling pin or a paper towel tube. As you wind, make sure the edges of the paper touch, but do not overlap. Tape the top and bottom ends of the paper strip to the rolling pin or tube. Lay the rolling pin or tube up and down or vertically on a table. Write a message going down, by placing one letter on each strip. Leave a strip blank between words. Each time you reach the end of the rolling pin or tube, start over at the top. When your message is complete, unwind the paper. Save it for Day 3.

Key Idea: The Spartans had a strong military.

Vocabulary — S

You may choose 3-5 of the following vocabulary words from *A Child's History of the World* to use for this lesson: *account* (p. 63), *obliged* (p. 64), *bitter* (p. 64), *luxuries* (p. 65), and/or *laconic* (p. 65). First, find the word in the text and read the sentence containing the word. Think about possible meanings. Next, find the word in a dictionary and select the correct meaning. Write the word at the top of an index card or at the top of the corresponding letter page in the notebook. Underneath the word, copy the correct definition from the dictionary. Then, use the word correctly in a sentence. The sentence may either be copied from the text or be one of your own creation. Last, draw a small picture to show the word's meaning. If you used an index card to record your word, file it under the correct alphabetical tab.

Key Idea: In ancient Greece, Sparta and Athens were the two main cities. The Spartans and the Athenians prized different things. The Spartans prized discipline and military strength. The Athenians prized the arts, beauty, and training the mind and body.

Independent History Study — I

★ Read *The Trojan Horse* p. 38-47. On lined paper, copy in cursive the **first** paragraph of *Draw and Write Through History* p. 55. Store your completed copywork with your completed drawings in the place you have chosen for them.

Key Idea: Along with the legend of the Trojan Horse, comes the saying, *Beware of Greeks bearing gifts.*

Learning the Basics

Focus: Language Arts, Math, Bible, and Science

Language Arts

T

Work with the students to complete **one** of the English options listed below:

★ *Beginning Wisely:* Lesson 36

★ *Building with Diligence:* Lesson 36 (half)

★ Your own grammar program

Say, *You will be doing a writing activity based on the poem, "My Shadow"* (see Appendix).

Say, *Personification means giving human actions or qualities to an object.* At the top of a markerboard or a paper, make 2 columns labeled *"Shadow"* and *"Wind"*. Say, *List the human actions or qualities that Robert Louis Stevenson gave to the shadow in the poem.* Write the students' responses under the *"Shadow"* heading (i.e. goes in and out, jump, grow, make a fool of me, stays close, coward, fast asleep in bed).

Ask, *What human actions or qualities could you give the wind?* Write down the students' ideas under the *"Wind"* column (i.e. sings in the heavens, whistles through the trees, roars over the sea, ruffles the bird's feathers, dries the puddles, etc.).

Say, *You will use the list we made about the wind to write your own poem or paragraph. It must be at least 4 lines or 4 sentences in length. You need to use personification in your writing so that the wind sounds like a real person.*

Have students share the poem or paragraph by reading it aloud.

Key Idea: Write creatively from classic poetry.

Bible Study

T

Have students say Psalm 34:1-6 using the hand motions they added on Day 1. Say, *A mood is a feeling, a sensation, or a state of mind. What is the mood of Psalm 34:6?* (Some examples of moods include frightened, worried, happy, peaceful, hopeful, sad, unhappy, angry, thankful, prayerful, joyful, and lonely.) Ask, *When would this Psalm help you, or when would you go to this Psalm?* (i.e. as an encouragement to cry out to the Lord in times of trouble, as a reminder that the Lord hears our prayers, to give us hope that the Lord will deliver us from our fears)

Last, pray with your children that they will cry out to the Lord when they are fearful. Pray that the Lord will hear their prayers and will deliver them from their fears.

✔ *Lead Me to the Rock* CD
Track 5; Song: "O Magnify the Lord" (vs. 1-6)

Key Idea: The Psalms reflect the many emotions and moods we have. They are a wonderful place to seek counsel from the Lord.

Math Exploration

S

Choose **one** of the math options listed below (see Appendix for details).

★ *Singapore Primary Mathematics 2A/2B, 3A/3B, or 4A/4B*

★ Your own math program

Key Idea: Use a step-by-step math program.

Science Exploration

I

★ Read *The Great Dinosaur Mystery and the Bible* p. 14-15. Orally retell or narrate to an adult the portion of text that you read today. Use the *Narration Tips* in the Appendix for help as needed.

Key Idea: There are many problems with fossils. Putting together a dinosaur skeleton is like putting together a puzzle, with many missing or damaged pieces! All descriptions of dinosaurs are based on guesses, which often turn out to be wrong as more information is found. Only God knows the answers.

Reading about History [T]

Read about history in the following resource:

★ *A Child's History of the World: Ch. 15* p. 67-70

After today's reading, have your students orally narrate or retell the portion of today's text that you read. Use the *Narration Tips* in the Appendix as needed.

Key Idea: The Greeks had a big, outdoor sports meet once every four years in Olympia. The best Greek men or boys came to compete in the games. A truce was declared in times of war, so the games could go on. All competitors were expected to show good sportsmanship. Winners were crowned with laurel wreaths.

History Project [S]

Get out the scytale message you wrote yesterday. Choose someone to read your message. Give them both the message and the same rolling pin or paper towel tube that you used when writing the message on Day 2. Help the receiver of your message wrap the paper strip around the rolling pin or tube. See if the message can be decoded. Try winding the message around a different-sized tube. Can the message still be read? Why not? Why would the Spartans need to make sure the receiver of the message had the same-sized cylinder used for writing the message?

Key Idea: Due to their harsh training, the Spartans often won many of the early athletic games held in Olympia.

Storytime [T]

Read aloud the following assigned passage:

★ *Aesop's Fables* p. 46-52

Ask, *In what does the main character place his faith? How would the story be different if the main character put his faith in God? Share a character, a story, or a verse from the Bible that you are reminded of by today's reading.*

Key Idea: Share a Biblical connection.

Geography [S]

Use a globe for today's activities. Olympia was the site of the first Olympics in Greece. *Find Olympia on p. 35 of A Child's History of the World. Then, find the same area on the globe where Olympia would be in modern-day Greece. Athens was the site where the new Olympic Games were first held in 1896. Find Athens on p. 35 of A Child's History of the World. Then, find Athens on the globe in modern-day Greece. On what continent is Greece located?*

Review the following concept: *Point to and name the 5 oceans.* Note: Many texts list the Southern Ocean at the South Pole as a 5th ocean.

Key Idea: The first recorded date we have for the Greek Olympiad is 776 B.C. After a long time, the Greeks no longer had the Olympiad. In 1896, the Olympic Games began again in Athens. Countries around the world were invited to participate.

Independent History Study [I]

★ On lined paper, copy in cursive the **first** paragraph from p. 61 of *Draw and Write Through History.* Store your completed copywork with your completed drawings in the place you have chosen for them.

Key Idea: The Olympic games were held in honor of the Greek god Zeus. Who do today's athletes honor? Since all gifts and abilities are given to us by our heavenly Father, who should receive the honor and glory?

Learning the Basics

Focus: Language Arts, Math, Bible, and Science

Unit 10 - Day 3

Poetry

T

Read aloud with the students the poem *"My Shadow"* (see Appendix). Say, *Describe a memory that the poem brought to mind. What can you learn about the poet from the poem?* Say, *Did you know that when Robert Louis Stevenson was a child, he had a nurse he called "Cummie"? She cared for him when he was sick, and he loved her very much. He dedicated the poems you are reading to her.* Have the students read the poem on their own.

Key Idea: Read and appreciate classic poetry.

Language Arts

S

Have students complete one studied dictation exercise (see Appendix for directions and passages).

Help students complete one lesson from the following reading program:

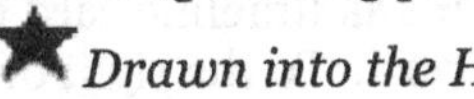

★ *Drawn into the Heart of Reading*

Work with the students to complete **one** of the English options listed below:

★ *Beginning Wisely:* Lesson 37

★ *Building with Diligence:* Lesson 36 (Half)

★ Your own grammar program

Key Idea: Practice language arts skills.

Bible Study

T

Say, *You will be having your own quiet time with God today. Choose a quiet place for this special time, where you can be alone with God. Then, do the following things:*

1. Read Psalm 34:1-6 in your Bible.
2. Pray about the Psalm using the following beginning for your prayer: *Thank you for hearing me when I pray. Help me to cry out to you when ________. Right now, I know that ________ really needs you, because ________. Please help ________.*
3. Recite Psalm 34:1-6 using the hand motions you added on Day 1.
4. Sing Psalm 34:1-6 along with the CD at the end of your quiet time.

✔ *Lead Me to the Rock* CD
Track 5; Song: "O Magnify the Lord" (vs. 1-6)

Key Idea: The Lord hears us when we pray.

Math Exploration

S

Choose **one** of the math options listed below (see Appendix for details).

★ *Singapore Primary Mathematics 2A/2B, 3A/3B*, or *4A/4B*

★ Your own math program

Key Idea: Use a step-by-step math program.

Science Exploration

I

★ Read *The Great Dinosaur Mystery and the Bible* p. 16-19. Write the answer to each numbered question on lined paper. You do not need to copy the question. Use the listed page to help you answer each question.

1. Where did dinosaurs come from? (p. 16)
2. Approximately how old is the book of Job? (p. 19)
3. Why do you think the book of Job has such clear descriptions of dinosaur-like animals? (p. 19)
4. Why would people have forgotten about the dinosaurs over time? (p. 19)
5. How is the behemoth described in Job 40:15-19? (p. 18)

Key Idea: God is the Creator of all living things. He created dinosaur-like creatures as described in Job.

Reading about History [T]

Read about history in the following resource:

★ *A Child's History of the World: Ch. 16* p. 71-73

After today's reading, say, *You will be writing a narration about part of the day's history reading. In order to remember the details very well, you will need to reread the part of today's reading from the sixth paragraph on p. 71 through p. 72 (on your own if possible).*

After students have finished reading the passage, ask them the questions below. If the students do not know the answers, help them find the answers in the passage they just read. Ask, *Today's story was about the founding of what city? Is the story of how Rome began true? Who fled from Troy as it was burning? According to the story, how and where did Aeneas meet Lavinia? What were the names of the twins that were eventually born within Aeneas' and Lavinia's family? What happened to Romulus and Remus when they were babies? How were the twins supposedly saved? When the twins grew up, what happened?*

After the questions have been answered, have students write a 3-5 sentence narration that begins, *The story of the founding of Rome...* When students have finished their narration, direct them to read the sentences out loud. Ask, *Did you include* ***who*** *the reading was mainly about? Did you include* ***what*** *important thing(s) happened? Did you include* ***how*** *it ended?* See the *Written Narration Skills* in the Appendix to guide students in editing their narrations.

Key Idea: The founding of Rome is a legend.

Storytime [T]

Read aloud the following assigned passage:

★ *Aesop's Fables* p. 53-55

Say, *Transport yourself back to the time of this story. Become one of the characters. Tell me what you see and do. (Make sure to use the word, "I", and to tell only what happened in today's reading.)*

Key Idea: Practice oral narration skills.

Timeline [S]

You will be adding 2 new cards to your staircase timeline today. On the first new card, draw and color a torch. Write, *First Olympiad (776 B.C.)*. On the second new card, draw and color a wolf. Write, *Founding of Rome (735 B.C.)*.

If you decided to tape your timeline cards to the back of a door, add a blank timeline card to the right of the *Solomon* card. To the right of the blank card, add the *First Olympiad* card. To the right of the *First Olympiad* card, add the *Founding of Rome* card. If you decided to tape the timeline cards side-by-side to accordion-fold them, use clear packing tape to tape the cards as described above.

Key Idea: The legend of the founding of Rome says that the twins Romulus and Remus were descended from the Trojan hero Aeneas. The story of the twin boys sounds similar to the Bible stories of baby Moses in the basket and of Cain killing Abel. Many myths and legends have parts that sound like stories from the Bible.

Independent History Study [I]

★ Read *The Young Christian's Introduction to the Bible: Ch. 1* p. 1-2. Then, read 2 Timothy 3:16-17 out loud to an adult and explain what the verses mean.

Key Idea: Legends exaggerate or stretch the truth of a real story or an event. The story of the founding of Rome is a legend. The Bible stories are true.

Learning the Basics

Focus: Language Arts, Math, Bible, and Science

Unit 10 - Day 4

Poetry

T

Read aloud with the students the poem *"My Shadow"* (see Appendix). Have students share this poem in a special way. Suggestions for sharing the poem include recording it to play for someone, reading it to someone on the telephone, photocopying the poem and adding illustrations, reading it to someone at home, putting the poem to a melody and singing it, using an instrument to tap out the meter or rhythm of the poem while reading it, or copying the poem on paper.

Key Idea: Share a variety of classic poetry.

Bible Study

T

Have students say Psalm 34:1-6 using the hand motions from Day 1.

Have students copy in cursive Psalm 34:6 beneath last unit's Psalm 34:4-5 in their *Common Place Book*. Students should leave the rest of the page blank to add to next week.

Students will add to the *Common Place Book* throughout the year.

✔ *Lead Me to the Rock* CD
Track 5; Song: "O Magnify the Lord" (vs. 1-6)

Key Idea: Copy in cursive a portion of a Psalm.

Language Arts

S

Have students complete one dictation exercise.

Guide students to complete one reading lesson.

★ *Drawn into the Heart of Reading*

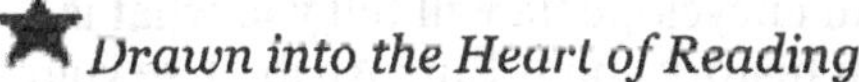

Help students complete **one** English lesson.

★ *Beginning Wisely:* Lesson 38

★ *Building with Diligence:* Lesson 37

★ Your own grammar program

Key Idea: Practice language arts skills.

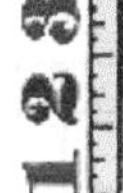

Math Exploration

S

Choose **one** math option listed below.

★ *Singapore Primary Mathematics 2A/2B, 3A/3B,* or *4A/4B*

★ Your own math program

Key Idea: Use a step-by-step math program.

Science Exploration

I

★ Read *The Great Dinosaur Mystery and the Bible* p. 20-21. Turn to the science experiment section in your science binder or sketchbook. At the top of a blank page, write: *What are the parts of an animal cell?* Under the question, write: *'Guess'*. Write down your guess. You will build a model of an animal cell today. First, mix ¾ cup corn starch and ½ cup water in a bowl. This will be the animal cell's **cytoplasm**. Cover a plate with a sheet of waxed paper. Spoon the mixture onto the plate. Animal cells have a **cell membrane**, which is a thin layer of protein and fat that surrounds the cytoplasm. Lift the cytoplasm to feel the membrane. Next, place a round object like a marble or a cherry in the center of the cell to be the **nucleus**. The nucleus of the cell contains the cell's chromosomes and controls the cell's activity. Place several pieces of macaroni or small marshmallows in the cytoplasm to be **vacuoles**. Vacuoles store food or waste. Place 3 or 4 jelly beans or blobs of jelly in the cytoplasm to be **mitochondria**. Mitochondria produce needed energy for the cell. On your paper, write: *'Procedure'*. Draw a picture of the experiment. Label the parts of the cell. At the bottom of the paper, write: *'Conclusion'*. Explain what you learned.

Key Idea: God designed every part of each animal including the very smallest cell. Isn't God amazing?!?

Learning through History
Focus: The Israelites Worship Idols

Unit 11 - Day 1

Reading about History **T**

Read about history in the following resource:
★ *Grandpa's Box: Ch. 18* p. 118-123

After today's reading, say, *Describe how Solomon's kingdom became divided after his death.* (comprehension) *Into what 2 parts was the kingdom divided?* (knowledge) *When Ahab was king in Israel, what wicked things did he do?* (knowledge) *Contrast the behavior of the prophets of Baal with what Elijah did.* (analysis) *Explain how God showed Israel that He is the one true God.* (evaluation)

Key Idea: After Solomon, the kings of Israel led the people in idol worship. When Ahab was king of Israel, he married Jezebel from the neighboring kingdom of Phoenicia. She brought the worship of Baal to Israel.

History Project **S**

In this unit you will make a flipbook of the contest that God set forth between Elijah on Mt. Carmel with the prophets of Baal. You will need 10 index cards or 10 small sheets of heavy paper. You will be drawing one continuous event which progresses in sequence on the cards. Each picture will vary slightly from the one on the card before it so that when the cards are stapled together and flipped you will see the moving pictures of the story. On the first card draw the stone altar on Mt. Carmel. On the second card, draw the same exact altar, but add a small stream of water pouring over it. Make the third card like the second card, with a larger stream of water. Save the rest for Day 2.

Key Idea: The contest revealed the true God.

Storytime **T**

Read aloud the following assigned passage:
★ 1 Kings 16:29-34; 17:1; and 18:16-46
Discuss today's reading in a "conversational way". Share about a person, time, event, or emotion from your life that today's reading brought to mind. Next, have your child share a connection.

Key Idea: Connect personally to the passage.

Research **S**

Solomon's kingdom was divided after his death into 2 parts, Israel and Judah. Was Ahab king of Israel or Judah? Where could you look to discover more about **King Ahab**? The index in your Bible or a Bible concordance will show you where in Scripture you can read about King Ahab. An encyclopedia will tell you what is known in history about King Ahab. Use your Bible, a reference book, or an online resource like www.wikipedia.org to look up *King Ahab*. Depending on the resource you use, you will have to type *King Ahab* in the search or look it up in the index alphabetically.

Orally answer one or more of the following questions from your research: *Was Ahab king of Israel or Judah? At the time of Ahab, what were the names of the ten tribes that made up Israel? Which two tribes made up Judah? What kind of king was Ahab? How did Baal worship become a practice in Israel when Ahab was king? When Ahab was king of Israel, who was king of Judah? Who was Ahab's wife?*

Key Idea: Ahab did many evil things as king.

Independent History Study **I**

★ Read *The Young Christian's Introduction to the Bible: Ch. 2* p. 3-6. Orally retell or narrate to an adult the portion of text that you read today. Use the *Narration Tips* in the Appendix for help as needed.

Key Idea: God used many different men to write the Bible. His Word is perfectly preserved for us today.

Learning the Basics

Focus: Language Arts, Math, Bible, and Science

Unit 11 - Day 1

Poetry

T

Guide students to choose one of Robert Louis Stevenson's poems from Units 1-10 to memorize. Students will have 2 weeks (units) to memorize the entire poem. So, students should have half of their chosen poem memorized by Day 4 of this unit. After students have chosen their poem, have them read it 3 times, adding actions.

Key Idea: Read and appreciate classic poetry.

Language Arts

S

Have students complete the first studied dictation exercise (see Appendix for directions and passages).

Help students complete one lesson from the following reading program:

 *Drawn into the Heart of Reading*

Work with the students to complete **one** of the English options listed below:

 *Beginning Wisely:* Lesson 39

 *Building with Diligence:* Lesson 38

 Your own grammar program

Key Idea: Practice language arts skills.

Bible Study

T

Say, *Find Psalm 34:1-7 in your Bible. This is the memory selection for this unit. Read the verses out loud.* Ask, *In Psalm 34:7, what is the angel of the Lord doing? How would you feel if the angels of the Lord were camped around you in a circle? Who does it say that the angel of the Lord encampeth around in Psalm 34:7? What does it say that the angel of the Lord does for those who fear the Lord? Who do the angels of the Lord stand against? How can knowing that the Lord directs His angels to stand against the powers of darkness for you help you be delivered from your fears?*

Have students say the verse 3 times, adding hand motions to help remember the words.

 *Lead Me to the Rock* CD
Track 5; Song: "O Magnify the Lord" (vs. 1-7)

Key Idea: The Lord's angels do His bidding.

Math Exploration

S

Choose **one** of the math options listed below (see Appendix for details).

 *Singapore Primary Mathematics 2A/2B, 3A/3B,* or *4A/4B*

 Your own math program

Key Idea: Use a step-by-step math program.

Science Exploration

I

Today you will add to your science notebook. At the top of an unlined paper, copy Job 40:15-19 in cursive. Beneath the verse, sketch a *Diplodocus* like the one shown on p. 18-19 of *The Great Dinosaur Mystery and the Bible*. Then, beneath your sketch write, *Behemoth means "kingly, gigantic beasts".*

Key Idea: The Bible describes several different kinds of very large creatures. The description of the behemoth sounds very similar to some of the dinosaur-like fossils that have been discovered. It is possible the Bible could be describing the *Diplodocus* or the *Apatosaurus*.

Learning through History

Focus: The Israelites Worship Idols

Unit 11 - Day 2

Reading about History [T]

Read about history in the following resource:

★ *Grandpa's Box: Ch. 19* p. 124-129

After today's reading, read aloud 1 Kings 22:28-35. Ask, *In 1 Kings 22:29, why does Ahab disguise himself, but tell Jehoshaphat to wear his royal robes? What reason does 1 Kings 22:31 give for Ahab's disguise? Why did the chariot commanders chase after Jehoshaphat in 1 Kings 22:32-33? Did Ahab's plan work? How was God's will done in spite of Ahab's plan in 1 Kings 22:34? Who was in control of the bowman in 1 Kings 22:34? How was the prophet Micaiah's prediction fulfilled in 1 Kings 22:35?*

Key Idea: King Ahab wanted to go to war to take back Aram. He asked Jehoshaphat, King of Judah, to fight with him. Jehoshaphat agreed, but he wanted to consult a prophet of God first. Ahab didn't like what God's prophet Micaiah had to say.

History Project [S]

Get your flipbook cards from Day 1. On the fourth card, draw the exact same altar as on the third card, but add an even larger stream of water pouring over the altar. On the fifth card, draw the exact same altar, but add water around the base of the altar and draw a bull on top of the altar. Make the sixth card like the fifth card, but add a streak of fire coming from heaven. Draw the seventh card like the sixth one, except add a larger streak of fire from heaven. Save the rest of the cards for Day 3.

Key Idea: Ahab didn't listen to God's prophets.

Storytime [T]

Read aloud the following assigned passage:

★ 1 Kings 22:1-37

Ask, *In what does the main character place his faith? How would the story be different if the main character put his faith in God? Share a character, a story, or a verse from the Bible that you are reminded of by today's reading.*

Key Idea: Share a Biblical connection.

Vocabulary [S]

You may choose 3-5 of the following vocabulary words from *Grandpa's Box* to use for this lesson: *obsidian* (p. 124), *predictions* (p. 126), *summoned* (p. 127), *prophecies* (p. 127), and/or *archer* (p. 129). First, find the word in the text and read the sentence containing the word. Think about possible meanings. Next, find the word in a dictionary and select the correct meaning. Write the word at the top of an index card or at the top of the corresponding letter page in the notebook. Underneath the word, copy the correct definition from the dictionary. Then, use the word correctly in a sentence. The sentence may either be copied from the text or be one of your own creation. Last, draw a small picture to show the word's meaning. If you used an index card to record your word, file it under the correct alphabetical tab.

Key Idea: King Ahab was an evil king in Israel. After the time of Solomon, all of Israel's kings were evil. Judah had some good kings and some bad kings. God eventually punished both Israel and Judah for idol worship.

Independent History Study [I]

★ At the top of an unlined paper, copy Luke 1:31-33 in cursive. Beneath the verse, draw the diagram from p. 6 of *The Young Christian's Introduction to the Bible* that shows the Old Testament and the New Testament both pointing to Christ. Store your completed page in the place you have chosen for it.

Key Idea: All of us are sinful by nature. God knew that we needed a savior, so He sent His Son to save us.

Learning the Basics
Focus: Language Arts, Math, Bible, and Science

Unit 11 - Day 2

Language Arts

T

Work with the students to complete **one** of the English options listed below:

★ *Beginning Wisely:* Lesson 40

★ *Building with Diligence:* Lesson 39

★ Your own grammar program

Say, *For today's writing session, you will copy half of the Robert Louis Stevenson poem that you have chosen to memorize this week* (see Appendix).

Say, *Copy the poem in cursive in your "Common Place Book". Leave the rest of the page blank to copy the remaining half of the poem during the next unit.*

Have students share the portion of the poem they copied by reading it aloud.

Key Idea: Write creatively from classic poetry.

Bible Study

T

Have students say Psalm 34:1-7 using the hand motions they added on Day 1. Say, *A mood is a feeling, a sensation, or a state of mind. What is the mood of Psalm 34:7?* (Some examples of moods include frightened, worried, happy, peaceful, hopeful, sad, unhappy, angry, thankful, prayerful, joyful, and lonely.) Ask, *When would this Psalm help you, or when would you go to this Psalm?* (i.e. to show us that the Lord uses His angels in answer to prayer, to remind us that we have heavenly hosts that we cannot see on our side if we respect and fear the Lord, to show us that deliverance comes from the Lord.)

Last, pray with your children that they will be surrounded by the Lord's angels in times of trouble. Pray that your children will respect and fear the Lord. Pray that they will feel God's protection over them, even in difficult times.

✔ *Lead Me to the Rock* CD
Track 5; Song: "O Magnify the Lord" (vs. 1-7)

Key Idea: The Psalms are a source of comfort.

Math Exploration

S

Choose **one** of the math options listed below (see Appendix for details).

★ *Singapore Primary Mathematics 2A/2B, 3A/3B,* or *4A/4B*

★ Your own math program

Key Idea: Use a step-by-step math program.

Science Exploration

I

★ Read *The Great Dinosaur Mystery and the Bible* p. 22-23. Orally retell or narrate to an adult the portion of text that you read today. Use the *Narration Tips* in the Appendix for help as needed.

Key Idea: There are many different ideas or theories to explain how dinosaurs became extinct. Many of these theories have been discarded due to problems. Some Christian scientists think that many dinosaurs were killed and buried quickly when the Earth was experiencing volcanoes erupting and earthquakes.

Learning through History
Focus: The Israelites Worship Idols

Unit 11 - Day 3

Reading about History — T

Read about history in the following resource:

★ *Grandpa's Box: Ch. 20* p. 130-135

After today's reading, have your students orally narrate or retell the portion of today's text that you read. Use the *Narration Tips* in the Appendix as needed.

Key Idea: Naaman had leprosy. His servant girl was an Israelite. She told Naaman that the prophet Elisha could cure him. Elisha told Naaman to wash in the Jordan River 7 times. Naaman almost refused to do it. But, his servants convinced him to obey Elisha.

History Project — S

Get your flipbook cards from Day 2. On the eighth card, draw the exact same altar as on the seventh card, but show the fire burning up the bull. On the ninth card, draw the exact same altar without the bull and show the fire burning up the water around the base of the altar. Make the tenth card showing the fire burning up the rocks so that nothing is left. Stack the 10 cards in order and staple them together on the left side. Flip the pages quickly with your thumb to see the story of Elijah on Mt. Carmel.

Key Idea: In the Old Testament, God often showed His power through His prophets. God used Elijah and Elisha to do miracles. God healed the Syrian captain Naaman in the Jordan River, and Naaman realized the God of Israel is the only true God.

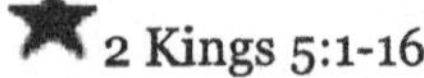

Storytime — T

Read aloud the following assigned passage:

★ 2 Kings 5:1-16

Ask, *In today's reading, how were people's lives different from your life? What would you have enjoyed or found difficult about living during that time?*

Key Idea: Compare and contrast the historical time period of the reading to your own life.

Geography — S

Use a globe for today's activities. *Find Assyria on p. 35 of A Child's History of the World. Then, find the area where Assyria would be on the modern-day globe. Finding the Black Sea, the Caspian Sea, and Mount Ararat on the globe will help you find the area where Assyria used to be. What modern-day countries are located where Assyria used to be? Can you find Syria and Turkey on the globe? Later, Assyria also conquered part of modern-day Egypt, and all of modern-day Israel, Jordan, and Iraq. Can you find those countries on the globe?*

Introduce the following concept: *In order to practice finding the 4 cardinal directions, point your right hand toward the rising sun. This is East. Point your left hand toward the setting sun. That is West. The direction you are facing is North. Your back is toward the South. North, South, East, and West are the 4 cardinal directions.*

Key Idea: The king of Syria had a strong army captain named Naaman.

Independent History Study — I

★ On white paper, follow the directions on p. 57-58 of *Draw and Write Through History* to draw a Phoenician merchant ship. If you enjoy a challenge, you may also add the details shown on p. 59. Wait to color your ship until Day 4. Store your drawing in the place you have chosen for it.

Key Idea: Phoenicia and Assyria were near Israel. Their practice of idol-worship moved into Israel.

Learning the Basics

Focus: Language Arts, Math, Bible, and Science

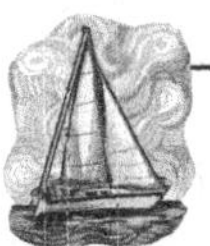

Poetry

T

Have students practice reading half of the poem that they have chosen to memorize, using the actions that they added. Have students do this 2 times. Then, have students recite half of the poem without looking at the words. Students have 2 weeks (units) to memorize the entire poem. So, they should have half of their chosen poem memorized by Day 4 of this unit.

Key Idea: Read and appreciate classic poetry.

Language Arts

S

Have students complete one studied dictation exercise (see Appendix for directions and passages).

Help students complete one lesson from the following reading program:

★ *Drawn into the Heart of Reading*

Work with the students to complete **one** of the English options listed below:

★ *Beginning Wisely:* Lesson 41

★ *Building with Diligence:* Lesson 40

★ Your own grammar program

Key Idea: Practice language arts skills.

Bible Study

T

Say, *You will be having your own quiet time with God today. Choose a quiet place for this special time, where you can be alone with God. Then, do the following things:*

1. Read Psalm 34:1-7 in your Bible.
2. Pray about the Psalm using the following beginning for your prayer: *Thank you for sending your angels to help me in times of need. Please surround ______ with your angels now, because ______. Help me to feel your protection when I am fearful.*
3. Recite Psalm 34:1-7 using the hand motions you added on Day 1.
4. Sing Psalm 34:1-7 along with the CD at the end of your quiet time.

✔ *Lead Me to the Rock* CD
Track 5; Song: "O Magnify the Lord" (vs. 1-7)

Key Idea: The Lord always hears us when we pray. He sends His angels to protect us.

Math Exploration

S

Choose **one** of the math options listed below (see Appendix for details).

★ *Singapore Primary Mathematics 2A/2B, 3A/3B,* or *4A/4B*

★ Your own math program

Key Idea: Use a step-by-step math program.

Science Exploration

I

★ Read *The Great Dinosaur Mystery and the Bible* p. 24-27. Write the answer to each numbered question on lined paper. You do not need to copy the question. Use the listed page to help you answer each question.

1. What was the greatest disaster in history? (p. 25)
2. What did Noah's Flood destroy? (p. 25)
3. Where did the floodwaters come from? (p. 25)
4. How do plants and animals fossilize? (p. 26)
5. What does Genesis 7:11-8:5 teach you about Noah's Flood?

Key Idea: Noah's Flood was the greatest disaster the world has ever known. Noah was in the ark a year!

Learning through History
Focus: The Israelites Worship Idols

Unit 11 - Day 4

Reading about History — T

Read about history in the following resource:

★ *Grandpa's Box: Ch. 21* p. 136-141

After today's reading, say, *You will be writing a narration about part of the day's history reading. In order to remember the details very well, you will need to reread p. 140 through the top of p. 141 (on your own if possible).*

After students have finished reading the passage, ask them the questions below. If the students do not know the answers, help them find the answers in the passage they just read. Ask, *Why would Satan want to destroy King David's family? Who tried to kill all the members of David's family line? In this story, who did God save? How did God use Jehosheba to keep God's promise that a Savior would come from King David's family line? How old was Joash when he became king? When Joash was 7, what did the priest Jehoida do?*

After the questions have been answered, have students write a 3-5 sentence narration that begins, *In Israel, Athaliah tried to...* When students have finished their narration, direct them to read the sentences out loud. Ask, *Did you include **who** the reading was mainly about? Did you include **what** important thing(s) happened? Did you include **how** it ended?*

See the *Written Narration Skills* in the Appendix to guide students in editing their narrations.

Key Idea: When Athaliah's son, King Ahaziah, was killed, Athaliah immediately put all of his children to death, so she could be queen.

Storytime — T

Read aloud the following assigned passage:

★ 1 Kings 22:39-40 and 2 Kings 11:1-21

After today's reading, have your students orally narrate or retell the portion of today's text that you read. Use the *Narration Tips* listed in the Appendix as needed.

Key Idea: Practice oral narration skills.

Timeline — S

If you decided to tape your timeline cards to the back of a door, then you will use the blank card that is next to the *Solomon* card for today's timeline entry. If you decided to tape the timeline cards side-by-side to accordion-fold them, then you will use the same blank card described above for today's entry.

On the blank card, draw and color an altar with fire surrounding it. Write, *Ahab becomes king of Israel. Elijah begins his ministry the following year. (874 B.C.).*

Key Idea: King Ahab and his queen, Jezebel, had a daughter named Athaliah. When King Jehoshaphat of Judah and Ahab went to war together against Aram, Jehoshaphat also allowed Athaliah to marry his son. The wickedness of Jezebel and Ahab in Israel followed Athaliah into Judah. As we can see throughout the Bible stories, it is very important who you marry!

Independent History Study — I

★ Take out your picture of the Phoenician ship. Follow the directions on p. 58 of *Draw and Write Through History* to color the ship. Store your drawing in the place you have chosen for it.

Key Idea: King Ahab's queen, Jezebel, was from Phoenicia. Their daughter, Athaliah, followed the same evil ways her parents had. But, God provided for Joash to be saved to become the next king of Judah.

Learning the Basics

Focus: Language Arts, Math, Bible, and Science

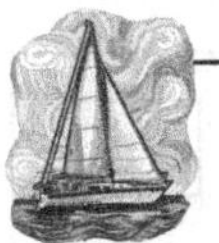

Poetry

T

Have students practice reading half of the poem that they have chosen to memorize, using the actions that they added. Have students do this 2 times. Then, have students recite half of the poem without looking at the words. Students have 2 weeks (units) to memorize the entire poem. So, they should have half of their chosen poem memorized by today.

Key Idea: Read and appreciate classic poetry.

Language Arts

S

Have students complete one dictation exercise.

Guide students to complete one reading lesson.

★ *Drawn into the Heart of Reading*

Help students complete **one** English lesson.

★ *Beginning Wisely:* Lesson 42

★ *Building with Diligence:* Lesson 41

★ Your own grammar program

Key Idea: Practice language arts skills.

Bible Study

T

Have students say Psalm 34:1-7 using the hand motions from Day 1.

Have students copy in cursive Psalm 34:7 beneath last unit's Psalm 34:6 in their *Common Place Book.* Students should leave the rest of the page blank to add to next week.

Students will add to the *Common Place Book* throughout the year.

✔ *Lead Me to the Rock* CD
Track 5; Song: "O Magnify the Lord" (vs. 1-7)

Key Idea: Copy in cursive a portion of a Psalm.

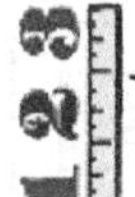

Math Exploration

S

Choose **one** math option listed below.

★ *Singapore Primary Mathematics 2A/2B, 3A/3B,* or *4A/4B*

★ Your own math program

Key Idea: Use a step-by-step math program.

Science Exploration

I

★ Read *The Great Dinosaur Mystery and the Bible* p. 28-29. Turn to the science experiment section in your science binder or sketchbook. At the top of a blank page, write: *How does something become fossilized?* Under the question, write: *'Guess'.* Write down your guess.

Place one piece of bread on a flat surface. This will be your soft, muddy earth. Place some objects to fossilize on top of your muddy earth (i.e. leaf, rock, coin, paperclip, etc.). Place another piece of bread on top of your objects to be more mud sweeping over the earth. Add several more objects to fossilize on top of your second slice of bread. Then, add a third slice of bread to be another layer of mud. Flatten all 3 layers by pressing down very hard and squishing them together. Then, slowly pull apart the layers to see how things were preserved. Which fossils showed the greatest detail in the earth? Which fossils were not very detailed? On your paper, write: *'Procedure'.* Draw a picture of the experiment. At the bottom of the paper, write: *'Conclusion'.* Explain what you learned.

Key Idea: Plants and animals could have been fossilized quite quickly after Noah's Flood.

Learning through History
Focus: The Israelites in Babylon

Unit 12 - Day 1

Reading about History — T

Read about history in the following resource:

★ *Grandpa's Box: Ch. 22* p. 142-147

After today's reading, ask, *Who was Sennacherib?* (knowledge) *Explain what the letter from the Assyrian commander said.* (knowledge) *Tell me about King Hezekiah.* (comprehension) *What examples can you give from today's reading that prove God is the only true God.* (application) *What might have happened if God hadn't continued proving to the Israelites that He is the one true God?* (synthesis)

Key Idea: When Sennacherib was king in Assyria, he began conquering all of the nations around him. He sent a threatening letter to King Hezekiah in Judah.

History Project — S

In this unit you will make a scroll like God's words were written on in the time of Hezekiah and Jeremiah. Lay a paper bag flat. Cut off the bottom of the bag and throw it away. Next, cut up one side of the bag to make one long strip of paper. Crumple and smooth the paper strip several times to make it soft like parchment. Then, use a paintbrush to paint water on one side of the paper. Lay it flat to dry until Day 2.

Key Idea: When King Hezekiah received Sennacherib's letter, he brought it to the temple and laid it out before God. Hezekiah prayed for God to deliver Judah, and God answered Hezekiah's prayer. Sennacherib's army was destroyed without setting foot in Jerusalem.

Storytime — T

Read aloud the following assigned passage:

★ 2 Kings 18:1-8, 13-16; and 19:9-19, 32-36

Discuss today's reading in a "conversational way". Share about a person, time, event, or emotion from your life that today's reading brought to mind. Next, have your child share a connection.

Key Idea: Connect personally to the passage.

Research — S

In Bible times, God's words were written down on scrolls. What is a **scroll**? Where could you look to discover more about a scroll? A dictionary will give you a definition of a scroll. An encyclopedia will tell you what a scroll is and show you a picture of it. Use a reference book or an online resource like www.wikipedia.org to look up *scroll*. Depending on the resource you use, you will have to type *scroll* in the search or look it up in the index.

Orally answer one or more of the following questions from your research: *What is a scroll? What was a scroll used for? How was a scroll made? How were scrolls stored? What are the names of some places that scrolls have been found? What are the Dead Sea Scrolls? Why are the Dead Sea Scrolls so important?*

Key Idea: Scrolls were used for writing important documents or for keeping records. At the time of the Old Testament, God's words were recorded on scrolls.

Independent History Study — I

★ On white paper, follow the directions on p. 60 of *Draw and Write Through History* to draw and color a big fish. Store your completed drawing in the place you have chosen for it.

Key Idea: Nineveh was the chief city of Assyria. The Israelites and the Assyrians were enemies, yet later God sent Jonah to preach to the Assyrians.

Learning the Basics

Focus: Language Arts, Math, Bible, and Science

Poetry

T

Guide students to continue memorizing the Robert Louis Stevenson poem they chose in Unit 11. Students should have half of their chosen poem memorized already. They should memorize the rest of the poem by Day 4 of this unit. Have students read the entire poem 3 times, adding actions to the last half of the poem to help them memorize the words more easily.

Key Idea: Read and appreciate classic poetry.

Language Arts

S

Have students complete the first studied dictation exercise (see Appendix for directions and passages).

Help students complete one lesson from the following reading program:

★ *Drawn into the Heart of Reading*

Work with the students to complete **one** of the English options listed below:

★ *Beginning Wisely:* Lesson 43

★ *Building with Diligence:* Lesson 42

★ Your own grammar program

Key Idea: Practice language arts skills.

Bible Study

T

Say, *Find Psalm 34:1-9 in your Bible. This is the memory selection for this unit. Read the verses out loud.* Ask, *What does Psalm 34:8 encourage us to do so we can know for ourselves the goodness of the Lord? If you have something good to eat but never taste it, do you really get to enjoy its goodness? How is this the same as having the opportunity to know the Lord but never really experiencing a relationship with Him? Why would we be blessed by trusting in the Lord? What does Psalm 34:9 tell us to do? How can we fear the Lord?* (i.e. keep His commands, show reverence to Him, respect His will, serve Him, be worried about offending Him). Have students say the verse 3 times, adding hand motions to help remember the words.

✔ *Lead Me to the Rock* CD
Track 5; Song: "O Magnify the Lord" (vs. 1-9)

Key Idea: We need to show fear of the Lord.

Math Exploration

S

Choose **one** of the math options listed below (see Appendix for details).

★ *Singapore Primary Mathematics 2A/2B, 3A/3B,* or *4A/4B*

★ Your own math program

Key Idea: Use a step-by-step math program.

Science Exploration

I

Today you will add to your science notebook. At the top of an unlined paper, copy Ecclesiastes 3:19-20 in cursive. Make a dinosaur border around the page. Beneath the verse, copy the following text:

Ingredients for a Fossil:

1. quick burial
2. water, in the right amounts
3. suitable materials

Key Idea: Although both man and beast will return to dust, man longs for an eternal home in heaven.

Learning through History
Focus: The Israelites in Babylon

Unit 12 - Day 2

Reading about History — T

Read about history in the following resource:

★ *A Child's History of the World: Ch. 17* p. 74-77

Note: There is some graphic content on p. 74.

After today's reading, read aloud 2 Kings 19:14-19. Ask, *In 2 Kings 19:14, how can you tell that King Hezekiah was a Godly man? How does Hezekiah describe God in 2 Kings 19:15? What does Hezekiah ask God in 2 Kings 19:16? What does Hezekiah say about Sennacherib in 2 Kings 19:16? In 2 Kings 19:18, what does Hezekiah say that shows He knows God is the only true living God? What reason does Hezekiah give for asking God to deliver Judah in 2 Kings 19:19? How does this request show respect for God?*

Key Idea: God sent the prophet Isaiah to let Hezekiah know God had heard Hezekiah's prayer.

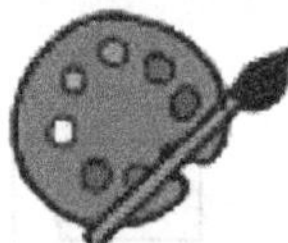

History Project — S

Get the paper you prepared for your scroll on Day 1. Using a black pen, carefully copy 2 Kings 19:32-34 on the center of your scroll in cursive. If you have difficulty copying in cursive, you may want to write in pencil instead. Save your scroll for Day 3.

Key Idea: God saved Judah and defeated Sennacherib as He promised. Sennacherib returned to Nineveh and was killed by his sons in the temple of his god Nisroch, just as God had foretold.

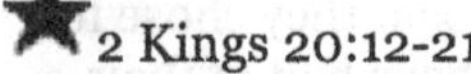

Storytime — T

Read aloud the following assigned passage:

★ 2 Kings 20:12-21

Ask, *In today's reading, how were people's lives different from your life? What would you have enjoyed or found difficult about living during that time?*

Key Idea: Compare and contrast the historical time period of the reading to your own life.

Vocabulary — S

You may choose 3-5 of the following vocabulary words from *A Child's History of the World* to use for this lesson: *corkscrew* (p. 74), *magnificence* (p. 75), *cherub* (p. 75), *cuneiform* (p. 76), and/or *reign* (p. 76). First, find the word in the text and read the sentence containing the word. Think about possible meanings. Next, find the word in a dictionary and select the correct meaning. Write the word at the top of an index card or at the top of the corresponding letter page in the notebook. Underneath the word, copy the correct definition from the dictionary. Then, use the word correctly in a sentence. The sentence may either be copied from the text or be one of your own creation. Last, draw a small picture to show the word's meaning. If you used an index card to record your word, file it under the correct alphabetical tab.

Key Idea: The Assyrians were feared by everyone, yet Hezekiah trusted God to protect His people. God delivered Judah from Sennacherib in an amazing way. We can learn much about trusting God from this story.

Independent History Study — I

★ On lined paper, copy in cursive the **second** paragraph from *Draw and Write Through History* p. 61. Store your completed copywork with your completed drawings in the place you have chosen for them.

Key Idea: It is easy to understand why Jonah didn't want to go to Nineveh as God had instructed him to do. The Israelites feared and hated the Assyrians. Yet, God used Jonah to help the Ninevites repent.

Learning the Basics

Focus: Language Arts, Math, Bible, and Science

Unit 12 - Day 2

Language Arts

T

Work with the students to complete **one** of the English options listed below:

 *Beginning Wisely:* Lesson 44

 *Building with Diligence:* Lesson 43

 Your own grammar program

Say, *For today's writing session, you will copy the last half of the Robert Louis Stevenson poem that you chose to memorize this week* (see Appendix).

Say, *Copy the rest of the poem in cursive in your "Common Place Book".*

Have students share the poem they copied by reading it aloud.

Key Idea: Write creatively from classic poetry.

Bible Study

T

Have students say Psalm 34:1-9 using the hand motions they added on Day 1. Say, *A mood is a feeling, a sensation, or a state of mind. What is the mood of Psalm 34:8-9?* (Some examples of moods include frightened, worried, happy, peaceful, hopeful, sad, unhappy, angry, thankful, prayerful, joyful, and lonely.) Ask, *When would this Psalm help you, or when would you go to this Psalm?* (i.e. to encourage us to enjoy a close relationship with the Lord, to remind us of the blessing of trusting in the Lord, to help us to remember to show fear of the Lord and reverence for the Lord).

Last, pray with your children that they will have a close relationship with the Lord. Pray that your children will show respect, reverence, and fear of the Lord. Pray that they will trust in the Lord and seek to do His will.

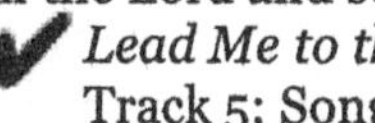

✔ *Lead Me to the Rock* CD
Track 5; Song: "O Magnify the Lord" (vs. 1-9)

Key Idea: The Psalms are a wonderful place to seek counsel from the Lord.

Math Exploration

S

Choose **one** of the math options listed below (see Appendix for details).

 *Singapore Primary Mathematics 2A/2B, 3A/3B,* or *4A/4B*

 Your own math program

Key Idea: Use a step-by-step math program.

Science Exploration

I

★ Read *The Great Dinosaur Mystery and the Bible* p. 30-33. Orally retell or narrate to an adult the portion of text that you read today. Use the *Narration Tips* in the Appendix for help as needed.

Key Idea: At the time of Noah the Bible says that every thought that man had was continually evil. So, God destroyed everyone except Noah, his family, and the animals on the ark. Before the flood, Noah spent 120 years building the ark and warning people about the coming flood. Everyone had a chance to be saved.

Learning through History
Focus: The Israelites in Babylon

Unit 12 - Day 3

Reading about History [T]

Read about history in the following resource:

★ *Grandpa's Box: Ch. 23* p. 148-154

After today's reading, have your students orally narrate or retell the portion of today's text that you read. Use the *Narration Tips* in the Appendix as needed.

Key Idea: God gave Jeremiah a message for His people. Jeremiah had Baruch write it down on a scroll. When King Jehoiakim heard God's words, he ignored them and cut up the scroll that contained the words. Then he sent his soldiers to find Jeremiah and Baruch, but God had hidden them.

History Project [S]

Get out the scroll from Day 2. Tape a straw or a pencil to each end of the scroll. Starting at one end, roll the scroll up until you reach the middle. Then, start at the other end and roll that side in to the middle. When the two rolls meet one another, tie a piece of string, yarn, or ribbon around the rolled scroll to hold it closed.

Key Idea: Even though King Jehoiakim cut up God's scroll, it didn't stop God's words from coming true. When we are doing something wrong, we need to listen to God's words, repent of our sin, and change our ways.

Storytime [T]

Read aloud the following assigned passage:

★ Jeremiah 36:1-7, 19-32; and 2 Kings 24:1-7

Ask, *In what do the people place their faith? How would the story be different if they had put their faith in God? Share a character, a story, or a verse from the Bible that you are reminded of by today's reading.*

Key Idea: Share a Biblical connection.

Geography [S]

Use a globe for today's activities. In 612 B.C., Nineveh was captured by the Babylonians and the Medes (or Persians). The Babylonians also conquered Judah in 586 B.C. *Find Babylon, Persia, and Nineveh on p. 35 of A Child's History of the World. Why would Nineveh have a hard time holding out against Babylon and Persia? What famous Bible story took place in Nineveh? Jonah preached in Nineveh over 150 years before Nineveh was destroyed. Find the area on the globe where Nineveh would be located in modern-day Iraq on the Tigris River.*

Review the following concept: *Find the 4 cardinal directions. Point your right hand toward the rising sun. This is East. Point your left hand toward the setting sun. That is West. The direction you are facing is North. Your back is toward the South. Which direction is the nearest town from your house? Which direction is your closest neighbor?*

Key Idea: God's prophets were often sent to warn people of the coming destruction if they failed to change their sinful ways.

Independent History Study [I]

★ Read *The Young Christian's Introduction to the Bible* p. 7-9. Then, copy Jeremiah 36:27-28 in cursive onto a clean page in your *Common Place Book*.

Key Idea: Even though men have tried to destroy God's word, God has preserved it for us to read today.

Learning the Basics
Focus: Language Arts, Math, Bible, and Science

Unit 12 - Day 3

Poetry
T

Have students practice reading the poem that they have chosen to memorize, using the actions that they added on Day 1. Have students do this 2 times. Then, have students recite the poem without looking at the words. Students should have their chosen poem memorized by Day 4 of this unit.

Key Idea: Read and appreciate classic poetry.

Language Arts
S

Have students complete one studied dictation exercise (see Appendix for directions and passages).

Help students complete one lesson from the following reading program:

★ *Drawn into the Heart of Reading*

Work with the students to complete **one** of the English options listed below:

★ *Beginning Wisely:* Lesson 45

★ *Building with Diligence:* Lesson 44

★ Your own grammar program

Key Idea: Practice language arts skills.

Bible Study
T

Say, *You will be having your own quiet time with God today. Choose a quiet place for this special time, where you can be alone with God. Then, do the following things:*

1. Read Psalm 34:1-9 in your Bible.
2. Pray about the Psalm using the following beginning to your prayer: *Thank you for the blessing of ______. Help me to show you the respect and reverence that you deserve by ______ and ______. Please forgive me when I ______. I love you Lord.*
3. Recite Psalm 34:1-9 using the hand motions you added on Day 1.
4. Sing Psalm 34:1-9 along with the CD at the end of your quiet time.

✔ *Lead Me to the Rock* CD
Track 5; Song: "O Magnify the Lord" (vs. 1-9)

Key Idea: The Lord deserves our respect.

Math Exploration
S

Choose **one** of the math options listed below (see Appendix for details).

★ *Singapore Primary Mathematics 2A/2B, 3A/3B,* or *4A/4B*

★ Your own math program

Key Idea: Use a step-by-step math program.

Science Exploration
I

★ Read *The Great Dinosaur Mystery and the Bible* p. 34-35. Write the answer to each numbered question on lined paper. You do not need to copy the question. Use the listed page to help you answer each question.

1. How much of the Earth is still under water today? (p. 34)
2. What plagued the animals and man after the Flood? (p. 34)
3. After the Flood, what happened to the temperatures in the world? (p. 34)
4. Why did animals become extinct? (p. 35)
5. Why are God's promises in Genesis 9:9-17 so important?

Key Idea: After the flood, the Earth was changed. Both man and animals had a harder time surviving.

Learning through History
Focus: The Israelites in Babylon

Reading about History **T**

Read about history in the following resource:

★ *A Child's History of the World: Ch. 18* p. 78-80 p. 111-114

After today's reading, say, *You will be writing a narration about part of the day's history reading. In order to remember the details very well, you will need to reread the part of today's reading from the last paragraph on p. 78 up to the last paragraph on p. 79 (on your own if possible).*

After students have finished reading the passage, ask them the questions below. If the students do not know the answers, help them find the answers in the passage they just read. Ask, *In today's story, who was the King of Babylon? How did Nebuchadnezzar make the city of Babylon strong? Where did Nebuchadnezzar go to find a wife? Why? What did Nebuchadnezzar build for his wife? Why were the gardens and the walls of Babylon known as one of the Seven Wonders of the World?*

After the questions have been answered, have students choose one of the following 3 topics about which to write a 3-5 sentence narration:

1. The design of the city of Babylon
2. The hanging gardens of Babylon
3. Tell about Nebuchadnezzar

Begin your narration, *When Nebuchadnezzar was king of Babylon...*

See the *Written Narration Skills* in the Appendix to guide students in editing their narrations.

Key Idea: Nebuchadnezzar burned Jerusalem.

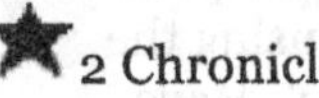

Storytime **T**

Read aloud the following assigned passage:

★ 2 Chronicles 36:9-21

After today's reading, have your students orally narrate or retell the portion of today's text that you read. Use the *Narration Tips* as needed.

Key Idea: Practice oral narration skills.

Timeline **S**

You will be adding 2 new cards to your staircase timeline today. On the first new card, draw and color chains. Write, *Assyria conquers Israel (720 B.C.)*. On the second new card, draw and color chains. Write, *Babylon conquers Judah (586 B.C.).*

If you decided to tape your timeline cards to the back of a door, add the *Assyria conquers Israel* card to the right of the *Founding of Rome* card. To the right of the *Assyria conquers Israel* card, add the *Babylon conquers Judah* card. If you decided to tape the timeline cards side-by-side to accordion-fold them, use clear packing tape to tape the cards as described above.

Key Idea: When God's chosen people in Israel and Judah refused to listen to Him, He allowed them to be captured. God had warned them over and over, but they did not heed His warnings. Israel was captured by the Assyrians. Later, Judah was captured by the Babylonians.

Independent History Study **I**

★ Read *The Young Christian's Introduction to the Bible* p. 10-13. Then, choose an interesting part from today's pages to read aloud and explain to an adult.

Key Idea: In history stories, there are often some inaccuracies or things that are not completely true. But, God's word is different. Since all of the Bible is inspired by God, He guards it to preserve it accurately.

Learning the Basics

Focus: Language Arts, Math, Bible, and Science

Unit 12 - Day 4

Poetry

T

Have students practice reading the poem that they have chosen to memorize, using the actions that they added. Have students do this 2 times. Then, have students recite the poem for you without looking at the words. They should have their chosen poem memorized today.

Key Idea: Read and appreciate classic poetry.

Language Arts

S

Have students complete one dictation exercise.

Guide students to complete one reading lesson.

★ *Drawn into the Heart of Reading*

Help students complete **one** English lesson.

★ *Beginning Wisely:* Lesson 46

★ *Building with Diligence:* Lesson 45

★ Your own grammar program

Key Idea: Practice language arts skills.

Bible Study

T

Have students say Psalm 34:1-9 using the hand motions from Day 1.

Have students copy in cursive Psalm 34:8-9 beneath last unit's Psalm 34:7 in their *Common Place Book.*.

Students will add to the *Common Place Book* throughout the year.

Lead Me to the Rock CD
Track 5; Song: "O Magnify the Lord" (vs. 1-9)

Key Idea: Copy in cursive a portion of a Psalm.

Math Exploration

S

Choose **one** math option listed below.

★ *Singapore Primary Mathematics 2A/2B, 3A/3B,* or *4A/4B*

★ Your own math program

Key Idea: Use a step-by-step math program.

Science Exploration

I

★ Read *The Great Dinosaur Mystery and the Bible* p. 36-37. Turn to the science experiment section in your science binder or sketchbook. At the top of a blank page, write: *Why is it difficult to correctly assemble a dinosaur skeleton?* Under the question, write: *'Guess'*. Write down your guess.

You will need a partner for this activity. Each of you will need a piece of paper. Both you and your partner will use a pencil to draw a new kind of dinosaur. The dinosaur should fill the paper. Do not color it. **It is important that you do not let your partner see your drawing.** After completing the drawing, both of you should cut your drawings into 12 pieces. Make sure you **do not** let your partner see your drawing before it is cut up. Then, mix your puzzle pieces together with your partner's pieces, and dump them out on the ground. Each of you must put together your partner's dinosaur. Your partner should not help you. Why was it difficult to assemble your partner's dinosaur? On your paper, write: *'Procedure'*. Draw a picture of the experiment. At the bottom of the paper, write: *'Conclusion'*. Explain what you learned.

Key Idea: There are many ancient stories told about reptile-like creatures all around the world.

Learning through History
Focus: Babylon Is Conquered by Medes and Persians

Unit 13 - Day 1

Reading about History T

Read about history in the following resource:

★ *Grandpa's Box: Ch. 24* p. 155-160

After today's reading, ask, *When King Jehoiakim cut up Jeremiah's scroll, did it stop God's plan from happening?* (knowledge) *How did God use Nebuchadnezzar's dream to show that God is still the ruler over all?* (analysis) *Why did King Nebuchadnezzar make a giant golden statue?* (comprehension) *Did Shadrach Meshach, and Abednego know God was going to save them? Explain.* (analysis) *What should Nebuchadnezzar have learned about God?* (evaluation)

Key Idea: God used Nebuchadnezzar to show Daniel and the Israelites that He was still in control. The Israelites would remain in Babylon 70 years as prophesied.

History Project S

In this unit you will use invisible ink to write a message that was revealed by God to one of the kings of Babylon after Nebuchadnezzar. In a small bowl, mix 1 Tablespoon baking soda with 1 Tablespoon water. Dip a cotton swab or a paintbrush in the invisible ink mixture and write the words, *Mene, Mene, Tekel, Uparsin* on white paper. Lay the paper flat to dry until Day 2.

Key Idea: God gave King Nebuchadnezzar a dream about a statue. God revealed the meaning of the dream to Daniel, so Daniel could interpret the dream for the king. Later, Daniel would interpret writing on the wall for Belshazzar, another king of Babylon.

Storytime T

Read aloud the following assigned passage:

★ Daniel 2:1-49

Discuss today's reading in a "conversational way". Share about a person, time, event, or emotion from your life that today's reading brought to mind. Next, have your child share a connection.

Key Idea: Connect personally to the passage.

Research S

In Bible times, God's words were revealed through dreams, angels, prophets, and even through writing on the wall. In what instance did God use writing on the wall to prophecy what was to come? Where could you look to discover more about this writing on the wall? The Bible tells about a time when God used Daniel to interpret words on the wall for Belshazzar, king of Babylon. Use the Bible, a reference book, or an online resource like www.wikipedia.org to read more of this story. Depending on the resource you use, you will have to type *writing on the wall* or *Daniel* or *Belshazzar* in the search or look in the index.

Orally answer one or more of the following questions from your research: *How did the writing get on the wall? What was Belshazzar doing when the hand wrote on the wall? What words were written on the wall? Who suggested that Belshazzar send for Daniel? What did Daniel say the words meant? Did God's words come true?*

Key Idea: God gave Daniel many talents.

Independent History Study I

★ Read *The Young Christian's Introduction to the Bible* p. 18-20. Orally retell or narrate to an adult the portion of text that you read today. Use the *Narration Tips* in the Appendix for help as needed.

Key Idea: Even though Daniel was a captive in the foreign land of Babylon, God used him in a mighty way. It is important that we read and study God's word so that we can understand what God wants us to do.

Learning the Basics

Focus: Language Arts, Math, Bible, and Science

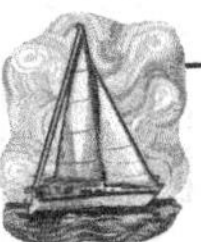

Poetry

T

Read aloud to the students the poem *"Where Go the Boats?"* (see Appendix). Ask, *What picture do you see in your mind when you listen to this poem? What words does the poet use to help paint a picture in your mind? Why do you think the poet titled the poem, "Where Go the Boats?" Explain the meaning of the last stanza of the poem.* Read the poem again with the students.

Key Idea: Read and appreciate classic poetry.

Language Arts

S

Have students complete the first studied dictation exercise (see Appendix for directions and passages).

Help students complete one lesson from the following reading program:

 *Drawn into the Heart of Reading*

Work with the students to complete **one** of the English options listed below:

 *Beginning Wisely:* Lesson 47

 *Building with Diligence:* Lesson 46

 Your own grammar program

Key Idea: Practice language arts skills.

Bible Study

T

Say, *Find Psalm 98:1 in your Bible. This is the memory selection for this unit. Read the verse out loud.* Ask, *What are we told to do in Psalm 98:1? In Psalm 98:1, why are we told to sing to the Lord? What marvelous things can you think of that the Lord has done? When Psalm 98:1 speaks of God's right hand and His holy arm, how does it show God's power? How did God work out our salvation through Christ Jesus? Look at God's plan from the beginning when the Savior was promised to Adam and Eve, until the promised Savior was born on Earth, died, rose from the dead, and ascended into heaven, until now as we wait for Christ to return. Can you see how marvelous God is?!?* Have students say the verse 3 times, adding hand motions to help remember the words.

 *Lead Me to the Rock* CD
Track 2; Song: "Sing Unto the Lord" (vs. 1)

Key Idea: God has done marvelous things!

Math Exploration

S

Choose **one** of the math options listed below (see Appendix for details).

 *Singapore Primary Mathematics 2A/2B, 3A/3B,* or *4A/4B*

 Your own math program

Key Idea: Use a step-by-step math program.

Science Exploration

I

Today you will add to your science notebook. At the top of an unlined paper, copy Revelation 4:11 in cursive. Beneath the verse, write the following heading: *Could these dragons be dinosaurs?* Underneath the heading, copy the **second** and **third** paragraphs of text from p. 36 of *The Great Dinosaur Mystery and the Bible*. Then, if you have a copy machine, photocopy and add the pictures and descriptions shown on p. 36. If you do not have a copy machine, choose one or more dinosaurs on p. 36 to sketch on your notebook page.

Key Idea: Most legends are based on some facts. Since there are many legends about dragons, could some have come from memories of real dinosaurs?

Learning through History

Focus: Babylon Is Conquered by Medes and Persians

Unit 13 - Day 2

Reading about History — T

Read about history in the following resource:

★ *A Child's History of the World: Ch. 19* p. 81-84

After today's reading, read aloud Daniel 5:18-30. Ask, *In Daniel 5:18, who did Daniel say had given Nebuchadnezzar sovereignty? In Daniel 5:20, what did Daniel say happened to Nebuchadnezzar when he became arrogant and proud? What did Nebuchadnezzar realize in Daniel 5:21? What sins did Belshazzar commit in Daniel 5:22-23? In Daniel 5:26-28, what did Daniel say the words on the wall meant? What happened to Belshazzar in Daniel 5:30? Who holds our lives in His hand?*

Key Idea: When Belshazzar became king of Babylon, he did not acknowledge God or His sovereignty. One night Belshazzar used the goblets from God's temple for a party.

History Project — S

Get the paper you prepared with your secret message on Day 1. Choose whether you want to reveal the message yourself, or whether you would rather have another person reveal it instead. In a bowl, mix 1 Tablespoon of water with 5 drops of food coloring. To reveal the secret message, use a paintbrush to paint the mixture over the paper. What does the message mean?

Key Idea: During the party, a hand wrote on the wall in Aramaic. Daniel was summoned to interpret the words for Belshazzar.

Storytime — T

Read aloud the following assigned passage:

★ Daniel 5:1-30

Ask, *In what does the main character place his faith? How would the story be different if the main character put his faith in God? Share a character, a story, or a verse from the Bible that you are reminded of by today's reading.*

Key Idea: Share a Biblical connection.

Vocabulary — S

You may choose 3-5 of the following vocabulary words from *A Child's History of the World* to use for this lesson: *Magi* (p. 82), *taxes* (p. 82), *seal* (p. 82), *engraved* (p. 83), and/or *riverbed* (p. 84). First, find the word in the text and read the sentence containing the word. Think about possible meanings. Next, find the word in a dictionary and select the correct meaning. Write the word at the top of an index card or at the top of the corresponding letter page in the notebook. Underneath the word, copy the correct definition from the dictionary. Then, use the word correctly in a sentence. The sentence may either be copied from the text or be one of your own creation. Last, draw a small picture to show the word's meaning. If you used an index card to record your word, file it under the correct alphabetical tab.

Key Idea: The writing on the wall showed God's judgment of Belshazzar. It said that God was bringing Belshazzar's reign to an end by dividing his kingdom between the Medes and Persians. It also said that God had weighed Belshazzar's motives and found him wanting.

Independent History Study — I

★ Read *The Young Christian's Introduction to the Bible* p. 21-22. Then, copy Psalm 119:11 in cursive onto a clean page in your *Common Place Book*.

Key Idea: It is obvious from what we know about Daniel that he had hidden God's words and commands in his heart from the time that he was a young boy. This helped Daniel throughout his whole life.

Learning the Basics

Focus: Language Arts, Math, Bible, and Science

Unit 13 - Day 2

Language Arts **T**

Work with the students to complete **one** of the English options listed below:

★ *Beginning Wisely:* Lesson 48

★ *Building with Diligence:* Lesson 47

★ Your own grammar program

Say, *You will be doing a writing activity based on the poem, "Where Go the Boats?"* (see Appendix).

Say, *To start with, you will draw and color a scene based on the first 8 lines of the poem. Refer to the poem as you draw, so you don't leave anything out.*

After students are done drawing and coloring their scene, ask them to list the items in the first 8 lines of the poem that they noticed and included in their picture (i.e. river, sand, trees, green leaves floating, castles of foam, a little boat). Write each item on a markerboard or a piece of paper.

Next, ask students to think of one additional item that would go well with their scene. Have them add it into their drawing. Add the item to the list as well.

Then, guide students to use the scene they drew and the listed items to write a description of the scene (i.e. The river is dark brown along the golden sand. It flows along past trees on both sides.) Make sure that students write a sentence to describe the item that they added to the scene too. Have students share their descriptions by reading them aloud.

Key Idea: Write creatively from classic poetry.

Bible Study **T**

Have students say Psalm 98:1 using the hand motions they added on Day 1. Say, *A mood is a feeling, a sensation, or a state of mind. What is the mood of Psalm 98:1?* (Some examples of moods include frightened, worried, happy, peaceful, hopeful, sad, unhappy, angry, thankful, prayerful, joyful, and lonely.) Ask, *When would this Psalm help you, or when would you go to this Psalm?* (i.e. as an encouragement to sing joyfully to the Lord, as a reminder of the marvelous things God has done, to remember the salvation we have in Jesus.)

Last, pray with your children that they will be filled with joy for the Lord when they sing. Pray that your children's eyes will be opened to the marvelous things God has done. Pray that they will be saved through Christ Jesus.

✔ *Lead Me to the Rock* CD
Track 2; Song: "Sing Unto the Lord" (vs. 1)

Key Idea: The Psalms reflect the many emotions and moods we have. They are a wonderful place to seek counsel from the Lord.

Math Exploration **S**

Choose **one** of the math options listed below (see Appendix for details).

★ *Singapore Primary Mathematics 2A/2B, 3A/3B, or 4A/4B*

★ Your own math program

Key Idea: Use a step-by-step math program.

Science Exploration **I**

★ Read *The Great Dinosaur Mystery and the Bible* p. 38-41. Orally retell or narrate to an adult the portion of text that you read today. Use the *Narration Tips* in the Appendix for help as needed.

Key Idea: There are mosaics, carvings, paintings, and many legends from the past that tell about unusual reptile-like animals. Dinosaurs that have been discovered often resemble these descriptions and stories.

Learning through History
Focus: Babylon Is Conquered by Medes and Persians

Unit 13 - Day 3

Reading about History T

Read about history in the following resource:

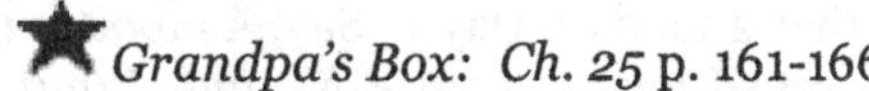

★ *Grandpa's Box: Ch. 25* p. 161-166

After today's reading, have your students orally narrate or retell the portion of today's text that you read. Use the *Narration Tips* in the Appendix as needed.

Key Idea: After 70 years of captivity in Babylon, King Cyrus allowed the Israelites to return to Jerusalem to rebuild God's temple. Ezra came with the first group of Israelites. The neighbors of the Israelites sent letters to the king to try to stop the building. So, God sent the prophets Haggai and Zechariah to encourage the people to finish the temple and to live according to God's laws.

History Project S

Make an invisible ink picture that goes with today's story. In a small bowl, mix 1 Tablespoon baking soda with 1 Tablespoon water. Dip a cotton swab or a paintbrush in the invisible ink mixture and draw your picture on white paper. Lay the paper flat to dry. After your picture is dry, mix 1 Tablespoon of water with 5 drops of food coloring. To reveal the invisible picture, use a paintbrush to paint the mixture over the paper.

Key Idea: Not all of the Israelites chose to return to Jerusalem from exile. The Israelites that did return joined with other Israelites who had been left behind in Jerusalem by Nebuchadnezzar. It was hard work to rebuild God's temple and to rebuild their city.

Storytime T

Read aloud the following assigned passage:

★ Ezra 1:1-11; 4:1-5 and Haggai 1:1-15

Ask, *In today's reading, how were people's lives different from your life? What would you have enjoyed or found difficult about living during that time?*

Key Idea: Compare and contrast the historical time period of the reading to your own life.

Geography S

Use a globe for today's activities. In 538 B.C., Babylon was captured by the Medes and Persians. *Find Babylon and Persia on p. 35 of A Child's History of the World. What modern-day city do you see on the globe that is near or on the site of Babylon? Can you find Baghdad, Iraq on the globe? What modern-day country is Persia? Can you find Iran on the Persian Gulf? Later, after Persia overtook Babylon, Cyrus allowed the Jews to go home to rebuild their temple. This was in accordance with God's prophecy.*

Review the following concept: *Find the 4 cardinal directions. Point your right hand toward the rising sun. This is East. Point your left hand toward the setting sun. That is West. The direction you are facing is North. Your back is toward the South. Which direction do your nearest relatives live from your house?*

Key Idea: In fulfillment of the prophecy, God brought His people back from exile. His temple was finally rebuilt once more.

Independent History Study I

★ Read *The Young Christian's Introduction to the Bible* p. 37-39. In the middle of an unlined paper, copy Psalm 119:105 in cursive. Make a decorative border around the verse. Add a corresponding picture if you'd like. Store your completed page in the place you have chosen for it.

Key Idea: God always keeps His promises. He will provide us strength to do whatever He requires of us.

Learning the Basics

Focus: Language Arts, Math, Bible, and Science

Unit 13 - Day 3

Poetry

T

Read aloud with the students the poem *"Where Go the Boats?"* (see Appendix). Say, *Describe a memory that the poem brought to mind. What can you learn about the poet from the poem?* Say, *Did you know that when Robert Louis Stevenson was older, he took a boat to the South Seas? He was looking for a warmer climate to help his health improve. He finally ended up on the Samoan island of Upolu.* Have the students read the poem on their own.

Key Idea: Read and appreciate classic poetry.

Language Arts

S

Have students complete one studied dictation exercise (see Appendix for directions and passages).

Help students complete one lesson from the following reading program:

★ *Drawn into the Heart of Reading*

Work with the students to complete **one** of the English options listed below:

★ *Beginning Wisely:* Lesson 49

★ *Building with Diligence:* Lesson 48

★ Your own grammar program

Key Idea: Practice language arts skills.

Bible Study

T

Say, *You will be having your own quiet time with God today. Choose a quiet place for this special time, where you can be alone with God. Then, do the following things:*

1. Read Psalm 98:1 in your Bible.
2. Pray about the Psalm using the following beginning to your prayer: *Thank you for the marvelous things you have done like ______, ______, and______. Help me to sing joyfully to honor you. Help me to know Jesus as my Savior in my heart.*
3. Recite Psalm 98:1 using the hand motions you added on Day 1.
4. Sing Psalm 98:1 along with the CD at the end of your quiet time.

✔ *Lead Me to the Rock* CD
Track 2; Song: "Sing Unto the Lord" (vs. 1)

Key Idea: The Lord loves our joyful singing.

Math Exploration

S

Choose **one** of the math options listed below (see Appendix for details).

★ *Singapore Primary Mathematics 2A/2B, 3A/3B,* or *4A/4B*

★ Your own math program

Key Idea: Use a step-by-step math program.

Science Exploration

I

★ Read *The Great Dinosaur Mystery and the Bible* p. 42-44. Write the answer to each numbered question on lined paper. You do not need to copy the question. Use the listed page to help you answer each question.

1. According to old Chinese books, how were dragons used by kings? (p. 42)
2. Who described small flying reptiles in ancient Egypt and Arabia? (p. 44)
3. What did Herodotus say about these animals? (p. 44)
4. Where else were these creatures said to exist according to Aristotle and Strabo? (p. 44)
5. What can we learn about the beasts and the birds from Genesis 2:19 ?

Key Idea: It is interesting to wonder how much of each "dragon" legend might be true.

Learning through History
Focus: Babylon Is Conquered by Medes and Persians

Unit 13 - Day 4

Reading about History T

Read about history in the following resource:

★ *Grandpa's Box: Ch. 26* p. 167-173

After today's reading, say, *You will be writing a narration about part of the day's history reading. In order to remember the details very well, you will need to reread the part of today's reading from the fourth paragraph on p. 171 through p. 173 (on your own if possible).*

After students have finished reading the passage, ask them the questions below. If the students do not know the answers, help them find the answers in the passage they just read. Ask, *Who is the story mainly about? What did Haman plan to do to the Jews? Who asked Esther to speak to the king on behalf of the Jews? Why was Esther worried about going to see the king? How did God take care of Esther? What did Haman do because he was upset with Mordecai? When Xerxes couldn't sleep, what story was read from the king's history book? How did God save the Israelites this time?*

After the questions have been answered, have students choose one of the following 3 topics about which to write a 3-5 sentence narration:

1. Esther
2. Xerxes
3. Haman

Begin your narration, *When Esther was queen of Persia...*

See the *Written Narration Skills* in the Appendix to guide students in editing their narrations.

Key Idea: God used Esther to save her people.

Storytime T

Read aloud the following assigned passage:

★ Esther 1:15-19; 2:17-23; 3:8-11; 4:6-17; 5:1-8; 7:1-10

After today's reading, have your students orally narrate or retell the portion of today's text that you read. Use the *Narration Tips* as needed.

Key Idea: Practice oral narration skills.

Timeline S

You will be adding 2 new cards to your staircase timeline today. On the first new card, draw and color a golden cup on its side spilling its drink. Write, *Fall of Babylon (538 B.C.).* On the second new card, draw and color a golden crown. Write, *Esther becomes Queen of Persia (479 B.C.).*

If you decided to tape your timeline cards to the back of a door, add the *Fall of Babylon* card to the right of the *Babylon conquers Judah* card. To the right of the *Fall of Babylon* card, add the *Esther becomes Queen of Persia* card. If you decided to tape the timeline cards side-by-side to accordion-fold them, use clear packing tape to tape the cards as described above.

Key Idea: In the same year that Babylon was captured by the Medes and Persians, the Jews were allowed to return to Jerusalem from Babylon. Not all of the Jewish people returned to Jerusalem, as it was a hard trip. So, many of the Jews remained in Babylon. They were still there at the time of Queen Esther.

Independent History Study I

★ Read *The Young Christian's Introduction to the Bible* p. 40-42. Then, choose an interesting part from today's pages to read aloud and explain to an adult.

Key Idea: As we read the Bible, we can see how God works out His plan for the good of His people. When we aren't sure why something is happening, we need to remember that God can see the big picture.

Learning the Basics

Focus: Language Arts, Math, Bible, and Science

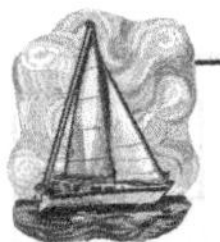

Poetry

T

Read aloud with the students the poem *"Where Go the Boats?"* (see Appendix). Have students share this poem in a special way. Suggestions for sharing the poem include recording it to play for someone, reading it to someone on the telephone, photocopying the poem and adding illustrations, reading it to someone at home, putting the poem to a melody and singing it, using an instrument to tap out the meter or rhythm of the poem while reading it, or copying the poem on paper.

Key Idea: Share a variety of classic poetry.

Language Arts

S

Have students complete one dictation exercise.

Guide students to complete one reading lesson.

★ *Drawn into the Heart of Reading*

Help students complete **one** English lesson.

★ *Beginning Wisely:* Lesson 50

★ *Building with Diligence:* Lesson 49 (Half)

★ Your own grammar program

Key Idea: Practice language arts skills.

Bible Study

T

Have students say Psalm 98:1 using the hand motions from Day 1.

Have students copy in cursive Psalm 98:1 on a new page in their *Common Place Book.* Students should leave the rest of the page blank to add to next week.

Students will add to the *Common Place Book* throughout the year.

✔ *Lead Me to the Rock* CD
Track 2; Song: "Sing Unto the Lord" (vs. 1)

Key Idea: Copy in cursive a portion of a Psalm.

Math Exploration

S

Choose **one** math option listed below.

★ *Singapore Primary Mathematics 2A/2B, 3A/3B,* or *4A/4B*

★ Your own math program

Key Idea: Use a step-by-step math program.

Science Exploration

I

★ Read *The Great Dinosaur Mystery and the Bible* p. 45-47. Turn to the science experiment section in your science binder or sketchbook. At the top of a blank page, write: *What would a dinosaur egg look and feel like?* Under the question, write: *'Guess'*. Write down your guess. We don't know if all dinosaurs laid eggs, but quite a few fossilized dinosaur eggs have already been found. Since dinosaurs are reptile-like creatures, we would guess that dinosaur eggs would be reptile-like. To learn what a reptile egg feels like, add 1 cup of vinegar to a glass. Gently place one chicken egg in the vinegar. Make sure the egg is completely submerged in the vinegar. Allow the egg to sit in the vinegar overnight. The next day, use a spoon to take the egg out. Gently squeeze the egg to learn how the shell feels. **The egg will break if you squeeze it too hard!** Reptile eggs have tough, leathery shells with a built-in food supply. The tough shell also allows the eggs to be fossilized. On your paper, write: *'Procedure'*. Draw a picture of the experiment. At the bottom of the paper, write: *'Conclusion'*. Explain what you learned.

Key Idea: We don't know for sure if real dinosaurs could still be alive somewhere in the world today.

Learning through History
Focus: India, China, Greece, and Rome

Unit 14 - Day 1

Reading about History — T

Read about history in the following resource:

★ *A Child's History of the World: Ch. 20* p. 85-87

★ *Hero Tales* p. 35-43 (omit p. 33-34)

After today's first reading, say, *Describe the castes or caste system.* (knowledge) *What might be some of the problems with a caste system?* (analysis) *Tell about the Indian prince Gautama.* (comprehension) *Even though Gautama was a good man, what was wrong with Buddhism?* (analysis) *Why is it wrong to think that a person is a god and wrong to worship that person?* (evaluation)

Key Idea: India has existed since ancient times. For a long time, it had a caste system, which separated the people in India. People from different castes did not associate with one another. Castes are illegal in India today.

History Project — S

In this unit you will be mapping the Silk Road and showing how silk was made. Use a reference book or an online resource such as www.wikipedia.org to view a map of the Silk Road. Then, either draw your own map of the Silk Road or print a map at: www.nationalgeographic.com/xpeditions/atlas and add colored lines to show the Silk Road.

Key Idea: In the Far East, India was known for its spices, just as China was known for its silk.

Storytime — T

Read aloud the following assigned story:

★ *Hero Tales* p. 45-55

Discuss today's reading in a "conversational way". Share about a person, time, event, or emotion from your life that today's reading brought to mind. Next, have your child share a connection.

Key Idea: Connect personally to the story.

Research — S

Both India and China had strong civilizations during ancient times. India was known for its spices, and China was known for its silk. Over time, a Spice Route and the Silk Road became paths for carrying spices and silk from the far East. Where could you look to discover more about the **Silk Road**? Use a reference book or an online resource like www.wikipedia.org to look up *Silk Road*. Depending on the resource you use, you will have to type *Silk Road* in the search or look it up in the index.

Orally answer one or more of the following questions from your research: *What was the Silk Road? What made the Silk Road dangerous? Why was silk so expensive? How was silk made? Why didn't China want anyone else to know the secret of how silk was made? What was the penalty for telling the secret?*

Key Idea: People all over the world wanted to get spices and silk through the trade routes.

Independent History Study — I

★ Read *The Young Christian's Introduction to the Bible* p. 43-44. Orally retell or narrate to an adult the portion of text that you read today. Use the *Narration Tips* in the Appendix for help as needed.

Key Idea: Through His word, God shows us how much worship of men or idols displeases Him. Even though Buddha was a good man, when Buddhists worship him, they are displeasing the one true God!

Learning the Basics

Focus: Language Arts, Math, Bible, and Science

Poetry

T

Read aloud to the students the poem *"My Kingdom"* (see Appendix). Ask, *What would you guess 'heather' and 'gorse' are? How did the two lines of the poem after 'heather' and 'gorse' help you guess their meaning? What is the child in this poem doing? After the child arrives back home, why would the nurse appear big? Explain why the child notices how "great and cool the rooms" seem.* Read the poem again with the students.

Key Idea: Read and appreciate classic poetry.

Language Arts

S

Have students complete the first studied dictation exercise (see Appendix for directions and passages).

Help students complete one lesson from the following reading program:

★ *Drawn into the Heart of Reading*

Work with the students to complete **one** of the English options listed below:

★ *Beginning Wisely:* Review One p. 123-125

★ *Building with Diligence:* Lesson 49 (Half)

★ Your own grammar program

Key Idea: Practice language arts skills.

Bible Study

T

Say, *Find Psalm 98:1-3 in your Bible. This is the memory selection for this unit. Read the verse out loud.* Ask, *Because we have a sinful nature, are we able to save ourselves? Who was sent to be a Savior for us? Since the coming of Jesus was foretold throughout the Old Testament, how does His coming fulfill God's promise of salvation to all nations in Psalm 98:2? Since the Israelites are God's chosen people, how did God keep His promise to them in Psalm 98:3? According to Psalm 98:3, where has the salvation of God been seen? Why should this make us sing a new, joyful song to the Lord?* Have students say the verse 3 times, adding hand motions to help remember the words.

✔ *Lead Me to the Rock* CD
Track 2; Song: "Sing Unto the Lord"
(vs. 1-3)

Key Idea: God sent His only Son to Earth to be the promised Savior.

Math Exploration

S

Choose **one** of the math options listed below (see Appendix for details).

★ *Singapore Primary Mathematics 2A/2B, 3A/3B,* or *4A/4B*

★ Your own math program

Key Idea: Use a step-by-step math program.

Science Exploration

I

Today you will add to your science notebook. At the top of an unlined paper, copy Psalm 104:25-26 in cursive. Beneath the verse, write the following heading: *God's Amazing Creatures.* Underneath the heading, draw and color a picture of a *Kronosaurus* and a *Plesiosaur* from p. 46-47 of *The Great Dinosaur Mystery and the Bible.* To read more about the leviathan, read Job chapter 41.

Key Idea: The Bible describes the leviathan in Job 41. King David mentions the leviathan again in Psalm 104. Although we are not sure exactly what a leviathan looked like, we do know this was a very large sea creature created by God, and it had no equal on Earth.

Learning through History
Focus: India, China, Greece, and Rome

Unit 14 - Day 2

Reading about History — T

Read about history in the following resource:

★ *A Child's History of the World: Ch. 21* p. 88-90

★ Also, read *Hero Tales* as scheduled in the *Storytime* box of the plans.

After today's first reading, read aloud Luke 6:27-36. Say, *Contrast what Jesus said in Luke 6:31 to Confucius' Golden Rule on p. 88 of* A Child's History of the World. *How are the 2 sayings different? Many religions say that we should not harm others, but Jesus says that we need to seek to do good for others and to have mercy on them. How is that different from what Confucius said? How can sayings that sound alike confuse us about other religions? Why is what Jesus said so much more important than what other men say?*

Key Idea: We need to be careful not to be confused by religions that sound like Christianity.

Storytime — T

Read aloud the following assigned passage:

★ *Hero Tales* p. 141-151

Ask, *In today's reading, how were people's lives different from your life? What would you have enjoyed or found difficult about living during that time?*

Key Idea: Compare and contrast the historical time period of the reading to your own life.

History Project — S

Get 8 index cards. You will be listing the steps for making silk. On the first card, write, *Silk moths lay eggs on special paper.* On the second card, write, *Silkworm caterpillars hatch from the eggs and feed on fresh mulberry leaves.* On the third card, write, *After a month of eating, the silkworms are very heavy.* On the fourth card, write, *The silkworms begin spinning their cocoons by moving their heads back and forth.* Save the rest of the cards for Day 3.

Key Idea: China kept the process of silk-making a secret for a long time.

Geography — S

Use a globe for today's activities. *Find China on the globe. On which continent do you find China? In China (on the globe), find the Huang River and the Yangtze River. Next, find the Himalaya Mountains. They are located south of Tibet. Last, find the Gobi Desert in southern Mongolia. You can also see a picture of the Gobi Desert in your* One Small Square: Cactus Desert *science book on p. 38.*

Review the following concept: *Find the 4 cardinal directions. Point your right hand toward the rising sun. This is East. Point your left hand toward the setting sun. That is West. The direction you are facing is North. Your back is toward the South. Try figuring out which direction you are going next time you are riding in your car or automobile.*

Key Idea: China is a very old civilization. Even though the country was not very connected to the rest of the world, the Chinese were inventing and using things like printing presses, compasses, immunizations, and gun powder long ago.

Independent History Study — I

★ On white paper, follow the directions on p. 29-30 of *Draw and Write Through History* to draw and color a silkworm moth. Store your completed drawing in the place you have chosen for it.

Key Idea: Ancient China was known for its production of silk. Silk moths were necessary to make silk.

Learning the Basics

Focus: Language Arts, Math, Bible, and Science

Language Arts

T

Work with the students to complete **one** of the English options listed below:

★ *Beginning Wisely:* Review Two p. 126-127

★ *Building with Diligence:* Lesson 50

★ Your own grammar program

Say, *You will be doing a writing activity based on the poem, "My Kingdom"* (see Appendix).

Say, *Think of a quiet place outdoors that you've been that you could describe well* (i.e. a backyard in summer, a garden in the spring, snow hills in the winter, on a river bank fishing, etc.). At the top of a markerboard or a paper, make 2 columns: *"Saw"* and *"Heard"*. Ask students to list things that they saw and heard, while they were in that quiet place outdoors. Write down the students' ideas under the appropriate column.

Next, say, *You will draw and color your outdoor scene based on the list we just made. Refer to the list as you draw, so you don't leave anything out.*

After students have finished drawing and coloring, guide students to use the scene they just drew and the items they listed to write a 5 sentence description of their scene (i.e. The yard was bathed in sunlight. The bright pink flower petals were opening sleepily, as bees buzzed through the air. The breeze smelled like fresh clover.).

Have students share their descriptions by reading them aloud.

Key Idea: Write creatively from classic poetry.

Bible Study

T

Have students say Psalm 98:1-3 using the hand motions they added on Day 1. Say, *A mood is a feeling, a sensation, or a state of mind. What is the mood of Psalm 98:2-3?* (Some examples of moods include frightened, worried, happy, peaceful, hopeful, sad, unhappy, angry, thankful, prayerful, joyful, and lonely.) Ask, *When would this Psalm help you, or when would you go to this Psalm?* (i.e. to understand that Jesus is the promised Savior, as a reminder that God keeps His promises, to help us see how blessed we are to know Jesus.)

Last, pray with your children that they may come to know Jesus personally. Pray that they will understand the gift of salvation through Christ Jesus.

✔ *Lead Me to the Rock* CD
Track 2; Song: "Sing Unto the Lord" (vs. 1-3)

Key Idea: The Psalms reflect the many emotions and moods we have. They are a wonderful place to seek counsel from the Lord.

Math Exploration

S

Choose **one** of the math options listed below (see Appendix for details).

★ *Singapore Primary Mathematics 2A/2B, 3A/3B,* or *4A/4B*

★ Your own math program

Key Idea: Use a step-by-step math program.

Science Exploration

I

★ Read *The Great Dinosaur Mystery and the Bible* p. 48-51. Orally retell or narrate to an adult the portion of text that you read today. Use the *Narration Tips* in the Appendix for help as needed.

Key Idea: The world after the Flood would have been much different than the world before the Flood. Food would have been much harder to find. Both man and animals would have had to work harder to survive.

Learning through History
Focus: India, China, Greece, and Rome

Unit 14 - Day 3

Reading about History — T

Read about history in the following resource:

★ *A Child's History of the World: Ch. 22* p. 91-94

After today's reading, have your students orally narrate or retell the portion of today's text that you read. Use the *Narration Tips* in the Appendix as needed.

Key Idea: In Athens, the rich and poor were often quarreling. They were tired of kings who always seem to side with the rich, so they chose a man named Draco to make rules for them instead. Draco's laws were so strong that a man named Solon was chosen to make fairer laws.

Storytime — T

Read aloud the following assigned passage:

★ *A Triumph for Flavius:* First ½ of Ch. I

Ask, *In what does the main character place his faith? How would the story be different if the main character put his faith in God? Share a character, a story, or a verse from the Bible that you are reminded of by today's reading.*

Key Idea: Share a Biblical connection.

History Project — S

Get your index cards from Day 1. You will be listing the last 4 steps for making silk. On the fifth card, write, *The worms shoot liquid silk out of small holes in their heads. The silk turns solid when it touches the air.* On the sixth card, write, *Within a few days the silkworm has spun one mile of silk that surrounds it in a cocoon.* On the seventh card, write, *The cocoons are heated to keep the caterpillars from turning into moths and destroying their cocoons as they emerge.* On the eighth card, write, *A few worms are allowed to turn into moths to lay eggs of their own.* Mix up the cards and see if you can put the steps in the correct order.

Key Idea: The process for making silk was kept a secret.

Vocabulary — S

You may choose 3-5 of the following vocabulary words from *A Child's History of the World* to use for this lesson: *aristocrat* (p. 91), *senators* (p. 92), *orally* (p. 93), *election* (p. 93), and/or *ostracism* (p. 93). First, find the word in the text and read the sentence containing the word. Think about possible meanings. Next, find the word in a dictionary and select the correct meaning. Write the word at the top of an index card or at the top of the corresponding letter page in the notebook. Underneath the word, copy the correct definition from the dictionary. Then, use the word correctly in a sentence. The sentence may either be copied from the text or be one of your own creation. Last, draw a small picture to show the word's meaning. If you used an index card to record your word, file it under the correct alphabetical tab.

Key Idea: In Athens, some rulers were chosen, and others just took over. Each ruler governed differently as the Greeks tried to find a system of government that would work for both rich and poor people.

Independent History Study — I

★ On lined paper, copy in cursive the **first** paragraph of *Draw and Write Through History* p. 34. Store your completed copywork with your completed drawings in the place you have chosen for them.

Key Idea: The Chinese civilization has a much longer history than the Greek civilization.

Poetry

T

Read aloud with the students the poem *"My Kingdom"* (see Appendix). Say, *Describe a time you have been somewhere like this or felt like this. What can you learn about the poet, Robert Louis Stevenson, from the poem?* Say, *Did you know that as Robert Louis Stevenson was traveling by boat around the South Seas, he visited Hawaii and became friends with the last King of Hawaii?* Have the students read the poem on their own.

Key Idea: Read and appreciate classic poetry.

Language Arts

S

Have students complete one studied dictation exercise (see Appendix for directions and passages).

Help students complete one lesson from the following reading program:

★ *Drawn into the Heart of Reading*

Work with the students to complete **one** of the English options listed below:

★ *Beginning Wisely:* A Poem to Enjoy p. 129

★ *Building with Diligence:* Lesson 51

★ Your own grammar program

Key Idea: Practice language arts skills.

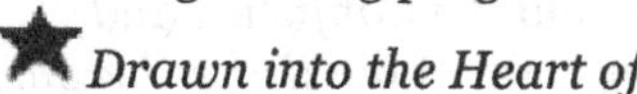

Bible Study

T

Say, *You will be having your own quiet time with God today. Choose a quiet place for this special time, where you can be alone with God. Then, do the following things:*

1. Read Psalm 98:1-3 in your Bible.
2. Pray about the Psalm using the following beginning to your prayer: *Thank you for sending your Son, Jesus, to Earth to be my Savior. Help me to honor Him by ______ and ______. Please fill ______ with a love for Jesus too.*
3. Recite Psalm 98:1-3 using the hand motions you added on Day 1.
4. Sing Psalm 98:1-3 along with the CD at the end of your quiet time.

✔ *Lead Me to the Rock* CD
Track 2; Song: "Sing Unto the Lord" (vs. 1-3)

Key Idea: Salvation is a gift through Jesus.

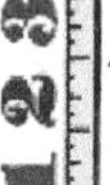

Math Exploration

S

Choose **one** of the math options listed below (see Appendix for details).

★ *Singapore Primary Mathematics 2A/2B, 3A/3B*, or *4A/4B*

★ Your own math program

Key Idea: Use a step-by-step math program.

Science Exploration

I

★ Read *The Great Dinosaur Mystery and the Bible* p. 52-54. Write the answer to each numbered question on lined paper. You do not need to copy the question. Use the listed page to help you answer each question.

1. How does the size of most dinosaurs' brains compare to the size of their bodies? (p. 52)
2. What is the name of one of the smallest dinosaurs? (p. 52)
3. Who was the oldest man in the Bible, and how old was he? (p. 53)
4. List some of the types of giant animals whose fossils have been discovered. (p. 53)
5. What major change happened after the flood according to Genesis 9:2?

Key Idea: We know God created Adam and Eve and the animals with perfect bodies, and they lived longer.

Learning through History
Focus: India, China, Greece, and Rome

Unit 14 - Day 4

Reading about History [T]

Read about history in the following resource:

★ *A Child's History of the World: Ch. 23* p. 95-98

After today's reading, say, *You will be writing a narration about part of the day's history reading. In order to remember the details very well, you will need to reread the part of today's reading from the fifth paragraph on p. 96 through the third paragraph on p. 97 (on your own if possible).*

After students have finished reading the passage, ask them the questions below. If the students do not know the answers, help them find the answers in the passage they just read. Ask, *In today's story, who commanded the Roman army? What did Horatius command his army to do? Over what river was the bridge? Why did Horatius give orders to break down the bridge over the Tiber River? While the Romans were chopping down the bridge, what did Horatius do? When the bridge began to crack, what did Horatius do then? How did everyone react?*

After the questions have been answered, have students write a 3-5 sentence narration that begins, *When Horatius was commander of the Roman army...* You may wish to write the names Horatius, Tiber River, Estruscans, and Tarquin for students to refer to as they write. When students have finished their narration, direct them to read the sentences out loud.

See the *Written Narration Skills* in the Appendix to guide students in editing their narrations.

Key Idea: In 509 B.C., Rome got rid of their king and became a republic.

Storytime [T]

Read aloud the following assigned passage:

★ *A Triumph for Flavius:* Last ½ of Ch. I

After today's reading, have your students orally narrate or retell the portion of today's text that you read. Use the *Narration Tips* in the Appendix as needed.

Key Idea: Practice oral narration skills.

Timeline [S]

You will be adding 2 new cards to your staircase timeline today. On the first new card, draw and color a silkworm moth. Write, *Shang Dynasty in China (1500 B.C.).* On the second new card, draw and color a golden crown. Write, *Confucius and Buddha (500 B.C.).*

If you decided to tape your timeline cards to the back of a door, add the *Confucius and Buddha* card to the right of the *Esther becomes Queen of Persia* card.

To add the *Shang Dynasty* card, you will need to go back and place it between the *Exodus* card and the *Fall of Jericho* card. If you decided to tape the timeline cards side-by-side to accordion-fold them, use clear packing tape to tape the cards as described above.

Key Idea: The Romans elected their rulers. These 2 men were called consuls. Each consul had a bodyguard of 12 men called lictors. When Rome's previous king Tarquin tried to take back Rome, Horatius prevented him by cutting down the bridge across the Tiber River.

Independent History Study [I]

★ On white paper, follow the directions on p. 31-33 of *Draw and Write Through History* to draw a giant panda. Wait to color it. Store your completed drawing in the place you have chosen for it.

Key Idea: Rome was growing into a powerful country while China remained separated from the world.

Learning the Basics

Focus: Language Arts, Math, Bible, and Science

Unit 14 - Day 4

Poetry

T

Read aloud with the students the poem *"My Kingdom"* (see Appendix). Have students share this poem in a special way. Suggestions for sharing the poem can be viewed in the "Poetry" box for Unit 13 – Day 4.

Key Idea: Share a variety of classic poetry.

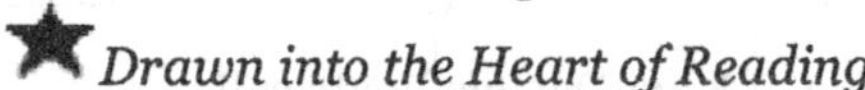

Language Arts

S

Have students complete one dictation exercise.

Guide students to complete one reading lesson.

★ *Drawn into the Heart of Reading*

Help students complete **one** English lesson.

★ *Beginning Wisely:* Lesson 51

★ *Building with Diligence:* Lesson 52

★ Your own grammar program

Key Idea: Practice language arts skills.

Bible Study

T

Have students say Psalm 98:1-3 using the hand motions from Day 1. Have students copy in cursive Psalm 98:2-3 beneath last unit's Psalm 98:1 in their *Common Place Book.* Students will add to the *Common Place Book* throughout the year.

✔ *Lead Me to the Rock* CD
Track 2; Song: "Sing Unto the Lord" (vs. 1-3)

Key Idea: Copy in cursive a portion of a Psalm.

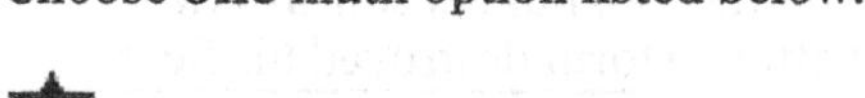

Math Exploration

S

Choose **one** math option listed below.

★ *Singapore Primary Mathematics 2A/2B, 3A/3B,* or *4A/4B*

★ Your own math program

Key Idea: Use a step-by-step math program.

Science Exploration

I

★ Read *The Great Dinosaur Mystery and the Bible* p. 55-57. Turn to the science experiment section in your science binder or sketchbook. At the top of a blank page, write: *How does the body design of a dinosaur affect its balance ?* Under the question, write: *'Guess'.* Write down your guess.

In order to be able to walk and run, your body must be balanced with your "center of gravity". To see how this works, stand up. You are balanced or centered. Keeping your body straight, lean forward. This makes you off-balance and pulls you forward. Did you reach out with your hands or feet to regain your balance?

Dinosaurs also needed balance. Use mini-marshmallows and cut up pieces of drinking straw to build the 4-legged dinosaur shown on p. 18-19. If needed, you can use bits of clay and toothpicks instead. Place one marshmallow on the ground to be the foot. Put a piece of straw into the marshmallow to be the leg. Add another marshmallow to be the knee. Above that add another piece of straw to be the thigh. Add another marshmallow to be the hip. Make 3 more legs like this one. Connect the legs together in pairs with short straws. Then, place one longer straw between two marshmallows to be the spine and connect the legs to it. Make sure your dinosaur is balanced. Now, add a long straw for the neck with a marshmallow on the end to be the head. What happened? To balance out your dinosaur, add a long straw tail with a marshmallow on the end. Write: *'Procedure'.* Draw the experiment. At the bottom, write: *'Conclusion'.* Explain.

Key Idea: God designed each dinosaur's body carefully to give it balance for walking and eating.

Learning through History
Focus: Coming into the Golden Age of Greece

Unit 15 - Day 1

Reading about History [T]

Read about history in the following resource:

★ *A Child's History of the World: Ch. 24* p. 99-104

After today's reading, say, *What two things did Darius order each Greek city to send him? Why did he ask for these two things?* (knowledge) *Explain why the Spartans didn't come right away when the Athenians sent for them.* (comprehension) *What does this tell you about the Spartans?* (analysis) *Describe the Battle of Marathon.* (comprehension) *Why is a Marathon race 26 miles long today?* (application)

Key Idea: Darius was the ruler of a vast Persian Empire. Yet, he wanted to conquer Greece to add to his empire. He sent his son-in-law to do the job, but his son-in-law returned after a storm destroyed his fleet.

History Project [S]

In this unit you will be building a miniature trireme, or boat, like the Persians and Greeks used in ancient times. On a heavy piece of paper or cardboard, draw an oval-shape that is 6" long and 2" wide and has pointed ends. Cut the oval out. This will be the bottom of your boat. Wrap the oval in aluminum foil. Take another piece of foil that is 12"x 12". Fold the foil in half. Place the boat bottom in the center of the folded foil so the long part of the foil sticks out on the ends. Pull the foil up around either side of the oval to make the sides of the boat. Fashion the prow and stern of the board by pinching the foil together at each end.

Key Idea: Triremes were ancient warships.

Storytime [T]

Read aloud the following assigned story:

★ *A Triumph for Flavius: Ch. II*

Discuss today's reading in a "conversational way". Share about a person, time, event, or emotion from your life that today's reading brought to mind. Next, have your child share a connection.

Key Idea: Connect personally to the story.

Research [S]

At the time of King Darius, boats called triremes were used. Where could you look to discover more about a **trireme**? Use a reference book or an online resource like www.wikipedia.org to look up *trireme*. Depending on the resource you use, you will have to type *trireme* in the search or look it up in the index.

Orally answer one or more of the following questions from your research: *What is a trireme? Describe a trireme. How did a trireme move? Was King Darius the only one who used triremes? Who else used triremes? What made triremes good for transporting armies and for fighting battles on the water?*

Key Idea: The next time Darius sailed to attack Greece, he went with his fleet to lead the attack himself. The Persian fleet landed near the plain of Marathon. Here the trained Greek soldiers beat the Persian soldiers, even though the Greeks were highly outnumbered. A runner ran 26 miles to share the good news.

Independent History Study [I]

★ Take out your picture of the giant panda. Follow the directions on p. 33 of *Draw and Write Through History* to color the panda. Store your drawing in the place you have chosen for it.

Key Idea: During the time period the Greeks battled the Persians, Confucius lived and taught in China.

Learning the Basics

Focus: Language Arts, Math, Bible, and Science

Poetry — T

Read aloud to the students the poem *"At the Sea-Side"* (see Appendix). Ask, *How do you know that this poem is being told by a child or from a child's perspective? Explain the meaning of the last stanza of the poem. Have you ever been to a beach? If so, what happened over time to any holes that had been dug in the sand? Explain.* Read the poem again with the students.

Key Idea: Read and appreciate classic poetry.

Language Arts — S

Have students complete the first studied dictation exercise (see Appendix for directions and passages).

Help students complete one lesson from the following reading program:

 *Drawn into the Heart of Reading*

Work with the students to complete **one** of the English options listed below:

★ *Beginning Wisely:* Lesson 52

★ *Building with Diligence:* Lesson 53

★ Your own grammar program

Key Idea: Practice language arts skills.

Bible Study — T

Say, *Find Psalm 98:1-5 in your Bible. This is the memory selection for this unit. Read the verse out loud.* Ask, *What kind of a noise does Psalm 98:4 say that we should make when we sing unto the Lord? Why should we sing heartily and with a strong voice when we are singing to the Lord? What does Psalm 98:4 say we are doing when we sing in this way? Why do you think there are so many examples in the Bible of God's people singing praises to Him? How can singing Psalms of praise to the Lord make your heart glad or give you courage and strength? What does this Psalm show us about how the Lord views singing praises to Him?* Have students say the verse 3 times, adding hand motions to help remember the words.

 *Lead Me to the Rock* CD
Track 2; Song: "Sing Unto the Lord" (vs. 1-5)

Key Idea: The Lord deserves our praise.

Math Exploration — S

Choose **one** of the math options listed below (see Appendix for details).

★ *Singapore Primary Mathematics 2A/2B, 3A/3B,* or *4A/4B*

★ Your own math program

Key Idea: Use a step-by-step math program.

Science Exploration — I

★ Read *The Great Dinosaur Mystery and the Bible* p. 58-59. Today you will add to your science notebook. At the top of an unlined paper, copy Job 41:33 in cursive. Beneath the verse, write the following heading: *What have you learned about dinosaurs?* You will need an adult to help you with this next part. Dictate your ideas to an adult, while he/she writes them down for you on your paper. Here are a few possible ideas: *Dinosaurs were created by God. They didn't evolve from reptiles or amphibians. Dinosaur-like animals are described in the Bible. Sin changed the way the dinosaurs behaved. Dinosaurs would have been on the ark. Dinosaur fossils have been found many places. Dragon stories could be describing dinosaurs. Both Job and David talk about the leviathan.* Then, decorate your paper.

Key Idea: There are many things that we do not know about the past, but we do know God's word is true.

Learning through History

Focus: Coming into the Golden Age of Greece

Unit 15 - Day 2

Reading about History **T**

Read about history in the following resource:

★ *A Child's History of the World: Ch. 25* p. 105-108

After today's reading, read aloud Daniel 10:12-11:2. Say, *Daniel lived at the time of the rulers Nebuchadnezzar, Belshazzar, Darius the Mede, and Cyrus. When the angelic messenger came to Daniel in Daniel 10:12, what reason did he give for coming? In Daniel 10:13, why didn't the messenger come right away when Daniel prayed? Who would come into power after Persia, according to Daniel 10:20? Who did the angel say he supported and protected in Daniel 11:1? The fourth Persian king that is mentioned in Daniel 11:2, is most likely Xerxes. In Daniel 11:2, in what does it say Xerxes will place his trust? What does it say Xerxes will do about Greece?*

Key Idea: The angelic messenger revealed to Daniel the future of the Israelites. Within this revelation, we can glimpse God's plan for history which happened later just as the messenger had said. God knows all of history, because He is the author.

History Project **S**

Take out your trireme that you made on Day 1. Use an index card or a 3 x 5 piece of paper to be your sail. Placing your card vertically, punch a hole 1" from the top and 1" from the bottom of the card. Poke a craft stick or a straw through the holes to be your mast. Place a chunk of clay on the inside floor of your boat and stick the mast into the clay. Save the trireme for Day 3.

Key Idea: Each trireme held hundreds of men.

Storytime **T**

Read aloud the following assigned passage:

★ *A Triumph for Flavius: Ch. III*

Ask, *In today's reading, how were people's lives different from your life? What would you have enjoyed or found difficult about living during that time?*

Key Idea: Compare and contrast the historical time period of the reading to your own life.

Geography **S**

Use a globe for today's activities. *Define the meaning of a 'strait' according to A Child's History of the World p. 107. On the globe, find the Hellespont (which is now called the Dardanelles) in modern-day Turkey. On the globe, trace the path that Xerxes' army took across land from near modern-day Baghdad in Iraq across the Dardanelles Strait and down into Greece.*

Review the following concept: *Find the 4 cardinal directions. Point your right hand toward the rising sun. This is East. Point your left hand toward the setting sun. That is West. The direction you are facing is North. Your back is toward the South. Find the compass rose on your globe that shows the 4 cardinal directions.*

Key Idea: Even though it would have been a shorter route to sail to Greece than to march across land, Xerxes didn't have enough triremes to carry his entire army. So, most of the army marched to Greece and the remaining army sailed on triremes. The battle was fought on both land and sea.

Independent History Study **I**

★ On lined paper, copy in cursive the **second** paragraph of *Draw and Write Through History* p. 34. Store your completed copywork with your completed drawings in the place you have chosen for them.

Key Idea: During the time of King Xerxes, China was divided into 7 kingdoms who were constantly at war.

Learning the Basics

Focus: Language Arts, Math, Bible, and Science

Unit 15 - Day 2

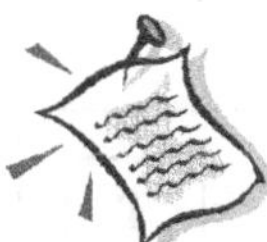

Language Arts

T

Work with the students to complete **one** of the English options listed below:

★ *Beginning Wisely:* Lesson 53

★ *Building with Diligence:* Lesson 54

★ Your own grammar program

Say, *You will be doing a writing activity based on the poem, "At the Sea-Side"* (see Appendix). *A meter in a poem is its beat or its rhythm. Let's read the first line of the poem and clap out the syllables* (When/I/was/down/be/side/the/sea). Then, write the number of syllables at the end of the first line (8). Repeat the activity with the next line (A/wood/en/spade/they/gave/to/me). Write the number of syllables at the end of line two (8). Repeat the activity with the rest of the poem to see a pattern emerge (8,8, 6). Explain that this is called the meter of a poem.

Next, have students point out the rhyming pattern they see in the poem (*sea* and *me, cup* and *up, shore* and *more).*

Tell students that they will be writing 6 more lines to add to the poem. Students need to try to follow the meter (and possibly the rhyming pattern) of the original poem. Guide students to think of things that they might see at the seashore. Make a web of their ideas by placing a circle in the middle of a markerboard or paper and writing, *Sea-side* in it. Then, draw lines coming out from the circle like spokes on a wheel. At the end of each spoke draw another circle. Write one idea in each circle. Have students begin their poem, *When I was down beside the sea.*

Key Idea: Write creatively from classic poetry.

Bible Study

T

Have students say Psalm 98:1-5 using the hand motions they added on Day 1. Say, *A mood is a feeling, a sensation, or a state of mind. What is the mood of Psalm 98:4-5?* (Some examples of moods include frightened, worried, happy, peaceful, hopeful, sad, unhappy, angry, thankful, prayerful, joyful, and lonely.) Ask, *When would this Psalm help you, or when would you go to this Psalm?* (i.e. as a reminder of how to sing praises to the Lord, to help us remember that we sing to rejoice and praise God, to help us rejoice in the Lord.)

Last, pray with your children that they will sing praises to the Lord in a joyous and mighty way. Pray that your children will realize the blessing of praising the Lord with singing as a way to honor Him as King over all. Pray that the Lord may be glorified today.

✔ *Lead Me to the Rock* CD
Track 2; Song: "Sing Unto the Lord" (vs. 1-5)

Key Idea: The Psalms reflect the many emotions and moods we have. They are a wonderful place to seek counsel from the Lord.

Math Exploration

S

Choose **one** of the math options listed below (see Appendix for details).

★ *Singapore Primary Mathematics 2A/2B, 3A/3B,* or *4A/4B*

★ Your own math program

Key Idea: Use a step-by-step math program.

Science Exploration

I

★ Read *Find the Constellations* p. 3-6. Orally retell or narrate to an adult the portion of text that you read today. Use the *Narration Tips* in the Appendix for help as needed.

Key Idea: Constellations are groups of stars that you can see in the night sky. Even shepherds thousands of years ago knew the stars and the constellations. They reveal God's handiwork.

Learning through History
Focus: Coming into the Golden Age of Greece

Unit 15 - Day 3

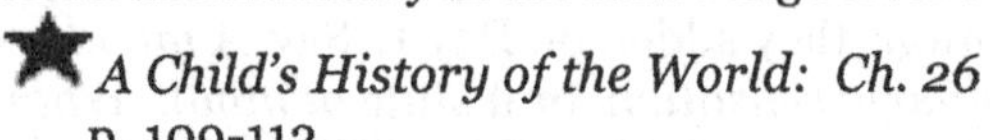

Reading about History — T

Read about history in the following resource:

★ *A Child's History of the World: Ch. 26* p. 109-112

After today's reading, have your students orally narrate or retell the portion of today's text that you read. Use the *Narration Tips* in the Appendix as needed.

Key Idea: When Xerxes' army arrived in Greece, they found their way blocked in the pass at Thermopylae by Leonidas and his much smaller army. Xerxes finally overtook Leonidas and his men by taking a secret path over the mountains. The Athenians deserted their city as the Persian army approached.

History Project — S

Get your trireme you made on Day 2. Fill a sink or tub partway full of water. Place your trireme in the water. If your boat tips to one side, you may need to reposition your clay to be more centered in the bottom of your boat. Experiment with sailing your trireme by blowing on the sail from various directions. Why would it be necessary to have oars and rowers in addition to the sail? Sometimes a flute would be played to help the rowers stay together. How would the music from the flute aid the rowers in this task?

Key Idea: When the Athenians deserted their city, they boarded their triremes in the bay of Salamis. Themistocles and the Greeks defeated Xerxes' army by dividing the Persian fleet in the bay and fighting them in two halves.

Storytime — T

Read aloud the following assigned passage:

★ *A Triumph for Flavius: Ch. IV*

Ask, *In what does the main character place his faith? How would the story be different if the main character put his faith in God? Share a character, a story, or a verse from the Bible that you are reminded of by today's reading.*

Key Idea: Share a Biblical connection.

Vocabulary — S

You may choose 3-5 of the following vocabulary words from *A Child's History of the World* to use for this lesson: *pass* (p. 110), *bleak* (p. 110), *bay* (p. 111), *rammed* (p. 112), and/or *hasty* (p. 112). First, find the word in the text and read the sentence containing the word. Think about possible meanings. Next, find the word in a dictionary and select the correct meaning. Write the word at the top of an index card or at the top of the corresponding letter page in the notebook. Underneath the word, copy the correct definition from the dictionary. Then, use the word correctly in a sentence. The sentence may either be copied from the text or be one of your own creation. Last, draw a small picture to show the word's meaning. If you used an index card to record your word, file it under the correct alphabetical tab.

Key Idea: Xerxes was defeated and the scene was set for a new leader in Greece to rise up. It happened just like the angelic messenger had said over 50 years earlier when Daniel had been given a glimpse into God's future plans.

Independent History Study — I

★ Read *The Young Christian's Introduction to the Bible* p. 23-25. Then, copy 1 John 3:4-5 in cursive onto a clean page in your *Common Place Book*.

Key Idea: God has a plan for all of history. We can be thankful that God planned for man's redemption.

Learning the Basics

Focus: Language Arts, Math, Bible, and Science

Unit 15 - Day 3

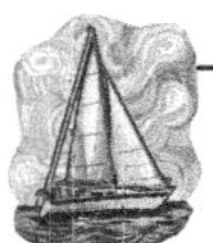

Poetry

T

Read aloud with the students the poem *"At the Sea-Side"* (see Appendix). *Describe a time you have been somewhere like this or felt like this. What can you learn about the poet, Robert Louis Stevenson, from the poem?* Say, *Did you know that Robert Louis Stevenson's father designed the lighthouse system used all over Scotland? It's not surprising that young Robert grew up to love the sea.* Have the students read the poem on their own.

Key Idea: Read and appreciate classic poetry.

Language Arts

S

Have students complete one studied dictation exercise (see Appendix for directions and passages).

Help students complete one lesson from the following reading program:

★ *Drawn into the Heart of Reading*

Work with the students to complete **one** of the English options listed below:

★ *Beginning Wisely:* Lesson 54

★ *Building with Diligence:* Lesson 55

★ Your own grammar program

Key Idea: Practice language arts skills.

Bible Study

T

Say, *You will be having your own quiet time with God today. Choose a quiet place for this special time, where you can be alone with God. Then, do the following things:*

1. Read Psalm 98:1-5 in your Bible.
2. Pray about the Psalm using the following beginning to your prayer: *Thank you for giving me a voice that I can use to praise you. Help me to sing in a ______ way, in order to honor you. Show me how to ______ so that I may glorify you with my life.*
3. Recite Psalm 98:1-5 using the hand motions you added on Day 1.
4. Sing Psalm 98:1-5 along with the CD at the end of your quiet time.

✔ *Lead Me to the Rock* CD
Track 2; Song: "Sing Unto the Lord" (vs. 1-5)

Key Idea: The Lord is worthy to be praised.

Math Exploration

S

Choose **one** of the math options listed below (see Appendix for details).

★ *Singapore Primary Mathematics 2A/2B, 3A/3B,* or *4A/4B*

★ Your own math program

Key Idea: Use a step-by-step math program.

Science Exploration

I

★ Read *Find the Constellations* p. 7-9. Write the answer to each numbered question on lined paper. You do not need to copy the question. Use the listed page to help you answer each question.

1. What are constellations? (p. 7)
2. Which constellation is the Big Dipper part of? (p. 7)
3. Draw The Great Bear constellation. (p. 7)
4. Draw either the Herdsman or the Lion constellation. (p. 8-9)
5. What constellations and stars do you see mentioned in Job 9:9?

Key Idea: Each star was placed in the heavens by the Lord. The names of the constellations and stars that we recognize today are mentioned in Scripture.

Learning through History
Focus: Coming into the Golden Age of Greece

Unit 15 - Day 4

Reading about History [T]

Read about history in the following resource:

★ *A Child's History of the World: Ch. 27* p. 113-118

After today's reading, say, *You will be writing a narration about part of the day's history reading. In order to remember the details very well, you will need to reread the part of today's reading from the third paragraph on p. 113 through the bottom of p. 114 (on your own if possible).*

After students have finished reading the passage, ask them the questions below. If the students do not know the answers, help them find the answers in the passage they just read. Ask, *What city was today's story about? Who burned Athens down? How did Xerxes' burning of Athens turn out to be a good thing? Who was the main leader in Athens at that time? What did Pericles do for Athens? During the Golden Age of Greece, what would you have seen in Athens? Pagan means to worship other gods or many gods, instead of worshiping the one true God of the Bible. How can you tell that the people of Ancient Greece were pagan?*

After the questions have been answered, have students write a 3-5 sentence narration that begins, *During the Golden Age of Greece...* You may wish to write the words *Athens, Pericles,* and *pagan* for students to refer to as they write. When students have finished their narration, direct them to read the sentences out loud. See the *Written Narration Skills* in the Appendix to guide students in editing their narrations.

Key Idea: Athens was rebuilt after the fire.

Storytime [T]

Read aloud the following assigned passage:

★ *A Triumph for Flavius: Ch. V*

Say, *Transport yourself back to the time of this story. Pretend you lived at this time. Tell me what you see and do. (Make sure to use the word, "I", and to tell only what was described in today's reading.)*

Key Idea: Practice oral narration skills.

Timeline [S]

You will be adding a new card to your staircase timeline today. On the first new card, draw and color a picture of the Parthenon. Use the picture on p. 115 of A Child's History of the World for help drawing the Parthenon. Write, *The Golden Age of Greece (480-430 B.C.).*

If you decided to tape your timeline cards to the back of a door, add the *Golden Age of Greece* card to the right of the *Confucius and Buddha* card. If you decided to tape the timeline cards side-by-side to accordion-fold them, use clear packing tape to tape the cards as described above.

Key Idea: Pericles was the chief leader in Greece during its Golden Age. He did much to encourage philosophy, architecture, sculpting, art, poetry, and plays. Athens was rebuilt to be much finer then it had been before. The Golden Age of Greece is also often called the Age of Pericles.

Independent History Study [I]

★ Read *The Young Christian's Introduction to the Bible* p. 26-28. Then, choose an interesting part from today's pages to read aloud and explain to an adult.

Key Idea: Since sin separates us from God, we needed someone to pay the penalty for our sin. God had a plan for his Son to pay that penalty for us, even though His Son was perfect. So, all of history since the first sin in the Garden of Eden, was leading up to the birth of our Savior.

Learning the Basics

Focus: Language Arts, Math, Bible, and Science

Unit 15 - Day 4

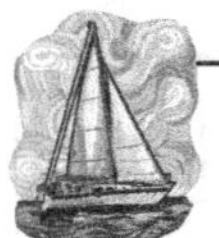

Poetry

T

Read aloud with the students the poem *"At the Sea-Side"* (see Appendix). Have students share this poem in a special way. Suggestions for sharing the poem include recording it to play for someone, reading it to someone on the telephone, photocopying the poem and adding illustrations, reading it to someone at home, putting the poem to a melody and singing it, using an instrument to tap out the meter or rhythm of the poem while reading it, or copying the poem on paper.

Key Idea: Share a variety of classic poetry.

Language Arts

S

Have students complete one dictation exercise.

Guide students to complete one reading lesson.

★ *Drawn into the Heart of Reading*

Help students complete **one** English lesson.

★ *Beginning Wisely:* Lesson 55

★ *Building with Diligence:* Lesson 56

★ Your own grammar program

Key Idea: Practice language arts skills.

Bible Study

T

Have students say Psalm 98:1-5 using the hand motions from Day 1.

Have students copy in cursive Psalm 98:4-5 beneath last unit's Psalm 98:2-3 in their *Common Place Book.* Students should leave the rest of the page blank to add to next week.

Students will add to the *Common Place Book* throughout the year.

✔ *Lead Me to the Rock* CD
Track 2; Song: "Sing Unto the Lord" (vs. 1-5)

Key Idea: Copy in cursive a portion of a Psalm.

Math Exploration

S

Choose **one** math option listed below.

★ *Singapore Primary Mathematics 2A/2B, 3A/3B,* or *4A/4B*

★ Your own math program

Key Idea: Use a step-by-step math program.

Science Exploration

I

★ Read *Find the Constellations* p. 10. Turn to the science experiment section in your science binder or sketchbook. At the top of a blank page, write: *How can the size of a star affect how bright it appears?* Under the question, write: *'Guess'.* Write down your guess. Lay a sheet of paper on a table. Cover a flashlight lens with a piece of aluminum foil. Make a small hole in the center of the aluminum foil. Turn off the lights to darken the room. Next, you will need a partner. Turn on the flashlight, and have your partner hold it 8 inches above the piece of paper. Use a ruler to makes sure it's 8 inches above the paper. Then, draw a circle around the ring of light formed on the paper. Next, turn off the flashlight, and make a larger hole in the aluminum foil. Repeat the experiment. For your third trial, make a very large hole in the foil. Repeat the experiment. On your paper, write: *'Procedure'.* Draw a picture of the experiment. At the bottom of the paper, write: *'Conclusion'.* Explain what you learned.

Key Idea: A star's brightness is known as its magnitude. Large, very hot stars shine brightly in the sky.

Learning through History
Focus: Alexander the Great Conquers the World

Unit 16 - Day 1

Reading about History — T

Read about history in the following resource:

★ *A Child's History of the World: Ch. 28* p. 119-122

After today's reading, say, *What caused the end of the Golden Age of Greece?* (comprehension) *Why were the Spartans and Athenians fighting?* (knowledge) *Tell what you know about Socrates.* (comprehension) *Do you think that listening to your conscience is the same thing as listening to the Holy Spirit? Explain.* (knowledge) *Is it only Christians that believe that your soul lives on after death?* (knowledge) *Then, what makes Christianity different?* (synthesis)

Key Idea: Socrates was known as a philosopher. He asked questions that led people to see what was right. This is still called Socratic questioning today!

History Project — S

In this unit you will be drawing a piece of Greek pottery called the amphora. This is a Greek vase. On an 8" x 8" piece of white paper, draw the outline of a Greek amphora. Add an ornamental design around the neck of the vase. Add a different ornamental design on the handles of the vase. Color in only the ornamental designs with a thick layer of brown crayon. Leave a white space in the center of the amphora to add a drawing on Day 2.

Key Idea: Greek vases, called amphoras, show pictures of Greek heroes, Greek stories, or Greek life. The glistening black background of the vases, showcases the brown designs and pictures. Many Greek vases have been found.

Storytime — T

Read aloud the following assigned story:

★ *A Triumph for Flavius: Ch. VI*

Discuss today's reading in a "conversational way". Share about a person, time, event, or emotion from your life that today's reading brought to mind. Next, have your child share a connection.

Key Idea: Connect personally to the story.

Research — S

At the time of Alexander the Great, Greek pottery was shiny and black with dark brown sketches and ornamental designs. Where could you look to discover more about **Greek pottery**? Use a reference book or an online resource like www.wikipedia.org to look up *Greek pottery*. Depending on the resource you use, you will have to type *Greek pottery* in the search or look it up in the index.

Orally answer one or more of the following questions from your research: *What is pottery? What were Greek vases called? Describe Greek pottery. Are there many pieces of Greek pottery left today? What can be learned about Greek life from studying their pottery? What were some of the uses for Greek vases?*

Key Idea: Athens was known for its beautiful buildings, its culture, its education, and its fleet. Sparta did not care for these fine things, but they were sorry not to have a fleet. Athens and Sparta fought a long war with one another because of their differences. Neither side won.

Independent History Study — I

★ Read *The Young Christian's Introduction to the Bible* p. 29-32. Read aloud and explain to an adult the different groupings of books in the Old Testament.

Key Idea: All of the Old Testament looked forward to the coming of Christ.

Learning the Basics

Focus: Language Arts, Math, Bible, and Science

Poetry

T

Read aloud to the students the poem *"The Hayloft"* (see Appendix). Ask, *Can you guess what a 'scythe' might be, using the clues given in lines 3 and 4 of the poem? How are the haystacks like mountains for mountaineers to climb? Where do you think the names of the 'Mounts' in the poem came from? Are these real mountains? Describe the mood in the last stanza of the poem.* Read the poem again with the students.

Key Idea: Read and appreciate classic poetry.

Language Arts

S

Have students complete the first studied dictation exercise (see Appendix for directions and passages).

Help students complete one lesson from the following reading program:

★ *Drawn into the Heart of Reading*

Work with the students to complete **one** of the English options listed below:

★ *Beginning Wisely:* Lesson 56

★ *Building with Diligence:* Lesson 57

★ Your own grammar program

Key Idea: Practice language arts skills.

Bible Study

T

Say, *Find Psalm 98:1-6 in your Bible. This is the memory selection for this unit. Read the verse out loud.* Ask, *What kind of noise do trumpets and coronets make? Since trumpets and coronets resound, what kind of praise and worship is described in Psalm 98:6? When a king arrives, he is heralded by a trumpet and by people cheering. Where do we see people cheering and clapping today? Since we need to show God reverence when we are in His house, how can we joyfully praise Him without cheering? How can we be sure that we do not show more praise and enthusiasm for earthly things than for God?* Have students say the verse 3 times, adding hand motions to help remember the words.

✔ *Lead Me to the Rock* CD
Track 2; Song: "Sing Unto the Lord" (vs. 1-6)

Key Idea: Our praise for the Lord should be hearty and resound like the trumpets.

Math Exploration

S

Choose **one** of the math options listed below (see Appendix for details).

★ *Singapore Primary Mathematics 2A/2B, 3A/3B,* or *4A/4B*

★ Your own math program

Key Idea: Use a step-by-step math program.

Science Exploration

I

Today you will begin a book about the stars. You will add to this book for the next 7 units. To make a cover for your book, fold a piece of black paper in half. Use a white colored pencil or crayon, or gel or glitter pens to write a title on your book cover. Next, cut out a square piece of white paper to glue beneath the title. Before gluing the white paper on the cover, copy Psalm 147:4-5 on it in cursive. Then, fold 8 sheets of white paper in half and place them inside your cover to make a book. Staple the side of the book to hold it together. On the first page inside the book, draw one or more of the following constellations: Big Dipper (p. 6), Great Bear (p. 7), Herdsman (p. 8), Lion (p. 9). Make sure to draw the brighter stars larger, like they are shown in the pictures. Label each constellation with its name.

Key Idea: While man cannot hope to count the stars, God knows each one and calls it by name!

Learning through History

Focus: Alexander the Great Conquers the World

Unit 16 - Day 2

Reading about History — T

Read about history in the following resource:

★ *A Child's History of the World: Ch. 29* p. 123-126

After today's reading, read aloud Daniel 11:2-4. Say, *Daniel was visited by an angelic messenger during the reign of Cyrus in Babylon. By this time, Cyrus had already allowed the Jews to return to Jerusalem. Yet, Daniel remained in Babylon. In Daniel 11:2, the messenger foretold about which king? After Xerxes, in Daniel 11:3, what is said about the next mighty king? We can look at Daniel 10:20 to see that as Persia is defeated, Greece will rise. This is the predicted reign of Alexander the Great (almost 180 years before he became king). In Daniel 11:4, what does it say will happen to Alexander the Great's kingdom upon his death? How can we know from reading this passage that God controls all of history?*

Key Idea: King Philip of Macedonia became king of Greece too. When he was killed, his young son, Alexander, become King of Greece at the age of 20.

History Project — S

Take out your amphora that you drew on Day 1. Add a simple outline drawing to the vase that shows Alexander the Great taming the black horse Bucephalus. Color Alexander with a thick layer of brown crayon. Outline Bucephalus in brown too, but do not color him in. Save the picture of the amphora for Day 3.

Key Idea: Alexander became King of Greece.

Storytime — T

Read aloud the following assigned passage:

★ *A Triumph for Flavius: Ch. VII*

Ask, *In today's reading, how were people's lives different from your life? What would you have enjoyed or found difficult about living during that time?*

Key Idea: Compare and contrast the historical time period of the reading to your own life.

Vocabulary — S

You may choose 3-5 of the following vocabulary words from *A Child's History of the World* to use for this lesson: *forefathers* (p. 123), *orator* (p. 124), *stammered* (p. 124), *lukewarm* (p. 125), and/or *pupils* (p. 126). First, find the word in the text and read the sentence containing the word. Think about possible meanings. Next, find the word in a dictionary and select the correct meaning. Write the word at the top of an index card or at the top of the corresponding letter page in the notebook. Underneath the word, copy the correct definition from the dictionary. Then, use the word correctly in a sentence. The sentence may either be copied from the text or be one of your own creation. Last, draw a small picture to show the word's meaning. If you used an index card to record your word, file it under the correct alphabetical tab.

Key Idea: When Alexander was young, he had a famous Greek teacher named Aristotle. Aristotle was a writer and a thinker. Alexander grew up to be a brilliant military commander. His years with Aristotle trained him well.

Independent History Study — I

★ Read *The Young Christian's Introduction to the Bible* p. 33-36. At the top of a lined paper, copy in cursive the first sentence of the paragraph on p. 36 which begins *During the 400 years between....* Then, copy the remaining part of the paragraph in cursive underneath the heading.

Key Idea: There is a period of 400 years between the end of the Old Testament and the birth of Christ.

Learning the Basics
Focus: Language Arts, Math, Bible, and Science

Language Arts
T

Work with the students to complete **one** of the English options listed below:

★ *Beginning Wisely:* Lesson 57

★ *Building with Diligence:* Lesson 58

★ Your own grammar program

Say, *You will be doing a writing activity based on the poem, "The Hayloft"* (see Appendix). Ask, *What words does the poet use to describe the hay in the poem "The Hayloft"? What are some places that had strong scents or smells that you can remember fondly?* List students' responses on a markerboard or a piece of paper (i.e. cotton candy at the circus, peanuts at the zoo, funnel cakes at the fair, freshly mown grass, geysers at Yellowstone Park, an ice cream parlor, a fudge shop, fried chicken at a picnic, the salty ocean spray on the beach, pine trees in the mountains, etc.)

Next, have students choose one idea off the list to be the topic of their descriptive paragraph or a poem.

Help students make a web of possible phrases to include in their writing by listing their topic in a circle in the middle of a markerboard or paper. Then, draw lines coming out from the circle like spokes on a wheel. As students share possible phrases to describe their topic, write one phrase on each spoke.

Have students use the phrases from the web in a paragraph or poem to describe their chosen topic. Students should read aloud their finished piece of writing.

Key Idea: Write creatively from classic poetry.

Bible Study
T

Have students say Psalm 98:1-6 using the hand motions they added on Day 1. Say, *A mood is a feeling, a sensation, or a state of mind. What is the mood of Psalm 98:6?* (Some examples of moods include frightened, worried, happy, peaceful, hopeful, sad, unhappy, angry, thankful, prayerful, joyful, and lonely.) Ask, *When would this Psalm help you, or when would you go to this Psalm?* (i.e. to remind us to sing heartily, to show us that the Lord is King and deserves our praise, to help us remember to enthusiastically praise our Lord more than we praise other things.)

Last, pray with your children that they will understand how important praise is in glorifying Jesus. Pray that their hearts will be filled with joy that bursts forth as singing. Pray that Jesus may be glorified through our praise.

✔ *Lead Me to the Rock* CD
Track 2; Song: "Sing Unto the Lord" (vs. 1-6)

Key Idea: The Psalms reflect the many emotions and moods we have. They are a wonderful place to seek counsel from the Lord.

Math Exploration
S

Choose **one** of the math options listed below (see Appendix for details).

★ *Singapore Primary Mathematics 2A/2B, 3A/3B,* or *4A/4B*

★ Your own math program

Key Idea: Use a step-by-step math program.

Science Exploration
I

★ Read *Find the Constellations* p. 11-13. Orally retell or narrate to an adult the portion of text that you read today. Use the *Narration Tips* in the Appendix for help as needed.

Key Idea: The first magnitude stars each have names. Arcturus is the bright star in the Herdsman constellation, and Regulus is the bright star in the Lion constellation.

Learning through History
Focus: Alexander the Great Conquers the World

Unit 16 - Day 3

Reading about History [T]

Read about history in the following resource:

★ *A Child's History of the World: Ch. 30* p. 127-130

After today's reading, have your students orally narrate or retell the portion of today's text that you read. Use the *Narration Tips* in the Appendix as needed.

Key Idea: Alexander wanted to rule the world, so he set out to conquer Persia, just as his father had planned to do. He was gone with his army for 10 years. When his army finally reached India, they wanted to go home. Alexander wept when there was nothing left for him to conquer.

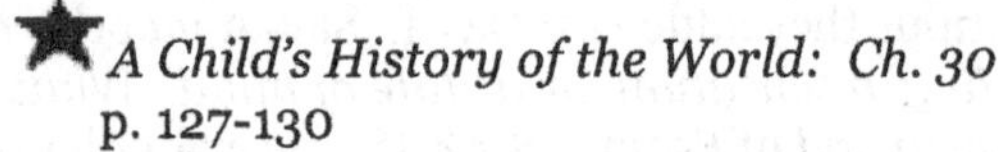

History Project [S]

Take out the picture of the Greek amphora that you made on Day 2. Paint over the entire amphora with black watercolor paint. The areas of brown crayon will resist the paint and show through. Lay the painting flat to dry. Cut the vase out when it is completely dry.

Key Idea: As Alexander the Great conquered the world, he taught the people he conquered to speak and read Greek, to learn about Greek sculpture and painting, to train athletically, and to learn the wise sayings of the Greek philosophers.

Storytime [T]

Read aloud the following assigned passage:

★ *A Triumph for Flavius: Ch. VIII- Epilogue*

Ask, *In what does the main character place his faith? How would the story be different if the main character put his faith in God? Share a character, a story, or a verse from the Bible that you are reminded of by today's reading.*

Key Idea: Share a Biblical connection.

Geography [S]

Use a globe for today's activities. *Find modern-day Macedonia on the globe. It is north of Greece. Trace Alexander's path on the globe from Greece across the Hellespont (which is called the Dardenelles today) into Persia (which is modern-day Turkey, Syria, Iraq, and Iran) up to India and China. Next, trace Alexander's path into Egypt. Alexander founded the city Alexandria and named it after himself. On the globe, find the location of Alexandria at the mouth of the Nile River in Egypt. Remember the mouth of a river is the place where the river empties.*

Introduce the following concept: *The equator divides the earth into the Northern and the Southern Hemispheres. Point to and name them. In which hemisphere do you live?*

Key Idea: When Alexander reached India, he had conquered the known world, so he started back to Greece. While feasting and drinking in Babylon, Alexander died. So, he never did return to Greece.

Independent History Study [I]

★ Choose one or more of the Alexander the Great quotes to copy in cursive in your *Common Place Book:*

1. There is nothing impossible to him who will try.
2. A tomb now suffices him for whom the whole world was not sufficient.
3. If my father wins any more battles, there won't be anything left for me to conquer.
4. I am indebted to my father for living, but to my teacher for living well.

Key Idea: When Alexander the Great died at age 33, he left it to his generals to fight over his empire.

Learning the Basics
Focus: Language Arts, Math, Bible, and Science

Poetry

T

Read aloud with the students the poem *"The Hayloft"* (see Appendix). *Describe a time you have been somewhere like this or felt like this. What can you learn about the poet, Robert Louis Stevenson, from the poem?* Say, *Did you know that Robert Louis Stevenson was an only child? Many of his poems are about a child playing alone or accompanied by his nurse.* Have the students read the poem on their own.

Key Idea: Read and appreciate classic poetry.

Language Arts

S

Have students complete one studied dictation exercise (see Appendix for directions and passages).

Help students complete one lesson from the following reading program:

★ *Drawn into the Heart of Reading*

Work with the students to complete **one** of the English options listed below:

★ *Beginning Wisely:* Lesson 58

★ *Building with Diligence:* Lesson 59

★ Your own grammar program

Key Idea: Practice language arts skills.

Bible Study

T

Say, *You will be having your own quiet time with God today. Choose a quiet place for this special time, where you can be alone with God. Then, do the following things:*

1. Read Psalm 98:1-6 in your Bible.
2. Pray about the Psalm using the following beginning to your prayer: *Thank you for being my Savior and my King. Help me to show you the honor you deserve by ______ and ______. Help me be more enthusiastic for you than I am about anything else in my life.*
3. Recite Psalm 98:1-6 using the hand motions you added on Day 1.
4. Sing Psalm 98:1-6 along with the CD at the end of your quiet time.

✔ *Lead Me to the Rock* CD
Track 2; Song: "Sing Unto the Lord" (vs. 1-6)

Key Idea: The Lord is our Savior and our King!

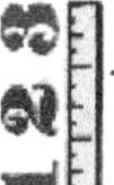

Math Exploration

S

Choose **one** of the math options listed below (see Appendix for details).

★ *Singapore Primary Mathematics 2A/2B, 3A/3B,* or *4A/4B*

★ Your own math program

Key Idea: Use a step-by-step math program.

Science Exploration

I

★ Read *Find the Constellations* p. 14-15. Write the answer to each numbered question on lined paper. You do not need to copy the question. Use the listed page to help you answer each question.

1. What is a light-year? (p. 14)
2. How fast does light travel? (p. 14)
3. What is the name of the star that is nearest to Earth? (p. 15)
4. How long does it take the light from the Sun to reach Earth? (p. 15)
5. How does Jeremiah 31:35 show that God rules over the Sun, Moon, stars, and sea?

Key Idea: Most stars are so far away from Earth that the distance is measured in light years. The Sun is our nearest star at 93 million miles away. God designed the Sun to give Earth the light and heat it needs.

Learning through History

Focus: Alexander the Great Conquers the World

Reading about History — T

Read about history in the following resource:

★ *A Child's History of the World: Ch. 31* p. 131-135

After today's reading, say, *You will be writing a narration about part of the day's history reading. In order to remember the details very well, you will need to reread the part of today's reading from the last two paragraphs on p. 132 through p. 135 (on your own if possible).*

After students have finished reading the passage, ask them the questions below. If the students do not know the answers, help them find the answers in the passage they just read. Ask, *What were the names of the two cities that began a war in today's story? Why were Rome and Carthage enemies? What was the war called? Describe the problems Rome had with fighting Carthage. What did the Romans find that really helped them? How did Rome solve their problems? Who won the First Punic War?*

After the questions have been answered, have students write a 3-5 sentence narration that begins, *First... Next... Then... Last...* When students have finished their narration, direct them to read the sentences out loud. Ask, *Did you include **who** the reading was mainly about? Did you include **what** important thing(s) happened? Did you include **how** it ended?*

See the *Written Narration Skills* in the Appendix to guide students in editing their narrations.

Key Idea: Rome and Carthage began a war.

Storytime — T

Read aloud the following assigned passage:

★ *Fountain of Life: Ch. 1*

Say, *Transport yourself back to the time of this story. Pretend you lived at this time. Tell me what you see and do. (Make sure to use the word, "I", and to tell only what was described in today's reading.)*

Key Idea: Practice oral narration skills.

Timeline — S

You will be adding 2 new cards to your staircase timeline today. On the first new card, draw and color a picture of a man thinking. Write, *Socrates (470 – 399 B.C.)* On the second new card, draw and color a black horse. Write, *Alexander the Great (356 - 323 B.C.).*

If you decided to tape your timeline cards to the back of a door, add the *Socrates* card to the right of *The Golden Age of Greece* card. To the right of the *Socrates* card, add the *Alexander the Great* card. If you decided to tape the timeline cards side-by-side to accordion-fold them, use clear packing tape to tape the cards as described above.

Key Idea: Both Rome and Carthage felt that the other city was becoming too powerful. So, they started the First Punic War. Since the Romans had no navy, they could not fight the Carthaginians at sea. When the Romans discovered a Carthaginian ship wrecked on the shore, they made a ship just like it. Soon, the Romans had a fleet of ships too.

Independent History Study — I

★ Read *Little Miriam of Galilee: Ch.1.* Then, choose an interesting part from today's pages to read aloud and explain to an adult.

Key Idea: After the death of Alexander the Great, Rome and Carthage began fighting for power. The Romans won the First Punic War.

Learning the Basics

Focus: Language Arts, Math, Bible, and Science

Unit 16 - Day 4

Poetry

T

Read aloud with the students the poem *"The Hayloft"* (see Appendix). Have students share this poem in a special way. Suggestions for sharing the poem include recording it to play for someone, reading it to someone on the telephone, photocopying the poem and adding illustrations, reading it to someone at home, putting the poem to a melody and singing it, using an instrument to tap out the meter or rhythm of the poem while reading it, or copying the poem on paper.

Key Idea: Share a variety of classic poetry.

Bible Study

T

Have students say Psalm 98:1-6 using the hand motions from Day 1.

Have students copy in cursive Psalm 98:6 beneath last unit's Psalm 98:4-5 in their *Common Place Book*. Students should leave the rest of the page blank to add to next week.

Students will add to the *Common Place Book* throughout the year.

✔ *Lead Me to the Rock* CD
Track 2; Song: "Sing Unto the Lord" (vs. 1-6)

Key Idea: Copy in cursive a portion of a Psalm.

Language Arts

S

Have students complete one dictation exercise.

Guide students to complete one reading lesson.

★ *Drawn into the Heart of Reading*

Help students complete **one** English lesson.

★ *Beginning Wisely:* Lesson 59

★ *Building with Diligence:* Lesson 60

★ Your own grammar program

Key Idea: Practice language arts skills.

Math Exploration

S

Choose **one** math option listed below.

★ *Singapore Primary Mathematics 2A/2B, 3A/3B,* or *4A/4B*

★ Your own math program

Key Idea: Use a step-by-step math program.

Science Exploration

I

★ Read *Find the Constellations* p. 16-17. Turn to the science experiment section in your science binder or sketchbook. At the top of a blank page, write: *Why do stars look like they are twinkling?* Under the question, write: *'Guess'*. Write down your guess. For today's experiment, you will need a room that will be dark when the lights are turned off. Fill a glass bowl partway full of water. Cut a circular piece of foil to place under the bowl of water. Crumple the foil gently to wrinkle it, before placing it under the bowl. Wait for the water in the bowl to be still, then turn off the lights. Hold the flashlight over the bowl and turn it on. What do you notice about the light projected out of the bowl and onto the ceiling? Next, touch your finger to the water's surface several times. What happens to the light? Does it appear to twinkle? On your paper, write: *'Procedure'*. Draw a picture of the experiment. At the bottom of the paper, write: *'Conclusion'*. Explain what you learned.

Key Idea: Stars appear to twinkle as their light rays are bent or refracted when the rays move through the Earth's atmosphere.

Learning through History
Focus: Rome Rises as Greece Falls

Unit 17 - Day 1

Reading about History T

Read about history in the following resource:

★ *A Child's History of the World: Ch. 32* p. 136-138

After today's reading, say, *How did Hannibal surprise the Romans?* (knowledge) *Why did Hannibal have to conquer Spain first? See the map on* A Child's History of the World *p. 133.* (knowledge) *What plan did the Romans come up with to stop Hannibal?* (comprehension) *After Scipio won at Zama, why didn't the Romans leave Carthage alone?* (analysis) *Once the Romans had beaten Carthage a third time, what do you think happened next?* (synthesis)

Key Idea: After Rome beat Carthage in the First Punic War, Hannibal crossed the Alps to attack and take the Romans by surprise. To stop Hannibal, the Romans attacked Carthage.

History Project S

In this unit you will make a Roman coin called a denarius. Remove the crusts from 2 slices of bread. Tear the bread into pieces and put the pieces in a bowl with 2 Tablespoons of white glue. Add ½ Tablespoon of coffee **or** a few drops of black and white paint to give the coins an antique look. Stir the mixture. Then, knead it with your hands until it is a soft dough and is no longer sticky. Roll a small ball of dough in between your hands. Place it on a piece of waxed paper and flatten it gently with the bottom of a glass. Use a toothpick to draw the head of a Roman emperor on the coin. Make other coins. Allow them to dry until Day 3.

Key Idea: The denarius was a Roman coin.

Storytime T

Read aloud the following assigned story:

★ *Fountain of Life: Ch. 2-3*

Discuss today's reading in a "conversational way". Share about a person, time, event, or emotion from your life that today's reading brought to mind. Next, have your child share a connection.

Key Idea: Connect personally to the story.

Research S

At the time of the Punic Wars, the Romans began making a coin called the denarius. Where could you look to discover more about the **denarius**? Use a reference book or an online resource like www.wikipedia.org to look up *denarius*. Depending on the resource you use, you will have to type *denarius* in the search or look it up in the index.

Orally answer one or more of the following questions from your research: *What did a denarius look like? Who were some of the people that were on the Roman coins? When was the denarius first used by the Romans in everyday life? What color was the denarius? How much was a denarius worth, compared to our money today?*

Key Idea: The Romans beat the Carthaginians in the Second and Third Punic Wars. At the time of the Punic Wars, the Romans made a coin called the denarius that could be used to do everyday business when buying and selling things.

Independent History Study I

★ Read *Little Miriam of Galilee: Ch. 2.* Orally retell or narrate to an adult the portion of text that you read today. Use the *Narration Tips* in the Appendix for help as needed.

Key Idea: At the time of this story, the Jews were under Roman rule, and they were not happy about it!

Learning the Basics

Focus: Language Arts, Math, Bible, and Science

Unit 17 - Day 1

Poetry

T

Read aloud to the students the poem *"The Moon"* (see Appendix). Ask, *How is the Moon's face like a clock in the hall? What does the Moon do in the poem? What kinds of animals are out in the light of the Moon? How does the poet give you the feeling of being out at night? What does it mean to "belong to the day"? List some things that are asleep during the night and awake when the Sun comes up.* Read the poem again with the students.

Key Idea: Read and appreciate classic poetry.

Language Arts

S

Have students complete the first studied dictation exercise (see Appendix for directions and passages).

Help students complete one lesson from the following reading program:

 *Drawn into the Heart of Reading*

Work with the students to complete **one** of the English options listed below:

★ *Beginning Wisely:* Lesson 60

★ *Building with Diligence:* Lesson 61

★ Your own grammar program

Key Idea: Practice language arts skills.

Bible Study

T

Say, *Find Psalm 98:1-9 in your Bible. This is the memory selection for this unit. Read the verse out loud.* Ask, *In Psalm 98:7, who is praising the Lord? What does this verse make you picture in your mind? Psalm 98:8 talks about the floods and the hills praising the Lord. Usually floods are rushing and roaring. What sound do the hills usually make? If even the usually silent hills break forth into praise, what are we expected to do? Why should the whole Earth praise the Lord? What does Psalm 98:9, say that Christ will do when He returns? How does Psalm 98:9 say that Christ will judge? What does equity mean?* Have students say the verse 3 times, adding hand motions to help remember the words.

✔ *Lead Me to the Rock* CD
Track 2; Song: "Sing Unto the Lord"
(vs. 1-9)

Key Idea: When Christ returns, the trumpets will sound, and all of Creation will praise Him.

Math Exploration

S

Choose **one** of the math options listed below (see Appendix for details).

★ *Singapore Primary Mathematics 2A/2B, 3A/3B*, or *4A/4B*

★ Your own math program

Key Idea: Use a step-by-step math program.

Science Exploration

I

★ Read *Find the Constellations* p. 18-19. Get your book about the stars that you began last unit. On the top of the next clean page in your book, copy in cursive Job 9:9. Beneath the verse, draw one or more of the following constellations: Twins (p. 12), Orion (p. 13), Big Dog (p. 16), Little Dog (p. 16), Charioteer (p. 16), Virgin (p. 17), or Scorpion (p. 17). Make sure to draw the brighter stars larger, and label them with their names, as shown in the pictures. Label each constellation with its name too. You may trace the constellations if you wish. Save your book for next week.

Key Idea: It takes us much practice to find the constellations in the night sky. Yet, God knows the location of each star!

Learning through History
Focus: Rome Rises as Greece Falls

Unit 17 - Day 2

Reading about History T

Read about history in the following resource:

★ *A Child's History of the World: Ch. 33* p. 139-143

After today's reading, read aloud Mark 1:1-5. Say, *In Rome at the time of Jesus' birth, there were many gods being worshiped. Why would there be a need for someone to come ahead of Jesus to prepare the way for Him? In Mark 1:4, who came to prepare the way for the Lord? What did John want the people to do in Mark 1:3? How would the roads that the Romans built help the good news of Jesus spread more quickly? Why was it helpful to the spread of the gospel that everyone in the Roman Empire could speak the same language? How were these things also helping prepare the way for the Lord?*

Key Idea: The Romans copied many things from the Greeks, but they also thought of new and practical ways to solve problems. The Romans built paved roads across their empire. They made laws that were followed throughout Rome. They also forced the people they conquered to become their slaves.

History Project S

Continue to let the coins from Day 1 dry. Get a coffee filter. Use a hole punch to make an even number of holes 2 inches apart around the outside of the filter. Place a cup of water in a bowl and add a few coffee grounds or tea leaves. Dip your coffee filter into the brown water. Then, lay it flat to dry for Day 3.

Key Idea: The Romans built strong cities.

Storytime T

Read aloud the following assigned passage:

★ *The Fountain of Life: Ch. 4*

Ask, *In today's reading, how were people's lives different from your life? What would you have enjoyed or found difficult about living during that time?*

Key Idea: Compare and contrast the historical time period of the reading to your own life.

Vocabulary S

You may choose 3-5 of the following vocabulary words from *A Child's History of the World* to use for this lesson: *citizen* (p. 139), *spigot* (p. 140), *plagues* (p. 140), *aqueduct* (p. 140), and/or *amphitheater* (p. 142). First, find the word in the text and read the sentence containing the word. Think about possible meanings. Next, find the word in a dictionary and select the correct meaning. Write the word at the top of an index card or at the top of the corresponding letter page in the notebook. Underneath the word, copy the correct definition from the dictionary. Then, use the word correctly in a sentence. The sentence may either be copied from the text or be one of your own creation. Last, draw a small picture to show the word's meaning. If you used an index card to record your word, file it under the correct alphabetical tab.

Key Idea: The Romans built water-carriers called aqueducts to bring fresh water to the cities. They also built sewers to carry away the dirty water.

Independent History Study I

★ Read *Little Miriam of Galilee: Ch. 3*. Make a notebook page that is titled, *Differences Between Roman and Jewish Children.* Make the following 2 columns under the title: *Chloe (Roman)* and *Miriam (Jewish)*. List differences between Chloe's and Miriam's lives under each girl's name.

Key Idea: Chloe and Miriam were growing up very differently from one another. Yet, they were friends.

Learning the Basics

Focus: Language Arts, Math, Bible, and Science

Language Arts

T

Work with the students to complete **one** of the English options listed below:

★ *Beginning Wisely:* Lesson 61

★ *Building with Diligence:* Lesson 62

★ Your own grammar program

Say, *You will be doing a writing activity based on the poem, "The Moon"* (see Appendix). *We will be taking ideas from the poem about the Moon to write our own poem or paragraph about the Sun.* At the top of a markerboard or a paper, make 3 columns: *"Has a face like..."* and *"Shines on..."* and *"Hears..."*.

Say, *In this poem the Moon is personified, or made to seem human.* Ask, *What is the Moon's face compared to in the poem? What could you compare the Sun's face to in your poem?* Write the students' responses under the *"Has a face like...."* column.

Next, ask, *On what does the Moon shine in the poem? On what could the Sun shine?* List the students' responses under the *"Shines on..."* column.

Then, ask students, *Which words in the poem describe what the Moon hears? What could the Sun hear?* List the students' responses under the *"Hears"* column.

Have students use the lists to write a paragraph or poem to describe the Sun, as if it were a person. Have them begin the first line, *The Sun has a face like a...* Students should read aloud their finished piece of writing.

Key Idea: Write creatively from classic poetry.

Bible Study

T

Have students say Psalm 98:1-9 using the hand motions they added on Day 1. Say, *A mood is a feeling, a sensation, or a state of mind. What is the mood of Psalm 98:7-9?* (Some examples of moods include frightened, worried, happy, peaceful, hopeful, sad, unhappy, angry, thankful, prayerful, joyful, and lonely.) Ask, *When would this Psalm help you, or when would you go to this Psalm?* (i.e. to remind us not to keep silent with our praise for the Lord, to give us hope that Jesus is returning some day, to show us the praise that Jesus deserves.)

Last, pray with your children that they will not keep silent with their praise for the Lord. Pray that they will be watchful, excited, and ready for the day that Jesus returns.

✔ *Lead Me to the Rock* CD
Track 2; Song: "Sing Unto the Lord" (vs. 1-9)

Key Idea: The Psalms reflect the many emotions and moods we have. They are a wonderful place to seek counsel from the Lord.

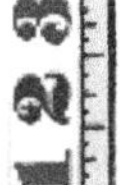

Math Exploration

S

Choose **one** of the math options listed below (see Appendix for details).

★ *Singapore Primary Mathematics 2A/2B, 3A/3B, or 4A/4B*

★ Your own math program

Key Idea: Use a step-by-step math program.

Science Exploration

I

★ Read *Find the Constellations* p. 20-21. Orally retell or narrate to an adult the portion of text that you read today. Use the *Narration Tips* in the Appendix for help as needed.

Key Idea: The 15 brightest stars in our sky each have a special name. These stars are 1st magnitude stars and are part of various constellations in the sky.

Learning through History
Focus: Rome Rises as Greece Falls

Unit 17 - Day 3

Reading about History

T

Read about history in the following resource:

★ *A Child's History of the World: Ch. 34* p. 144-149

After today's reading, have your students orally narrate or retell the portion of today's text that you read. Use the *Narration Tips* in the Appendix as needed.

Key Idea: When Julius Caesar was young, he fought pirates on the sea. As he grew up, his fame as a commander spread. He was given command of a large Roman army, which won battles in Spain, Britain, and Gaul. When Caesar was asked to give up his command of his troops, Caesar instead marched on Rome.

Storytime

T

Read aloud the following assigned passage:

★ *The Fountain of Life: Ch. 5-6*

Ask, *In what do the main characters place their faith? Even though the characters put their faith in God, how would the story be different if they believed Jesus is the Son of God? Share a character, a story, or a verse from the Bible that you are reminded of by today's reading.*

Key Idea: Share a Biblical connection.

History Project

S

Today you will make a pouch for your coins. Take out your filter from Day 2. Cut two pieces of string or yarn that each measure 1 yd. Thread one piece of string or yarn through the holes in the filter, going up and down to make stitches until the two ends of string or yarn meet. Then, with the second piece of yarn, start stitching around the filter from the opposite side until the ends of the second piece of string or yarn meet. Gather together the 4 ends of the string or yarn and tie a knot at the top. While holding the filter with one hand, gently pull the strands of string or yarn up by the knot to close the pouch. Place your coins in your pouch.

Key Idea: When there was talk of making Caesar king, some of Caesar's friends and enemies stabbed him as he entered the Senate.

Geography

S

Use a globe for today's activities. Say, *Find Spain, Britain, and Gaul (France) on the map on p. 133 of A Child's History of the World. These were the first countries conquered by Caesar. Find these same countries on the globe. Next, find Rome in Italy, which Julius Caesar conquered next. Rome was the ruler of almost all of the countries bordering the Mediterranean Sea, although Cleopatra was allowed to rule in Egypt under Caesar. Trace the Roman Empire on the modern-day globe.*

Review the following concept: *The equator divides the earth into the Northern and the Southern Hemisphere. Which continents are in the Northern Hemisphere? Point to North America, Europe, Asia, and half of Africa. Which continents are in the Southern Hemisphere? Point to Australia, Antarctica, South America, and half of Africa.*

Key Idea: When Caesar crossed the Rubicon, he disobeyed the Senate and took over Rome.

Independent History Study

I

★ Read *Little Miriam of Galilee* p. 29-32. Then, copy Luke 2:1 in cursive onto a clean page in your *Common Place Book*. You will copy more verses beneath Luke 2:1 tomorrow, so save some room.

Key Idea: Caesar took a census, or a count of the people of the land, in order to be able to tax them. Miriam's family might lose their fields, since they are not able to pay the high taxes the Romans demand.

Learning the Basics

Focus: Language Arts, Math, Bible, and Science

Unit 17 - Day 3

Poetry

T

Read aloud with the students the poem *"The Moon"* (see Appendix). *Describe a memory that the poem brought to mind. What can you learn about the poet, Robert Louis Stevenson, from the poem?* Say, *Did you know that as a child Robert Louis Stevenson had many nights where he watched the Moon and the night-time animals out his bedroom window? His coughing often kept him awake.* Have the students read the poem on their own.

Key Idea: Read and appreciate classic poetry.

Language Arts

S

Have students complete one studied dictation exercise (see Appendix for directions and passages).

Help students complete one lesson from the following reading program:

★ *Drawn into the Heart of Reading*

Work with the students to complete **one** of the English options listed below:

★ *Beginning Wisely:* Lesson 62

★ *Building with Diligence:* Lesson 63 (Half)

★ Your own grammar program

Key Idea: Practice language arts skills.

Bible Study

T

Say, *You will be having your own quiet time with God today. Choose a quiet place for this special time, where you can be alone with God. Then, do the following things:*

1. Read Psalm 98:1-9 in your Bible.
2. Pray about the Psalm using the following beginning to your prayer: *Thank you for the beautiful things in Creation that glorify you, like the ______, ______, and ______. Help me be ready for your return by ______. Help me to live my life for you.*
3. Recite Psalm 98:1-9 using the hand motions you added on Day 1.
4. Sing Psalm 98:1-9 along with the CD at the end of your quiet time.

✔ *Lead Me to the Rock* CD
Track 2; Song: "Sing Unto the Lord" (vs. 1-9)

Key Idea: The Lord is coming back some day!

Math Exploration

S

Choose **one** of the math options listed below (see Appendix for details).

★ *Singapore Primary Mathematics 2A/2B, 3A/3B*, or *4A/4B*

★ Your own math program

Key Idea: Use a step-by-step math program.

Science Exploration

I

★ Cover the answers on the bottom of *Find the Constellations* p. 22. Write the answer to each numbered question on lined paper. You do not need to copy the question. Use the listed page to check your answer.

1. Which constellation is shown in number 1? What is the name of its brightest star? (p. 17)
2. Which constellation is shown in number 2? What is the name of its brightest star? (p. 20)
3. Which constellation is shown in number 3? What is the name of its brightest star? (p. 17)
4. Which constellation is shown in number 4? What is the name of its brightest star? (p. 20)
5. Which constellation is shown in number 5? What is the name of its brightest star? (p. 20)
6. Which constellation is shown in number 6? What is the name of its brightest star? (p. 21)
7. Last, do the quiz on p. 23, but just say the answers, rather than writing them down.

Key Idea: Are you starting to be able to recognize some of the constellations in the pictures?

Reading about History | T

Read about history in the following resource:

★ *A Child's History of the World: Ch. 35* p. 150-154

Note: You may wish to reword p. 151 (as it pertains to Antony's and Cleopatra's suicide).

After today's reading, say, *You will be writing a narration about part of the day's history reading. In order to remember the details well, you will need to reread today's reading from the last paragraph on p. 151 through the third paragraph on p. 153 (on your own if possible).*

After students have finished reading the passage, ask the questions below. If students do not know the answers, help them find the answers in the passage. Ask, *Who was ruler of Rome in today's story? How did Augustus make Rome a beautiful city? What was the Pantheon? Why is Rome called The Eternal City? Can Rome truly be an eternal city? Why not? If you visited ancient Rome, what would you have seen? Describe the Forum. Describe the amphitheater, Circus Maximus. How can you tell that ancient Rome was pagan? Could Caesar really be made a god? Explain.*

After the questions have been answered, have students write a 3-5 sentence narration that begins, *At the time of Augustus Caesar, Rome...* When students have finished their narration, direct them to read the sentences out loud. Help students write a good closing sentence to summarize their paragraph. See the *Written Narration Skills* in the Appendix to guide students in editing their narrations.

Key Idea: After the death of Caesar, Antony and Octavius fought for control of Rome.

Storytime | T

Read aloud the following assigned passage:

★ *Fountain of Life: Ch. 7*

Say, *Transport yourself back to the time of this story. Pretend you lived at this time. Tell me what you see and do. (Make sure to use the word, "I", and to tell only what was described in today's reading.)*

Key Idea: Practice oral narration skills.

Timeline | S

You will be adding 2 new cards to your staircase timeline today. On the first new card, draw and color a picture of an elephant. Write, *Hannibal crosses the Alps (202 B.C.).* On the second new card, draw and color a crown of golden leaves. Write, *Julius Caesar (100 - 44 B.C.).*

If you decided to tape your timeline cards to the back of a door, add the *Hannibal crosses the Alps* card to the right of the *Socrates* card. To the right of the *Hannibal crosses the Alps* card, add the *Julius Caesar* card. If you decided to tape the timeline cards side-by-side to accordion-fold them, use clear packing tape to tape the cards as described above.

Key Idea: After Caesar's death, Antony ruled the eastern part of the Roman Empire (along with Cleopatra), and Octavius ruled the west. Octavius finally beat Antony and Cleopatra, and won control of Rome. Then, Octavian changed his name to Augustus Caesar. Rome was his beautiful capitol city. The month of August is named after Augustus Caesar.

Independent History Study | I

★ Read *Little Miriam of Galilee* p. 33-37. Then, copy Luke 2:4 and Luke 2:11 in cursive (beneath Luke 2:1 that you copied on Day 3) in your *Common Place Book.*

Key Idea: Jesus was born during the reign of Augustus Caesar. The Bible tells of Mary and Joseph traveling to Bethlehem to be counted for the census. This is how Jesus came to be born in Bethlehem.

Learning the Basics

Focus: Language Arts, Math, Bible, and Science

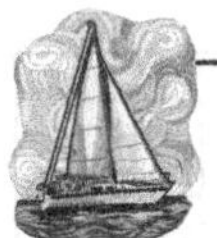

Poetry

T

Read aloud with the students the poem *"The Moon"* (see Appendix). Have students share this poem in a special way. Suggestions for sharing the poem include recording it to play for someone, reading it to someone on the telephone, photocopying the poem and adding illustrations, reading it to someone at home, putting the poem to a melody and singing it, using an instrument to tap out the meter or rhythm of the poem while reading it, or copying the poem on paper.

Key Idea: Share a variety of classic poetry.

Bible Study

T

Have students say Psalm 98:1-9 using the hand motions from Day 1.

Have students copy in cursive Psalm 98:7-9 beneath last unit's Psalm 98:6 in their *Common Place Book.*

Students will add to the *Common Place Book* throughout the year.

✔ *Lead Me to the Rock* CD
Track 2; Song: "Sing Unto the Lord" (vs. 1-9)

Key Idea: Copy in cursive a portion of a Psalm.

Language Arts

S

Have students complete one dictation exercise.

Guide students to complete one reading lesson.

★ *Drawn into the Heart of Reading*

Help students complete **one** English lesson.

★ *Beginning Wisely:* Lesson 63

★ *Building with Diligence:* Lesson 63 (Half)

★ Your own grammar program

Key Idea: Practice language arts skills.

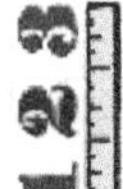

Math Exploration

S

Choose **one** math option listed below.

★ *Singapore Primary Mathematics 2A/2B, 3A/3B,* or *4A/4B*

★ Your own math program

Key Idea: Use a step-by-step math program.

Science Exploration

I

★ Read *Find the Constellations* p. 24-25. Turn to the science experiment section in your science binder or sketchbook. At the top of a blank page, write: *Why do the constellations only show up in the night sky?* Under the question, write: *'Guess'*. Write down your guess.

Place an index card on a pile of old newspaper or on a folded up rag. Use a pencil or a nail to poke holes in the index card in the shape of one of the constellations from *Find the Constellations.* Place the index card inside an envelope. Leave the lights on, and hold the envelope in front of you. Can you see the constellation very well? But, is it still there? Now, turn the lights off and hold a flashlight behind the envelope. Can you see the constellation now? On your paper, write: *'Procedure'*. Draw a picture of the experiment. At the bottom of the paper, write: *'Conclusion'*. Explain what you learned.

Key Idea: The stars and the constellations are still shining even in the day, but the Sun's light is so bright that you cannot see the other stars. When the Earth turns away from the Sun, you can see the other stars.

Learning through History
Focus: The Savior Arrives on Earth

Unit 18 - Day 1

Reading about History — T

Read about history in the following resource:

★ *Grandpa's Box: Ch. 27* p. 174-179

After today's reading, say, *Was Satan able to stop God's Son from being born? Why not?* (knowledge) *In what unusual ways did God announce his Son's birth?* (knowledge) *Tell about King Herod.* (comprehension) *Do you think King Herod realized he was trying to kill God's Son? Explain.* (evaluation) *How do you know that God wasn't surprised by King Herod's plan?* (analysis)

Key Idea: When the magi asked Herod where the King of the Jews was to be born, Herod became worried. He asked the magi to let him know where the child was, so he could worship Him too. But, God warned the magi not to return to Herod. He also warned Mary and Joseph to take Jesus to safety in Egypt.

History Project — S

In this unit you will be drawing and painting the Star of Bethlehem. On an 9" x 12" sheet of paper, use a pencil to lightly draw a star that fills the paper. Erase the lines inside the star so that only the outline remains. Cut the star out. Lightly sketch a line around the outside of the star to make a border that you can paint on Day 2. Then, with your pencil sketch 5-10 shapes inside the star. Make sure none of the shapes touch one another. Save it for Day 2.

Key Idea: Jesus' birth was announced with a special star, visits by shepherds and magi, and a heavenly host of angels. The Savior had come to earth just as it had been prophesied.

Storytime — T

Read aloud the following assigned story:

★ *Fountain of Life: Ch. 8*

Discuss today's reading in a "conversational way". Share about a person, time, event, or emotion from your life that today's reading brought to mind. Next, have your child share a connection.

Key Idea: Connect personally to the story.

Research — S

At the time of Jesus' birth, a star appeared that led magi from the East to worship Jesus. We do not know how many magi there were or which countries they came from. The magi could have been Medes that came from Persia who were priests and astrologers. They may have known Daniel's prophecies surrounding Christ's birth from the Jewish people's time of captivity in Babylon. Where could you look to discover more about the **Jesus Star**? Use the Bible passage Matthew 2:1-12 or an online resource like www.wikipedia.org to look up *Jesus Star* or *Star of Bethlehem* in the search.

Orally answer one or more of the following questions from your research: *What reason did the magi give for their trip? Why did the magi visit King Herod in Jerusalem? Why did Herod ask the magi when the star had appeared? How did the magi know where to find Jesus? Where did the star stop?*

Key Idea: A star led the magi from the East to worship Jesus in Bethlehem.

Independent History Study — I

★ Read *Little Miriam of Galilee: Ch. 5*. Orally retell or narrate to an adult the portion of text that you read today. Use the *Narration Tips* in the Appendix for help as needed.

Key Idea: The Jewish people were very careful to follow God's laws, yet it was hard for many of them to accept that Jesus was the promised Savior.

Learning the Basics

Focus: Language Arts, Math, Bible, and Science

Unit 18 - Day 1

Poetry

T

Read aloud to the students the poem *"Escape at Bedtime"* (see Appendix). Ask, *Why do you think this poem is titled "Escape at Bedtime"? What two things does the poet compare to the number of stars in the sky? What are the Dog, the Plough, and the Hunter? How can the pail be "half-full of water and stars"? Explain the meaning of the last 2 lines of the poem.* Read the poem again with the students.

Key Idea: Read and appreciate classic poetry.

Language Arts

S

Have students complete the first studied dictation exercise (see Appendix for directions and passages).

Help students complete one lesson from the following reading program:

★ *Drawn into the Heart of Reading*

Work with the students to complete **one** of the English options listed below:

★ *Beginning Wisely:* Lesson 64

★ *Building with Diligence:* Lesson 64

★ Your own grammar program

Key Idea: Practice language arts skills.

Bible Study

T

Say, *Find Psalm 119:169-170 in your Bible. This is the memory selection for this unit. Read the verses out loud.* Ask, *What does the Psalmist ask for in Psalm 119:169? In Psalm 119:169-170 what phrase is repeated twice? What does the phrase "according to thy word" mean? Why is this phrase so important? How can we know that God hears our prayers? When the Psalmist asks to be delivered, what does that mean? What things might we need to be delivered from?* Have students say the verse 3 times, adding hand motions to help remember the words.

✔ *Lead Me to the Rock* CD
Track 3; Song: "According to Thy Word" (vs. 169-170)

Key Idea: We know that the Lord hears our prayers, because He says so in His word. The Lord always keeps His promises.

Math Exploration

S

Choose **one** of the math options listed below (see Appendix for details).

★ *Singapore Primary Mathematics 2A/2B, 3A/3B,* or *4A/4B*

★ Your own math program

Key Idea: Use a step-by-step math program.

Science Exploration

I

Get your book about the stars that you began in Unit 16. On the top of the next clean page in your book, copy in cursive Psalm 8:3-4. Beneath the verse, draw one or more of the following constellations: The Lyre (p. 20), The Swan (p. 20), The Eagle (p. 20), The Bull (p. 21), or The Southern Fish (p. 21). Make sure to draw the brighter stars larger, and label them with their names, as shown in the pictures. Label each constellation with its name too. You may trace the constellations if you wish. Save your book for next week.

Key Idea: By now, you have read about the different constellations that contain the 15 brightest stars in the sky. Are you beginning to recognize some of their names?

Learning through History

Focus: The Savior Arrives on Earth

Unit 18 - Day 2

Reading about History — T

Read about history in the following resource:

★ *Grandpa's Box: Ch. 28* p. 180-186

After today's reading, read aloud Luke 4:1-13. Ask, *In Luke 4:1, who does it say led Jesus into the desert? For what purpose was Jesus led by the Spirit into the desert in Luke 4:2? Why did Satan want Jesus to sin? If Jesus would have sinned, could He have saved us from our sins? Why not? What did Jesus do each time that Satan tempted Him in Luke 4:4, 8, and 12? Why is it important for us to read and memorize Scripture? What can we learn about facing temptation from the way Jesus responded to Satan?*

Key Idea: After Jesus was baptized by John the Baptist, He was sent by the Holy Spirit to the desert to be tempted by Satan. Satan must have wanted Jesus to fall into sin just like Adam and Eve had in the Garden of Eden.

History Project — S

Take out your star from Day 1. Get blue and white paint, a thin paintbrush, and a paper plate or waxed paper to mix paint. First, paint the outside border around the edge of the star with blue paint. Next, place blue paint on your mixing surface and add a little white paint. Paint 2 shapes in the middle of your star with the new color. Then, add a little more white paint to the previous color and paint 2 other shapes. Continue adding a little white paint at a time and painting shapes until they are all painted. Leave the space between shapes white.

Key Idea: Jesus resisted Satan's temptations.

Storytime — T

Read aloud the following assigned passage:

★ *Fountain of Life: Ch. 9-10*

Ask, *In what does the main character place his faith? How has Eli's father put so much faith in the law that he is missing the Savior? Share a character, a story, or a verse from the Bible that you are reminded of by the reading.*

Key Idea: Share a Biblical connection.

Vocabulary — S

You may choose 3-5 of the following vocabulary words from *Grandpa's Box* to use for this lesson: *representative* (p. 181-182), *temptation* (p. 182-183), *propaganda* (p. 184), *quoting* (p. 184), and/or *symbolized* (p. 186). First, find the word in the text and read the sentence containing the word. Think about possible meanings. Next, find the word in a dictionary and select the correct meaning. Write the word at the top of an index card or at the top of the corresponding letter page in the notebook. Underneath the word, copy the correct definition from the dictionary. Then, use the word correctly in a sentence. The sentence may either be copied from the text or be one of your own creation. Last, draw a small picture to show the word's meaning. If you used an index card to record your word, file it under the correct alphabetical tab.

Key Idea: Although Satan tempted Jesus three times, Jesus did not fall for Satan's schemes. Jesus quoted God's words in response to each temptation. Even when Satan quoted from Scripture, Jesus was not fooled.

Independent History Study — I

★ Read *Little Miriam of Galilee* p. 47-53. Then, copy 1 Thessalonians 5:16-18 in cursive onto a clean page in your *Common Place Book*.

Key Idea: The Pharisees were strict followers of God's laws, so they should have been the first to realize that Jesus is God's promised Son. Do you realize that Jesus is the Son of God?

Learning the Basics

Focus: Language Arts, Math, Bible, and Science

Language Arts

T

Work with the students to complete **one** of the English options listed below:

★ *Beginning Wisely:* Lesson 65

★ *Building with Diligence:* Lesson 65

★ Your own grammar program

Say, *You will be doing a writing activity based on the poem, "Escape at Bedtime"* (see Appendix).

Say, *Name some of the beautiful evening skies that you have seen* (i.e. a rainbow in the sky after a storm, stars at night, fireworks on the 4th of July, silent snow falling on a clear winter night, a humid summer evening thunderstorm, a full harvest moon, an autumn night with blowing leaves, the clean mountain air after a rain, dew on the grass in the evening, etc.). Write the students' ideas down on a markerboard or a paper. Then, help students choose one idea off the list to use as a topic for a descriptive paragraph.

Next, on a markerboard or a paper, make 4 columns: *"Saw", "Felt", "Heard",* and *"Smelled".* Guide students to list details that they remember from the evening they chose to describe (i.e. "Saw" – rainbow shimmering, raindrops glistening, clouds shining; "Felt" – breeze blowing, humid night air; "Heard" – crickets chirping, dogs barking; "Smelled" – clean air, damp dirt).

Have students use the lists to write a paragraph that describes the evening they chose as a topic.

Key Idea: Write creatively from classic poetry.

Bible Study

T

Have students say Psalm 119:169-170 using the hand motions they added on Day 1. Say, *A mood is a feeling, a sensation, or a state of mind. What is the mood of Psalm 119:169-170?* (Some examples of moods include frightened, worried, happy, peaceful, hopeful, sad, unhappy, angry, thankful, prayerful, joyful, and lonely.) Ask, *When would this Psalm help you, or when would you go to this Psalm?* (i.e. to remind us that the Lord always hears our prayers, to remember that we need to speak to the Lord with reverence, to show us that we can trust in the Lord's word and His promises.)

Last, pray with your children that they might trust God's word. Pray that they will realize the blessing of being able to speak directly to the Lord and will speak to the Lord reverently.

✔ *Lead Me to the Rock* CD
Track 3; Song: "According to Thy Word" (vs. 169-170)

Key Idea: The Psalms reflect the many emotions and moods we have. They are a wonderful place to seek counsel from the Lord.

Math Exploration

S

Choose **one** of the math options listed below (see Appendix for details).

★ *Singapore Primary Mathematics 2A/2B, 3A/3B,* or *4A/4B*

★ Your own math program

Key Idea: Use a step-by-step math program.

Science Exploration

I

★ Read *Find the Constellations* p. 26-29. Orally retell or narrate to an adult the portion of text that you read today. Use the *Narration Tips* in the Appendix for help as needed.

Key Idea: Use Sky-View 1 to practice finding some of the constellations you've learned so far.

Learning through History

Focus: The Savior Arrives on Earth

Unit 18 - Day 3

Reading about History T

Read about history in the following resource:

★ *Grandpa's Box: Ch. 29* p. 187-193

After today's reading, have your students orally narrate or retell the portion of today's text that you read. Use the *Narration Tips* in the Appendix as needed.

Key Idea: When Jesus was teaching by the Sea of Galilee one day, He saw a man who was tormented by evil spirits. Even the spirits recognized Jesus as the Son of God. Jesus commanded the spirits to leave the man and allowed them to go into a herd of wild pigs. As God's Son, Jesus has power over all things.

History Project S

Take out your star that you painted on Day 2. On the back of the star, copy in cursive Luke 2:14. This is what the angels said to praise God upon the birth of Jesus!

Key Idea: No problem is too great for Jesus to solve. Even the demon-possessed man in today's story was healed by Jesus. When we become a Christian we still have to work hard to overcome our sins, but Jesus will help us become more and more like Him. It is our job to read His Word, pray, and work to glorify Him with the way we live our lives.

Storytime T

Read aloud the following assigned passage:

★ *Fountain of Life: Ch. 11*

Ask, *In today's reading, how were people's lives different from your life? What would you have enjoyed or found difficult about living during that time?*

Key Idea: Compare and contrast the historical time period of the reading to your own life.

Geography S

Use a globe or a Bible atlas for today's activities. *Find the city of Bethlehem where Jesus was born just south of Jerusalem in modern-day Israel. After the birth of Jesus, why did Mary and Joseph go to Egypt? Trace the route from Bethlehem to Egypt on the globe. After King Herod died, Mary and Joseph left Egypt to settle in Nazareth. Find Nazareth on the globe, just north of Jerusalem in modern-day Israel. Find the Sea of Galilee where Jesus healed the man in today's story. It is located in Israel. The Jordan River flows into it.*

Review the following concept: *The Prime Meridian is an imaginary line running from the North to the South Pole that divides the earth into Eastern and Western Hemispheres. Which continents are in the Eastern Hemisphere? Find Australia, Asia, Europe, and Africa. Which continents are in the Western Hemisphere? Find North and South America. Antarctica is in both hemispheres.*

Key Idea: You can still visit these places today.

Independent History Study I

★ Read *Little Miriam of Galilee* p. 54-60. Then, on white paper, **either** photocopy the picture on p. 54 and color it **or** trace the picture to outline it. At the bottom or top of the picture, write the caption, *Jesus is coming soon!* File your picture in the place you have chosen for it.

Key Idea: Miriam was praying for a miracle to save their fields from the Romans. God hears our prayers.

Learning the Basics

Focus: Language Arts, Math, Bible, and Science

Unit 18 - Day 3

Poetry

T

Read aloud with the students the poem *"Escape at Bedtime"* (see Appendix). Say, *Describe a time you have been somewhere like this or felt like this. What can you learn about the poet, Robert Louis Stevenson, from the poem?* Say, *Did you know that Robert Louis Stevenson saw the same constellations in the night sky that you see? The stars continue moving in the same patterns year after year.* Have the students read the poem on their own.

Key Idea: Read and appreciate classic poetry.

Language Arts

S

Have students complete one studied dictation exercise (see Appendix for directions and passages).

Help students complete one lesson from the following reading program:

 *Drawn into the Heart of Reading*

Work with the students to complete **one** of the English options listed below:

★ *Beginning Wisely:* Lesson 66

★ *Building with Diligence:* Lesson 66

★ Your own grammar program

Key Idea: Practice language arts skills.

Bible Study

T

Say, *You will be having your own quiet time with God today. Choose a quiet place for this special time, where you can be alone with God. Then, do the following things:*

1. Read Psalm 119:169-170 in your Bible.
2. Pray about the Psalm using the following beginning to your prayer: *Thank you for letting me come before you in prayer, Lord. I ask for help with _______ and _______. I trust that you will _______ according to your word.*
3. Recite Psalm 119:169-170 using the hand motions you added on Day 1.
4. Sing Psalm 119:169-170 along with the CD at the end of your quiet time.

✔ *Lead Me to the Rock* CD
Track 3; Song: "According to Thy Word" (vs. 169-170)

Key Idea: The Lord hears your prayers.

Math Exploration

S

Choose **one** of the math options listed below (see Appendix for details).

 *Singapore Primary Mathematics 2A/2B, 3A/3B,* or *4A/4B*

 Your own math program

Key Idea: Use a step-by-step math program.

Science Exploration

I

★ Read *Find the Constellations* p. 30-31. Write the answer to each numbered question on lined paper. You do not need to copy the question. Use the listed page to help you answer each question.

1. Why is Polaris, the Pole Star, so important? (p. 30)
2. What is another name for Polaris? Why is it called that? (p. 30)
3. Draw how you can find Polaris by using the Big Dipper. (p. 30-31)
4. Why do the stars appear to move, rise, and set in the night sky? (p. 31)
5. As God speaks to Job in Job 38:31-33, what do God's questions show Job about the constellations?

Key Idea: God controls the constellations as they "move" through the sky. He brings forth each star and keeps it maintaining its pattern. The movements of these heavenly bodies are very regular.

Learning through History

Focus: The Savior Arrives on Earth

Unit 18 - Day 4

Reading about History **T**

Read about history in the following resource:

★ *Grandpa's Box: Ch. 30* p. 194-200

After today's reading, say, *You will be writing a narration about part of the day's history reading. In order to remember the details very well, you will need to reread the part of today's reading from the last half of p. 196 through p. 197 (on your own if possible).*

After students have finished reading the passage, ask them the questions below. If the students do not know the answers, help them find the answers in the passage they just read. Ask, *What are some of the miracles that Jesus did? How did the miracles act as signs to show who Jesus is? Who is Jesus? Why was it so hard for people to understand that Jesus is the Son of God? What is the Trinity?*

After the questions have been answered, have students write a 3-5 sentence narration that begins, *When Jesus was alive, He....*

When students have finished their narration, direct them to read the sentences out loud. Ask, *Did you include* ***who*** *the reading was mainly about? Did you include* ***what*** *important thing(s) happened? Did you include* ***how*** *it ended?*

Help students underline or highlight the main topic sentence in their narration.

See the *Written Narration Skills* in the Appendix to guide students in editing their narrations.

Key Idea: It was hard for people to understand how Jesus could be both man and God.

Storytime **T**

Read aloud the following assigned passage:

★ *Fountain of Life: Ch. 12-13*

Say, *Transport yourself back to the time of this story. Pretend you lived at this time. Tell me what you see and do. (Make sure to use the word, "I", and to tell only what was described in today's reading.)*

Key Idea: Practice oral narration skills.

Timeline **S**

You will be adding 2 new cards to your staircase timeline today. On the first new card, draw and color a picture of a crown of golden leaves. Write, *Caesar Augustus (Octavian) (63 B.C.- 14 A.D.).* On the second new card, draw and color a manger with a star over it. Write, *Birth of Christ (5 B.C.).*

If you decided to tape your timeline cards to the back of a door, add the *Caesar Augustus* card to the right of the *Julius Caesar* card. To the right of the *Caesar Augustus* card, add the *Birth of Christ* card. If you decided to tape the timeline cards side-by-side to accordion-fold them, use clear packing tape to tape the cards as described above.

Key Idea: Jesus did many miracles as signs that He is indeed God's Son. Yet, people had a difficult time believing God had come down to earth in human form through Jesus. Satan tried to have Jesus killed more than once, but Jesus would only die at God's appointed time. God's plan would be carried out so that mankind could be saved.

Independent History Study **I**

★ Read *Little Miriam of Galilee: Ch. 7.* Then, choose an interesting part from today's pages to read aloud and explain to an adult.

Key Idea: Miriam had to stay home from the Jewish festival because of her broken foot. She was lucky to see Chloe and to spend time with her grandmother. Miriam still prayed for a miracle to save their fields.

Learning the Basics

Focus: Language Arts, Math, Bible, and Science

Poetry

T

Read aloud with the students the poem *"Escape at Bedtime"* (see Appendix). Have students share this poem in a special way. Suggestions for sharing the poem include recording it to play for someone, reading it to someone on the telephone, photocopying the poem and adding illustrations, reading it to someone at home, putting the poem to a melody and singing it, using an instrument to tap out the meter or rhythm of the poem while reading it, or copying the poem on paper.

Key Idea: Share a variety of classic poetry.

Language Arts

S

Have students complete one dictation exercise.

Guide students to complete one reading lesson.

★ *Drawn into the Heart of Reading*

Help students complete **one** English lesson.

★ *Beginning Wisely:* Lesson 67

★ *Building with Diligence:* Lesson 67

★ Your own grammar program

Key Idea: Practice language arts skills.

Bible Study

T

Have students say Psalm 119:169-170 using the hand motions from Day 1.

Have students copy in cursive Psalm 119:169-170 onto a clean page in their *Common Place Book*. Students should leave the rest of the page blank to add to next week.

Students will add to the *Common Place Book* throughout the year.

✔ *Lead Me to the Rock* CD
Track 3; Song: "According to Thy Word" (vs. 169-170)

Key Idea: Copy in cursive a portion of a Psalm.

Math Exploration

S

Choose **one** math option listed below.

★ *Singapore Primary Mathematics 2A/2B, 3A/3B,* or *4A/4B*

★ Your own math program

Key Idea: Use a step-by-step math program.

Science Exploration

I

★ Read *Find the Constellations* p. 32-33. Turn to the science experiment section in your science binder or sketchbook. At the top of a blank page, write: *Why do the constellations appear to move, while Polaris stays in one place?* Under the question, write: *'Guess'*. Write down your guess. For today's experiment, you will need an adult partner. Open your *Find the Constellations* book to p. 33. Stand up. Have your partner hold your book open to p. 33 high over your head so that you are standing and looking directly up at Polaris, the North Star. You will be the Earth, slowly rotating. As you slowly spin, keep your eyes on Polaris. What do you notice? It does not appear to move in the sky. Now, as you rotate this time, watch the other constellations. What do you see? The constellations appear to move, while Polaris appears to stand still. On your paper, write: *'Procedure'*. Draw a picture of the experiment. At the bottom of the paper, write: *'Conclusion'*. Explain what you learned.

Key Idea: Polaris stays in the north while the constellations seem to go around it in circles. This is due to the Earth's rotation as it spins on its axis. The constellations farther from Polaris seem to rise and set.

Learning through History

Focus: Jesus' Death and Resurrection

Unit 19 - Day 1

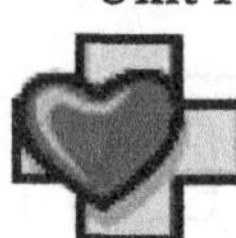

Reading about History T

Read about history in the following resource:

★ *Grandpa's Box: Ch. 31* p. 201-206

After today's reading, say, *Why didn't Jesus come right away when He knew that Lazarus was very sick?* (analysis) *When Jesus finally came, describe what happened.* (comprehension) *Explain why Jesus wept.* (synthesis) *How did Jesus use Lazarus to show that God has power over death?* (application) *What can we learn about Jesus from today's story?* (analysis)

Key Idea: When Jesus was told that Lazarus was dying, He did not go immediately to see Lazarus. Instead, He waited knowing that Lazarus would die. When Jesus saw Mary and Martha, He wept with them. After that, Jesus raised Lazarus from the dead, even though he had been dead for 4 days. God has power over all things, even death.

History Project S

In this unit you will be making perfume like they used long ago. Fill a baby food jar (or a container with a tight lid) ¾ full with rubbing alcohol. Drop in 15-20 whole spices such as cloves, cinnamon sticks, or allspice. Allow the perfume to sit undisturbed for one week. Then, remove the lid and dab a little on your wrist. Wave your wrist in the air to smell the scent. The alcohol dissolves the aromatic oil of the spices so that when the alcohol evaporates from your wrist, the scented oil is left.

Key Idea: Perfumes and colognes are made in a similar way today.

Storytime T

Read aloud the following assigned story:

★ *Fountain of Life: Ch. 14*

Discuss today's reading in a "conversational way". Share about a person, time, event, or emotion from your life that today's reading brought to mind. Next, have your child share a connection.

Key Idea: Connect personally to the story.

Research S

At the time of Jesus, perfume made of spices such as myrrh was used to prepare a body for burial. Where could you look to discover more about the **anointing of Jesus**? Use a reference book or an online resource like www.wikipedia.org to look up *anointing of Jesus* or *perfume*. Depending on the resource you use, you will have to type *anointing of Jesus* or *perfume* in the search or look it up in the index.

Orally answer one or more of the following questions from your research: *What are some of the uses for perfume? What kinds of things are used in perfume to make different scents? Why did Mary anoint Jesus with perfume? How do we know it was an expensive perfume? What did Judas say should have been done with the perfume? How did Jesus respond to Judas? Why was perfume used for anointing in preparation for burial?*

Key Idea: At the time Jesus was alive, myrrh was a very expensive perfume. It was one of the gifts given to Jesus by the wise men who visited Him to celebrate His birth.

Independent History Study I

★ Read *Little Miriam of Galilee: Ch. 8.* Orally retell or narrate to an adult the portion of text that you read today. Use the *Narration Tips* in the Appendix for help as needed.

Key Idea: During her visit to Chloe's, Miriam got to see how different life was for a wealthy Roman soldier.

Learning the Basics
Focus: Language Arts, Math, Bible, and Science

Unit 19 - Day 1

Poetry
T

Read aloud to the students the poem *"The Sun's Travels"* (see Appendix). Say, *Explain the meaning of the first stanza. When the child in the poem is playing in the sunny garden, what are the children on the other side of the world in India doing? After the child in the poem has had his evening tea and is getting ready for bed, what are the children on the other side of the world doing?* Read the poem again with the students.

Key Idea: Read and appreciate classic poetry.

Language Arts
S

Have students complete the first studied dictation exercise (see Appendix for directions and passages).

Help students complete one lesson from the following reading program:

★ *Drawn into the Heart of Reading*

Work with the students to complete **one** of the English options listed below:

★ *Beginning Wisely:* Lesson 68

★ *Building with Diligence:* Lesson 68

★ Your own grammar program

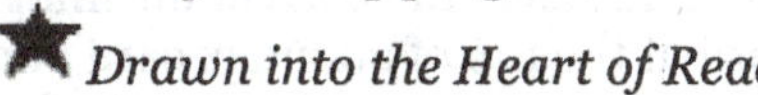

Key Idea: Practice language arts skills.

Bible Study
T

Say, *Find Psalm 119:169-173 in your Bible. This is the memory selection for this unit.* Read the verses out loud. Ask, *What does Psalm 119:171 say we should do when God has helped us become more like Him? Why is it important to thank God for His help? What are we told to do in Psalm 119:172? Why is it important to speak to others about God's word? What is the Psalmist asking God for in Psalm 119:173? Why should we ask for God's hand to be with us? What does Psalm 119:173 say the Psalmist has chosen? Why is it important to make sure we are choosing God's ways, rather than our own?* Have students say the verse 3 times, adding hand motions to help remember the words.

✔ *Lead Me to the Rock* CD
Track 3; Song: "According to Thy Word" (vs. 169-173)

Key Idea: We need to remember to ask God for His help and to thank Him for helping us.

Math Exploration
S

Choose **one** of the math options listed below (see Appendix for details).

★ *Singapore Primary Mathematics 2A/2B, 3A/3B,* or *4A/4B*

★ Your own math program

Key Idea: Use a step-by-step math program.

Science Exploration
I

Get your book about the stars that you began in Unit 16. On the top of the next clean page in your book, copy in cursive 1 Corinthians 15:41. Beneath the verse, draw one or more of the following constellations: The Little Dipper (p. 32), The Dragon (p. 32), Cassiopeia (p. 32), Cepheus (p. 32), or The Giraffe (p. 32). Make sure to draw the brighter stars larger, and label them with their names, as shown in the pictures. Label each constellation with its name too. You may trace the constellations if you wish. Save your book for next week.

Key Idea: The constellations you studied today are located near the North Star, or Polaris. The Big Dipper is also located near the North Star.

Learning through History

Focus: Jesus' Death and Resurrection

Unit 19 - Day 2

Reading about History — T

Read about history in the following resource:

★ *Grandpa's Box: Ch. 32* p. 207-212

After today's reading, read aloud Luke 23:6-43. Then, go over the events listed in the "History Project" box of today's plans. Ask, *Which person are you like, the thief who ridiculed and mocked Jesus or the one who repented? Explain. What reward will you be given if you believe in the Lord Jesus Christ? Does that mean you will have a life free from suffering on earth? Why not?*

Key Idea: Jesus chose to die for our sins. He could have easily called the angels to save Him.

Storytime — T

Read aloud the following assigned passage:

★ *Fountain of Life: Ch. 15*

Ask, *In what does the main character place his faith? How has Eli's father put so much faith in the law and customs that He is missing out on the Savior? Share a character, a story, or a verse from the Bible that you are reminded of by the reading.*

Key Idea: Share a Biblical connection.

History Project — S

On white paper, trace around a dinner plate to make 2 large circles. Cut the circles out. The first circle will be a clock face. Write the hours on the clock, starting with '12' at the top. Make a dot in the center of the clock. Copy the following hourly steps like spokes on a wheel coming out from the center dot for the day of Jesus' death. You will do the rest on Day 3.

6 A.M. Jesus goes before Pilate and is sent to Herod. (Luke 23:6-10)

7 A.M. Jesus is returned to Pilate and sentenced. (Luke 23:11-25)

8 A.M. Jesus is led to Calvary. (Luke 23:26)

9 A.M. Jesus is crucified. (Luke 23:33)

10 A.M. Jesus asks for forgiveness for His enemies. (Luke 23:34)

11 A.M. Jesus tells the thief he will be with Him in paradise. (Luke 23:35-43)

Key Idea: Jesus died in God's perfect timing.

Vocabulary — S

You may choose 3-5 of the following vocabulary words from *Grandpa's Box* to use for this lesson: *jealous* (p. 209), *blasphemy* (p. 210), *obstacle* (p. 210), *fickle* (p. 211), and/or *grim* (p. 211). First, find the word in the text and read the sentence containing the word. Think about possible meanings. Next, find the word in a dictionary and select the correct meaning. Write the word at the top of an index card or at the top of the corresponding letter page in the notebook. Underneath the word, copy the correct definition from the dictionary. Then, use the word correctly in a sentence. The sentence may either be copied from the text or be one of your own creation. Last, draw a small picture to show the word's meaning. If you used an index card to record your word, file it under the correct alphabetical tab.

Key Idea: How difficult it must have been for a sinless man to carry the weight of the world's sin on the cross at Calvary! Yet, Jesus was willing to do that for you and for me. What are we willing to do to serve Jesus?

Independent History Study — I

★ Read *Little Miriam of Galilee* p. 91-98. Then, on white paper, **either** photocopy the picture on p. 97 and color it **or** trace the picture. At the bottom, write a caption. File your picture in the chosen place.

Key Idea: Miriam's family was thankful for what they had, even though it looked like they'd have to move.

Learning the Basics

Focus: Language Arts, Math, Bible, and Science

Language Arts

T

Work with the students to complete **one** of the English options listed below:

★ *Beginning Wisely:* Lesson 69

★ *Building with Diligence:* Lesson 69

★ Your own grammar program

Say, *You will be doing a writing activity based on the poem, "The Sun's Travels"* (see Appendix).

Draw a circle in the middle of a piece of paper. Draw a line down the center of the paper to divide the circle in half. Write, "Day" at the top of the left half of the paper and "Night" at the top of the right half of the paper. Say, *This is a picture of the Earth, showing one half having day while the other half is having night. Let's make a list of sights, sounds, and activities that go with "Day" and "Night".* As students share their ideas, write them down under the correct heading (i.e. Day: light, playing, Sun shining, laughing, eating, biking, walking, clouds, birds chirping. Night: dark, sleeping, dreaming, crickets chirping, Moon shining, stars, quiet).

Next, say, *You will be using the lists we made to help you write a paragraph that contrasts or shows the differences between the night and the day.*

Begin your paragraph, *Did you know that while it is day on one side of the world, on the other side of the world it is night?* Provide as much help as needed for students to write their paragraph well.

Key Idea: Write creatively from classic poetry.

Bible Study

T

Have students say Psalm 119:169-173 using the hand motions they added on Day 1. Say, *A mood is a feeling, a sensation, or a state of mind. What is the mood of Psalm 119:171-173?* (Some examples of moods include frightened, worried, happy, peaceful, hopeful, sad, unhappy, angry, thankful, prayerful, joyful, and lonely.) Ask, *When would this Psalm help you, or when would you go to this Psalm?* (i.e. to remind us to thank the Lord for His help, to give us courage to speak about God's word to others, to help us to remember to ask for God's hand to be with us as we follow His word.)

Last, pray with your children that they will ask for God's hand to be upon them. Pray that they will remember to thank the Lord for His help. Pray for them to have courage to speak about God's word.

✔ *Lead Me to the Rock* CD
Track 3; Song: "According to Thy Word" (vs. 169-173)

Key Idea: The Psalms reflect the many emotions and moods we have. They are a wonderful place to seek counsel from the Lord.

Math Exploration

S

Choose **one** of the math options listed below (see Appendix for details).

★ *Singapore Primary Mathematics 2A/2B, 3A/3B,* or *4A/4B*

★ Your own math program

Key Idea: Use a step-by-step math program.

Science Exploration

I

★ Read *Find the Constellations* p. 34-35. Orally retell or narrate to an adult the portion of text that you read today. Use the *Narration Tips* in the Appendix for help as needed.

Key Idea: The part of the sky where the planets can be seen is called the Zodiac. Twelve constellations are located in the Zodiac.

Learning through History
Focus: Jesus' Death and Resurrection

Unit 19 - Day 3

Reading about History — T

Read about history in the following resource:

★ *Grandpa's Box: Ch. 33* p. 213-218

After today's reading, have your students orally narrate or retell the portion of today's text that you read. Use the *Narration Tips* in the Appendix as needed.

Key Idea: John and Peter saw the empty tomb. The resurrection shows us Jesus is God's Son.

Storytime — T

Read aloud the following assigned passage:

★ *Fountain of Life: Ch. 16-17*

Ask, *In today's reading, how were people's lives different from your life? What would you have enjoyed or found difficult about living during that time?*

Key Idea: Compare and contrast the historical time period of the reading to your own life.

History Project — S

Get the clock face you made on Day 2. Copy the following steps on the clock like spokes on a wheel. Note: These are only general times.
12 P.M. Darkness falls over the land for 3 hours. (Mark 15:33)
1 P.M. Jesus cries out, *My God, my God, why hast Thou forsaken me?* (Mark 15:34)
2 P.M. Jesus says, *I thirst.* (John 19:28)
3 P.M. Jesus cries, *It is finished,* and breathes His last. (John 19:30 or Luke 23:46)
4 P.M. Right after Jesus' death, the temple curtain tore in two, and the earth quaked. (Matthew 27:51)
5 P.M. The tombs broke open, and many holy people were raised to life. (Matthew 27:52-54)

Last cut out a thin, pie-shaped slice from the blank circle from Day 2. Place the blank circle on top of the clock face and attach the two circles together with a paper fastener in the center. Turn the top circle to view the events of Jesus' death written on the bottom circle.

Key Idea: Jesus had prophesied His own resurrection. When He rose from the dead, it showed that everything He said is true.

Geography — S

Use a globe or a Bible atlas for today's lesson. *All of Jesus' last days centered around the city of Jerusalem. Find Jerusalem in modern-day Israel on the globe. When Herod the Great died, Mary and Joseph returned from Egypt with Jesus. Then, Herod's kingdom was divided among his 3 sons. At the time of Jesus' death, Pontius Pilate was ruling for Rome in Judea (in place of Herod the Great's son Archelaus). So, Jesus stood trial before Pilate. Judea was on the west side of the Dead Sea. Find the location of Judea on the globe.*

Review the following concept: *The equator is an imaginary line running east and west around the center of the earth dividing it into the Northern and Southern Hemispheres. The Prime Meridian is an imaginary line running from the North to the South Pole dividing the earth into Eastern and Western Hemispheres. Which continents are in each hemisphere? Look back at the "Geography" box of Unit 17 – Day 3 and Unit 18 – Day 3 for help as needed.*

Key Idea: Jesus' resurrection was at the time of the Passover. Jerusalem was full of people.

Independent History Study — I

★ Read *Little Miriam of Galilee* p. 99-102. Then, copy James 5:13 in cursive onto a clean page in your *Common Place Book.*

Key Idea: Miriam was sad to miss the Passover trip - but glad her foot healed in time for the wedding.

Learning the Basics

Focus: Language Arts, Math, Bible, and Science

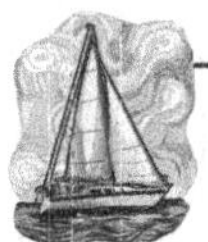

Poetry

T

Read aloud with the students the poem *"The Sun's Travels"* (see Appendix). Say, *Describe a time you have felt like this. What can you learn about the poet, Robert Louis Stevenson, from the poem?* Say, *Did you know that Robert Louis Stevenson loved adventure and loved to travel? He enjoyed thinking about what was going on around the world and imagining what others might be doing.* Have the students read the poem on their own.

Key Idea: Read and appreciate classic poetry.

Language Arts

S

Have students complete one studied dictation exercise (see Appendix for directions and passages).

Help students complete one lesson from the following reading program:

★ *Drawn into the Heart of Reading*

Work with the students to complete **one** of the English options listed below:

★ *Beginning Wisely:* Lesson 70

★ *Building with Diligence:* Lesson 70

★ Your own grammar program

Key Idea: Practice language arts skills.

Bible Study

T

Say, *You will be having your own quiet time with God today. Choose a quiet place for this special time, where you can be alone with God. Then, do the following things:*

1. Read Psalm 119:169-173 in your Bible.
2. Pray about the Psalm using the following beginning to your prayer: *Thank you for hearing my prayer. Help me to speak about your word when I ______. Please let your hand be upon me as I ______.*
3. Recite Psalm 119:169-173 using the hand motions you added on Day 1.
4. Sing Psalm 119:169-173 along with the CD at the end of your quiet time.

✔ *Lead Me to the Rock* CD
Track 3; Song: "According to Your Word" (vs. 169-173)

Key Idea: It is good to ask for the Lord's help.

Math Exploration

S

Choose **one** of the math options listed below (see Appendix for details).

★ *Singapore Primary Mathematics 2A/2B, 3A/3B,* or *4A/4B*

★ Your own math program

Key Idea: Use a step-by-step math program.

Science Exploration

I

★ Read *Find the Constellations* p. 36-39. Write the answer to each numbered question on lined paper. You do not need to copy the question. Use the listed page to help you answer each question.

1. What are the names of the five 1st magnitude stars shown on p. 37? (Hint: They are labeled.)
2. Name two new figures on these charts that are shown to have risen in the east. (p. 38)
3. Where is the Northern Crown located? (p. 38)
4. In late spring, what is the first star you'll see coming out high in the sky? (p. 39)
5. What does God say about worshiping the Sun, Moon, and stars in Deuteronomy 4:19?

Key Idea: God created the Sun, the Moon, and stars. We are never to worship the things that God created, we are only to worship the Creator. The stars cannot predict our future, only God knows that!

Learning through History
Focus: Jesus' Death and Resurrection

Unit 19 - Day 4

Reading about History — T

Read about history in the following resource:

★ *Grandpa's Box: Ch. 34* p. 219-225

After today's reading, say, *You will be writing a narration about part of the day's history reading. In order to remember the details very well, you will need to reread the part of today's reading from the last half of p. 223 through p. 224 (on your own if possible).*

After students have finished reading the passage, ask them the questions below. If the students do not know the answers, help them find the answers in the passage they just read. Ask, *What is the Trinity?* (If needed, review "Trinity" from *Grandpa's Box* p. 197.) Ask, *Who did God send to comfort the disciples? What signs did God send along with the Holy Spirit? Which feast was going on at this time in Jerusalem? Why was it the perfect time for the disciples to share the good news of Jesus with others? Who preached to the crowds? How was Peter able to preach boldly about Jesus? What happened after his preaching? Why did people repent and believe in Jesus?*

After the questions have been answered, have students write a 3-5 sentence narration that begins, *After Jesus' death....* When students have finished their narration, direct them to read the sentences out loud. Ask, *Did you include* ***who*** *the reading was mainly about? Did you include* ***what*** *important thing(s) happened? Did you include* ***how*** *it ended?*

Help students underline or highlight the main topic sentence in their narration. See the *Written Narration Skills* in the Appendix to guide students in editing their narrations.

Key Idea: The disciples were changed men.

Storytime — T

Read aloud the following assigned passage:

★ *Fountain of Life: Ch. 18*

After today's reading, have your students orally narrate or retell the portion of today's text that you read. Use the *Narration Tips* in the Appendix as needed.

Key Idea: Practice oral narration skills.

Timeline — S

You will be adding a new card to your staircase timeline today. On your new card, draw a line down the center of it. On the left side, draw a cross. On the right side, draw the empty tomb. Write, *Death and Resurrection of Jesus (30 A.D)*.

If you decided to tape your timeline cards to the back of a door, begin a new row above the row you just made (like a staircase). On the right side of the door, tape the *Death and Resurrection of Jesus* card. If you decided to tape the timeline cards side-by-side to accordion-fold them, use clear packing tape to tape the cards as described above.

Key Idea: God equipped the disciples to spread the Good News of Jesus by giving them the Holy Spirit at Pentecost. The disciples were also able to speak to many visitors in Jerusalem in their own languages. They told everyone about Jesus being God's Son and His resurrection from the dead. The disciples changed from fearful men, to men who preached boldly for the Lord.

Independent History Study — I

★ Read *Little Miriam of Galilee: Ch. 10.* Then, choose an interesting part from today's pages to read aloud and explain to an adult.

Key Idea: Jesus changed Jachan's heart so that instead of collecting money, Jachan repaid it.

Learning the Basics

Focus: Language Arts, Math, Bible, and Science

Unit 19 - Day 4

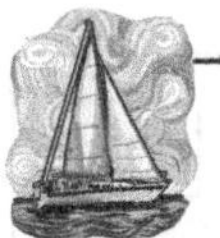

Poetry

T

Read aloud with the students the poem *"The Sun's Travels"* (see Appendix). Have students share this poem in a special way. Suggestions for sharing the poem are mentioned in the "Poetry" box of Unit 18 – Day 4.

Key Idea: Share a variety of classic poetry.

Language Arts

S

Have students complete one dictation exercise.

Guide students to complete one reading lesson.

★ *Drawn into the Heart of Reading*

Help students complete **one** English lesson.

★ *Beginning Wisely:* Lesson 71

★ *Building with Diligence:* Lesson 71

★ Your own grammar program

Key Idea: Practice language arts skills.

Bible Study

T

Have students say Psalm 119:169-173 using the hand motions from Day 1. Have students copy in cursive Psalm 119:171-173 beneath last unit's Psalm 119:169-170 in their *Common Place Book*. Students should leave the rest of the page blank to add to next week. Students will add to the *Common Place Book* throughout the year.

✔ *Lead Me to the Rock* CD
Track 3; Song: "According to Thy Word" (vs. 169-173)

Key Idea: Copy in cursive a portion of a Psalm.

Math Exploration

S

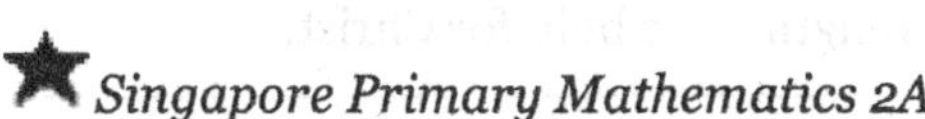

Choose **one** math option listed below.

★ *Singapore Primary Mathematics 2A/2B, 3A/3B,* or *4A/4B*

★ Your own math program

Key Idea: Use a step-by-step math program.

Science Exploration

I

Turn to the science experiment section in your science binder or sketchbook. At the top of a blank page, write: *Why does the Sun appear to move through the Zodiac constellations each year?* Under the question, write: *'Guess'*. Write down your guess.

You will need 12 index cards. Refer to p. 34 in *Find the Constellations* as you write a different one of the following Zodiac constellations on each card: The Ram (Aries), The Bull (Taurus), The Twins (Gemini), The Crab (Cancer), The Lion (Leo), The Virgin (Virgo), The Scales (Libra), The Scorpion (Scorpio), The Archer (Sagittarius), The Goat (Capricorn), The Water Carrier (Aquarius), The Fishes (Pisces). Go to a room with open space on the floor. Place a flashlight on the floor in the center of the room to be the Sun. Place the cards around the Sun in a circle, beginning with The Ram at the top, and going around counter-clockwise. You will be the Earth. Walk around the outside of the cards, going counterclockwise. Watch how the Sun appears to move through the Zodiac constellations, even though the Earth is the one moving. On your paper, write: *'Procedure'*. Draw a picture of the experiment. At the bottom, write *'Conclusion'*. Explain what you learned.

Key Idea: The ancient Babylonians studied the stars and used the 12 Zodiac constellations to describe the movement of the Sun. As the Earth orbits around the Sun, the Sun appears to move through the 12 constellations in the Zodiac. The Babylonians also worshiped the stars, which God tells us never to do!

Learning through History
Focus: The Spread of the Gospel

Unit 20 - Day 1

Reading about History — T

Read about history in the following resource:

★ *Grandpa's Box: Ch. 35* p. 226-232

After today's reading, say, *How did Peter explain what had happened to the lame man?* (knowledge) *Why did the priests have Peter and John arrested?* (comprehension) *Describe what happened the next morning to Peter and John.* (comprehension) *Compare God's ways to Satan's ways.* (analysis) *Explain how God's plan was being carried out by the apostles.* (evaluation)

Key Idea: After the apostles received the Holy Spirit, they boldly preached about Jesus throughout Jerusalem. Many people's hearts were changed, and they became believers in Christ. The apostles were imprisoned and beaten, but they continued preaching the Good News about Jesus. The Holy Spirit gave them the strength to be bold for Christ.

History Project — S

In this unit you will make an ichthys, which is a Christian symbol for the followers of Jesus. Add ¼ cup applesauce and ¼ cup cinnamon to a ziploc bag. Seal the bag. Mix the applesauce and cinnamon by gently kneading the bag. Then, dump the mixture onto a piece of waxed paper. Form a fish shape, or the ichthys, with the mixture. Use the circular end of a pen or pencil to make a hole near the top of the fish to thread yarn or string later. Let the fish dry until Day 3.

Key Idea: The ichthys was one of the first Christian symbols used to identify Christians.

Storytime — T

Read aloud the following assigned story:

★ *Fountain of Life: Ch. 19-20*

Discuss today's reading in a "conversational way". Share about a person, time, event, or emotion from your life that today's reading brought to mind. Next, have your child share a connection.

Key Idea: Connect personally to the story.

Research — S

After the resurrection of Jesus, early Christians often identified themselves by using a fish symbol. Where could you look to discover more about the **fish symbol**? Use a reference book or an online resource like www.wikipedia.org to look up *fish symbol.* Depending on the resource you use, you will have to type *fish symbol* or *ichthys* (which is the Greek word for fish) in the search or look it up in the index.

Orally answer one or more of the following questions from your research: *What does the fish symbol look like? How was the fish symbol used by early Christians? What was the meaning of the fish symbol? What is the fish symbol known as now? Why would early Christians have needed a symbol? How did Christians use the symbol to tell whether a person they met was also a Christian?*

Key Idea: The early Christians met secretly in order to protect themselves from persecution. The ichthys symbol was scratched on walls and rocks to signal a meeting place.

Independent History Study — I

★ Read *Little Miriam of Galilee: Ch. 11.* Orally retell or narrate to an adult the portion of text that you read today. Use the *Narration Tips* in the Appendix for help as needed.

Key Idea: Miriam was thankful to Jehovah for saving their home. She was hoping to see Jesus one day.

Learning the Basics

Focus: Language Arts, Math, Bible, and Science

Unit 20 - Day 1

Poetry

T

Read aloud to the students the poem *"The Lamplighter"* (see Appendix). Say, *What time of day does the first line say it is? What job does Leerie have? Why would towns have needed a lamplighter? Who do you think Tom and Marcia are? Why do you think the poet says, "...when I am stronger and can choose what to do"? Why would a sickly child long to be the lamplighter he sees outside his window?* Read the poem again with the students.

Key Idea: Read and appreciate classic poetry.

Language Arts

S

Have students complete the first studied dictation exercise (see Appendix for directions and passages).

Help students complete one lesson from the following reading program:

★ *Drawn into the Heart of Reading*

Work with the students to complete **one** of the English options listed below:

★ *Beginning Wisely:* Lesson 72

★ *Building with Diligence:* Lesson 72

★ Your own grammar program

Key Idea: Practice language arts skills.

Bible Study

T

Say, *Find Psalm 119:169-175 in your Bible. This is the memory selection for this unit. Read the verses out loud.* Ask, *What does David say he longs for in Psalm 119:174? According to Psalm 119:174, if we long for salvation as David did, then in what will we delight? How can we delight in God's word? In Psalm 119:175, what does David ask for? Where do our souls live while we are on Earth? Where will our souls live when we die? How will our souls always be able to praise the Lord? How can the Lord's judgments help us overcome our sin in order to glorify the Lord more?* Have students say the verse 3 times, adding hand motions to help remember the words.

✔ *Lead Me to the Rock* CD
Track 3; Song: "According to Thy Word" (vs. 169-175)

Key Idea: We should work to glorify the Lord with our lives through prayer and praise.

Math Exploration

S

Choose **one** of the math options listed below (see Appendix for details).

★ *Singapore Primary Mathematics 2A/2B, 3A/3B,* or *4A/4B*

★ Your own math program

Key Idea: Use a step-by-step math program.

Science Exploration

I

Get your book about the stars that you began in Unit 16. On the top of the next clean page in your book, copy in cursive Genesis 1:16. Beneath the verse, draw one or more of the following constellations: The Archer (p. 34), The Ram (p. 35), The Crab (p. 35), The Scales (p. 35), The Goat (p. 35), The Water Carrier (p. 35), or The Fishes (p. 35). Make sure to draw the brighter stars larger as shown in the pictures. Label each constellation with its name. You may trace the constellations if you wish. Save your book for next week.

Key Idea: Half of the constellations in the Zodiac have very faint stars, making them difficult to see.

Unit 20 - Day 2

Reading about History T

Read about history in the following resource:
★ *Grandpa's Box: Ch. 36* p. 233-239

After today's reading, read aloud Acts 7:55-60. Ask, *In Acts 7:55, what does it say filled Stephen? What did Stephen see in Acts 7:55-56? How did this prove that Christ is in heaven seated at the right hand of God? What happened to Stephen in Acts 7:58-59? Who does it mention was there at the stoning of Stephen in Acts 7:58?*

Next, read aloud Acts 11:19-24. Ask, *What happened because of the death of Stephen in Acts 11:19? How did Stephen's death help spread the gospel of Jesus? Why do you think Stephen's death was so important?*

Key Idea: After Stephen's death, Christians were persecuted. Many left Jerusalem and fled for their lives. As they moved, they helped spread the gospel of Christ throughout Judea and Samaria, just as Jesus had commanded.

History Project S

Continue to let your fish dry until Day 3. Meanwhile, cut a piece of paper to fit on the body of the fish. Copy Matthew 4:19 on the paper. Glue the verse on the body of the fish. Let it dry until Day 3.

Key Idea: Being a Christian shortly after Jesus' death wasn't easy. Yet, God made sure the gospel was spread quickly as people returned to their hometowns after celebrating the Passover in Jerusalem. Then, persecuted Christians moved and spread the gospel even further.

Storytime T

Read aloud the following assigned passage:
★ *Fountain of Life: Ch. 21*
Ask, *In what does the main character place his faith? How is Eli's faith different from his father's faith? Share a character, a story, or a verse from the Bible that you are reminded of by the reading.*

Key Idea: Share a Biblical connection.

Vocabulary S

You may choose 3-5 of the following vocabulary words from *Grandpa's Box* to use for this lesson: *research* (p. 234), *martyr* (p. 235), *accusations* (p. 236), *gnash* (p. 236), and/or *persecution* (p. 238). First, find the word in the text and read the sentence containing the word. Think about possible meanings. Next, find the word in a dictionary and select the correct meaning. Write the word at the top of an index card or at the top of the corresponding letter page in the notebook. Underneath the word, copy the correct definition from the dictionary. Then, use the word correctly in a sentence. The sentence may either be copied from the text or be one of your own creation. Last, draw a small picture to show the word's meaning. If you used an index card to record your word, file it under the correct alphabetical tab.

Key Idea: We are so blessed to live in a country where we are allowed to worship Jesus. Many countries today do not allow their people to worship Jesus. Christians still endure persecution all over the world.

Independent History Study I

★ Read *The Young Christian's Introduction to the Bible* p. 45-46. Then, copy Hebrews 9:27-28 in cursive onto a clean page in your *Common Place Book*.

Key Idea: Christ only needed to die once to save us from our sin. He was willing to be a sacrifice for us.

Learning the Basics

Focus: Language Arts, Math, Bible, and Science

Unit 20 - Day 2

Language Arts

T

Work with the students to complete **one** of the English options listed below:

★ *Beginning Wisely:* Lesson 73

★ *Building with Diligence:* Lesson 73

★ Your own grammar program

Say, *You will be doing a writing activity based on the poem, "The Lamplighter"* (see Appendix). Ask, *What does the child in the poem see as he's looking out the window? What are some things that you've watched out your window?* (i.e. children playing, cows in the pasture, pigeons on a building, baby robins in the yard, the postman bringing the mail, the ice cream truck delivering ice cream, a neighbor washing his car, etc.) Have the students choose one of the ideas that they shared to describe.

At the top of a markerboard or a paper, draw a large box divided into 4 sections. Label the sections "When?", "What?", "Saw?", "Heard?" Ask students to share words or phrases to describe their chosen topic. As students share the words and phrases, write them under the correct heading.

Next, say, *Use the words we listed to help you write a paragraph describing what you saw outside your window. Begin your paragraph with a sentence like the first line of "The Lamplighter" that tells "When" you saw this scene. For the second sentence, write, "It's time to take to the window to see...". Finish the sentence with words that tell "What" you saw. Then, finish the paragraph with details that describe what you "Saw" and "Heard".*

Key Idea: Write creatively from classic poetry.

Bible Study

T

Have students say Psalm 119:169-175 using the hand motions they added on Day 1. Say, *A mood is a feeling, a sensation, or a state of mind. What is the mood of Psalm 119:174-175?* (Some examples of moods include frightened, worried, happy, peaceful, hopeful, sad, unhappy, angry, thankful, prayerful, joyful, and lonely.) Ask, *When would this Psalm help you, or when would you go to this Psalm?* (i.e. to give each of us a glimpse of the perfect salvation we'll have in heaven one day, to show us that we can delight in God's word and His law, to remind us that our soul is meant to praise and glorify God)

Last, pray with your children that they will long for heaven and perfect salvation. Pray that they will delight in God's word and that their souls may glorify and praise the Lord.

✔ *Lead Me to the Rock* CD
Track 3; Song: "According to Thy Word" (vs. 169-175)

Key Idea: The Psalms reflect the many emotions and moods we have. They are a wonderful place to seek counsel from the Lord.

Math Exploration

S

Choose **one** of the math options listed below (see Appendix for details).

★ *Singapore Primary Mathematics 2A/2B, 3A/3B,* or *4A/4B*

★ Your own math program

Key Idea: Use a step-by-step math program.

Science Exploration

I

★ Read *Find the Constellations* p. 40-41. Orally retell or narrate to an adult the portion of text that you read today. Use the *Narration Tips* in the Appendix for help as needed.

Key Idea: This Greek myth about Andromeda and Cassiopeia shows the Greeks' pagan beliefs in other gods. The Greeks often took stories from the Bible and twisted them into tales of mortal human beings interacting with the gods. The Bible warns us not to create other gods or to worship them.

Learning through History
Focus: The Spread of the Gospel

Unit 20 - Day 3

Reading about History **T**

Read about history in the following resource:

★ *Grandpa's Box: Ch. 37* p. 240-246
Note: You may want to reword or omit some of the more graphic content on p. 241.

After today's reading, have your students orally narrate or retell the portion of today's text that you read. Use the *Narration Tips* in the Appendix as needed.

Key Idea: While Saul was growing up, he was a student of the Pharisees. He knew God's laws and did not believe that Jesus was the Son of God.

Storytime **T**

Read aloud the following assigned passage:

★ *Fountain of Life: Ch. 22*
Ask, *In today's reading, how were people's lives different from your life? What would you have enjoyed or found difficult about living during that time?*

Key Idea: Compare and contrast the historical time period of the reading to your own life.

History Project **S**

Once your fish from Days 1-2 is dry, thread a piece of string or yarn through the hole at the top of your fish. Then, tie the string or yarn into a knot. Hang the fish somewhere you can see it and enjoy its scent. Possible places for hanging your fish might be on a drawer knob, from a light fixture, or on a doorknob. You could also tape it to a window or give it as a gift.

Key Idea: Saul was blind for 3 days after Jesus spoke to him on the road to Damascus. Then, God sent a believer named Ananias to visit Saul. He prayed with Saul and baptized him, and Saul's eyes were opened. God used Saul to spread the gospel of Jesus to Gentiles all over the Roman empire. If God can use Saul, God can use you.

Geography **S**

Use a globe or a Bible atlas for today's lesson. *Damascus was northeast of the Dead Sea and the Sea of Galilee. Find Damascus on the globe in modern-day Syria. On the globe, trace Paul's first missionary journey with Barnabas from Syria, to the island of Cyprus, and up into Turkey, and then back to the Mediterranean Sea to Syria. Then, trace Paul's second missionary journey with Silas from Antioch in Syria, across Turkey, around Greece and the Aegean Sea, across the Mediterranean Sea to modern-day Israel, and north on land to Syria.*

Review the following concept: *The equator divides the earth into the Northern and Southern Hemispheres. The Prime Meridian divides the earth into the Eastern and Western Hemispheres. Which continents are in each hemisphere? Look back at the "Geography" box of Unit 17 – Day 3 and Unit 18 – Day 3 for help as needed.*

Key Idea: When Jesus spoke to Saul on the road to Damascus, Saul realized he'd been wrong. He became a Christian and a new man.

Independent History Study **I**

★ Read *The Young Christian's Introduction to the Bible* p. 47-48. Then, copy Romans 10:9 in cursive onto a clean page in your *Common Place Book*.

Key Idea: Saul's name changed to Paul when he became a Christian. He wrote many books of the Bible.

Learning the Basics

Focus: Language Arts, Math, Bible, and Science

Unit 20 - Day 3

Poetry

T

Read aloud with the students the poem *"The Lamplighter"* (see Appendix). Say, *Describe a time you have been somewhere like this or felt like this. What can you learn about the poet, Robert Louis Stevenson, from the poem?* Say, *Did you know that at the time of Robert Louis Stevenson there wasn't any electricity, and so there really were lamplighters? I wonder if the lamplighter's name really was Leerie?* Have the students read the poem on their own.

Key Idea: Read and appreciate classic poetry.

Language Arts

S

Have students complete one studied dictation exercise (see Appendix for directions and passages).

Help students complete one lesson from the following reading program:

★ *Drawn into the Heart of Reading*

Work with the students to complete **one** of the English options listed below:

★ *Beginning Wisely:* Lesson 74

★ *Building with Diligence:* Lesson 74

★ Your own grammar program

Key Idea: Practice language arts skills.

Bible Study

T

Say, *You will be having your own quiet time with God today. Choose a quiet place for this special time, where you can be alone with God. Then, do the following things:*

1. Read Psalm 119:169-175 in your Bible.
2. Pray about the Psalm using the following beginning to your prayer: *Thank you for this special prayer time with you. Help me to delight in your word by ______ and ______. Help my soul to praise you by ______. Give me a longing for salvation.*
3. Recite Psalm 119:169-175 using the hand motions you added on Day 1.
4. Sing Psalm 119:169-175 along with the CD at the end of your quiet time.

✔ *Lead Me to the Rock* CD
Track 3; Song: "According to Your Word" (vs. 169-175)

Key Idea: Our souls were made to praise God.

Math Exploration

S

Choose **one** of the math options listed below (see Appendix for details).

★ *Singapore Primary Mathematics 2A/2B, 3A/3B,* or *4A/4B*

★ Your own math program

Key Idea: Use a step-by-step math program.

Science Exploration

I

★ Read *Find the Constellations* p. 42-43. Write the answer to each numbered question on lined paper. You do not need to copy the question. Use the listed page to help you answer each question.

1. What was the name of the great hunter in this myth, and about what did he brag? (p. 42)
2. What did Aesculapius the physician supposedly do? Could this really be true? (p. 42)
3. Why was Pluto, King of the Dead, so worried? (p. 42)
4. Which characters from the myth were put into the sky among the stars? (p. 42)
5. What can we learn about the constellations in Isaiah 40:25-26?

Key Idea: The gods of the Greek myths do not begin to compare to the living God who created all things. There is no one who is His equal. His word shows that He brings forth each star and calls it by name.

Reading about History [T]

Read about history in the following resource:

★ *Grandpa's Box: Ch. 38* p. 247-253

After today's reading, say, *You will be writing a narration about part of the day's history reading. In order to remember the details very well, you will need to reread the part of today's reading from p. 251 through p. 252 (on your own if possible).*

After students have finished reading the passage, ask them the questions below. If the students do not know the answers, help them find the answers in the passage they just read. Ask, *What is a Gentile?* (If needed, look this up in a dictionary.) Ask, *Who came to see Peter? When the 3 Gentile men came to the door, why did Peter go with them? Why did the Roman centurion send for Peter? As Peter shared the gospel of Jesus, what happened? How did God show that the gospel of Jesus was for everyone? Why was Peter so amazed? Would you be considered a Gentile?*

After the questions have been answered, have students write a 3-5 sentence narration. You may wish to list the key words *Gentiles, Peter, Cornelius, centurion,* and *Holy Spirit* for students. When students have finished their narration, direct them to read the sentences out loud. Ask, *Did you include **who** the reading was mainly about? Did you include **what** important thing(s) happened? Did you include **how** it ended?*

Help students underline or highlight the main idea sentence in their narration. See the *Written Narration Skills* in the Appendix to guide students in editing their narrations.

Key Idea: Peter did as the Spirit directed him.

Storytime [T]

Read aloud the following assigned passage:

★ *Fountain of Life: Ch. 23-24*

After today's reading, have your students orally narrate or retell the portion of today's text that you read. Use the *Narration Tips* in the Appendix as needed.

Key Idea: Practice oral narration skills.

Timeline [S]

You will be adding a new card to your staircase timeline today. On your new card, draw and color a bright light shining from heaven. Write, *Saul's conversion on the Road to Damascus (35 A.D).*

If you decided to tape your timeline cards to the back of a door, then add *Saul's conversion on the Road to Damascus* card to the left of the *Death and Resurrection of Jesus* card. If you decided to tape the timeline cards side-by-side to accordion-fold them, use clear packing tape to tape the cards as described above. Then, accordion-fold the timeline to store it.

Key Idea: After the vision Peter received from God, he went with the 3 Gentile men who were sent by the Roman centurion. Peter was amazed that God wanted the Gentiles to believe and receive the Holy Spirit just like the Jews. The good news of Jesus is for everyone. At first, this was difficult for Jewish Christians to understand, and it caused some problems within the church. But, God's message is clear. Salvation is available to all.

Independent History Study [I]

★ Read *The Young Christian's Introduction to the Bible* p. 49-51. Then, choose an interesting part from today's pages to read aloud and explain to an adult.

Key Idea: At first, Peter and the disciples preached only to the Jews. But, later they preached to everyone.

Learning the Basics

Focus: Language Arts, Math, Bible, and Science

Unit 20 - Day 4

Poetry

T

Read aloud with the students the poem *"The Lamplighter"* (see Appendix). Have students share this poem in a special way. Suggestions for sharing the poem include recording it to play for someone, reading it to someone on the telephone, photocopying the poem and adding illustrations, reading it to someone at home, putting the poem to a melody and singing it, using an instrument to tap out the meter or rhythm of the poem while reading it, or copying the poem on paper.

Key Idea: Share a variety of classic poetry.

Bible Study

T

Have students say Psalm 119:169-175 using the hand motions from Day 1.

Have students copy in cursive Psalm 119:174-175 beneath last unit's Psalm 119:171-173 in their *Common Place Book*. Students should leave the rest of the page blank to add to next week.

Students will add to the *Common Place Book* throughout the year.

 *Lead Me to the Rock* CD
Track 3; Song: "According to Thy Word" (vs. 169-175)

Key Idea: Copy in cursive a portion of a Psalm.

Language Arts

S

Have students complete one dictation exercise.

Guide students to complete one reading lesson.

★ *Drawn into the Heart of Reading*

Help students complete **one** English lesson.

★ *Beginning Wisely:* Lesson 75

★ *Building with Diligence:* Lesson 75

★ Your own grammar program

Key Idea: Practice language arts skills.

Math Exploration

S

Choose **one** math option listed below.

★ *Singapore Primary Mathematics 2A/2B, 3A/3B,* or *4A/4B*

★ Your own math program

Key Idea: Use a step-by-step math program.

Science Exploration

I

★ Read *Find the Constellations* p. 44-45. Turn to the science experiment section in your science binder or sketchbook. At the top of a blank page, write: *Why do the stars appear to rise and set?* Under the question, write: *'Guess'*. Write down your guess. Tape a tiny toy person to a ball. The ball will be Earth, and the person will be you. Place a 4" square piece of foil on several layers of paper towels. Use a toothpick to poke holes in the foil to outline the constellation "The Scorpion" as shown on p. 17 of *Find the Constellations*. Then, place the foil over the end of a flashlight. This will be a constellation in the night sky. Place the ball in the center of a table in a darkened room. Lay the flashlight on the table and turn it on facing the ball. Make sure the person on the Earth is turned away the flashlight. Since the Earth rotates from west to east, slowly turn the ball counterclockwise. As the person begins to see the constellation it appears to be rising in the east. As the Earth continues to rotate, the constellation appears to set in the west. On your paper, write: *'Procedure'*. Draw a picture of the experiment. At the bottom of the paper, write: *'Conclusion'*. Explain what you learned.

Key Idea: The stars appear to rise and set in the night sky due to the rotation of the Earth.

Learning through History
Focus: The Christians Are Persecuted

Unit 21 - Day 1

Reading about History [T]

Read about history in the following resource:

★ *Grandpa's Box: Ch. 39* p. 254-260

Note: You may want to reword the content on p. 259.

After today's reading, say, *Why did Herod go after the followers of Jesus?* (analysis) *Who was the first of Jesus' 12 apostles to die for his faith?* (knowledge) *Tell how God miraculously saved Peter.* (comprehension) *How did God make use of Herod to show Christians His power?* (application) *Can you explain why Herod was struck down dead?* (synthesis)

Key Idea: Herod began persecuting Christians. He put the apostle James to death. But, God saved Peter from Herod with a miraculous prison escape. Later, Herod was struck down.

History Project [S]

In this unit you will make a mosaic picture of the cross. The Romans used brightly colored glass to make their mosaics. You will use paper instead. On black paper, use your pencil to lightly make a large outline of a cross. Then, behind the cross outline large clouds with sunshine rays coming out of them. Decide what color you would like the cross to be. From a magazine, cut out color squares that match the color you chose. The mosaic squares should all be shades of that same color. Glue the squares on the outline of the cross, leaving black space between each square. Save the rest for Day 2.

Key Idea: After Christ's death, the apostles persevered in spite of much persecution.

Storytime [T]

Read aloud the following assigned story:

★ *Fountain of Life: Ch. 25*

Discuss today's reading in a "conversational way". Share about a person, time, event, or emotion from your life that today's reading brought to mind. Next, have your child share a connection.

Key Idea: Connect personally to the story.

Research [S]

During Roman times, mosaics were a common type of art. Where could you look to discover more about **mosaics**? Use a reference book or an online resource like www.wikipedia.org to look up *mosaic*. Depending on the resource you use, you will have to type *mosaic* in the search or look it up in the index.

Orally answer one or more of the following questions from your research: *What are mosaics? What types of pictures were often used in mosaics? During what time period were mosaics popular? In which cultures were mosaics popular? Where could mosaics be found? What popular mosaic was used on the threshold to Roman villas? At the time of the Renaissance, what replaced mosaics as an art form?*

Key Idea: In Rome, mosaics were a popular art form. *Beware of the dog,* was one common mosaic used in entrances. Later, many mosaics were used in churches and cathedrals. These mosaics often showed stories from the Bible or images of Christ.

Independent History Study [I]

★ Choose one story from the list on p. 52-54 of *The Young Christian's Introduction to the Bible* to read from your Bible. Then, orally retell or narrate to an adult the portion of text that you read today. Use the *Narration Tips* in the Appendix for help as needed.

Key Idea: Christianity spread even during times of persecution. People were willing to die for their Lord.

Learning the Basics

Focus: Language Arts, Math, Bible, and Science

Poetry

T

Read aloud to the students the poem *"The Wind"* (see Appendix). Say, *How does the way the child speaks about the wind make you feel like it's a person? What lines do you see repeated in the poem? Why do you think the poet chose to repeat those lines? How does the child in the poem know when the wind is near, even though he cannot see the wind? In the last stanza, what questions does the child ask?* Read the poem again with the students.

Key Idea: Read and appreciate classic poetry.

Language Arts

S

Have students complete the first studied dictation exercise (see Appendix for directions and passages).

Help students complete one lesson from the following reading program:

★ *Drawn into the Heart of Reading*

Work with the students to complete **one** of the English options listed below:

★ *Beginning Wisely:* Review One p. 186-188

★ *Building with Diligence:* Lesson 76 (half)

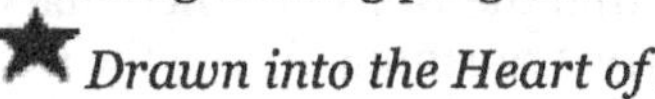

★ Your own grammar program

Key Idea: Practice language arts skills.

Bible Study

T

Say, *Find Psalm 119:169-176 in your Bible. This is the memory selection for this unit. Read the verses out loud.* Ask, *What does David say he has done in Psalm 119:176? Why do we "go astray like lost sheep" even though we are Christians? Even though he has sinned, what does David ask God to do for him in Psalm 119:176? Why would the Lord seek us, even when we are sinning? Why is it important to remember the Lord's commandments and His word? How does remembering the Lord's words show us what is right? What can we learn from Psalm 119:176 about how to act when we have sinned?* Have students say the verse 3 times, adding hand motions to help remember the words.

✔ *Lead Me to the Rock* CD
Track 3; Song: "According to Thy Word" (vs. 169-176)

Key Idea: The Lord seeks us and forgives us.

Math Exploration

S

Choose **one** of the math options listed below (see Appendix for details).

★ *Singapore Primary Mathematics 2A/2B, 3A/3B,* or *4A/4B*

★ Your own math program

Key Idea: Use a step-by-step math program.

Science Exploration

I

★ Read *Find the Constellations* p. 46-47. Get your book about the stars that you began in Unit 16. On the top of the next clean page in your book, copy in cursive Job 26:13. Beneath the verse, draw one or more of the following constellations: Andromeda (p. 41), Pegasus (p. 41), The Whale (p. 41), The Serpent Holder (p. 43), The Hare (p. 43), Hercules (p. 47), or The Dolphin (p. 47). Make sure to draw the brighter stars larger as shown in the pictures. Label each constellation with its name. You may trace the constellations if you wish. Save your book for next week.

Key Idea: The serpent constellation is mentioned in Job. God formed each star and its pattern in the sky.

Learning through History

Focus: The Christians Are Persecuted

Unit 21 - Day 2

Reading about History

T

Read about history in the following resource:

★ *Grandpa's Box: Ch. 40* p. 261-267

After today's reading, read aloud Acts 13:2-12. Ask, *In Acts 13:2, who does it say was set apart for ministry? On this first missionary journey, Saul was now called Paul. Where were Barnabas and Paul preaching in Acts 13:5? Whom did they meet in Acts 13:6? What did the sorcerer do in Acts 13:8? What did Paul say about the sorcerer in Acts 13:10? What consequence was given to the sorcerer by God in Acts 13:11? What effect did that have on the proconsul or deputy in Acts 13:12? What can we learn about how God views sorcery from this passage?*

Key Idea: God chose Paul and other disciples for ministry. He equipped them to be strong in the face of the opposition that surrounded them daily. The Holy Spirit guided and directed the disciples as they shared the gospel with others.

History Project

S

Get your cross mosaic that you began on Day 1. Decide what color you would like the clouds to be. Make sure to choose a different color than the cross. From a magazine, cut out color squares that match the color you chose. The mosaic squares should all be shades of that same color. Glue the squares on the outline of the clouds, leaving black space between each square. Wait to do the sunshine rays on Day 3.

Key Idea: Paul endured beatings, prison, earthquakes, shipwrecks, and stonings while spreading the news of Christ.

Storytime

T

Read aloud the following assigned passage:

★ *Fountain of Life: Ch. 26*

Ask, *In what does the main character place his faith? If you were alive at the time of Jesus, why would it be difficult to understand the resurrection? Share a character, a story, or a verse from the Bible that you are reminded of by the reading.*

Key Idea: Share a Biblical connection.

Vocabulary

S

You may choose 3-5 of the following vocabulary words from *Grandpa's Box* to use for this lesson: *correspondent* (p. 262), *gospel* (p. 263), *skeptically* (p. 263), *eyewitnesses* (p. 263), and/or *stocks* (p. 266). First, find the word in the text and read the sentence containing the word. Think about possible meanings. Next, find the word in a dictionary and select the correct meaning. Write the word at the top of an index card or at the top of the corresponding letter page in the notebook. Underneath the word, copy the correct definition from the dictionary. Then, use the word correctly in a sentence. The sentence may either be copied from the text or be one of your own creation. Last, draw a small picture to show the word's meaning. If you used an index card to record your word, file it under the correct alphabetical tab.

Key Idea: Luke wrote the book of Acts. He was a Greek, Gentile physician (or doctor). He was a companion and close friend of Paul's. Luke also wrote the gospel of Luke.

Independent History Study

I

★ Read *The Young Christian's Introduction to the Bible* p. 14-17. Then, copy 1 Peter 1:24-25 in cursive onto a clean page in your *Common Place Book*.

Key Idea: We are so blessed to have God's Word to read. We should never forget that it is very special.

Learning the Basics

Focus: Language Arts, Math, Bible, and Science

Language Arts

T

Work with the students to complete **one** of the English options listed below:

★ *Beginning Wisely:* Review Two p. 188-190

★ *Building with Diligence:* Lesson 76 (half)

★ Your own grammar program

Say, *You will be doing a writing activity based on the poem, "The Wind"* (see Appendix). Say, *Personification means giving human qualities to something that is not human. What human qualities were given to the wind in the poem?* (i.e. toss the kites, heard you pass, hid, push, call, young or old, beast of field and tree)

Say, *You will choose rain, snow, or fog to describe using personification.* At the top of a markerboard or a paper, make 3 columns labeled *"I saw you...", "I heard you....',* and *"I felt you...".* Say, *List human actions or qualities that you could give to the type of weather that you chose to describe* (rain, snow, or fog). Write the students' responses under the correct heading as they share their ideas. For example for rain, students might list, *I saw you running down the window panes. I heard you thundering through the sky. I felt you slipping down into the Earth's cracks and crevices.*

Next, say, *Use the words we listed to help you write your poem or paragraph. Begin your first line, "I saw you....". Refer to the poem "The Wind" for ideas as needed.* Students may also wish to have a repetitive line like the one in the poem.

Key Idea: Write creatively from classic poetry.

Bible Study

T

Have students say Psalm 119:169-176 using the hand motions they added on Day 1. Say, *A mood is a feeling, a sensation, or a state of mind. What is the mood of Psalm 119:176?* (Some examples of moods include frightened, worried, happy, peaceful, hopeful, sad, unhappy, angry, thankful, prayerful, joyful, and lonely.) Ask, *When would this Psalm help you, or when would you go to this Psalm?* (i.e. to remind us that it is easy to go astray from the Lord all throughout our lives, to show us that we need to continually seek the Lord, to help us know how important God's words and His commandments are in keeping us from straying too far from the Lord.)

Last, pray with your children that they will not stray far from the Lord. Pray that they will keep God's word in their hearts. Pray that they will seek God and that God will seek them.

✔ *Lead Me to the Rock* CD
Track 3; Song: "According to Thy Word"
(vs. 169-176)

Key Idea: The Psalms reflect the many emotions and moods we have.

Math Exploration

S

Choose **one** of the math options listed below (see Appendix for details).

★ *Singapore Primary Mathematics 2A/2B, 3A/3B, or 4A/4B*

★ Your own math program

Key Idea: Use a step-by-step math program.

Science Exploration

I

★ Read *Find the Constellations* p. 48-49. Orally retell or narrate to an adult the portion of text that you read today. Use the *Narration Tips* in the Appendix for help as needed.

Key Idea: Each star in the sky appears to rise and set about 4 minutes earlier than it did on the previous day. This means that after one year, the stars are back to rising and setting at the same time they did a year ago.

Learning through History
Focus: The Christians Are Persecuted

Unit 21 - Day 3

Reading about History | T

Read about history in the following resource:

★ *Grandpa's Box: Ch. 41* p. 268-274

After today's reading, have your students orally narrate or retell the portion of today's text that you read. Use the *Narration Tips* in the Appendix as needed.

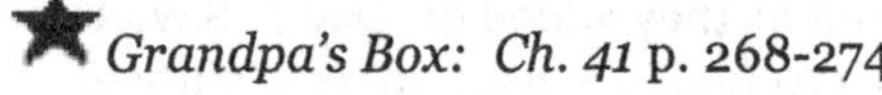

Key Idea: When Paul returned to Jerusalem the Jews tried to kill him. They were upset that he was preaching to Gentiles, and they thought he was encouraging disobedience to the Jewish law. Paul used his rights as a Roman citizen to eventually request a trial before Caesar.

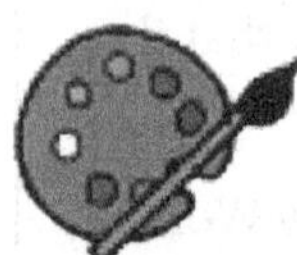

History Project | S

Get your cross mosaic that you began on Days 1-2. Decide what color you would like the sunshine rays coming out of the clouds to be. Make sure to choose a different color than the clouds or the cross. From a magazine, cut out color squares that match the color you chose. The mosaic squares should all be shades of that same color. Glue the squares on the outline of the sunshine rays, leaving black space between each square. Lay your mosaic flat to dry.

Key Idea: Even though Paul waited for his trial for 2 years in Rome, he was allowed to rent a small house, have visitors, and send letters. Paul continued to spread the gospel of Jesus and His resurrection during his time in Rome. Paul trusted in God's plan.

Storytime | T

Read aloud the following assigned passage:

★ *Fountain of Life: Ch. 27-28*

Ask, *In today's reading, how were people's lives different from your life? What would you have enjoyed or found difficult about living during that time?*

Key Idea: Compare and contrast the historical time period of the reading to your own life.

Geography | S

Use a globe or a Bible atlas for today's lesson. *Trace Paul's voyage to Rome. Start from Caesarea in Israel (between modern-day Tel-Aviv and Haifa) on the Mediterranean Sea. Go up the coast of Syria and west across the coast of Turkey. Next, travel around the south side of the island of Crete to Malta (which is a tiny island off the coast of Italy). This is where the ship Paul was on was wrecked. Next, travel up the eastern coast of Sicily and through the Strait of Messina (which is a narrow section of water between Sicily and Italy). Then, travel up the western coast of Italy to Rome. As you trace Paul's journey, what do you notice about how far the gospel was spread compared to where it had been shared before?*

Introduce the following concept: *Lines of latitude are parallel to the equator. They are also called parallels. Find the lines of latitude on the globe.*

Key Idea: Paul traveled to Rome from Caesarea. God had revealed to Paul that he would go to Rome to share the gospel.

Independent History Study | I

★ Read Revelations 22:1-5. Then, on white paper, draw and color a picture of heaven that matches the Biblical description you just read. Store your completed picture with your other notebooking assignments.

Key Idea: Paul knew that one day all believers will be with Jesus in heaven. Do you believe in Jesus?

Learning the Basics

Focus: Language Arts, Math, Bible, and Science

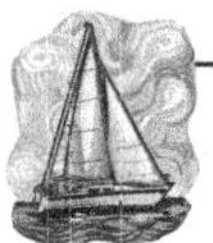

Poetry

T

Read aloud with the students the poem *"The Wind"* (see Appendix). Say, *Describe a time you have been somewhere like this or felt like this. What can you learn about the poet, Robert Louis Stevenson, from the poem?* Say, *Did you know that Robert Louis Stevenson loved the outdoors? He also loved thinking and pondering about things. Many of his poems are filled with wondering questions.* Have the students read the poem on their own.

Key Idea: Read and appreciate classic poetry.

Language Arts

S

Have students complete one studied dictation exercise (see Appendix for directions and passages).

Help students complete one lesson from the following reading program:

★ *Drawn into the Heart of Reading*

Work with the students to complete **one** of the English options listed below:

★ *Beginning Wisely:* A Poem... p. 192-193

★ *Building with Diligence:* Lesson 77

★ Your own grammar program

Key Idea: Practice language arts skills.

Bible Study

T

Say, *You will be having your own quiet time with God today. Choose a quiet place for this special time, where you can be alone with God. Then, do the following things:*

1. Read Psalm 119:169-176 in your Bible.
2. Pray about the Psalm using the following beginning to your prayer: *Thank you for seeking me even when I sin. I'm sorry for _______. When I sin, help me to _______. Keep me close to you by _______.*
3. Recite Psalm 119:169-176 using the hand motions you added on Day 1.
4. Sing Psalm 119:169-176 along with the CD at the end of your quiet time.

✔ *Lead Me to the Rock* CD
Track 3; Song: "According to Your Word" (vs. 169-176)

Key Idea: We need to seek the Lord when we have sinned. His word draws us closer to Him.

Math Exploration

S

Choose **one** of the math options listed below (see Appendix for details).

★ *Singapore Primary Mathematics 2A/2B, 3A/3B,* or *4A/4B*

★ Your own math program

Key Idea: Use a step-by-step math program.

Science Exploration

I

★ Read *Find the Constellations* p. 50-53. **Note: Skip the first sentence on p. 52.** Write the answer to each numbered question on lined paper. You do not need to copy the question. Use the listed page to help you answer each question.

1. What is the most distant object that can be seen with the naked eye? (p. 50-51)
2. Where can the Nebula be found? (p. 50)
3. What is a Galaxy? (p. 51)
4. What is on the rim of our Galaxy? (p. 53)
5. How does Jeremiah 33:22 describe the stars and to what are they compared?

Key Idea: We can barely see the Nebula as a faint, hazy light near Andromeda. It's actually a Galaxy!

Learning through History
Focus: The Christians Are Persecuted

Unit 21 - Day 4

Reading about History [T]

Read about history in the following resource:

★ *Grandpa's Box: Ch. 42* p. 275-280

After today's reading, say, *You will be writing a narration about part of the day's history reading. In order to remember the details very well, you will need to reread the part of today's reading from the second paragraph on p. 279 through p. 280 (on your own if possible).*

After students have finished reading the passage, ask them the questions below. If the students do not know the answers, help them find the answers in the passage they just read. Ask, *What things make it hard for Christians to trust in God? What did John see? In John's vision, how was evil punished? How was Jesus shown in John's vision? What was Jesus doing in the vision? What can we learn from John's vision?*

After the questions have been answered, have students write a 3-5 sentence narration. When students have finished their narration, direct them to read the sentences out loud. Ask, *Did you include **who** the reading was mainly about? Did you include **what** important thing(s) happened? Did you include **how** it ended?*

Help students underline or highlight the main idea sentence in their narration. See the *Written Narration Skills* in the Appendix to guide students in editing their narrations.

Key Idea: John was exiled, or sent away, to the island of Patmos. While he was there, God gave him the vision that we find in the book of Revelations. Through Revelations, we can get a glimpse of heaven.

Storytime [T]

Read aloud the following assigned passage:

★ *Fountain of Life: Ch. 29*

After today's reading, have your students orally narrate or retell the portion of today's text that you read. Use the *Narration Tips* in the Appendix as needed.

Key Idea: Practice oral narration skills.

Timeline [S]

You will be adding 2 new cards to your staircase timeline today. On the first new card, draw and color a little house. Write, *Apostle Paul is martyred (approximately 67 A.D.).* On the second new card, draw and color blackness to stand for the angry persecution of Christians. Write, *Nero is emperor of Rome (37 – 68 A.D.)*

If you decided to tape your timeline cards to the back of a door, then add the *Apostle Paul is martyred* card to the left of the *Saul's conversion on the Road to Damascus* card. To the left of the *Apostle Paul is martyred* card, add the *Nero is emperor of Rome* card. If you decided to tape the timeline cards side-by-side to accordion-fold them, use clear packing tape to tape the cards as described above. Then, accordion-fold the timeline to store it.

Key Idea: God gives us assurance through His Word that He is in charge of all of history. Even though Satan is working hard to fight it, God's plan is still unfolding right on schedule. We can trust in God, no matter how evil the world becomes around us.

Independent History Study [I]

★ Read Revelations 21:3-4 and 22:6-21. Then, choose an interesting part from today's pages to read aloud and explain to an adult.

Key Idea: As believers of Jesus Christ, we can trust that one day we will be in heaven with Him.

Learning the Basics

Focus: Language Arts, Math, Bible, and Science

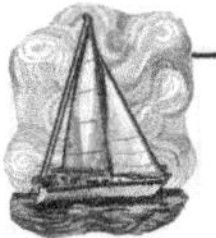

Poetry

T

Read aloud with the students the poem *"The Wind"* (see Appendix). Have students share this poem in a special way. Suggestions for sharing the poem include recording it to play for someone, reading it to someone on the telephone, photocopying the poem and adding illustrations, reading it to someone at home, putting the poem to a melody and singing it, using an instrument to tap out the meter or rhythm of the poem while reading it, or copying the poem on paper.

Key Idea: Share a variety of classic poetry.

Language Arts

S

Have students complete one dictation exercise.

Guide students to complete one reading lesson.

★ *Drawn into the Heart of Reading*

Help students complete **one** English lesson.

★ *Beginning Wisely:* Lesson 76

★ *Building with Diligence:* Lesson 78

★ Your own grammar program

Key Idea: Practice language arts skills.

Bible Study

T

Have students say Psalm 119:169-176 using the hand motions from Day 1.

Have students copy in cursive Psalm 119:176 beneath last unit's Psalm 119:174-175 in their *Common Place Book.*

Students will add to the *Common Place Book* throughout the year.

✔ *Lead Me to the Rock* CD
Track 3; Song: "According to Thy Word" (vs. 169-176)

Key Idea: Copy in cursive a portion of a Psalm.

Math Exploration

S

Choose **one** math option listed below.

★ *Singapore Primary Mathematics 2A/2B, 3A/3B,* or *4A/4B*

★ Your own math program

Key Idea: Use a step-by-step math program.

Science Exploration

I

★ Read *Find the Constellations* p. 54-55. Turn to the science experiment section in your science binder or sketchbook. At the top of a blank page, write: *If the Sun is not the largest star, then why does it look so big?* Under the question, write: *'Guess'.* Write down your guess. Place a medium-sized plate face down on a sheet of white paper, and trace around it. Cut out the circle. Next, fold your paper circle in half, and cut a half-circle out of the folded side. Then, open both papers. You should have a large circular frame and a smaller circle. Color the smaller circle yellow to be the Sun. Now, you will need a partner for this next part. Have your partner stand a few feet away from you, holding up the circle to be the Sun. Then, you hold the frame at arm's length, moving it until you can see the Sun within the frame. Notice the size of the Sun. Next, have your partner back up across the room and hold up the Sun again. You hold your frame at arm's length again, moving it until you can see the Sun within the frame. What do you notice about the size of the Sun? Why does it appear smaller? Is it really any smaller? Write: *'Procedure'.* Draw a picture of the experiment. At the bottom of the paper, write: *'Conclusion'.* Explain what you learned.

Key Idea: The Sun appears larger than other stars because it is closer to Earth.

Learning through History

Focus: Roman Emperors and Christianity

Unit 22 - Day 1

Reading about History — T

Read about history in the following resource:

★ *A Child's History of the World: Ch. 36* p. 155-158

After today's reading, say, *How were Augustus Caesar and Jesus different?* (analysis) *Can a man really become a god? Explain.* (analysis) *How do we know that Jesus is the Son of the one true God?* (evaluation) *Why were there so many different religions in the Roman Empire?* (analysis) *Are there still many religions today?* (knowledge) *Then, how do we know that Christianity is the one true religion of the living God?* (application)

Key Idea: Jesus and Augustus Caesar lived at the same time. Who was the true king?

History Project — S

In this unit you will make a golden laurel wreath like the one that the commander or emperor would wear in a triumph. Cut a narrow strip of heavy paper that is long enough to circle your head. You may have to tape two strips of paper together to make it long enough. Staple the ends of the strip together in a circle. Make sure it fits on your head. On heavy paper, draw an outline of a laurel leaf and cut it out to use for a pattern. The bay leaf is the type of laurel leaf that was often used in wreaths. Trace the leaf pattern on yellow or gold paper to make 10-15 leaves. You will need enough to cover the paper strip. Cut the leaves out. Save them for Day 2.

Key Idea: Jesus will be King over all the earth.

Storytime — T

Read aloud the following assigned story:

★ *Fountain of Life: Ch. 30*

Discuss today's reading in a "conversational way". Share about a person, time, event, or emotion from your life that today's reading brought to mind. Next, have your child share a connection.

Key Idea: Connect personally to the story.

Research — S

During Roman times, a triumph was held to honor conquering military generals upon their return home. Where could you look to discover more about a **triumph**? Use a reference book or an online resource like www.wikipedia.org to look up *Roman triumph*. Depending on the resource you use, you will have to type *Roman triumph* in the search or look it up in the index.

Orally answer one or more of the following questions from your research: *What was a triumph? How was it decided who received a triumph? What was the order of the parade for the triumph? Describe what the army wore in the triumph. What was held above the imperator's, or commander's, head throughout the triumph? Why would a slave whisper in the commander's ear throughout the triumph?*

Key Idea: In Rome, conquering commanders were sometimes given triumphs to celebrate their military victory. Later, it became law that only Roman emperors could have a triumph. The golden laurel wreath eventually became a crown, symbolizing royalty and power.

Independent History Study — I

★ Read Matthew 28:1-20. Then, orally retell or narrate to an adult the portion of text that you read today. Use the *Narration Tips* in the Appendix for help as needed.

Key Idea: Jesus told the apostles to spread the news of salvation to all nations. It wasn't just for the Jews.

Learning the Basics

Focus: Language Arts, Math, Bible, and Science

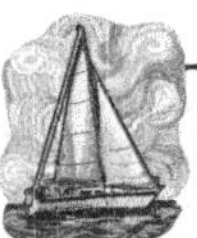

Poetry

T

Read aloud to the students the poem *"Block City"* (see Appendix). Say, *What is the child in the poem doing? Describe the city the child is building out of blocks. What happens to the city in the fifth stanza of the poem? How does the child feel at the end of the poem? What things can you fondly remember building?* Read the poem again with the students.

Key Idea: Read and appreciate classic poetry.

Language Arts

S

Have students complete the first studied dictation exercise (see Appendix for directions and passages).

Help students complete one lesson from the following reading program:

★ *Drawn into the Heart of Reading*

Work with the students to complete **one** of the English options listed below:

★ *Beginning Wisely:* Lesson 77

★ *Building with Diligence:* Lesson 79

★ Your own grammar program

Key Idea: Practice language arts skills.

Bible Study

T

Say, *Find Psalm 8:1 in your Bible. This is the memory selection for this unit. Read the verse out loud.* Ask, *How is the Lord's name described in Psalm 8:1? What does it mean if something is truly excellent? How can the Lord's name be excellent throughout all the Earth? How does this show the greatness of the Lord? What does Psalm 8:1 say that the Lord has done? Can anyone else do what the Lord has done? Why not?*

Have students say the verse 3 times, adding hand motions to help remember the words.

✔ *Lead Me to the Rock* CD
Track 8; Song: "How Excellent Is Thy Name" (vs. 1)

Key Idea: God is the all-powerful Creator. His majesty is all around us.

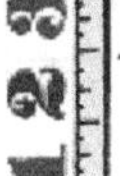

Math Exploration

S

Choose **one** of the math options listed below (see Appendix for details).

★ *Singapore Primary Mathematics 2A/2B, 3A/3B,* or *4A/4B*

★ Your own math program

Key Idea: Use a step-by-step math program.

Science Exploration

I

★ Read *Find the Constellations* p. 56. Get your book about the stars that you began in Unit 16. On the top of the next clean page in your book, copy in cursive 1 Corinthians 15:40. Beneath the verse, write the heading, *"The Solar System"*. Beneath the heading, draw a picture of the planets and their orbits from p. 57 of *Find the Constellations*. Make sure to label each planet. You may leave Pluto off your drawing, since it is no longer considered to be a planet.

Key Idea: Planets are different from stars. They are much closer to us than the stars. They do not have any light of their own. Instead, they reflect the Sun's light. The planets circle the Sun in paths called orbits.

Learning through History
Focus: Roman Emperors and Christianity

Unit 22 - Day 2

Reading about History **T**

Read about history in the following resource:

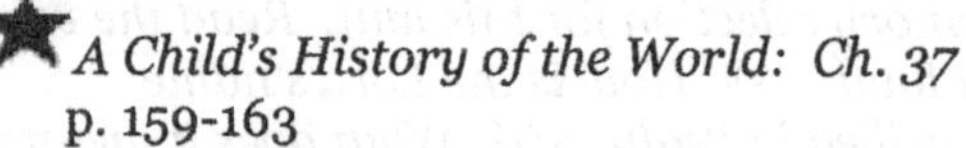

★ *A Child's History of the World: Ch. 37* p. 159-163

After today's reading, read aloud Luke 19:32-44. Ask, *What event is being described in Luke 19:32-38? Do you think the people understood that Jesus was not an earthly king? Why do you think the Pharisees told Jesus to quiet the people in Luke 19:39? Explain Jesus' answer in Luke 19:40. What does Jesus reveal about Jerusalem in Luke 19:43? What reason does Jesus give for the coming fall of Jerusalem in Luke 19:44? How did Jesus know that Titus would come to destroy Jerusalem almost 40 years later? What does this show us about God's plans?*

<u>Key Idea</u>: When Nero was emperor of Rome, he persecuted Christians. He blamed them for supposedly setting fire to Rome. Nero is remembered for his extravagance and violence.

History Project **S**

Get your golden leaves that you cut out on Day 1. Use a fine-tipped paintbrush and golden or light brown paint to outline each leaf. On each leaf, also paint a thin stem down the center and a few veins coming out from the stem. Lay the leaves flat to dry until Day 3.

<u>Key Idea</u>: During his time as emperor of Rome, Nero had a palace built that was known as Nero's House of Gold. He also had a huge bronze statue built of himself.

Storytime **T**

Read aloud the following assigned passage:

★ *Raiders from the Sea: Ch. 1*

Ask, *In today's reading, how were people's lives different from your life? What would you have enjoyed or found difficult about living during that time?*

<u>Key Idea</u>: Compare and contrast the historical time period of the reading to your own life.

Geography **S**

Use a globe for today's activities. *When the Jews rebelled against Roman rule, the Roman emperor's son, Titus, was sent from Rome to Jerusalem to stop the rebellion. He destroyed Jerusalem and the temple in 70 A.D. On the globe, trace the path from Rome to Jerusalem. Later, when Titus became emperor of Rome, Mt. Vesuvius erupted and buried the city of Pompeii. Find Mt. Vesuvius on the globe near Naples, Italy. Notice how close Mt. Vesuvius is to the city of Rome.*

Introduce the following concept: *Lines of latitude are parallel to the equator, so they are also called parallels. Find the following important parallels on the globe: Antarctic Circle, Arctic Circle, Equator, Tropic of Cancer (located 23 degrees north of the equator), Tropic of Capricorn (located 23 degrees south of the equator).*

<u>Key Idea</u>: Jesus prophesied the fall of Jerusalem long before it happened. He wept when He shared of the coming destruction.

Independent History Study **I**

★ Read 2 Corinthians 11:24-31 and 12:7-10. Then, copy 2 Corinthians 12:10 in cursive in your *Common Place Book.*

<u>Key Idea</u>: Paul was awaiting trial in Rome at the time of Nero. Nero is most likely the one who put both Peter and Paul to death, although we do not know for sure.

Learning the Basics

Focus: Language Arts, Math, Bible, and Science

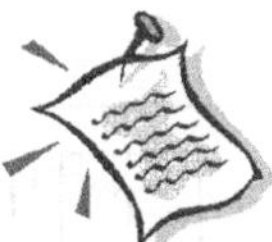

Language Arts

T

Work with the students to complete **one** of the English options listed below:

★ *Beginning Wisely:* Lesson 78

★ *Building with Diligence:* Lesson 80

★ Your own grammar program

Say, *You will be doing a writing activity based on the poem, "Block City"* (see Appendix). Say, *In the poem "Block City", Robert Louis Stevenson gives a very detailed description of how his block city looked. You will be writing a poem or a paragraph that gives a detailed picture of something that you have built for playtime in the past.*

On a markerboard or a paper, help students list some playscenes that they have built in the past (i.e. castle and knights, mountain with mountain climbers, doll house with dolls, barracks and soldiers, wild west town and cowboys, roads with vehicles, stables with horses, etc.).

Say, *Choose one of the ideas off the list to describe in detail in a poem or a paragraph. Begin your first line, "Once I built a....". Start your second sentence, "It was...". Refer to the poem "Block City" for ideas as needed.*

Help students as much as needed to be successful with their writing. Have students share their poem or their paragraph by reading it aloud.

Key Idea: Write creatively from classic poetry.

Bible Study

T

Have students say Psalm 8:1 using the hand motions they added on Day 1. Say, *A mood is a feeling, a sensation, or a state of mind. What is the mood of Psalm 8:1?* (Some examples of moods include frightened, worried, happy, peaceful, hopeful, sad, unhappy, angry, thankful, prayerful, joyful, and lonely.) Ask, *When would this Psalm help you, or when would you go to this Psalm?* (i.e. to remind us of the Lord's greatness and majesty, to show us that there is no one like Him, to help us to remember to praise Him.)

Last, pray with your children that they will see God's majesty all around them. Pray that they will glimpse how great our God is and how worthy He is to be praised.

✔ *Lead Me to the Rock* CD
Track 8; Song: "How Excellent Is Thy Name" (vs. 1)

Key Idea: The Psalms reflect the many emotions and moods we have. They are a wonderful place to seek counsel from the Lord.

Math Exploration

S

Choose **one** of the math options listed below (see Appendix for details).

★ *Singapore Primary Mathematics 2A/2B, 3A/3B,* or *4A/4B*

★ Your own math program

Key Idea: Use a step-by-step math program.

Science Exploration

I

★ Read *Find the Constellations* p. 57. Orally retell or narrate to an adult the portion of text that you read today. Use the *Narration Tips* in the Appendix for help as needed.

Key Idea: The planets are fixed in their orbits around the Sun. The amount of time it takes a planet to orbit the Sun is called a year. Each planet's year varies from another planet's year.

Learning through History

Focus: Roman Emperors and Christianity

Unit 22 - Day 3

Reading about History

T

Read about history in the following resource:

★ *A Child's History of the World: Ch. 38* p. 164-167

After today's reading, have your students orally narrate or retell the portion of today's text that you read. Use the *Narration Tips* in the Appendix as needed.

Key Idea: Marcus Aurelius was a famous Roman emperor. He was a Stoic who tried to do what was right, pursued wisdom, and tried to bear hardship or pain in silence. He wrote down his thoughts on how to live his life. He wanted to obey the laws of God. People can still read his words today.

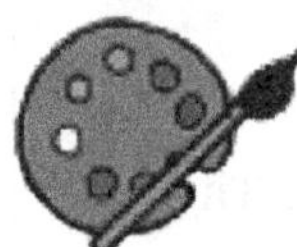

History Project

S

Get the golden leaves and the band you made for your crown on Days 1-2. Punch two holes about 2 inches apart in the center of the headband. Thread a ribbon or colored piece of yarn through the two holes and tie it in a bow that hangs down. This ribbon will be in the back when you place the wreath on your head. Then, use clear tape to tape the golden leaves around the outside of the band, alternating the angle of the leaves to cover the wreath. Your wreath is finished. Try it on! Do you feel like royalty?

Key Idea: Even though Marcus Aurelius was a good man, he was not a Christian. During his reign, Christians were still punishable by law, although they were not persecuted as much during this time.

Storytime

T

Read aloud the following assigned passage:

★ *Raiders from the Sea: Ch. 2-3*

Ask, *In what does the main character place her faith? How would the story be different if the main character didn't put her faith in God? Share a character, a story, or a verse from the Bible that you are reminded of by the reading.*

Key Idea: Share a Biblical connection.

Vocabulary

S

You may choose 3-5 of the following vocabulary words from *A Child's History of the World* to use for this lesson: *stoic* (p. 164), *murmur* (p. 165), *dissipated* (p. 166), *philosopher* (p. 166), and/or *superstition* (p. 167). First, find the word in the text and read the sentence containing the word. Think about possible meanings. Next, find the word in a dictionary and select the correct meaning. Write the word at the top of an index card or at the top of the corresponding letter page in the notebook. Underneath the word, copy the correct definition from the dictionary. Then, use the word correctly in a sentence. Last, draw a small picture to show the word's meaning. If you used an index card to record your word, file it under the correct alphabetical tab.

Key Idea: Marcus Aurelius's son, Commodus, was not like his father. He wanted to be worshiped as if he were a god. He was known for living a wild life and for seeking personal pleasure above all else.

Independent History Study

I

★ Copy one of the following quotes by Marcus Aurelius in your *Common Place Book:*

*For a man can lose neither the past nor the future; for how can one take from him that which is not his?

*How much time he gains who does not look to see what his neighbor says or does or thinks, but only at what he does himself, to make it just and holy.

Key Idea: There are good men who are not Christians. Goodness is not enough. Salvation is not earned.

Learning the Basics

Focus: Language Arts, Math, Bible, and Science

Poetry

T

Read aloud with the students the poem *"Block City"* (see Appendix). Say, *Describe a memory that the poem brought to mind. What can you learn about the poet, Robert Louis Stevenson, from the poem?* Say, *Did you know that as a child Robert Louis Stevenson loved adventure stories and enjoyed playing them out in his vivid imagination. When he grew up he wrote several very famous adventure stories.* Have the students read the poem on their own.

Key Idea: Read and appreciate classic poetry.

Language Arts

S

Have students complete one studied dictation exercise (see Appendix for directions and passages).

Help students complete one lesson from the following reading program:

★ *Drawn into the Heart of Reading*

Work with the students to complete **one** of the English options listed below:

★ *Beginning Wisely:* Lesson 79

★ *Building with Diligence:* Lesson 81

★ Your own grammar program

Key Idea: Practice language arts skills.

Bible Study

T

Say, *You will be having your own quiet time with God today. Choose a quiet place for this special time, where you can be alone with God. Then, do the following things:*

1. Read Psalm 8:1 in your Bible.
2. Pray about the Psalm using the following beginning to your prayer: *Thank you, Lord, for allowing me to see your majesty all around me in your creation. I praise you for the _____, _____, and _____. Help me to praise you with _____ and _____.*
3. Recite Psalm 8:1 using the hand motions you added on Day 1.
4. Sing Psalm 8:1 along with the CD at the end of your quiet time.

✔ *Lead Me to the Rock* CD
Track 8; Song: "How Excellent Is Thy Name" (vs. 1)

Key Idea: The Lord's greatness surrounds us.

Math Exploration

S

Choose **one** of the math options listed below (see Appendix for details).

★ *Singapore Primary Mathematics 2A/2B, 3A/3B,* or *4A/4B*

★ Your own math program

Key Idea: Use a step-by-step math program.

Science Exploration

I

★ Read *Find the Constellations* p. 58-59. **Note: Pluto is no longer considered to be a planet.** Write the answer to each numbered question on lined paper. You do not need to copy the question. Use the listed page to help you answer each question.

1. List the planets in order according to their distance from the Sun. (p. 58-59)
2. Which two planets are closest to Earth? (p. 58-59)
3. Name the planets that have moons. (p. 58-59)
4. Write two interesting facts about any of the planets. (p. 58-59)
5. What does Psalm 89:11 tell us about the heavens, the Earth, and all that is in them?

Key Idea: The planets in our solar system revolve around the Sun in a year. The Earth's year is 365 days.

Learning through History
Focus: Roman Emperors and Christianity

Unit 22 - Day 4

Reading about History | T

Read about history in the following resource:

★ *A Child's History of the World: Ch. 39* p. 168-170

Note: Omit the graphic content on p. 168.

After today's reading, say, *You will be writing a narration about part of the day's history reading. In order to remember the details very well, you will need to reread the part of today's reading from the last two paragraphs on p. 168 through p. 169 (on your own if possible).*

After students have finished reading the passage, ask them the questions below. If the students do not know the answers, help them find the answers in the passage they just read. Ask, *Who was the emperor of Rome in today's story? What dream did Constantine have? Why did Constantine make Christianity legal in the Roman Empire? Who was Constantine's mother? What did Constantine's mother, Helena, do? Where did Constantine build a church? What was the name of Constantine's main city, Byzantium, changed to instead?*

After the questions have been answered, have students write a 3-5 sentence narration about what they remember about Constantine. When students have finished their narration, direct them to read the sentences out loud. Ask, *Did you include **who** the reading was mainly about? Did you include **what** important thing(s) happened? Did you include **how** it ended?* Help students underline or highlight the main idea sentence in their narration. See the *Written Narration Skills* in the Appendix to guide students in editing their narrations.

Key Idea: Constantine made Christianity legal.

Storytime | T

Read aloud the following assigned passage:

★ *Raiders from the Sea: Ch. 4*

After today's reading, have your students orally narrate or retell the portion of today's text that you read. Use the *Narration Tips* as needed.

Key Idea: Practice oral narration skills.

Timeline | S

You will be adding 3 new cards to your staircase timeline today. On the first new card, draw and color a volcano erupting. Write, *Mt. Vesuvius erupts (79 A.D.).* On the second new card, draw and color a golden wreath. Write, *Marcus Aurelius is emperor of Rome (161-180 A.D.).* On the third new card, draw and color a cross. Write, *Constantine makes Christianity legal (approximately 300 A.D.).*

If you decided to tape your timeline cards to the back of a door, then add the *Mt. Vesuvius erupts* to the left of the *Apostle Paul is martyred* card. To the left of the *Mt. Vesuvius erupts* card, add the *Marcus Aurelius is emperor of Rome* card. To the left of the *Marcus Aurelius* card, add the *Constantine makes Christianity legal* card. If you decided to tape the timeline cards side-by-side to accordion-fold them, use clear packing tape to tape the cards as described above. Then, accordion-fold the timeline to store it.

Key Idea: Constantine had a dream with a flaming cross. He placed crosses on his soldier's shields and won a great victory in battle. After that he made Christianity legal in the Roman Empire.

Independent History Study | I

★ Read *Leif the Lucky* p. 1-9. Then, choose an interesting part from today's pages to read aloud and explain to an adult.

Key Idea: The Vikings began raiding parts of the Roman Empire. They were very superstitious.

Poetry

T

Read aloud with the students the poem *"Block City"* (see Appendix). Have students share this poem in a special way. Suggestions for sharing the poem include recording it to play for someone, reading it to someone on the telephone, photocopying the poem and adding illustrations, reading it to someone at home, putting the poem to a melody and singing it, using an instrument to tap out the meter or rhythm of the poem while reading it, or copying the poem on paper.

Key Idea: Share a variety of classic poetry.

Bible Study

T

Have students say Psalm 8:1 using the hand motions from Day 1.

Have students copy in cursive Psalm 8:1 onto a clean page in their *Common Place Book*. Students should leave the rest of the page blank to add to next week.

Students will add to the *Common Place Book* throughout the year.

✔ *Lead Me to the Rock* CD
Track 8; Song: "How Excellent Is Thy Name" (vs. 1)

Key Idea: Copy in cursive a portion of a Psalm.

Language Arts

S

Have students complete one dictation exercise.

Guide students to complete one reading lesson.

★ *Drawn into the Heart of Reading*

Help students complete **one** English lesson.

★ *Beginning Wisely:* Lesson 80

★ *Building with Diligence:* Lesson 82

★ Your own grammar program

Key Idea: Practice language arts skills.

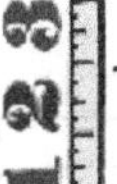

Math Exploration

S

Choose **one** math option listed below.

★ *Singapore Primary Mathematics 2A/2B, 3A/3B,* or *4A/4B*

★ Your own math program

Key Idea: Use a step-by-step math program.

Science Exploration

I

★ Read *Find the Constellations* p. 60-64. Turn to the science experiment section in your science binder or sketchbook. At the top of a blank page, write: *Why does the Moon shine in the night sky?* Under the question, write: *'Guess'*. Write down your guess.

You will need a flashlight, a handheld mirror, and a ball. Go into a large room. Place the mirror on the floor propped up against a wall or a piece of furniture, so it's facing out. Then, place the ball and the flashlight on the floor to form a large triangle with the mirror. Turn off the overhead light. Then, turn on the flashlight, and shine it on the mirror. Move the ball so that the light from the mirror is reflected on the ball. The ball represents the Earth, the flashlight represents the Sun, and the mirror represents the Moon's surface. What do you notice about the Moon's light? On your paper, write: *'Procedure'*. Draw a picture of the experiment. At the bottom of the paper, write: *'Conclusion'*. Explain what you learned.

Key Idea: The Moon gets its light from the Sun. When we see moonlight, we are actually seeing a reflection of the Sun's light off the surface of the Moon.

Learning through History
Focus: Barbarians Attack

Unit 23 - Day 1

Reading about History [T]

Read about history in the following resource:

★ *A Child's History of the World: Ch. 40* p. 171-175

After today's reading, say, *What was a barbarian?* (knowledge) *Describe what the barbarians valued or thought was good.* (comprehension) *Explain how you know the barbarians weren't Christians.* (synthesis) *Name some of the Germanic tribes.* (knowledge) *Tell what you know about the barbarians.* (comprehension)

Key Idea: The Romans were continually fighting the Germanic tribes from the north to keep them from crossing over the border into Roman territory.

History Project [S]

In this unit you will make a Viking brooch. If you have access to the internet, you may want to type *photo Viking brooch* in the search engine to see pictures of various brooches before designing your own. On heavy paper or cardboard, trace around the bottom of a glass to make a circle. Cut the circle out. This will be your brooch. Then, use pencil to draw a pattern on your brooch. Save your brooch for Day 2.

Key Idea: The Vikings wore brooches to fasten their cloaks and dresses. Depending on how wealthy a Viking was, brooches could be made of bronze, gold, silver, wood, or animal bones. They often had beautiful designs carved on them.

Storytime [T]

Read aloud the following assigned story:

★ *Raiders from the Sea: Ch. 5*

Discuss today's reading in a "conversational way". Share about a person, time, event, or emotion from your life that today's reading brought to mind. Next, have your child share a connection.

Key Idea: Connect personally to the story.

Research [S]

Viking men and women wore jewelry. One common type of Viking jewelry was the brooch. Where could you look to discover more about a **brooch**? Use a reference book or an online resource like www.wikipedia.org to look up *Viking brooch.* Depending on the resource you use, you will have to type *Viking brooch* in the search or look it up in the index.

Orally answer one or more of the following questions from your research: *What is a brooch? Of what were brooches made? With what were brooches often decorated? What was the purpose of a brooch? Describe some of the designs found on brooches. What did Viking women use brooches to do? Why did Viking men often only wear one brooch, instead of two, like the women?*

Key Idea: Romans called the invaders from the north barbarians. Many of the barbarians were very fierce. They prized bravery among all else. They chose their own chiefs and worshiped their own gods. Woden was their god of war. Thor was their god of thunder and lightning.

Independent History Study [I]

★ Read *Leif the Lucky* p. 10-17. Orally retell or narrate to an adult the portion of text that you read today. Use the *Narration Tips* in the Appendix for help as needed.

Key Idea: The Vikings made up stories about their gods battling and racing across the sky. In truth, they saw the Northern Lights, or *aurora borealis,* which are natural light displays in the polar nighttime sky.

Learning the Basics

Focus: Language Arts, Math, Bible, and Science

Unit 23 - Day 1

Poetry

T

Guide students to choose one of Robert Louis Stevenson's poems from Units 13-22 to memorize. Students will have 2 weeks (units) to memorize the entire poem. So, students should have half of their chosen poem memorized by Day 4 of this unit. After students have chosen their poem, have them read it 3 times, adding actions.

Key Idea: Read and appreciate classic poetry.

Language Arts

S

Have students complete the first studied dictation exercise (see Appendix for directions and passages).

Help students complete one lesson from the following reading program:

★ *Drawn into the Heart of Reading*

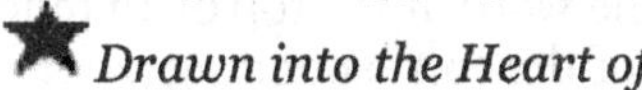

Work with the students to complete **one** of the English options listed below:

★ *Beginning Wisely:* Lesson 81

★ *Building with Diligence:* Lesson 83

★ Your own grammar program

Key Idea: Practice language arts skills.

Bible Study

T

Say, *Find Psalm 8:1-2 in your Bible. This is the memory selection for this unit. Read the verses out loud.* Ask, *What are some differences between the way children praise the Lord and the way adults praise the Lord? Why do you think Psalm 8:2 mentions the praise of babes and infants? What does it mean to have faith like a child? How can we keep that childlike trust and enthusiasm for the Lord, even as we grow up to be adults? In Psalm 8:2, who is the enemy or avenger? How can our praising God silence or still Satan, our enemy?*

Have students say the verse 3 times, adding hand motions to help remember the words.

✔ *Lead Me to the Rock* CD
Track 8; Song: "How Excellent Is Thy Name" (vs. 1-2)

Key Idea: Childlike faith means trusting the Lord and praising Him without holding back.

Math Exploration

S

Choose **one** of the math options listed below (see Appendix for details).

★ *Singapore Primary Mathematics 2A/2B, 3A/3B*, or *4A/4B*

★ Your own math program

Key Idea: Use a step-by-step math program.

Science Exploration

I

★ Read *One Small Square: Coral Reef* p. 3-5 and p. 38-39. Today you will add to your science notebook. At the top of an unlined paper, copy Psalm 24:1-2 in cursive. Beneath the verse, draw or trace the map from p. 38-39 of *One Small Square: Coral Reef*. Color the coral reefs light green. Copy the **first** paragraph shown on p. 38 beneath your picture. Look on a real globe to see where the coral reefs are found.

Key Idea: The Great Barrier Reef is located off the coast of Australia. It is a "barrier" reef because it is out in the sea, separated from land by a lagoon. It is like a wall or a barrier to passing ships or submarines.

Unit 23 - Day 2

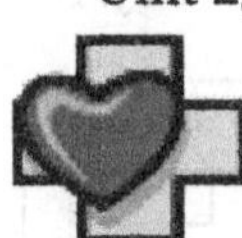

Reading about History T

Read about history in the following resource:

★ *A Child's History of the World: Ch. 41* p. 176-179

After today's reading, read aloud 2 Peter 1:12 – 2:1. Ask, *In 2 Peter 1:16, what is Peter reminding us to remember when we read God's Word? How does Peter know in 2 Peter 1:17-18 that the stories of Jesus are not invented fables? Explain how this is different from the stories of other gods such as the Greek gods, Roman gods, and Norse gods? What does Peter also point out in 2 Peter 1:20-21? Why is it important to know that the prophets did not write down their own version of Gods' words or interpret God's will? Many religions do this today. Why is this dangerous? How might false teachers try to trick us by belittling Christ's life, death, and resurrection, according to 2 Peter 2:1?*

Key Idea: Even the German tribes were no match for the fierce tribe from the northeast called the Huns. Everyone feared their leader Attila the Hun.

History Project S

Get your Viking brooch that you began on Day 1. Outline the pattern you drew in pencil on the brooch with a thick line of white glue. Leave the brooch flat to dry until Day 3.

Key Idea: As soon as Attila the Hun headed home with his army, the Vandals in Africa sailed up the Tiber River and attacked Rome. The western part of the Roman Empire was broken apart.

Storytime T

Read aloud the following assigned passage:

★ *Raiders from the Sea: Ch. 6*

Ask, *In what does the main character place her trust? How does the main character's faith in Jesus help comfort her? Share a character, a story, or a verse from the Bible that you are reminded of by the reading.*

Key Idea: Share a Biblical connection.

Vocabulary S

You may choose 3-5 of the following vocabulary words from *A Child's History of the World* to use for this lesson: *barbarians* (p. 176), *pomp* (p. 177), *era* (p. 178), *unity* (p. 178), and/or *classical* (p. 179). First, find the word in the text and read the sentence containing the word. Think about possible meanings. Next, find the word in a dictionary and select the correct meaning. Write the word at the top of an index card or at the top of the corresponding letter page in the notebook. Underneath the word, copy the correct definition from the dictionary. Then, use the word correctly in a sentence. The sentence may either be copied from the text or be one of your own creation. Last, draw a small picture to show the word's meaning. If you used an index card to record your word, file it under the correct alphabetical tab.

Key Idea: A Roman and Germanic army finally beat the Huns in Chalons, which is close to the city of Paris, France. After that the Huns went after the Romans in Italy instead. As the Huns approached Rome, everyone thought all was lost. But, Attila left without attacking Rome.

Independent History Study I

★ Read *Leif the Lucky* p. 18-26. Then, copy the **first three** sentences from the top of p. 26 in cursive onto a clean page in your *Common Place Book*.

Key Idea: Leif was christened a Christian on his visit to Norway. King Olav, of Norway, asked him to return to Greenland to spread Christianity there.

Learning the Basics

Focus: Language Arts, Math, Bible, and Science

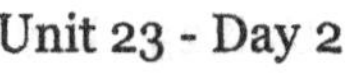

Language Arts

T

Work with the students to complete **one** of the English options listed below:

★ *Beginning Wisely:* Lesson 82

★ *Building with Diligence:* Lesson 84

★ Your own grammar program

Say, *For today's writing session, you will copy half of the Robert Louis Stevenson poem that you have chosen to memorize this week* (see Appendix).

Say, *Copy the poem in cursive in your "Common Place Book". Leave the rest of the page blank to copy the remaining half of the poem next unit.*

Have students share the portion of the poem they copied by reading it aloud.

Key Idea: Write creatively from classic poetry.

Bible Study

T

Have students say Psalm 8:1-2 using the hand motions they added on Day 1. Say, *A mood is a feeling, a sensation, or a state of mind. What is the mood of Psalm 8:2?* (Some examples of moods include frightened, worried, happy, peaceful, hopeful, sad, unhappy, angry, thankful, prayerful, joyful, and lonely.) Ask, *When would this Psalm help you, or when would you go to this Psalm?* (i.e. to remind us to enthusiastically praise the Lord, to show us that the Lord values childlike faith, to help us remember that the Lord is on our side in the battle against Satan)

Last, pray with your children that they will always keep their childlike faith. Pray that they will enthusiastically praise the Lord and that the Lord will be with them as they struggle against Satan's temptations.

✔ *Lead Me to the Rock* CD
Track 8; Song: "How Excellent Is Thy Name" (vs. 1-2)

Key Idea: The Psalms reflect the many emotions and moods we have. They are a wonderful place to seek counsel from the Lord.

Math Exploration

S

Choose **one** of the math options listed below (see Appendix for details).

★ *Singapore Primary Mathematics 2A/2B, 3A/3B, or 4A/4B*

★ Your own math program

Key Idea: Use a step-by-step math program.

Science Exploration

I

★ Read *One Small Square: Coral Reef* p. 6-7. Orally retell or narrate to an adult the portion of text that you read today. Use the *Narration Tips* in the Appendix for help as needed.

Key Idea: The coral reef you will be reading about is part of the Great Barrier Reef. This reef is located facing the open sea with a lagoon separating it from land. There are many new animals to explore in the reef.

Learning through History

Focus: Barbarians Attack

Unit 23 - Day 3

Reading about History [T]

Read about history in the following resource:

★ *A Child's History of the World: Ch. 42* p. 180-182

After today's reading, have your students orally narrate or retell the portion of today's text that you read. Use the *Narration Tips* in the Appendix as needed.

Key Idea: The Roman Emperor Justinian built the church Santa Sophia in Constantinople. He also brought the secret of making silk to Europe from China.

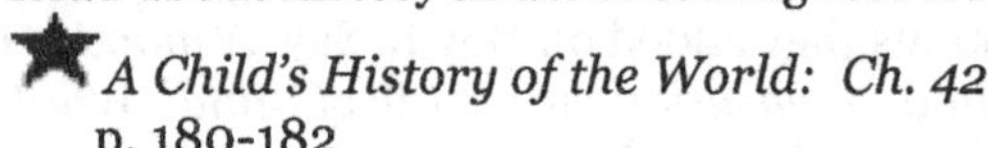

History Project [S]

Get your Viking brooch that you outlined with glue on Day 2. Make sure the glue is very dry. Then, cover the brooch with a small piece of aluminum foil, gently pressing the foil on the glue lines so that the design appears on the brooch. Cut off the excess foil, leaving a small edge to wrap around the back of the brooch. Tape the foil edges to the back of the brooch with clear tape. Attach a safety pin to the back of the brooch with tape. Put your brooch on and see how it looks.

Key Idea: At the time that Justinian was ruling over the Roman Empire, Clovis was ruling the Franks in France, and Arthur was supposedly ruling in England. Since there were many Celtic kings named Arthur near this time, it is difficult to know whether any of the stories about the legendary King Arthur are really true.

Storytime [T]

Read aloud the following assigned passage:

★ *Raiders from the Sea: Ch. 7*

Ask, *In today's reading, how were people's lives different from your life? What would you have enjoyed or found difficult about living during that time?*

Key Idea: Compare the historical time periods.

Geography [S]

Use a globe for today's activities. *The Emperor Constantine moved the capitol from Rome to a city called Byzantium. He changed the city's name to Constantinople. The Roman Justinian ruled from there too. Today the city is called Istanbul. Find Istanbul on the globe in modern-day Turkey. When the Franks began ruling Gaul, it became France after the Franks. Find France on the globe. Clovis made Paris his capitol city in France. It is still the capitol of France. Find it on the globe. Look at* A Child's History of the World *p. 172. Match the numbered areas on the map to the same locations on the globe.*

Review the following concept: *Find the Tropic of Cancer 23 degrees north of the equator and the Tropic of Capricorn 23 degrees south of the equator. The area between these two tropics is the tropic or torrid zone. Which countries are located in this zone? Describe the climate.*

Key Idea: Justinian ruled in Constantinople, and Clovis ruled in Paris.

Independent History Study [I]

★ On white paper, draw or trace the portion of the world shown on the map in the opening pages of *Leif the Lucky*. Draw a colored line to show Erik the Red's voyage from Norway to Iceland, and from Iceland to Brattali, Greenland. Draw a different colored line to show Leif the Lucky's voyage from Brattali, Greenland to Nidaros, Norway and from Norway to Vinland or Wineland in America. Last, draw a line showing Leif's return to Brattali, Greenland. Make a key for your map.

Key Idea: Leif the Lucky found the continent of America when he got off course on his way to Greenland.

Learning the Basics
Focus: Language Arts, Math, Bible, and Science

Unit 23 - Day 3

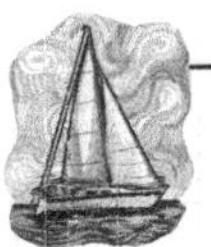

Poetry [T]

Have students practice reading half of the poem that they have chosen to memorize, using the actions that they added. Have students do this 2 times. Then, have students recite half of the poem without looking at the words. Students have 2 weeks (units) to memorize the entire poem. So, they should have half of their chosen poem memorized by Day 4 of this unit.

Key Idea: Read and appreciate classic poetry.

Language Arts [S]

Have students complete one studied dictation exercise (see Appendix for directions and passages).

Help students complete one lesson from the following reading program:

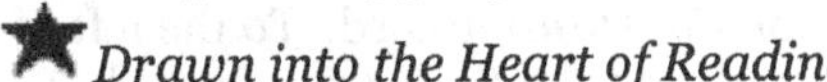
★ *Drawn into the Heart of Reading*

Work with the students to complete **one** of the English options listed below:

★ *Beginning Wisely:* Lesson 83

★ *Building with Diligence:* Lesson 85

★ Your own grammar program

Key Idea: Practice language arts skills.

Bible Study [T]

Say, *You will be having your own quiet time with God today. Choose a quiet place for this special time, where you can be alone with God. Then, do the following things:*

1. Read Psalm 8:1-2 in your Bible.
2. Pray about the Psalm using the following beginning to your prayer: *Thank you for this quiet time where I can be close to you. Help me as I struggle with ______. Be with me as I ______, and guide me to live my life for you.*
3. Recite Psalm 8:1-2 using the hand motions you added on Day 1.
4. Sing Psalm 8:1-2 along with the CD at the end of your quiet time.

✔ *Lead Me to the Rock* CD
Track 8; Song: "How Excellent Is Thy Name" (vs. 1-2)

Key Idea: The Lord's greatness surrounds us.

Math Exploration [S]

Choose **one** of the math options listed below (see Appendix for details).

★ *Singapore Primary Mathematics 2A/2B, 3A/3B,* or *4A/4B*

★ Your own math program

Key Idea: Use a step-by-step math program.

Science Exploration [I]

★ Read *One Small Square: Coral Reef* p. 8-9. Write the answer to each numbered question on lined paper. You do not need to copy the question. Use the listed page to help you answer each question.

1. What is most of the reef made of? (p. 8)
2. How do reefs grow? (p. 8)
3. What are sea anemones? (p. 9)
4. Describe hard corals. (p. 9)
5. What does Genesis 1:20-22 tell us about the creatures that live in the sea?

Key Idea: God made all of the sea creatures. The beautiful-colored coral reef is another example of God's incredible creativity and of His amazing attention to even the smallest details.

Learning through History
Focus: Barbarians Attack

Unit 23 - Day 4

Reading about History [T]

Read about history in the following resource:

★ *A Child's History of the World: Ch. 43* p. 183-186

After today's reading, say, *You will be writing a narration about part of the day's history reading. In order to remember the details very well, you will need to reread the part of today's reading from the last paragraph on p. 184 through p. 186 (on your own if possible).*

After students have finished reading the passage, ask them the questions below. If the students do not know the answers, help them find the answers in the passage they just read. Ask, *What is a monk? Where did the monks live? What was a monastery like? What kind of work did monks do? How did monks make manuscripts and diaries? Why were monks and monasteries so important during this time in history?*

After the questions have been answered, have students write a 3-5 sentence narration about the monks. When students have finished their narration, direct them to read the sentences out loud. Ask, *Did you include **who** the reading was mainly about? Did you include **what** important thing(s) happened? Did you include **how** it ended?*

Help students underline or highlight the main idea sentence in their narration. See the *Written Narration Skills* in the Appendix to guide students in editing their narrations.

Key Idea: Men and women who desired to live holy lives gathered together in monasteries or abbeys. The men were called monks, and the women were called nuns.

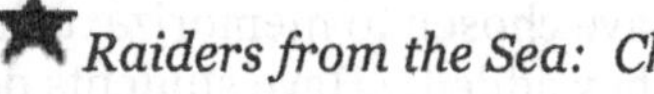

Storytime [T]

Read aloud the following assigned passage:

★ *Raiders from the Sea: Ch. 8*

After today's reading, have your students orally narrate or retell the portion of today's text that you read. Use the *Narration Tips* as needed.

Key Idea: Practice oral narration skills.

Timeline [S]

You will be adding 3 new cards to your staircase timeline today. Leave the first new card blank. On the second new card, draw and color a sword. Write, *Fall of Rome (476 A.D.).* On the third new card, draw and color a cross. Write, *St. Benedict (480-547 A.D.).*

If you decided to tape your timeline cards to the back of a door, then add the blank card to the left of the *Constantine* card. To the left of the blank card, add the *Fall of Rome* card. To the left of the *Fall of Rome* card, add the *St. Benedict* card. If you decided to tape the timeline cards side-by-side to accordion-fold them, use clear packing tape to tape the cards as described above. Then, accordion-fold the timeline to store it.

Key Idea: Monks and nuns carefully copied many old books, including the Bible. In this way, important books were carefully preserved for us today. The monks and nuns also cared for the poor and the sick, and provided lodging for weary travelers. Monasteries and abbeys were very important during this time.

Independent History Study [I]

★ Read *Leif the Lucky* p. 28-35. Then, choose an interesting part from today's pages to read aloud and explain to an adult.

Key Idea: Leif returned home from Vinland to share Christianity all over Greenland. His father, Erik the Red, did not want to become a Christian. His mother did though, and she built a church at Brittali.

Learning the Basics

Focus: Language Arts, Math, Bible, and Science

Poetry — T

Have students practice reading half of the poem that they have chosen to memorize, using the actions that they added. Have students do this 2 times. Then, have students recite half of the poem without looking at the words. Students have 2 weeks (units) to memorize the entire poem. So, they should have half of their chosen poem memorized by today.

Key Idea: Read and appreciate classic poetry.

Language Arts — S

Have students complete one dictation exercise.

Guide students to complete one reading lesson.

★ *Drawn into the Heart of Reading*

Help students complete **one** English lesson.

★ *Beginning Wisely:* Lesson 84

★ *Building with Diligence:* Lesson 86 (half)

★ Your own grammar program

Key Idea: Practice language arts skills.

Bible Study — T

Have students say Psalm 8:1-2 using the hand motions from Day 1.

Have students copy in cursive Psalm 8:2 beneath last unit's Psalm 8:1 in their *Common Place Book*. Students should leave the rest of the page blank to add to next week.

Students will add to the *Common Place Book* throughout the year.

✔ *Lead Me to the Rock* CD
Track 8; Song: "How Excellent Is Thy Name" (vs. 1-2)

Key Idea: Copy in cursive a portion of a Psalm.

Math Exploration — S

Choose **one** math option listed below.

★ *Singapore Primary Mathematics 2A/2B, 3A/3B,* or *4A/4B*

★ Your own math program

Key Idea: Use a step-by-step math program.

Science Exploration — I

★ Read *One Small Square: Coral Reef* p. 10-11. Turn to the science experiment section in your science binder or sketchbook. At the top of a blank page, write: *How do the parts of the coral polyp help it survive?* Under the question, write: *'Guess'*. Write down your guess.

Today you will make an edible model of a coral polyp. First, wash your hands with soap and warm water. Next, get out a plate and a piece of waxed paper. Place one large marshmallow on the waxed paper. This is the coral polyp's body. If you do not have a marshmallow, use a 2-inch piece of banana instead. Now, poke a ring of 4 holes in the top of your coral polyp. These are for your polyp's tentacles, which you will add later. Next, roll only the sides of your coral polyp in a thin coat of strawberry jelly or melted chocolate. This is the calcium carbonate coating, which creates the skeletons of the coral reef. Then, dust candy sprinkles on the coating to be the helper algae found in the coral's tissue. Last, insert 4 pieces of either string licorice, gummy worms, slices of fruit roll-up, or chow-mein noodles into the 4 holes to be tentacles. Place your coral polyp on a plate. If more than one person made a polyp, join your two polyps together on the plate. On your paper, write: *'Procedure'*. Draw a picture of the experiment. At the bottom of the paper, write: *'Conclusion'*. Explain what you learned. Then, enjoy eating your coral polyp!

Key Idea: Coral polyps are invertebrates protected by a hard coating and stinging tentacles.

Learning through History

Focus: World Religions Spread

Unit 24 - Day 1

Reading about History

T

Read about history in the following resource:

★ *A Child's History of the World: Ch. 44* p. 187-190

After today's reading, say, *Describe the kingdom of Axum.* (comprehension) *Explain how we know that the Queen of Sheba really did visit King Solomon. See 1 Kings 10:1-13.* (evaluation) *Tell about King Ezana.* (comprehension) *How was King Ezana converted to Christianity?* (knowledge) *What modern-day country is Axum today?* (knowledge) *How was Christianity spread to Axum?* (analysis) *Ethiopia, or Axum, is mentioned in Acts 8:26-39.*

Key Idea: Axum was a trading port in Africa. Merchants from Axum also traveled by land to trade with the Romans. So, Axum became rich.

History Project

S

In this unit you will make an illuminated manuscript of Psalm 1:2. In the upper left corner of a white piece of paper, outline a neat rectangle that is 5 inches long and 3 inches wide. You will place the illuminated letter *'B'* in this space later, since this is the first letter of Psalm 1:2. Then, leaving off the first letter *'B'*, copy the rest of Psalm 1:2 very neatly in black letters using a black ink pen. Save for Day 2.

Key Idea: King Ezana was a famous king of Axum. He became a Christian while he was king. Then, he made Christianity the religion of Axum. The Bible was translated into the Ge'ez language, and churches were built.

Storytime

T

Read aloud the following assigned story:

★ *Raiders from the Sea: Ch. 9*

Discuss today's reading in a "conversational way". Share about a person, time, event, or emotion from your life that today's reading brought to mind. Next, have your child share a connection.

Key Idea: Connect personally to the story.

Research

S

During the Middle Ages special manuscripts were often decorated with beautiful lettering or pictures. These were called **illuminations.** Where could you look to discover more about illuminated manuscripts? Use a reference book or an online resource like www.wikipedia.org to type *illuminated manuscript* in the search or look it up in the index.

Orally answer one or more of the following questions from your research: *What does the word illuminate mean? Describe an illuminated manuscript. On what were the manuscripts written? How was an illumination added to a manuscript? What were some of the different types of illuminations? Why were illuminated manuscripts considered to be very valuable?*

Key Idea: After King Ezana, Axum was a Christian kingdom for several centuries. Then, when the Arabs conquered North Africa, Islam became the religion.

Independent History Study

I

★ Read *Leif the Lucky* p. 36-45. Orally retell or narrate to an adult the portion of text that you read today. Use the *Narration Tips* in the Appendix for help as needed.

Key Idea: Although both of Leif's brothers tried to sail to Vinland, neither made it. Later, his brother's widow remarried, and she and her new husband settled in Vinland. They traded with the Skraellingers.

Learning the Basics

Focus: Language Arts, Math, Bible, and Science

Unit 24 - Day 1

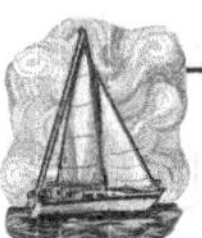

Poetry

T

Guide students to continue memorizing the Robert Louis Stevenson poem they chose in Unit 23. Students should have half of their chosen poem memorized already. They should memorize the rest of the poem by Day 4 of this unit. Have students read the entire poem 3 times, adding actions to the last half of the poem to help them memorize the words more easily.

Key Idea: Read and appreciate classic poetry.

Language Arts

S

Have students complete the first studied dictation exercise (see Appendix for directions and passages).

Help students complete one lesson from the following reading program:

 *Drawn into the Heart of Reading*

Work with the students to complete **one** of the English options listed below:

 *Beginning Wisely:* Lesson 85

 *Building with Diligence:* Lesson 86 (half)

 Your own grammar program

Key Idea: Practice language arts skills.

Bible Study

T

Say, *Find Psalm 8:1-3 in your Bible. This is the memory selection for this unit. Read the verses out loud.* Ask, *How does Psalm 8:3 describe the heavens? In Psalm 8:3, whom does it say ordained the Sun, Moon, and stars? How do the Sun, Moon, and stars show God's majesty? When we compare ourselves to God's greatness, how do we feel? Why is it important to realize how great God is, and how small we are? When we consider that we are one small part of God's creation, how should we feel about God valuing us so highly?*

Have students say the verse 3 times, adding hand motions to help remember the words.

 *Lead Me to the Rock* CD
Track 8; Song: "How Excellent Is Thy Name" (vs. 1-3)

Key Idea: God's majesty shows throughout His creation. Although we are one small part of His creation, He loves us and values us.

Math Exploration

S

Choose **one** of the math options listed below (see Appendix for details).

 *Singapore Primary Mathematics 2A/2B, 3A/3B,* or *4A/4B*

 Your own math program

Key Idea: Use a step-by-step math program.

Science Exploration

I

Today you will add to your science notebook. At the top of an unlined paper, copy Psalm 95:5 in cursive. Beneath the verse, draw and color the picture of the hard coral polyps (including the circled picture of the stinging cell and alga) from p. 9 of *One Small Square: Coral Reef.* Color the hard coral light green and pink as shown in the picture. Then, label the parts of the picture as shown on p. 9. Copy the first 3 sentences of the paragraph at the bottom of p. 9 under your picture.

Key Idea: Hard coral polyps make stone cups, which form the coral reefs. The polyps usually hide in their stone "pits" with their tentacles pulled inside.

Learning through History
Focus: World Religions Spread

Unit 24 - Day 2

Reading about History — T

Read about history in the following resource:

★ *A Child's History of the World: Ch. 45* p. 191-195

Ask, *After the coming of Jesus Christ, how did Judaism become a separate religion from Christianity? How did Islam begin? What do followers of Islam think Jesus was? What does God say about Jesus in Matthew 3:13-17? If Muslims believe that Jesus was a prophet, instead of the Son of God, is that in keeping with what God says in the Bible? Since part of Muhammad's teaching was that he was a prophet and that Jesus was a prophet, do you think it really was Gabriel who visited him with a message from God? What does 2 Peter 2:1-2 warn us against? The teachings of Muhammad were written down in a Muslim holy book called the Qur'an, or Koran, which also contains Bible passages. Did God intend for His word to be added to or altered? Why would studying the Qur'an, in place of the Bible, not match what 2 Timothy 3:15-17 says?*

Key Idea: Much of the Middle East is Islamic.

History Project — S

Get Psalms 1:2 that you copied on Day 1. Outline a large *'B'* in the rectangle at the top left of the page. Choose pictures to draw within the *'B'* that go along with the verse (i.e. an open Bible, day, night, a child studying God's Word, praying hands). In gold pen, marker, or paint, outline the *'B'* and add gold to parts of the pictures to make them illuminate. Save the rest of the coloring for Day 3.

Key Idea: Bibles often had illuminations.

Storytime — T

Read aloud the following assigned passage:

★ *Raiders from the Sea: Ch. 10-11*

Ask, *In what does the main character place her trust? How does the main character's faith in Jesus help comfort her? Share a character, a story, or a verse from the Bible that you are reminded of by the reading.*

Key Idea: Share a Biblical connection.

Vocabulary — S

You may choose 3-5 of the following vocabulary words from *A Child's History of the World* to use for this lesson: *unjust* (p. 192), *migration* (p. 193), *caliph* (p. 193), *mosque* (p. 194), and/or *minaret* (p. 194). First, find the word in the text and read the sentence containing the word. Think about possible meanings. Next, find the word in a dictionary and select the correct meaning. Write the word at the top of an index card or at the top of the corresponding letter page in the notebook. Underneath the word, copy the correct definition from the dictionary. Then, use the word correctly in a sentence. The sentence may either be copied from the text or be one of your own creation. Last, draw a small picture to show the word's meaning. If you used an index card to record your word, file it under the correct alphabetical tab.

Key Idea: Muhammad's teachings led to a new religion called Islam. Those who follow Islam are called Muslims. Muslim armies captured much of the Roman Empire, until they were turned back at Constantinople and in Tours, France.

Independent History Study — I

★ Read *Leif the Lucky* p. 46-54. Then, copy the **first two** sentences from p. 50 in cursive onto a clean page in your *Common Place Book*.

Key Idea: As the Skraellingers and the Vikings fought more and more, the Vikings decided to sail home.

Learning the Basics

Focus: Language Arts, Math, Bible, and Science

Language Arts

T

Work with the students to complete **one** of the English options listed below:

★ *Beginning Wisely:* Lesson 86

★ *Building with Diligence:* Lesson 87

★ Your own grammar program

Say, *For today's writing session, you will copy the last half of the Robert Louis Stevenson poem that you chose to memorize this week* (see Appendix).

Say, *Copy the rest of the poem in cursive in your "Common Place Book".*

Have students share the poem they copied by reading it aloud.

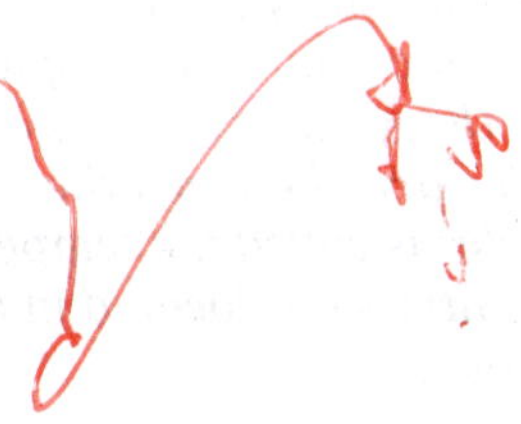

Key Idea: Write creatively from classic poetry.

Bible Study

T

Have students say Psalm 8:1-3 using the hand motions they added on Day 1. Say, *A mood is a feeling, a sensation, or a state of mind. What is the mood of Psalm 8:3?* (Some examples of moods include frightened, worried, happy, peaceful, hopeful, sad, unhappy, angry, thankful, prayerful, joyful, and lonely.) Ask, *When would this Psalm help you, or when would you go to this Psalm?* (i.e. to remind us that God created the heavens and all that is in them, to help us remember God's majesty, to show us that He cares for us)

Last, pray with your children that they will recognize God's majesty. Pray that they will treat God with the respect He deserves and will know how much God cares for them.

 *Lead Me to the Rock* CD
Track 8; Song: "How Excellent Is Thy Name" (vs. 1-3)

Key Idea: The Psalms reflect the many emotions and moods we have. They are a wonderful place to seek counsel from the Lord.

Math Exploration

S

Choose **one** of the math options listed below (see Appendix for details).

 *Singapore Primary Mathematics 2A/2B, 3A/3B, or 4A/4B*

 Your own math program

Key Idea: Use a step-by-step math program.

Science Exploration

I

★ Read *One Small Square: Coral Reef* p. 12-13. Orally retell or narrate to an adult the portion of text that you read today. Use the *Narration Tips* in the Appendix for help as needed.

Key Idea: In the coral reef, algae are very important, so the damselfish protects her seaweed patch from big algae eaters. The coral cups also have algae inside their bodies. The algae are protected by the coral's stinging tentacles because they share food and oxygen with the coral and recycle the coral's waste.

Reading about History — T

Read about history in the following resource:

★ *A Child's History of the World: Ch. 46* p. 196-200

After today's reading, have your students orally narrate or retell the portion of today's text that you read. Use the *Narration Tips* in the Appendix as needed.

Key Idea: The Muslim Empire eventually became larger than the Roman Empire had been. However, Europe was not conquered by the Muslims.

Storytime — T

Read aloud the following assigned passage:

★ *Raiders from the Sea: Ch. 12-13*

Ask, *In today's reading, how were people's lives different from your life? What would you have enjoyed or found difficult about living during that time?*

Key Idea: Compare the historical time periods.

History Project — S

Get your illuminated Psalm that you began on Days 1-2. Draw berries and leaves, branches, scrolls, or other designs to surround the white space around your *'B'*. Then, use brightly colored markers or crayons to completely color the pictures within the *'B'* and surrounding the *'B'*. When you are finished, there should be no white space showing within the rectangle that you outlined around the illuminated letter.

Key Idea: The Arabs of long ago were famous for many things such as their beautiful churches, sharp swords, making coffee, weaving cotton into cloth, and the numbering system that we still use today. The Muslims also believe women must be completely covered, and men may have several wives.

Geography — S

Use a globe for today's activities. *Look at the map of the Muslim Empire on p. 192 of A Child's History of the World. Find the black-shaded areas on the globe. These areas included Spain, North Africa, the Middle East, and Persia (up to India and China). Next on the globe, find the Muslims' eastern capitol, which was in Baghdad, Iraq. Then, find the Muslims western capitol, which was in Cordova, Spain. Last, find Damascus, in Syria, where the Arabs made their famous swords.*

Introduce the following concept: *Find the Tropic of Cancer and the Tropic of Capricorn. Then find the Antarctic Circle and the Arctic Circle. The area between the tropic and the arctic circles is called the temperate zone. Which countries are located in this zone? Describe the climate.*

Key Idea: The Muslim Empire was so large that it needed two capitol cities.

Independent History Study — I

★ On white paper, list Erik the Red's family. Make an oval at the top of the paper. In it, write, *Erik the Red 950-1003 A.D. (founded first Nordic settlement in Greenland)*. Under the top oval, draw 4 ovals going across the paper in a row. Draw a line from the top oval to each of the 4 ovals beneath it. Write the following names of Erik the Red's children, one in each oval: *Freydis (daughter), Torstein (sailed for Vinland and never returned), Torvald (sailed for Vinland and never found it), Leif (explored Vinland and became high chief)*. Add a decorative border around the page like those shown in *Leif the Lucky*.

Key Idea: Leif the Lucky became the chief after his father Erik the Red died. His travels were legendary.

Learning the Basics
Focus: Language Arts, Math, Bible, and Science

Poetry

T

Have students practice reading the poem that they have chosen to memorize, using the actions that they added on Day 1. Have students do this 2 times. Then, have students recite the poem without looking at the words. Students should have their chosen poem memorized by Day 4 of this unit.

Key Idea: Read and appreciate classic poetry.

Language Arts

S

Have students complete one studied dictation exercise (see Appendix for directions and passages).

Help students complete one lesson from the following reading program:

★ *Drawn into the Heart of Reading*

Work with the students to complete **one** of the English options listed below:

★ *Beginning Wisely:* Lesson 87

★ *Building with Diligence:* Lesson 88

★ Your own grammar program

Key Idea: Practice language arts skills.

Bible Study

T

Say, *You will be having your own quiet time with God today. Choose a quiet place for this special time, where you can be alone with God. Then, do the following things:*

1. Read Psalm 8:1-3 in your Bible.
2. Pray about the Psalm using the following beginning to your prayer: *Thank you for letting me come into your holy presence. I praise you for your majesty, which I see all around me in _____, _____, and _____. Thank you for taking time for me.*
3. Recite Psalm 8:1-3 using the hand motions you added on Day 1.
4. Sing Psalm 8:1-3 along with the CD at the end of your quiet time.

✔ *Lead Me to the Rock* CD
Track 8; Song: "How Excellent Is Thy Name" (vs. 1-3)

Key Idea: The Lord is holy and deserves praise.

Math Exploration

S

Choose **one** of the math options listed below (see Appendix for details).

★ *Singapore Primary Mathematics 2A/2B, 3A/3B,* or *4A/4B*

★ Your own math program

Key Idea: Use a step-by-step math program.

Science Exploration

I

★ Read *One Small Square: Coral Reef* p. 14-15. Write the answer to each numbered question on lined paper. You do not need to copy the question. Use the listed page to help you answer each question.

1. Describe the size of the giant clam. (p. 14)
2. How does a giant clam see you? (p. 15)
3. How do the giant clam's tubes work? (p. 15)
4. Why is the octopus dangerous? (p. 15)
5. What does Jeremiah 5:22 say about the sea to show us the respect and awe God deserves from us?

Key Idea: The giant clam can weigh more than 500 pounds! God created the sea and all of the creatures in it. He set boundaries for the sea and contained it.

Reading about History [T]

Read about history in the following resource:

★ *A Child's History of the World: Ch. 47* p. 201-205

After today's reading, say, *You will be writing a narration about part of the day's history reading. In order to remember the details very well, you will need to reread the part of today's reading from the last half of p. 202 up to the last paragraph on p. 203 (on your own if possible).*

After students have finished reading the passage, ask them the questions below. If the students do not know the answers, help them find the answers in the passage they just read. Ask, *Who was king of the Franks in today's story? Why do you think the time when Charlemagne lived was called the Dark Ages? Could very many people read or write in Charlemagne's time? Why did Charlemagne invite the monk Alcuin to come from England? What is one thing Charlemagne could never learn? Tell what Charlemagne wore and ate, and how he raised his children. Describe Charlemagne's home.*

After the questions have been answered, have students write a 3-5 sentence narration about Charlemagne. When students have finished their narration, direct them to read the sentences out loud.

Help students underline or highlight the main idea sentence in their narration. See the *Written Narration Skills* in the Appendix to guide students in editing their narrations.

Key Idea: Charlemagne was a Frank who was king of France. His name meant Charles the Great. Eventually, he became king of Germany and part of Spain too.

Storytime [T]

Read aloud the following assigned passage:

★ *Raiders from the Sea: Ch. 14-15*

After today's reading, have your students orally narrate or retell the portion of today's text that you read. Use the *Narration Tips* as needed.

Key Idea: Practice oral narration skills.

Timeline [S]

You will be adding 3 new cards to your staircase timeline today. For the first new card, use the blank card already taped on your timeline from Unit 23. Draw and color a picture of the outline of Africa. Write, *King Ezana – African King (330 A.D.)* On the second new card, draw and color a mosque like on p. 193 of *A Child's History of the World.* Write, *Muhammad's Hegira (622 A.D.).* On the third new card, draw and color a golden crown. Write, *Charlemagne crowned by Pope Leo (800 A.D.).*

If you decided to tape your timeline cards to the back of a door, then add the *Muhammad's Hegira* card to the left of the *St. Benedict* card. To the left of the *Muhammad's Hegira* card, add the *Charlemagne crowned by Pope Leo* card. If you decided to tape the timeline cards side-by-side to accordion-fold them, use clear packing tape to tape the cards as described above. Then, accordion-fold the timeline to store it.

Key Idea: After helping the pope gain control back in Italy, the pope crowned Charlemagne Emperor of Italy as well. Charlemagne was now ruling over an empire.

Independent History Study [I]

★ Read *Minstrel in the Tower: Ch. I.* Then, choose an interesting part from today's pages to read aloud and explain to an adult.

Key Idea: Life during medieval times was full of war and sickness. Clothes and homes were often dirty.

Learning the Basics

Focus: Language Arts, Math, Bible, and Science

Unit 24 - Day 4

Poetry

T

Have students practice reading the poem that they have chosen to memorize, using the actions that they added. Have students do this 2 times. Then, have students recite the poem without looking at the words for you. They should have their chosen poem memorized today.

Key Idea: Read and appreciate classic poetry.

Language Arts

S

Have students complete one dictation exercise.

Guide students to complete one reading lesson.

★ *Drawn into the Heart of Reading*

Help students complete **one** English lesson.

★ *Beginning Wisely:* Lesson 88

★ *Building with Diligence:* Lesson 89

★ Your own grammar program

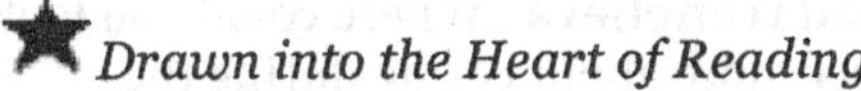

Key Idea: Practice language arts skills.

Bible Study

T

Have students say Psalm 8:1-3 using the hand motions from Day 1. Have students copy in cursive Psalm 8:3 beneath last unit's Psalm 8:2 in their *Common Place Book*. Students should leave the rest of the page blank to add to next week.

Students will add to the *Common Place Book* throughout the year.

✔ *Lead Me to the Rock* CD
Track 8; Song: "How Excellent Is Thy Name" (vs. 1-3)

Key Idea: Copy in cursive a portion of a Psalm.

Math Exploration

S

Choose **one** math option listed below.

★ *Singapore Primary Mathematics 2A/2B, 3A/3B,* or *4A/4B*

★ Your own math program

Key Idea: Use a step-by-step math program.

Science Exploration

I

Turn to the science experiment section in your science binder or sketchbook. At the top of a blank page, write: *How do different fishes' mouths help them take in their food?* Under the question, write: *'Guess'*. Write down your guess. Look at the pictures of the different fishes' mouths on p. 14-15 of *One Small Square: Coral Reef.*

Set out a tweezers, a pliers, and a clothespin (or a chip bag clip). These will be 3 different types of fishes' mouths. Next, set up a reef for your fish. On the counter, pile several blocks or building bricks in a heap. This will be a coral reef. Scatter a few grains of rice or thin cereal pieces in the cracks among the blocks to be food. Next, scatter several pieces of dry pasta or nuts on the counter to be snails. Then, get out a rock to be a coral cup skeleton. Dip it in water and then in sugar to be the algae growing on the cup. Test the tweezer, pliers, and clothespin on each type of food to see which type of fish's mouth works best for each type of food. Why would the tweezers work best for the bits of food among the coral reef cracks? Why would the clothespin work best for the snails? Why would the pliers work best for scraping algae form the coral cup skeleton? On your paper, write: *'Procedure'*. Draw a picture of the experiment. At the bottom of the paper, write: *'Conclusion'*. Explain what you learned.

Key Idea: Each fish has a mouth that is well-suited for getting the food it needs to survive.

Reading about History T

Read about history in the following resource:

★ *A Child's History of the World: Ch. 48* p. 206-209

After today's reading, say, *How did Alfred first learn to read?* (knowledge) *Tell about Alfred as a king.* (comprehension) *Judge whether it worked to give the Danes part of England. Explain.* (evaluation) *Explain how we know that the English were quite ignorant during the time of King Alfred.* (analysis) *Identify what good things Alfred did for England.* (application)

Key Idea: When Alfred was king of England, the Danes were coming across the border and raiding the English towns and villages. So, Alfred finally gave them a piece of England.

History Project S

In this unit you will make a medieval trencher. In a bowl, mix 1 cup of flour, 1 teaspoon salt, and 1 ½ teaspoons baking powder. Add 1/8 cup shortening to the mixture. Then, scrape the mixture with a fork to cut it into crumbs. Make a well in the center of the mixture and pour in 1/3 cup milk. Stir the mixture with a fork to form a dough. Place a sheet of aluminum foil on the table. Divide the dough into 4 equal pieces on the foil. Knead each piece of dough 10-15 times with the palms of your hands. Then, flatten each piece, so it is about ½ inch thick. Place the foil and trenchers on the baking sheet and bake for 12 minutes at 450 degrees. Store the trenchers for Day 3, so they will be hard and stale.

Key Idea: After the meal, trenchers were eaten.

Storytime T

Read aloud the following assigned story:

★ *Raiders from the Sea: Ch. 16-18*

Discuss today's reading in a "conversational way". Share about a person, time, event, or emotion from your life that today's reading brought to mind. Next, have your child share a connection.

Key Idea: Connect personally to the story.

Research S

During the Middle Ages pieces of hard, stale bread were used as plates during meals. These were called **trenchers**. Where could you look to discover more about eating during the Middle Ages? Use a reference book or an online resource like www.wikipedia.org to type *Medieval cuisine* or *trenchers* in the search or look it up in the index.

Orally answer one or more of the following questions from your research: *What was a trencher? How many meals were eaten a day during medieval times? At what times of day were the meals usually eaten? What types of utensils were used when eating? Why were cups and knives often shared at meals? How did medieval meals differ between the wealthy and the poor? What were some of the foods eaten in medieval times?*

Key Idea: Food was often scarce during medieval times. The English were kept busy fighting with their neighbors and trying to keep their families safe from raiders. Many people couldn't read or write, so Alfred started schools to teach them.

Independent History Study I

★ Read *Minstrel in the Tower: Ch. II.* Orally retell or narrate to an adult the portion of text that you read today. Use the *Narration Tips* in the Appendix for help as needed.

Key Idea: Roger and Alice are trying to find their uncle because mother is sick, and father is dead.

Learning the Basics

Focus: Language Arts, Math, Bible, and Science

Poetry

T

Read aloud to the students the poem *"Windy Nights"* (see Appendix). Say, *What kind of mood is set in the poem's first stanza? Do you think there really is a man who goes galloping by on a horse when the nights are dark and wet? What do you think the poet meant when he wrote about that? What kind of sounds do you hear on a rainy, windy night? Could it sound like a man galloping on his horse?* Read the poem again with the students.

Key Idea: Read and appreciate classic poetry.

Language Arts

S

Have students complete the first studied dictation exercise (see Appendix for directions and passages).

Help students complete one lesson from the following reading program:

★ *Drawn into the Heart of Reading*

Work with the students to complete **one** of the English options listed below:

★ *Beginning Wisely:* Lesson 89

★ *Building with Diligence:* Lesson 90

★ Your own grammar program

Key Idea: Practice language arts skills.

Bible Study

T

Say, *Find Psalm 8:1-5 in your Bible. This is the memory selection for this unit. Read the verses out loud.* Ask, *In Psalm 8:4, what does David wonder about? As we look at the majesty of God's creation, is it easy to wonder why God would care so much about us? In Psalm 8:5, how does God show us that He cares for us? What does it mean to be crowned with glory and honor? Are we deserving of such praise? Why not? In whose image were we created? Since we are created in God's image, how does that make us different from the rest of God's creation?* Have students say the verse 3 times, adding hand motions to help remember the words.

✔ *Lead Me to the Rock* CD
Track 8; Song: "How Excellent Is Thy Name" (vs. 1-5)

Key Idea: We were created in God's image, which makes us different from the rest of God's creation. We are valued more highly by God.

Math Exploration

S

Choose **one** of the math options listed below (see Appendix for details).

★ *Singapore Primary Mathematics 2A/2B, 3A/3B*, or *4A/4B*

★ Your own math program

Key Idea: Use a step-by-step math program.

Science Exploration

I

★ Read *One Small Square: Coral Reef* p. 16-19. Study the pictures of the fish on p. 18-19 to see how they are camouflaged. Today you will add to your science notebook. At the top of an unlined paper, copy Amos 5:8 in cursive. Beneath the verse, draw and color one fish from p. 40-41 of *One Small Square: Coral Reef.* Then, draw and color some stinging-cell animals, from p. 41, and some other invertebrates, from p. 42-43, around your fish to camouflage it. Label each animal that you drew with the correct name.

Key Idea: Camouflage can help predators sneak up on their prey and help the prey escape from a predator. Camouflage is an important adaptation for survival in a coral reef.

Learning through History
Focus: The Middle Ages

Unit 25 - Day 2

Reading about History [T]

Read about history in the following resource:

★ *A Child's History of the World: Ch. 49* p. 210-212

After today's reading, read aloud Matthew 24:36-44. Say, *In the Year 1000, many people thought the world would end. What does Matthew 24:36, say about this? According to this verse, can man predict when the world will end? What is Christ's return compared to in Matthew 24:37-39? How does Matthew 24:40-41 describe what will happen when Christ returns? In Matthew 24:42, what are we warned to do? How are we to be ready for Christ's return?*

Key Idea: Each 1000 year period is a millennium. Many people in the tenth century thought the world would end in the year 1000. In the year 2000, people again wondered if the world might end. But, it did not.

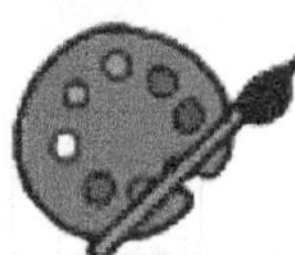

History Project [S]

Have a parent help you plan your medieval feast for Day 3. This usually included cheese, a choice of fruits tossed with cinnamon and sugar (such as pears, apples, figs, grapes, oranges, or lemons), peas or beans, a meat or stew of some kind, and a dessert (such as almond pudding, pastries, or marzipan). Write your menu on a sheet of paper. Your meal does not need to include all of these things. Keep it simple.

Key Idea: During medieval times, life was hard. Large groups of people often ate together in one large hall. Food and drink were shared.

Storytime [T]

Read aloud the following assigned passage:

★ *Door in the Wall* p. 7-17

Ask, *In today's reading, how were people's lives different from your life? What would you have enjoyed or found difficult about living during that time?*

Key Idea: Compare and contrast the historical time period of the reading to your own life.

Geography [S]

Use a globe for today's activities. *On the globe, trace the places the Vikings traveled. The Vikings started out in Norway. Then, they sailed to Iceland and on to Greenland. From Greenland, they sailed to Newfoundland, Canada. From there, they may have even sailed on to Cape Cod, Massachusetts.*

Review the following concept: *Lines of latitude are parallel to the equator, so they are also called parallels. Find the following important parallels on the globe: Antarctic Circle, Arctic Circle, Equator, Tropic of Cancer (located 23 degrees north of the equator), Tropic of Capricorn (located 23 degrees south of the equator).*

The areas near the Antarctic and Arctic Circles are called the frigid or polar zones. Which countries are located in this zone? Describe the climate.

Key Idea: The Vikings were brave sea-faring explorers. Leif Ericson is known for reaching the coast of the Americas. Columbus may have known stories about these explorers.

Independent History Study [I]

★ Read *Minstrel in the Tower: Ch III.* Then, copy in cursive paragraphs 3 and 4 from p. 25 onto a clean page in your *Common Place Book.*

Key Idea: Roger and Alice's father had gone with the Crusaders and had never returned.

Learning the Basics

Focus: Language Arts, Math, Bible, and Science

Unit 25 - Day 2

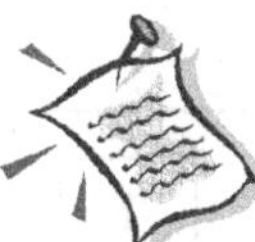

Language Arts — T

Work with the students to complete **one** of the English options listed below:

★ *Beginning Wisely:* Lesson 90

★ *Building with Diligence:* Lesson 91

★ Your own grammar program

Say, *You will be doing a writing activity based on the poem, "Windy Nights"* (see Appendix). Say, *Onomatopoeia is using sound words to add mood and drama to writing. Which word in "Windy Nights" makes the sound of hooves pounding against the ground? How does repeating the word "gallop" in the poem make it sound like the rhythmic pounding of hooves is getting faster and closer? What type of mood does this poem have? What are some of the words in the poem that help create that mood?* (i.e. wind is high, dark, wet, late in the night, fires are out, trees are crying, ships are tossed, low and loud)

Help students choose whether to describe a summer thunderstorm or a winter blizzard at night. At the top of a markerboard or a paper, make 3 columns labeled "Feel, "See", and "Hear". Guide students to list words and phrases to describe the type of weather that they chose. The list must include at least one example of onomatopoeia. For example, a summer thunderstorm might include the following ideas: "Feel" - air is heavy and damp; "See" - lightning flashes, sky is pea-green, clouds are churning; "Hear" - eerie silence before the wind begins to howl, thunder crashes, hail is pounding. Next, guide students to write a paragraph or a poem using their descriptive words.

Key Idea: Write creatively from classic poetry.

Bible Study — T

Have students say Psalm 8:1-5 using the hand motions they added on Day 1. Say, *A mood is a feeling, a sensation, or a state of mind. What is the mood of Psalm 8:4-5?* (Some examples of moods include frightened, worried, happy, peaceful, hopeful, sad, unhappy, angry, thankful, prayerful, joyful, and lonely.) Ask, *When would this Psalm help you, or when would you go to this Psalm?* (i.e. to remind us of God's love for us, to make us grateful that God cares for us in spite of our sin, to show us how important we are to God)

Last, pray with your children that they will know how important they are to God. Pray that they will feel how much God loves them and will strive to glorify Him with their lives.

Lead Me to the Rock CD
Track 8; Song: "How Excellent Is Thy Name" (vs. 1-5)

Key Idea: The Psalms reflect the many emotions and moods we have. They are a wonderful place to seek counsel from the Lord.

Math Exploration — S

Choose **one** of the math options listed below (see Appendix for details).

★ *Singapore Primary Mathematics 2A/2B, 3A/3B,* or *4A/4B*

★ Your own math program

Key Idea: Use a step-by-step math program.

Science Exploration — I

★ Read *One Small Square: Coral Reef* p. 20-21. Orally retell or narrate to an adult the portion of text that you read today. Use the *Narration Tips* in the Appendix for help as needed.

Key Idea: Clownfish spend much of their time in the middle of the sea anemone's tentacles. The body of the clownfish is covered with a mucus that protects it from the poison of the sea anemone.

Learning through History
Focus: The Middle Ages

Unit 25 - Day 3

Reading about History [T]

Read about history in the following resource:

★ *A Child's History of the World: Ch. 50* p. 213-217

After today's reading, have your students orally narrate or retell the portion of today's text that you read. Use the *Narration Tips* in the Appendix as needed.

Key Idea: In the Feudal System, the serfs had to give their time, their work, and much of their crops to the lord on whose manor they lived. In return the lord gave them protection.

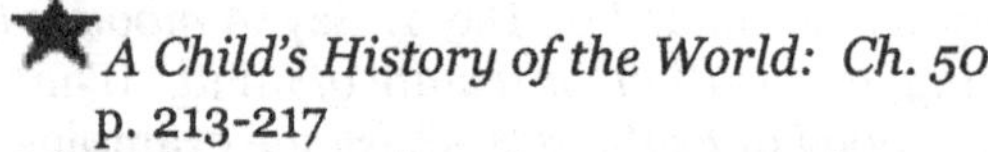

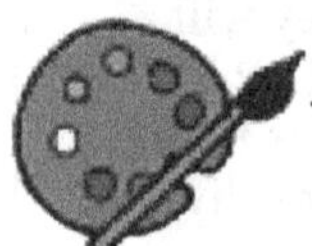

History Project [S]

Set up your medieval feast. Place your menu in the center of the table. Place the trenchers from Day 1 like plates on the table. Each person may have a blunt knife (but no fork). Spoons were sometimes used for dessert. Present the salt in a bowl to the seated guests as a welcome. Then, pour water over the guests' hands while they wash them over a basin and dry them. Place each course of food on the trenchers to be eaten. Serve the foods one course at a time. Between courses guests may play an instrument, juggle, sing, or recite a poem. At the end of the meal, guests must try a bite of their trencher. They may then choose to give it to the poor, eat it themselves, or give it to the dogs.

Key Idea: Meals were served on long wooden boards in the Great Hall of the castle.

Storytime [T]

Read aloud the following assigned passage:

★ *Door in the Wall* p. 18-31

Ask, *In what does the main character place his faith? How would the story be different if the main character put his faith in God? Share a character, a story, or a verse from the Bible that you are reminded of by today's reading.*

Key Idea: Share a Biblical connection.

Vocabulary [S]

You may choose 3-5 of the following vocabulary words from *A Child's History of the World* to use for this lesson: *vassal* (p. 213), *homage* (p. 214), *portcullis* (p. 216), *serf* (p. 217), and/or *feudal system* (p. 217). First, find the word in the text and read the sentence containing the word. Think about possible meanings. Next, find the word in a dictionary and select the correct meaning. Write the word at the top of an index card or at the top of the corresponding letter page in the notebook. Underneath the word, copy the correct definition from the dictionary. Then, use the word correctly in a sentence. The sentence may either be copied from the text or be one of your own creation. Last, draw a small picture to show the word's meaning. If you used an index card to record your word, file it under the correct alphabetical tab.

Key Idea: In medieval times, most people were poor. Only the lords and nobles were rich.

Independent History Study [I]

★ Read *Minstrel in the Tower: Ch. IV*. On white paper, draw a castle and label the following parts: *keep, Great Hall, portcullis, drawbridge, moat,* and *manor*. The lord of the castle lived in the main building called the *keep*. The main room in the keep was the *Great Hall*. This is where the meals were served. The castle had an iron gate at the entrance called a *portcullis*. The castle had a trench of water around it called a *moat*. A drawbridge went across the moat. The area outside the castle walls was called the *manor*. Serfs lived outside the castle in small one-room huts. Color your picture if you have time.

Key Idea: In the Feudal System, rulers gave land to their generals, and the generals gave land to lords or nobles. These lords or nobles built a castle on their land. The people who worked for the lord were serfs.

Learning the Basics

Focus: Language Arts, Math, Bible, and Science

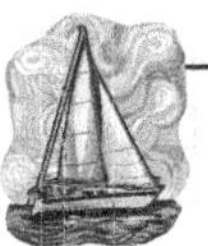

Poetry

T

Read aloud with the students the poem *"Windy Nights"* (see Appendix). Say, *Describe a memory that the poem brought to mind. What can you learn about the poet, Robert Louis Stevenson, from the poem?* Say, *Did you know that Robert Louis Stevenson's grandfather built lighthouses in impossible places where ships had often crashed on windy, stormy nights? Robert often mentions ships at sea when he writes about stormy weather.* Have the students read the poem on their own.

Key Idea: Read and appreciate classic poetry.

Language Arts

S

Have students complete one studied dictation exercise (see Appendix for directions and passages).

Help students complete one lesson from the following reading program:

★ *Drawn into the Heart of Reading*

Work with the students to complete **one** of the English options listed below:

★ *Beginning Wisely:* Lesson 91

★ *Building with Diligence:* Lesson 92

★ Your own grammar program

Key Idea: Practice language arts skills.

Bible Study

T

Say, *You will be having your own quiet time with God today. Choose a quiet place for this special time, where you can be alone with God. Then, do the following things:*

1. Read Psalm 8:1-5 in your Bible.
2. Pray about the Psalm using the following beginning to your prayer: *Thank you for always loving me. Help me to show your love to others by ______ and ______. Guide me to be more like you by ______.*
3. Recite Psalm 8:1-5 using the hand motions you added on Day 1.
4. Sing Psalm 8:1-5 along with the CD at the end of your quiet time.

✔ *Lead Me to the Rock* CD
Track 8; Song: "How Excellent Is Thy Name" (vs. 1-5)

Key Idea: The Lord always loves us. We need to try to be more like Him.

Math Exploration

S

Choose **one** of the math options listed below (see Appendix for details).

★ *Singapore Primary Mathematics 2A/2B, 3A/3B,* or *4A/4B*

★ Your own math program

Key Idea: Use a step-by-step math program.

Science Exploration

I

★ Read *One Small Square: Coral Reef* p. 22-23. Write the answer to each numbered question on lined paper. You do not need to copy the question. Use the listed page to help you answer each question.

1. How are coral caves formed? (p. 22)
2. What do stone breakers do? (p. 22)
3. What happens if a feather star's arms break off? (p. 23)
4. Where might the sea squirt have gotten its name? (p. 23)
5. Explain what you can learn about the sea from Ecclesiastes 1:7.

Key Idea: A coral cave is filled with sponges and coral that grow in the dark. Fish hide or nap in the cave.

Reading about History T

Read about history in the following resource:

★ *A Child's History of the World: Ch. 51* p. 218-221

After today's reading, say, *You will be writing a narration about part of the day's history reading. In order to remember the details very well, you will need to reread the part of today's reading from the second paragraph on p. 218 up to the last paragraph of p. 219 (on your own if possible).*

After students have finished reading the passage, ask them the questions below. If the students do not know the answers, help them find the answers in the passage they just read. Ask, *What two things were the son of a lord taught? Explain the steps for becoming a knight. First, explain being a page. Next, explain being a squire. Then, explain the knighting ceremony. Finally, describe what a knight swore to do.*

After the questions have been answered, have students write a 5 sentence narration about the steps for becoming a knight. Write and complete the following sentence starters: *First... Next... Then... Finally... A knight swore...* Students may look back in the text for help as needed. When students have finished their narration, direct them to read the sentences out loud.

Help students underline or highlight the main idea sentence in their narration. See the *Written Narration Skills* in the Appendix to guide students in editing their narrations.

Key Idea: The son of a lord was brought up to become a knight. First, he was a page, then a squire, and finally a knight.

Storytime T

Read aloud the following assigned passage:

★ *Door in the Wall* p. 32-41

Say, *Transport yourself back to the time of this story. Become one of the characters. Tell me what you see and do. (Make sure to use the word, "I", and to tell only what happened in today's reading.)*

Key Idea: Practice oral narration skills.

Timeline S

You will be adding 2 new cards to your staircase timeline today. On the first new card, draw and color a candle. Write, *Alfred the Great (900 A.D.)*. For the second new card, draw and color a Viking ship. Write, *Leif Erickson (1000 A.D.)*

If you decided to tape your timeline cards to the back of a door, then add the *Alfred the Great* card to the left of the *Charlemagne crowned by Pope Leo* card. To the left of the *Alfred the Great* card, add the *Leif Erickson* card. If you decided to tape the timeline cards side-by-side to accordion-fold them, use clear packing tape to tape the cards as described above. Then, accordion-fold the timeline to store it.

Key Idea: During the days of chivalry, reading and writing were not often taught. Instead, a knight was taught how to fight and how to be a gentleman. Knights often competed in tournaments where they practiced jousting and sword-fighting. Knights also enjoyed using dogs or falcons to hunt wild boar.

Independent History Study I

★ Read *Minstrel in the Tower: Ch. V.* Then, choose an interesting part from today's pages to read aloud and explain to an adult.

Key Idea: Alice and Roger overheard the thieves saying that their mother was the daughter of a noble. The children wondered how this could be true, since they had grown up living like serfs.

Learning the Basics
Focus: Language Arts, Math, Bible, and Science

Unit 25 - Day 4

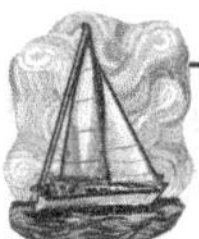

Poetry

T

Read aloud with the students the poem *"Windy Nights"* (see Appendix). Have students share this poem in a special way. Suggestions for sharing the poem include recording it to play for someone, reading it to someone on the telephone, photocopying the poem and adding illustrations, reading it to someone at home, putting the poem to a melody and singing it, using an instrument to tap out the meter or rhythm of the poem while reading it, or copying the poem on paper.

Key Idea: Share a variety of classic poetry.

Language Arts

S

Have students complete one dictation exercise.

Guide students to complete one reading lesson.

★ *Drawn into the Heart of Reading*

Help students complete **one** English lesson.

★ *Beginning Wisely:* Lesson 92

★ *Building with Diligence:* Lesson 93

★ Your own grammar program

Key Idea: Practice language arts skills.

Bible Study

T

Have students say Psalm 8:1-5 using the hand motions from Day 1.

Have students copy in cursive Psalm 8:4-5 beneath last unit's Psalm 8:3 in their *Common Place Book.* Students should leave the rest of the page blank to add to next week.

Students will add to the *Common Place Book* throughout the year.

✔ *Lead Me to the Rock* CD
Track 8; Song: "How Excellent Is Thy Name" (vs. 1-5)

Key Idea: Copy in cursive a portion of a Psalm.

Math Exploration

S

Choose **one** math option listed below.

★ *Singapore Primary Mathematics 2A/2B, 3A/3B,* or *4A/4B*

★ Your own math program

Key Idea: Use a step-by-step math program.

Science Exploration

I

Turn to the science experiment section in your science binder or sketchbook. At the top of a blank page, write: *How do sponges get their food out of the water?* Under the question, write: *'Guess'.* Write down your guess. Fill a clear glass partway full of water. Fold two paper towels together to make a "sponge". Hold the paper towels behind the glass of water. Look through the front of the glass to magnify the paper towel. Do you see the pores in the paper towel? A live sponge has pores which it squeezes water through to filter out the food. Sprinkle glitter or sequins into your glass of water to be food. Stir them into the water. Stand over a sink or tub, hold your paper sponge over the top of the glass, and pour the water onto the sponge. Then, squeeze the paper sponge over the glass, so the water in the sponge is pushed out. What is left on the sponge? How did the sponge filter the food out of the water? On your paper, write: *'Procedure'.* Draw a picture of the experiment. At the bottom of the paper, write: *'Conclusion'.* Explain what you learned.

Key Idea: Sponges are invertebrates that take in water and filter out their food through their pores.

Learning through History
Focus: Pirates, Pilgrimages, and Princes

Unit 26 - Day 1

Reading about History T

Read about history in the following resource:

★ *A Child's History of the World: Ch. 52* p. 222-227

After today's reading, say, *Why did the king of France give the Norsemen part of the French coast?* (comprehension) *What is that part of France called today?* (knowledge) *Tell about William the Conqueror, Duke of Normandy.* (comprehension) *What facts can you share that show William the Conqueror was good for England?* (synthesis) *Explain why the English were so upset about the New Forest.* (analysis) *What is your opinion about the New Forest?* (evaluation)

Key Idea: The king of France gave the Norsemen part of France. That part is called Normandy. When William became Duke of Normandy, he decided to conquer England.

History Project S

In this unit you will decorate a small box to hold an imaginary relic. To begin, you will need a small box with a lid. If you don't have a small box with a lid, you may use a pudding, gelatin, or rice box and cut one side of the box open on three sides, so you can lift the side like a lid on a hinge. Cover the inside and outside of your box carefully with aluminum foil. Use a pencil to lightly sketch swirls and geometric designs on the foil to decorate it beautifully. You will paint the designs on Day 2.

Key Idea: Relics were considered to be holy. People often worshiped relics, because they thought relics brought them closer to God.

Storytime T

Read aloud the following assigned story:

★ *Door in the Wall* p. 42-61

Discuss today's reading in a "conversational way". Share about a person, time, event, or emotion from your life that today's reading brought to mind. Next, have your child share a connection.

Key Idea: Connect personally to the story.

Research S

In medieval times, items that were considered holy were called **relics.** Where could you look to discover more about *relics*? Use a reference book or an online resource like www.wikipedia.org to type *relic* in the search or look it up in the index.

Orally answer one or more of the following questions from your research: *What was a relic? Why would people in the Middle Ages often purchase a relic from a shrine while they were on a pilgrimage? Name some things that were considered to be relics in the Middle Ages. What did people do with a relic? As Christians, how do we know that worshiping a relic is wrong?*

Key Idea: William, the Duke of Normandy, made Harold, the future king of England, promise to give England to him whenever Harold became king. William made Harold take an oath on it over the relics of bones of the saints. Later, Harold refused to give England to William, so William attacked England. After William won, he was called William the Conqueror.

Independent History Study I

★ Read *Minstrel in the Tower: Ch. VI.* Orally retell or narrate to an adult the portion of text that you read today. Use the *Narration Tips* in the Appendix for help as needed.

Key Idea: Alice finally reached Lord Raimond's castle. She needed to convince him that she was his neice.

Learning the Basics

Focus: Language Arts, Math, Bible, and Science

Unit 26 - Day 1

Poetry

T

Read aloud to the students the poem *"Young Night Thought"* (see Appendix). Say, *Who is the child picturing in his mind as he's going to sleep? What are they doing? Why would they move slowly at first? How do they move, as the child gets closer to falling asleep? Where does the child picture himself? What does the child do at the end of the poem? What do you picture at night as you're falling asleep?* Read the poem again with the students.

Key Idea: Read and appreciate classic poetry.

Language Arts

S

Have students complete the first studied dictation exercise (see Appendix for directions and passages).

Help students complete one lesson from thc following reading program:

 *Drawn into the Heart of Reading*

Work with the students to complete **one** of the English options listed below:

★ *Beginning Wisely:* Lesson 93

★ *Building with Diligence:* Lesson 94

★ Your own grammar program

Key Idea: Practice language arts skills.

Bible Study

T

Say, *Find Psalm 8:1-8 in your Bible. This is the memory selection for this unit. Read the verses out loud.* Ask, *What responsibility does Psalm 8:6 say God has given to us? What does it mean to have dominion over something? According to Psalm 8:7-8, what things do we have dominion over? Why is this a very important responsibility? Who created all things? By caring for God's creation, what are we doing?*

Have students say the verse 3 times, adding hand motions to help remember the words.

 *Lead Me to the Rock* CD
Track 8; Song: "How Excellent Is Thy Name" (vs. 1-8)

Key Idea: By giving us dominion over the Earth, God also gives us the responsibility of caring for His creation.

Math Exploration

S

Choose **one** of the math options listed below (see Appendix for details).

 *Singapore Primary Mathematics 2A/2B, 3A/3B,* or *4A/4B*

 Your own math program

Key Idea: Use a step-by-step math program.

Science Exploration

I

★ Read *One Small Square: Coral Reef* p. 24-25. Today you will add to your science notebook. At the top of an unlined paper, copy Job 26:10 in cursive. Beneath the verse, draw and label the parts of the sea anemone shown in the circle on p. 21 of *One Small Square: Coral Reef.* Copy the paragraph below the sea anemone onto your notebook page. Then, draw and label the parts of the sea squirt shown in the circle on p. 23 of *One Small Square: Coral Reef.* Copy the paragraph below the sea squirt onto your notebook page.

Key Idea: As the Sun sinks, the reef shark will often attack just as the schools of fishes are swimming out to sea for the night. Other fish disappear inside sponges or among coral branches for the night.

Learning through History
Focus: Pirates, Pilgrimages, and Princes

Unit 26 - Day 2

Reading about History **T**

Read about history in the following resource:

★ *A Child's History of the World: Ch. 53* p. 228-231

After today's reading, read aloud Proverbs 19:2-3. Say, *People were very zealous about going on a crusade, yet they often didn't stop to count the cost first. There was even a crusade of children that expected the waters to part for them on their way to Jerusalem. What does Proverbs 19:2 say about knowledge? Why is it important to have knowledge, or to think things through, before becoming zealous? What does Proverbs 19:3 say about a man's folly or foolishness? Why do you think the children's crusade wasn't a very knowledgeable decision? How do hasty decisions often turn out? How can we tell what things God wants us to do?*

Key Idea: There were many different Crusades.

History Project **S**

Get your relic box that you made on Day 1. Using a thin paintbrush and brightly colored paints, carefully paint the designs you drew on the box on Day 1. Allow the paint on your box to dry until Day 3.

Key Idea: Jerusalem is the site of the Church of the Holy Sepulcher. This is 3 connected churches built originally for Helena, mother of Constantine, over sites that have to do with Jesus' death and resurrection. The churches are said to be built over Golgatha, where Jesus was crucified, and over the tomb where Jesus was buried. The church also is said to contain the true cross on which Christ was crucified.

Storytime **T**

Read aloud the following assigned passage:

★ *Door in the Wall* p. 62-75

Ask, *In today's reading, how were people's lives different from your life? What would you have enjoyed or found difficult about living during that time?*

Key Idea: Compare and contrast the historical time period of the reading to your own life.

Vocabulary **S**

You may choose 3-5 of the following vocabulary words from *A Child's History of the World* to use for this lesson: *sepulcher* (p. 228), *pilgrimage* (p. 228), *hermit* (p. 229), *Crusader* (p. 230), and/or *pious* (p. 230). First, find the word in the text and read the sentence containing the word. Think about possible meanings. Next, find the word in a dictionary and select the correct meaning. Write the word at the top of an index card or at the top of the corresponding letter page in the notebook. Underneath the word, copy the correct definition from the dictionary. Then, use the word correctly in a sentence. The sentence may either be copied from the text or be one of your own creation. Last, draw a small picture to show the word's meaning. If you used an index card to record your word, file it under the correct alphabetical tab.

Key Idea: The purpose of the Crusades was for Christians to recapture Jerusalem from the Muslims. Since the Muslims, the Jews, and the Christians consider Jerusalem to be a holy city, there has been much fighting over it.

Independent History Study **I**

★ Read *Minstrel in the Tower: Ch VII-VIII.* Then, copy in cursive paragraph 2 from p. 58 onto a clean page in your *Common Place Book*.

Key Idea: Lord Raimond and his knights reminded Roger of when his father left for the Crusades long ago.

Language Arts

T

Work with the students to complete **one** of the English options listed below:

★ *Beginning Wisely:* Lesson 94

★ *Building with Diligence:* Lesson 95 (half)

★ Your own grammar program

Say, *You will be doing a writing activity based on the poem, "Young Night Thought"* (see Appendix). Say, *What are some things that you see or think of as you're going to sleep at night?* (i.e. counting sheep, thinking of things from the day, imagining a character from a book you've read before bed, singing a song, or listening to night sounds outside). On paper, write the lines listed below, one under the other. Say, *Use the ideas we discussed to help you finish the missing lines from the following poem:*

All night long and every night,
When my mama puts out the light,
I see...
As plain as day, before my eye.

______ *and* ______ *and* _____,
All carrying different kinds of things,
And ________ *in so* _______ *a way,*
You never saw the like by day.

So fine a show was never seen
At....
For every kind of ______ *and* ______
Is _______ *in that* _______.

At first they move a little slow,
But still the faster on they go,
And still beside them close I keep
Until we reach the Town of Sleep.

Key Idea: Write creatively from classic poetry.

Bible Study

T

Have students say Psalm 8:1-8 using the hand motions they added on Day 1. Say, *A mood is a feeling, a sensation, or a state of mind. What is the mood of Psalm 8:6-8?* (Some examples of moods include frightened, worried, happy, peaceful, hopeful, sad, unhappy, angry, thankful, prayerful, joyful, and lonely.) Ask, *When would this Psalm help you, or when would you go to this Psalm?* (i.e. to show us how much authority God has given us over the Earth, to remind us of the responsibility we have to care for God's creation, to know that we are accountable to God for our actions)

Last, pray with your children that they will take good care of God's creation. Pray that they will use the authority they have been given over the Earth wisely and will realize that they are accountable to God for their actions.

✔ *Lead Me to the Rock* CD
Track 8; Song: "How Excellent Is Thy Name" (vs. 1-8)

Key Idea: The Psalms reflect the many emotions and moods we have. They are a wonderful place to seek counsel from the Lord.

Math Exploration

S

Choose **one** of the math options listed below (see Appendix for details).

★ *Singapore Primary Mathematics 2A/2B, 3A/3B*, or *4A/4B*

★ Your own math program

Key Idea: Use a step-by-step math program.

Science Exploration

I

★ Read *One Small Square: Coral Reef* p. 26-27. Orally retell or narrate to an adult the portion of text that you read today. Use the *Narration Tips* in the Appendix for help as needed.

Key Idea: As night falls, it is almost completely dark in the coral reef. Only experienced divers should explore the reef at night, since it is a wild place filled with predators stalking their prey in the dark water.

Unit 26 - Day 3

Reading about History T

Read about history in the following resource:

★ *A Child's History of the World: Ch. 54* p. 232-236

After today's reading, have your students orally narrate or retell the portion of today's text that you read. Use the *Narration Tips* in the Appendix as needed.

Key Idea: The 3 kings were a part of the Third Crusade. Later, a crusade of children attempted the trip to Jerusalem too. They were tricked and sold as slaves.

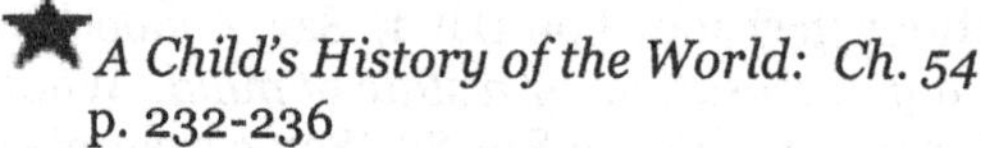

History Project S

Get the relic box that you painted on Day 2. Place a folded up tissue in the bottom of your relic box. Think of an imaginary relic that you could place inside your box. You may place an actual object in the box or cut a relic out of paper to place in the box. Write a note to put inside the lid of the box that explains what your relic is and why it is considered special.

Key Idea: It is important not to worship the creation, rather than the Creator. We are told in God's word to only worship God and never to worship created beings, such as the angels or saints, or created things such as the relics.

Storytime T

Read aloud the following assigned passage:

★ *Door in the Wall* p. 76-85

Ask, *In what does the main character place his faith? How would the story be different if the main character put his faith in God? Share a character, a story, or a verse from the Bible that you are reminded of by today's reading.*

Key Idea: Share a Biblical connection.

Geography S

Use a globe for today's activities. *The Third Crusade was led by three kings. On the globe, find the countries that these three kings ruled. The first king was King Richard of England. Find England on the globe. The second king was King Philip of France. Find France on the globe. The third king was King Frederick Barbarossa of Germany. Find Germany on the globe. Trace the path from these 3 countries to Jerusalem in Israel.*

Introduce the following concept: *Lines of longitude run north and south from the North Pole to the South Pole. They are called meridians of longitude. Point to the lines, or meridians, of longitude on the globe.*

Key Idea: When King Richard arrived in Jerusalem, he fought the Muslim King Saladin. Richard and Saladin reached an agreement.

Independent History Study I

★ On white paper, make a page about King Richard of England. At the top of the paper, write: *Richard the Lion-Hearted (King of England).* Draw King Richard's coat of arms, (which was 3 yellow lions, one on top of the other) on a red background. Add other facts about King Richard, such as the following:

1. Lived from 1157-1199 A.D.
2. Fought Saladin for Jerusalem on the Third Crusade in 1192
3. Was held for ransom by the German king (Legend says the minstrel Blondel found Richard.)
4. Was supposed to have forgiven Robin Hood and his men for their actions

Key Idea: King Richard was loved by many as a leader. He is the topic of many legends and stories.

Learning the Basics

Focus: Language Arts, Math, Bible, and Science

Unit 26 - Day 3

Poetry

T

Read aloud with the students the poem *"Young Night Thought"* (see Appendix). Say, *Describe a memory that the poem brought to mind. What can you learn about the poet, Robert Louis Stevenson, from the poem?* Say, *Did you know that Robert Louis Stevenson was known for his vivid imagination? He is still famous for his imaginative stories and poems. The way he writes helps readers clearly picture things in their minds, just as he intended.* Have the students read the poem on their own.

Key Idea: Read and appreciate classic poetry.

Language Arts

S

Have students complete one studied dictation exercise (see Appendix for directions and passages).

Help students complete one lesson from the following reading program:

★ *Drawn into the Heart of Reading*

Work with the students to complete **one** of the English options listed below:

★ *Beginning Wisely:* Lesson 95

★ *Building with Diligence:* Lesson 95 (half)

★ Your own grammar program

Key Idea: Practice language arts skills.

Bible Study

T

Say, *You will be having your own quiet time with God today. Choose a quiet place for this special time, where you can be alone with God. Then, do the following things:*

1. Read Psalm 8:1-8 in your Bible.
2. Pray about the Psalm using the following beginning to your prayer: *Thank you for trusting me to care for your creation. Help me care for it by _______, _______, and _______. I pray that I will be a good steward over the things that you entrust to me.*
3. Recite Psalm 8:1-8 using the hand motions you added on Day 1.
4. Sing Psalm 8:1-8 along with the CD at the end of your quiet time.

✔ *Lead Me to the Rock* CD
Track 8; Song: "How Excellent Is Thy Name" (vs. 1-8)

Key Idea: The Lord trusts us with His creation. We need to be good stewards.

Math Exploration

S

Choose **one** of the math options listed below (see Appendix for details).

★ *Singapore Primary Mathematics 2A/2B, 3A/3B,* or *4A/4B*

★ Your own math program

Key Idea: Use a step-by-step math program.

Science Exploration

I

★ Read *One Small Square: Coral Reef* p. 28-31. Write the answer to each numbered question on lined paper. You do not need to copy the question. Use the listed page to help you answer each question.

1. How does the coral reef change at night? (p. 28)
2. What are coral wars? (p. 29)
3. Draw a diagram to show how the flashlight-fish's eye pouches shine at night. (p. 30)
4. How do predators find their prey at night in the coral reef? (p. 31)
5. What do the sailors who sail in deep waters see in Psalm 107:23-24?

Key Idea: At night the coral reef is changed, as corals use tentacles to catch their food and fight other coral for space. Other predators, like the lion fish, hunt at night too.

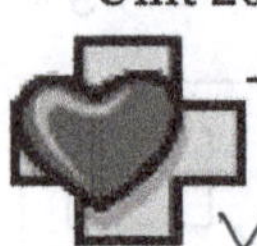

Reading about History T

Read about history in the following resource:

★ *A Child's History of the World: Ch. 56* p. 242-246

After today's reading, say, *You will be writing a narration about part of the day's history reading. In order to remember the details very well, you will need to reread the part of today's reading from the middle of p. 243 through the bottom of p. 245 (on your own if possible).*

After students have finished reading the passage, ask them the questions below. If the students do not know the answers, help them find the answers in the passage they just read. Ask, *How were the churches in Europe built differently from the buildings of the Greeks and Romans? What was this style of building called? Why was this style of building called Gothic? What was a flying buttress? What was drawn on the ground to start the building of a Gothic church? Describe other ways in which Gothic churches were different.*

After the questions have been answered, have students write a 5 sentence narration about the Gothic style of building. Students may look back in the text for help as needed. When students have finished their narration, direct them to read the sentences out loud.

Help students underline or highlight the main idea sentence in their narration. See the *Written Narration Skills* in the Appendix to guide students in editing their narrations.

Key Idea: The churches in Europe were built with braces called flying buttresses. The people in Italy called this style of building Gothic, because the building style was so wild looking.

Storytime T

Read aloud the following assigned passage:

★ *Door in the Wall* p. 86-94

Say, *Transport yourself back to the time of this story. Become one of the characters. Tell me what you see and do. (Make sure to use the word, "I", and to tell only what happened in today's reading.)*

Key Idea: Practice oral narration skills.

Timeline S

You will be adding 2 new cards to your staircase timeline today. On the first new card, draw and color a golden crown. Write, *William the Conqueror (1066 A.D.)*. For the second new card, draw and color a red cross. Write, *The Crusades (1095-1272 A.D.)*

If you decided to tape your timeline cards to the back of a door, begin a new row above the row you just made (like a staircase). On the left side of the door, tape the *William the Conqueror* card. To the right of the *William the Conqueror* card, add *The Crusades* card. If you decided to tape the timeline cards side-by-side to accordion-fold them, use clear packing tape to tape the cards as described above. Then, accordion-fold the timeline to store it.

Key Idea: Each Gothic church was built in the shape of a cross with its head facing Jerusalem. The windows in Gothic style churches were made of stained glass. Pictures in the stained glass showed stories from the Bible. Gargoyles were placed on the corners of the church buildings to scare away evil spirits.

Independent History Study I

★ Read *Pedro's Journal: Aug. 3 - Aug. 27.* Then, choose an interesting part from today's pages to read aloud and explain to an adult.

Key Idea: Churches in Europe were very important to everyone. All Christians went to the same church, and most attended church daily. Before a sea-voyage, sailors prayed for safe travel and a safe return home.

Learning the Basics

Focus: Language Arts, Math, Bible, and Science

Poetry

T

Read aloud with the students the poem *"Young Night Thought"* (see Appendix). Have students share this poem in a special way. Suggestions for sharing the poem are given in the "Poetry" box of Unit 25 – Day 4.

Key Idea: Share a variety of classic poetry.

Language Arts

S

Have students complete one dictation exercise.

Guide students to complete one reading lesson.

★ *Drawn into the Heart of Reading*

Help students complete **one** English lesson.

★ *Beginning Wisely:* Lesson 96

★ *Building with Diligence:* Lesson 96

★ Your own grammar program

Key Idea: Practice language arts skills.

Bible Study

T

Have students say Psalm 8:1-8 using the hand motions from Day 1. Have students copy in cursive Psalm 8:6-8 beneath last unit's Psalm 8:5 in their *Common Place Book.* Students should leave the rest of the page blank to add to next week. Students will add to the *Common Place Book* throughout the year.

✔ *Lead Me to the Rock* CD
Track 8; Song: "How Excellent Is Thy Name" (vs. 1-8)

Key Idea: Copy in cursive a portion of a Psalm.

Math Exploration

S

Choose **one** math option listed below.

★ *Singapore Primary Mathematics 2A/2B, 3A/3B,* or *4A/4B*

★ Your own math program

Key Idea: Use a step-by-step math program.

Science Exploration

I

★ Read *One Small Square: Coral Reef* p. 32-35. Turn to the science experiment section in your science binder or sketchbook. At the top of a blank page, write: *How are colonies of hard coral formed?* Under the question, write: *'Guess'.* Write down your guess. Get out two mounds of clay. Scratch the bottom of the clay mounds with a fork to make them rough. Press the clay mounds down in two separate places inside a rectangular pan. Make sure the mounds are attached well. These will form the base of your coral colonies. Add water to your pan to cover the tip of the mounds. Either use pipe cleaners cut into small pieces or pasta noodles to be your coral larvae (and later adults). Plant the bottom of one coral larvae in each mound, and place two larvae in the water. Then, add another coral next to the implanted one, showing your coral growing into an adult and reproducing.

Swish the water back and forth to be a current. The current should carry the larvae in the water over to the coral mounds. Implant the coral from the water in a new spot on your mound to start another coral community. Each time you swish the water, have each adult coral reproduce and make another coral. So, with each swish of the water, you will be doubling the number of coral in each spot. For example, 2 coral will become 4 coral. 4 coral will become 8 coral. Can you see how the coral community grows? On your paper, write: *'Procedure'.* Draw a picture of the experiment. At the bottom of the paper, write: *'Conclusion'.* Explain what you learned.

Key Idea: Coral polyps squeeze off part of their bodies and grow an exact copy, which makes its own cup.

Reading about History [T]

Read about history in the following resource:

★ *A Child's History of the World: Ch. 57* p. 247-249

Note: There is some graphic content on p. 248 that you may wish to omit or reword.

After today's reading, say, *Share what you know about King John.* (comprehension) *Why was it so upsetting to the English people that the churches were closed?* (analysis) *Tell about the Magna Carta.* (comprehension) *How did the Magna Carta change the way English kings ruled?* (evaluation) *The Magna Carta later helped influence the American Constitution and the Bill of Rights. Why would Americans look back at the Magna Carta as a guide for how to govern?* (application)

Key Idea: England suffered under King John.

History Project [S]

In this unit you will make a picture of a stained glass window. Look through some pictures of stained glass windows at www.wikipedia.org under the *stained glass windows* search by scrolling down to the *gallery of windows* heading. Decide whether you want to make an arched window or a circular rose window. Outline your window on a piece of white paper. Sketch your picture or design inside the window first. Then, color the outside of your window in heavy black crayon. Add thick, black crayon lines around your design to make it stand out. Wait to color the rest on Days 2-3.

Key Idea: The pope closed the churches.

Storytime [T]

Read aloud the following assigned story:

★ *Door in the Wall* p. 95-107

Discuss today's reading in a "conversational way". Share about a person, time, event, or emotion from your life that today's reading brought to mind. Next, have your child share a connection.

Key Idea: Connect personally to the story.

Research [S]

In medieval times, churches had beautiful stained glass windows. Where could you look to discover more about **stained glass windows**? Use a reference book or an online resource like www.wikipedia.org to type *stained glass windows* in the search or look it up in the index.

Orally answer one or more of the following questions from your research: *What are stained glass windows? Where were stained glass windows mainly used? What types of scenes did stained glass windows show most often? How were stained glass windows like a Bible for the poor people of Europe who could not read? How were stained glass windows made?*

Key Idea: Richard the Lion-Heart's brother, John, became king. King John refused to listen to the pope or to anyone else. After the pope closed the churches in England, the people became so upset that King John feared for his life. King John was finally forced to sign the Magna Carta, which guaranteed the people their rights and some protection from the king.

Independent History Study [I]

★ Read *Pedro's Journal: Sept. 3 – Sept. 21.* Orally retell or narrate to an adult the portion of text that you read today. Use the *Narration Tips* in the Appendix for help as needed.

Key Idea: Columbus set sail about 280 years after King John signed the Magna Carta.

Learning the Basics
Focus: Language Arts, Math, Bible, and Science

Poetry — T

Read aloud to the students the poem *"The Land of Story-Books"* (see Appendix). Say, *What time of day is it in the poem? What are the child's parents doing during the evening hours? As the parents are sitting and talking by the fire, what is the child doing? How does the child "play at books" that he has read? When the child's nurse comes in, what happens?* Read the poem again with the students.

Key Idea: Read and appreciate classic poetry.

Language Arts — S

Have students complete the first studied dictation exercise (see Appendix for directions and passages).

Help students complete one lesson from the following reading program:

 *Drawn into the Heart of Reading*

Work with the students to complete **one** of the English options listed below:

★ *Beginning Wisely:* Lesson 97

★ *Building with Diligence:* Lesson 97

★ Your own grammar program

Key Idea: Practice language arts skills.

Bible Study — T

Say, *Find Philippians 4:8 in your Bible. This is the memory selection for this unit. Read the verse out loud.* Ask, *What things does Paul tell us to think upon in Philippians 4:8? Why is it important to be careful what thoughts we put into our minds? How does what we read, watch, and hear affect what we think, do, and say? If we are not surrounding ourselves with wholesome material, what will happen to our thoughts and our daydreams? How can we focus our mind on what is good and pure? Why is it so important to read God's word and to pray?*

Have students say the verse 3 times, adding hand motions to help remember the words.

 *Lead Me to the Rock* CD
Track 7; Song: "Think on These Things" (vs. 8)

Key Idea: What we read, watch, and hear affects what we think, do, and say.

Math Exploration — S

Choose **one** of the math options listed below (see Appendix for details).

 *Singapore Primary Mathematics 2A/2B, 3A/3B,* or *4A/4B*

★ Your own math program

Key Idea: Use a step-by-step math program.

Science Exploration — I

Today you will add to your science notebook. At the top of an unlined paper, copy Psalm 95:4-5 in cursive. Beneath the verse, draw and label the parts of the coral life cycle shown in the circle on p. 33 of *One Small Square: Coral Reef.* Copy the paragraph below the coral life cycle diagram onto your notebook page. Color the coral life cycle drawing to match the picture on p. 33.

Key Idea: In the late spring, a few days after the full moon, coral polyps cloud the water by letting go bundles of sperm and eggs. In order for the life cycle of the polyps to continue, the sperm must find an egg of its own kind to join with and then grow into a coral larvae.

Reading about History T

Read about history in the following resource:

★ *A Child's History of the World: Ch. 60* p. 257-261

After today's reading, read aloud Luke 14:28-33. Say, *What does Luke 14:28-31 say about counting the cost? Do you think the King of England counted the cost before beginning the Hundred Years' War? If he had known it would go on over 100 years, do you think he would have started it? What does Luke 14:33 say about being a disciple of Jesus? Joan of Arc was known to be a devout Christian, yet she had visions that were out of the ordinary for a peasant girl. When she died, she called upon Jesus. Do you think Joan of Arc counted the cost of her faith? Are we guaranteed a trouble-free life if we are followers of Christ?*

Key Idea: Edward the III, King of England, started the Hundred Years' War by attacking France. Many people died throughout the war.

History Project S

Get your stained glass window that you began on Day 1. Draw pencil lines to divide your design or drawing into pieces. Each piece will have its own color. Use crayons to brightly color each part of your stained glass window. You will finish coloring your window on Day 3.

Key Idea: While England and France were fighting the Hundred Years' War, the bubonic plague swept across Europe. It killed many millions of people, and there was no medicine or cure for the disease. In sorrowful times, remember that God is in control of history. Our hope is in Him instead of in the world.

Storytime T

Read aloud the following assigned passage:

★ *Door in the Wall* p. 108-121

Ask, *In today's reading, how were people's lives different from your life? What would you have enjoyed or found difficult about living during that time?*

Key Idea: Compare and contrast the historical time period of the reading to your own life.

Vocabulary S

You may choose 3-5 of the following vocabulary words from *A Child's History of the World* to use for this lesson: *clad* (p. 257), *longbow* (p. 258), *bubonic plague* (p. 258), *peasant* (p. 259), and/or *visions* (p. 259). First, find the word in the text and read the sentence containing the word. Think about possible meanings. Next, find the word in a dictionary and select the correct meaning. Write the word at the top of an index card or at the top of the corresponding letter page in the notebook. Underneath the word, copy the correct definition from the dictionary. Then, use the word correctly in a sentence. The sentence may either be copied from the text or be one of your own creation. Last, draw a small picture to show the word's meaning. If you used an index card to record your word, file it under the correct alphabetical tab.

Key Idea: The war continued on over 100 years, until Joan of Arc led the French in finally driving out the English army. Joan of Arc was captured and killed by the English. Later, she was found not guilty of the charges against her and was declared a saint by the pope in 1920.

Independent History Study I

★ Read *Pedro's Journal: Sept. 25 - Oct. 5*. Then, copy in cursive paragraph 2 from p. 26 onto a clean page in your *Common Place Book*.

Key Idea: As Columbus and his men sailed on, they all began to worry that they might never see land.

Learning the Basics

Focus: Language Arts, Math, Bible, and Science

Unit 27 - Day 2

Language Arts

T

Work with the students to complete **one** of the English options listed below:

★ *Beginning Wisely:* Lesson 98

★ *Building with Diligence:* Lesson 98

★ Your own grammar program

Say, *You will be doing a writing activity based on the poem, "The Land of Story-Books"* (see Appendix). Say, *In the poem "The Lands of Story-Books", the poet used one main topic per stanza.* Guide students to share the following main topics from the poem by stanza, as you list them on a markerboard or a paper:

1. Parents are around the fire.
2. I crawl with a play gun.
3. I pretend to be in a hunter's camp.
4. I pretend there are hills, woods, a river, and lions.
5. I pretend to be an Indian scout.
6. My nurse comes and takes me to bed.

Ask, *What are some things that you have acted out or pretended about from storybooks? Make a list to outline a possible poem patterned after "The Land of Story-Books" that begins with your parents sitting and talking somewhere in your house in the evening hours. Next, in the middle stanzas on the list, describe the pretend things you could act out from your storybooks. Then, for the last stanza on your list, end with your mother or father coming to send you to bed. When the list is complete, retell the scene orally to an adult following the sequence of topics on your list.*

Key Idea: Write creatively from classic poetry.

Bible Study

T

Have students say Philippians 4:8 using the hand motions they added on Day 1. Say, *A mood is a feeling, a sensation, or a state of mind. What is the mood of Philippians 4:8?* (Some examples of moods include frightened, worried, happy, peaceful, hopeful, sad, unhappy, angry, thankful, prayerful, joyful, and lonely.) Ask, *When would this verse help you, or when would you go to this verse?* (i.e. as a reminder of the things that God wishes us to think about, to guide us to surround ourselves with wholesome things, to be careful with what we put into our minds)

Last, pray with your children that they will carefully guard what they put into their minds. Pray for the Lord to help them focus their minds on what is good and pure. Pray for them to desire wholesome things.

✔ *Lead Me to the Rock* CD
Track 7; Song: "Think on These Things" (vs. 8)

Key Idea: Scripture reflects the many emotions and moods we have. They are a wonderful place to seek counsel from the Lord.

Math Exploration

S

Choose **one** of the math options listed below (see Appendix for details).

★ *Singapore Primary Mathematics 2A/2B, 3A/3B,* or *4A/4B*

★ Your own math program

Key Idea: Use a step-by-step math program.

Science Exploration

I

★ Read *One Small Square: Coral Reef* p. 36-37. Orally retell or narrate to an adult the portion of text that you read today. Use the *Narration Tips* in the Appendix for help as needed.

Key Idea: Since more and more coral reefs are being destroyed or polluted, some countries are turning their reefs into national marine parks.

Learning through History

Focus: East Meets West

Unit 27 - Day 3

Reading about History **T**

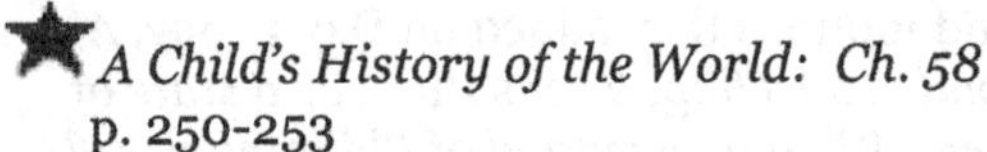

Read about history in the following resource:

★ *A Child's History of the World: Ch. 58* p. 250-253

★ Also, read *Hero Tales* as scheduled in the *Storytime* box of the plans.

After today's first reading, have your students orally narrate or retell the portion of today's first text that you read. Use the *Narration Tips* in the Appendix as needed.

Key Idea: Genghis Khan was ruler over the fierce Mongols in Cathay. Both he and his army were strong fighters. He had an empire larger than Alexander the Great's empire.

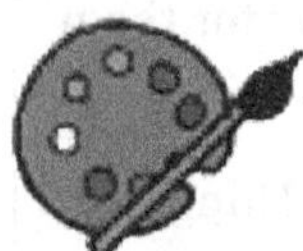

History Project **S**

Get the stained glass window that you began on Days 1-2. Finish coloring the stained glass window in crayon. Then, cut it out. Place the picture of the window face down on a paper towel. Dip a cotton ball in baby oil or vegetable oil. Lightly swipe the cotton across the back of the paper. Lay the paper flat to dry. When your window is dry, tape it to a real window to let the light shine through your "stained glass".

Key Idea: Genghis Khan's grandson, Kublai Khan, built beautiful palaces and gardens. He met two brothers from Italy named Nicolo and Maffeo Polo. Later, Nicolo's son, Marco, also visited China. Marco Polo told many amazing stories about his time in China.

Storytime **T**

Read aloud the following assigned passage:

★ *Hero Tales* p. 9-13

Ask, *In what does the main character place her faith? How would the story be different if the main character didn't put her faith in God? Share a character, a story, or a verse from the Bible that you are reminded of by today's reading.*

Key Idea: Share a Biblical connection.

Geography **S**

Use a globe for today's activities. *Cathay is the same thing as modern-day China. Find China on the globe. Trace Genghis Khan's empire from the Pacific Ocean all the way to Eastern Europe. Find Kublai Khan's capitol of Peiping, which in now called Beijing. It is located in eastern China. Last, find Venice, Italy where the Polos originally departed from on their trip to China. What a long trip that was!*

Introduce the following concept: *Lines of longitude run north and south from the North Pole to the South Pole. They are called meridians of longitude. The Prime Meridian is at 0 degrees longitude. It passes through Greenwich in the United Kingdom. Find the Prime Meridian on the globe. What other countries does it pass through?*

Key Idea: Kublai Khan ruled over a vast empire. He was more peaceful than his father and grandfather had been.

Independent History Study **I**

★ On white paper, make a page about Marco Polo. At the top of the paper, write: *Marco Polo (1254-1324 A.D.).* Then, copy in cursive the last paragraph on p. 253 from *A Child's History of the World.* Draw small pictures to go along with Marco's descriptions.

Key Idea: Christopher Columbus owned a copy of Marco Polo's book. We can see that he had written many notes in it. Columbus was most likely inspired by the book to find a new way in which to reach the riches of the Far East.

Learning the Basics

Focus: Language Arts, Math, Bible, and Science

Unit 27 - Day 3

Poetry

T

Read aloud with the students the poem *"The Land of Story-Books"* (see Appendix). Say, *Describe a memory that the poem brought to mind. What can you learn about the poet, Robert Louis Stevenson, from the poem?* Say, *Did you know that Robert Louis Stevenson was an only child in a very close, loving family? Through the words of this poem, you can picture his childhood evenings, ending with his nurse hustling him off to bed.* Have the students read the poem on their own.

Key Idea: Read and appreciate classic poetry.

Language Arts

S

Have students complete one studied dictation exercise (see Appendix for directions and passages).

Help students complete one lesson from the following reading program:

 *Drawn into the Heart of Reading*

Work with the students to complete **one** of the English options listed below:

 *Beginning Wisely:* Lesson 99

 *Building with Diligence:* Lesson 99

 Your own grammar program

Key Idea: Practice language arts skills.

Bible Study

T

Say, *You will be having your own quiet time with God today. Choose a quiet place for this special time, where you can be alone with God. Then, do the following things:*

1. Read Philippians 4:8 in your Bible.
2. Pray about the verse using the following beginning to your prayer: *Thank you for showing me how to live my life for you. Help me to think on things that are ______, ______, and ______. Guide me to carefully guard what I put into my mind.*
3. Recite Philippians 4:8 using the hand motions you added on Day 1.
4. Sing Philippians 4:8 along with the CD at the end of your quiet time.

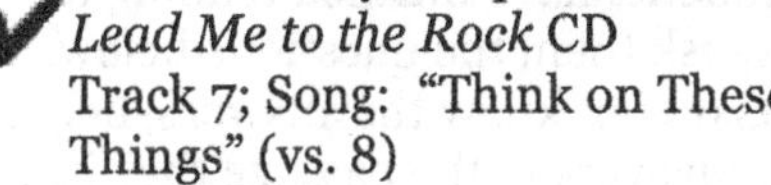

✔ *Lead Me to the Rock* CD
Track 7; Song: "Think on These Things" (vs. 8)

Key Idea: The Lord can help you keep your mind on things that are good and pure.

Math Exploration

S

Choose **one** of the math options listed below (see Appendix for details).

 *Singapore Primary Mathematics 2A/2B, 3A/3B,* or *4A/4B*

 Your own math program

Key Idea: Use a step-by-step math program.

Science Exploration

I

★ Read *One Small Square: Coral Reef* p. 40-43. Write the answer to each numbered question on lined paper. You do not need to copy the question. Use the listed page to help you answer each question.

1. What is a vertebrate? (p. 40)
2. How can you tell a hard coral apart from other stinging-celled animals? (p. 41)
3. Since most of the animals living on the reef do not have bones, what are they called? (p. 42)
4. Name some of the protists that are important food for small reef creatures. (p. 43)
5. How does Nehemiah 9:6 show that all life comes from God and continues on because of Him?

Key Idea: Most of the animals living in the coral reef are invertebrates. Many small creatures in the coral reef live on algae and plankton that can be found in the water.

Learning through History
Focus: East Meets West

Unit 27 - Day 4

Reading about History — T

Read about history in the following resource:

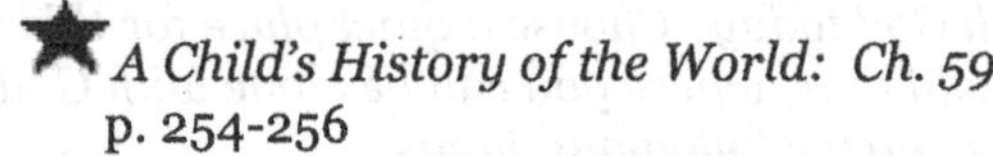

★ *A Child's History of the World: Ch. 59* p. 254-256

★ Also, read *Hero Tales* as scheduled in the *Storytime* box of the plans.

After today's first reading, say, *You will be writing a narration about part of the day's first history reading. In order to remember the details very well, you will need to reread the part of today's reading from the second paragraph on p. 254 up to the last paragraph on p. 255 (on your own if possible).*

After students have finished reading the passage, ask them the questions below. If the students do not know the answers, help them find the answers in the passage they just read. Ask, *What new invention was of great help to sailors? Before the compass, how did sailors know which way to go? Why did sailors get off course during cloudy or stormy weather? How did the compass solve the sailors' problems? Explain why it was a long time before sailors used the compass. What does it mean to be superstitious? Should Christians be superstitious? Why not?*

After the questions have been answered, have students write a 3-5 sentence narration about the compass. When students have finished their narration, direct them to read the sentences out loud.

Help students underline or highlight the main idea sentence in their narration. See the *Written Narration Skills* in the Appendix to guide students in editing their narrations.

Key Idea: A compass was a needed invention.

Storytime — T

Read aloud the following assigned passage:

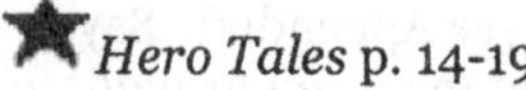

★ *Hero Tales* p. 14-19

Say, After today's reading, have your students orally narrate or retell the portion of today's text that you read. Use the *Narration Tips* in the Appendix as needed.

Key Idea: Practice oral narration skills.

Timeline — S

You will be adding 3 new cards to your staircase timeline today. On the first new card, draw and color a quill pen. Write, *Magna Carta (1215 A.D.).* For the second new card, draw and color jewels. Write, *Marco Polo (returned home 1271 A.D.).* On the third new card, draw a big '100'. Write, *Hundred Years' War (1337-1453 A.D.).*

If you decided to tape your timeline cards to the back of a door, then add the *Magna Carta* card to the right of *The Crusades* card. To the right of the *Magna Carta* card, add the *Marco Polo* card. To the right of the *Marco Polo* card, add the *Hundred Years' War* card. If you decided to tape the timeline cards side-by-side to accordion-fold them, use clear packing tape to tape the cards as described above. Then, accordion-fold the timeline to store it.

Key Idea: The Arab sailors carried many of the new inventions from the Far East to Europe. Inventions such as the compass changed the way sailors navigated. Inventions such as gunpowder changed the way wars were fought.

Independent History Study — I

★ Read *Pedro's Journal: Oct. 7 – Oct. 11.* Then, choose an interesting part from today's pages to read aloud and explain to an adult.

Key Idea: It took European sailors awhile before they were willing to use a compass, because Europeans were very superstitious of anything that seemed like magic. Columbus sailed by the stars and the compass.

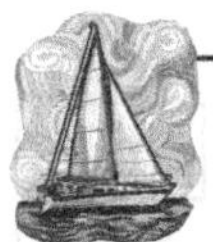

Poetry

T

Read aloud with the students the poem *"The Land of Story-Books"* (see Appendix). Have students share this poem in a special way. Suggestions for sharing the poem are given in the "Poetry" box of Unit 25 – Day 4.

Key Idea: Share a variety of classic poetry.

Bible Study

T

Have students say Philippians 4:8 using the hand motions from Day 1. Have students copy in cursive Philippians 4:8 onto **the bottom** of a clean page in their *Common Place Book*. Students should leave the **top** of the page blank to add to next week. Students will add to the *Common Place Book* throughout the year.

✔ *Lead Me to the Rock* CD
Track 7; Song: "Think on These Things" (vs. 8)

Key Idea: Copy in cursive a portion of a Bible verse from Philippians..

Language Arts

S

Have students complete one dictation exercise.

Guide students to complete one reading lesson.

★ *Drawn into the Heart of Reading*

Help students complete **one** English lesson.

★ *Beginning Wisely:* Lesson 100

★ *Building with Diligence:* Lesson 100

★ Your own grammar program

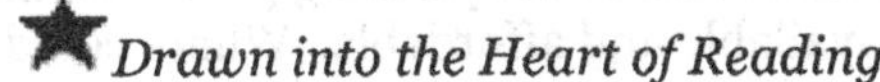

Key Idea: Practice language arts skills.

Math Exploration

S

Choose **one** math option listed below.

★ *Singapore Primary Mathematics 2A/2B, 3A/3B,* or *4A/4B*

★ Your own math program

Key Idea: Use a step-by-step math program.

Science Exploration

I

★ Read *Columbus* p. 4-12. Turn to the science experiment section in your science binder or sketchbook. At the top of a blank page, write: *Is seawater heavier or lighter than fresh water? Explain.* Under the question, write: *'Guess'*. Write down your guess. Place 4 glasses in a row on the counter. Make sure the fourth glass is clear, so you can see through it. Fill the first 3 glasses one-quarter full of water. Place a piece of masking tape on the counter in front of the first 3 glasses to label their contents. Add 2 tsp. of salt to the first glass of water, and stir it until it is dissolved. On the masking tape in front of the first glass, write "2 tsp. salt". Add 1 tsp. of salt to the second glass of water, and stir until it is dissolved. On the masking tape in front of the second glass, write "1 tsp. salt". Leave the third glass of water plain. On the masking tape in front of the third glass, write "no salt". Add 2 drops of red food coloring to the first glass, 2 drops of yellow to the second glass, and 2 drops of blue to the third glass. The fourth glass is empty.

Place a straw into the red water. Put your finger over the top opening of the straw, pick the straw up, and place it over the empty glass. Remove your finger from the top of the straw to let the water run into the glass. Rinse out the straw, and repeat the activity, this time using the yellow water. Allow it to run into the empty glass on top of the red water. Rinse out the straw, and repeat the activity one more time using the blue water. Why would the saltiest water stay on the bottom? On your paper, write: *'Procedure'*. Draw a picture of the experiment. At the bottom of the paper, write: *'Conclusion'*. Explain what you learned.

Key Idea: Seawater is very salty, making it heavier than plain water. This also makes it more buoyant.

Learning through History
Focus: Age of Exploration

Unit 28 - Day 1

Reading about History — T

Read about history in the following resource:

★ *A Child's History of the World: Ch. 61* p. 262-264

★ Also, read *Hero Tales* as scheduled in the *Storytime* box of the plans.

After today's first reading, say, *Why weren't there many books in Europe before Gutenberg invented the printing press?* (comprehension) *How did the printing press change Europe?* (analysis) *Describe how the Turks changed the way that battles were fought.* (knowledge) *Tell why castles, armor, and bows and arrows weren't useful in this new kind of fighting.* (application) *Explain why 1453 is often called the end of the Middle Ages.* (synthesis)

Key Idea: Gunpowder ended the Middle Ages.

History Project — S

In this unit you will learn how the Bible is structured and make a braided bookmark. First, practice opening your Bible to Genesis, which is the first book. Then, practice opening your Bible to the middle, which is Psalms. Last practice opening your Bible halfway between Psalms and the end of the Bible, which is Matthew. This is the first book in the New Testament. Repeat the activity until you can find those 3 places in your Bible easily. Then, measure and cut 9 pieces of yarn 13" long. Tie them together at the top with a knot. Group 3 pieces of yarn together and braid them. Tie a knot at the bottom. Repeat the activity to make 2 more braids. Place one braid in Genesis, one in Psalms, and one in Matthew.

Key Idea: The Bible became more available.

Storytime — T

Read aloud the following assigned story:

★ *Hero Tales* p. 164-169

Discuss today's reading in a "conversational way". Share about a person, time, event, or emotion from your life that today's reading brought to mind. Next, have your child share a connection.

Key Idea: Connect personally to the story.

Research — S

With the invention of the printing press, books became available and affordable. Where could you look to discover more about the **printing press?** Use a reference book or an online resource like www.wikipedia.org to type *printing press* in the search or look it up in the index.

Orally answer one or more of the following questions from your research: *Where was movable type and block printing first invented? Who invented the first printing press? Describe how the printing press worked. What were some of the first books printed by Gutenberg? How did the printing press change people's lives? How did the printing press change religious practices and church services? Why would the invention of the printing press cause more people to learn to read?*

Key Idea: Gutenberg spent five years printing the first Bible made with movable type. The Bible was the most important book in Europe at that time. We are blessed to be able to have our own copy of the Bible.

Independent History Study — I

★ Read *Pedro's Journal: Oct. 12 – Nov. 6.* Orally retell or narrate to an adult the portion of text that you read today. Use the *Narration Tips* in the Appendix for help as needed.

Key Idea: As Columbus and his ships finally reached land, the crew met many different groups of natives.

Learning the Basics

Focus: Language Arts, Math, Bible, and Science

Unit 28 - Day 1

Poetry

T

Read aloud to the students the poem *"Nest Eggs"* (see Appendix). Say, *Where are the children at the beginning of the poem? What are they watching? After the baby birds hatch, what does the poet say will eventually happen? Why won't the children be looking down on the birds after awhile? Explain the humor in the last stanza.* Read the poem again with the students.

<u>Key Idea</u>: Read and appreciate classic poetry.

Language Arts

S

Have students complete the first studied dictation exercise (see Appendix for directions and passages).

Help students complete one lesson from the following reading program:

 *Drawn into the Heart of Reading*

Work with the students to complete **one** of the English options listed below:

★ *Beginning Wisely:* Review One p. 250-252

★ *Building with Diligence:* Lesson 101

★ Your own grammar program

<u>Key Idea</u>: Practice language arts skills.

Bible Study

T

Say, *Find Philippians 4:6-8 in your Bible. This is the memory selection for this unit. Read the verses out loud.* Ask, *In Philippians 4:6, what are we told to do with our cares and our worries? What does Philippians 4:7 say will happen if we pray and make our worries known to God? How can knowing that God is in control give us peace? When we believe in Christ Jesus, what can we be assured of having one day? How can this help us to worry less?*

Have students say the verse 3 times, adding hand motions to help remember the words.

 *Lead Me to the Rock* CD
Track 7; Song: "Think on These Things" (vs. 6-8)

<u>Key Idea</u>: The Lord wants us to turn to Him in prayer during times of worry. He wants to give us His peace.

Math Exploration

S

Choose **one** of the math options listed below (see Appendix for details).

★ *Singapore Primary Mathematics 2A/2B, 3A/3B,* or *4A/4B*

★ Your own math program

<u>Key Idea</u>: Use a step-by-step math program.

Science Exploration

I

★ Read *Columbus* p. 14-23. Today you will add to your science notebook. At the top of an unlined paper, copy Isaiah 40:22 in cursive. Beneath the verse, draw the picture of the orange and the butterfly from p. 9 of *Columbus*. Then, copy the first paragraph from p. 8 to go along with your picture of the orange and the butterfly.

<u>Key Idea</u>: Columbus believed the stories about Leif Erikson traveling to new lands. He decided to sail west to try to reach the riches of the East. He spent many years waiting for the King of Portugal, and later the King and Queen of Spain, to finance his voyage. At long last, Columbus received 3 small ships and money for the journey.

Learning through History
Focus: Age of Exploration

Unit 28 - Day 2

Reading about History [T]

Read about history in the following resource:

★ *A Child's History of the World: Ch. 62* p. 265-271

★ Also, read *Hero Tales* as scheduled in the *Storytime* box of the plans.

After today's first reading, read aloud Acts 27:10-11, 21-26. Say, *What warning did Paul give the crew before they sailed in Acts 27:10-11? In Acts 27:21, what was Paul showing the crew? How could Paul have known that there would be trouble on the voyage? What did Paul say in Acts 27:22? In Acts 27:23-24, what reason did Paul give for knowing that this was true? What was God's plan for Paul in Acts 27:24? Since God was protecting Paul for a later purpose, how did God's plan for Paul impact the other men on the ship? Do you think that God had a plan for Columbus? Are God's plans always carried out?*

Key Idea: Columbus finally set sail from Palos.

History Project [S]

Place one braid of your bookmark in the middle of Joshua. The books to the left of Joshua are books of the law. The books to the right of Joshua (up to Job) are books of history. Open your Bible at the halfway point. Place one braid in Psalms. Job, Psalms, Proverbs, Ecclesiastes, and Song of Solomon are books of poetry. Find Matthew halfway between Psalms and the end of the Bible. Place your third bookmark braid there. From Isaiah to Matthew are books of the prophets.

Key Idea: God used Columbus for His purpose.

Storytime [T]

Read aloud the following assigned passage:

★ *Hero Tales* p. 170-175

Ask, *In what does the main character place his faith? How would the story be different if the main character didn't put his faith in God? Share a character, a story, or a verse from the Bible that you are reminded of by the reading.*

Key Idea: Share a Biblical connection.

Vocabulary [S]

You may choose 3-5 of the following vocabulary words from *A Child's History of the World* to use for this lesson: *yarns* (p. 265), *ambition* (p. 265), *navigators* (p. 266), *vast* (p. 267), and/or *ingratitude* (p. 270). First, find the word in the text and read the sentence containing the word. Think about possible meanings. Next, find the word in a dictionary and select the correct meaning. Write the word at the top of an index card or at the top of the corresponding letter page in the notebook. Underneath the word, copy the correct definition from the dictionary. Then, use the word correctly in a sentence. The sentence may either be copied from the text or be one of your own creation. Last, draw a small picture to show the word's meaning. If you used an index card to record your word, file it under the correct alphabetical tab.

Key Idea: Even though Columbus planned for the voyage, God's plan brought him to the New World. Our plans don't always turn out like we expect them to, but God's plans do. God has a purpose for each one of us, just as He had a purpose for Columbus.

Independent History Study [I]

★ Read *Pedro's Journal: Nov. 19 – Dec. 16.* Then, copy in your *Common Place Book* a paragraph of your choice from the pages you read today. Make sure to copy the paragraph in cursive.

Key Idea: Columbus didn't know there were other continents in his path as he tried to sail to the Indies.

Learning the Basics
Focus: Language Arts, Math, Bible, and Science

Language Arts
T

Work with the students to complete **one** of the English options listed below:

★ *Beginning Wisely:* Review Two p. 252-253

★ *Building with Diligence:* Lesson 102

★ Your own grammar program

Say, *You will be doing a writing activity based on the poem, "Nest Eggs"* (see Appendix). Say, *In the poem "Nest Eggs", the poet listed the steps for hatching an egg.* Guide students to share the following steps from the poem, as you list them on a markerboard or a paper:

1. The mother bird sits on the eggs to keep them warm.
2. The eggs hatch.
3. The baby birds sing.
4. The baby birds learn to fly.
5. The birds are flying above the tree - tops, while we are still walking.

Say, *What are some other living things in nature that go through stages or steps as they grow?* (i.e. plants, frogs, butterflies, trees, moths, insects, etc.) Say, *Choose one living thing and make a list to outline the stages or steps it goes through as it grows. You may need to use a science book or an encyclopedia to help you list the various stages. Then, write a poem or several paragraphs to describe the growth process in an interesting way.*

Share the poem or paragraphs by reading them out loud when you are finished writing.

Key Idea: Write creatively from classic poetry.

Bible Study
T

Have students say Philippians 4:6-8 using the hand motions they added on Day 1. Say, *A mood is a feeling, a sensation, or a state of mind. What is the mood of Philippians 4:6-7?* (Some examples of moods include frightened, worried, happy, peaceful, hopeful, sad, unhappy, angry, thankful, prayerful, joyful, and lonely.) Ask, *When would this passage help you, or when would you go to this passage?* (i.e. as a reminder to pray about all of our worries and concerns, to give us the assurance that God is in control of our lives, to show us the peace that comes from trusting the Lord)

Last, pray with your children that they will turn to God with their cares and their worries. Pray that God will give them His perfect peace and that they will take comfort in knowing that God is in control.

Lead Me to the Rock CD
Track 7; Song: "Think on These Things" (vs. 6-8)

Key Idea: Scripture reflects the many emotions and moods we have. They are a wonderful place to seek counsel from the Lord.

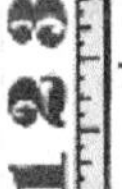

Math Exploration
S

Choose **one** of the math options listed below (see Appendix for details).

★ *Singapore Primary Mathematics 2A/2B, 3A/3B,* or *4A/4B*

★ Your own math program

Key Idea: Use a step-by-step math program.

Science Exploration
I

★ Read *Columbus* p. 24-33. Orally retell or narrate to an adult the portion of text that you read today. Use the *Narration Tips* in the Appendix for help as needed.

Key Idea: Columbus sailed west, using the stars, his maps, and his compass as his guides. When his compass stopped pointing to the North Star, and the seaweed was thick in the sea, the sailors panicked. When Columbus saw the light of a fire that must have meant land, he dropped anchor to avoid the reef.

Learning through History
Focus: Age of Exploration

Unit 28 - Day 3

Reading about History [T]

Read about history in the following resource:

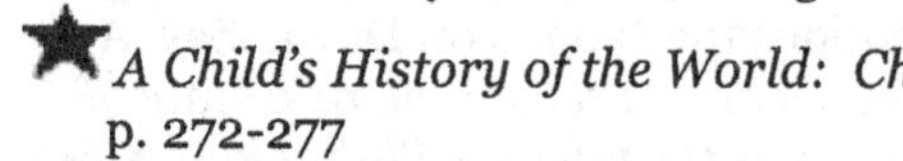

★ *A Child's History of the World: Ch. 63* p. 272-277

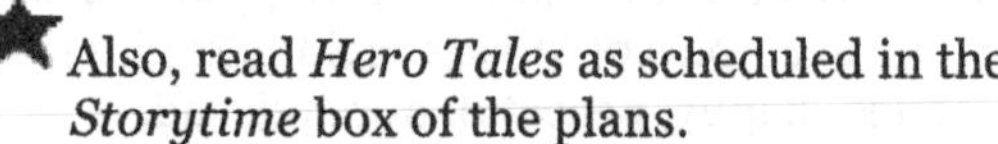

★ Also, read *Hero Tales* as scheduled in the *Storytime* box of the plans.

After today's first reading, have your students orally narrate or retell the portion of today's first text that you read. Use the *Narration Tips* in the Appendix as needed.

Key Idea: After Columbus, many more explorers made voyages searching for water routes to the East.

History Project [S]

Open your Bible in the middle to Psalms. Place one braid of your bookmark there. Then, open up halfway between Psalms and the end of the Bible to Matthew. Place a second braid there. Then, open your Bible halfway between Matthew and the end of your Bible to Romans. Place the third braid of your bookmark there. The book of Matthew is the beginning of the New Testament. From Matthew to Romans are the 4 gospels and the book of Acts. The 4 gospels are Matthew, Mark, Luke, and John. To the right of the book of Romans, are the letters to the churches. The last book, Revelation, is a book of prophecy.

Key Idea: Everything before the New Testament is B.C. because it is before Christ.

Storytime [T]

Read aloud the following assigned passage:

★ *Hero Tales* p. 57-61

Ask, *In today's reading, how were people's lives different from your life? What would you have enjoyed or found difficult about living during that time?*

Key Idea: Compare historical time periods.

Geography [S]

Use a globe for today's activities. *Trace Vasco da Gama's route on the globe from Portugal, down the coast of Africa, and around the tip of the Cape of Good Hope to India. Next, trace one of Cabot's routes on the globe from England, west to Canada, and along the coast of the United States (which he claimed for England). Last, trace Magellan's route around the world, from Spain to South America, down around Cape Horn through the Straits of Magellan, across the Pacific Ocean to the Philippine Islands. This is where Magellan was killed. His crew continued on to the west across the Pacific Ocean toward Africa, around the Cape of Good Hope, and up the western coast of Africa to Spain.*

Introduce the following concept: *Meridians of longitude run north and south. There are 15 degrees between each line of longitude, because Earth turns 15 degrees every hour. If you add up the 15 degree increments, you get 360 degrees. After 24 hours, or 1 day, earth has turned 360 degrees (or 1 complete turn).*

Key Idea: Magellan's crew circled the world.

Independent History Study [I]

★ On white paper, photocopy or draw the map from p. 275 of *A Child's History of the World*. If you drew the map, label it *The New World*. Circle the islands where Columbus landed in the Bahamas, one of which is called San Salvador. Circle the Isthmus of Panama where Balboa traveled. Draw and label a line to show where Cabot sailed along the eastern coast of North America. Make a key to explain your map.

Key Idea: Columbus ushered in the Age of Exploration. Many other explorers followed his lead.

Learning the Basics
Focus: Language Arts, Math, Bible, and Science

Unit 28 - Day 3

Poetry

T

Read aloud with the students the poem *"Nest Eggs"* (see Appendix). Say, *Describe a memory that the poem brought to mind. What can you learn about the poet, Robert Louis Stevenson, from the poem?* Say, *Did you know that Robert Louis Stevenson's mother and father both came from large families? Robert loved playing with his many cousins outdoors in the beautiful gardens at his grandfather's house.* Have the students read the poem on their own.

Key Idea: Read and appreciate classic poetry.

Language Arts

S

Have students complete one studied dictation exercise (see Appendix for directions and passages).

Help students complete one lesson from the following reading program:

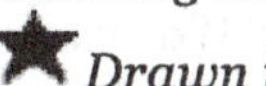 *Drawn into the Heart of Reading*

Work with the students to complete **one** of the English options listed below:

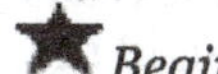 *Beginning Wisely:* A Poem to Enjoy p. 255

 *Building with Diligence:* Lesson 103

 Your own grammar program

Key Idea: Practice language arts skills.

Bible Study

T

Say, *You will be having your own quiet time with God today. Choose a quiet place for this special time, where you can be alone with God. Then, do the following things:*

1. Read Philippians 4:6-8 in your Bible.
2. Pray about the verse using the following beginning to your prayer: *Thank you for being in control of my life. Right now, I am worried about ______ and ______. I pray that you will give me your peace so that I will be less worried. Please watch over ______, who needs you today.*
3. Recite Philippians 4:6-8 using the hand motions you added on Day 1.
4. Sing Philippians 4:6-8 along with the CD at the end of your quiet time.

✔ *Lead Me to the Rock* CD
Track 7; Song: "Think on These Things" (vs. 6-8)

Key Idea: The Lord hears your prayers.

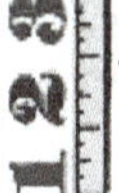

Math Exploration

S

Choose **one** of the math options listed below (see Appendix for details).

 *Singapore Primary Mathematics 2A/2B, 3A/3B,* or *4A/4B*

★ Your own math program

Key Idea: Use a step-by-step math program.

Science Exploration

I

★ Read *Columbus* p. 34-43. Write the answer to each numbered question on lined paper. You do not need to copy the question. Use the listed page to help you answer each question.

1. What was the land like where Columbus and his men first went ashore? (p. 34)
2. As Columbus sailed on to Haiti, what happened to the *Santa Maria*? (p. 38)
3. What did Columbus do after the wreck of the *Santa Maria*? (p. 38)
4. As Columbus sailed for Spain, what happened on the way home? (p. 40)
5. What does Job 28:12-18 say about wisdom compared to gold?

Key Idea: Columbus searched for gold along the coast of Cuba and Haiti. The *Santa Maria* wrecked when it hit a coral reef. As Columbus sailed back to Spain, his ships were in a terrible storm.

Learning through History
Focus: Age of Exploration

Unit 28 - Day 4

Reading about History T

Read about history in the following resource:

★ *A Child's History of the World: Ch. 64* p. 278-281

★ Also, read *Hero Tales* as scheduled in the *Storytime* box of the plans.

After today's first reading, say, *You will be writing a narration about part of the day's first history reading. In order to remember the details, you will reread part of today's reading from the second paragraph on p. 279 through the first paragraph on p. 280 (on your own).*

After students have finished reading the passage, ask them the questions below. Ask, *Where were the Aztec cities located? Describe the Aztec cities. In what terrible way did the Aztecs worship their idols? What does the Bible tell us about that? How did Cortes keep the Spanish soldiers from turning back to Spain? What did the Spaniards bring to Mexico that the Aztecs had never seen before? Who was the Aztec king at the time of Cortes? How did Montezuma welcome Cortes? When Montezuma would not become a Christian what happened?*

After the questions have been answered, have students write a 3-5 sentence narration about the Aztecs and Cortes. When students have finished their narration, direct them to read the sentences out loud.

Help students underline or highlight the main idea sentence in their narration. See the *Written Narration Skills* in the Appendix to guide students in editing their narrations.

Key Idea: The Aztec Indians lived in Mexico.

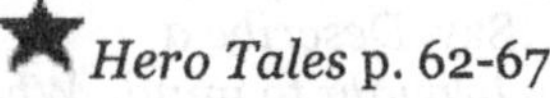

Storytime T

Read aloud the following assigned passage:

★ *Hero Tales* p. 62-67

Say, After today's reading, have your students orally narrate or retell the portion of today's text that you read. Use the *Narration Tips* as needed.

Key Idea: Practice oral narration skills.

Timeline S

You will be adding 2 new cards to your staircase timeline today. On the first new card, draw and color a ship. Write, *Columbus (1451-1506 A.D.)*. For the second new card, draw and color another ship. Write, *Magellan (1480-1521 A.D.)*.

If you decided to tape your timeline cards to the back of a door, then add the *Columbus* card to the right of *The Hundred Years' War* card. To the right of the *Columbus* card, add the *Magellan* card. If you decided to tape the timeline cards side-by-side to accordion-fold them, use clear packing tape to tape the cards as described above. Then, accordion-fold the timeline to store it.

Key Idea: Cortes was a Spanish conquistador who was sent to colonize the Americas. When he arrived in Mexico, he burned his ships so that his men could not sail back to Spain. The Spaniards used their guns to fight their way into the Aztec's capital city. Cortes later took the Aztec's King, Montezuma, as a prisoner. After awhile Montezuma was killed, and the Spanish took over the Aztecs.

Independent History Study I

★ Read *Pedro's Journal: Dec. 25 – Jan. 9.* Then, choose an interesting part from today's pages to read aloud and explain to an adult.

Key Idea: The Santa Maria had run aground near the island of Haiti and could not sail back to Spain.

Learning the Basics

Focus: Language Arts, Math, Bible, and Science

Unit 28 - Day 4

Poetry

T

Read aloud with the students the poem *"Nest Eggs"* (see Appendix). Have students share this poem in a special way. Suggestions for sharing the poem include recording it to play for someone, reading it to someone on the telephone, photocopying the poem and adding illustrations, reading it to someone at home, putting the poem to a melody and singing it, using an instrument to tap out the meter or rhythm of the poem while reading it, or copying the poem on paper.

Key Idea: Share a variety of classic poetry.

Bible Study

T

Have students say Philippians 4:6-8 using the hand motions from Day 1.

Have students copy in cursive Philippians 4:6-7 **above** last unit's Philippians 4:8 in their *Common Place Book*.

Students will add to the *Common Place Book* throughout the year.

 *Lead Me to the Rock* CD
Track 7; Song: "Think on These Things" (vs. 6-8)

Key Idea: Copy in cursive a portion of a Bible verse.

Language Arts

S

Have students complete one dictation exercise.

Guide students to complete one reading lesson.

★ *Drawn into the Heart of Reading*

Help students complete **one** English lesson.

★ *Beginning Wisely:* Lesson 101

★ *Building with Diligence:* Lesson 104

★ Your own grammar program

Key Idea: Practice language arts skills.

Math Exploration

S

Choose **one** math option listed below.

 *Singapore Primary Mathematics 2A/2B, 3A/3B,* or *4A/4B*

 Your own math program

Key Idea: Use a step-by-step math program.

Science Exploration

I

★ Read *Columbus* p. 44-57. Turn to the science experiment section in your science binder or sketchbook. At the top of a blank page, write: *How does a waterspout, like the one Columbus saw in the ocean, pull objects toward it?* Under the question, write: *'Guess'*. Write down your guess.

You will need a plastic bottle with a lid. If there is a label on the bottle, remove it. Fill the bottle ¾ of the way full with water. Add 1 spoonful of dishwashing detergent to the water in the bottle. Next, add several drops of blue food coloring and several small sequins, beads, or buttons. Screw the lid tightly on the bottle. Swirl the bottle using a circular motion for 15 seconds. Then, set it on the table. Do you see something like a waterspout? What do you notice about the objects in the bottle? Are they drawn into the waterspout? On your paper, write: *'Procedure'*. Draw a picture of the experiment. At the bottom of the paper, write: *'Conclusion'*. Explain what you learned.

Key Idea: On Columbus' fourth voyage to the west, he saw a waterspout twisting like a whirlwind in the ocean. Its circular motion was drawing the water up into the clouds!

Learning through History

Focus: The Renaissance Begins

Unit 29 - Day 1

Reading about History **T**

Read about history in the following resource:

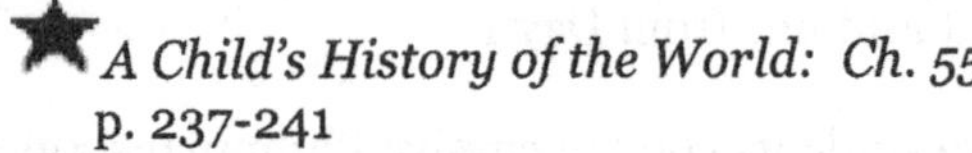

★ *A Child's History of the World: Ch. 55* p. 237-241

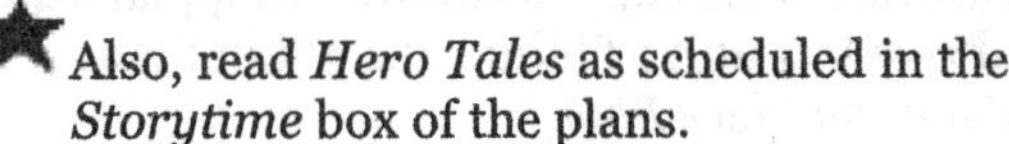

★ Also, read *Hero Tales* as scheduled in the *Storytime* box of the plans.

After today's first reading, say, *Use the map on p. 238 to tell where Ghana, Mali, and Songhay were located.* (knowledge) *Tell how trading was done with the gold miners in West Africa.* (comprehension) *Explain why salt was so valuable in Africa.* (analysis) *Why did Mansa Musa's pilgrimage to Mecca make him famous?* (evaluation) *Describe what you learned about Timbuktu.* (knowledge)

Key Idea: West Africa had strong kingdoms.

History Project **S**

In this unit you will be making a chart of spices, drawing a map of the spice route, and pretending to be a ship captain trading for spices. India was, and still is, known for its spices. Look in your cupboard and get out any of the following spices from India that you have: cinnamon, cassia, cardamom, ginger, turmeric, garlic, cumin, nutmeg, cloves, dill, mint, coriander, and saffron. At the top of a piece of paper write, *Spices from India.* Underneath the heading, make a chart of the spices you have by placing a dot of glue on the paper, sprinkling the spice on the glue, and writing the name of the spice under it. Decorate your chart and lay it flat to dry.

Key Idea: Spices were very important items for trade throughout much of history.

Storytime **T**

Read aloud the following assigned story:

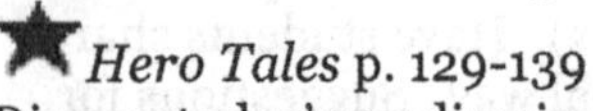

★ *Hero Tales* p. 129-139

Discuss today's reading in a "conversational way". Share about a person, time, event, or emotion from your life that today's reading brought to mind. Next, have your child share a connection.

Key Idea: Connect personally to the story.

Research **S**

Spices and salt were very important in the days before refrigerators and electricity. They were used to keep food from spoiling and for covering up the taste of food that was spoiled. Africa became known for its ports of trade for spices from India. Where could you look to discover more about the **Spice Route?** Use a reference book or an online resource like www.wikipedia.org to type *Spice Route* in the search or look it up in the index.

Orally answer one or more of the following questions from your research: *What was the spice route? Why were spices so important? Where did most of the spices come from? Where do most spices come from today? What types of spices were popular? Describe the spice route that went over land. Who was the first explorer to go around Africa by sea to get to India? Describe the sea route he took.*

Key Idea: When Vasco da Gama sailed around Africa to reach India, a whole new water route opened up for the spice trade. It was safer and faster than the land route had been. Africa's port cities became important trade centers.

Independent History Study **I**

★ Read *Pedro's Journal: Jan. 16 - end.* Orally retell or narrate to an adult the portion of text that you read today. Use the *Narration Tips* in the Appendix for help as needed.

Key Idea: After Columbus discovered the "New World", other explorers voyaged to find out more about it.

Learning the Basics

Focus: Language Arts, Math, Bible, and Science

Poetry

T

Read aloud to the students the poem "Keepsake Mill" (see Appendix). Say, *In the first stanza, what is the sin without pardon that the children are committing? What sounds does the mill make? What does the mill wheel do as time is passing? How does the poet show that the mill seems unchanged, even though time has gone by? In the last stanza, as the boys have become men, what are they remembering? Why would the poem be titled "Keepsake Mill"?* Read the poem again with the students.

Key Idea: Read and appreciate classic poetry.

Language Arts

S

Have students complete the first studied dictation exercise (see Appendix for directions and passages).

Help students complete one lesson from the following reading program:

 *Drawn into the Heart of Reading*

Work with the students to complete **one** of the English options listed below:

★ *Beginning Wisely:* Lesson 102

★ *Building with Diligence:* Lesson 105

★ Your own grammar program

Key Idea: Practice language arts skills.

Bible Study

T

Say, *Find Psalm 148:1-3 in your Bible. This is the memory selection for this unit. Read the verses out loud.* Ask, *What are we told to do in Psalm 148:1? In Psalm 148:1, where is the Lord being praised? In Psalm 148:2, who is praising the Lord? What can we learn about praising the Lord from this verse? In Psalm 148:3, what created things are praising the Lord? Since we were also created by God to glorify Him, what should we be doing?*

Have students say the verse 3 times, adding hand motions to help remember the words.

 *Lead Me to the Rock* CD
Track 9; Song: "Praise Ye Him"
(vs. 1-3)

Key Idea: All things in creation praise God. We need to lift our voices in praise to the Lord too.

Math Exploration

S

Choose **one** of the math options listed below (see Appendix for details).

 *Singapore Primary Mathematics 2A/2B, 3A/3B*, or *4A/4B*

 Your own math program

Key Idea: Use a step-by-step math program.

Science Exploration

I

★ Read *Who Was Leonardo da Vinci?* p. 1-12. Today you will add to your science notebook. At the top of an unlined paper, copy Psalm 119:130 in cursive. Beneath the verse, draw one or more of the pictures from p. 8-9 of *Who Was Leonardo da Vinci?* Then, copy the first paragraph from p. 8 **and** the first two sentences from p. 9 to go along with your picture.

Key Idea: Leonardo was born in 1452 in Italy. He came from the town of Vinci. During this time, paper was very valuable. It was first made with bark from mulberry trees in China about 2000 years ago.

Learning through History
Focus: The Renaissance Begins

Unit 29 - Day 2

Reading about History **T**

Read about history in the following resource:

★ *A Child's History of the World: Ch. 65* p. 282-287

★ Also, read *Hero Tales* as scheduled in the *Storytime* box of the plans.

After today's first reading, read aloud Ecclesiastes 2:1-11. Say, *What does Solomon say that he filled his life with in Ecclesiastes 2:1? List some of the things that King Solomon says he sought after in Ecclesiastes 2:3-8. When Solomon considered his life in Ecclesiastes 2:11, what did he think of it? Fortune hunters came to Africa from Portugal in search of gold and trade routes. Is gold or money the most important thing in life? Does it bring people true happiness? What can we learn from Solomon in Ecclesiastes 12:13-14?*

Key Idea: Vasco da Gama sailed from Portugal around Africa, five years after Columbus left from Spain.

History Project **S**

Today, you will make a map of Vasco daGama's water route to India for spices. You may print a map of the world at the following address: www.nationalgeographic.com/xpeditions/atlas

Then, use www.wikipedia.org or another resource to view the spice route. Draw a line on your map to show the route. Make a key for your map.

Key Idea: Ibn Battuta was a Muslim traveler from Tangier. He traveled for 25 years.

Storytime **T**

Read aloud the following assigned passage:

★ *Hero Tales* p. 93-103

Ask, *In what does the main character place his faith? How would the story be different if the main character didn't put his faith in God? Share a character, a story, or a verse from the Bible that you are reminded of by the reading.*

Key Idea: Share a Biblical connection.

Geography **S**

Use a globe for today's activities. *On p. 283 of A Child's History of the World, trace the Portuguese explorers' route with your finger down the coast of West Africa to the mouth of the Senegal River. Then, continue the route to Benin (which is Nigeria) and on to Kongo. Next, on the globe, trace Vasco da Gama's route from Portugal, down the West African coast, around the tip of Africa (and the Cape of Good Hope), up the coast of East Africa, and on to India. This became the new spice route to India. Last, on the globe, find the following port cities in East Africa that became important stops along the spice route: Mogadishu (Somalia), Malindi (Kenya), Mombasa (Kenya), and Kilwa (Tanzania).*

Review the following concept: *Meridians of longitude run north and south. Find which meridian of longitude is closest to where you live. Name the other places in the world that are on the same meridian of longitude where you live.*

Key Idea: East African cities were wealthy.

Independent History Study **I**

★ Read *William Shakespeare and the Globe* p. 9-15. Then, copy in cursive the quote from *As You Like It* (which is shown on the page next to the Table of Contents in *William Shakespeare and the Globe*) onto a clean page in your *Common Place Book*.

Key Idea: While sailors were still exploring the world, Shakespeare was born in 1564 in England.

Learning the Basics

Focus: Language Arts, Math, Bible, and Science

Language Arts

T

Work with the students to complete **one** of the English options listed below:

★ *Beginning Wisely:* Lesson 103

★ *Building with Diligence:* Lesson 106

★ Your own grammar program

Say, *You will be doing a writing activity based on the poem, "Keepsake Mill"* (see Appendix). Say, *In the poem "Keepsake Mill", the poet used one main topic per stanza.* Guide students to share the following main topics from the poem by stanza, as you list them on a markerboard or a paper:

1. The children sneak out of the garden to the river.
2. They see the mill with the wheel turning.
3. The noisy mill is by the quiet river.
4. The wheel of the mill goes on turning as time passes.
5. When the children are older, they return to see the mill still running.
6. The friends then meet again when they are much older and remember the past.

Say, *What are some other things that continue on without changing very much as time passes?* (i.e. a windmill turning, a tree blowing or swaying, a river running, an oil well pumping, etc.) Say, *Choose one thing that remains almost unchanged over time, and make a list to outline ways to show it remaining the same as time passes. When the list is complete, retell the scene orally to an adult following the sequence of topics on the list.*

Key Idea: Write creatively from classic poetry.

Bible Study

T

Have students say Psalm 148:1-3 using the hand motions they added on Day 1. Say, *A mood is a feeling, a sensation, or a state of mind. What is the mood of Psalm 148:1-3?* (Some examples of moods include frightened, worried, happy, peaceful, hopeful, sad, unhappy, angry, thankful, prayerful, joyful, and lonely.) Ask, *When would this Psalm help you, or when would you go to this Psalm?* (i.e. to show us that the Lord is worthy of praise in heaven and on Earth, to remind us that the angels and the heavenly hosts praise the Lord, to help us realize that we need to praise the Lord)

Last, pray with your children that they will praise the Lord with joy in their hearts. Pray that they will let their voices be heard as they use them to glorify the Lord in heaven.

✔ *Lead Me to the Rock* CD
Track 9; Song: "Praise Ye Him"
(vs. 1-3)

Key Idea: The Psalms reflect the many emotions and moods we have. They are a wonderful place to seek counsel from the Lord.

Math Exploration

S

Choose **one** of the math options listed below (see Appendix for details).

★ *Singapore Primary Mathematics 2A/2B, 3A/3B,* or *4A/4B*

★ Your own math program

Key Idea: Use a step-by-step math program.

Science Exploration

I

★ Read *Who Was Leonardo da Vinci?* p. 13-24. Orally retell or narrate to an adult the portion of text that you read today. Use the *Narration Tips* in the Appendix for help as needed.

Key Idea: Leonardo's father apprenticed him in Florence to an artist, named Andrea del Verrocchio. As an apprentice, Leonardo made paintbrushes from animal hair, made tempera paint from eggs, and prepared wood for painting. He was also allowed to paint parts of various paintings for patrons.

Learning through History

Focus: The Renaissance Begins

Unit 29 - Day 3

Reading about History **T**

Read about history in the following resource:

★ *A Child's History of the World: Ch. 67* p. 292-296

★ Also, read *Hero Tales* as scheduled in the *Storytime* box of the plans.

After today's first reading, have your students orally narrate or retell the portion of today's first text that you read. Use the *Narration Tips* in the Appendix as needed.

Key Idea: Martin Luther was a monk who made a list of 95 things he thought should be changed in the Catholic church. The pope ordered Luther to stop, but Luther did not obey.

History Project **S**

If you have access to the internet, go to the following website to see what it would be like to make decisions as an explorer or a ship captain on the spice route:
www.learner.org/interactives/renaissance/spicetrade

If you do not have access to the internet, or the link above does not work, then color the map of the spice route that you made on Day 2 instead.

Key Idea: The reformation that was happening in the church happened about the same time as the renaissance in Italy. Both the renaissance and the reformation swept across Europe.

Storytime **T**

Read aloud the following assigned passage:

★ *Hero Tales* p. 68-79

Ask, *In today's reading, how were people's lives different from your life? What would you have enjoyed or found difficult about living during that time?*

Key Idea: Compare historical time periods.

Vocabulary **S**

You may choose 3-5 of the following vocabulary words from *A Child's History of the World* to use for this lesson: *denomination* (p. 292), *religion* (p. 292), *reformed* (p. 294), *abdicated* (p. 294), and/or *divorce* (p. 295). First, find the word in the text and read the sentence containing the word. Think about possible meanings. Next, find the word in a dictionary and select the correct meaning. Write the word at the top of an index card or at the top of the corresponding letter page in the notebook. Underneath the word, copy the correct definition from the dictionary. Then, use the word correctly in a sentence. The sentence may either be copied from the text or be one of your own creation. Last, draw a small picture to show the word's meaning. If you used an index card to record your word, file it under the correct alphabetical tab.

Key Idea: Luther was summoned to stand trial before Charles V. Even though Luther was later allowed to go free, his friends hid him for safety's sake. While Luther was hidden, he translated the Bible into German.

Independent History Study **I**

★ At the top of a sheet of white paper, write, *Young William Shakespeare*. Beneath this heading, copy facts about William Shakespeare from p. 12-13 of *William Shakespeare and the Globe*.

Key Idea: Shakespeare was born about 50 years after Martin Luther pounded his 95 thesis on the church's door. Shakespeare was born in England, and Luther lived in Germany. However, the English king, Henry VIII, had brought the controversy about religion over to England too, during his reign. His daughter, Elizabeth, was Queen of England at the time of Shakespeare.

Learning the Basics
Focus: Language Arts, Math, Bible, and Science

Poetry
T

Read aloud with the students the poem *"Keepsake Mill"* (see Appendix). Say, *Describe a time you have been somewhere like this or felt like this. What can you learn about the poet, Robert Louis Stevenson, from the poem?* Say, *Did you know that in the garden of Robert's grandfather's home in Colington, there was a gap in the wall that led to the Water of Leith? As a child, Robert could slip through the gap into the wet world beyond.* Have the students read the poem on their own.

Key Idea: Read and appreciate classic poetry.

Language Arts
S

Have students complete one studied dictation exercise (see Appendix for directions and passages).

Help students complete one lesson from the following reading program:

 *Drawn into the Heart of Reading*

Work with the students to complete **one** of the English options listed below:

 *Beginning Wisely:* Lesson 104

 *Building with Diligence:* Lesson 107 (half)

 Your own grammar program

Key Idea: Practice language arts skills.

Bible Study
T

Say, *You will be having your own quiet time with God today. Choose a quiet place for this special time, where you can be alone with God. Then, do the following things:*

1. Read Psalm 148:1-3 in your Bible.
2. Pray about the verse using the following beginning to your prayer: *Thank you for creating me to glorify you. Help me to ______ in order to praise you more. Work in my heart so that I am ______ in praising you.*
3. Recite Psalm 148:1-3 using the hand motions you added on Day 1.
4. Sing Psalm 148:1-3 along with the CD at the end of your quiet time.

✔ *Lead Me to the Rock* CD
Track 9; Song: "Praise Ye Him"
(vs. 1-3)

Key Idea: The Lord hears your prayers.

Math Exploration
S

Choose **one** of the math options listed below (see Appendix for details).

 *Singapore Primary Mathematics 2A/2B, 3A/3B,* or *4A/4B*

 Your own math program

Key Idea: Use a step-by-step math program.

Science Exploration
I

★ Read *Who Was Leonardo da Vinci?* p. 25-36. Write the answer to each numbered question on lined paper. You do not need to copy the question. Use the listed page to help you answer each question.

1. What important invention changed Leonardo's life? (p. 26-27)
2. Explain the meaning of "painting in perspective". (p. 28-29)
3. What was the Renaissance? (p. 30-31)
4. Why did Leonardo finish so few paintings in his lifetime? (p. 34)
5. What does Ecclesiastes 1:4 remind us about man's accomplishments when they are compared to the Lord's accomplishments?

Key Idea: In his lifetime, Leonardo completed only 10 paintings that we know of. They are very beautiful.

Learning through History
Focus: The Renaissance Begins

Unit 29 - Day 4

Reading about History — T

Read about history in the following resource:

★ *A Child's History of the World: Ch. 66* p. 288-291

★ *Hero Tales* p. 117-127

After today's reading, say, *You will be writing a narration about part of today's history reading. In order to remember the details well, you will reread part of today's reading from the last paragraph of p. 288 through the first half of p. 290 (on your own if possible).*

After students have finished reading the passage, ask them the questions below. Ask, *Who was the famous sculptor in today's reading? How was Michelangelo different from other sculptors? Why does the statue of Moses have a crack in the marble? What is the name of the famous building whose ceiling Michelangelo painted? Describe how Michelangelo painted the ceiling of the Sistine Chapel. What did Michelangelo do when the pope came to see him while he was working? Explain what this shows about Michelangelo.*

After the questions have been answered, have students write a 5 sentence narration about Michelangelo. When students have finished their narration, direct them to read the sentences out loud.

Help students underline or highlight the main idea sentence in their narration. See the *Written Narration Skills* in the Appendix to guide students in editing their narrations.

Key Idea: The Renaissance was a time of renewed interest in sculpting, writing, painting, and building. Michelangelo, Leonardo DaVinci, and Raphael were all famous Italian artists who lived during this period.

Storytime — T

Read aloud the following assigned passage:

★ *The Wonderful Winter* p. 13-31

Say, After today's reading, have your students orally narrate or retell the portion of today's text that you read. Use the *Narration Tips* in the Appendix as needed.

Key Idea: Practice oral narration skills.

Timeline — S

You will be adding 2 new cards to your staircase timeline today. On the first new card, draw and color a paper with a nail in it. Write, *Martin Luther's 95 Theses (1517 A.D.).* For the second new card, draw and color a quill pen. Write, *William Shakespeare (1564-1616 A.D.).*

If you decided to tape your timeline cards to the back of a door, then add the *Martin Luther's 95 Theses* card to the right of the *Magellan* card. To the right of the *Martin Luther's 95 Thesis* card, add the *William Shakespeare* card. If you decided to tape the timeline cards side-by-side to accordion-fold them, use clear packing tape to tape the cards as described above. Then, accordion-fold the timeline to store it.

Key Idea: The 1500's was a time of great change and excitement in religion and the fine arts. It was the time of the Reformation in the church, and a time of the Renaissance in the fine arts. The Reformation and the Renaissance both changed history, and we are still impacted by these changes today.

Independent History Study — I

★ Read *William Shakespeare and the Globe* p. 16-25. Then, choose an interesting part from today's pages to read aloud and explain to an adult.

Key Idea: In 1592, as Shakespeare was in London, a terrible plague raged. The theaters closed for 2 years.

Learning the Basics

Focus: Language Arts, Math, Bible, and Science

Unit 29 - Day 4

Poetry

T

Read aloud with the students the poem *"Keepsake Mill"* (see Appendix). Have students share this poem in a special way. Suggestions for sharing the are listed in the "Poetry" box in Unit 28 – Day 4.

Key Idea: Share a variety of classic poetry.

Language Arts

S

Have students complete one dictation exercise.

Guide students to complete one reading lesson.

★ *Drawn into the Heart of Reading*

Help students complete **one** English lesson.

★ *Beginning Wisely:* Lesson 105

★ *Building with Diligence:* Lesson 107 (half)

★ Your own grammar program

Key Idea: Practice language arts skills.

Bible Study

T

Have students say Psalm 148:1-3 using the hand motions from Day 1. Have students copy in cursive Psalm 148:1-3 onto a clean page in their *Common Place Book*. Students should leave the rest of the page blank to add to next week. Students will add to the *Common Place Book* throughout the year.

✔ *Lead Me to the Rock* CD
Track 9; Song: "Praise Ye Him"
(vs. 1-3)

Key Idea: Copy in cursive a portion of a Psalm.

Math Exploration

S

Choose **one** math option listed below.

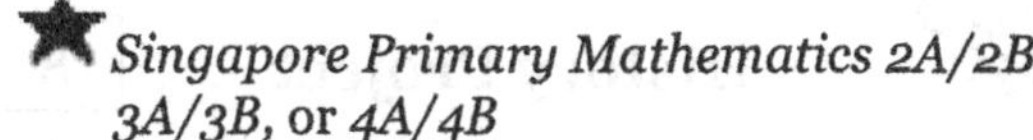

★ *Singapore Primary Mathematics 2A/2B, 3A/3B,* or *4A/4B*

★ Your own math program

Key Idea: Use a step-by-step math program.

Science Exploration

I

★ Read *Who Was Leonard da Vinci?* p. 37-45. Turn to the science experiment section in your science binder or sketchbook. At the top of a blank page, write: *How can we use the Earth's rotation to explain the Sun's rising and setting?* Under the question, write: *'Guess'*. Write down your guess. Get 4 index cards. Write, "south", on a card, and tape it to the front of your body. Write, "east" on a card, and tape it to the outside of your left shoulder. Write, "north" on a card, and tape it to your back. Write, "west" on a card, and tape it to the outside of your right shoulder. You will need a partner with a flashlight for this next part. Turn out the lights. Have your partner stand near the center of one wall with the flashlight pointing out. The partner is the Sun. Stand with your back to the Sun. You are the Earth. Right now it is early morning, and the Sun isn't up yet. It will be daytime, when the Sun shines on your face. Very slowly rotate or turn your body to the left, without turning your head. When you see the Sun's light shining in the side of your eye, stop rotating. In which direction is the Sun rising? Do you see it in the east, according to the card on your left arm? Now, continue slowly rotating your body to the left, until you are facing the Sun. In what direction is the Sun now? Has the Sun moved? Has the Earth rotated? Continue rotating left until the flashlight has almost disappeared from your sight. In which direction is the Sun setting, according to the card on your right arm? Continue turning left until your back is to the Sun. This represents the rotation of the Earth for one complete day. On your paper, write: *'Procedure'*. Draw a picture of the experiment. At the bottom of the paper, write: *'Conclusion'*. Explain what you learned.

Key Idea: The Sun appears to move from east to west during the day, but the Earth is actually rotating.

Learning through History
Focus: Age of Elizabeth

Unit 30 - Day 1

Reading about History [T]

Read about history in the following resource:

★ *A Child's History of the World: Ch. 68* p. 297-300

Note: There is some graphic content on p. 298. After today's reading, say, *When Mary became queen of England after Henry the VIII's young son died, how did things change in England?* (comprehension) *How was Elizabeth different from Mary?* (analysis) *Why did Philip II of Spain send the Spanish Armada to attack England?* (knowledge) *Tell how the Spanish Armada was defeated.* (comprehension) *Explain how Elizabeth made England powerful.* (evaluation)

Key Idea: Elizabeth became queen after Mary.

History Project [S]

In this unit you will be making a Renaissance-style pendant. A pendant is a hanging object attached to a chain. Men and women wore pendants. Make air dry clay by mixing together 2 Tbsp. white glue, 4 Tbsp. cornstarch, 1 Tbsp. water, and 1 Tbsp. toothpaste. This clay dries quickly in 20 minutes or less. First, roll the clay into small balls to make beads. Then, slide a straw or a toothpick through the center of the balls making a large enough hole to thread a piece of yarn through the beads. Allow the beads to dry overnight on the straw or toothpick. Next, roll a large ball of clay and flatten it to make a pendant. Use your straw or toothpick to make a hole through the top of the pendant, so it will hang facing forward on the yarn chain you'll add on Day 3.

Key Idea: Elizabeth became queen at age 25.

Storytime [T]

Read aloud the following assigned story:

★ *The Wonderful Winter* p. 32-50

Discuss today's reading in a "conversational way". Share about a person, time, event, or emotion from your life that today's reading brought to mind. Next, have your child share a connection.

Key Idea: Connect personally to the story.

Research [S]

During the Renaissance time period, jewelry became very ornate. Where could you look to discover more about Renaissance **jewelry?** Use a reference book or an online resource like www.wikipedia.org to type *jewelry* in the search and then look under the category *Renaissance* or look it up in the index.

Orally answer one or more of the following questions from your research: *Describe the jewelry at the time of the Renaissance. What are the names of some of the gemstones that were used in the jewelry? How was the use of gemstones different from the way that jewelry had been made before? What kinds of jewelry were worn during the Renaissance? When looking at a picture of Queen Elizabeth I of England, what can you learn about the jewelry of the Renaissance?*

Key Idea: When Elizabeth became queen, the Catholics and Protestants were fighting and killing one another. Mary was a strong Catholic, and Elizabeth had been raised Protestant. The two queens were very different.

Independent History Study [I]

★ Read *William Shakespeare and the Globe* p. 26-33. Orally retell or narrate to an adult the portion of text that you read today. Use the *Narration Tips* in the Appendix for help as needed.

Key Idea: Queen Elizabeth enjoyed plays and music. She invited Shakespeare to the palace to perform.

Learning the Basics

Focus: Language Arts, Math, Bible, and Science

Unit 30 - Day 1

Poetry

T

Read aloud to the students the poem *"The Dumb Soldier"* (see Appendix). Say, *What does the child do in the first stanza of the poem? What does the soldier look like? When will the soldier be found again? What does the word "dumb" mean in the poem? Why would the soldier be "silent" or "dumb"? What things does the child imagine that the soldier has seen? Why must the child make up the tale?* Read the poem again with the students.

Key Idea: Read and appreciate classic poetry.

Language Arts

S

Have students complete the first studied dictation exercise (see Appendix for directions and passages).

Help students complete one lesson from the following reading program:

 *Drawn into the Heart of Reading*

Work with the students to complete **one** of the English options listed below:

- ★ *Beginning Wisely:* Lesson 106
- ★ *Building with Diligence:* Lesson 108
- ★ Your own grammar program

Key Idea: Practice language arts skills.

Bible Study

T

Say, *Find Psalm 148:1-5 in your Bible. This is the memory selection for this unit. Read the verses out loud.* Ask, *In Psalm 148:4, what created things are praising the Lord? In Psalm 148:5, what reason does it give for this praise? Are we able to create something, just by our command? How does this show the Lord's power? If the Lord is to be praised by each part of creation, what should we be doing? Why is it important that we praise the Lord?*

Have students say the verse 3 times, adding hand motions to help remember the words.

 *Lead Me to the Rock* CD
Track 9; Song: "Praise Ye Him"
(vs. 1-5)

Key Idea: We were created to glorify our Lord, so it is very important that we praise Him!

Math Exploration

S

Choose **one** of the math options listed below (see Appendix for details).

 *Singapore Primary Mathematics 2A/2B, 3A/3B,* or *4A/4B*

 Your own math program

Key Idea: Use a step-by-step math program.

Science Exploration

I

★ Read *Who Was Leonardo da Vinci?* p. 46-54 and p. 88-89. Today you will add to your science notebook. At the top of an unlined paper, copy Proverbs 9:9 in cursive. Beneath the verse, follow the steps to draw your own cartoon from p. 88-89 of *Who Was Leonardo da Vinci?* First, draw the simple outline of an object on a piece of white paper. Next, place your paper on a pile of newspapers or several folded paper towels. Use a toothpick, a nail, or the pointed end of a paper clip to punch small holes along the outline of the drawing. Then, place your drawing over your notebooking page, and color over the holes with a pencil to make an outline of the sketch in your notebook. Last, copy onto your notebook page the 4 steps for making a Renaissance cartoon from p. 88-89 of *Who Was Leonardo da Vinci?*.

Key Idea: During the Renaissance, a cartoon was used to plan a fresco before it was painted on the wall.

Learning through History

Focus: Age of Elizabeth

Unit 30 - Day 2

Reading about History [T]

Read about history in the following resource:

★ *A Child's History of the World: Ch. 69* p. 301-304

After today's reading, read aloud Psalm 2:10-11. Say, *What warning is given to kings and rulers in Psalm 2:10-11? Who were all of us created to serve? How does Psalm 2:11 say we are to serve the Lord? Why is it important to serve the Lord reverently and with trembling? Even though Elizabeth was a strong queen, from whom did her power come? Who is the ruler over us all? What can we learn from Psalm 2:10-11 about being a wise ruler or leader?*

Key Idea: Elizabeth became a strong queen in England. Sir Walter Raleigh once placed his velvet cloak on the ground so that the queen could walk across it without getting her shoes muddy. He became a favorite friend of the queen's and was knighted by her.

History Project [S]

Get the pendant that you made on Day 1. Paint a design on the pendant so that it looks as if it is covered with various colored gemstones. Make it very ornate and decorative. Lay the pendant flat to dry until Day 3.

Key Idea: Men such as Sir Walter Raleigh and William Shakespeare wore pearl earrings and pendants. Jewelry was very ornate during the Renaissance, and both men and women wore it.

Storytime [T]

Read aloud the following assigned passage:

★ *The Wonderful Winter* p. 51-71

Ask, *In today's reading, how were people's lives different from your life? What would you have enjoyed or found difficult about living during that time?*

Key Idea: Compare historical time periods.

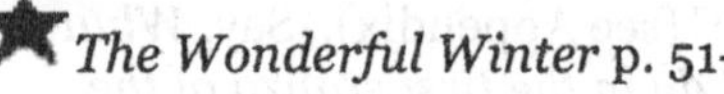

Vocabulary [S]

You may choose 3-5 of the following vocabulary words from *A Child's History of the World* to use for this lesson: *gentlemanly* (p. 301), *soiling* (p. 301), *tobacco* (p. 302), *fortune* (p. 303), and/or *remarkable* (p. 304). First, find the word in the text and read the sentence containing the word. Think about possible meanings. Next, find the word in a dictionary and select the correct meaning. Write the word at the top of an index card or at the top of the corresponding letter page in the notebook. Underneath the word, copy the correct definition from the dictionary. Then, use the word correctly in a sentence. The sentence may either be copied from the text or be one of your own creation. Last, draw a small picture to show the word's meaning. If you used an index card to record your word, file it under the correct alphabetical tab.

Key Idea: Sir Walter Raleigh started a settlement in Roanoke, Virginia. It didn't survive. However, tobacco was brought back to England from Virginia, and smoking became fashionable.

Independent History Study [I]

★ Read *William Shakespeare and the Globe* p. 34 - end. Then, choose a quote from the bottom of one of the pages in *William Shakespeare and the Globe* to copy in cursive in your *Common Place Book*. Copy it.

Key Idea: Sam Wanamaker worked hard to have William Shakespeare's playhouse, *The Globe*, rebuilt.

Learning the Basics

Focus: Language Arts, Math, Bible, and Science

Unit 30 - Day 2

Language Arts

T

Work with the students to complete **one** of the English options listed below:

★ *Beginning Wisely:* Lesson 107

★ *Building with Diligence:* Lesson 109

★ Your own grammar program

Say, *You will be doing a writing activity based on the poem, "The Dumb Soldier"* (see Appendix). Say, *Have you ever lost something, and then found it again? What did you lose?* (i.e. stuffed toy, glasses, favorite hat, purse, money, backpack, etc.) *Where did you find it? If it could talk, what things would it tell you it had seen and heard? Use your ideas to finish the following sentence starters:*

Once when...
I lost...
I shall find him/her, never fear.
I shall find my...

She/he has lived...
In the....
Done....
Just as...

And has seen...
And the...
And the....
In the...

In the silence she/he has heard...
And the...
And the...
Over him/her as she/he...

Not a word will he/she disclose,
Not a word of all he/she knows.
I must lay him/her upon my shelf,
And make up the tale myself.

Key Idea: Write creatively from classic poetry.

Bible Study

T

Have students say Psalm 148:1-5 using the hand motions they added on Day 1. Say, *A mood is a feeling, a sensation, or a state of mind. What is the mood of Psalm 148:4-5?* (Some examples of moods include frightened, worried, happy, peaceful, hopeful, sad, unhappy, angry, thankful, prayerful, joyful, and lonely.) Ask, *When would this Psalm help you, or when would you go to this Psalm?* (i.e. to remind us of the things that the Lord created, to show us the Lord's power in commanding all of creation, to help us join with creation in praising the Lord)

Last, pray with your children that they will join with all of creation in praising the Lord. Pray that they will realize this is very important to the Lord and that it should bring them joy to praise our Lord.

✔ *Lead Me to the Rock* CD
Track 9; Song: "Praise Ye Him"
(vs. 1-5)

Key Idea: The Psalms reflect the many emotions and moods we have. They are a wonderful place to seek counsel from the Lord.

Math Exploration

S

Choose **one** of the math options listed below (see Appendix for details).

★ *Singapore Primary Mathematics 2A/2B, 3A/3B,* or *4A/4B*

★ Your own math program

Key Idea: Use a step-by-step math program.

Science Exploration

I

★ Read *Who Was Leonardo da Vinci?* p. 55-63. Orally retell or narrate to an adult the portion of text that you read today. Use the *Narration Tips* in the Appendix for help as needed.

Key Idea: Leonardo began keeping notebooks full of sketches. He also wrote in mirror writing.

Learning through History
Focus: Age of Elizabeth

Unit 30 - Day 3

Reading about History

T

Read about history in the following resource:

★ *A Child's History of the World: Ch. 70* p. 305-308

After today's reading, have your students orally narrate or retell the portion of today's text that you read. Use the *Narration Tips* in the Appendix as needed.

Key Idea: After Elizabeth died, the English people asked King James of Scotland to be their king too. He believed in the Divine Right of Kings and this didn't fit well with what the English people wanted.

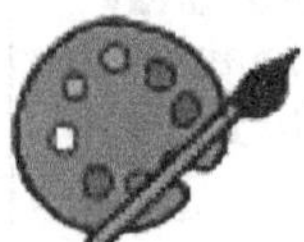

History Project

S

Choose a piece of yarn, ribbon, or string to use as a chain for the beads and pendant you made on Days 1-2. Make sure the chain is long enough to go over your head, once it is tied in a circle. Place a piece of clear tape around one end of your yarn, ribbon, or string, to make it easier to thread it through the holes in your beads and pendant. Thread half of your beads on the chain first. Then, thread your pendant on the chain. It should be in the middle. Last, thread the other half of your beads on the chain. Tie the two ends of your chain together in a knot. Place your pendant around your neck.

Key Idea: During King James' reign, the Bible was translated into English. This is the version we have today which is called the *King James Bible.*

Storytime

T

Read aloud the following assigned passage:

★ *The Wonderful Winter* p. 72-84

Ask, *In what does the main character place his faith? How would the story be different if the main character put his faith in God? Share a character, a story, or a verse from the Bible that you are reminded of by the reading.*

Key Idea: Share a Biblical connection.

Geography

S

Use a globe for today's activities. *During the historical time period of today's story, the Stuarts were reigning in Scotland. Find Scotland on the globe. It is part of the present day United Kingdom. James I ruled in England after Elizabeth. Find England on the globe. Remember that Cabot had claimed much of America for England. So, let's find two of the first successful English settlements in America. Trace a path on the globe from England to Jamestown, Virginia. Then, trace a path on the globe from England to Plymouth, Massachusetts.*

Review the following concept: *Lines of latitude are parallel to the equator, so they are also called parallels. Lines of longitude run north and south from the North Pole to the South Pole. They are called meridians of longitude. Choose a place in the world to point to on the globe. Then, tell which lines of longitude and latitude are closest to that place.*

Key Idea: England became very powerful.

Independent History Study

I

★ At the top of a white piece of paper, write *Shakespeare's Later Years*. Then, copy in cursive **some** of the facts about Shakespeare from p. 29 and p. 33 of *William Shakespeare and the Globe*. You may also photocopy p. 44 and glue that on the back of your paper to include a listing of Shakespeare's plays. Decorate your page with drawings or designs which remind you of Shakespeare.

Key Idea: King James loved the theater and plays, and Shakespeare's players became The King's Men.

Learning the Basics

Focus: Language Arts, Math, Bible, and Science

Unit 30 - Day 3

Poetry

T

Read aloud with the students the poem *"The Dumb Soldier"* (see Appendix). Say, *Describe a time you have been somewhere like this or felt like this. What can you learn about the poet, Robert Louis Stevenson, from the poem?* Say, *Did you know that when Robert Louis Stevenson was a child, he and his nurse, Cummie, went on many walks? I wonder if he ever buried one of his toy soldiers, and then found it again later?* Have the students read the poem on their own.

Key Idea: Read and appreciate classic poetry.

Language Arts

S

Have students complete one studied dictation exercise (see Appendix for directions and passages).

Help students complete one lesson from the following reading program:

 *Drawn into the Heart of Reading*

Work with the students to complete **one** of the English options listed below:

 *Beginning Wisely:* Lesson 108

 *Building with Diligence:* Lesson 110

 Your own grammar program

Key Idea: Practice language arts skills.

Bible Study

T

Say, *You will be having your own quiet time with God today. Choose a quiet place for this special time, where you can be alone with God. Then, do the following things:*

1. Read Psalm 148:1-5 in your Bible.
2. Pray about the verse using the following beginning to your prayer: *Thank you for your beautiful creation. Help me to join in with creation in praising you by _____ and ______. Even when I am sad, help me to praise you for being _____ and ______.*
3. Recite Psalm 148:1-5 using the hand motions you added on Day 1.
4. Sing Psalm 148:1-5 along with the CD at the end of your quiet time.

✔ *Lead Me to the Rock* CD
Track 9; Song: "Praise Ye Him"
(vs. 1-5)

Key Idea: We can praise God even in times of sorrow, for His love and for His great power.

Math Exploration

S

Choose **one** of the math options listed below (see Appendix for details).

 *Singapore Primary Mathematics 2A/2B, 3A/3B,* or *4A/4B*

★ Your own math program

Key Idea: Use a step-by-step math program.

Science Exploration

I

★ Read *Who Was Leonardo da Vinci?* p. 64-71. Write the answer to each numbered question on lined paper. You do not need to copy the question. Use the listed page to help you answer each question.

1. Name three of Leonardo's ideas for inventions. (p. 64-65)
2. How did Leonardo study flight? (p. 66-67)
3. Describe what Leonardo invented for Cesare Borgia. (p. 70-71)
4. Why was Leonardo a "man way ahead of his time"? (p. 69)
5. What does Proverbs 2:6 say about wisdom?

Key Idea: Leonardo was also an inventor. He sketched many inventions that we have today. We know he was very interested in birds and flight. He may even have tested some man-made wings!

Learning through History
Focus: Age of Elizabeth

Unit 30 - Day 4

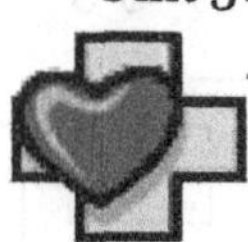

Reading about History — T

Read about history in the following resource:

★ *A Child's History of the World: Ch. 71* p. 309-312

After today's reading, say, *You will be writing a narration about part of today's history reading. In order to remember the details well, you will reread part of today's reading from p. 309 through p. 310 (on your own if possible).*

After students have finished reading the passage, ask them the questions below. If the students do not know the answers, help them find the answers in the passage they just read. Ask, *Who was the king that upset the Parliament in today's reading? Why did the people gather an army to fight against King Charles I? When King Charles lost, what did Parliament do? How did the English people feel about what the Parliament had done? Who ruled England next? What kind of ruler was Oliver Cromwell?*

After the questions have been answered, have students write a 5 sentence narration about the time of Charles I and Oliver Cromwell. When students have finished their narration, direct them to read the sentences out loud.

Help students underline or highlight the main idea sentence in their narration. See the *Written Narration Skills* in the Appendix to guide students in editing their narrations.

Key Idea: The English people were tired of the Divine Right of Kings. So, an army led by Oliver Cromwell fought and defeated King Charles I. A small part of the English Parliament had King Charles put to death. Then, Oliver Cromwell became ruler.

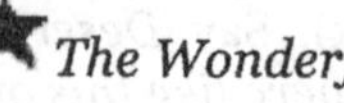

Storytime — T

Read aloud the following assigned passage:

★ *The Wonderful Winter* p. 85-110

Say, After today's reading, have your students orally narrate or retell the portion of today's text that you read. Use the *Narration Tips* in the Appendix as needed.

Key Idea: Practice oral narration skills.

Timeline — S

You will be adding a new card to your staircase timeline today. On the new card, draw and color a golden crown or tiara for a queen. Write, *Queen Elizabeth (1558-1603 A.D.).*

If you decided to tape your timeline cards to the back of a door, then add the *Queen Elizabeth* card to the right of the *William Shakespeare* card. If you decided to tape the timeline cards side-by-side to accordion-fold them, use clear packing tape to tape the cards as described above. Then, accordion-fold the timeline to store it.

Key Idea: After Oliver Cromwell died, his son could not carry on his father's role and resigned. Then, the English people asked Charles II to be king. During the reign of Charles II, a plague and a fire both broke out in London. After Charles II, William and Mary became king and queen. Parliament became the English governing body, after William and Mary signed the Bill of Rights.

Independent History Study — I

★ Read *Peter the Great* p. 4-11. Then, choose an interesting part from today's pages to read aloud and explain to an adult.

Key Idea: During the time of the Stuarts' reign in England, Peter the Great was growing up in Russia.

Learning the Basics

Focus: Language Arts, Math, Bible, and Science

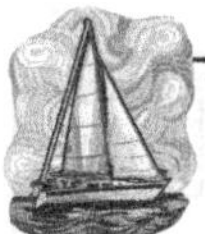

Poetry

T

Read aloud with the students the poem *"The Dumb Soldier"* (see Appendix). Have students share this poem in a special way. Suggestions for sharing the are listed on Day 28 – Day 4.

Key Idea: Share a variety of classic poetry.

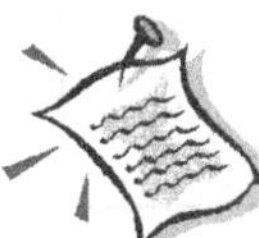

Language Arts

S

Have students complete one dictation exercise.

Guide students to complete one reading lesson.

★ *Drawn into the Heart of Reading*

Help students complete **one** English lesson.

★ *Beginning Wisely:* Lesson 109

★ *Building with Diligence:* Lesson 111

★ Your own grammar program

Key Idea: Practice language arts skills.

Bible Study

T

Have students say Psalm 148:1-5 using the hand motions from Day 1. Have students copy in cursive Psalm 148:4-5 beneath last unit's Psalm 148:1-3 in their *Common Place Book.* Students should leave the rest of the page blank to add to next week. Students will add to the *Common Place Book* throughout the year.

✔ *Lead Me to the Rock* CD
Track 9; Song: "Praise Ye Him"
(vs. 1-5)

Key Idea: Copy in cursive a portion of a Psalm.

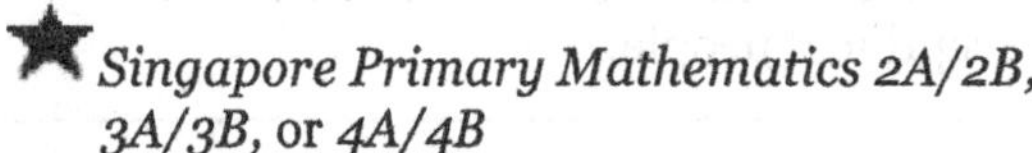

Math Exploration

S

Choose **one** math option listed below.

★ *Singapore Primary Mathematics 2A/2B, 3A/3B,* or *4A/4B*

★ Your own math program

Key Idea: Use a step-by-step math program.

Science Exploration

I

★ Read *Who Was Leonardo da Vinci* p. 72-77. Turn to the science experiment section in your science binder or sketchbook. At the top of a blank page, write: *What is the difference between a voluntary muscle and an involuntary muscle?* Under the question, write: *'Guess'.* Write down your guess.

All movement in the body requires the use of muscles. To demonstrate the difference between voluntary and involuntary muscles, you will do two different experiments. First, squeeze a clothespin or a baster as fast as possible for 2 minutes. Count the number of times that you squeeze it. Rest for one minute, and then repeat the experiment. Why couldn't you squeeze the clothespin or baster as many times on the second try? You used voluntary muscles, or those you consciously control. Voluntary muscles get tired!

For the next experiment, begin by feeling the rhythm of your heart. Then, place a strip of masking tape on the floor. Keeping your feet together jump quickly back and forth across the tape for one minute. Feel your heart again. What happened to the rhythm of your heart? Your heart is an involuntary muscle, so you do not consciously control it. It is designed so it doesn't get tired, even when it is working harder than usual. On your paper, write: *'Procedure'.* Draw a picture of the experiment. At the bottom of the paper, write: *'Conclusion'.* Explain what you learned.

Key Idea: Leonardo studied the way that bones and muscles work. He drew detailed sketches of them. In his sketches, he showed the different muscles, and how they work.

Unit 31 - Day 1

Reading about History T

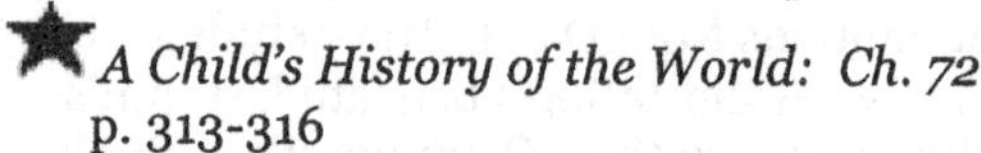

Read about history in the following resource:

★ *A Child's History of the World: Ch. 72* p. 313-316

After today's reading, say, *What two sides fought against one another in the Thirty Years' War?* (knowledge) *Why is the Passion Play given in Oberammergau Germany every 10 years?* (comprehension) *Describe Louis XIV, the Grand Monarch of France.* (analysis) *Tell about Louis XIV's court.* (comprehension) *What problems can you predict France may have after what you read today?* (synthesis)

Key Idea: While the Stuarts were reigning in England, Louis XIV was ruling in France. He was called the Grand Monarch. He loved grandeur and parading about in expensive clothes. His palace at Versailles was richly decorated, and his court was filled with exceptional people.

History Project S

In this unit you will be making an engraving using paint and paper. Today, sketch a picture or a design on paper that you will be able to engrave in paint on Day 2. Do not color the sketch. You may wish to sketch a vase with flowers, a portrait of a person or a pet, a scene from the Bible or favorite story, or a design of some kind.

Key Idea: Prior to the use of photography, engraving was a popular method of printmaking. It was used to decorate jewelry, glassware, and metalwork. It was also used to reproduce paintings or pictures.

Storytime T

Read aloud the following assigned story:

★ *The Wonderful Winter* p. 111-136

Discuss today's reading in a "conversational way". Share about a person, time, event, or emotion from your life that today's reading brought to mind. Next, have your child share a connection.

Key Idea: Connect personally to the story.

Research S

During the time of the American and French revolutions, engraving was the method used to produce pictures. Where could you look to discover more about **engraving?** Use a reference book or an online resource like www.wikipedia.org to type *engraving* in the search or look it up in the index.

Orally answer one or more of the following questions from your research: *What is an engraving? How was engraving used to produce pictures? Which types of things were engraved? What are some of the references in the Bible to engraving? As time passed, what replaced engravings? Is engraving used very much today? Why not?*

Key Idea: Louis XIV ruled France for over 70 years. He succeeded in making France one of the most powerful nations in Europe. Yet, the people of France began to grow tired of paying for the king's expensive lifestyle. Trouble was waiting for the French nobility.

Independent History Study I

★ Read *Peter the Great* p. 12-17. Orally retell or narrate to an adult the portion of text that you read today. Use the *Narration Tips* in the Appendix for help as needed.

Key Idea: Peter the Great was ruling Russia at the same time that Louis XIV was ruling France.

Learning the Basics

Focus: Language Arts, Math, Bible, and Science

Unit 31 - Day 1

Poetry

T

Read aloud to the students the poem *"My Treasures"* (see Appendix). Say, *Why do you think the poem is titled "My Treasures"? What are some of the treasures that the boy has gathered? Where did the boy find his treasures? What are some of the treasures that you've gathered? Do you think that the boy's stone is really gold? Explain. Why would different children treasure different things?* Read the poem again together.

Key Idea: Read and appreciate classic poetry.

Language Arts

S

Have students complete the first studied dictation exercise (see Appendix for directions and passages).

Help students complete one lesson from the following reading program:

★ *Drawn into the Heart of Reading*

Work with the students to complete **one** of the English options listed below:

★ *Beginning Wisely:* Lesson 110

★ *Building with Diligence:* Lesson 112

★ Your own grammar program

Key Idea: Practice language arts skills.

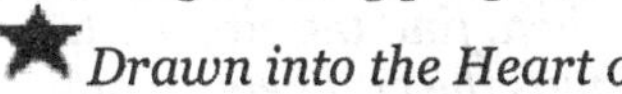

Bible Study

T

Say, *Find Psalm 148:1-8 in your Bible. This is the memory selection for this unit. Read the verses out loud.* Ask, *When you read Psalm 148:3-6, what do you think the word "them" is referring to in verse 6? Who set the Sun, Moon, and stars in motion and gave them the laws they must follow? What can we learn from Psalm 148:6? In Psalm 148:7, where is the praise for the Lord coming from? In Psalm 148:1, where was the praise for the Lord coming from? Together, what do these 2 verses show? What huge and imposing things are listed in Psalm 148:7-8? Yet, whose design and laws must all of these things obey?* Have students say the verse 3 times, adding hand motions to help remember the words.

✔ *Lead Me to the Rock* CD
Track 9; Song: "Praise Ye Him"
(vs. 1-8)

Key Idea: All things in nature must follow the laws that the Lord has designed for them.

Math Exploration

S

Choose **one** of the math options listed below (see Appendix for details).

★ *Singapore Primary Mathematics 2A/2B, 3A/3B,* or *4A/4B*

★ Your own math program

Key Idea: Use a step-by-step math program.

Science Exploration

I

★ Read *Who Was Leonardo da Vinci?* p. 78-87. Today you will add to your science notebook. At the top of an unlined paper, copy Proverbs 23:12 in cursive. Beneath the verse, write, *"Sketches like these were in Leonardo da Vinci's Notebooks:"*. Under the heading, either photocopy and glue in some of Leonardo's sketches from p. 56-63 and p. 72-75, or sketch some of his drawings yourself from the listed pages. Then, copy the first paragraph from the top of p. 62. You may wish to include some mirror writing on your notebook page, like Leonardo did.

Key Idea: Other talented sculptors and painters were also creating their masterpieces at the same time that Leonardo da Vinci was alive. Both Raphael and Michelangelo lived during the Italian Renaissance.

Learning through History
Focus: Wars and Revolutions

Unit 31 - Day 2

Reading about History [T]

Read about history in the following resource:

★ *A Child's History of the World: Ch. 73* p. 317-320

After today's reading, read aloud Ecclesiastes 2:12-16. Say, *Peter the Great was known for his pursuit of wisdom. What does King Solomon say about wisdom in Ecclesiastes 2:13? Even though Solomon says wisdom is better than folly, what does he say that he realized in Ecclesiastes 2:14? Why does Solomon say wisdom is meaningless in Ecclesiastes 2:15? What does Ecclesiastes 2:16 say happens to all men? Does this mean that we should act foolishly? Then, what is Solomon trying to say is even more important than wisdom? Since Solomon was one of the wisest men to ever live, what does that tell you about pursuing wisdom instead of pursuing God? Which is important for eternity?*

Key Idea: Peter the Great brought the wisdom and knowledge he had gained home to Russia. He built a new capitol named St. Petersburg.

History Project [S]

Get the sketch that you made for your engraving on Day 1. Add white glue to dark colored paint to thicken it. Then, brush a thick layer of the paint onto a piece of white paper. Use a toothpick or the pointed end of a paperclip to engrave your sketch into the paint. Lay your engraving flat to dry until Day 3.

Key Idea: Peter the Great brought western fashion and customs to Russia. He decided to help Russia change so that it could become more like the rest of Europe.

Storytime [T]

Read aloud the following assigned passage:

★ *The Wonderful Winter* p. 137-157

Ask, *In today's reading, how were people's lives different from your life? What would you have enjoyed or found difficult about living during that time?*

Key Idea: Compare historical time periods.

Geography [S]

Use a globe for today's activities. *Peter the Great was from Russia. Find Russia on the globe. Trace a path with your finger on the globe from Russia to Holland, or the Netherlands as its called today. This is where Peter went to study shipbuilding. Then, trace a path to England where Peter went next. Then, find Sweden, where Peter fought to conquer a piece of seashore for Russia. Last, find the city of Moscow, which was the first capitol of Russia. Then, find the city of St. Petersburg, which was the city Peter made Russia's new capitol. Which city is the capitol of Russia today?*

Introduce the following concept: *The meridians of longitude divide Earth into 24 sections. Each section is a different time zone. Each time zone differs one hour from the time zone on either side of it. Look at the section of Earth where you live. Which other places are in the same time zone as you are?*

Key Idea: Peter the Great went to Holland and England to learn about the western world. He fought Charles XII of Sweden for a portion of the seashore. Eventually, Peter won, and then he built a fleet of ships.

Independent History Study [I]

★ Read *Peter the Great* p. 18-25. Then, copy the first two paragraphs from p. 20 of *Peter the Great* in cursive into your *Common Place Book.*

Key Idea: Peter the Great began educating the Russian people and changing the way they did everything.

Learning the Basics

Focus: Language Arts, Math, Bible, and Science

Language Arts

T

Work with the students to complete **one** of the English options listed below:

★ *Beginning Wisely:* Lesson 111

★ *Building with Diligence:* Lesson 113

★ Your own grammar program

Say, *You will be doing a writing activity based on the poem, "My Treasures"* (see Appendix).

Say, *On paper, list 3-4 of your favorite treasures that you have gathered, saving the best treasure for last* (i.e. rock, feather, seashell, coin, ticket, ribbon, postcard, stamp, medal, brochure, picture, ring, card, letter, sticker, or a creation)

After students have finished listing their treasures, say, *You will write one paragraph about each of your treasures, much like the poem "My Treasures". In each paragraph, you need to explain where you got the treasure, and why you think it's special.*

Say, *Make sure to start a new paragraph each time you begin talking about a new treasure. Your written piece will be 3-4 paragraphs long. If you prefer to tell about your treasures by writing a poem, you may do that instead.*

When students have finished writing their piece, have them title it *"My Treasures"*. Then, have students share it by reading it aloud.

Key Idea: Write creatively from classic poetry.

Bible Study

T

Have students say Psalm 148:1-8 using the hand motions they added on Day 1. Say, *A mood is a feeling, a sensation, or a state of mind. What is the mood of Psalm 148:6-8?* (Some examples of moods include frightened, worried, happy, peaceful, hopeful, sad, unhappy, angry, thankful, prayerful, joyful, and lonely.) Ask, *When would this Psalm help you, or when would you go to this Psalm?* (i.e. to comfort us by showing that the Lord is in control of all things, to remind us that nature must follow God's design and decrees, to show us God's great power)

Last, pray with your children that they will recognize God's great power. Pray that they will see that nature must follow God's design and that God is in control of all things.

✔ *Lead Me to the Rock* CD
Track 9; Song: "Praise Ye Him"
(vs. 1-8)

Key Idea: The Psalms reflect the many emotions and moods we have. They are a wonderful place to seek counsel from the Lord.

Math Exploration

S

Choose **one** of the math options listed below (see Appendix for details).

★ *Singapore Primary Mathematics 2A/2B, 3A/3B*, or *4A/4B*

★ Your own math program

Key Idea: Use a step-by-step math program.

Science Exploration

I

★ Read *Who Was Leonardo da Vinci?* p. 90-102. Orally retell or narrate to an adult the portion of text that you read today. Use the *Narration Tips* in the Appendix for help as needed.

Key Idea: When Leonardo finished the *Mona Lisa,* he decided to keep it. The *Mona Lisa* is one of the most famous paintings in the world today. The expression on the woman's face is full of mystery.

Learning through History
Focus: Wars and Revolutions

Unit 31 - Day 3

Reading about History — T

Read about history in the following resource:

★ *A Child's History of the World: Ch. 74* p. 321-324

After today's reading, have your students orally narrate or retell the portion of today's text that you read. Use the *Narration Tips* in the Appendix as needed.

Key Idea: Frederick the Great fought Maria Theresa in the Seven Years' War to acquire part of Austria. Frederick was a smart general, and he beat Maria Theresa.

Storytime — T

Read aloud the following assigned passage:

★ *The Wonderful Winter* p. 158-169

Ask, *In what does the main character place his faith? How would the story be different if the main character put his faith in God? Share a character, a story, or a verse from the Bible that you are reminded of by the reading.*

Key Idea: Share a Biblical connection.

History Project — S

Make a frame for your engraving that you made on Day 2. First, choose a piece of colored construction paper for your frame. Next fold the colored paper in half and cut out a rectangle shape from the center, leaving an equal border of paper around the outside. This will be your frame. Open the paper up. Tape or glue the colored frame around your engraving.

Key Idea: Even though Frederick did not always treat other countries fairly, he did try to treat the people in Prussia fairly. He felt that his people had rights, which the king should not overstep.

Vocabulary — S

You may choose 3-5 of the following vocabulary words from *A Child's History of the World* to use for this lesson: *hobby* (p. 321), *collect* (p. 321), *account* (p. 322), *miller* (p. 323), and/or *uneducated* (p. 324). First, find the word in the text and read the sentence containing the word. Think about possible meanings. Next, find the word in a dictionary and select the correct meaning. Write the word at the top of an index card or at the top of the corresponding letter page in the notebook. Underneath the word, copy the correct definition from the dictionary. Then, use the word correctly in a sentence. The sentence may either be copied from the text or be one of your own creation. Last, draw a small picture to show the word's meaning. If you used an index card to record your word, file it under the correct alphabetical tab.

Key Idea: England had taken Frederick's side, and France had taken Maria Theresa's side. So, when Frederick won in Europe, the English also beat the French in America.

Independent History Study — I

★ At the top of a white piece of paper, write *Peter the Great: Tsar of Russia (1672-1725)*. Then, draw and color a series of small pictures all over the page to tell about his life and interests. Some possible ideas for pictures include a sailboat (p. 11), tools (p. 15), a watch (p. 16), a bridge (p. 17), and a human body (p. 16).

Key Idea: Just as Peter the Great made Russia Great, Frederick the Great made Prussia great.

Learning the Basics

Focus: Language Arts, Math, Bible, and Science

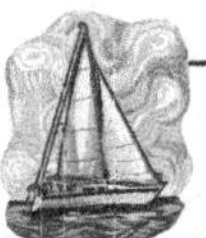

Poetry

T

Read aloud with the students the poem *"My Treasures"* (see Appendix). Say, *Describe a memory that the poem brought to mind. What can you learn about the poet, Robert Louis Stevenson, from the poem?* Say, *Did you know that Robert Louis Stevenson dedicated his poetry book "A Child's Garden of Verse" to his nurse, Cummie, who he said was "My second mother, my first wife". What do you think he meant by that?* Have the students read the poem on their own.

Key Idea: Read and appreciate classic poetry.

Language Arts

S

Have students complete one studied dictation exercise (see Appendix for directions and passages).

Help students complete one lesson from the following reading program:

★ *Drawn into the Heart of Reading*

Work with the students to complete **one** of the English options listed below:

★ *Beginning Wisely:* Lesson 112

★ *Building with Diligence:* Lesson 114

★ Your own grammar program

Key Idea: Practice language arts skills.

Bible Study

T

Say, *You will be having your own quiet time with God today. Choose a quiet place for this special time, where you can be alone with God. Then, do the following things:*

1. Read Psalm 148:1-8 in your Bible.
2. Pray about the verse using the following beginning to your prayer: *Thank you for designing your amazing creation to follow your laws. I praise you for the way you designed the _____, _____, and _____. These are wonderfully made and show your _____ and _____.*
3. Recite Psalm 148:1-8 using the hand motions you added on Day 1.
4. Sing Psalm 148:1-8 along with the CD at the end of your quiet time.

✔ *Lead Me to the Rock* CD
Track 9; Song: "Praise Ye Him" (vs. 1-8)

Key Idea: God's creation praises their Creator.

Math Exploration

S

Choose **one** of the math options listed below (see Appendix for details).

★ *Singapore Primary Mathematics 2A/2B, 3A/3B,* or *4A/4B*

★ Your own math program

Key Idea: Use a step-by-step math program.

Science Exploration

I

★ Read the first 8 pages (counting pictures as pages) of *Pasteur's Fight Against Microbes*. Stop at "The little drop was full of swimming *things!*" Write the answer to each numbered question on lined paper. You do not need to copy the question. Use the listed page to help you answer each question.

1. Explain the problem that Pasteur was asked to solve. (p. 3)
2. What did Pasteur do first? (p. 6)
3. Why did Pasteur decide to look at the contents of the bottles under a microscope? (p. 7)
4. Describe what Pasteur saw when he looked into the microscope. (p. 7)
5. What does Colossians 1:16 say about things too tiny to be seen, except for under a microscope?

Key Idea: When Pasteur was teaching in Lille, he began working on a problem at the sugarbeet factory.

Learning through History
Focus: Wars and Revolutions

Unit 31 - Day 4

Reading about History — T

Read about history in the following resource:

★ *A Child's History of the World: Ch. 75* p. 325-331

★ *Hero Tales* p. 177-187

After today's reading, say, *You will be writing a narration about part of today's history reading. In order to remember the details well, you will need to reread part of today's reading from p. 329 through the second paragraph on p. 330 (on your own if possible).*

After students have finished reading the passage, ask them the questions below. If the students do not know the answers, help them find the answers in the passage they just read. Ask, *Who was the king of England in today's story? Why did the Americans begin to fight the English? When the English would not give the Americans the same rights as the English, what did the Americans do next? What was the Declaration of Independence? Who wrote it? Who was general of the Continental (or American) Army? What hard times did the Continental Army have? Who went to France to get help for America? What happened then?* After the questions have been answered, have students write a 5 sentence narration about how the Americans gained their independence from England.

When students have finished their narration, direct them to read the sentences out loud. Help students underline or highlight the main idea sentence in their narration. See the *Written Narration Skills* in the Appendix to guide students in editing their narrations.

Key Idea: The colonists in America were tired of paying heavy taxes to the king of England.

Storytime — T

Read aloud the following assigned passage:

★ *The Wonderful Winter* p. 170-184

Say, After today's reading, have your students orally narrate or retell the portion of today's text that you read. Use the *Narration Tips* in the Appendix as needed.

Key Idea: Practice oral narration skills.

Timeline — S

You will be adding 2 new cards to your staircase timeline today. On the first new card, draw and color a ship. Write, *Peter the Great (1672-1725 A.D.).* On the second new card, draw and color an American flag. Write, *American Revolution (1775-1783 A.D.)*

If you decided to tape your timeline cards to the back of a door, then add the *Peter the Great* card to the right of the *Queen Elizabeth* card. To the right of the *Peter the Great* card, add the *American Revolution* card. If you decided to tape the timeline cards side-by-side to accordion-fold them, use clear packing tape to tape the cards as described above. Then, accordion-fold the timeline to store it.

Key Idea: Benjamin Franklin was sent to work with the king of England to come to a fair agreement about taxing the people in the colonies. When that failed, the Americans gathered an army to fight for their rights. Later, Thomas Jefferson wrote the Declaration of Independence to declare that the colonies wanted to be free of English rule.

Independent History Study — I

★ Read *Peter the Great* p. 26-32. Then, choose an interesting part from today's pages to read aloud and explain to an adult.

Key Idea: By the time Peter the Great died, the Russians were tired of all of the taxes they were paying.

Learning the Basics

Focus: Language Arts, Math, Bible, and Science

Unit 31 - Day 4

Poetry

T

Read aloud with the students the poem *"My Treasures"* (see Appendix). Have students share this poem in a special way. Suggestions for sharing the poem are given in the "Poetry" box of Unit 30 – Day 4.

Key Idea: Share a variety of classic poetry.

Language Arts

S

Have students complete one dictation exercise.

Guide students to complete one reading lesson.

★ *Drawn into the Heart of Reading*

Help students complete **one** English lesson.

★ *Beginning Wisely:* Lesson 113

★ *Building with Diligence:* Lesson 115 (half)

★ Your own grammar program

Key Idea: Practice language arts skills.

Bible Study

T

Have students say Psalm 148:1-8 using the hand motions from Day 1. Have students copy in cursive Psalm 148:6-8 beneath last unit's Psalm 148:4-5 in their *Common Place Book*. Students should leave the rest of the page blank to add to next week. Students will add to the *Common Place Book* throughout the year.

✔ *Lead Me to the Rock* CD
Track 9; Song: "Praise Ye Him"
(vs. 1-8)

Key Idea: Copy in cursive a portion of a Psalm.

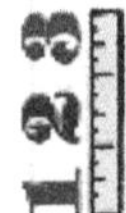

Math Exploration

S

Choose **one** math option listed below.

★ *Singapore Primary Mathematics 2A/2B, 3A/3B,* or *4A/4B*

★ Your own math program

Key Idea: Use a step-by-step math program.

Science Exploration

I

★ Read the next 10 pages (counting pictures as pages) of *Pasteur's Fight Against Microbes*. Stop at "A war had been fought and won." Turn to the science experiment section in your science binder or sketchbook. At the top of a blank page, write: *What causes mold or fungus to grow?* Under the question, write: *'Guess'*. Write down your guess. **Have an adult help you with this first part.** Stir ¼ cup of sugar and ¼ cup of water in a microwave safe dish or in a saucepan. Heat the mixture one minute at a time until the sugar dissolves. The mixture does not need to boil. Allow the mixture to cool for 5 minutes.

Seal one piece of bread in a bag, labeled, *Plain bread*. Next, sprinkle 20 drops of water on a different piece of bread. Seal it in a different bag, labeled, *Bread with water*. Then, sprinkle 20 drops of sugar water on the last piece of bread. Seal it in a fourth bag, labeled, *Bread with sugar water*. Place all 3 bags in a dark, warm place where they will not be disturbed.

Check the bags in 1 week. **Do not open the bags.** Write down your conclusion. Then, throw away the bags without opening them. On your paper, write: *'Procedure'*. Draw a picture of the experiment. At the bottom of the paper, write: *'Conclusion'*. Explain what you learned.

Key Idea: The fungus needs water and food, such as sugar, to grow. The fungus can also use the starch and sugar inside the bread as food, but the more food there is, the more the fungus can grow. So, the sugar water provides the best growing environment for the fungus.

Learning through History
Focus: Napoleon Arrives on the Scene

Unit 32 - Day 1

Reading about History T

Read about history in the following resource:

★ *A Child's History of the World: Ch. 76* p. 332-337 (Note: This reading contains some graphic content that you may wish to omit.)

After today's reading, say, *Why was there a revolution in France?* (analysis) *What was the Bastille?* (knowledge) *Tell about the Reign of Terror.* (comprehension) *How was the French Revolution different from the American Revolution?* (analysis) *What happened when Christ and Christianity were removed from France?* (evaluation)

Key Idea: Shortly after the American Revolution, the French people also had a revolution. They were rebelling against high taxes, rich nobility, lack of rights, and starvation. The storming of the Bastille was the beginning of the French Revolution.

History Project S

In this unit you will be making a French tricolor flag. Begin by folding a piece of white paper in half from top to bottom. Measure and divide the folded paper into 3 equal sections. Color the section farthest left royal blue. Leave the middle section white. Color the section on the farthest right red. Save the flag for Day 2.

Key Idea: The French Revolution took a terrible turn when the worship of Christ, attending church, and Sundays were done away with. The Reign of Terror finally ended with the death of Robespierre, one of the main leaders during the Reign of Terror.

Storytime T

Read aloud the following assigned story:

★ *The Wonderful Winter* p. 185-199

Discuss today's reading in a "conversational way". Share about a person, time, event, or emotion from your life that today's reading brought to mind. Next, have your child share a connection.

Key Idea: Connect personally to the story.

Research S

During the time of the French Revolution, the French tricolor was very popular. Where could you look to discover more about the **French tricolor?** Use a reference book or an online resource like www.wikipedia.org to type *French tricolor* in the search or look it up in the index.

Orally answer one or more of the following questions from your research: *What was the French tricolor? Why is the flag called the tricolor? What did the colors stand for? When did this flag become popular? Before the French Revolution, what was the emblem of France? Describe what the French flag looks like today. Is it the same as the French tricolor?*

Key Idea: After the storming of the Bastille, the angry mob marched to the palace of the French queen and king in Versailles. Later, the king and queen both lost their lives to the guillotine. The Reign of Terror began next, when anyone who might be in favor of the king was beheaded.

Independent History Study I

★ Read *Mozart the Wonder Boy* p. 11-24 and listen to the optional CD Track 16, *"Minuet in G"*. Orally retell to an adult the portion of text that you read today. Use the *Narration Tips* in the Appendix for help.

Key Idea: During the French Revolution, many wanted to attack Austria. Mozart was born in Austria.

Learning the Basics

Focus: Language Arts, Math, Bible, and Science

Unit 32 - Day 1

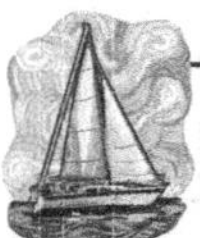

Poetry

T

Read aloud to the students the poem *"Historical Associations"* (see Appendix). Say, *What is the child telling his Uncle Jim about the garden? Name some of the things the children have imagined the garden has become. What are some of the adventures the children have pretended to have in the garden? Explain the meaning of the last stanza.* Read the poem again with the students.

Key Idea: Read and appreciate classic poetry.

Bible Study

T

Say, *Find Psalm 148:1-12 in your Bible. This is the memory selection for this unit. Read the verses out loud.* Ask, *What is the difference between mountains and hills? In Psalm 148:9, both the mountains and the hills praise the Lord. Why do you think Psalm 148:9 lists two opposite kinds of trees? How are wild beasts and domesticated cattle opposite from one another? What other opposites do you notice in Psalm 148:10-12? How does this part of the Psalm use opposites to show that all things join together in praising the Lord?*

Have students say the verse 3 times, adding hand motions to help remember the words.

✔ *Lead Me to the Rock* CD
Track 9; Song: "Praise Ye Him"
(vs. 1-12)

Key Idea: All things in nature praise their Maker, whether they are great or small.

Language Arts

S

Have students complete the first studied dictation exercise (see Appendix for directions and passages).

Help students complete one lesson from the following reading program:

 *Drawn into the Heart of Reading*

Work with the students to complete **one** of the English options listed below:

★ *Beginning Wisely:* Lesson 114

★ *Building with Diligence:* Lesson 115 (half)

★ Your own grammar program

Key Idea: Practice language arts skills.

Math Exploration

S

Choose **one** of the math options listed below (see Appendix for details).

★ *Singapore Primary Mathematics 2A/2B, 3A/3B,* or *4A/4B*

★ Your own math program

Key Idea: Use a step-by-step math program.

Science Exploration

I

★ Read the next 10 pages (counting pictures as pages) of *Pasteur's Fight Against Microbes.* Stop at "But when he tipped the microbe-free soup into the swan-neck to rinse trapped dust back into the flask, microbes appeared, growing energetically." Today you will add to your science notebook. At the top of an unlined paper, copy Hebrews 11:1 in cursive. Beneath the verse, on the left side of the paper, draw a picture of a flask with liquid in it. Under the flask, write, *yeast with sugar = yeast soup.* Next to the flask, make a "+" sign. Next to the "+" sign, draw bits of dust. Under the dust, write, *dust in air.* Next to the dust, draw an "=" sign. Next to the "=" sign, draw the flask of yeast soup with black rods in it. Under the last flask, write, *black rods or microbes.* Then, at the bottom, write, *Less dust in the air = less microbes.*

Key Idea: Pasteur discovered that microbes are in the dust in the air. This was a new idea.

Learning through History
Focus: Napoleon Arrives on the Scene

Unit 32 - Day 2

Reading about History [T]

Read about history in the following resource:

★ *A Child's History of the World: Ch. 77* p. 338-343

After today's reading, read aloud Psalm 33:12-19. Say, *What kind of nation does Psalm 33:12 say will be blessed? What can we learn about God in Psalm 33:13-15? Although Napoleon had a very great army, did it save him? What does Psalm 33:16-17 tell us about that. Where do we need to place our hope? What does Psalm 33:20-22 say about hoping in the Lord? Does Psalm 33:18-19 mean that as Christians we won't have to worry about death or famine? Then, how will the Lord deliver us from these things? Why is our heavenly home much more important than our earthly home? How can you spend eternity in heaven?*

Key Idea: Napoleon became a general by the time he was 26 years old. He crossed the Alps into Italy and conquered that country. Then, he went to Egypt to conquer that too. Napoleon's fleet was destroyed in Egypt by the English admiral Lord Nelson.

History Project [S]

Get the French tricolor flag that you began on Day 1. Cut on the lines between the blue, white, and red sections of the flag to make three flaps that you can lift. Then, use a marker to write, *Liberte,* on the blue flap, *egalite,* on the white flap, and *fraternite,* on the red flap. Save the flag for Day 3.

Key Idea: The reign of Napoleon ended the French Revolution.

Storytime [T]

Read aloud the following assigned passage:

★ *The Wonderful Winter* p. 200-215

Ask, *In today's reading, how were people's lives different from your life? What would you have enjoyed or found difficult about living during that time?*

Key Idea: Compare historical time periods.

Vocabulary [S]

You may choose 3-5 of the following vocabulary words from *A Child's History of the World* to use for this lesson: *mob* (p. 338), *fleet* (p. 340), *consul* (p. 340), *retreating* (p. 341), and/or *tyrant* (p. 341). First, find the word in the text and read the sentence containing the word. Think about possible meanings. Next, find the word in a dictionary and select the correct meaning. Write the word at the top of an index card or at the top of the corresponding letter page in the notebook. Underneath the word, copy the correct definition from the dictionary. Then, use the word correctly in a sentence. The sentence may either be copied from the text or be one of your own creation. Last, draw a small picture to show the word's meaning. If you used an index card to record your word, file it under the correct alphabetical tab.

Key Idea: After Napoleon returned from Egypt to France, he became first consul. Later he became emperor of France and king of Italy. All of Europe began to worry that Napoleon would attack them next. So, when Napoleon sailed to attack England, the English admiral Lord Nelson fought him near Trafalgar, Spain. Napoleon's fleet was destroyed.

Independent History Study [I]

★ Read *Mozart the Wonder Boy* p. 27-36 and listen to the optional CD Track 17, *"Minuet in F"*. Then, copy the last sentence from p. 36 of *Mozart the Wonder Boy* in cursive into your *Common Place Book*.

Key Idea: Mozart and his sister Nannerl gave concerts in Munich and Vienna. They played for the prince.

Learning the Basics

Focus: Language Arts, Math, Bible, and Science

Unit 32 - Day 2

Language Arts

T

Work with the students to complete **one** of the English options listed below:

★ *Beginning Wisely:* Lesson 115

★ *Building with Diligence:* Lesson 116 (half)

★ Your own grammar program

Say, *You will be doing a writing activity based on the poem, "Historical Associations"* (see Appendix). Say, *Let's make a list of all of the things you can remember pretending in your backyard.* As students share their ideas, list them on a markerboard or a piece of paper (i.e. castles with knights and princesses, forts with soldiers, cattle drives with cowboys, rodeos with bucking broncoes, races with racecars, horse races, baseball games, house with babies to care for, firemen and fire stations, wagon trains going west, camping in tents, Indians in teepees, circuses with circus acts, lemonade stands, airplanes flying, acting out Bible stories, etc.)

Next, say, *You will write one long poem that lists the many things you have pretended in your backyard. The poem does not need to rhyme. Include the things from your list in your poem. Refer to the poem, "Historical Associations" for ideas on how to begin and end your poem.*

When students have finished writing their poem, have them title it. Then, have students share it by reading it aloud.

Key Idea: Write creatively from classic poetry.

Bible Study

T

Have students say Psalm 148:1-12 using the hand motions they added on Day 1. Say, *A mood is a feeling, a sensation, or a state of mind. What is the mood of Psalm 148:9-12?* (Some examples of moods include frightened, worried, happy, peaceful, hopeful, sad, unhappy, angry, thankful, prayerful, joyful, and lonely.) Ask, *When would this Psalm help you, or when would you go to this Psalm?* (i.e. to give us the feeling that all of nature is joining together to praise the Lord, to help us feel like praising our Maker, to celebrate life)

Last, pray with your children that they will praise their Maker with joy! Pray that they will know that the Lord has a plan for their life and know that He is never taken by surprise.

✔ *Lead Me to the Rock* CD
Track 9; Song: "Praise Ye Him"
(vs. 1-12)

Key Idea: The Psalms reflect the many emotions and moods we have. They are a wonderful place to seek counsel from the Lord.

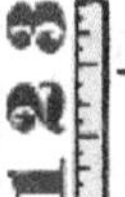

Math Exploration

S

Choose **one** of the math options listed below (see Appendix for details).

★ *Singapore Primary Mathematics 2A/2B, 3A/3B,* or *4A/4B*

★ Your own math program

Key Idea: Use a step-by-step math program.

Science Exploration

I

★ Read the last 12 pages (counting pictures as pages) of *Pasteur's Fight Against Microbes*. Orally retell or narrate to an adult the portion of text that you read today. Use the *Narration Tips* in the Appendix for help as needed.

Key Idea: Pasteur shared what he had discovered about microbes with other scientists in Paris. Doctors began to understand that microbes cause infections and diseases. Foods began being heated to kill the microbes by a process called pasteurization (named after Pasteur). Later, Pasteur developed vaccination.

Learning through History
Focus: Napoleon Arrives on the Scene

Unit 32 - Day 3

Reading about History — T

Read about history in the following resource:

★ *A Child's History of the World: Ch. 78* p. 344-352

After today's reading, have your students orally narrate or retell the portion of today's text that you read. Use the *Narration Tips* in the Appendix as needed.

Key Idea: After the American and French Revolutions, many other colonies began to revolt to gain their independence too.

History Project — S

Get out your French tricolor flag that you began on Days 1-2. Lift the blue flap and write, *Liberty,* on the paper under the flap. Lift the white flap, and write, *equality,* on the paper under the flap. Lift the red flap and write, *brotherhood,* on the paper under the flap. The words on top of the flaps are written in French, and the words under the flaps are the same words written in English. *Liberty, equality, and brotherhood* became the cry for freedom everywhere as countries struggled for independence.

Key Idea: During the time of the French Revolution, Touissant led a revolt in Haiti against the French government. He helped govern Haiti until Napoleon had him imprisoned in France. Haiti eventually won their independence. When Napoleon conquered Spain, the Spanish colony in Peru revolted against Napoleon's new king.

Storytime — T

Read aloud the following assigned passage:

★ *The Wonderful Winter* p. 216-227

Ask, *In what does the main character place his faith? How would the story be different if the main character put his faith in God? Share a character, a story, or a verse from the Bible that you are reminded of by the reading.*

Key Idea: Share a Biblical connection.

Geography — S

Use a globe for today's activities. *Look on the map on p. 346 of A Child's History of the World. Find the area owned by Portugal or the Portuguese. Find this same area in Brazil on the globe. Next, on p. 346, find the area conquered by Spain starting with Mexico all the way down to the tip of South America. This is why Spanish is the main language spoken in these countries. Find this same area on the globe. Shortly after the American and French Revolutions, revolutions broke out in Spanish colonies too. Compare the map on p. 346 to the map on p. 349. Name the countries shown on p. 349 that revolted against Spain to win their freedom.*

Review the following concept: *The meridians of longitude divide Earth into 24 sections. Each section is a different time zone. Each time zone differs one hour from the time zone on either side of it. Look at the section to the right of where you live. This time zone is one hour ahead of you. Explain why this is true.*

Key Idea: Many countries won their freedom.

Independent History Study — I

★ Make a notebook page with the following heading at the top: *Mozart's Younger Years.* If you have a copy machine, photocopy p. 60-61 from *Mozart the Wonder Boy* and color it. Listen to the optional CD Tracks 24-34 while you color. If you do not have a copy machine, write facts about Mozart instead (i.e. Born in Salzburg, Austria. Sister Nannerl (Marianne). Wrote "*Minuet in F*" at age 6.)

Key Idea: Mozart and Nannerl gave concerts all over Austria, Germany, Belgium, France, and England.

Learning the Basics

Focus: Language Arts, Math, Bible, and Science

Unit 32 - Day 3

Poetry

T

Read aloud with the students the poem "*Historical Associations*" (see Appendix). Say, *Describe a memory that the poem brought to mind. What can you learn about the poet, Robert Louis Stevenson, from the poem?* Say, *Did you know that Robert loved imagining tales even as an adult? In his short life, he wrote many different kinds of tales. He died at the age of 44 in the South Seas on the island of Samoa, where he lived with his wife, Fanny.* Have the students read the poem on their own.

Key Idea: Read and appreciate classic poetry.

Language Arts

S

Have students complete one studied dictation exercise (see Appendix for directions and passages).

Help students complete one lesson from the following reading program:

★ *Drawn into the Heart of Reading*

Work with the students to complete **one** of the English options listed below:

★ *Beginning Wisely:* Lesson 116

★ *Building with Diligence:* Lesson 116 (half)

★ Your own grammar program

Key Idea: Practice language arts skills.

Bible Study

T

Say, *You will be having your own quiet time with God today. Choose a quiet place for this special time, where you can be alone with God. Then, do the following things:*

1. Read Psalm 148:1-12 in your Bible.
2. Pray about the verse using the following beginning to your prayer: *Thank you for giving me a voice so that I can join with creation in praising you! I see examples of your power all around me in the ______, ______, and ______. Help me to live my life in a way that praises you.*
3. Recite Psalm 148:1-12 using the hand motions you added on Day 1.
4. Sing Psalm 148:1-12 along with the CD at the end of your quiet time.

✔ *Lead Me to the Rock* CD
Track 9; Song: "Praise Ye Him"
(vs. 1-12)

Key Idea: God's power is all around us.

Math Exploration

S

Choose **one** of the math options listed below (see Appendix for details).

★ *Singapore Primary Mathematics 2A/2B, 3A/3B*, or *4A/4B*

★ Your own math program

Key Idea: Use a step-by-step math program.

Science Exploration

I

★ Read *Albert Einstein: Young Thinker* p. 1-13. Write the answer to each numbered question on lined paper. You do not need to copy the question. Use the listed page to help you answer each question.

1. What gift did Mr. Einstein bring five-year old Albert? (p. 1)
2. What are some of the questions Albert asked about the compass? (p. 6)
3. Explain how a compass works. (p. 9-11)
4. What other questions did Albert have about magnets? (p. 13)
5. In Job 38:18, what does God ask Job about the Earth?

Key Idea: When Albert was sick, his father bought him a magnet. He explained that the Earth acts like a big magnet, so the small magnetic needle inside the compass turns until the south end is pointing north.

Learning through History

Focus: Napoleon Arrives on the Scene

Unit 32 - Day 4

Reading about History [T]

Read about history in the following resource:

★ *A Child's History of the World: Ch. 79* p. 353-358

After today's reading, say, *You will be writing a narration about part of today's history reading. In order to remember the details well, you will reread part of today's reading from p. 355 through the second paragraph on p. 356 (on your own if possible).*

After students have finished reading the passage, ask them the questions below. If the students do not know the answers, help them find the answers in the passage they just read. Ask, *Who was the first musician to write popular music? In which country was Handel born? What did Handel's father want him to be when he grew up? Describe the instrument that Handel learned to play. How did Handel's family discover his love for music? Where did Handel go to live? What famous music did Handel write?*

After the questions have been answered, have students write a 5 sentence narration about Handel. When students have finished their narration, direct them to read the sentences out loud.

Help students underline or highlight the main idea sentence in their narration. See the *Written Narration Skills* in the Appendix to guide students in editing their narrations.

Key Idea: Around 1700 A.D., a German named Handel began composing music on the clavichord. He wrote *The Messiah,* which is sung everywhere at Christmas. Bach was another German musician, living at the same time as Handel. He wrote music for the organ.

Storytime [T]

Read aloud the following assigned passage:

★ *The Wonderful Winter* p. 228-248 and the *Author's Note*

Say, After today's reading, have your students orally narrate or retell the portion of today's text that you read. Use the *Narration Tips* in the Appendix as needed.

Key Idea: Practice oral narration skills.

Timeline [S]

You will be adding 2 new cards to your staircase timeline today. On the first new card, draw and color a music note. Write, *Mozart (1756-1791 A.D.)*. On the second new card, draw and color a French tricolor flag. Write, *Napoleon (1769-1821 A.D.)*.

If you decided to tape your timeline cards to the back of a door, then add the *Mozart* card to the right of the *American Revolution* card. To the right of the *Mozart* card, add the *Napoleon* card. If you decided to tape the timeline cards side-by-side to accordion-fold them, use clear packing tape to tape the cards as described above. Then, accordion-fold the timeline to store it.

Key Idea: Mozart was an Austrian composer who was born near the time of Bach and Handel's deaths. Mozart wrote operas and symphonies. Yet, he made very little money and died as a pauper. Today, we still play Mozart's music! Beethoven was a German composer who lived at the same time as Mozart. As he grew older, he became deaf, yet he still continued to write beautiful music.

Independent History Study [I]

★ Read *Mozart the Wonder Boy* p. 39-52 and listen to the optional CD Track 18, *"Allegro"*. Then, choose an interesting part from today's pages to read aloud and explain to an adult.

Key Idea: Mozart and Nannerl played for King Francis, Queen Maria Theresa, and little Marie Antoinette.

Learning the Basics

Focus: Language Arts, Math, Bible, and Science

Unit 32 - Day 4

Poetry

T

Read aloud with the students the poem *"Historical Associations"* (see Appendix). Have students share this poem in a special way. Suggestions for sharing the poem include recording it to play for someone, reading it to someone on the telephone, photocopying the poem and adding illustrations, reading it to someone at home, putting the poem to a melody and singing it, using an instrument to tap out the meter or rhythm of the poem while reading it, or copying the poem on paper.

Key Idea: Share a variety of classic poetry.

Language Arts

S

Have students complete one dictation exercise.

Guide students to complete one reading lesson.

★ *Drawn into the Heart of Reading*

Help students complete **one** English lesson.

★ *Beginning Wisely:* Lesson 117

★ *Building with Diligence:* Lesson 117 (half)

★ Your own grammar program

Key Idea: Practice language arts skills.

Bible Study

T

Have students say Psalm 148:1-12 using the hand motions from Day 1.

Have students copy in cursive Psalm 148:9-12 beneath last unit's Psalm 148:6-8 in their *Common Place Book.* Students should leave the rest of the page blank to add to next week.

Students will add to the *Common Place Book* throughout the year.

 *Lead Me to the Rock* CD
Track 9; Song: "Praise Ye Him"
(vs. 1-12)

Key Idea: Copy in cursive a portion of a Psalm.

Math Exploration

S

Choose **one** math option listed below.

 *Singapore Primary Mathematics 2A/2B, 3A/3B,* or *4A/4B*

 Your own math program

Key Idea: Use a step-by-step math program.

Science Exploration

I

★ Read *Albert Einstein: Young Thinker* p. 14-28. Turn to the science experiment section in your science binder or sketchbook. At the top of a blank page, write: *Why do helium-filled balloons rise up into the air?* Under the question, write: *'Guess'.* Write down your guess. Blow up a balloon. What have you filled your balloon with? You have filled your balloon with carbon dioxide. Set your balloon on the table. Does it rise up into the air? Why not? What is keeping the balloon on the table? Now, toss your balloon into the air. Why did it go up? Why didn't it stay in the air? If you had a balloon filled with helium, why do you think it would go up and stay in the air longer than this balloon? Helium is a very light gas, which makes helium lighter than air. This is why it floats up. But, the molecules of helium are so tiny that after awhile they start to leak out of the balloon. The shrinking balloon gets heavier than air, and gravity eventually pulls it back down. On your paper, write: *'Procedure'.* Draw a picture of the experiment. At the bottom of the paper, write: *'Conclusion'.* Explain what you learned.

Key Idea: Albert wondered what was beyond the Earth's surface. He wondered why the balloons rose into the air and where the balloons went.

Reading about History **T**

Read about history in the following resource:

★ *A Child's History of the World: Ch. 80* p. 359-363

★ Also, read *Hero Tales* as scheduled in the *Storytime* box of the plans.

After today's first reading, say, *Describe Queen Victoria of England.* (comprehension) *Explain what you learned about Florence Nightingale.* (knowledge) *Tell about Abraham Lincoln.* (knowledge) *Why was the outcome of the Civil War so important?* (analysis) *What do you think would have happened if the South had won the Civil War?* (application)

Key Idea: At the time of the Civil War in America, England was fighting the Crimean War with Russia. Florence Nightingale went to Crimea to help care for the English soldiers. She became the first professional nurse and was known as the Lady of the Lamp.

History Project **S**

In this unit you will be making a map of the United States that shows which states sided with the Union and which states sided with the Confederacy during the Civil War. Print a United States map at one of the following links and save it for Day 2.
www.50states.com/maps/usamap.htm

www.eduplace.com/ss/maps/index.html

www.printablemaps.net/north-america-maps/usa-maps/index.php

Key Idea: The Civil War lasted 4 long years.

Storytime **T**

Read aloud the following assigned story:

★ *Hero Tales* p. 153-163

Discuss today's reading in a "conversational way". Share about a person, time, event, or emotion from your life that today's reading brought to mind. Next, have your child share a connection.

Key Idea: Connect personally to the story.

Research **S**

The conflict in the United States between the North and the South turned into a Civil War when South Carolina seceded from the Union in 1860. Where could you look to discover more about the **Civil War?** Use a reference book or an online resource like www.wikipedia.org to type *American Civil War* in the search or look it up in the index.

Orally answer one or more of the following questions from your research: *What is a Civil War? What does it mean to secede? Why did the Southern states secede from the Union? Who was President of the United States during the Civil War? Who was President of the Confederate States during the Civil War? In what year did the Civil War begin? In what year did it end? What was the outcome of the Civil War?*

Key Idea: Abraham Lincoln was President of the United States during the Civil War. He succeeded in preserving the Union. When the Civil War ended, slavery was abolished in the United States.

Independent History Study **I**

★ Read *Mozart the Wonder Boy* p. 55-63 and listen to the optional CD Tracks 35-37. Orally retell to an adult the portion of text that you read today. Use the *Narration Tips* in the Appendix for help.

Key Idea: Before the French Revolution, Mozart played at the palace in Versailles for King Louis XV.

Learning the Basics

Focus: Language Arts, Math, Bible, and Science

Unit 33 - Day 1

Poetry

T

Guide students to choose one of Robert Louis Stevenson's poems from Units 25-32 to memorize. Students will have 3 weeks (units) to memorize the entire poem. So, students should have one-third of their chosen poem memorized by Day 4 of this unit. After students have chosen their poem, have them read it 3 times, adding actions.

Key Idea: Read and appreciate classic poetry.

Language Arts

S

Have students complete the first studied dictation exercise (see Appendix for directions and passages).

Help students complete one lesson from the following reading program:

★ *Drawn into the Heart of Reading*

Work with the students to complete **one** of the English options listed below:

★ *Beginning Wisely:* Lesson 118

★ *Building with Diligence:* Lesson 117 (half)

★ Your own grammar program

Key Idea: Practice language arts skills.

Bible Study

T

Say, *Find Psalm 148:1-14 in your Bible. This is the memory selection for this unit. Read the verses out loud.* Ask, *What does Psalm 148:13 say about the Lord's name? What does excellent mean? Why does Psalm 148:13 say that the Lord's name "alone" is excellent? How is His glory above the heaven and Earth? God is good to all, but what does it say in Psalm 148:14 that He does for His people? How does God raise up, or exalt, His people? What is the result of this? According to Psalm 148:14, who are the people that are near to the Lord? If you are a believer in Christ, are you near to the Lord? Why should this fill you with reverence and praise for the Lord?*
Have students say the verse 3 times, adding hand motions to help remember the words.

✔ *Lead Me to the Rock* CD
Track 9; Song: "Praise Ye Him"
(vs. 1-14)

Key Idea: The Lord is exalted above all things.

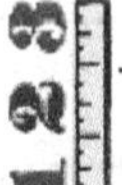

Math Exploration

S

Choose **one** of the math options listed below (see Appendix for details).

★ *Singapore Primary Mathematics 2A/2B, 3A/3B,* or *4A/4B*

★ Your own math program

Key Idea: Use a step-by-step math program.

Science Exploration

I

★ Read *Albert Einstein: Young Thinker* p. 29-44. Today you will add to your science notebook. At the top of an unlined paper, copy Proverbs 1:7 in cursive. Beneath the verse, write, *Albert Einstein: Young Thinker*. Then, list the following information down the left side of the paper (leaving the rest of the page blank to add more quotes in Units 34-35):

Place of Birth: Ulm, Germany
Birth/Death: March 14, 1879 – April 18, 1955
Family: Hermann and Pauline (parents) and Maja (sister)
Quotes: "The important thing is to never stop questioning."

Key Idea: When he was young, Albert was known for asking questions. He didn't fit in well at school.

Learning through History
Focus: The Age of Inventions

Unit 33 - Day 2

Reading about History T

Read about history in the following resource:

★ *A Child's History of the World: Ch. 81* p. 364-367

After today's reading, read aloud Ecclesiastes 9:13-18. Say, *How was the city saved in Ecclesiastes 9:15? What did Solomon conclude in Ecclesiastes 9:16? How could wisdom be better than strength? Was it wise for Napoleon III to attack Prussia? Why not? What can we learn about the difference between those who speak quietly and those who are loud in Ecclesiastes 9:17? What does Solomon say about weapons of war in Ecclesiastes 9:18? Why would wisdom be better than weapons of war? What can we learn from this passage? Why is the wise man often not heard by others?*

Key Idea: Napoleon III became president of France. A war broke out between Prussia and France called the Franco-Prussian War. Napoleon III eventually was beaten by Prussia. Prussia joined the German states together.

History Project S

Get the United States map that you printed on Day 1. Label it, *Civil War Map (1861-1865)*. Then, color the following Confederate States grey: South Carolina, Mississippi, Florida, Alabama, Georgia, Louisiana, Texas, Virginia, Arkansas, North Carolina, and Tennessee. Make a key that shows a grey square labeled *Confederate States*. Save the map for Day 3.

Key Idea: Napoleon III ruled in France during the time of the Civil War in America.

Storytime T

Read aloud the following assigned passage:

★ *The Family Under the Bridge: Ch. 1-2*

Ask, *In today's reading, how were people's lives different from your life? What would you have enjoyed or found difficult about living during that time?*

Key Idea: Compare historical time periods.

Geography S

Use a globe for today's activities. *Look on the map on p. 341 of A Child's History of the World to find the area that was Prussia. Find that same area on the modern-day globe. Prussia is now separated among Poland, Russia, and Lithuania. At the time of the Franco-Prussian War, the German states joined together to form the country of Germany. Find Germany on the modern-day globe. When Austria lost to Prussia in the Austro-Prussian War, it was excluded from becoming a part of unified Germany. See p. 341 to see the Austrian Empire. Austria and Hungary then joined together to form the Austro-Hungarian Empire. Find Austria and Hungary on the modern-day globe.*

Review the following concept: *The meridians of longitude divide Earth into 24 sections. Each section is a different time zone. Each time zone differs one hour from the time zone on either side of it. Look at the section to the left of where you live. This time zone is one hour behind you. Explain why this is true.*

Key Idea: In Europe, states united into single countries to form Germany and Italy.

Independent History Study I

★ Read *Mozart the Wonder Boy* p. 64-74. Listen to the optional CD Tracks 19-20 titled *"Theme"* and *"A Little Waltz"*. Then, copy the first paragraph from p. 65 of *Mozart the Wonder Boy* in cursive on a clean sheet of your *Common Place Book*.

Key Idea: Mozart and Nannerl gave concerts in Paris, France on their way back to their home in Salzburg.

Learning the Basics

Focus: Language Arts, Math, Bible, and Science

Language Arts

T

Work with the students to complete **one** of the English options listed below:

★ *Beginning Wisely:* Lesson 119

★ *Building with Diligence:* Lesson 118

★ Your own grammar program

Say, *For today's writing session, you will copy one-third of the Robert Louis Stevenson poem that you have chosen to memorize this week* (see Appendix).

Say, *Copy the poem in cursive in your "Common Place Book". Leave the rest of the page blank to copy the remaining two-thirds of the poem during the next units.*

Have students share the portion of the poem they copied by reading it aloud.

Key Idea: Write creatively from classic poetry.

Bible Study

T

Have students say Psalm 148:1-14 using the hand motions they added on Day 1. Say, *A mood is a feeling, a sensation, or a state of mind. What is the mood of Psalm 148:13-14?* (Some examples of moods include frightened, worried, happy, peaceful, hopeful, sad, unhappy, angry, thankful, prayerful, joyful, and lonely.) Ask, *When would this Psalm help you, or when would you go to this Psalm?* (i.e. to show how special the Lord's name is, to remind us that the Lord is above all of heaven and Earth, to realize how blessed we are to be close to the Lord) Last, pray with your children that they will show reverence to the Lord and His name. Pray that they will understand that there is no one like the Lord and that it is a blessing to be close to Him.

✔ *Lead Me to the Rock* CD
Track 9; Song: "Praise Ye Him"
(vs. 1-14)

Key Idea: The Psalms reflect the many emotions and moods we have. They are a wonderful place to seek counsel from the Lord.

Math Exploration

S

Choose **one** of the math options listed below (see Appendix for details).

★ *Singapore Primary Mathematics 2A/2B, 3A/3B,* or *4A/4B*

★ Your own math program

Key Idea: Use a step-by-step math program.

Science Exploration

I

★ Read *Albert Einstein: Young Thinker* p. 45-55. Orally retell or narrate to an adult the portion of text that you read today. Use the *Narration Tips* in the Appendix for help as needed.

Key Idea: When Albert had a holiday break from school, he enjoyed watching his father and his uncle work in their electrical shop where they made electric batteries. Uncle Jacob was an electrical engineer. Albert loved asking him questions about electricity. Uncle Jacob taught Albert about algebra too.

Learning through History
Focus: The Age of Inventions

Unit 33 - Day 3

Reading about History T

Read about history in the following resource:

★ *A Child's History of the World: Ch. 82* p. 368-372

★ *Hero Tales* p. 81-91

Have your students orally narrate or retell today's first reading. Use the *Narration Tips* in the Appendix as needed.

Key Idea: In the last 100 years, there have been many inventions. During the time of George Washington and Napoleon there were no cars, airplanes, televisions, or radios.

Storytime T

Read aloud the following assigned passage:

★ *The Family Under the Bridge: Ch. 3-4*

Ask, *In what do the main characters place their faith? How would the story be different if they put their faith in God? Share a character, a story, or a verse from the Bible that you are reminded of by the reading.*

Key Idea: Share a Biblical connection.

History Project S

Get the United States map that you printed on Day 1. Color the following Union States dark blue: California, Connecticut, Delaware, Illinois, Indiana, Iowa, Kansas, Kentucky, Maine, Maryland, Massachusetts, Michigan, Minnesota, Missouri, New Hampshire, New Jersey, New York, Ohio, Oregon, Pennsylvania, Rhode Island, Vermont, and Wisconsin. During the Civil War, Nevada and West Virginia joined the United States as new states on the Union side. The territories of Colorado, both the Dakotas, Nebraska, New Mexico, Utah, and Washington also fought for the Union. Make a key that shows a dark blue square labeled *Union States*.

Key Idea: At the time of the Civil War, the North and the South disagreed about where the transcontinental railroad should be built. Both the northern and the southern states wanted the railroad to run through their area.

Vocabulary S

You may choose 3-5 of the following vocabulary words from *A Child's History of the World* to use for this lesson: *diesel* (p. 368), *radar* (p. 369), *piston* (p. 369), *locomotive* (p. 369), and/or *phonograph* (p. 371). First, find the word in the text and read the sentence containing the word. Think about possible meanings. Next, find the word in a dictionary and select the correct meaning. Write the word at the top of an index card or at the top of the corresponding letter page in the notebook. Underneath the word, copy the correct definition from the dictionary. Then, use the word correctly in a sentence. The sentence may either be copied from the text or be one of your own creation. Last, draw a small picture to show the word's meaning. If you used an index card to record your word, file it under the correct alphabetical tab.

Key Idea: Inventions like the steamship, the telegraph, and the locomotive changed the world. Inventors like Thomas Edison and the Wright brothers became famous.

Independent History Study I

★ Make a notebook page with the following heading at the top: *Mozart Grows Up*. If you have a copy machine, photocopy p. 76 from *Mozart the Wonder Boy* and color it. Listen to the optional CD Tracks 38-45 while you color. If you do not have a copy machine, write facts about Mozart instead (i.e. played for kings and queens, composed a symphony at age 8, moved to Chelsea when Leopold was ill, etc.).

Key Idea: Mozart and Nannerl were glad to finally return home once more to Salzburg.

Learning the Basics

Focus: Language Arts, Math, Bible, and Science

Poetry

T

Have students practice reading one-third of the poem that they have chosen to memorize, using the actions that they added. Have students do this 2 times. Then, have students recite one-third of the poem without looking at the words. Students have 3 weeks (units) to memorize the entire poem. So, they should have one-third of their chosen poem memorized by Day 4 of this unit.

Key Idea: Read and appreciate classic poetry.

Bible Study

T

Say, *You will be having your own quiet time with God today. Choose a quiet place for this special time, where you can be alone with God. Then, do the following things:*

1. Read Psalm 148:1-14 in your Bible.
2. Pray about the verse using the following beginning to your prayer: *Thank you for the chance to be near to you, Lord. Help me to show reverence to you by _____ and _____. Forgive me when I _____ and _____. I praise your name Lord, for it is excellent above the heaven and the Earth!*
3. Recite Psalm 148:1-14 using the hand motions you added on Day 1.
4. Sing Psalm 148:1-14 along with the CD at the end of your quiet time.

Lead Me to the Rock CD
Track 9; Song: "Praise Ye Him"
(vs. 1-14)

Key Idea: It is a blessing to be near to God.

Language Arts

S

Have students complete one studied dictation exercise (see Appendix for directions and passages).

Help students complete one lesson from the following reading program:

★ *Drawn into the Heart of Reading*

Work with the students to complete **one** of the English options listed below:

★ *Beginning Wisely:* Lesson 120

★ *Building with Diligence:* Lesson 119

★ Your own grammar program

Key Idea: Practice language arts skills.

Math Exploration

S

Choose **one** of the math options listed below (see Appendix for details).

★ *Singapore Primary Mathematics 2A/2B, 3A/3B,* or *4A/4B*

★ Your own math program

Key Idea: Use a step-by-step math program.

Science Exploration

I

★ Read *Albert Einstein: Young Thinker* p. 56-66. Write the answer to each numbered question on lined paper. You do not need to copy the question. Use the listed page to help you answer each question.

1. In the beginning of today's story, what did Maja bring home? (p. 56)
2. Why did Albert say that Gertrude, the cat, and Laura, the parrot, were like the ends of a magnet? (p. 58)
3. On the evening of Albert's birthday, what did Gertrude do? (p. 60-61)
4. What happened when Gertrude and Laura were left alone? (p. 64-65)
5. According to 1 Peter 3:8-11,what lesson can be learned from today's story?

Key Idea: The Einstein family learned the hard way that cats and birds do not get along well!

Learning through History
Focus: The Age of Inventions

Unit 33 - Day 4

Reading about History — T

Read about history in the following resource:

★ *A Child's History of the World: Ch. 83* p. 373-377

★ *Hero Tales* p. 105-115

After today's first reading, say, *You will be writing a narration about part of today's first history reading. In order to remember the details well, you will need to reread part of today's reading from the third paragraph on p. 374 through half of p. 375 of A Child's History of the World (on your own if possible).*

After students have finished reading the passage, ask them the questions below. If the students do not know the answers, help them find the answers in the passage they just read. Ask, *When people began to work in factories, what happened to the farms? How did factories put family businesses out of business? What happened to the cities as more people came to work in the factories? Why were cities so crowded? How did cities spread out as time passed?*

After the questions have been answered, have students write a 5 sentence narration about how factories changed the world. When students have finished their narration, direct them to read the sentences out loud.

Help students underline or highlight the main idea sentence in their narration. See the *Written Narration Skills* in the Appendix to guide students in editing their narrations.

Key Idea: Inventions caused an industrial revolution. Factories began making all sorts of new things. People moved to the city to work in the factories. Children began working in factories too. Factories produced many of the things that had been made at home in the past.

Storytime — T

Read aloud the following assigned passage:

★ *The Family Under the Bridge: Ch. 5-6*

Say, *Transport yourself back to the time of this story. Pretend you lived at this time. Tell me what you see and do. (Make sure to use the word, "I", and to tell only what was described in today's reading.)*

Key Idea: Practice oral narration skills.

Timeline — S

You will be adding a new card to your staircase timeline today. On the new card, draw and color an American flag. Write, *U.S. Civil War and Abolition of Slavery (1861-1865 A.D.).*

If you decided to tape your timeline cards to the back of a door, then add the *U.S Civil War* card to the right of the *Napoleon* card. If you decided to tape the timeline cards side-by-side to accordion-fold them, use clear packing tape to tape the cards as described above. Then, accordion-fold the timeline to store it.

Key Idea: When the Civil War ended, America needed time to heal and to rebuild. As America rebuilt, big cities sprung up around factories. America became an industrialized nation.

Independent History Study — I

★ Read *Mozart the Wonder Boy* p. 77-85. Listen to the optional CD Tracks 21-22 *("Wiegenlied"* and *"Longing for Spring")*. Then, choose an interesting part to read aloud and explain to an adult.

Key Idea: Mozart was able to remember and write down music he had heard only once. He was amazing!

Learning the Basics

Focus: Language Arts, Math, Bible, and Science

Unit 33 - Day 4

Poetry

T

Have students practice reading one-third of the poem that they have chosen to memorize, using the actions that they added. Have students do this 2 times. Then, have students recite one-third of the poem without looking at the words. Students have 3 weeks (units) to memorize the entire poem. So, they should have one-third of their chosen poem memorized by today.

Key Idea: Read and appreciate classic poetry.

Bible Study

T

Have students say Psalm 148:1-14 using the hand motions from Day 1.

Have students copy in cursive Psalm 148:13-14 beneath last unit's Psalm 148:9-12 in their *Common Place Book.*

Students will add to the *Common Place Book* throughout the year.

✔ *Lead Me to the Rock* CD
Track 9; Song: "Praise Ye Him"
(vs. 1-14)

Key Idea: Copy in cursive a portion of a Psalm.

Language Arts

S

Have students complete one dictation exercise.

Guide students to complete one reading lesson.

★ *Drawn into the Heart of Reading*

Help students complete **one** English lesson.

★ *Beginning Wisely:* Lesson 121

★ *Building with Diligence:* Lesson 120

★ Your own grammar program

Key Idea: Practice language arts skills.

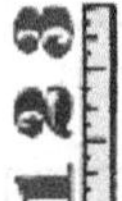

Math Exploration

S

Choose **one** math option listed below.

★ *Singapore Primary Mathematics 2A/2B, 3A/3B,* or *4A/4B*

★ Your own math program

Key Idea: Use a step-by-step math program.

Science Exploration

I

★ Read *Albert Einstein: Young Thinker* p. 67-82. Turn to the science experiment section in your science binder or sketchbook. At the top of a blank page, write: *How does a stork's skinny legs support the weight of its body?* Under the question, write: *'Guess'.* Write down your guess. Roll up a sheet of 8½" x 11" paper to make a hollow cylinder about 1" wide. Tape the cylinder, so it doesn't unroll. This will be the stork's leg bone. Make another leg, just like the first one. Stand the legs up on their ends, and place a book on top of the two legs to be the stork's body. Add books one at a time, until the weight collapses the bones. Now, repeat the experiment, but use 2 sheets of paper rolled tightly with no hollow section in the middle for the stork's legs this time. What did you notice? How were the hollow bones able to support more weight? How might the hollow center make the bones stronger? Why would the hollow bones be lighter-weight, making it easier for the stork to fly? On your paper, write: *'Procedure'.* Draw a picture of the experiment. At the bottom of the paper, write: *'Conclusion'.* Explain what you learned.

Key Idea: Albert found a stork with a broken leg. His new friend, Max, helped him set the stork's leg, so it would heal. When the leg was healed, the stork flew away.

Learning through History
Focus: World War I and II

Unit 34 - Day 1

Reading about History [T]

Read about history in the following resource:

★ *A Child's History of the World: Ch. 84* p. 378-382

★ *Hero Tales* p. 21-31

After today's reading, say, *How did the war between Austria and Serbia begin?* (knowledge) *Look at the map on p. 379. Point to Russia and France, who both sided with Serbia. Point to Germany, who sided with Austria. Why would Germany attack France?* (analysis) *How did the Battle of Marne near Paris, France make a big difference in the war?* (comprehension) *When Great Britain entered the war on the side of France, what happened?* (synthesis) *Why did Russia have a revolution?* (knowledge)

Key Idea: Austria declared war on Serbia after the Austrian prince was shot.

Storytime [T]

Read aloud the following assigned story:

★ *The Family Under the Bridge* p. 78-98

Discuss today's reading in a "conversational way". Share about a person, time, event, or emotion from your life that today's reading brought to mind. Next, have your child share a connection.

Key Idea: Connect personally to the story.

History Project [S]

In this unit you will make a paper Zeppelin and a submarine diver. To make the Zeppelin, cut a strip of paper that is 1" wide and 8" long. Cut a notch starting at the bottom of the paper strip 1" from the end. Make sure the notch does not go all of the way through the strip. On the opposite end of the strip, cut a notch starting at the top of the paper strip 1" from the other end. Bend the strip and slip the two notches together, sliding one notch into the other. Make sure the Zeppelin is curved rather than folded at the front. Lift the Zeppelin high in the air and drop it parallel to the ground. It will spin as it falls toward the ground.

Key Idea: Germany used Zeppelins in WWI.

Research [S]

During WWI, Germany used Zeppelins for bombing and scouting missions. Where could you look to discover more about the **Zeppelin?** Use a reference book or an online resource like www.wikipedia.org to type *Zeppelin* in the search or look it up in the index.

Orally answer one or more of the following questions from your research: *What is a Zeppelin? Describe the design of a Zeppelin. How did Germany use Zeppelins during World War I? Tell about the inventor of the Zeppelin. How were Zeppelins used after WWI? When did Germany stop using Zeppelins? What is another word for Zeppelin? Is something like the Zeppelin ever used today?*

Key Idea: Russia joined Serbia in its fight, and Germany joined Austria. When Russia joined Serbia, France followed. So, the Germans marched through Belgium to attack Paris, France. However, the Germans were stopped at the Battle of Marne.

Independent History Study [I]

★ Read *Mozart the Wonder Boy* p. 86-92. Listen to the optional CD Tracks 47-51. Orally retell to an adult the portion of text that you read today. Use the *Narration Tips* in the Appendix for help.

Key Idea: Mozart's beautiful sonatas, quartets, operas, and symphonies are still played and enjoyed today.

Learning the Basics
Focus: Language Arts, Math, Bible, and Science

Unit 34 - Day 1

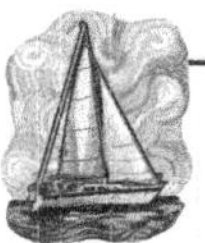

Poetry

T

Guide students to continue memorizing the Robert Louis Stevenson poem they chose in Unit 33. Students should have one-third of their chosen poem memorized already. They should memorize two-thirds of the poem by Day 4 of this unit. Have students read the entire poem 3 times, adding actions to the last part of the poem to help them memorize the words more easily.

Key Idea: Read and appreciate classic poetry.

Language Arts

S

Have students complete the first studied dictation exercise (see Appendix for directions and passages).

Help students complete one lesson from the following reading program:

 *Drawn into the Heart of Reading*

Work with the students to complete **one** of the English options listed below:

★ *Beginning Wisely:* Lesson 122

★ *Building with Diligence:* Lesson 121

★ Your own grammar program

Key Idea: Practice language arts skills.

Bible Study

T

Say, *Find Psalm 61:1-2 in your Bible. This is the memory selection for this unit. Read the verses out loud.* Ask, *What does David ask God to do in Psalm 61:1? Where does David say he is, in Psalm 61:2, when he is calling out to God? When we are away from home, does God still hear us when we pray? According to Psalm 61:2, how is David feeling? What does David ask God to do for him in Psalm 61:2? What do you think David means when he asks God to lead him "to a rock that is higher than I"? A high rock would be a place of safety or refuge. What lesson can we learn from Psalm 61:1-2?* Have students say the verse 3 times, adding hand motions to help remember the words.

 *Lead Me to the Rock* CD
Track 1; Song: "Lead Me to the Rock" (vs. 1-2)

Key Idea: The Lord is our refuge at all times.

Math Exploration

S

Choose **one** of the math options listed below (see Appendix for details).

★ *Singapore Primary Mathematics 2A/2B, 3A/3B,* or *4A/4B*

★ Your own math program

Key Idea: Use a step-by-step math program.

Science Exploration

I

Get your notebook page about Albert Einstein that you began in Unit 33. Choose two or more of the following Albert Einstein quotes to add to your notebook page by copying them in cursive:

1. Before God we are all equally wise – and equally foolish.
2. I never think of the future – it comes soon enough.
3. Imagination is more important than knowledge.
4. We should take care not to make intellect our god; it has, of course, powerful muscles, but no personality.
5. At any rate, I am convinced that He (God) does not play dice with the universe.

Key Idea: Albert loved talking with Max about things he'd read from *Popular Books on Natural Science.*

Reading about History T

Read about history in the following resource:

★ *A Child's History of the World: Ch. 85* p. 383-389

After today's reading, read aloud Psalm 33:6-11. Say, *How does Psalm 33:6-7 show the Lord's power? What does Psalm 33:8 say that man should do? How does Psalm 33:10 show that the Lord's purpose prevails over man's purposes? What does Psalm 33:11 say about the Lord's plans? Why is it important to honor the Lord with our plans instead of honoring ourselves? How does today's passage show that the Lord is in control of all things?*

Key Idea: There were only 20 years between WWI and WWII.

History Project S

Today you will make a submarine. Either use a straw cut in half or a pen cap as the submarine. Place a ball of clay on the end of the straw or pen cap. Add water to an empty plastic bottle until it is full. Place the submarine in the bottle with the clay facing down. Remove clay until the submarine is floating just below the water's surface. This is called neutral buoyancy. Put the lid on and squeeze the bottle. When the sealed bottle is squeezed, water flows into the straw or cap and the air bubble is compressed. The buoyancy of the submarine is reduced when the air bubble is squashed, making the submarine sink. When the bottle is not being squeezed, the air bubble inside the sub expands back to its original size, and the sub surfaces.

Key Idea: Submarines have chambers that are filled with water or air to control buoyancy.

Storytime T

Read aloud the following assigned passage:

★ *The Family Under the Bridge* p. 99-123

Ask, *In today's reading, how were people's lives different from your life? What would you have enjoyed or found difficult about living during that time?*

Key Idea: Compare historical time periods.

Vocabulary S

You may choose 3-5 of the following vocabulary words from *A Child's History of the World* to use for this lesson: *league* (p. 384), *armed* (p. 384), *industrial* (p. 385), *artillery* (p. 386), and/or *depression* (p. 387). First, find the word in the text and read the sentence containing the word. Think about possible meanings. Next, find the word in a dictionary and select the correct meaning. Write the word at the top of an index card or at the top of the corresponding letter page in the notebook. Underneath the word, copy the correct definition from the dictionary. Then, use the word correctly in a sentence. The sentence may either be copied from the text or be one of your own creation. Last, draw a small picture to show the word's meaning. If you used an index card to record your word, file it under the correct alphabetical tab.

Key Idea: After WWI, peace didn't last very long. Japan became an industrialized nation and attacked China. Italy attacked Ethiopia. Spain began a civil war, and other countries began taking sides.

Independent History Study I

★ Read *The Little Riders: Ch. 1.* Then, copy part of the second paragraph from p. 9 that begins, *For the people of Holland, who had always loved...* Copy it in cursive into your *Common Place Book.*

Key Idea: The people of Holland were used to being free. It was difficult when Hitler conquered them.

Learning the Basics
Focus: Language Arts, Math, Bible, and Science

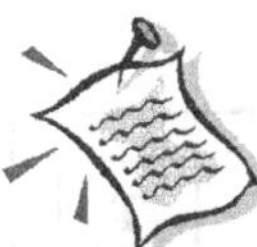

Language Arts

T

Work with the students to complete **one** of the English options listed below:

★ *Beginning Wisely:* Lesson 123

★ *Building with Diligence:* Lesson 122

★ Your own grammar program

Say, *For today's writing session, you will copy the next one-third of the Robert Louis Stevenson poem that you chose to memorize this week* (see Appendix).

Say, *Copy the poem in cursive in your "Common Place Book". Leave the rest of the page blank to copy the remaining one-third of the poem during the next unit.*

Have students share the portion of the poem they copied by reading it aloud.

Key Idea: Write creatively from classic poetry.

Bible Study

T

Have students say Psalm 61:1-2 using the hand motions they added on Day 1. Say, *A mood is a feeling, a sensation, or a state of mind. What is the mood of Psalm 61:1-2?* (Some examples of moods include frightened, worried, happy, peaceful, hopeful, sad, unhappy, angry, thankful, prayerful, joyful, and lonely.) Ask, *When would this Psalm help you, or when would you go to this Psalm?* (i.e. to remind you that the Lord is always with you, to guide you to call upon the Lord when you are overwhelmed, to show you that the Lord is your refuge)

Last, pray with your children that they will know the Lord is always with them. Pray that they will call upon the Lord and seek refuge in Him.

Lead Me to the Rock CD
Track 1; Song: "Lead Me to the Rock" (vs. 1-2)

Key Idea: The Psalms are a wonderful place to seek counsel from the Lord.

Math Exploration

S

Choose **one** of the math options listed below (see Appendix for details).

★ *Singapore Primary Mathematics 2A/2B, 3A/3B,* or *4A/4B*

★ Your own math program

Key Idea: Use a step-by-step math program.

Science Exploration

I

★ Read *Albert Einstein: Young Thinker* p. 83-101. Orally retell or narrate to an adult the portion of text that you read today. Use the *Narration Tips* in the Appendix for help as needed.

Key Idea: At the circus Albert saw an Australian bushman do tricks with a boomerang. Albert worked hard at building his own boomerang, but his father had him put it away because it was keeping Albert from working hard on his studies for school. Later, the boomerang came in handy, when the Einsteins needed to get rid of a bat.

Reading about History T

Read about history in the following resource:

★ *A Child's History of the World: Ch. 86* p. 390-395

After today's reading, have your students orally narrate or retell the portion of today's text that you read. Use the *Narration Tips* in the Appendix as needed.

Key Idea: Hitler became the dictator in Germany. As he gained power, he built up Germany's army and prepared for war.

History Project T

Today you will explore one or more websites devoted to the attack on Pearl Harbor. This attack prompted the United States to get involved in WWII. Watch a short video about the Pearl Harbor attack at the following link: http://www.history.com/topics/world-war-ii/world-war-ii-history/videos/attack-pearl-harbor

Read more about the attack at the link below. http://www.socialstudiesforkids.com/articles/ushistory/pearlharborattack1.htm

If the above link doesn't work, try this link: http://www.ducksters.com/history/world_war_ii/pearl_harbor_attack.php

If you do not have Internet access, read about the attack on Pearl Harbor in another resource.

Key Idea: Although the German government had signed the Treaty of Versailles at the end of WWI (saying they wouldn't build a large army or air force), Hitler ignored the treaty and did it anyway. Hitler's followers were called NAZIS.

Storytime T

Read aloud the following assigned passage:

★ *Twenty and Ten* p. 11-30

Ask, *In what do the main characters place their faith? How is Sister Gabriel teaching the children to put their faith in God? Share a character, a story, or a verse from the Bible that you are reminded of by the reading.*

Key Idea: Share a Biblical connection.

Geography S

Use a globe for today's activities. *Look on the map on p. 393 of A Child's History of the World to find the countries that Hitler's German army conquered: Austria, Czechoslovakia, Albania, Poland, Norway, Denmark, France, Belgium, Holland (Netherlands), Yugoslavia, and Greece. As the Battle of Britain was fought over England, Hitler had his first defeat. He would never conquer Great Britain. Find these same countries on the modern-day globe. Italy, Bulgaria, Romania, and Finland sided with Germany until partway through the war. Find these countries on the globe.*

Review the following concept: *The meridians of longitude divide Earth into 24 sections. Each section is a different time zone. Each time zone differs one hour from the time zone on either side of it. How many hours ahead or behind your time zone are the countries that we read about today?*

Key Idea: Hitler did not conquer England.

Independent History Study I

★ Read *The Little Riders: Ch. 2.* Make a notebook page about WWII. Copy the quote in cursive from Winston Churchill on p. 394 of *A Child's History of the World* that begins, *"We shall defend our island, whatever the cost..."* If you have internet access, view the following WWII map link, watching the black color to see Hitler and his Axis forces progress: http://commons.wikimedia.org/wiki/File:Ww2_allied_axis_1939_sep.PNG

Key Idea: The United States did not enter WWII until 1941, after the Japanese bombed Pearl Harbor.

Learning the Basics

Focus: Language Arts, Math, Bible, and Science

Poetry

T

Have students practice reading the two-thirds of the poem that they have chosen to memorize, using the actions that they added. Have students do this 2 times. Then, have students recite two-thirds of the poem without looking at the words. Students have 3 weeks (units) to memorize the entire poem. So, they should have two-thirds of their chosen poem memorized by Day 4 of this unit.

Key Idea: Read and appreciate classic poetry.

Language Arts

S

Have students complete one studied dictation exercise (see Appendix for directions and passages).

Help students complete one lesson from the following reading program:

★ *Drawn into the Heart of Reading*

Work with the students to complete **one** of the English options listed below:

★ *Beginning Wisely:* Lesson 124

★ *Building with Diligence:* Lesson 123

★ Your own grammar program

Key Idea: Practice language arts skills.

Bible Study

T

Say, *You will be having your own quiet time with God today. Choose a quiet place for this special time, where you can be alone with God. Then, do the following things:*

1. Read Psalm 61:1-2 in your Bible.
2. Pray about the verse using the following beginning to your prayer: *Thank you for being my refuge in times of trouble. Help me to call upon you when ______ or ______. I'm so glad that you're with me when I'm ______ or ______. You are my rock.*
3. Recite Psalm 61:1-2 using the hand motions you added on Day 1.
4. Sing Psalm 61:1-2 along with the CD at the end of your quiet time.

✔ *Lead Me to the Rock* CD
Track 1; Song: "Lead Me to the Rock" (vs. 1-2)

Key Idea: The Lord is always with us. He is our solid rock and our place of refuge.

Math Exploration

S

Choose **one** of the math options listed below (see Appendix for details).

★ *Singapore Primary Mathematics 2A/2B, 3A/3B*, or *4A/4B*

★ Your own math program

Key Idea: Use a step-by-step math program.

Science Exploration

I

★ Read *Albert Einstein: Young Thinker* p. 102-118. Write the answer to each numbered question on lined paper. You do not need to copy the question. Use the listed page to help you answer each question.

1. Why was Albert looking forward to school in 1891? (p. 103)
2. What is the study of geometry? (p. 106)
3. Describe the geometry game that the Einstein family played. (p. 107)
4. Give some examples of shapes that the Einstein family found in nature. (p. 108-110)
5. How does Romans 1:20 say that nature reveals God to all mankind?

Key Idea: Although Albert usually did not like school, he was excited to study geometry. The whole Einstein family enjoyed looking for examples of geometry in nature.

Learning through History
Focus: World War I and II

Unit 34 - Day 4

Reading about History — T

Read about history in the following resource:

★ *A Child's History of the World: Ch. 87* p. 396-401

After today's reading, say, *You will be writing a narration about part of today's history reading. In order to remember the details well, you will reread part of today's reading from the second paragraph on p. 400 through p. 401 (on your own if possible).*

After students have finished reading the passage, ask them the questions below. If the students do not know the answers, help them find the answers in the passage they just read. Ask, *What war was this chapter about? Who was the American President during WWII? Who was the British Prime Minister during this war? Who were the Allied forces fighting against? What did the American and British armies do? How did Russia help defeat Germany? What ended the war with Japan? After the war ended, what problems were there?*

After the questions have been answered, have students write a 5 sentence narration about World War II. When students have finished their narration, direct them to read the sentences out loud.

Help students underline or highlight the main idea sentence in their narration. See the *Written Narration Skills* in the Appendix to guide students in editing their narrations.

Key Idea: After the U.S. fleet was bombed at Pearl Harbor, the United States needed time to rebuild its fleet and prepare its troops for war. So, the United States supplied the English and Russian troops in Egypt and got ready to fight.

Storytime — T

Read aloud the following assigned passage:

★ *Twenty and Ten* p. 31-46

Say, *Transport yourself back to the time of this story. Pretend you lived at this time. Tell me what you see and do. (Make sure to use the word, "I", and to tell only what was described in today's reading.)*

Key Idea: Practice oral narration skills.

Timeline — S

You will be adding 2 new cards to your staircase timeline today. On the first new card, draw and color a Zeppelin. Write, *World War I (1914-1918 A.D.).* On the second new card, draw and color a German swastika. Write, *World War II (1937-1945 A.D.).*

If you decided to tape your timeline cards to the back of a door, then add the *World War I* card to the right of the *U.S. Civil War* card. Then, add the *World War II* card to the right of the *World War I* card. If you decided to tape the timeline cards side-by-side to accordion-fold them, use clear packing tape to tape the cards as described above. Then, accordion-fold the timeline to store it.

Key Idea: The Allied forces fought Hitler and his armies first. The main attack was on the coast of Normandy in France. As the United States and England chased the German armies back across Europe, the Russian army pushed from the other side. Finally, the German army was forced back into Germany. Then, the Allied forces fought Japan. WWII ended after 2 nuclear bombs were dropped on Japan.

Independent History Study — I

★ Read *The Little Riders: Ch. 3.* Then, choose an interesting part to read aloud and explain to an adult. Use the *Narration Tips* in the Appendix for help as needed.

Key Idea: Johanna and her grandfather hid the Little Riders so that the Germans wouldn't find them.

Learning the Basics

Focus: Language Arts, Math, Bible, and Science

Unit 34 - Day 4

Poetry

T

Have students practice reading the two-thirds of the poem that they have chosen to memorize, using the actions that they added. Have students do this 2 times. Then, have students recite two-thirds of the poem for you without looking at the words. Students have 3 weeks (units) to memorize the entire poem. So, they should have two-thirds of their chosen poem memorized by today.

Key Idea: Read and appreciate classic poetry.

Bible Study

T

Have students say Psalm 61:1-2 using the hand motions from Day 1.

Have students copy in cursive Psalm 61:1-2 onto a clean page in their *Common Place Book*.

Students will add to the *Common Place Book* throughout the year.

✔ *Lead Me to the Rock* CD
Track 1; Song: "Lead Me to the Rock" (vs. 1-2)

Key Idea: Copy in cursive a portion of a Psalm.

Language Arts

S

Have students complete one dictation exercise.

Guide students to complete one reading lesson.

★ *Drawn into the Heart of Reading*

Help students complete **one** English lesson.

★ *Beginning Wisely:* Lesson 125

★ *Building with Diligence:* Lesson 124

★ Your own grammar program

Key Idea: Practice language arts skills.

Math Exploration

S

Choose **one** math option listed below.

★ *Singapore Primary Mathematics 2A/2B, 3A/3B*, or *4A/4B*

★ Your own math program

Key Idea: Use a step-by-step math program.

Science Exploration

I

★ Read *Albert Einstein: Young Thinker* p. 119-136. Turn to the science experiment section in your science binder or sketchbook. At the top of a blank page, write: *How does light travel?* Under the question, write: *'Guess'*. Write down your guess. Get out 3 index cards. Punch a hole in the center of each card. To find the center, use a ruler to draw a diagonal line from the top left corner to the bottom right corner of the card. Then, draw a second diagonal line from the top right corner to the bottom left corner of the card. This should form an 'X'. Punch a hole in the center of the 'X' where the two lines cross one another on each card. Next, stand the cards one behind the other several inches apart by placing the bottom of each card in a bit of clay. The holes must be arranged so you can see through them in a straight line. Place a flashlight at one end, and shine it through the holes. What do you notice? Does the light travel in a straight line? On your paper, write: *'Procedure'*. Draw a picture of the experiment. At the bottom of the paper, write: *'Conclusion'*. Explain what you learned.

Key Idea: In 1905, Albert Einstein discovered that a ray of light is actually the path taken by *photons*, or light particles, that travel in a straight line. This study of light is called optics.

Reading about History [T]

Read about history in the following resource:

★ *A Child's History of the World: Ch. 88* p. 402-406

After today's reading, say, *What is the United Nations, or the U.N.?* (knowledge) *How did Gandhi cleverly protest against English rule in India?* (comprehension) *After WWII, why were so many countries given their independence?* (evaluation) *Did becoming independent solve each country's problems? Explain.* (analysis) *Why is freedom from being ruled by another country so important?* (application)

Key Idea: After WWII ended, many countries wanted their independence. Gandhi led the people in India in non-violent protest against British rule. India won their independence.

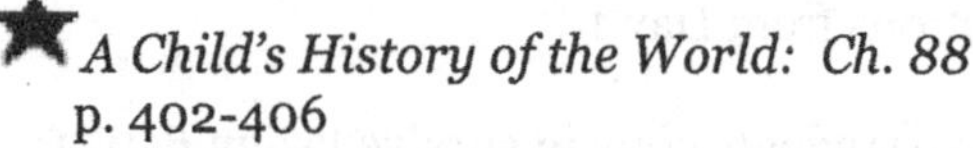

History Project [S]

In this unit you will be making a tri-fold brochure for the Olympic games. Divide a piece of white paper into 3 equal sections. Then, fold the paper on the lines to make a brochure. On the front of the brochure, copy the following Olympic motto: *Citius, Altius, Fortius* which means *Faster, Higher, Stronger*. On the back of the front flap, add the symbol for the Olympics, which is 5 interlocking rings. Color the top 3 rings blue, black, then red from left to right. Color the bottom 2 rings yellow, and then green from left to right. Save the brochure for Day 2.

Key Idea: The Olympics unites countries.

Storytime [T]

Read aloud the following assigned story:

★ *Twenty and Ten* p. 47-61

Discuss today's reading in a "conversational way". Share about a person, time, event, or emotion from your life that today's reading brought to mind. Next, have your child share a connection.

Key Idea: Connect personally to the story.

Research [S]

Neither the League of Nations nor the United Nations has been successful in uniting the world. However, once every 4 years, the Olympics unites the world in peaceful competition. Where could you look to discover more about the **Olympics?** Use a reference book or an online resource like www.wikipedia.org to type *Olympics* in the search or look it up in the index.

Orally answer one or more of the following questions from your research: *What is the Olympics? When and where were the first Olympic games held? What is the Olympic Truce? What is the Olympic Creed? Describe the Olympic symbols. What are some of the past cities that have hosted the Olympics? Why have the Olympic games now been divided into summer and winter games? Who are some of the famous Olympic athletes from your country?*

Key Idea: Other nations won their independence too. Many of these countries are very poor, but they are glad to be free.

Independent History Study [I]

★ Read *The Little Riders* p. 37-46. Orally retell to an adult the portion of text that you read today. Use the *Narration Tips* in the Appendix for help.

Key Idea: Johanna hid the riders in the German captain's room. The German officers would soon be back.

Learning the Basics

Focus: Language Arts, Math, Bible, and Science

Poetry

T

Guide students to continue memorizing the Robert Louis Stevenson poem they chose in Unit 33. Students should have two-thirds of their chosen poem memorized already. They should memorize the rest of the poem by Day 4 of this unit. Have students read the entire poem 3 times, adding actions to the poem to help them memorize the words more easily.

Key Idea: Read and appreciate classic poetry.

Language Arts

S

Have students complete the first studied dictation exercise (see Appendix for directions and passages).

Help students complete one lesson from the following reading program:

★ *Drawn into the Heart of Reading*

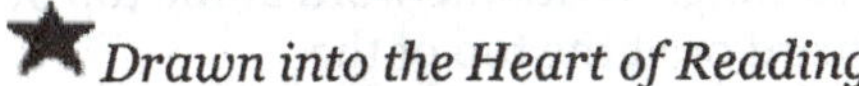

Work with the students to complete **one** of the English options listed below:

★ *Beginning Wisely:* Review One p. 310-311

★ *Building with Diligence:* Lesson 125

★ Your own grammar program

Key Idea: Practice language arts skills.

Bible Study

T

Say, *Choose any Psalm from the previous units to review this week. Read over the Psalm, and say as much of it as you can from memory.*

Say, *Then, listen to the Psalm on the accompanying CD.*

✔ *Lead Me to the Rock* CD

Key Idea: The Psalms are a wonderful source of comfort and joy.

Math Exploration

S

Choose **one** of the math options listed below (see Appendix for details).

★ *Singapore Primary Mathematics 2A/2B, 3A/3B,* or *4A/4B*

★ Your own math program

Key Idea: Use a step-by-step math program.

Science Exploration

I

★ Read *Albert Einstein: Young Thinker* p. 137-147. Get out your notebook page about Albert Einstein that you began in Unit 33. Choose two or more of the following Albert Einstein quotes to copy in cursive:

1. I want to know God's thoughts; the rest are details.
2. Try not to become a man of success but rather to become a man of value.
3. Do not worry about your difficulties in mathematics, I can assure you mine are still greater.
4. Insanity: Doing the same thing over and over and expecting different results.
5. I know not with what weapons WWIII will be fought, but WWIV will be fought with sticks and stones.

Key Idea: Albert loved Switzerland. While traveling in the countryside, he saw a shower of falling stars. Albert decided to go to Munich to study physics. He was very interested in light.

Learning through History
Focus: Nations Rise and Nations Fall

Unit 35 - Day 2

Reading about History T

Read about history in the following resource:

★ *A Child's History of the World: Ch. 89* p. 407-410

After today's reading, read aloud Matthew 16:26-28. Say, *As Russia worked to become a strong communist country, it closed its churches. What warning does Jesus give in Matthew 16:26 about this? Why is a person's soul much more important than any earthly gains? What determines where a person will spend eternity? How would the spread of communism hurt Christians? What does Matthew 16:27 say will happen when Jesus returns? Will all of us be judged? What is the meaning of Matthew 16:28? Do we know when Christ will return? How can we be ready?*

Key Idea: After WWII, Russia was ruled by harsh dictators like Stalin.

History Project S

Get the Olympic brochure that you started on Day 1. On the inside middle flap, copy the Olympic Creed which is the following: *"The most important thing in the Olympic Games is not to win, but to take part, just as the most important thing in life is not the triumph but the struggle. The essential thing is not to have conquered but to have fought well."* On the right inside flap of the brochure, draw and color the gold (1st place), silver (2nd place), and bronze (3rd place) medals. Save the brochure for Day 3.

Key Idea: Communism was spreading.

Storytime T

Read aloud the following assigned passage:

★ *Twenty and Ten: Ch. 5*

Ask, *In today's reading, how were people's lives different from your life? What would you have enjoyed or found difficult about living during that time?*

Key Idea: Compare historical time periods.

Vocabulary S

You may choose 3-5 of the following vocabulary words from *A Child's History of the World* to use for this lesson: *destruction* (p. 407), *rivals* (p. 407), *czar* (p. 408), *communism* (p. 408), and/or *dictator* (p. 409). First, find the word in the text and read the sentence containing the word. Think about possible meanings. Next, find the word in a dictionary and select the correct meaning. Write the word at the top of an index card or at the top of the corresponding letter page in the notebook. Underneath the word, copy the correct definition from the dictionary. Then, use the word correctly in a sentence. The sentence may either be copied from the text or be one of your own creation. Last, draw a small picture to show the word's meaning. If you used an index card to record your word, file it under the correct alphabetical tab.

Key Idea: Under dictators like Lenin and Stalin, Russia became a Communist country. Everything belonged to the state. Travel in and out of Russia was controlled by the government. The newspapers could only print what the government allowed. Churches were closed, and religion was unlawful.

Independent History Study I

★ Read *The Little Riders* p. 47-57. Then, copy the fourth paragraph from p. 51 of *The Little Riders* which begins, *"The little riders will be my guests for as long as they want to be..."*. Copy the paragraph in cursive into your *Common Place Book*.

Key Idea: Johanna was surprised by Captain Braun's kind help in hiding the little riders.

Learning the Basics

Focus: Language Arts, Math, Bible, and Science

Language Arts **T**

Work with the students to complete **one** of the English options listed below:

★ *Beginning Wisely:* Review Two p. 312-313

★ *Building with Diligence:* Lesson 126

★ Your own grammar program

Say, *For today's writing session, you will copy the last one-third of the Robert Louis Stevenson poem that you chose to memorize this week* (see Appendix).

Say, *Copy the rest of the poem in cursive in your "Common Place Book".*

Have students share the poem they copied by reading it aloud.

Key Idea: Write creatively from classic poetry.

Bible Study **T**

Have students review one of the previous unit's Psalms using the hand motions they added, if they can remember them. Ask, *What have you learned this year about the Psalms? When will you turn to the Psalms throughout your life?*

Last, pray with your children that they will keep God's word hidden in their hearts. Pray that they will turn to God's word when they are frightened or worried, when they are joyful or happy, if they are lonely or unhappy, or when they are feeling hopeful or thankful. Pray that they will be drawn closer to God through His word.

Have students listen to their favorite Psalms on the CD:

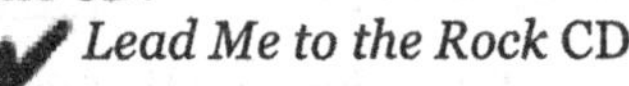
✔ *Lead Me to the Rock* CD

Key Idea: The Psalms reflect the many emotions and moods we have. They are a wonderful place to seek counsel from the Lord.

Math Exploration **S**

Choose **one** of the math options listed below (see Appendix for details).

★ *Singapore Primary Mathematics 2A/2B, 3A/3B,* or *4A/4B*

★ Your own math program

Key Idea: Use a step-by-step math program.

Science Exploration **I**

★ Read *Albert Einstein: Young Thinker* p. 148-160. Orally retell or narrate to an adult the portion of text that you read today. Use the *Narration Tips* in the Appendix for help as needed.

Key Idea: Albert tried to get into the Swiss Federal Institute of Technology, but he didn't pass his entrance tests. He had to go back to school to get his diploma first. Albert found the schools in Switzerland were much better suited to his personality. He enjoyed his classes at the school at Aarau. He made a new friend named Karl Winteler.

Learning through History
Focus: Nations Rise and Nations Fall

Unit 35 - Day 3

Reading about History — T

Read about history in the following resource:

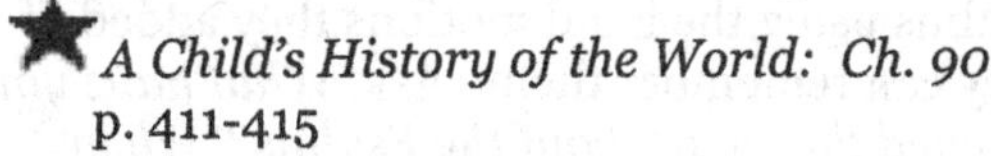

A Child's History of the World: Ch. 90 p. 411-415

After today's reading, have your students orally narrate or retell the portion of today's text that you read. Use the *Narration Tips* in the Appendix as needed.

Key Idea: Communism began to spread. Russia helped both North Korea and Vietnam become communist too.

Storytime — T

Read aloud the following assigned passage:

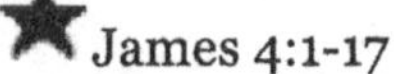

James 4:1-17

Ask, *In what does this passage say you should place your faith? How would the world be different if people put their faith in God? Share a character, a story, or a verse from the Bible that you are reminded of by the reading.*

Key Idea: Share a Biblical connection.

History Project — S

Get out the brochure of the Olympics that you began on Days 1-2. On the back of the brochure, draw the lighted torch, which is an Olympic symbol. Then, copy the following facts around the torch: *The Olympic torch is a symbol of the truce between countries. It means that all countries will put aside their differences for the Olympic games. Ever since 1936, the torch has been carried from the original Olympic site in Greece to the new Olympic site before the start of the games. Once lighted, the torch and flame travel to each continent, until arriving back at the chosen site for the games.*

Key Idea: Over time, Russians could see that communism was not working in their country. So, they gave up communism and freed the countries under their rule.

Geography — S

Use a globe for today's activities. *Look on the globe to find the following communist nations: the former Soviet Union (or Russia), China, North Korea, Cuba, Laos, and Vietnam. Later, when the Soviet Union (Russia) gave up communism, many of the countries they had controlled gained their freedom. On the globe find the following countries that gained their freedom: Latvia, Lithuania, Estonia, Ukraine, Kazakhstan, Uzbekistan, Turkmenistan, Afghanistan, Tajikistan, and Kyrgzstan.*

Review the following concept: *The meridians of longitude divide Earth into 24 sections. Each section is a different time zone. Each time zone differs one hour from the time zone on either side of it. How many different time zones are there in the United States?*

Key Idea: After WWII, the United Nations sent troops to South Korea to fight the North Koreans so that all of Korea wouldn't become communist. The United States also fought in Vietnam to limit the spread of communism.

Independent History Study — I

★ Read *The Little Riders* p. 58-67. Make a notebook page titled, *The End of WWII.* Copy the following: *Germany surrendered to Allied forces in May of 1945. Japan surrendered to Allied forces in August of 1945.* Photocopy the map on p. 399 and color the following countries that had been taken by Japan: the Philippines, Singapore, East Indies, Siam, Burma, Malay Peninsula, French Indo-China, Korea, outer part of Manchuria, part of eastern China, Guam, Wake, New Guinea, Bougainville, Guadalcanal, and Kiska.

Key Idea: After WWII, there was a period of "Cold War" between the United States and the Soviet Union.

Learning the Basics

Focus: Language Arts, Math, Bible, and Science

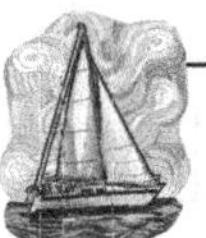

Poetry

T

Have students practice reading the poem that they have chosen to memorize, using the actions that they added on Day 1. Have students do this 2 times. Then, have students recite the poem without looking at the words. Students should have their chosen poem memorized by Day 4 of this unit.

Key Idea: Read and appreciate classic poetry.

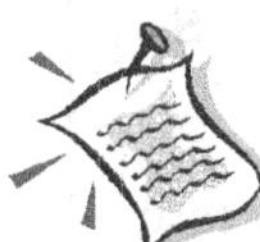

Language Arts

S

Have students complete one studied dictation exercise (see Appendix for directions and passages).

Help students complete one lesson from the following reading program:

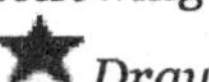

★ *Drawn into the Heart of Reading*

Work with the students to complete **one** of the English options listed below:

★ *Beginning Wisely:* Extra Activity p. 314

★ *Building with Diligence:* Lesson 127 (half)

★ Your own grammar program

Key Idea: Practice language arts skills.

Bible Study

T

Say, *You will be having your own quiet time with God today. Choose a quiet place for this special time, where you can be alone with God. Then, do the following things:*

1. Read one of your favorite Psalms in the Bible.
2. Pray about the Psalm using the following beginning to your prayer: *Thank you Lord for giving me your word. Help me to want to learn more about you by _____ and _____. Keep your word in my heart and my mind.*
3. Recite one of the Psalms you learned this year.
4. Sing the Psalm along with the CD at the end of your quiet time.

✔ *Lead Me to the Rock* CD

Key Idea: The Lord gave us His word so that we can know His will and be drawn closer to Him.

Math Exploration

S

Choose **one** of the math options listed below (see Appendix for details).

★ *Singapore Primary Mathematics 2A/2B, 3A/3B,* or *4A/4B*

★ Your own math program

Key Idea: Use a step-by-step math program.

Science Exploration

I

★ Read *Albert Einstein: Young Thinker* p. 161-177. Write the answer to each numbered question on lined paper. You do not need to copy the question. Use the listed page to help you answer each question.

1. What did Albert believe about the Sun? (p. 166)
2. What did Albert believe about the speed of light? (p. 167)
3. How did Albert describe light? (p. 167)
4. In 1912, what new idea did Albert have about light? (p. 170)
5. When you think about light, how does Genesis 1:3-4 show you God's greatness?

Key Idea: Albert wrote some interesting papers about light and energy while he was a patent officer. Then, he became a professor at the University of Zurich. He also continued working on his theories.

Learning through History
Focus: Nations Rise and Nations Fall

Unit 35 - Day 4

Reading about History [T]

Read about history in the following resource:

★ *A Child's History of the World: Ch. 91* p. 416-418

After today's reading, say, *You will be writing a narration about part of today's history reading. In order to remember the details well, you will reread part of today's reading from the second paragraph on p. 417 through the first paragraph on p. 419 (on your own if possible).*

After students have finished reading the passage, ask them the questions below. If the students do not know the answers, help them find the answers in the passage they just read. Ask, *What is the difference between a discovery and an invention? Name some of the important discoveries that have been found. Name some of the important inventions that have been made. How is history like a continuing story? Who is the only one that knows how long history will go on?*

After the questions have been answered, have students write a 5 sentence narration about some of the discoveries and inventions. When students have finished their narration, direct them to read the sentences out loud.

Help students underline or highlight the main idea sentence in their narration. See the *Written Narration Skills* in the Appendix to guide students in editing their narrations.

Key Idea: History has been filled with wars.

Storytime [T]

Read aloud the following assigned passage:

★ Revelation 22:1-21

Say, *What does Revelation 22:18-19, say about changing or adding to God's word, the Bible? Why is this important? What does Revelation 22:20 say about Christ's return? How does this give us hope in times of war and trials?*

Key Idea: Discuss questions using Scripture.

Timeline [S]

You will be adding 2 new cards to your staircase timeline today. On the first new card, write *North Korea / South Korea.* Under that write *Korean Conflict (1950-1953 A.D.).* On the second new card, write *North Vietnam / South Vietnam.* Under that write *Vietnam War (1959-1975 A.D.).*

If you decided to tape your timeline cards to the back of a door, then add the *Korean Conflict* card to the right of the *World War I* card. Then, add the *Vietnam War* card to the right of the *Korean Conflict* card. If you decided to tape the timeline cards side-by-side to accordion-fold them, use clear packing tape to tape the cards as described above. Then, accordion-fold the timeline to store it.

Key Idea: As long as there is sin in the world, there will be wars. There will be no perfect peace until Christ returns. We need to be thankful for the men and women who defend our country's freedom each day. It is important to be patriotic and to honor those who have died to keep us free.

Independent History Study [I]

★ Read *The Little Riders:* p. 68-end. Then, choose an interesting part to read aloud and explain to an adult. Use the *Narration Tips* in the Appendix for help as needed.

Key Idea: The people of Holland were grateful to be given back their freedom at the end of WWII.

Learning the Basics

Focus: Language Arts, Math, Bible, and Science

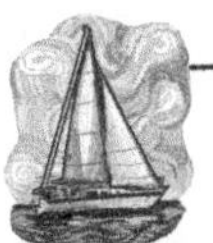

Poetry — T

Have students practice reading the poem that they have chosen to memorize, using the actions that they added. Have students do this 2 times. Then, have students recite the poem for you without looking at the words. They should have their chosen poem memorized today.

Key Idea: Read and appreciate classic poetry.

Language Arts — S

Have students complete one dictation exercise.

Guide students to complete one reading lesson.

★ *Drawn into the Heart of Reading*

Help students complete **one** English lesson.

★ *Beginning Wisely:* A Poem to Enjoy p. 315

★ *Building with Diligence:* Lesson 127 (half)

★ Your own grammar program

Key Idea: Practice language arts skills.

Bible Study — T

Have students review one of their favorite Psalms from this year by reading it from their *Common Place Book.*

Then, listen to the corresponding Psalm on the CD:

✔ *Lead Me to the Rock* CD

Key Idea: Copy in cursive a portion of a Psalm.

Math Exploration — S

Choose **one** math option listed below.

★ *Singapore Primary Mathematics 2A/2B, 3A/3B,* or *4A/4B*

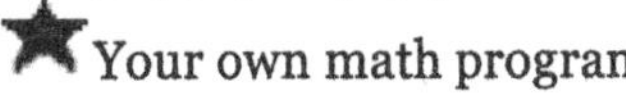

★ Your own math program

Key Idea: Use a step-by-step math program.

Science Exploration — I

★ Read *Albert Einstein: Young Thinker* p. 178-195. Turn to the science experiment section in your science binder or sketchbook. At the top of a blank page, write: *How does light bend?* Under the question, write: *'Guess'*. Write down your guess.

Cut a slit that is ½" wide and 1" long in the center of an index card. Tape the card over the end of a flashlight so that the beam of the flashlight will shine through the slit. Fill a glass bowl with water. Add a few drops of milk to the water and stir it well. Turn out the lights. Hold the flashlight beside the glass bowl at an angle, so it will shine through the outside of the bowl into the water. Do you see the light beam bending as it passes through the milky water? Experiment with changing the angle of the flashlight to see the path of the light inside the milky water change.

On your paper, write: *'Procedure'*. Draw a picture of the experiment. At the bottom of the paper, write: *'Conclusion'*. Explain what you learned.

Key Idea: In 1912, Albert Einstein wrote a paper about the bending of light, called *refraction*. Refraction happens because light travels at different speeds through different materials, causing it to bend when it passes from one transparent material to another (like air to milky water). The change in direction is called refraction.

Appendix

Bibliography: Storytime Titles

This list includes 10 great resources that provide meaningful text connections with the history theme in *Preparing Hearts for His Glory.* Each book was very carefully chosen as an excellent read-aloud selection for this listening level. This package of read-alouds is highly recommended, unless you need to economize. These Storytime titles are all part of the *Preparing Hearts for His Glory* **Basic Package**: *The True Story of Noah's Ark, Tirzah, Classic Treasury of Aesop's Fables, Triumph for Flavius, Fountain of Life, Viking Quest I: Raiders of the Sea, Door in the Wall, The Wonderful Winter, The Family Under the Bridge,* and *Twenty and Ten.*

For your convenience, these resources may be purchased from Heart of Dakota either as an entire set called the *Preparing Hearts for His Glory* **Basic Package,** or as individual titles. View packages on the website www.heartofdakota.com or call (605) 428-4068 for more information. Otherwise, please feel free to use your library in order to economize. Book descriptions are taken from the book or card catalog listing.

The True Story of Noah's Ark by Tom Dooley, 2003 Master Books
ISBN: 0890513880
This thrilling adventure of Noah's Ark comes to life through dazzling, detailed illustrations! The images of the interior of the ark are like nothing you've ever seen before. The people and cities depicted here are certainly quite advanced. They invented metals, musical instruments, and were skilled craftsmen too. This book and CD set is all biblically and historically based.

Tirzah by Lucille Travis, 1991 Herald Press
ISBN: 0836135466
Twelve-year-old Tirzah and her family are slaves in Egypt. Pharaoh forces them to make mud bricks without straw, so Tirzah cuts grass for her family to use. If only Moses could persuade Pharaoh to let them go. Surely God will hear their prayers to leave Egypt for a better life; they hope.

Classic Treasury of Aesop's Fable by Don Daily, 2007 Running Book Press Publishers
ISBN: 0762428767
This treasury has twenty tales, each told through a series of lush, colorful pictures, which end with a simple moral. Children will love to see what befalls Aesop's cast of creatures that includes dogs, mice, and lions – proving that no one is too big or small to learn a thing or two.

Triumph for Flavius by Caroline Dale Snedeker, 2004 American Home-School Publishing
ISBN: 0966706714
Here is a touching story of a young Roman boy, Flavius, and his developing compassion for his captured Greek slave Ariphron. Drama, personal development, tragedy, hope, compassion, triumph – this story is a wonderful introduction to the study of classical Rome and Greece!

Bibliography: Storytime Titles
(continued)

Fountain of Life by Rebecca Martin, 2001 Christian Light Publications
ISBN: 0-87813-595-2
Eli had heard about Jesus' profound teachings and amazing miracles, but he had never seen Jesus. He wondered, "Was Jesus the Messiah who would deliver the Jews from Rome?" Set in New Testament times and including a wealth of information about Jewish life and customs, this is an inspiring story of blossoming faith, seeking and finding the truth, and drinking deeply at the Fountain of Life.

Viking Quest I – Raiders of the Sea by Lois Walfrid Johnson, 2003 Moody Publishers
ISBN: 0802431127
In one harrowing day, Viking raiders capture Bree and her brother Devin from their home in Ireland. After the young Viking prince sets Devin free on the Irish coast far from home, Bree sails to Norway on the Viking ship, and Devin travels the dangerous road home. They both must trust their all-powerful God in the midst of difficult situations!

Door in the Wall by Marguerite De Angeli, 1998 Laurel Leaf
ISBN: 978-0-440-22779-3 (0-440-22779-8)
Ever since he can remember, Robin has been told what is expected of him as the son of a nobleman: he must become a knight. But Robin's destiny is changed forever, when he falls ill and loses the use of his legs!

The Wonderful Winter by Marchette Chute, 2002 Green Mansion Press LLC
ISBN: 097146121X
The year is 1597 and, more than anything else in the world, Sir Robert Wakefield wants a companion. Life can be lonely for an orphan boy, and when a lost puppy turns up, Robin is determined to keep him. When his aunt refuses, Robin runs away from home, puppy in hand. As he makes his way to London, he finds a wonderful winter there. What a treasure to have this classic book back in print!

The Family Under the Bridge by Natalie Savage Carlson, 1989 HarperTrophy
ISBN: 0064402509
Armand relished his solitary life, but the children who lived under the bridge still recognized a true friend in him, even if he was a trifle unwilling at the start. Armand soon came to realize that he had gotten himself a ready-made family; one that he loved with all his heart, and one for whom he would have to find a better home than under the bridge.

Twenty and Ten by Claire Huchet Bishop and Janet Joly, 1978 Penguin Group USA, Inc.
ISBN: 0140310762
During the Nazi occupation of France, 20 ordinary French kids in a boarding school agree to hide 10 Jewish children. Then, German soldiers arrive. Will the children be able to keep their secret? *Twenty and Ten* is based on a true story – one of many similar incidents that took place all over Europe during World War II.

Bibliography: Deluxe Package

This **Deluxe Package** gives your children 12 incredible books to read independently using the self-study plans in *Preparing Hearts for His Glory*. Daily independent reading assignments for your third or fourth graders use books that correspond with the time period. Reading material is meant to be easy and short enough for children to complete on their own. This is an optional package, but it greatly enhances the study of history.

For your convenience, these resources may be purchased from Heart of Dakota either as an entire set called the *Preparing Hearts for His Glory* **Deluxe Package,** or as individual titles. View packages on the website www.heartofdakota.com or call (605) 428-4068 for more information. Otherwise, please feel free to use your library in order to economize. Each resource of the **Deluxe Package** is listed below. Book descriptions are taken from the book or card catalog listing.

<u>Units 1-16, 20-21:</u> *Draw and Write Through History: Creation Through Jonah* by Carylee Gressman, 2006 CPR Publishing
ISBN: 0-9778597-0-3
Take your students on an exciting journey through time as you draw and write your way from Creation all the way to Jonah, learning about the ark and animals on it, the Trojan horse, Egypt and the plagues, quail in the desert, David, the Olympics and more! Each drawing is broken down into steps, and each step is illustrated in full-color. Writing samples are written out in cursive for copywork.

<u>Units 5-6:</u> *5000 Year-Old Puzzle: Solving a Mystery of Ancient Egypt* by Claudia Logan, 2002 Farrar, Straus and Giroux (BYR)
ISBN: 0374323356
When King Tut's tomb was discovered in Egypt in 1922, the world was abuzz. What would be the next big, newsworthy archaeological find? Might it be Giza 7000X, a secret Egyptian tomb buried deep within the earth? This book answers that question and asks a few more. Readers follow a fictional family to Egypt in 1924 to an actual expedition led by Dr. George Reisner. Written in diary form from the perspective of young Will Hunt, the book is engaging, communicating the mystery and excitement of an archaeological dig like nothing we've seen.

<u>Units 9-10:</u> *The Trojan Horse: How the Greeks Won the War* by Emily Little, 1988 Random House Children's Books
ISBN: 0394896742
An ancient history lesson emerges from this account of the way the Greeks tricked the Trojans and rescued Helen of Troy. The book is well tailored to younger readers with careful explanations and short sentences. Drawings portray the story's main events. This is a nice supplement to units on ancient Greece.

<u>Units 10-21:</u> *The Young Christian's Introduction to the Bible* by Charles C. Ryrie, 2003 Charles C. Ryrie
ISBN: 1-880960-56-7
This is an excellent introduction to the Bible for young Christians. Chapters included are: "What Is the Bible?" "How Did We Get the Bible?" "Can I Really Understand the Bible?" "The Structure of the Bible." "The Order of Events in the Bible." "What Each Book of the Bible Is All About." Each section is written in a way that the young reader can understand.

Bibliography: Deluxe Package

(continued)

Units 16-20: *Little Miriam of Galilee* by Edith Martin, 2005 Christian Light Publications
ISBN: 0-87813-624-X
Through her window Miriam watched the bright yellow sun begin its climb into the blue dome of sky above Galilee. Father, Nahum, and Grandmother were discussing the day's plans. This was Miriam's home in Galilee, and everything was just right... until later that day, when Father explained that they might have to leave their home. With little rain, there was hardly any wheat to harvest. "Jehovah will provide," said Father – but Miriam wasn't sure. It would take a miracle!

Units 22-24: *Leif the Lucky* by Ingri and Edgar D'Aulaire, 1995 Beautiful Feet Books
ISBN: 0964380307
When the Vikings roamed the seas, there lived a man in Norway called Erik the Red. He was able and strong, but his temper was wild. After a fight he was banned from Norway, and later fled from Iceland too. Erik the Red had three sons named Torstein, Torvald, and Leif. This is the story of Leif who sailed with his father to Greenland, and who later sailed still farther west and found there the continent of America. Originally published in 1941, this oversized book is beautifully illustrated.

Units 24-26: *The Minstrel in the Tower* by Gloria Skurzynski, 2004 Random House Children's Books
ISBN: 0394895983
In this gripping medieval page-turner, Alice and Roger search for their uncle and are then held for ransom in an ancient tower. To escape and find their uncle, the children must summon all their courage and imagination. Designed as easy-reading material for middle-graders, this has the virtues of an attractive format and illustrations, and a fast plot.

Units 26-29: *Pedro's Journal* by Pam Conrad, 1992 Scholastic, Incorporated
ISBN: 0590462067
Written in a diary format, this mesmerizing tale brings to life the story of Columbus' voyage, as seen through the eyes of a young boy named Pedro. As a ship's boy aboard Columbus' *Santa Maria*, Pedro captures the danger and excitement of his experiences in the pages of his journal – so if he didn't return alive, someone might find it and learn of his incredible journey to the New World.

Units 29-30: *William Shakespeare and the Globe* by Aliki, 2000 HarperCollins Publishers
ISBN: 0064437221
William Shakespeare was perhaps the greatest English playwright ever. Take a tour of Shakespeare's life and times, through the crowded streets of sixteenth-century London, to the boisterous Globe theater, and to other playhouses where his work flourished. Then follow Shakespeare's legacy to the present day and to the Globe's glorious reopening. Learn, step-by-step, how the theater was reconstructed using the same methods builders used to construct the original Globe.

Units 30-31: *Peter the Great* by Diane Stanley, 1999 HarperCollins Publishers
ISBN: 068816708X
This biography of Peter the Great, Tsar of Russia, begins with his childhood surrounded by servants, trained monkeys, and dancing bears; moves on to his youthful fascination with ships and the culture of Europe; and concludes with his

Bibliography: Deluxe Package
(continued)

transformation of Russia into a European country and his building of St. Petersburg before his death. The paintings display wonderfully detailed interiors, architectural details, and clothing. Peter's insatiable curiosity and energy are emphasized.

Units 32-34: *Mozart the Wonder Boy* by Opal Wheeler and Sybil Deucher, 2005 Zeezok Publishing
ISBN: 0974650536
This book offers a clear, simple, upbeat story of Mozart's seemingly charmed childhood and his musical genius. He was truly a "wonder boy," and his musical abilities were apparent at the tender age of three. He traveled to play in the concert halls of Europe and for royalty as well, but he was always composing.

Units 34-35: *The Little Riders* by Margaretha Shemin, 1993 HarperCollins Publishers
ISBN: 0688124992
"Take care of the little riders," says Johanna's father to the 11-year-old when he leaves her with his parents in their Dutch village. Johanna loves the 12 metal figures on horseback who ride forth when the clock in the church tower strikes each hour - and one night she risks her life to protect them. Set during WWII when the German army occupied Holland, *The Little Riders* is an exciting adventure story.

Bibliography: Extension Package

When to use this Extension Package Schedule: This reading schedule is recommended if you wish to extend the area of history to include more advanced material. This will allow your older students to learn along with your younger students. Books are at a mid-fifth to upper seventh grade reading level.

Older students should first listen along with younger students to the scheduled history readings in *Preparing Hearts for His Glory*. Then, older students will independently read the assigned text and literature from the Extension Package for each unit. These readings will provide more details about people and events already being studied as well as immersing older students in the time period being studied.

Books for the Extension Package Schedule:
Note: The books listed below are required in order to use the Extension Package Schedule. For ease of use, Heart of Dakota Publishing sells the books listed below as a set called **Self-Study Extension Package for Older Students** on the website www.heartofdakota.com or by telephone at (605) 428-4068. Book descriptions are from the publisher or book reviewer.

Units 1-3: *Uncovering the Mysterious Woolly Mammoth: Life at the End of the Great Ice Age* by Michael Oard, 2007 Master Books
ISBN-10: 0890515085
How did woolly mammoths get preserved in ice, why did they go extinct, and how did they live? The answers given are usually in line with an evolutionary world view, but is this the only answer? Is there a better explanation for the evidences found in the remains of these unique creatures? Author Mike Oard gives answers to these questions for young readers. He also gives fascinating facts about these hairy, elephant-like creatures in this sequel to *Life in the Great Ice Age*.

Units 4-9, 12, 14-17, 22: *Usborne Internet-Linked Ancient World Encyclopedia* by Fiona Chandler, 2004 EDC Publishing
ISBN: 0794508162
From the Old Testament cities to the fall of Rome, from enormous empires to humble homes, this lavishly illustrated book is packed with fascinating facts about the ancient world. Follow the rise and fall of great civilizations across the globe and explore everyday life for ancient people. Find out about Egyptian mummies, when the Great Wall of China was built, and why Celtic warriors painted themselves blue.

Units 10-15: *Aesop's Fables* by Ann McGovern, 1963 Scholastic, Incorporated
ISBN: 0590438808
This collection of stories attributed to a Greek slave named Aesop contains 67 tales. Each one illustrates the failings and virtues of human nature in a simple, humorous way and ends with a proverb that teaches a moral.

Bibliography: Extension Package
(continued)

Units 17-21: *The Bronze Bow* by Elizabeth George Speare, 1997 Houghton Mifflin Company Trade & Reference Division
ISBN: 0395137195
Set in Galilee in the time of Jesus, this story tells of a young Jewish rebel who is won over to the gentle teachings of Jesus. *The Bronze Bow* is a dramatic, deeply felt narrative whose characters and message will long be remembered.

Units 22-24: *Beorn the Proud* by Madeleine A. Polland, 1999 Bethlehem Books
ISBN: 1883937086
Beorn, a pagan Viking from Denmark, becomes a better ruler as a result of the influence of Ness, a Christian girl he took from Ireland as his slave.

Units 25-27: *Adam of the Road* by Elizabeth J. Gray, 1987 Penguin Group (USA) Incorporated
ISBN: 014032464X
This engaging book describes the adventures of eleven-year-old Adam as he travels the open roads of thirteenth-century England. As Adam searches for his missing father and his stolen red spaniel, you'll be cheering him on and feel like you're traveling right along with him. This book was the winner of the Newbery Medal in 1943.

Units 28-29: *Who Was Marco Polo?* by Joan Holub, 2007 Penguin Group (USA)
ISBN: 0448445409
Marco Polo was seventeen when he set out for China ... and forty-one when he came back! He traveled from the medieval city of Venice to the fabled kingdom of the great Kublai Khan, seeing new sights and riches that no Westerner had ever before seen. But did Marco Polo experience the things he wrote about... or was it all made-up? Readers are presented with the facts in this entertaining, highly readable book.

Units 29-32: *Shakespeare Stealer* by Gary L. Blackwood, 2000 Penguin Group (USA) Incorporated
ISBN: 0141305959
Widge is an orphan with a rare talent for shorthand. His fearsome master demands he steal Shakespeare's play "Hamlet", and Widge has no choice but to follow orders, so he works his way into the heart of the Globe Theatre, where Shakespeare's players perform. Once at the Globe Theatre, Widge makes friends with some of the actors and, for the first time in his life, experiences a sense of family. Widge now has a new problem: How can he fulfill his task of stealing the play for his master and not betray his friends? As full of twists and turns as a London alleyway, this entertaining novel is rich in period details, colorful characters, villainy, and drama.

Units 32-34: *Louis Pasteur: Founder of Modern Medicine* by John Hudson Tiner, 1999 Mott Media
ISBN: 0-88062-159-1
If you listed the top ten scientists of all time, you would include Louis Pasteur. This great man was a Christian, and many times, he stated his belief that spiritual and religious values go beyond scientific knowledge. Learn about Pasteur's early life as the son of a country tanner. Experience his years of struggle as an unknown scientist and enjoy his triumph as one of the world's most celebrated heroes.

Bibliography: Extension Package
(continued)

Units 34-35: *Journey to America* by Sonia Levitin, 1987 Simon & Schuster Children's Publishing
ISBN: 0689711301
It was 1938, and suddenly, there were more and more restrictions for Jews: yellow stars they had to wear, schools they could not attend, things they were forbidden to do. The Nazis were in power, and Lisa Platt was scared. Her father knew they had to escape, and he left for America in the middle of the night. He promised to send for Lisa, her mother, and her two sisters when there was enough money. Until then, they were to live in Switzerland. So they did, waiting, in unforeseen hardship.

Note: History readings are broken down into manageable daily assignments that coordinate with the various time periods in *Preparing Hearts for His Glory*. The reading assignments are meant for your older students to read independently.

Depending on your goals for your older students' independent readings, you may want to assess their reading comprehension in some way. Some suggestions for assessment of your older students' reading could include having them do a combination of the following things:

- orally retell what they've read (suggested once during each unit; use the "Narration Tips" found in the Appendix for help as needed)
- write a two to three paragraph summary of the reading (suggested twice during each unit; use the "Written Narration Skills" found in the Appendix for help in editing)
- draw a picture about the reading and write a one paragraph summary about what you read that goes along with your picture (suggested once during each unit)

Extension Package Schedule

Unit 1:

Day 1: *Uncovering the Mysterious Woolly Mammoth: Life at the End of the Great Ice Age* p. 6-7 and p. 44
Day 2: *Uncovering the Mysterious Woolly Mammoth: Life at the End of the Great Ice Age* p. 8-9 and p. 45-46
Day 3: *Uncovering the Mysterious Woolly Mammoth: Life at the End of the Great Ice Age* p. 10-12 and p. 47 – half of p. 48
Day 4: *Uncovering the Mysterious Woolly Mammoth: Life at the End of the Great Ice Age* p. 13-15

Extension Package Schedule
(continued)

Unit 2:

Day 1: *Uncovering the Mysterious Woolly Mammoth: Life at the End of the Great Ice Age* p. 16- middle of p. 18
Day 2: *Uncovering the Mysterious Woolly Mammoth: Life at the End of the Great Ice Age* middle of p. 18-21
Day 3: *Uncovering the Mysterious Woolly Mammoth: Life at the End of the Great Ice Age* p. 22 – middle of p. 27
Day 4: *Uncovering the Mysterious Woolly Mammoth: Life at the End of the Great Ice Age* middle of p. 27 – p. 29 and the purple box only on p. 49

Unit 3:

Day 1: *Uncovering the Mysterious Woolly Mammoth: Life at the End of the Great Ice Age* p. 30 – top of p. 32 and p. 50 – half of p. 51
Day 2: *Uncovering the Mysterious Woolly Mammoth: Life at the End of the Great Ice Age* p. 32 – top of p. 35 and p. 57
Day 3: *Uncovering the Mysterious Woolly Mammoth: Life at the End of the Great Ice Age* p. 35-36 and the purple box only on p. 53
Day 4: *Uncovering the Mysterious Woolly Mammoth: Life at the End of the Great Ice Age* p. 38-40 and the purple box only on p. 58

Unit 4:

Day 1: *Usborne Internet-Linked Ancient World Encyclopedia* p. 16-17
Day 2: *Usborne Internet-Linked Ancient World Encyclopedia* p. 18-19
Day 3: *Usborne Internet-Linked Ancient World Encyclopedia* p. 6-7 and p. 14-15
Day 4: *Usborne Internet-Linked Ancient World Encyclopedia* p. 8-9

Unit 5:

Day 1: *Usborne Internet-Linked Ancient World Encyclopedia* p. 10-11
Day 2: *Usborne Internet-Linked Ancient World Encyclopedia* p. 12-13
Day 3: *Usborne Internet-Linked Ancient World Encyclopedia* p. 28
Day 4: *Usborne Internet-Linked Ancient World Encyclopedia* p. 29

Unit 6:

Day 1: From a Bible of your choice – Genesis 22:1-19
Day 2: From a Bible of your choice – Genesis 25:19-34 and 27:1-40
Day 3: *Usborne Internet-Linked Ancient World Encyclopedia* p. 30-31
Day 4: *Usborne Internet-Linked Ancient World Encyclopedia* p. 34-35

Unit 7:

Day 1: *Usborne Internet-Linked Ancient World Encyclopedia* p. 32-33
Day 2: *Usborne Internet-Linked Ancient World Encyclopedia* p. 36
Day 3: From a Bible of your choice – Exodus Chapters 19-20
Day 4: From a Bible of your choice – Exodus 23:20-33 and Numbers 13:17-33; 14:1-24

Unit 8:

Day 1: *Usborne Internet-Linked Ancient World Encyclopedia* p. 5
Day 2: From a Bible of your choice – Judges 6:36-40 and 7:1-22
Day 3: From a Bible of your choice – Ruth 2:1-23 and 4:13-17
Day 4: *Usborne Internet-Linked Ancient World Encyclopedia* p. 38

Extension Package Schedule
(continued)

Unit 9:

Day 1: From a Bible of your choice – Psalm Chapter 51
Day 2: *Usborne Internet-Linked Ancient World Encyclopedia* p. 20-23
Day 3: *Usborne Internet-Linked Ancient World Encyclopedia* p. 24-27
Day 4: *Usborne Internet-Linked Ancient World Encyclopedia* p. 37

Unit 10:

Day 1: *Usborne Internet-Linked Ancient World Encyclopedia* p. 40-41
Day 2: *Aesop's Fables*: Read the last page of the book and p. 5-8
Day 3: *Aesop's Fables* p. 9-13
Day 4: *Aesop's Fables* p. 14-17

Unit 11:

Day 1: *Aesop's Fables* p. 19-23
Day 2: *Aesop's Fables* p. 24-27
Day 3: *Aesop's Fables* p. 28-31
Day 4: *Aesop's Fables* p. 33-37

Unit 12:

Day 1: *Usborne Internet-Linked Ancient World Encyclopedia* p. 42-43 and *Aesop's Fables* p. 38-39
Day 2: *Usborne Internet-Linked Ancient World Encyclopedia* p. 44-45 and *Aesop's Fables* p. 40-41
Day 3: *Usborne Internet-Linked Ancient World Encyclopedia* p. 46 and *Aesop's Fables* p. 42-43
Day 4: *Usborne Internet-Linked Ancient World Encyclopedia* p. 47 and *Aesop's Fables* p. 44-45

Unit 13:

Day 1: *Aesop's Fables* p. 46-50
Day 2: *Aesop's Fables* p. 51-54
Day 3: *Usborne Internet-Linked Ancient World Encyclopedia* p. 48-49 and *Aesop's Fables* p. 55
Day 4: *Aesop's Fables* p. 56-59

Unit 14:

Day 1: *Usborne Internet-Linked Ancient World Encyclopedia* p. 70-71 and *Aesop's Fables* p. 60-61
Day 2: *Usborne Internet-Linked Ancient World Encyclopedia* p. 60-65
Day 3: *Aesop's Fables* p. 62-65
Day 4: *Usborne Internet-Linked Ancient World Encyclopedia* p. 41 and *Aesop's Fables* p. 66-68

Unit 15:

Day 1: *Aesop's Fables* p. 69-71
Day 2: *Aesop's Fables* p. 72-74
Day 3: *Usborne Internet-Linked Ancient World Encyclopedia* p. 50-51 and *Aesop's Fables* p. 75
Day 4: *Usborne Internet-Linked Ancient World Encyclopedia* p. 52-53 and *Aesop's Fables* p. 77

Extension Package Schedule
(continued)

Unit 16:

Day 1: *Usborne Internet-Linked Ancient World Encyclopedia* p. 54-55 and *Aesop's Fables* p. 78
Day 2: *Usborne Internet-Linked Ancient World Encyclopedia* p. 58-59
Day 3: *Usborne Internet-Linked Ancient World Encyclopedia* p. 56-57
Day 4: *Usborne Internet-Linked Ancient World Encyclopedia* p. 80-81

Unit 17:

Day 1: *Usborne Internet-Linked Ancient World Encyclopedia* p. 82-83
Day 2: *Usborne Internet-Linked Ancient World Encyclopedia* p. 84-85 and p. 86-87
Day 3: *The Bronze Bow* Chapter 1
Day 4: *The Bronze Bow* Chapter 2

Unit 18:

Day 1: *The Bronze Bow* Chapter 3
Day 2: *The Bronze Bow* Chapter 4
Day 3: *The Bronze Bow* Chapter 5
Day 4: *The Bronze Bow* Chapter 6

Unit 19:

Day 1: *The Bronze Bow* Chapter 7
Day 2: *The Bronze Bow* Chapter 8
Day 3: *The Bronze Bow* Chapter 9-10
Day 4: *The Bronze Bow* Chapter 11

Unit 20:

Day 1: *The Bronze Bow* Chapter 12-13
Day 2: *The Bronze Bow* Chapter 14
Day 3: *The Bronze Bow* Chapter 15
Day 4: *The Bronze Bow* Chapter 16

Unit 21:

Day 1: *The Bronze Bow* Chapter 17-18
Day 2: *The Bronze Bow* Chapter 19-20
Day 3: *The Bronze Bow* Chapter 21-22
Day 4: *The Bronze Bow* Chapter 23-24

Unit 22:

Day 1: *Usborne Internet-Linked Ancient World Encyclopedia* p. 88-89
Day 2: *Usborne Internet-Linked Ancient World Encyclopedia* p. 90-91
Day 3: *Beorn the Proud* Chapter 1
Day 4: *Beorn the Proud* Chapter 2

Unit 23:

Day 1: *Beorn the Proud* Chapter 3 and *Usborne Internet-Linked Ancient World Encyclopedia* p. 78-79
Day 2: *Beorn the Proud* Chapter 4-5
Day 3: *Beorn the Proud* Chapter 6
Day 4: *Beorn the Proud* Chapter 7

Extension Package Schedule
(continued)

Unit 24:

Day 1: *Beorn the Proud* Chapter 8 and *Usborne Internet-Linked Ancient World Encyclopedia* p. 68-69
Day 2: *Beorn the Proud* Chapter 9
Day 3: *Beorn the Proud* Chapter 10 and *Usborne Internet-Linked Ancient World Encyclopedia* p. 67
Day 4: *Beorn the Proud* Chapter 11-12

Unit 25:

Day 1: *Adam of the Road* Chapters 1-2
Day 2: *Adam of the Road* Chapters 3-4
Day 3: *Adam of the Road* Chapter 5
Day 4: *Adam of the Road* Chapters 6-7

Unit 26:

Day 1: *Adam of the Road* Chapters 8-9
Day 2: *Adam of the Road* Chapters 10-11
Day 3: *Adam of the Road* Chapter 12-13
Day 4: *Adam of the Road* Chapters 14-15

Unit 27:

Day 1: *Adam of the Road* Chapters 16-17
Day 2: *Adam of the Road* Chapters 18-19
Day 3: *Adam of the Road* Chapter 20-21
Day 4: *Adam of the Road* Chapters 22-23

Unit 28:

Day 1: *Who Was Marco Polo?* p. 1-17
Day 2: *Who Was Marco Polo?* p. 18-38; Note: On p. 20, we do not agree that Muhammod rose to heaven.
Day 3: *Who Was Marco Polo?* p. 39-56
Day 4: *Who Was Marco Polo?* p. 56-71 and *Usborne Internet-Linked Ancient World Encyclopedia* p. 74 and p. 76-77

Unit 29:

Day 1: *Who Was Marco Polo?* p. 72-83; Note: On p. 74, we do not agree that the hairy apelike creatures were "people".
Day 2: *Who Was Marco Polo?* p. 84-103
Day 3: *Shakespeare Stealer* Chapters 1-3
Day 4: *Shakespeare Stealer* Chapters 4-6

Unit 30:

Day 1: *Shakespeare Stealer* Chapters 7-9
Day 2: *Shakespeare Stealer* Chapters 10-11
Day 3: *Shakespeare Stealer* Chapters 12-13
Day 4: *Shakespeare Stealer* Chapters 14-15

Unit 31:

Day 1: *Shakespeare Stealer* Chapters 16-17
Day 2: *Shakespeare Stealer* Chapters 18-19
Day 3: *Shakespeare Stealer* Chapters 20-21
Day 4: *Shakespeare Stealer* Chapters 22-24

Extension Package Schedule
(continued)

Unit 32:

Day 1: *Shakespeare Stealer* Chapters 25-27
Day 2: *Louis Pasteur: Founder of Modern Medicine* p. 1-24
Day 3: *Louis Pasteur: Founder of Modern Medicine* p. 25-49
Day 4: *Louis Pasteur: Founder of Modern Medicine* p. 50-75

Unit 33:

Day 1: *Louis Pasteur: Founder of Modern Medicine* p. 76-90
Day 2: *Louis Pasteur: Founder of Modern Medicine* p. 91-103
Day 3: *Louis Pasteur: Founder of Modern Medicine* p. 104-126
Day 4: *Louis Pasteur: Founder of Modern Medicine* p. 127-147

Unit 34:

Day 1: *Louis Pasteur: Founder of Modern Medicine* p. 148-176
Day 2: *Journey to America* p. 3-28
Day 3: *Journey to America* p. 29-53
Day 4: *Journey to America* p. 54-79

Unit 35:

Day 1: *Journey to America* p. 80-94
Day 2: *Journey to America* p. 95-108
Day 3: *Journey to America* p. 109-123
Day 4: *Journey to America* p. 124-150

Science Lab

Question:

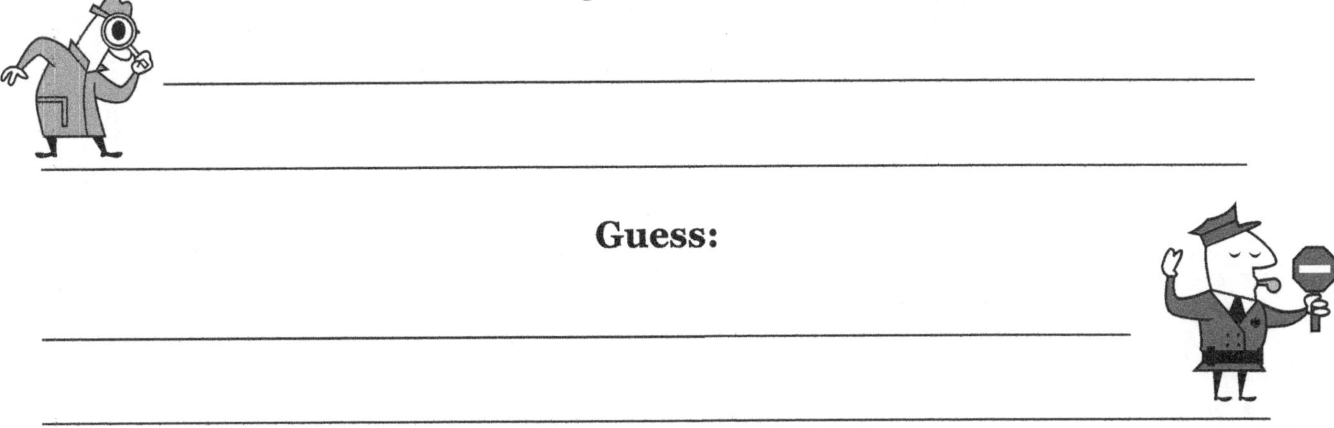

Guess:

Procedure:

Conclusion:

NARRATION TIPS: TEACHER'S LIST

Notes: When children narrate, they tell back in their own words what they have just read or heard. It allows them to share their own version of the passage with accuracy, individual personality, spirit, and originality.

Narrating is an essential skill in life. To be able to give an opinion of a book, relay a telephone message, summarize a letter, give driving directions, write an article, or share a doctor's instructions – are all examples of practical applications of narration skills. Narrating is an important skill to learn. You can begin to teach your children to narrate by following the steps listed below. Just be patient, and have fun with it! Narration is a way of life.

BEFORE NARRATING:

1. **Choose a living book.** Living books are alive with ideas and have a story aspect to them. The books read in this curriculum are living books.

2. **Skim the section your child will use for narration.** Children's narrations usually show how well they understand the book, but sometimes a child gives a confident, articulate narration that is eloquently wrong.

3. **Introduce the section being read.** Review **briefly** what was read last time. Other **optional** ideas: Use Charlotte Mason's "informing idea" (i.e. *The Pilgrims weren't allowed to worship God. I wonder what they'll do? Let's read to find out.*). Or, write a list of difficult names or words and pronounce them. Children may use the list during narrating.

4. **Tell children they will narrate after the reading.** When children know they will narrate, they will attend the reading with sharper attention.

5. **Read the selected passage once.** The teacher or the child may read it. Move toward having children do their own reading by age 9. This will help improve narrations. Have only one child narrate at a time. Keep the readings short at first. You can even read a bit, ask for a narration, read some more, and narrate some more. Don't define words during the reading.

DURING NARRATING:

1. **Have children tell you all they remember about the reading.** Say, *Tell me all you can about what you just read.* They should not be looking at the book. Do not interrupt a narration. It distracts the train of thought. Do not correct children while they are narrating.

2. **The teacher is a listener; not a lecturer.** Let the child's mind do the sorting, rejecting, and classifying of what should be shared.

3. **Children may use exact phrasing from the book.** They may pick up phrasing and vocabulary that strikes them. This allows children to make the language of good living books their own.

4. **Children may share connections made.** Children may compare what was read to another book, situation, or memory of their own. However, the connection should not take over the narration.

5. **The length of the narration is not the point.** If children can retell the most pertinent information in a few sentences, that may be enough. The purpose of narration is the process of ordering and selecting what to tell. Every narration doesn't need to be in full detail.

6. **There is not one "right" narration.** A dozen children could read the same section and give a dozen different good narrations. A teacher should not listen for a long list of words to be shared from the text.

AFTER NARRATING:

1. **Share comments or details.** You can ask questions, correct misinformation, and ask for clarification at this point. However, avoid being overly critical. Limit what you say to a few important points.

2. **Do not grade narrations.** Grading a narration gives the impression that there is only one right way to do it. Children are left searching for the elusive "one right narration", rather than using their own originality.

OTHER HELPFUL NARRATING TIPS:

1. **Be patient with your child.** If your child is frustrated or seems to be missing the meaning of the reading, shorten the sections he narrates on or take a turn narrating yourself. Try to be as encouraging as possiible; make sure not to be overly critical or to give too lengthy advice.

2. **Help your children develop the habits of listening and attention**. If your children have been used to "gobbling up" books instead of giving focused attention to reading, shorten the sections used for narration and focus on what they know – not on what they don't know.

3. **Children begin written narrations at age 10**. They need extensive practice in oral narrations first. Instructions for written narrations will be included in the next level of this curriculum.

HOW TO NARRATE: STUDENT'S LIST

1. Listen carefully to what your teacher tells you about the book.

2. If you are in the middle of a book, think about what was read last time.

3. During the reading, think carefully about what is being read. Pay attention to names, places, events, and things that grab your attention.

4. Be ready to tell all you can remember when the reading is done.

5. Retell what was read with as much detail as you can. There is not one right way to do this.

6. It's fine to repeat words or phrases that sound just like the book. It's fine to share connections you made with what was read.

7. Do not make things up or begin everything you say with, "And then…".

8. Listen to what your teacher says after you narrate. Try to do these things the next time you narrate.

WRITTEN NARRATION SKILLS: TEACHER'S LIST

Notes: When children do written narrations, they use their writing to tell back in their own words what they have just read or heard. Written narrations allow children to use their writing to share their own version of the passage they have just read or heard with accuracy, individual personality, spirit, and originality.

You can begin to help your children edit their written narrations by following the steps listed below. If you are new to Heart of Dakota and have not yet worked through the copywork, oral narration, and dictation in the guides, then you should plan to spend longer moving through the list of skills below. This is quite normal, so don't be surprised if you do not get through all of the skills in the list this year.

The skills listed below range from beginning writing skills to more difficult writing skills which require knowledge of higher levels of grammar, usage, and punctuation. Skills are based on a continuum of increasing difficulty, so related skills may be spread out to be placed where they each fall best on the overall continuum. For example, the third skill on the list is beginning and ending sentences correctly, as well as correcting sentence fragments. But, fixing run-on sentences, which is a related skill, is not addressed until the seventh skill. For this reason, it is best to read the list over in its entirety, so you can see the overall flow of the continuum. Focusing on teaching one new numbered skill at time in the order it is listed will help you to avoid overwhelming your child with too many skills at once, and will give your child a manageable plan for successfully learning to do written narrations.

For new or struggling writers, you should start with the skill listed first on the list below. Once that skill is mastered, move on to the next skill. The skills should be cumulative, meaning each time a new skill is added, the old skills are still required. You may either make gentle comments that guide students to use the listed skills as they are writing their narration, or wait until the narration is complete to make your gentle comments then.

If your child already routinely does the beginning skills on the list, you should jump to the first skill on the list that your child has not mastered. Before editing, always have your children read the narration aloud to you so they can catch any of their own mistakes first.

The skills list below is for the teacher's use. There is also a list for students' use that can be used for their reference; however, it should not be used in place of the teacher's list since written narration is a new skill being taught.

WRITTEN NARRATION SKILLS LIST:

1. **Indent each paragraph.** Leave a space about the size of one thumb tip at the beginning of the first sentence in each paragraph.

2. **Make sure the first sentence is on the right topic.** Reword it if necessary.

3. **Begin each sentence with a capital letter, and end each sentence with the correct punctuation mark (. ! ?).** To do this you will also need to correct any sentence fragments to make complete sentences.

4. **Begin working on writing with correct spelling by using a combination of the following options.** Note: Option 1 is a better habit for students to acquire than Option 2, and Option 2 is a better habit for students to acquire than Option 3, and so on. Option 4 should only be used for very poor spellers, as it is not the same as having students write something in their own words.

   Option 1: Have students look back in the book to copy the correct spelling of key words.
   Option 2: Write words that students ask you to spell for them on a markerboard or paper while they are writing. Then, they can copy the word(s) as they write.
   Option 3: Spell orally any words the students ask you to spell for them while they are writing.
   Option 4: Allow students to dictate the narration to you for you to write, and have them copy it at the end.

   Spelling will also be addressed more fully later on in the skills list.

5. **Make sure that sentences do not all start with the same word or words.** Vary the first word of the sentences within each paragraph as much as possible.

6. **Use correct capitalization within each sentence.** Check to be sure all proper nouns, titles, etc. are capitalized.

7. **While students are writing, fix any sentences that are run-ons by providing a gentle reminder to start a new sentence or to add a comma and a joining word.** For example, "That's the start of a new sentence now."

8. **Write a good closing sentence.** This sentence should wrap up the paragraph in an interesting way, and make the reader feel like your writing is coming to a close. Ideas for a strong closing sentence include the following:
   * restating the introduction using different words
   * using a quote
   * asking a question
   * stating the main theme or idea
   * giving your personal opinion

9. **Use correct spelling within your writing.** Edit the student's narration for spelling by underlining incorrectly spelled words in pencil and writing the correct spelling of the word in the margin of their paper or on a markerboard.

10. **Use correct punctuation within the sentences**. Check to be sure students have properly used commas in a series, commas between two sentences, apostrophes, etc.

WRITTEN NARRATION SKILLS: STUDENT'S LIST

1. Indent each paragraph by leaving a thumb tip space at the beginning.

2. Make sure the first sentence is on the right topic.

3. Begin each sentence with a capital letter, and end each sentence with the correct punctuation mark: . ? !

4. Begin working on writing with correct spelling by using the different options your teacher suggests.

5. Make sure that sentences do not all start with the same word or words.

6. Use correct capitalization within each sentence, like for special names or places.

7. Fix any sentences that are run-ons.

8. Write a good closing sentence.

9. Use correct spelling within your writing.

10. Use correct punctuation within the sentences.

Dictation Passages – Level 2

Special instructions for the dictation passages: Each student needs a notebook for dictation. A wide-lined notebook is best. On each dictation day, your student will study the dictation passage. It is helpful to write any difficult words on markerboard or paper for the students to focus on. New words are in bold. Also, call attention to any capital letters and punctuation marks in the passage. Discuss them briefly as needed.

When students feel ready, remove the dictation passage from the students' sight. Call out the passage one phrase at a time. Pause after each phrase for students to repeat it back to you and write it. Continue until the entire passage has been dictated.

Give students a moment to look over their passage for mistakes. Then, have them compare their sentences with the key. Students should circle any mistakes they made on the key and correct the mistakes in their own notebook. If the passage was correct, place a checkmark next to the passage in the key. All items in the sentence must be correct, including punctuation marks, before going on to the next passage. If students made any mistakes, they'll repeat the same passage as many days as it takes to get it right.

Always begin the next session where the student left off. If your child is repeatedly stuck on passages, he or she may not be ready for dictation. Then, it is best to go back to using the spelling lists and activities provided in our *Bigger Hearts for His Glory* guide instead.

*Dictation passages are taken from *Dictation Day by Day: Book One* by Kate Van Wagenen. (MacMillan Company 1916, 1923).

Level 2 – Dictation Passages Key

1

Sue has a **bird**.

It can call and **sing**.

king ring wing

2

Sue can sing and play.

Sam **does not** like to sing.

cot got jot pot

dot hot lot rot

3

I have a **pet** bird.

It can sing **you** a **song**.

bet let net wet

get met set long

4

That bird has a **nest**.

It is **in** the wood.

best lest rest vest

jest pest test west

5

The **cow gives milk.**

Sue does not like milk.

now vow silk

6

The cow **eats hay**.

Ned fed the cow and the pig.

bay jay pay way

day lay ray

gay may say

7

See the red cow.

She **loves her calf**.

half

8

See the **old** cow.

Dan is **kind** to her.

bind mind

find rind

9

I have a **dog** and a cat.

The dog can **run** and play.

fog log bun gun

hog jog fun sun

10

I love my pet dog.

See **me** pat **him**.

11

I call my dog **Jack**.

I like the **name of** Jack.

back pack came lame

rack tack game same

12

Jack can lap milk.

Jack loves milk.

cap map rap tap

gap nap sap

13

Ned has a **sled**.

He has fun with it.

bed led red

cell Nell wed

14

The **snow** is **soft**.

My cap **fell** in the snow.

bell dell sell well

cell Nell tell yell

15

The dog likes the snow.

It is fun **for** him to **roll** in it.

nor

16

All boys like the snow.

Ned has fun on the ice.

dice mice nice rice

17

Snow **keeps** the **roots warm.**

Nell does not like the snow.

boots

18

The **bean** is a seed.

You can eat this seed.

deed heed reed

feed need weed

19

We can eat roots, too.

We eat the **beet**.

feet meet

20

The red beets **are ripe**.

May does not like **them**.

pipe wipe

21

The sun has set.

Now my bird **will** sing

very low.

bill hill mill rill

fill kill pill sill

22

That is the **last** bell.

Now Jack **must** run.

cast mast dust just

fast past gust rust

23

Anna can not find her new hat.

She does not like to **be late**.

date gate Kate rate

fate hate mate

24

I have a **nut** and a date.

The date has a **pit**.

cut hut bit hit

but rut fit lit

25

That bird has **two** wings.

She can **fly** to her nest.

sly

26

My bird has **sand** in **his cage**.

I feed seeds to my bird.

band hand land

27

The ice is **thin**.

We must not **step on** it.

28

Here is Ned in the snow.

The snow is **cold** and wet.

bold gold mold told

fold hold sold

29

The old **hen** is here.

She has **left** her nest.

Ben men ten

den pen

30

This hen **laid** an **egg**.

We must **try** to feed her now.

maid paid raid

cry dry fry

31

Fill the **cup** with milk.

Our cat and dog like milk.

32

The cow **gave** a **pail** of milk.

I **saw** her give it.

cave rave bail mail

Dave save fail nail

pave wave jail rail

33

I saw the bird in the **tree**.

I must not hit the **poor** bird.

free

34

Ben does not run **or jump**.

He is too lame.

bump hump lump

dump pump

35

Ned **goes** for the mail.

He must **walk** fast.

talk

36

I did not stop the ball.

It fell in the snow.

bid hid kid lid rid

37

John hid in the hay.

Anna saw him **hide**.

bide side tide

ride wide

38

Ned **had** a red cap.

It **was** too big for him.

bad mad

lad sad

39

Mary made a new hat.

It was very big for her.

fade wade

40

Ruth saw the sun **rise**.

It **was** like a big red ball.

41

I saw the **moon** rise.

It was **up** in the **sky**.

42

The **stars were near** the moon. The sun had set.

dear hear rear

fear year

43

See the **fish** in the **pond**.

I see a **duck**.

dish bond

wish fond

44

That **box** is made of **tin**.

Ned told me **so**.

bin fin pin win

din grin sin fox

45

Ruth must **go home** now.

Her doll fell into the **mud**.

bud cud

46

Anna will **make** a cake.

I **hope** it will be good.

bake rake wake mope

cake sake Pope

lake take rope

47

The **flag** is on the pole.

It is a **fine** big flag.

dine mine pine

line nine vine

48

The **boat** is a big **one**.

It will sail **out** with the tide.

coat goat

49

It is a new year. I must **begin** it well.

bass mass brass

glass pass grass

50

We have a big **horse**. My **brother** and I feed him **sugar**.

51

Kate goes to the **store**. She gets **bread** and **butter**.

bore more sore

core pore tore

52

Do you love the **baby**? Then **kiss** her.

hiss miss bliss

53

My **father** keeps his horse very **clean**. He feeds him well.

bean lean mean

54

Our horse eats hay and **oats**. He eats grass and **apples when** he can get them.

55

Do not **drive** the horse so fast. You will hurt him.

kick pick dive

lick sick five

nick wick hive

56

John has a new cart. He bought it from my father.

dart part tart

57

The robin came north in the spring. She made her nest in the old apple tree.

king ring sing wing

58

The nest was made of mud and straw. The robin laid four blue eggs.

pour glue

59

The father robin gets **food** for the baby robins. Robins like **worms** and **fruit**.

60

Did you see the **young** robin eat the **cherry**? The **farmer** does not like the robin.

61

Half of **these grapes** are **green**. Do not eat such fruit.

keen seen

62

I have a **bright** new **coin**. I can **buy** an apple.

fight night tight sent
light right dent tent
might sight lent went

63

On Friday I shall sail my new boat. Will my mother let you go with me?

64

The milkman has come. Shall I buy a pint, a quart, or a gallon of milk?

65

My **thick** coat is made of wool. We get **wool** from the **sheep**.

deep peep brick click
keep weep chick stick

66

The wool is cut **off** in the spring, **before** it is very hot. It is soft and **white**.

67

A young sheep is **called** a **lamb**. It bleats softly.

fresh

68

The man **who tends** the sheep has a dog to **help** him. The sheep dog **knows** all the sheep and lambs.

bend mend

lend send

69

After the rain in the winter, we can slide on the ice.

gain main pain vain chain

drain grain stain train

70

See the black clouds in the west. The rain is near. Let us run.

dear fear hear rear year

71

The rain keeps me from my plan, but it makes the grass grow. Can you catch the drops of rain?

batch hatch latch

match patch snatch

72

The baby can not use a fork or spoon, so we feed her fresh milk. We get it from a farm.

cork pork harm

73

Last Sunday I saw a deer in the park. He was eating grass.

bark dark hark lark mark

74

The deer is reddish brown. He feeds on grass and moss.

boss loss toss cross floss

75

Did you **ever** see a deer run to **cover**? He runs and jumps with a **swift** light step.

76

I am going out to pick the corn. It is ripe now. Two women will help me.

born horn

77

May we play in the park? You may if you go home before six or seven in the evening.

fix mix

78

In winter the days are very short. we sometimes have supper after dark.

fort port sort

79

In **school** we use **paper** and **pencil**. We must keep all papers clean.

80

Our long days are in **June**. I **often** dig in my **garden** until seven at night.

tune

81

We should give all plants sun, light, and water. Then they will grow.

could would

82

Snow keeps the roots of many plants warm. They do not feel the cold.

heel peel reel kneel steel

83

At the end of the path is a big oak tree. Let us walk to it and rest.

84

In the fall the oak leaves turn red and brown and yellow. Dick and I keep them off the lawn.

burn churn fellow mellow

dawn fawn pawn yawn

85

Whose watch is this? I think it is mine. It is like the one I bought last March.

link pink rink sink wink

86

I must study my lesson before I go out to play. Does your brother study at night?

87

This week I am going out to lunch and to supper. I shall take my sister with me.

bunch leek peek cheek

punch meek seek creek

88

Kate is a good child. She will not get one spot on her new dress.

blot knot shot trot

89

Sister and I call our dog **Sport**. His brown **hair** is soft and **curly**.

fair pair chair

90

The dog has soft **pads** on his feet like the cat. Can the dog **pull** in his claws and hide them?

bull full

91

Dogs eat meat and lap milk. The teeth of the dog are very sharp.

beat heat neat seat

92

The father and his son will stay in the city till April. The days will be warm then.

93

Every **summer** I go out of the city in **July** and **August**. Is it very hot in the city in summer?

94

You must **look** at the **pretty** blue hat which **papa** bought me. The baby tore my old one.

book hook took shook

cook nook brook

95

The stars were near the moon. I saw three very bright ones.

96

I saw two men in the yard. They were busy with a fire.

card hard lard tire

hire mire sire wire

97

Last week I found the nest of an owl. It was in the top of an old tree.

bound mound round

hound pound sound

98

In the nest which I found were four **little** eggs. Shall I **show** them to you **some** day?

blow glow crow snow

flow slow grow come

99

Some owls are **gray,** and some are white. They never make a loud **noise** when they fly.

100

The claws of the owl are very **strong**. He eats **both** mice and **small** birds.

fall hall wall

call tall stall

101

How much **money** do you have? I have ten **dollars**, five cents, and a **dime**.

lime time honey

102

Fred takes a lesson on Monday and Friday. Do you take your lessons on those days?

bed led red bled sled

fed Ned wed fled shed

Dictation Passages – Level 3

Special instructions for the dictation passages: Each student needs a notebook for dictation. A wide-lined notebook is best. On each dictation day, your student will study the dictation passage. It is helpful to write any difficult words on markerboard or paper for the students to focus on. New words are in bold. Also, call attention to any capital letters and punctuation marks in the passage. Discuss them briefly as needed.

When students feel ready, remove the dictation passage from the students' sight. Call out the passage one phrase at a time. Pause after each phrase for students to repeat it back to you and write it. Continue until the entire passage has been dictated.

Give students a moment to look over their passage for mistakes. Then, have them compare their sentences with the key. Students should circle any mistakes they made on the key and correct the mistakes in their own notebook. If the passage was correct, place a checkmark next to the passage in the key. All items in the sentence must be correct, including punctuation marks, before going on to the next passage. If students made any mistakes, they'll repeat the same passage as many days as it takes to get it right.

Always begin the next session where the student left off. If your child is repeatedly stuck on passages, he or she may need to move to an easier level of dictation passages. Three different levels of passages are provided in this guide.

*Dictation passages are taken from *Dictation Day by Day: Book One* by Kate Van Wagenen. (MacMillan Company 1916, 1923).

Level 3 – Dictation Passages Key

1

The **children** who did not study **their** lessons last year are **sorry** now. Are you one of these **lazy** children?

2

Do you want a **flower** in the **schoolroom**? If you have **none**, you must plant some seeds in a pot of **earth**.

3

All plants have a root, a **stem**, and leaves. **Most** plants **also** have flowers, fruit, and seeds. Can you find **each** part?

4

Please open the **door**. I want to take a peep at the snow. Here is the **key**.

5

In March, April, May and June the farmer is very busy. **There** are a **dozen things** to be **done** on a farm.

6

Next Saturday I shall go to the farm to see my **aunt**. I like to take **dinner** with her.

7

How much **salt** did you **put** in the **soup**? Come here and I shall show you.

8

I **always** help my mother before I come to school. As soon as I **reach** home, I help her **again**.

9

Every Monday **morning** we begin a new week. We must **learn** each lesson well.

10

In **September** and **October** the leaves of the **maple** turn red and yellow and brown. They look pretty in a glass.

11

September, October, and **November** are the three **autumn months**. Then the birds fly to their winter home.

12

The **eagle** feeds on **rabbits**, small birds, and fish. He makes his nest in some **high** spot.

13

We can see an eagle on every **quarter** and **fifty**-cent **piece**. On **what** other piece do we find the eagle?

14

The **ox** is useful to the farmer. It **moves** very slowly. **Its neck** is big and strong.

15

Please **bring** me the **orange** which is on the **table**. I bought it for my dinner. It came from the **south**.

16

Dogs and sheep **carry** seeds around and drop them. Some seeds are **carried away** by **wind** and water.

17

The **butcher** and the **baker** call at our home every **Tuesday** and Saturday. **Julia** buys meat and bread for our dinner.

18

I like to play with Kate's doll very much. It can **lie** down and **shut** its **eyes**. Can you **guess** its name?

19

My mother and sister have **been** away from home **since** Friday, and we shall be **happy** to see them **once** more.

20

We feed Anna's **canary** every day at **twelve o'clock.** He likes all kinds of seeds, and he eats fruit **too**.

21

When my father was sick, we called a **doctor** who lives in **New York**. He **said** that father must have rest and **sleep**.

22

As Julia's home was a **mile** away, I took the **car** at **First Street**. I did not get the right one, so I was not on time.

23

Helen gave a **party** to **thirty** little boys and girls. They had cakes and ices and many nice things to eat.

24

When Jack hurt his **finger**, he could not help his father. He was such a good boy that his sister told him a **story almost** every day.

25

When I go into our **parlor**, I can hear the **clock** tick. My mother will not let me **touch** this clock.

26

My father gave my brother and me **silver** pencils. Fred's pencil was soon **broken**, but I **kept** mine a month.

27

How many **inches** are there in a **foot**, **George**? There are twelve inches in a foot, and three feet in a yard.

28

December, **January**, and **February** are the winter months. Then we have many storms, but we also have **skating**.

29

Does John go out **early** in the morning? Yes, he wants to **earn** money for his **mama**.

30

There are three classes of **bees**. They all live **together** in a hive and feed on honey, which they **collect** in the summer.

31

The **queen** bee lays the eggs. The **drones** do no work and have no **sting**.

32

The **workers** get food for the **entire** hive. They get this honey from the flowers. They like **clover** very much.

33

Friday noon I went to the store **myself** and bought a large **squash**, a quart of **pears**, and a pound of **tea**.

34

While mother was busy, I **read** to my little sister near the old **elm** tree. Did you ever try to keep a little sister **quiet**?

35

Do you read **word** by word? If you do, read a **page** a day for a month, and you will soon **improve**.

36

When we **raise** plants, we must give them sun and **air** and water. By the **middle** of March some of them may begin to bloom.

37

Last Saturday I saw **twenty merry children** on their way to the park. Can you tell me **why** they **smiled** and were so happy?

38

Frogs lay their eggs in a kind of **jelly**. It takes about a month for these eggs to hatch. Then we see the tadpole.

39

A tadpole is all **head** and tail. Did you ever watch the **gills disappear** and the legs grow?

40

As the **legs** of the tadpole grow, the tail disappears. Then the tadpole is **changed** to a **perfect** little frog. It feeds on **insects**.

41

Everything **else** one can turn and turn about, and make old look like new, but there's no **coaxing** boots and **shoes** to look better **than** they do.

42

I don't like the cold days of winter. Jack **Frost bites** my fingers and my **toes**. I like April and May better.

43

Nearly every day the rose's pretty **face** was **washed** by the dew. Was the dear little flower happy when it **felt** the drops of dew?

44

Said young **Dandelion**
With a sweet air,
I have my eye on
Miss **Daisy** fair.

- Miss Mulock

45

Do you see those black clouds **coming** up in the west? I think it will rain in **fifteen** or twenty **minutes**.

46

I **tried** to drive my **uncle's** big black horse to the **barn**. I soon found I could not **whip** him.

47

Is it too early to light the **lamp**? No, I wish to **write** a letter, and it must be done by nine o'clock **tonight**.

48

Do not **forget** to **speak** to your uncle **today** about the fruit which I bought for him. I have grapes, peaches, and pears.

49

Mother took me to the **circus**. I was **afraid** when the **lion roared**.

50

We went for a sail, but the wind **drove** the ship **along** very fast. When the water **dashed** into our boat, we were in great **danger**.

51

The horse helps men in their work. He is also **useful** in **war**. Did you ever look at his **iron shoes**?

52

Alice is a **gentle loving** child. She has a kind **heart**, and always does her very best to please both father and mother.

53

We get silk from the **tiny** silkworm. It feeds upon the **leaf** of the **mulberry** tree. It eats every leaf it can find.

54

Then the silkworm **spins** a little ball of silk **around** its **body** and goes to sleep. Did you ever see **any** of these balls of silk?

55

May I go with you on **Thursday** to see the **beaver** dams? **Henry** and I were there last Monday and saw **eight**.

56

The beaver **builds** these dams so that the door of his **house** will be **under** water. Did you ever see any of these **queer** houses?

57

Mr. Beaver does not make his house **until** September. I am **sure** he wants the coat of mud to **freeze** so hard that it will be quite **safe.**

58

Can the beavers cut **down** trees? **Yes**, it is **true** that they do this with their teeth **unless** the wood is too hard.

59

The fox and the **wolf** are **about** as **large** as dogs. Their teeth are very sharp, as they are made to **tear** their food.

60

The **nose** of both the wolf and the fox is more **pointed** than a dog's nose. Their tails are much more **bushy**.

61

The **puppies** of the fox do not open their eyes till they are **between** ten and twelve days old. They are **twice** as fond of play as a dog's puppies.

62

Here are **eighteen lemons** to make a **cool** drink for the children. Are they coming on Tuesday or **Wednesday**?

63

Did Harry **break** his **arm** some time **ago**? His mother told me he cried with pain when he fell from his **pony**.

64

When I pull the **string**, the **kitten follows** it from place to place. She likes to jump up in the air for it too.

65

We live in **America**, and we love our home. Every day when we **behold** the flag, we say that it is good to be an **American**.

66

In the summer months, June, July, and August, we use very little **coal**. Sometimes we get a **bushel**, which the coal man sends in a **bag**.

67

How many eggs does your sister **Emma** get for a dollar? I bought **fourteen** last Wednesday at our **own grocer's**.

68

The **lily grew** under glass till we could put it with the other flowers. We want it as a gift for Aunt **Ellen**, who will soon be **seventy** years old.

69

At home I have my own **soap**, **brush**, and **comb**. I never go away in summer **without** them.

70

Have you ever seen an **ostrich**? Yes, my **cousin** and I saw some of these big birds **yesterday** in **Central** Park. They are very strong and can run fast.

71

Among the flowers sent to **church** were **nineteen** or twenty **lilies**. We've never before seen such pretty white ones.

72

Some of **grandma's friends** took a long ride to see her on her seventy-**ninth birthday**. Did Emma show you the fruit which the children gave to grandma?

73

The **butterfly** lives only for one summer. It does not fly at night. It goes to rest about five o'clock in the **afternoon**. I **caught** a live one today down **beside** the brook.

74

I learned to add and **subtract** very well, but I cannot **multiply** and **divide** so **easily**. I **spent** months trying to learn.

75

You've been out to **gather wild** flowers, I am sure. Did you **climb** the rocks for them, or did you find them near the **river**?

76

Frank's father, Dr. West, sent him one **hundred** dollars for **Christmas**. What do you think he will do with that **amount** of money?

77

My rabbit likes to run in the **field**. When I feed him **carrots** or **tender cabbage** leaves, he looks at me as if he would like to **thank** me.

78

The **earthworm** bores **through** the **soil** and **softens** it. Then the rain can reach the roots of plants, and also any seeds which **happen** to be in the ground.

79

What did you see in the country? I saw a number of things, but I liked the lovely flowers best of all. One day I picked an apron full before six o'clock in the morning.

80

Woodpeckers have strong bills so that they can bore for insects. The farmer does not like these birds, **because** they **sample** his best fruit and often **hammer** his trees full of holes.

81

Dr. White and his **wife** spent **Easter** week at the **seashore**. Their home is in **Boston**, but they do not live there **during** June, July, or August.

82

Does Ruth's **music teacher** let her play by **ear**? No, she doesn't, because she wishes Ruth to play every piece as it is **written**.

83

All **parents** like to have **people praise** their children. They like to feel that their children never forget to be **polite**.

84

Sarah studies her lessons at night. She has **breakfast** early and is always **ready** for school at eight o'clock.

85

One day in September my sister's **husband wrote** me a letter saying he **expected** to come to the city in October. He also said he hoped I would not leave until he came.

86

The teacher told her children, when they worked an **example** in **division**, to be sure that the **remainder** was smaller than the **divisor**.

87

James asked whose **candy** he had found **lying** on the **shelf**. As no one said a word, he ate it.

88

Any child who wants to **become** strong and **healthy** must have **plenty** of **sunshine**. How much time do you **spend** in the air each day?

89

A **hungry** fox saw some grapes on a vine. He **sprang** up and tried to get them. Finding them **beyond** his reach, he said that he **thought** those grapes were **sour**.

90

Our **family** is so very large that we eat a loaf of bread at each **meal**. Can you tell me how many **loaves** we shall use in **December**?

91

Every Saturday Henry did the **different errands** very **quickly**. Then he had **nothing** else to do the remainder of the day.

92

The robin and the **bluebird**
Soon after flew away,
But as they left the **treetop**,
I think I **heard** them say,
"If birds and flowers have work
to do,
Why, so have the little children
too."

- Helen C. Bacon

93

The **poplar** tree is so tall and **straight** that it doesn't give much **shade**. When the wind blows, the leaves shake and shiver as **though** they would fall to the ground.

94

The **fir**, pine, **cedar**, and **spruce** trees **wear** their green leaves during the entire year. Their **twigs** are as green in February and March as they are in May.

95

The American **bison**, called by most people the **buffalo**, is a wild ox. Years ago it was found in our country from ocean to **ocean**, but now none is to be seen.

96

Buffaloes feed on grass and chew a cud like the cow. They always seek a **valley** near the **edge** of some **stream** so that the **herd** may get both food and drink.

97

When the white men came to this country, they **built** their homes on the **plains** near streams. Then they **began** to kill these **animals** for their fur and their flesh.

98

The buffaloes went West, where the **Indians** caught many of them by **throwing** a rope **over** their horns. Now we have no buffaloes **except** those found in our parks.

99

As I passed the grocer's, I saw **thirteen** or fourteen **melons** in the **window**. I did not see any **berries**.

100

Agnes has a small **place** in her garden where she is raising **tomatoes**. We all like them much better than those we buy in the **market**.

101

The **policeman** at our **corner** is quick to see people who do wrong. We **trust** him, because he is a friend of the children. He helps them to **avoid** all danger.

102

Firemen are **brave** and quick to **act**. They **rush** into **blazing** buildings and carry out helpless women and children.

103

All things **whatsoever** ye would that men should do to you, do ye **even** so to them, for this is the **law** and the **prophets**.

- The Bible

Dictation Passages – Level 4

Special instructions for the dictation passages: Each student needs a notebook for dictation. A lined composition book is best. On each dictation day, your student will study the dictation passage. It is helpful to write any difficult words on markerboard or paper for the students to focus on. New words are in bold. Also, call attention to any capital letters and punctuation marks in the passage. Discuss them briefly as needed.

When students feel ready, remove the dictation passage from the students' sight. Call out the passage one phrase at a time. Pause after each phrase for students to repeat it back to you and write it. Continue until the entire passage has been dictated.

Give students a moment to look over their passage for mistakes. Then, have them compare their sentences with the key. Students should circle any mistakes they made on the key and correct the mistakes in their own notebook. If the passage was correct, place a checkmark next to the passage in the key. All items in the sentence must be correct, including punctuation marks, before going on to the next passage. If students made any mistakes, they'll repeat the same passage as many days as it takes to get it right.

Always begin the next session where the student left off. If your child is repeatedly stuck on passages, he or she may need to move to an easier level of dictation passages. Three different levels of passages are provided in this guide.

*Dictation passages are taken from *Dictation Day by Day: Book One* by Kate Van Wagenen. (MacMillan Company 1916, 1923).

Level 4 – Dictation Passages Key

1

Let us take **pride** in our school. Children who make it a **rule** not to **scatter** papers, and who pick up such things when they find them, are **forming** good **habits**.

2

Our room must be clean and **cheerful**. Then a glass **vase** filled with a few **sweet** flowers will **brighten** our entire day.

3

What a **blessing** to have a policeman on the **avenue**! He **warns drivers** to go slowly around corners. He takes lost children home or finds their parents.

4

A fireman's **life** is often in **great** danger. He dashes into the **flames** and never thinks of **himself**. He must be brave to do this.

5

William bent the **blade** of his **knife** so much that he broke it. He's very sorry now, because his grandma gave it to him on his birthday.

6

Last Wednesday we went to **Coney Island** by boat. It's only a short sail from New York, but the **ship** was **loaded** with people, and we had a very **rough** trip.

7

On Sunday and every **holiday** we have **either turkey** or **chicken** for dinner. We all like these dinners very much.

8

When **Emily** is nineteen, her father has **promised** to let her **travel** for a year. Isn't it **strange** that he will let her stay away from home for such a long time?

9

In winter I get up at night
And dress by the yellow **candle** light.
In summer, quite the **other** way,
I have to go to bed by day.

- Robert Louis Stevenson

10

There were **forty angry geese** flying here and there, trying to get away from the dog. He wanted to drive them into that **dirty** water.

11

Hear the **steam** cars **whistle** as they fly down the **track**! I am sure that **eighty** trains pass here each day. Sometimes the noise almost makes me **deaf**.

12

When I went to market on Saturday, I bought a **peck** of **potatoes**, some **onions**, and a few **peppers**. The grocer very politely said he would send them home.

13

"I cannot stay the **east** wind
Or **thaw** its **icy smart**;
But I can keep a corner warm
In mother's loving heart."

14

This is the sixth lace collar I have made since April. I hope to finish making it by Tuesday. Your friend, Miss Lamb, said she would give me seventy cents for it, but I think that is not enough.

15

I'm going to **Brooklyn** at four o'clock. It is a great **distance** from home, and I fear I **cannot** go to the party. I shall be too **tired**.

16

In June we sold **ninety** yards of red, white, and blue **ribbon**. It was useful both for Flag Day and for **Fourth** of July.

17

All the **front** rooms in our house are much **larger** than the rear rooms. I know that it takes an **hour** to **sweep** each one, and it is not **easy** work.

18

Alice and Helen were on the lake during the **heavy shower**. Whose **fault** was it that they were caught in the storm and nearly **drowned**?

19

Tomorrow I expect to go to a small town **sixty** miles from here. I hope it will be **pleasant**, so that Frank and I may go down to the beach and gather **shells**.

20

When I brushed my **clothing**, I found that my **sleeve** was **loose** and torn about an inch above the **elbow**. Please wait until I find some **thread** to mend it.

21

Some time during Sunday night a **thief** went into our garden and picked all the ripe **vegetables**. Monday morning it **seemed** as though he had also **destroyed** every leaf and flower.

22

Boughs are **daily rifled**
By the gusty thieves,
And the book of **Nature**
Getteth short of leaves.
- Thomas Hood

23

The **sparrow's** eggs have many colors. She lays five or six. They hatch in sixteen or seventeen days. Did you ever see one?

24

The mother bird feeds her young ones **only** for a week. Then they must pick up their own food from the **ground** or **wherever** they can find it.

25

Last Friday Uncle Henry left New York at 2:30 P.M. and reached Chicago at 9:30 A.M. on Saturday. As he had most **important business** to **attend** to, he was very glad to pay an **extra price** to travel on this fast train.

26

Did you ever see a bird picking up grains of **wheat** in the farmer's field? We eat the same food, but the **miller grinds** it into **flour** for us, and **finally** it is baked into bread.

27

Martha went to the **kitchen** to see what she could do. Her mother, who **stood** near the table, asked her to put the oranges and melons on the shelf near the **pineapple**.

28

"I love little **Pussy**,
Her coat is so warm;
And if I don't hurt her,
She'll do me no harm.

So I'll not pull her tail,
Nor drive her away,
But Pussy and I
Very **gently** will play."

29

When **Richard** I was king of **England**, Robin Hood and his merry men lived in the **beautiful** Sherwood **Forest**. They dearly loved its hills, its valleys, its flowers, and its **carpet** of bright green.

30

These men **searched** people passing through the woods, and killed four or five of the king's deer every day. Robin Hood never **robbed** a **woman**. He **shared everything** with his men.

31

Robin Hood was **captain** of the band. Little John was **second** in **command.** Friar Tuck was **another** one of Robin Hood's men. Maid Marian also lived in the forest and **cheered** them all with her sweet music.

32

As the **ruler desired** to see Robin Hood, whose men did so much **mischief**, he went to their forest home. The bold robber stopped the king's horses with **ease**. Then he blew three times on his horn.

33

When Robin blew his horn, all his men **appeared** in **answer** to his call. The king saw he was not **frightened**, and he **admired** Robin's wit and **wisdom** so much that he told him it was King Richard who stood before him.

34

Then the king **invited** the entire band to go home with him. Robin **ordered** his men to **mount** and go **forward**, and as they **departed**, Robin Hood rode beside the king.

35

Alfred's manners are quite different from those of **David**. When Alfred meets me on the street, he raises his hat and **bows** very politely. David passes as though he were **ashamed** to see me.

36

Philip's mother, who saw him looking down the **road**, **knew** he could not finish his lessons that way; so she told him not to sit there **idly dreaming**.

37

Captain Church has a **cargo** of **hickory** logs which he is **obliged** to **deliver** in England. If all goes well, he may reach the other side before the first of the year.

38

When I am **grown** to man's **estate**,
I shall be very **proud** and great,
And tell the other girls and boys
Not to **meddle** with my toys.

- Robert Louis Stevenson

39

Amy, if you saw a **greedy spider** on the **branch** of a tree, wouldn't you **believe** that you were looking at an insect? And yet the spider is not a true insect, because it has eight legs and its body is divided into two parts.

40

Doesn't that spider look queer, **running** to a place of **safety** with a big white **bundle**! This holds **several** eggs; and her young, when hatched, are **content** to ride on her back.

41

If you spend a few minutes looking **closely** at a spider, you will **certainly** see that there are six points on its back. From these points comes the **sticky** **fluid** which makes the spider's **dainty** web.

42

"If Mother Nature **patches**
The leaves of trees and vines,
I'm sure she does her **darning**
With the **needles** of the pines."

43

Robert Bruce, king of **Scotland**, was **defeated** in six battles. At last his men disappeared, and **escaping alone** he hid himself in a barn. He thought he would give up the fight.

44

One **forenoon** as Bruce lay on a **blanket** in the barn, he **noticed** a spider trying to **fasten** its threads from one beam to another. Six times the spider failed. The next time it caught the beam.

45

When Bruce saw what the spider did, he sprang to his feet and cried that he would not give up and be beaten by a spider. He gathered his **soldiers** together, met the **enemy**, and **won** back his **kingdom**.

46

Last Tuesday, as we neared the **shore**, the **gulls surrounded** our ship. I **threw** half of my orange into the sea, and several birds tried to **seize** it at once.

47

When Mr. and Mrs. Miller went to the country, **Thomas** remained with friends until their **return**. He **meant** to be good, but I'm afraid he was often very **naughty**.

48

When George **Washington** was a boy at school, he was fond of **sport**, but he also liked his lessons. He never **broke** his word and always took **care** to speak the **truth**.

49

One Thursday in September the farmer put a load of **celery** and **lettuce** in his **wagon** and went to the **village**. After he sold these vegetables, he bought some fresh meat and a few yards of **cloth**.

50

In October and November, before our **furnace** is lighted, we have a **grate** fire in our **sitting** room. Here we gather every evening for a pleasant hour, and each one **describes** the **pictures** he sees in the fire.

51

Bertha's mother **taught** her to mend her own **stockings**. It was not easy for her to learn to **sew**, because her needle always broke and her thread always **knotted**.

52

When I go to see my aunt, I always take an **express** train. Before I get on the train, I **check** in my **trunk**. The man who gives me my check stands **behind** a **counter**.

53

Washington **planned** our flag. It was **begun** in May, 1777, by Mrs. **Betsey** Ross, and her **task** was **completed** in June of the same year.

54

June 14, 1777, **Congress approved** the flag **submitted** by Mrs. Ross. **Everyone** admired the red, white, and blue then, as we love and admire our flag today.

55

Dr. White gave **Isabel** a **couple** of plants for her birthday. She knew that to **produce** flowers, one must give them **sunshine**, and as it was cold **outside** she put them in her window.

56

Children, sing to Him whose care
Makes the land so rich and fair;
Raise your tuneful voices high
To our Father in the sky.

- Margaret Sangster

57

Isabel soon noticed the **effect** of the sun. The buds began to **swell**, and the entire plant bent toward the light. If you wish to know **whether** this is true, you can **prove** it at any time.

58

The peas became yellow, and the shell turned yellow. "All the world's turning yellow," said they. Suddenly the shell was torn off and put in to the pocket of a jacket.

- Andersen

59

Columbus went to **Spain** because no one in his **native** land had **faith** in him. He believed that the earth was round. The people in those days **imagined** it was flat.

60

The people of Spain were looking for a short way to **Asia**, because they wanted to **trade** with that **distant** place. The queen **granted** Columbus three ships and made him **commander** of the fleet.

61

Columbus and his men spent days of **terror** on the sea, but finally, by means of the **compass**, they **succeeded** in reaching land. When they first saw land, they **exclaimed** that hey had reached **India**.

62

Last June I was the **guest** of Dr. Frank's **nephew**, whose **cottage** stands near the **margin** of a large lake. We had great fun playing in the water. Each little wave seemed to **murmur**, "Catch me if you can."

63

One day in April as **Joseph hurried toward** the garden, he called to his sister, “Please help me dig some **angleworms**. Father is going to take Dick and me fishing. We are sure to catch nine or ten **perch**.”

64

Only a tender flower
Sent us to rear;
Only a life to love
While we are here.
Only a baby small,
Never at rest,
Small, but how dear to us,
God knoweth best.

- Matthias Barr

65

Bright little **dandelion**,
Downy, yellow face,
Peeping up among the grass
With such gentle grace;
Minding not the April wind,
Blowing rude and cold,
Bravc little dandelion,
With a heart of gold.

66

As Miss Roberts left the **classroom** to meet the Reverend George King, who called to see about his son **Albert**, she said, “I do not wish to leave a **monitor**. I am quite sure you will all **behave** well when I am **absent**.”

67

Oysters are **protected** from high waves by living at the **bottom** of small bays. From the first of May to the last of August they lay their eggs. During that time we eat **clams instead** of oysters.

68

When I was down beside the sea,
A **wooden spade** they gave to me
To dig the **sandy** shore.
My holes were **empty** like a cup.
In every hole the sea came up
Till it could come no more.

- Robert Louis Stevenson

69

Last Wednesday when **Jane** came home from the South and called, "**Prince**, come here!" the dog tried to give her both **paws** at once, and showed by his **joyful actions** that he was glad to see her.

70

The **wheels** of the farmer's wagon caught in the mud. In his **trouble** he called for help. He heard a voice say: "Put your **shoulder** to the wheel, and then I may **aid** you. Heaven helps those who help **themselves**."

71

There once lived in **Rome** a lady named **Cornelia**. She was a woman of great **intelligence** and spent all her time in **educating** her two sons, who grew up wise and strong.

72

One day a lady called upon Cornelia and asked to see her **jewels**. Cornelia, instead of showing **rubies** or **diamonds**, sent for her two sons and, when they **approached**, said, "These are my jewels."

73

Everybody who lived near the northern woods tells us that each **season** has its own **beauty**. Would you believe that the **dull** winter colors are as lovely as those of the spring and summer?

74

In July the **Atlantic** Ocean is often so **calm** that it looks like a **mirror**. If you cross in February or March, however, there is a **chance** that you may run into a **blinding** snowstorm.

75

Our teacher, Miss Wild, **refused** to call upon the **pupils** who always guessed the answers. She was most **careful** during the **grammar** and **arithmetic** lessons.

76

"Look! Here's a pretty pigeon house!
In every narrow cell
A **pigeon** with his little wife
And family may **dwell**."

77

The little flower **listened** to the **oriole's** song until she **understood** its **language**. She knew the bird was saying: "**Rejoice**! Rejoice!"

78

Switzerland is a small country in **Europe**. It is **famous** for its high mountains and its many lovely lakes. The Swiss are fond of **freedom**, and for that **reason** love the story of William Tell.

79

Switzerland was once ruled by the **cruel** Gessler. To show the Swiss that they must **obey** him, he placed his hat on a pole in the **public square**, and ordered everyone who passed to bow the **knee**.

80

Several men obeyed. At **length** Tell passed **beneath** the hat, and his friends were **dismayed** to see that he did not even bend his head. Tell said, "Does Gessler **suppose** he can make all the Swiss obey him?"

81

The soldiers near the pole at once **reported** Tell's **conduct** to Gessler, who **directed** Tell to be **brought** before him. Then Gessler said, "You're a very fine **archer**, and you shall have a chance to save your life by your skill."

82

Tell was **informed** that, if he could **shoot** an apple from his son's head, his life would be **spared**. However, if he failed or **injured** his son in any way, he should die **instantly**.

83

Tell **selected** two **arrows**, and after **putting** one in his belt, **aimed** at the apple and cut it in half. Gessler asked why he had selected two arrows. Tell replied, "The second arrow was for you **tyrant**, in case I missed my first shot."

84

My country, 'tis of **thee**,
Sweet land of **liberty**,
Of thee I sing;
Land where my fathers died,
Land of the **pilgrim's** pride,
From every mountain side,
Let freedom ring.
- Samuel F. Smith

85

Those who visited Mrs. Archer saw at once what an **excellent housekeeper** she was. The rooms were clean, the **furniture** was **polished**, and the flowers, books and pictures gave an air of **comfort** to her home.

86

In the fall when many of my **favorite** flowers are **dying**, I think that the woods are pleasanter than the **meadows**. If I find good **company**, I **enjoy** walking until the snow flies.

87

The first snowfall has **arrived**. The children have watched **eagerly** for it. Now they are **anxious** to leave their **cozy** room, and join some boys who are making a snow man on the **sidewalk**.

88

The wind blows a gale, but the boys are so **excited** that their mother has promised to allow them to go out in the **bitter** cold. The **largest** boy is twelve, and he will not find it very **difficult** to care for his brothers.

89

The snow had begun in the **gloaming**,
And **busily** all the night
Had been **heaping** field and **highway**
With a **silence** deep and white.
- James Russell Lowell

90

Did you ever read anything about **Florence Nightingale**? Both her parents were **English**, but as she was born in 1820 in Florence, **Italy**, she was named for the city of her **birth**.

91

When she was a child, she often **pretended** that her dolls had been injured, and she would **nurse** and **bandage** them. She was very fond of animals too, and her first living **patient** was a **shepherd's** dog.

92

From nursing animals, she passed to **human beings**, and her **chief pleasure** was caring for the sick and **suffering**. Her family had a great deal of money, but she did not care for the **enjoyments** of the rich.

93

In 1854 there appeared in the papers long **accounts** of the suffering of the **wounded** soldiers in **eastern** Europe. These men lacked not only **medicines** but the **commonest** things needed by the sick and dying.

94

Florence Nightingale collected a large amount of **hospital supplies**, and with thirty or forty nurses **prepared** to leave England at once. When she reached the Crimea, both **officers** and men gave her a hearty **welcome**.

95

She soon had ten **thousand invalids** under her care and had **general** charge of all the hospitals on the **peninsula**. Her **labors** finally **affected** her health, and she was obliged to return to England.

96

Here she lived for many years and wrote on the **subjects** of light, fresh air, **warmth**, and quiet in **dealing** with the sick. Longfellow has written a **poem** on her **relief** work in the East.

97

In our home we obey the **law** about fire escapes. We know that, if there is an **alarm** of fire and fire escapes are **blocked**, our lives and the lives of people on the **upper floors** may be in danger.

98

A good king of Atri once hung a bell in the market place. He **allowed** any **person** to ring the bell who had been harmed in a way he did not **deserve**. The king told his people to **remember** that he would always **answer** their call.

99

In Atri lived a man who loved his **wealth** more than anything else. He said he did not **intend** to **waste** it feeding useless animals, so his **faithful** old horse was turned out to die. This horse happened to go in the **direction** of the bell.

100

A passing **traveler** had once mended the rope of the bell with a vine growing **against** a neighboring wall. The horse seeing the vines **rapidly** ate them, with the **result** that the bell began to ring. A **group** of people gathered, and for the **honor** of the town forced the owner to care for his horse.

101

The soldiers marched up the avenue in regular **columns**, and were **reviewed** by the mayor. Our **nation** owes a **debt** of **gratitude** to these men who stand ready to give their lives for the **union**.

102

When we go to our country place everyone arrives in an ill **humor**, because the **journey** is a long one and can be made only by a **local** train. This year we **solved** our difficulties by making the trip in an **automobile**.

103

My brother's return home always gives us great **happiness**. This year he wanted to visit a **secret** place in the woods where he played as a boy, so we **borrowed** a big lunch basket and planned a **picnic**. Then the **steady** rain came and stopped our fun.

Math Schedule

Singapore Primary Mathematics 2A & 2B (U.S. Edition)
(Times Media Private Limited, 2003)

NOTE: This schedule is a five day plan. If you want to make it a four day plan instead, two days each week may be combined.

Unit 1:

Day 1: *Textbook 2A* p. 6-8; *Workbook 2A* p. 7-9
Day 2: *Textbook 2A* p. 9; *Workbook 2A* p. 10-11
Day 3: *Textbook 2A* p. 10-11; *Workbook 2A* p. 12-14
Day 4: *Textbook 2A* p. 12
Day 5: *Textbook 2A* p. 13-14; *Workbook 2A* p. 15-16

Unit 2:

Day 1: *Textbook 2A* p. 15-16; *Workbook 2A* p. 17-18
Day 2: *Textbook 2A* p. 17-19; *Workbook 2A* p. 19-21
Day 3: *Workbook 2A* p. 22-23
Day 4: *Textbook 2A* p. 20; *Workbook 2A* p. 24
Day 5: *Textbook 2A* p. 21

Unit 3:

Day 1: *Textbook 2A* p. 22-24 (middle); *Workbook 2A* p. 25
Day 2: *Textbook 2A* p. 24; *Workbook 2A* p. 26-27
Day 3: *Textbook 2A* p. 25-27; *Workbook 2A* p. 28-29
Day 4: *Textbook 2A* p. 28-29 (middle); *Workbook 2A* p. 30
Day 5: *Workbook 2A* p. 31

Unit 4:

Day 1: *Textbook 2A* p. 29-30; *Workbook 2A* p. 32-34
Day 2: *Textbook 2A* p. 31-32 (middle); *Workbook 2A* p. 35-36
Day 3: *Textbook 2A* p. 32-33; *Workbook 2A* p. 37
Day 4: *Workbook 2A* p. 38-39
Day 5: *Workbook 2A* Choose **either** p. 34 **or** p. 35

Unit 5:

Day 1: *Textbook 2A* p. 36-37 (middle); *Workbook 2A* p. 40-41
Day 2: *Textbook 2A* p. 37-38 (numbers 3-7); *Workbook 2A* p. 42-43
Day 3: *Textbook 2A* p. 38 (numbers 8-10) - p. 39; *Workbook 2A* p. 44-45
Day 4: *Textbook 2A* p. 39-40; *Workbook 2A* p. 46
Day 5: *Workbook 2A* p. 47-48

Math Schedule
Singapore Primary Mathematics 2A & 2B (U.S. Edition)
(Times Media Private Limited, 2003)

Unit 6:
Day 1: *Workbook 2A* p. 49-50
Day 2: *Textbook 2A* Choose **either** p. 41 **or** p. 42
Day 3: *Textbook 2A* p. 43-44; *Workbook 2A* p. 51
Day 4: *Textbook 2A* p. 45; *Workbook 2A* p. 52-53
Day 5: *Textbook 2A* p. 46 (top); *Workbook 2A* p. 54-55

Unit 7:
Day 1: *Textbook 2A* p. 46-47 (middle); *Workbook 2A* p. 56-58
Day 2: *Textbook 2A* p. 47 (numbers 15-16); *Workbook 2A* p. 59-60
Day 3: *Workbook 2A* p. 61-62
Day 4: *Textbook 2A* Choose **either** p. 48 **or** p. 49
Day 5: *Workbook 2A* p. 63-66

Unit 8:
Day 1: *Textbook 2A* Choose **either** p. 50 **or** p. 51
Day 2: *Textbook 2A* p. 52-54; *Workbook 2A* p. 67
Day 3: *Textbook 2A* p. 55-56; *Workbook 2A* p. 68-71
Day 4: *Textbook 2A* p. 57-58; *Workbook 2A* p. 72-73
Day 5: *Textbook 2A* p. 59-62; *Workbook 2A* p. 74

Unit 9:
Day 1: *Workbook 2A* p. 75-78
Day 2: *Textbook 2A* p. 63
Day 3: *Textbook 2A* p. 64-67; *Workbook 2A* p. 79-80
Day 4: *Textbook 2A* p. 68-69; *Workbook 2A* p. 81-82
Day 5: *Workbook 2A* p. 83 and 85

Unit 10:
Day 1: *Workbook 2A* p. 84 and 86
Day 2: *Workbook 2A* p. 87-90
Day 3: *Textbook 2A* p. 70-73
Day 4: *Textbook 2A* Choose **either** p. 74 **or** p. 75
Day 5: *Textbook 2A* p. 76-77; *Workbook 2A* p. 91-92

Unit 11:
Day 1: *Textbook 2A* p. 78 (top); *Workbook 2A* p. 93-96
Day 2: *Textbook 2A* p. 78 (bottom); *Workbook 2A* p. 97-98
Day 3: *Textbook 2A* p. 79-82; *Workbook 2A* p. 99-102
Day 4: *Textbook 2A* p. 83-84; *Workbook 2A* p. 103-106
Day 5: *Textbook 2A* p. 85; *Workbook 2A* p. 107-109

Math Schedule
Singapore Primary Mathematics 2A & 2B (U.S. Edition)
(Times Media Private Limited, 2003)

Unit 12:
Day 1: *Workbook 2A* p. 110-111
Day 2: *Workbook 2A* p. 112-113
Day 3: *Textbook 2A* p. 86-87
Day 4: *Textbook 2A* p. 88-89; *Workbook 2A* p. 114-117
Day 5: *Textbook 2A* p. 90 (top); *Workbook 2A* p. 118-119

Unit 13:
Day 1: *Textbook 2A* p. 90 (bottom); *Workbook 2A* p. 120-121
Day 2: *Textbook 2A* p. 91 (top); *Workbook 2A* p. 122
Day 3: *Workbook 2A* p. 123-124
Day 4: *Workbook 2A* p. 125-126
Day 5: *Textbook 2A* p. 91-92; *Workbook 2A* p. 127-128

Unit 14:
Day 1: *Textbook 2A* p. 93
Day 2: *Textbook 2A* p. 94-95; *Workbook 2A* p. 129-131
Day 3: *Workbook 2A* p. 132-133
Day 4: *Textbook 2A* p. 96 (top); *Workbook 2A* p. 134-135
Day 5: *Textbook 2A* p. 96 (bottom); *Workbook 2A* p. 136-137

Unit 15:
Day 1: *Textbook 2A* p. 97 (number 5); *Workbook 2A* p. 138-139
Day 2: *Textbook 2A* p. 97 (number 6); *Workbook 2A* p. 140-141
Day 3: *Textbook 2A* p. 97 (number 7); *Workbook 2A* p. 142-144
Day 4: *Workbook 2A* p. 145-147
Day 5: *Textbook 2A* Choose **either** p. 98 **or** p. 99

Unit 16:
Day 1: *Textbook 2A* p. 100-101; *Workbook 2A* p. 148-149
Day 2: *Textbook 2A* p. 102-103; *Workbook 2A* p. 150-151
Day 3: *Textbook 2A* p. 104
Day 4: *Textbook 2A* p. 105; *Workbook 2A* p. 152-153
Day 5: *Textbook 2A* p. 106; *Workbook 2A* p. 154-156

Unit 17:
Day 1: *Workbook 2A* p. 157-159
Day 2: *Workbook 2A* p. 160-162
Day 3: *Textbook 2A* Choose **either** p. 107 **or** p. 108
Day 4: *Workbook 2A* p. 163-165
Day 5: *Workbook 2A* p. 166-168

Math Schedule
Singapore Primary Mathematics 2A & 2B (U.S. Edition)
(Times Media Private Limited, 2003)

Unit 18:

Day 1: *Textbook 2A* Choose **either** p. 109-110 **or** p. 111-112
Day 2: *Workbook 2A* p. 169-171
Day 3: *Workbook 2A* p. 172-174
Day 4: *Textbook 2B* p. 6-middle of 9; *Workbook 2B* p. 7-8
Day 5: *Textbook 2B* p. 9-10; *Workbook 2B* p. 9-10

Unit 19:

Day 1: *Textbook 2B* p. 11
Day 2: *Textbook 2B* p. 12-13 (top); *Workbook 2B* p. 11
Day 3: *Workbook 2B* p. 12
Day 4: *Textbook 2B* p. 13 (middle); *Workbook 2B* p. 13
Day 5: *Workbook 2B* p. 14

Unit 20:

Day 1: *Textbook 2B* p. 13 (bottom); *Workbook 2B* p. 15
Day 2: *Textbook 2B* p. 14 (top); *Workbook 2B* p. 16
Day 3: *Textbook 2B* p. 14 (bottom); *Workbook 2B* p. 17
Day 4: *Textbook 2B* p. 15-16 (top); *Workbook 2B* p. 18-19
Day 5: *Textbook 2B* p. 16 (middle); *Workbook 2B* p. 20

Unit 21:

Day 1: *Workbook 2B* p. 21
Day 2: *Textbook 2B* p. 16 (bottom); *Workbook 2B* p. 22-23
Day 3: *Textbook 2B* p. 17 (top); *Workbook 2B* p. 24
Day 4: *Textbook 2B* p. 17 (bottom); *Workbook 2B* p. 25
Day 5: *Textbook 2B* Choose **either** p. 18 **or** p. 19

Unit 22:

Day 1: *Workbook 2B* p. 26-29
Day 2: *Textbook 2B* p. 20-21; *Workbook 2B* p. 30-33
Day 3: *Textbook 2B* p. 22-23 (top); *Workbook 2B* p. 34-35
Day 4: *Workbook 2B* p. 36-39
Day 5: *Textbook 2B* p. 23-24; *Workbook 2B* p. 40-42

Unit 23:

Day 1: *Textbook 2B* p. 25
Day 2: *Textbook 2B* p. 26-27 (top); *Workbook 2B* p. 43
Day 3: *Textbook 2B* p. 27 (bottom); *Workbook 2B* p. 44-45
Day 4: *Textbook 2B* p. 28; *Workbook 2B* p. 46-48
Day 5: *Textbook 2B* p. 29

Math Schedule
Singapore Primary Mathematics 2A & 2B (U.S. Edition)
(Times Media Private Limited, 2003)

Unit 24:
Day 1: *Textbook 2B* p. 30-31 (top); *Workbook 2B* p. 49-51
Day 2: *Textbook 2B* p. 31 (bottom); *Workbook 2B* p. 52-54
Day 3: *Textbook 2B* Choose **either** p. 32 **or** p. 33 **or** p. 34
Day 4: *Textbook 2B* Choose **either** p. 35 **or** *Workbook 2B p. 55-58*
Day 5: *Textbook 2B* p. 36-38; *Workbook 2B* p. 59-61

Unit 25:
Day 1: *Textbook 2B* p. 38 (number 3); *Workbook 2B* p. 62-63
Day 2: *Workbook 2B* p. 64-65
Day 3: *Textbook 2B* p. 38 (numbers 4-5) and p. 39; *Workbook 2B* p. 66-67
Day 4: *Textbook 2B* p. 40; *Workbook 2B* p. 68-69
Day 5: *Workbook 2B* p. 70-72

Unit 26:
Day 1: *Textbook 2B* p. 41
Day 2: *Textbook 2B* p. 42-43 (top); *Workbook 2B* p. 73
Day 3: *Textbook 2B* p. 43 (bottom); *Workbook 2B* p. 74
Day 4: *Textbook 2B* p. 44; *Workbook 2B* p. 75-76
Day 5: *Textbook 2B* p. 45-47 (top); *Workbook 2B* p. 77

Unit 27:
Day 1: *Textbook 2B* p. 47 (bottom); *Workbook 2B* p. 78
Day 2: *Textbook 2B* p. 48 (numbers 6-8); *Workbook 2B* p. 79-80
Day 3: *Textbook 2B* p. 49; *Workbook 2B* p. 81-82
Day 4: *Textbook 2B* Choose **either** p. 50 **or** p. 51
Day 5: *Workbook 2B* p. 83-86

Unit 28:
Day 1: *Workbook 2B* p. 87-90
Day 2: *Textbook 2B* p. 52-53; *Workbook 2B* p. 91-92
Day 3: *Textbook 2B* p. 54-55; *Workbook 2B* p. 93-94
Day 4: *Textbook 2B* p. 56; *Workbook 2B* p. 95-98
Day 5: *Textbook 2B* p. 57 (top); *Workbook 2B* p. 99-101

Unit 29:
Day 1: *Textbook 2B* p. 57 (bottom); *Workbook 2B* p. 102-103
Day 2: *Textbook 2B* Choose **either** p. 58 **or** p. 59
Day 3: *Textbook 2B* p. 60-62; *Workbook 2B* p. 104-107
Day 4: *Textbook 2B* p. 63; *Workbook 2B* p. 108-110
Day 5: *Textbook 2B* p. 64-67 (top); *Workbook 2B* p. 111-114

Math Schedule
Singapore Primary Mathematics 2A & 2B (U.S. Edition)
(Times Media Private Limited, 2003)

Unit 30:

Day 1: *Textbook 2B* p. 67 (numbers 5-6); *Workbook 2B* p. 115-116
Day 2: *Textbook 2B* Choose **either** p. 68 **or** p. 69
Day 3: *Workbook 2B* p. 117-120
Day 4: *Textbook 2B* p. 70-71; *Workbook 2B* p. 121-125
Day 5: *Textbook 2B* p. 72-75; *Workbook 2B* p. 126-128

Unit 31:

Day 1: *Textbook 2B* p. 76
Day 2: *Textbook 2B* p. 77-80; *Workbook 2B* p. 129-130
Day 3: *Textbook 2B* p. 81
Day 4: *Textbook 2B* p. 82-85; *Workbook 2B* p. 131-134
Day 5: *Textbook 2B* p. 86; *Workbook 2B* p. 135-136

Unit 32:

Day 1: *Textbook 2B* p. 87; *Workbook 2B* p.137-138
Day 2: *Textbook 2B* Choose **either** p. 88 **or** p. 89
Day 3: *Textbook 2B* p. 90-92; *Workbook 2B* p. 139-142
Day 4: *Textbook 2B* p. 93-94; *Workbook 2B* p. 143-145
Day 5: *Textbook 2B* p. 95-97; *Workbook 2B* p. 146-149

Unit 33:

Day 1: *Textbook 2B* p. 98-99; *Workbook 2B* p. 150-151
Day 2: *Textbook 2B* p.100-101
Day 3: *Workbook 2B* p. 152-155
Day 4: *Textbook 2B* p. 102-104; *Workbook 2B* p. 156-158
Day 5: *Textbook 2B* p. 105; *Workbook 2B* p. 159-160

Unit 34:

Day 1: *Workbook 2B* p. 161-162
Day 2: *Textbook 2B* p. 106-108
Day 3: *Workbook 2B* p. 163-168
Day 4: *Workbook 2B* p. 169-172
Day 5: *Textbook 2B* Choose **either** p. 109-112 **or** *Workbook 2B* p. 173-176

Math Schedule

Singapore Primary Mathematics 3A & 3B (U.S. Edition)
(Times Media Private Limited, 2003)

NOTE: This schedule is a five day plan. If you want to make it a four day plan instead, two days each week may be combined.

Unit 1:

Day 1: *Textbook 3A* p. 6-8; *Workbook 3A* p. 7-9
Day 2: *Textbook 3A* p. 9; *Workbook 3A* p. 10-11
Day 3: *Textbook 3A* p. 10-11; *Workbook 3A* p. 12-13
Day 4: *Textbook 3A* p. 12
Day 5: *Textbook 3A* p. 13

Unit 2:

Day 1: *Textbook 3A* p. 14-15; *Workbook 3A* p. 14-15
Day 2: *Textbook 3A* p. 16; *Workbook 3A* p. 16
Day 3: *Textbook 3A* p. 17
Day 4: *Textbook 3A* p. 18-19; *Workbook 3A* p. 17-18
Day 5: *Textbook 3A* p. 20 – top of p. 21; *Workbook 3A* p. 19-21

Unit 3:

Day 1: *Textbook 3A* bottom of p. 21; *Workbook 3A* p. 22-24
Day 2: *Textbook 3A* Choose **either** p. 22 **or** p. 23
Day 3: *Textbook 3A* p. 24 – top of p. 26; *Workbook 3A* p. 25-27
Day 4: *Textbook 3A* bottom of p. 26 – p. 27; *Workbook 3A* p. 28-29
Day 5: *Textbook 3A* p. 28-29; *Workbook 3A* p. 31-32

Unit 4:

Day 1: *Textbook 3A* p. 30-31; *Workbook 3A* p. 33
Day 2: *Textbook 3A* p. 32-33; *Workbook 3A* p. 34-35
Day 3: *Textbook 3A* Choose **either** p. 34 **or** p. 35
Day 4: *Textbook 3A* p. 36-37; *Workbook 3A* p. 36-38
Day 5: *Workbook 3A* p. 39-42

Unit 5:

Day 1: *Textbook 3A* p. 38
Day 2: *Textbook 3A* p. 39 – top of p. 40; *Workbook 3A* p. 43-46
Day 3: *Textbook 3A* bottom of p. 40-41; *Workbook 3A* p. 47-49
Day 4: *Workbook 3A* p. 50-51
Day 5: *Textbook 3A* p. 42; *Workbook 3A* p. 52-53

Math Schedule
Singapore Primary Mathematics 3A & 3B (U.S. Edition)
(Times Media Private Limited, 2003)

Unit 6:

Day 1: *Textbook 3A* p. 43
Day 2: *Textbook 3A* p. 44-45; *Workbook 3A* p. 54-56
Day 3: *Textbook 3A* p. 46; *Workbook 3A* p. 57-58
Day 4: *Textbook 3A* Choose **either** p. 47 **or** p. 48
Day 5: *Textbook 3A* p. 49 – top of p. 50; *Workbook 3A* p. 59-60

Unit 7:

Day 1: *Textbook 3A* bottom of p. 50 – top of p. 51; *Workbook 3A* p. 61-63
Day 2: *Textbook 3A* bottom of p. 51 – p. 52; *Workbook 3A* p. 64-65
Day 3: *Textbook 3A* p. 53; *Workbook 3A* p. 66-68
Day 4: *Textbook 3A* Choose **either** p. 54 **or** p. 55
Day 5: *Textbook 3A* p. 56

Unit 8:

Day 1: *Textbook 3A* p. 57 – top of p. 60; *Workbook 3A* p. 69
Day 2: *Textbook 3A* bottom of p. 60; *Workbook 3A* p. 70
Day 3: *Workbook 3A* p. 71-74
Day 4: *Workbook 3A* p. 75-78
Day 5: *Textbook 3A* p. 61-63; *Workbook 3A* p. 79-80

Unit 9:

Day 1: *Textbook 3A* p. 64; *Workbook 3A* p. 81-82
Day 2: *Textbook 3A* Choose **either** p. 65 **or** p. 66
Day 3: *Textbook 3A* p. 67
Day 4: *Textbook 3A* p. 68; *Workbook 3A* p. 83 – top of p. 84
Day 5: *Textbook 3A* p. 69; *Workbook 3A* bottom of p. 84 - 85

Unit 10:

Day 1: *Textbook 3A* p. 70 – top of p. 73; *Workbook 3A* p. 86-87
Day 2: *Textbook 3A* bottom of p. 73; *Workbook 3A* p. 88-89
Day 3: *Textbook 3A* top of p. 74; *Workbook 3A* p. 90-91
Day 4: *Textbook 3A* bottom of p. 74; *Workbook 3A* p. 92, 94
Day 5: *Workbook 3A* p. 93, 95-96

Math Schedule
Singapore Primary Mathematics 3A & 3B (U.S. Edition)
(Times Media Private Limited, 2003)

Unit 11:

Day 1: *Textbook 3A* p. 75
Day 2: *Textbook 3A* p. 76 – top of p. 78; *Workbook 3A* p. 97-98
Day 3: *Textbook 3A* bottom of p. 78 – number 4 on p. 79; *Workbook 3A* p. 99-100
Day 4: *Textbook 3A* numbers 5 and 6 on p. 79; *Workbook 3A* p. 101-102, 104
Day 5: *Textbook 3A* numbers 7 and 8 on p. 79; *Workbook 3A* p. 103, 105-106

Unit 12:

Day 1: *Textbook 3A* Choose **either** p. 80 **or** p. 81
Day 2: *Workbook 3A* p. 107-110
Day 3: *Textbook 3A* p. 82 – numbers 1 & 2 on p. 83; *Workbook 3A* p. 111-112
Day 4: *Textbook 3A* numbers 3 & 4 on p. 83; *Workbook 3A* p. 113-114, 117
Day 5: *Textbook 3A* number 5 on p. 83; *Workbook 3A* p. 115-116, 118-119

Unit 13:

Day 1: *Textbook 3A* p. 84
Day 2: *Textbook 3A* p. 85
Day 3: *Textbook 3A* p. 86-87; *Workbook 3A* p. 120
Day 4: *Textbook 3A* numbers 3-5 on p. 88; *Workbook 3A* p. 121
Day 5: *Textbook 3A* number 6 on p. 88; *Workbook 3A* p. 122-123

Unit 14:

Day 1: *Textbook 3A* number 7 on p. 88; *Workbook 3A* p. 124-125
Day 2: *Workbook 3A* p. 126-128
Day 3: *Textbook 3A* p. 89
Day 4: *Textbook 3A* p. 90
Day 5: *Textbook 3A* number 6 on p. 91-92; *Workbook 3A* p. 129-130

Unit 15:

Day 1: *Textbook 3A* p. 93
Day 2: *Textbook 3A* p. 94-95; *Workbook 3A* p. 131-132
Day 3: *Textbook 3A* p. 96-97; *Workbook 3A* p. 133-135
Day 4: *Textbook 3A* p. 98-99; *Workbook 3A* p. 136-137
Day 5: *Textbook 3A* p. 100; *Workbook 3A* p. 138-139

Math Schedule

Singapore Primary Mathematics 3A & 3B (U.S. Edition)
(Times Media Private Limited, 2003)

Unit 16:

Day 1: *Textbook 3A* p. 101; *Workbook 3A* p. 140-142
Day 2: *Textbook 3A* Choose **either** p. 102 **or** p. 103
Day 3: *Workbook 3A* p. 143-146
Day 4: *Textbook 3A* p. 104
Day 5: *Workbook 3A* p. 147-150

Unit 17:

Day 1: *Textbook 3B* p. 6 – top of p. 7; *Workbook 3B* p. 7
Day 2: *Textbook 3B* bottom of p. 7; *Workbook 3B* p. 8-9
Day 3: *Textbook 3B* p. 8-9; *Workbook 3B* p. 10-11
Day 4: *Textbook 3B* p. 10; *Workbook 3B* p. 12-13
Day 5: *Textbook 3B* p. 11; *Workbook 3B* p. 14-15

Unit 18:

Day 1: *Textbook 3B* p. 12
Day 2: *Textbook 3B* p. 13
Day 3: *Textbook 3B* p. 14-16; *Workbook 3B* p. 16-17
Day 4: *Textbook 3B* p. 17; *Workbook 3B* p. 18-19
Day 5: *Textbook 3B* p. 18

Unit 19:

Day 1: *Textbook 3B* p. 19 – number 1 on p. 20; *Workbook 3B* p. 20-21
Day 2: *Textbook 3B* number 2 on p. 20 – p. 21; *Workbook 3B* p. 22-23
Day 3: *Textbook 3B* p. 22; *Workbook 3B* p. 24-26
Day 4: *Textbook 3B* p. 23
Day 5: *Textbook 3B* p. 24-25; *Workbook 3B* p. 27-28

Unit 20:

Day 1: *Textbook 3B* p. 26-27; *Workbook 3B* p. 29-30
Day 2: *Textbook 3B* p. 28
Day 3: *Textbook 3B* p. 29-30; *Workbook 3B* p. 31-32
Day 4: *Textbook 3B* p. 31; *Workbook 3B* p. 33-35
Day 5: *Workbook 3B* p. 36-37

Math Schedule
Singapore Primary Mathematics 3A & 3B (U.S. Edition)
(Times Media Private Limited, 2003)

Unit 21:

Day 1: *Textbook 3B* p. 32; *Workbook 3B* p. 38-39
Day 2: *Textbook 3B* p. 33
Day 3: *Textbook 3B* p. 34-35; *Workbook 3B* p. 40-41
Day 4: *Textbook 3B* p. 36-37; *Workbook 3B* p. 42
Day 5: *Textbook 3B* p. 38

Unit 22:

Day 1: *Textbook 3B* p. 39-41; *Workbook 3B* p. 43-44
Day 2: *Textbook 3B* p. 42
Day 3: *Workbook 3B* p. 45-48
Day 4: *Textbook 3B* p. 43
Day 5: *Workbook 3B* p. 49-52

Unit 23:

Day 1: *Textbook 3B* p. 44
Day 2: *Textbook 3B* p. 45-46; *Workbook 3B* p. 53-54
Day 3: *Textbook 3B* p. 47; *Workbook 3B* p. 55-56
Day 4: *Textbook 3B* number 5 on p. 48; *Workbook 3B* p. 57-58
Day 5: *Textbook 3B* numbers 6 – 9 on p. 48; *Workbook 3B* p. 59-60

Unit 24:

Day 1: *Textbook 3B* p. 49; *Workbook 3B* p. 61-62
Day 2: *Textbook 3B* p. 50; *Workbook 3B* p. 63-66
Day 3: *Textbook 3B* p. 51
Day 4: *Textbook 3B* p. 52
Day 5: *Textbook 3B* p. 53-55; *Workbook 3B* p. 67-68

Unit 25:

Day 1: *Textbook 3B* p. 56
Day 2: *Textbook 3B* p. 57
Day 3: *Textbook 3B* p. 58-61; *Workbook 3B* p. 69-71
Day 4: *Textbook 3B* p. 62-63; *Workbook 3B* p. 72-74
Day 5: *Workbook 3B* p. 75-78

Unit 26:

Day 1: *Workbook 3B* p. 79-80
Day 2: *Workbook 3B* p. 81-82
Day 3: *Textbook 3B* p. 64; *Workbook 3B* p. 83-84
Day 4: *Textbook 3B* p. 65-66; *Workbook 3B* p. 85-86
Day 5: *Workbook 3B* p. 87-88

Math Schedule
Singapore Primary Mathematics 3A & 3B (U.S. Edition)
(Times Media Private Limited, 2003)

Unit 27:
Day 1: *Textbook 3B* p. 67; *Workbook 3B* p. 89, 91
Day 2: *Textbook 3B* p. 68; *Workbook 3B* p. 90, 92
Day 3: *Textbook 3B* p. 69
Day 4: *Textbook 3B* p. 70-71; *Workbook 3B* p. 93-94
Day 5: *Textbook 3B* p. 72; *Workbook 3B* p. 95-96

Unit 28:
Day 1: *Textbook 3B* numbers 4 and 5 on p. 73; *Workbook 3B* p. 97-98
Day 2: *Textbook 3B* number 6 on p. 73 – number 7 on p. 74; *Workbook 3B* p. 99-100
Day 3: *Textbook 3B* numbers 8 – 12 on p. 74; *Workbook 3B* p. 101
Day 4: *Textbook 3B* p. 75
Day 5: *Workbook 3B* p. 102-105

Unit 29:
Day 1: *Textbook 3B* p. 76-77
Day 2: *Workbook 3B* p. 106-108
Day 3: *Textbook 3B* p. 78-79; *Workbook 3B* p. 109-110
Day 4: *Textbook 3B* p. 80-81; *Workbook 3B* p. 111-112
Day 5: *Textbook 3B* p. 82; *Workbook 3B* p. 113-114

Unit 30:
Day 1: *Textbook 3B* p. 83-84; *Workbook 3B* p. 115-116
Day 2: *Textbook 3B* p. 85; *Workbook 3B* p. 117-118
Day 3: *Textbook 3B* p. 86
Day 4: *Textbook 3B* p. 87; *Workbook 3B* p. 119-120
Day 5: *Textbook 3B* number 2 on p. 88; *Workbook 3B* p. 121-123

Unit 31:
Day 1: *Textbook 3B* number 3 on p. 88; *Workbook 3B* p. 124-125
Day 2: *Textbook 3B* number 4 on p. 88; *Workbook 3B* p. 126-127
Day 3: *Textbook 3B* p. 89
Day 4: *Workbook 3B* p. 128-129
Day 5: *Textbook 3B* p. 90-91

Math Schedule
Singapore Primary Mathematics 3A & 3B (U.S. Edition)
(Times Media Private Limited, 2003)

Unit 32:

Day 1: *Textbook 3B* p. 92-93; *Workbook 3B* p. 130
Day 2: *Textbook 3B* p. 94-95; *Workbook 3B* p. 131-133
Day 3: *Textbook 3B* p. 96-97; *Workbook 3B* p. 134-135
Day 4: *Textbook 3B* p. 98-99; *Workbook 3B* p. 136-137
Day 5: *Textbook 3B* p. 100; *Workbook 3B* p. 138

Unit 33:

Day 1: *Textbook 3B* p. 101-102; *Workbook 3B* p. 139
Day 2: *Textbook 3B* p. 103-104; *Workbook 3B* p. 140-141
Day 3: *Textbook 3B* p. 105; *Workbook 3B* p. 142-143
Day 4: *Textbook 3B* p. 106; *Workbook 3B* p. 144-145
Day 5: *Textbook 3B* p. 107

Unit 34:

Day 1: *Workbook 3B* p. 146-147
Day 2: *Workbook 3B* p. 148-149
Day 3: *Textbook 3B* p. 108-109
Day 4: *Workbook 3B* p. 150-152
Day 5: *Textbook 3B* p. 110-112

Math Schedule

Singapore Primary Mathematics 4A & 4B (U.S. Edition)
(Times Media Private Limited, 2003)

NOTE: This schedule is written to coincide with the **four** day a week plan used in *Preparing Hearts for His Glory*. If you find you need to use the fifth day for math, you can easily do so by spreading out this schedule. When using this plan, remember that the "Textbook" pages are meant to be used as a teaching tool with your child. We highly recommend that, as much as possible, the Textbook portion be done together with your child on a markerboard with markers. This will help your child understand that each math lesson has 2 parts; the Textbook portion completed with your teaching and assistance, and the Workbook portion completed independently. On days that there is only a Textbook portion assigned, part of it can be done on markerboard and part of it can be done on notebook paper.

Each "Textbook" page has segments of skills on each day. Once your child has shown proficiency with a skill in the Textbook portion, simply move on to the next segment of skills on that day – there is no need to do all of the problems in each Textbook segment if the child already shows a good understanding of that type of problem. The workbook portion will adequately reinforce the textbook portion and provide enough practice with each skill. If you wish to give the end-of-the-year review, plan an extra week at the end of this schedule to do so. Time is not allotted for the end-of-the-year review in this schedule.

Unit 1:

- Day 1: *Textbook 4A* p. 6-8; *Workbook 4A* p. 7-8
- Day 2: *Textbook 4A* p. 9; *Workbook 4A* p. 9-10
- Day 3: *Textbook 4A* p. 10 – numbers 8 and 9 on p. 11; *Workbook 4A* p. 11
- Day 4: *Textbook 4A* number 10 on p. 11; *Workbook 4A* p. 12-13

Unit 2:

- Day 1: *Textbook 4A* p. 12-14; *Workbook 4A* p. 14-15
- Day 2: *Textbook 4A* p. 15-16; *Workbook 4A* p. 16-17
- Day 3: *Textbook 4A* p. 17; *Workbook 4A* p. 18-19
- Day 4: *Textbook 4A* p. 18

Unit 3:

- Day 1: *Textbook 4A* p. 19-20; *Workbook 4A* p. 20-21
- Day 2: *Textbook 4A* p. 21-22; *Workbook 4A* p. 22-23
- Day 3: *Textbook 4A* p. 23-26; *Workbook 4A* p. 24-25
- Day 4: *Textbook 4A* p. 27

Math Schedule
Singapore Primary Mathematics 4A & 4B (U.S. Edition)
(Times Media Private Limited, 2003)

Unit 4:

Day 1: *Textbook 4A* p. 28-30; *Workbook 4A* p. 26
Day 2: *Textbook 4A* p. 31-32; *Workbook 4A* p. 27-28
Day 3: *Textbook 4A* p. 33-34; *Workbook 4A* p. 29-30
Day 4: *Textbook 4A* p. 35

Unit 5:

Day 1: *Textbook 4A* p. 36-37 and number 4 on p. 38; *Workbook 4A* p. 31
Day 2: *Textbook 4A* numbers 5 and 6 on p. 38 – p. 39; *Workbook 4A* p. 32-34
Day 3: *Workbook 4A* p. 35-36
Day 4: *Textbook 4A* p. 40

Unit 6:

Day 1: Choose **either** *Textbook 4A* p. 41 **or** *Workbook 4A* p. 37-38
Day 2: *Textbook 4A* p. 42-43; *Workbook 4A* p. 39-41
Day 3: *Textbook 4A* p. 44-45; *Workbook 4A* p. 42-43
Day 4: *Textbook 4A* p. 46-47; *Workbook 4A* p. 44-46

Unit 7:

Day 1: *Textbook 4A* p. 48-49; *Workbook 4A* p. 47-50
Day 2: Choose **either** *Textbook 4A* p. 50 **or** *Textbook 4A* p. 51
Day 3: *Textbook 4A* p. 52-53; *Workbook 4A* p. 51-52
Day 4: *Textbook 4A* p. 54-55; *Workbook 4A* p. 53-54

Unit 8:

Day 1: *Textbook 4A* numbers 3, 4, and 5 on p. 56; *Workbook 4A* p. 55-56
Day 2: *Textbook 4A* number 6 on p. 56 – numbers 7, 8, and 9 on p. 57; *Workbook 4A* p. 57-59
Day 3: *Textbook 4A* numbers 10, 11, and 12 on p. 57; *Workbook 4A* p. 60-61
Day 4: *Workbook 4A* p. 62, 64

Unit 9:

Day 1: *Workbook 4A* p. 63, 65-66
Day 2: *Textbook 4A* p. 58 – number 1 on p. 59; *Workbook 4A* p. 67-68
Day 3: *Textbook 4A* numbers 2 and 3 on p. 59 – number 4 on p. 60; *Workbook 4A* p. 69-70
Day 4: *Workbook 4A* p. 71-72

Math Schedule
Singapore Primary Mathematics 4A & 4B (U.S. Edition)
(Times Media Private Limited, 2003)

Unit 10:

Day 1: *Textbook 4A* numbers 5 and 6 on p. 60; *Workbook 4A* p. 73-75
Day 2: *Textbook 4A* number 7 on p. 61; *Workbook 4A* p. 76-78
Day 3: *Textbook 4A* number 8 on p. 61 – numbers 9 and 10 on p. 62; *Workbook 4A* p. 79-80
Day 4: *Textbook 4A* number 11 on p. 62; *Workbook 4A* p. 81-83

Unit 11:

Day 1: *Textbook 4A* p. 63-64; *Workbook 4A* p. 84-87
Day 2: *Textbook 4A* p. 65
Day 3: Choose **either** *Textbook 4A* p. 66-67 **or** *Workbook 4A* p. 88-89
Day 4: Choose **either** *Textbook 4A* p. 68-69 **or** *Workbook 4A* p. 90-91

Unit 12:

Day 1: *Textbook 4A* p. 70-71; *Workbook 4A* p. 92-93
Day 2: *Textbook 4A* p. 72; *Workbook 4A* p. 94-95
Day 3: *Workbook 4A* p. 96-97
Day 4: *Textbook 4A* p. 73; *Workbook 4A* p. 98-100

Unit 13:

Day 1: *Workbook 4A* p. 101-102
Day 2: *Textbook 4A* p. 74 – number 1 on p. 75; *Workbook 4A* p. 103-105
Day 3: *Textbook 4A* numbers 2 and 3 on p. 75; *Workbook 4A* p. 106-109
Day 4: *Textbook 4A* p. 76 – numbers 6, 7, and 8 on p. 77; *Workbook 4A* p. 110-113

Unit 14:

Day 1: *Textbook 4A* number 9 on p. 77; *Workbook 4A* p. 114
Day 2: *Textbook 4A* p. 78-79; *Workbook 4A* p. 115-116
Day 3: *Textbook 4A* p. 80; *Workbook 4A* p. 117-118
Day 4: *Textbook 4A* p. 81-82; *Workbook 4A* p. 119-120

Unit 15:

Day 1: *Textbook 4A* p. 83; *Workbook 4A* p. 121-122
Day 2: *Textbook 4A* p. 84-86; *Workbook 4A* p. 123-124
Day 3: *Textbook 4A* p. 87-88; *Workbook 4A* p. 125-126
Day 4: *Textbook 4A* p. 89; *Workbook 4A* p. 127

Math Schedule

Singapore Primary Mathematics 4A & 4B (U.S. Edition)
(Times Media Private Limited, 2003)

Unit 16:

Day 1: *Textbook 4A* p. 90; *Workbook 4A* p. 128-129
Day 2: *Textbook 4A* p. 91-93
Day 3: *Textbook 4A* p. 94-96
Day 4: *Workbook 4A* p. 130-134

Unit 17:

Day 1: *Textbook 4B* p. 6-8; *Workbook 4B* p. 7-9
Day 2: *Textbook 4B* p. 9; *Workbook 4B* p. 10-11
Day 3: *Textbook 4B* p. 10; *Workbook 4B* p. 12-13
Day 4: *Textbook 4B* p. 11; *Workbook 4B* p. 14-15

Unit 18:

Day 1: *Textbook 4B* p. 12-14; *Workbook 4B* p. 16-18
Day 2: *Textbook 4B* p. 15-16; *Workbook 4B* p. 19-20
Day 3: *Textbook 4B* p. 17; *Workbook 4B* p. 21-22
Day 4: *Workbook 4B* p. 23-24

Unit 19:

Day 1: *Textbook 4B* p. 18 – numbers 16 and 17 on p. 19; *Workbook 4B* p. 25-26
Day 2: *Textbook 4B* numbers 18 through 23 on p. 19; *Workbook 4B* p. 27-28
Day 3: *Textbook 4B* p. 20 – numbers 2, 3, and 4 on p. 21; *Workbook 4B* p. 29-30
Day 4: *Textbook 4B* numbers 5 and 6 on p. 21; *Workbook 4B* p. 31

Unit 20:

Day 1: *Textbook 4B* p. 22; *Workbook 4B* p. 32-33
Day 2: *Textbook 4B* p. 23
Day 3: *Textbook 4B* p. 24
Day 4: *Textbook 4B* p. 25 – number 4 on p. 27; *Workbook 4B* p. 34-35

Unit 21:

Day 1: *Textbook 4B* numbers 5, 6, and 7 on p. 27; *Workbook 4B* p. 36
Day 2: *Textbook 4B* p. 28 – numbers 9, 10, and 11 on p. 29
Day 3: *Workbook 4B* p. 37 – numbers 9 through 14 on p. 38
Day 4: *Textbook 4B* numbers 12 through 15 on p. 29 – p. 30

Math Schedule

Singapore Primary Mathematics 4A & 4B (U.S. Edition)
(Times Media Private Limited, 2003)

Unit 22:

Day 1: *Workbook 4B* numbers 15 and 16 on p. 38 and p. 39, 40, and 41
Day 2: *Workbook 4B* p. 42-43
Day 3: *Workbook 4B* p. 44-46
Day 4: *Workbook 4B* p. 47-48

Unit 23:

Day 1: *Workbook 4B* p. 49-51
Day 2: *Textbook 4B* p. 31 – number 4 on p. 33; *Workbook 4B* p. 52
Day 3: *Textbook 4B* numbers 5, 6, and 7 on p. 33; *Workbook 4B* p. 53
Day 4: *Textbook 4B* p. 34 – numbers 11 and 12 on p. 35; *Workbook 4B* p. 54-55

Unit 24:

Day 1: *Textbook 4B* numbers 13 and 14 on p. 35; *Workbook 4B* p. 56
Day 2: *Textbook 4B* p. 36; *Workbook 4B* p. 57
Day 3: *Textbook 4B* p. 37 – numbers 21 and 22 on p. 38; *Workbook 4B* p. 58-59
Day 4: *Textbook 4B* numbers 23 and 24 on p. 38, *Workbook 4B* p. 60

Unit 25:

Day 1: *Textbook 4B* numbers 25 and 26 on p. 39; *Workbook 4B* p. 61
Day 2: *Textbook 4B* number 27 on p. 39; *Workbook 4B* p. 62
Day 3: *Textbook 4B* p. 40; *Workbook 4B* p. 63
Day 4: *Textbook 4B* p. 41-42; *Workbook 4B* p. 64-66

Unit 26:

Day 1: *Textbook 4B* p. 43
Day 2: *Textbook 4B* p. 44
Day 3: *Textbook 4B* p. 45-47; *Workbook 4B* p. 67-68
Day 4: *Textbook 4B* p. 48 – numbers 9, 10, and 11 on p. 49; *Workbook 4B* p. 69-70

Unit 27:

Day 1: *Textbook 4B* numbers 12, 13, and 14 on p. 49; *Workbook 4B* p. 71
Day 2: *Textbook 4B* p. 50; *Workbook 4B* p. 72
Day 3: *Textbook 4B* p. 51; *Workbook 4B* p. 73-74
Day 4: *Textbook 4B* p. 52

Math Schedule
Singapore Primary Mathematics 4A & 4B (U.S. Edition)
(Times Media Private Limited, 2003)

Unit 28:

Day 1: *Textbook 4B* p. 53-55; *Workbook 4B* p. 75-76
Day 2: *Textbook 4B* p. 56; *Workbook 4B* p. 77-78
Day 3: *Textbook 4B* p. 57; *Workbook 4B* p. 79-80
Day 4: *Textbook 4B* p. 58; *Workbook 4B* p. 81-82

Unit 29:

Day 1: *Textbook 4B* p. 59; *Workbook 4B* p. 83
Day 2: *Textbook 4B* p. 60-61; *Workbook 4B* p. 84-86
Day 3: *Textbook 4B* p. 62
Day 4: *Textbook 4B* p. 63

Unit 30:

Day 1: *Textbook 4B* p. 64
Day 2: *Textbook 4B* p. 65 – numbers 8 through 11 on p. 66
Day 3: *Textbook 4B* numbers 12 through 16 on p. 66 – p. 67
Day 4: *Textbook 4B* p. 68-69; *Workbook 4B* p. 87

Unit 31:

Day 1: *Textbook 4B* on p. 70-71; *Workbook 4B* p. 88-89
Day 2: *Textbook 4B* p. 72-73
Day 3: *Workbook 4B* p. 90 – numbers 6, 7, and 8 on p. 91
Day 4: *Workbook 4B* numbers 9 through 12 on p. 91 – p. 93

Unit 32:

Day 1: *Workbook 4B* p. 94, 96
Day 2: *Workbook 4B* p. 95, 97-98
Day 3: *Textbook 4B* p. 74-75; *Workbook 4B* p. 99-100
Day 4: *Textbook 4B* p. 76 – number 8 on p. 79; *Workbook 4B* p. 101-102

Unit 33:

Day 1: *Textbook 4B* number 9 on p. 79; *Workbook 4B* p. 103-104
Day 2: *Textbook 4B* p. 80 – numbers 9 and 10 on p. 81
Day 3: *Textbook 4B* numbers 11 through 15 on p. 81 – p. 82
Day 4: *Textbook 4B* p. 83 – numbers 6, 7, and 8 on p. 84

Unit 34:

Day 1: *Textbook 4B* numbers 9 and 10 on p. 84 – p. 85
Day 2: *Textbook 4B* p. 86-87; *Workbook 4B* p. 105-106
Day 3: *Textbook 4B* p. 88 – number 6 on p. 89; *Workbook 4B* p. 107-108
Day 4: *Textbook 4B* numbers 7 and 8 on p. 89; *Workbook 4B* p. 109-110

Math Schedule
Singapore Primary Mathematics 4A & 4B (U.S. Edition)
(Times Media Private Limited, 2003)

Unit 35:

Day 1: *Textbook 4B* p. 90-92; *Workbook 4B* p. 111-112
Day 2: *Textbook 4B* p. 93-96; *Workbook 4B* p. 113-114
Day 3: *Textbook 4B* p. 97; *Workbook 4B* p. 115-116
Day 4: *Textbook 4B* p. 98-99

NOTE: If you would like to give the **optional** end-of-the-year review, we suggest first reviewing the Textbook portion together with your child; perhaps partially orally, partially on markerboard, and partially on notebook paper. Then, we suggest having your child do the Workbook portion independently. The following is a sample schedule and pacing for this.

Optional Unit 36:

Day 1: *Textbook 4B* p. 100-101
Day 2: *Textbook 4B* p. 102-104
Day 3: *Workbook 4B* p. 117-119
Day 4: *Workbook 4B* p. 120-123
Day 5: *Workbook 4B* p. 124-128

Index of Poetry by Robert Louis Stevenson

Index of Poetry by Robert Louis Stevenson
(continued)

Poetry

Unit 1 – All Days

The Swing

How do you like to go up in a swing,
    Up in the air so blue?
Oh, I do think it the pleasantest thing
    Ever a child can do!

Up in the air and over the wall,
    Till I can see so wide,
Rivers and trees and cattle and all
    Over the countryside –

Till I look down on the garden green,
    Down on the roof so brown –
Up in the air I go flying again,
    Up in the air and down!

Robert Louis Stevenson

Poetry

Unit 2 – All Days

Bed in Summer

In winter I get up at night
And dress by yellow candle-light.
In summer, quite the other way,
I have to go to bed by day.

I have to go to bed and see
The birds still hopping on the tree,
Or hear the grown-up people's feet
Still going past me in the street.

And does it not seem hard to you,
When all the sky is clear and blue,
And I should like so much to play,
To have to go to bed by day?

Robert Louis Stevenson

Poetry

Unit 3 – All Days

Rain

The rain is raining all around,
It falls on field and tree,
It rains on the umbrellas here,
And on the ships at sea.

Robert Louis Stevenson

Poetry

Unit 4 – All Days

To Any Reader

As from the house your mother sees
You playing round the garden trees,
So you may see, if you will look
Through the windows of this book,
Another child, far, far away,
And in another garden, play.
But do not think you can at all,
By knocking on the window, call
That child to hear you. He intent
Is all on his play-business bent.
He does not hear; he will not look,
Nor yet be lured out of this book.
For, long ago, the truth to say,
He has grown up and gone away,
And it is but a child of air
That lingers in the garden there.

Robert Louis Stevenson

Poetry

Unit 5 – All Days

A Good Play

We built a ship upon the stairs
All made of the back-bedroom chairs,
And filled it full of sofa pillows
To go a-sailing on the billows.

We took a saw and several nails,
And water in the nursery pails;
And Tom said, "Let us also take
An apple and a slice of cake;" –
Which was enough for Tom and me
To go a-sailing on, till tea.

We sailed along for days and days,
And had the very best of plays;
But Tom fell out and hurt his knee,
So there was no left but me.

Robert Louis Stevenson

Poetry

Unit 6 – All Days

Summer Sun

Great is the sun, and wide he goes
Through empty heaven without repose;
And in the blue and glowing days
More thick than rain he showers his rays.

Though closer still the blinds we pull
To keep the shady parlour cool,
Yet he will find a chink or two
To slip his golden fingers through.

The dusty attic spider-clad
He, through the keyhole, maketh glad;
And through the broken edge of tiles,
Into the laddered hayloft smiles.

Meantime his golden face around
He bares to all the garden ground,
And sheds a warm and glittering look
Among the ivy's inmost nook.

Above the hills, along the blue,
Round the bright air with footing true,
To please the child, to paint the rose,
The gardener of the World, he goes.

Robert Louis Stevenson

Poetry

Unit 7 – All Days

Foreign Lands

Up into the cherry tree
Who should climb but little me?
I held the trunk with both my hands
And looked abroad on foreign lands.

I saw the next door garden lie,
Adorned with flowers, before my eye,
And many pleasant places more
That I had never seen before.

I saw the dimpling river pass
And by the sky's blue looking-glass;
The dusty roads go up and down
With people tramping into town.

If I could find a higher tree
Farther and farther I should see,
To where the grown-up river slips
Into the sea among the ships.

To where the roads on either hand
Lead onward into fairy land,
Where all the children dine at five,
And all the playthings come alive.

Robert Louis Stevenson

Poetry

Unit 8 – All Days

Looking-Glass River

Smooth it slides upon its travel,
    Here a wimple, there a gleam –
        O the clean gravel!
        O the smooth stream!

Sailing blossoms, silver fishes,
    Paven pools as clear as air –
        How a child wishes
        To live down there!

We can see our coloured faces
    Floating on the shaken pool
        Down in cool places,
        Dim and very cool;

Till a wind or water wrinkle,
    Dipping marten, plumping trout,
        Spreads in a twinkle
        And blots all out.

See the rings pursue each other;
    All below grows black as night,
        Just as if mother
        Had blown out the light!

Patience, children, just a minute –
    See the spreading circles die;
        The stream and all in it
        Will clear by-and-by.

Robert Louis Stevenson

Poetry

Unit 9 – All Days

Autumn Fires

In the other gardens
And all up the vale,
From the autumn bonfires
See the smoke trail!

Pleasant summer over
And all the summer flowers,
The red fire blazes,
The grey smoke towers.

Sing a song of seasons!
Something bright in all!
Flowers in the summer,
Fires in the fall!

Robert Louis Stevenson

Poetry

Unit 10 – All Days

My Shadow

I have a little shadow that goes in and out with me,
And what can be the use of him is more than I can see.
He is very, very like me from the heels up to the head;
And I see him jump before me, when I jump into my bed.

The funniest thing about him is the way he likes to grow –
Not at all like proper children, which is always very slow;
For he sometimes shoots up taller like an india-rubber ball,
And he sometimes gets so little that there's none of him at all.

He hasn't got a notion of how children ought to play,
And can only make a fool of me in every sort of way.
He stays so close beside me, he's a coward you can see;
I'd think, shame to stick to nursie as that shadow sticks to me!

One morning, very early, before the sun was up,
I rose and found the shining dew on every buttercup;
But my lazy little shadow, like an arrant sleepy-head,
Had stayed at home behind me and was fast asleep in bed.

Robert Louis Stevenson

Poetry

Unit 13 – All Days

Where Go the Boats?

Dark brown is the river,
Golden is the sand.
It flows along for ever,
With trees on either hand.

Green leaves a-floating,
Castles of the foam,
Boats of mine a-boating –
Where will all come home?

On goes the river
And out past the mill,
Away down the valley,
Away down the hill.

Away down the river,
A hundred miles or more,
Other little children
Shall bring my boats ashore.

Robert Louis Stevenson

Poetry

Unit 14 – All Days

My Kingdom

Down by a shining water well
I found a very little dell,
    No higher than my head.
The heather and the gorse about
In summer bloom were coming out,
    Some yellow and some red.

I called the little pool a sea;
The little hills were big to me;
    For I am very small.
I made a boat, I made a town,
I searched the caverns up and down,
    And named them one and all.

And all about was mine, I said,
The little sparrows overhead,
    The little minnows too.
This was the world and I was king;
For me the bees came by to sing,
    For me the swallows flew.

(continued on the next page)

Poetry
(continued)

I played there were no deeper seas,
Nor any wider plains than these,
        Nor other kings than me.
At last I heard my mother call
Out from the house at evenfall,
        To call me home to tea.

And I must rise and leave my dell,
And leave my dimpled water well,
        And leave my heather blooms.
Alas! and as my home I neared,
How very big my nurse appeared,
        How great and cool the rooms!

Robert Louis Stevenson

Poetry

Unit 15 – All Days

At the Sea-Side

When I was down beside the sea
A wooden spade they gave to me
    To dig the sandy shore.

My holes were empty like a cup.
In every hole the sea came up,
    Till it could come no more.

Robert Louis Stevenson

Poetry

Unit 16 – All Days

The Hayloft

Through all the pleasant meadow-side
The grass grew shoulder-high,
Till the shining scythes went far and wide
And cut it down to dry.

These green and sweetly smelling crops
They led in wagons home;
And they piled them here in mountain-tops
For mountaineers to roam.

Here is Mount Clear, Mount Rusty-Nail,
Mount Eagle and Mount High; –
The mice that in these mountains dwell,
No happier are than I!

O what a joy to clamber there,
O what a place for play,
With the sweet, the dim, the dusty air,
The happy hills of hay!

Robert Louis Stevenson

Poetry

Unit 17 – All Days

The Moon

The moon has a face like the clock in the hall;
She shines on thieves on the garden wall,
On streets and fields and harbour quays,
And birdies asleep in the forks of the trees.

The squalling cat and the squeaking mouse,
The howling dog by the door of the house,
The bat that lies in bed at noon,
All love to be out by the light of the moon.

But all of the things that belong to the day
Cuddle to sleep to be out of her way;
And flowers and children close their eyes
Till up in the morning the sun shall arise.

Robert Louis Stevenson

Poetry

Unit 18 – All Days

Escape at Bedtime

The lights from the parlour and kitchen shone out
Through the blinds and the windows and bars;
And high overhead and all moving about,
There were thousands of millions of stars.
There ne'er were such thousands of leaves on a tree,
Nor of people in church or the Park,
As the crowds of the stars that looked down upon me,
And that glittered and winked in the dark.

The Dog, and the Plough, and the Hunter, and all,
And the star of the Sailor, and Mars,
These shone in the sky, and the pail by the wall
Would be half full of water and stars.
They saw me at last, and they chased me with cries,
And they soon had me packed into bed;
But the glory kept shining and bright in my eyes,
And the stars going round in my head.

Robert Louis Stevenson

Poetry

Unit 19 – All Days

The Sun's Travels

The sun is not a-bed, when I
At night upon my pillow lie;
Still round the earth his way he takes,
And morning after morning makes.

While here at home, in shining day,
We round the sunny garden play,
Each little Indian sleepy-head
Is being kissed and put to bed.

And when at eve I rise from tea,
Day dawns beyond the Atlantic Sea;
And all the children in the West
Are getting up and being dressed.

Robert Louis Stevenson

Poetry

Unit 20 – All Days

The Lamplighter

My tea is nearly ready and the sun has left the sky;
It's time to take to the window to see Leerie going by;
For every night at teatime and before you take your seat,
With lantern and with ladder he comes posting up the street.

Now Tom would be a driver and Maria go to sea,
And my papa's a banker and as rich as he can be;
But I, when I am stronger and can choose what I'm to do,
O Leerie, I'll go round at night and light the lamps with you!

For we are very lucky, with a lamp before the door,
And Leerie stops to light it as he lights so many more;
And O! before you hurry by with ladder and with light,
O Leerie, see a little child and nod to him to-night.

Robert Louis Stevenson

Poetry

Unit 21 – All Days

The Wind

I saw you toss the kites on high
And blow the birds about the sky;
And all around I heard you pass,
Like ladies' skirts across the grass –
O wind, a-blowing all day long,
O wind, that sings so loud a song!

I saw the different things you did,
But always you yourself you hid.
I felt you push, I heard you call,
I could not see yourself at all –
O wind, a-blowing all day long,
O wind, that sings so loud a song!

O you that are so strong and cold,
O blower, are you young or old?
Are you a beast of field and tree,
Or just a stronger child than me?
O wind, a-blowing all day long,
O wind, that sings so loud a song!

Robert Louis Stevenson

Poetry

Unit 22 – All Days

Block City

What are you able to build with your blocks?
Castles and palaces, temples and docks.
Rain may keep raining, and others go roam,
But I can be happy and building at home.

Let the sofa be mountains, the carpet be sea,
There I'll establish a city for me:
A kirk and a mill and a palace beside,
And a harbour as well where my vessels may ride.

Great is the palace with pillar and wall,
A sort of a tower on the top of it all,
And steps coming down in an orderly way
To where my toy vessels lie safe in the bay.

This one is sailing and that one is moored:
Hark to the song of the sailors on board!
And see on the steps of my palace, the kings
Coming and going with presents and things!

Now I have done with it, down let it go!
All in a moment the town is laid low.
Block upon block lying scattered and free,
What is there left of my town by the sea?

Yet as I saw it, I see it again,
The kirk and the palace, the ships and the men,
And as long as I live and where'er I may be,
I'll always remember my town by the sea.

Robert Louis Stevenson

Poetry

Unit 25 – All Days

Windy Nights

Whenever the moon and stars are set,
Whenever the wind is high,
All night long in the dark and wet,
A man goes riding by.
Late in the night when the fires are out,
Why does he gallop and gallop about?

Whenever the trees are crying aloud,
And ships are tossed at sea,
By, on the highway, low and loud,
By at the gallop goes he.
By at the gallop he goes, and then
By he comes back at the gallop again.

Robert Louis Stevenson

Poetry

Unit 26 – All Days

Young Night Thought

All night long and every night,
When my mama puts out the light,
I see the people marching by,
As plain as day, before my eye.

Armies and emperors and kings,
All carrying different kinds of things,
And marching in so grand a way,
You never saw the like by day.

So fine a show was never seen
At the great circus on the green;
For every kind of beast and man
Is marching in that caravan.

At first they move a little slow,
But still the faster on they go,
And still beside them close I keep
Until we reach the Town of Sleep.

Robert Louis Stevenson

Poetry

Unit 27 – All Days

The Land of Story-Books

At evening when the lamp is lit,
Around the fire my parents sit;
They sit at home and talk and sing.
And do not play at anything.

Now, with my little gun, I crawl
All in the dark along the wall,
And follow round the forest track
Away behind the sofa back.

There, in the night, where none can spy,
All in my hunter's camp I lie,
And play at books that I have read
Till it is time to go to bed.

These are the hills, these are the woods,
These are my starry solitudes;
And there the river by whose brink
The roaring lions come to drink.

I see the others far away
As if in firelit camp they lay,
And I, like to an Indian scout,
Around their party prowled about.

So, when my nurse comes in for me,
Home I return across the sea,
And go to bed with backward looks
At my dear Land of Story-books.

Robert Louis Stevenson

Poetry

Nest Eggs

Birds all the sunny day
Flutter and quarrel
Here in the arbour-like
Tent of laurel.

Here in the fork
The brown nest is seated;
Four little blue eggs
The mother keeps heated.

While we stand watching her,
Staring like gabies,
Safe in each egg are the
Bird's little babies.

Soon the frail eggs they shall
Chip, and upspringing,
Make all the April woods
Merry with singing.

(continued on the next page)

Unit 28 – All Days

Younger than we are,
O children, and frailer,
Soon in blue air they'll be,
Singer and sailor.

We, so much older,
Taller and stronger,
We shall look down on the
Birdies no longer.

They shall go flying
With musical speeches
High overhead in the
Tops of the beeches.

In spite of our wisdom
And sensible talking,
We on our feet must go
Plodding and walking.

Robert Louis Stevenson

Poetry

Unit 29 – All Days

Keepsake Mill

Over the borders, a sin without pardon,
Breaking the branches and crawling below,
Out through the breach in the wall of the garden,
Down by the banks of the river, we go.

Here is the mill with the humming of thunder,
Here is the weir with the wonder of foam,
Here is the sluice with the race running under –
Marvelous places, though handy to home!

Sounds of the village grow stiller and stiller,
Stiller the note of the birds on the hill;
Dusty and dim are the eyes of the miller,
Deaf are his ears with the moil of the mill.

Years may go by, and the wheel in the river
Wheel as it wheels for us, children, to-day,
Wheel and keep roaring and foaming for ever –
Long after all of the boys are away.

Home from the Indies and home from the ocean,
Heroes and soldiers we all shall come home;
Still we shall find the old mill wheel in motion,
Turning and churning that river to foam.

You with the bean that I gave when we quarreled,
I with your marble of Saturday last,
Honoured and old and all gaily appareled,
Here we shall meet and remember the past.

Robert Louis Stevenson

Poetry

Unit 30 – All Days

The Dumb Soldier

When the grass was closely mown,
Walking on the lawn alone,
In the turf hole I found
And hid a soldier underground.

Spring and daisies came apace;
Grasses hide my hiding place;
Grasses run like a green sea
O'er the lawn up to my knee.

Under grass alone he lies,
Looking up with leaden eyes,
Scarlet coat and pointed gun,
To the stars and to the sun.

When the grass is ripe like grain,
When the scythe is stoned again,
When the lawn is shaven clear,
Then my hole shall reappear.

I shall find him, never fear,
I shall find my grenadier;
But for all that's gone and come,
I shall find my soldier dumb.

(continued on the next page)

He has lived, a little thing,
In the grassy woods of spring;
Done, if he could tell me true,
Just as I should like to do.

He has seen the starry hours
And the springing of the flowers;
And the fairy things that pass
In the forests of the grass.

In the silence he has heard
Talking bee and ladybird,
And the butterfly has flown
O'er him as he lay alone.

Not a word will he disclose,
Not a word of all he knows.
I must lay him on the shelf,
And make up the tale myself.

Robert Louis Stevenson

Poetry

Unit 31 – All Days

My Treasures

These nuts, that I keep in the back of the nest
Where all my lead soldiers are lying at rest,
Were gathered in autumn by nursie and me
In a wood with a well by the side of the sea.

This whistle we made (and how clearly it sounds!)
By the side of a field at the end of the grounds.
Of a branch of a plane, with a knife of my own,
It was nursie who made it, and nursie alone!

The stone, with the white and the yellow and grey,
We discovered I cannot tell *how* far away;
And I carried it back although weary and cold,
For though father denies it, I'm sure it is gold.

But of all my treasures the last is the king,
For there's very few children possess such a thing;
And that is a chisel, both handle and blade,
Which a man who was really a carpenter made.

Robert Louis Stevenson

Poetry

Unit 32 – All Days

Historical Associations

Dear Uncle Jim, this garden ground
That now you smoke your pipe around,
Has seen immortal actions done
And valiant battles lost and won.

Here we had best on tip-toe tread,
While I for safety march ahead,
For this is that enchanted ground
Where all who loiter slumber sound.

Here is the sea, here is the sand,
Here is simple Shepherd's Land,
Here are the fairy hollyhocks,
And there are Ali Baba's rocks.

But yonder, see! apart and high,
Frozen Siberia lies; where I,
With Robert Bruce and William Tell,
Was bound by an enchanter's spell.

There, then, awhile in chains we lay,
In wintry dungeons, far from day;
But ris'n at length, with might and main,
Our iron fetters burst in twain.

(continued on the next page)

Poetry
(continued)

Unit 32 – All Days

Then all the horns were blown in town;
And to the ramparts clanging down,
All the giants leaped to horse
And charged behind us through the gorse.

On we rode, the others and I,
Over the mountains blue, and by
The Silver River, the sounding sea,
And the robber woods of Tartary.

A thousand miles we galloped fast
And down the witches' lane we passed,
And rode amain, with brandished sword,
Up to the middle, through the ford.

Last we drew rein – a weary three –
Upon the lawn, in time for tea,
And from our steeds alighted down
Before the gates of Babylon.

Robert Louis Stevenson

Books by This Author:

Little Hands to Heaven
A preschool program for ages 2-5

Little Hearts for His Glory
An early learning program for ages 5-7

Beyond Little Hearts for His Glory
An early learning program for ages 6-8

Bigger Hearts for His Glory
A learning program for ages 7-9
With extensions for ages 10-11

Preparing Hearts for His Glory
A learning program for ages 8-10
With extensions for ages 11-12

Hearts for Him Through Time: Creation to Christ
A learning program for ages 9-11
With extensions for ages 12-13

Hearts for Him Through Time: Resurrection to Reformation
A learning program for ages 10-12
With extensions for ages 13-14

Hearts for Him Through Time: Revival to Revolution
A learning program for ages 11-13
With extensions for ages 14-15

Hearts for Him Through Time: Missions to Modern Marvels
A learning program for ages 12-14
With extensions for ages 15-16

Drawn into the Heart of Reading
A literature program for ages 7-15 that
Works with any books you choose

Hearts for Him Through High School: World Geography
A learning program for ages 13-15
Extending to 11th and 12th grades with adjustments

These books are published by Heart of Dakota Publishing, Inc.
See the website for placement help, product details, and catalog orders: www.heartofdakota.com
For ordering questions, email: carmikeaustin@msn.com
Or, call: 605-428-4068